JAMES IV

NORMAN MACDOUGALL

Senior Lecturer in Scottish History
University of St. Andrews

TUCKWELL PRESS

FOR SIMONE AND BONNIE
(not forgetting Alice)

Published in 1997 by Tuckwell Press Ltd,
The Mill House, Phantassie, East Linton
East Lothian EH40 3DG
Scotland

Originally published by
John Donald Publishers Ltd

The publishers acknowedge subsidy from
The Scottish Arts Council towards the publication of
this volume

ISBN 1 86232 006 3 (hardback)
ISBN 1 898410 41 0 (paperback)

British Library Cataloguing-in-Publication Data
A catalogue record for this book is available
from the British Library

*The endpapers of the hardcover edition show a signature of
James IV taken from a letter written from Edinburgh to
Emperor Maximilian on 17 March 1495, the King's
22nd birthday. The original is in the Tyrolean State
Archive, Innsbruck*

Printed and bound by
Biddles Ltd, Guildford

Acknowledgements

In 1982, shortly after completing a biography of James III, I decided not to be afraid of doing the obvious, and was easily seduced by the prospect of turning my attention from a ruler who proved a disaster in personal and public life alike to one who was clearly a resounding success. My path throughout has been smoothed by assistance from a large number of individuals, friends, colleagues, and students — the categories frequently overlap — who have made valuable suggestions or prevented me from falling into serious error.

I am grateful to many members of the Conference of Scottish Medievalists, above all to Dr Trevor Chalmers, Professor Ian Cowan, Dr Rod Lyall, Dr Michael Lynch, Dr David Caldwell, and Mr Geoffrey Stell. Amongst the Conference's 'elder statesmen', I have greatly benefited from the formidable scholarship and wise advice generously proffered by Dr John Durkan and Dr Leslie Macfarlane, whose kindnesses to me stretch back a quarter of a century. Scholars from further afield whose expertise I have greatly valued include Dr Thomas Riis from Copenhagen and Dr Ian Arthurson, whose important thesis on Henry VII's political and military schemes in 1497 sheds new light on Anglo-Scottish relations during that critical year; and nearer home, I should like to acknowledge the generous assistance of Dr Jane Dawson, of the Department of Modern History at St Andrews. Dr Jenny Wormald, a friend of very long standing, has patiently endured my wildly fluctuating views of the political events of 1488 and the early 'nineties over many years, and made constructive comments on these; and I should have been very much the poorer without the sage advice of Dr Ronald Cant, who long ago expressed in succinct form what many of us have taken volumes to discover about Stewart kingship.

My colleagues within the Scottish History department at St Andrews, Professor Christopher Smout, Dr Colin Martin, Dr Roger Mason and Dr Keith Brown, have been unfailingly generous with time, comments and suggestions; and I also record with pleasure the courtesy and assistance which I have invariably received from the staff of St Andrews University Library, above all those in charge of the muniments, Mr Robert Smart, Mr Geoffrey Hargreaves, and Mrs Christine Gascoigne. Most of all, perhaps, I have been fortunate in the able and enthusiastic array of students who over the years have graced my James IV Special Subject class, and it is only proper to name them all: Kathy Broun, Jamie Cameron, Ken Emond, Dorothy Husband, Leanda Thornton, Steve

Boardman, Fiona Chambers, Geoff Don, Moira Dunn, Ian Dutton, Stephen Major, Maureen Steven, Christine Stewart, Campbell Brady, Michael Brown, Marianne Gilchrist, Susan Neilands, Crispin Oliver, Ed Wallace, Fiona Watson, Edward Clark, Martha Leishman, Fiona McIntyre, Louise Macpherson, Justine Morgan, Gavin Rome, Doug Russell, and Sue Ward. No less than six of these have gone on to postgraduate research in Scottish History at St Andrews itself, at Glasgow, and at Oxford; all of them were a pleasure to teach, in the process contributing enormously to my own understanding of the subject; and all of them have walked from the parish church of Ladykirk down to the farm gate at the corner and gazed south across the Tweed, as James IV must have done, at the massive pile of Norham castle.

Amongst the galaxy above, I owe special debts to Steve Boardman, currently researching Scottish politics and the feud in the late medieval period, both for his overall perception and for his uncovering of minutiae in the Lords of Council records; to Jamie Cameron and Michael Brown for many helpful suggestions made in the course of lengthy monthly meetings; and to Dr Ken Emond for his scholarly thesis on the minority of James V, much of which will, I hope, soon appear in print. At the business end, John Tuckwell of John Donald publishers has been, as ever, an author's dream — patient to a fault, efficient, courteous, a good friend who is also keenly interested in the subject; and I would run out of superlatives to praise Mrs Margaret Richards, who has processed my untidy manuscript from beginning to end with great skill and immense patience, displaying throughout a marvellous combination of committed concern and cheerful enthusiasm.

Finally, I must record two vitally important contributions. My wife Simone has not only proof-read the entire book and made a number of valuable suggestions, but has also contrived to keep me happy during the writing-up process by spoiling me shamelessly, and by knowing when *not* to talk shop about medieval or Scottish history; and our labrador Bonnie, seven years older but hardly less enthusiastic about exercise than she was when she distracted me from work on James III, has throughout been a persuasive advocate of the need to have great historical thoughts in Tentsmuir Forest rather than at the desk at home. To Simone and Bonnie, with love and affection, this book is dedicated.

St Andrews, October 1989

Preface

More than thirty years have gone by since the appearance of R L Mackie's scholarly and immensely readable biography of James IV.[1] Mackie's king strides confidently through the book, an active, popular, effective ruler — war lord, patron of the arts, firm enforcer of the law, generously endowed with the kingly virtues of piety and liberality, for much of the reign the ideal Stewart king. Few would disagree with this overall estimate of James IV. Indeed it has become enshrined in histories of the king throughout the five centuries since his reign, an unbroken tradition, stretching from the works of Adam Abell, Sir David Lindsay of the Mount, Bishop John Lesley, and Robert Lindesay of Pitscottie,[2] through the seventeenth-century elaborations of Drummond of Hawthornden and Hume of Godscroft,[3] the romantic nineteenth-century excesses of Sir Walter Scott in *Tales of a Grandfather* and *Marmion*,[4] the painstaking scholarship of Tytler and Andrew Lang,[5] down to our own century, with the histories of Hume Brown, Taylor, and the biographies of King James's brother and illegitimate son Alexander by Herkless and Hannay.[6] Mackie's biography is firmly rooted in this tradition, and carries the added authority of extensive recourse to that indispensable treasure-chest of information about the king and reign, the first four volumes of the Treasurer's accounts, together with the very full treatment of foreign diplomacy which one would expect from the editor of King James's letters.[7]

There are, however, problems about the traditional view of the king which Mackie does little or nothing to resolve. Broadly these fall into two categories: first, with the benefit of hindsight we know that James IV was a highly successful ruler, and there is therefore a tendency to play down the political traumas of the late 1480s and early 1490s in the desire to have the king emerge, adult, able, and popular, as quickly as possible. Thus the famous parliamentary comment on the death of James III — that the king had 'happened' to be slain — is seized upon, the late king is shovelled into his grave and swiftly forgotten, and James IV emerges without difficulty in 1493 from the tutelage of those magnates who had eliminated his father to dominate all of them with ease and earn the much-used but singularly unhelpful title of 'Renaissance Prince'. Such a view is difficult to sustain. Of all decades of the fifteenth century, the 'eighties were the most politically troubled, with no less than three major rebellions — in 1482, 1488, and 1489 — in all of which James, as youthful prince or adolescent king, played

v

a prominent part together with a large, but constantly changing, proportion of the Scottish political community. The shock waves which followed in the wake of these major political upheavals did not subside for many years, and it seems unlikely that James IV was able to assert himself as an effective ruler until at least 1494, or more probably the spring of 1495.

Secondly, many writers have the problem of knowing what to do with King James once they have him launched on his adult career. A reign which is marked by a long period of domestic peace — the sixteen years between 1497 and 1513 are remarkably untroubled — does not lend itself easily to dramatic stories of intrigue, unrest, and masterful kingship. One solution to this problem is to pillage the Treasurer's accounts for evidence of the king's breadth of interests — his amateurish experiments in dentistry and medicine make excellent copy[8] — and to seize upon Somerset Herald's vivid account of James's marriage to Margaret Tudor in August 1503,[9] the follow-up to the grandly-named Treaty of Perpetual Peace of the previous year, which, despite its significance in making possible the Union of the Crowns a century later, was in terms of its immediate effects one of the least convincing of all Anglo-Scottish treaties.

In any event, few writers on James are content to leave him for long on his precarious pedestal as a paragon of Scottish kingly virtues. As soon as 1503 is safely past, there is a stampede towards the seemingly inevitable disaster of Flodden. Mackie devotes about one-third of his biography of James to the king's supposedly maladroit diplomacy, asserting rather than proving that King James was out of his depth in dealing with the powerful European rulers of his day, that he was blinded to diplomatic realities by his vision of a crusade against the infidel which he himself might lead, and that his growing megalomania was simply used by allies and enemies alike to drag him to his ruin. In Mackie's memorable and oft-quoted phrase, James IV was a 'moonstruck romantic'. But Mackie also believed that the young Henry VIII was a realist. A different view of both kings is offered below.

Discarding both the 'Renaissance' and 'moonstruck' tags as unhelpful in forming any useful estimate of the king's character and policies, I have attempted to chart James's development from the unpleasant, mistrusted, and neglected youth who successfully opposed his father in 1488 to the adult king of seven years later, and then developed a number of the themes which made James's kingship popular and successful — committed military leadership, an effective fiscal policy, firm control of the national church, delegation of royal authority to trustworthy men in the localities, the construction of a royal navy, and — above all — a personal itinerary which in terms of the speed and energy involved would do credit to a modern member of parliament defending a wafer-thin majority at election time. In pursuing these themes, I have benefitted enormously from the veritable explosion of scholarly activity which has transformed our knowledge of late medieval Scotland since Mackie's time. The work of Drs Athol Murray and Craig Madden — on the workings of the Scottish exchequer and royal fiscal policies respectively[10] — has added very substantially to our understanding of the size of income which a medieval Scottish king might hope to receive, and the many methods by which he might seek to augment it. Dr Trevor Chalmers' magisterial thesis on the royal council, patronage, and administration in the reigns of James III and IV[11] should be read by anyone wishing to understand the workings of royal government in the late medieval period; and Dr Leslie Macfarlane's scholarly biography of Bishop William Elphinstone, Privy Seal for twenty-two years, the most eminent legal mind in Scotland, and James IV's loyal servant throughout the reign, is a treasure-house of information, not only about the bishop, but on such varied subjects as government, administration, law, and education.[12] Then in 1986 the eagerly awaited edition of the acts of the Lords of the Isles, superbly edited by R W and Dr Jean Munro, appeared to illuminate the relative darkness of the medieval Highlands and Islands, the difficult relationships which developed amongst the leaders of Highland society, and between all of them and the Crown.[13]

In the generation since Mackie wrote, our understanding of how the medieval Scottish Crown and magnates viewed their respective roles in government — national and local — diplomacy, and war, has been transformed by the work of Drs Wormald[14] and Grant,[15] carrying us convincingly away from the traditional interpretation of weak — or strong — kings endlessly confronted by over-mighty magnates to a much more balanced assessment of the period, with king and nobility cooperating for much of the fifteenth century because both sought broadly the same objectives. For Dr Wormald in particular, the Stewart kings were more powerful than has often been suggested, for while they could not afford to spend the vast sums available to their much richer European neighbours, they had sufficient wealth to govern Scotland, to distribute patronage — generally in lands or offices — on a scale far greater than that possible to their wealthiest magnates. On the other hand, the Crown could not normally afford a contract army, so that it was bound to rely heavily on loyal members of the nobility in far-flung parts of the kingdom, and to reward them appropriately. Only in this way could royal government be at all effective, or the Scottish host be expected to appear at the muster point on those occasions when warfare on the borders or elsewhere had to be undertaken. The current orthodoxy in historical thinking about government in the late medieval period, then, stresses Crown-magnate cooperation rather than confrontation, an overall political equilibrium upset only by James I's assault on the Albany Stewarts, James II's systematic destruction of the Black Douglases, and one highly unsatisfactory king, James III.

In his extensive overview of late medieval Scotland, first published in 1974, Dr Ranald Nicholson is to some extent at odds with this new orthodoxy, portraying a fifteenth century in which violence directed at the Crown by its subjects, general disorder, and palace revolutions, often seem the norm rather than the exception. Dr Nicholson's major contribution to late medieval Scottish history, however, is surely to be found in his revisionist view of James IV, an estimate of the king which is significantly different from that of Mackie. In place of Mackie's genial, fearless, but ultimately stupid prince, Nicholson portrays a shrewd and occasionally devious ruler, skilled in foreign political intrigues and in screwing as much money out of his subjects as possible without inciting general unrest in the process. This is a stimulating — and broadly convincing — portrayal of successful royal Stewart government; indeed, Dr Nicholson's study of the entire late medieval period seems to increase in stature each time I return to it, and its contribution to the growing historical debate on the nature of late medieval Scottish government and society has been immense.[16]

Moving from the scholarly to the bizarre, in 1970 Scottish historians were confronted with the problem of assessing the validity of an autobiography of James IV, written by a lady who claimed — and claims — to be the reincarnation of the king.[17] Initial scholarly response to the challenge presented by this lady, Ada Kay or Stewart, was understandably cautious, for if she was indeed the reborn James IV, then her knowledge of the period was obviously unchallengeable. Surprisingly, there was a reluctance at the time to test what her racy and readable account of her former life said about people and events which are very fully described in contemporary official records. Even a casual glance at these swiftly reveals that the memory of the reincarnated king seems to be playing him/her false about incidents in his life which must have been important to him at the time. To take only one example, the James IV of the 1490s would have remembered his first two mistresses, Marion Boyd and Margaret Drummond, much more clearly than his reincarnation of the 1970s, who appears to have had recourse to later histories to jog his/her memory. This is not to deny the patent honesty of Ada Kay's conviction that she is the reincarnation of James IV; but it is to say that her 'autobiography' of the king is most safely read as a highly colourful and entertaining historical novel.[18]

Perhaps, therefore, the time is ripe for a further attempt to understand the career of the most successful of the late medieval Stewarts. No single volume could encompass all aspects of his life and reign, and there are significant and deliberate omissions from this one. For example, those primarily interested in Middle Scots poetry, in the makars who flourished in and around James's court, will find that they receive scant attention here, largely because they are extensively treated elsewhere. Similarly, I have little to add to Dr Macfarlane's scholarly treatment of the development of Scots law during the period, or to Dr Chalmers' unparalleled understanding of the workings of the royal administration; and late medieval feuds, including some in which the king was directly involved, are touched upon rather than discussed at length, because they form the subject of research currently being undertaken by Stephen Boardman.

Thus what follows is a biography of James IV which lays strong emphasis on political and diplomatic affairs. That these fields still offer the widest scope for debate as to the nature of James's kingship can be proved by asking a few apparently straightforward questions. Why was there a major rebellion, lasting no less than nine months from April 1489, only six months after the parliament of October 1488 had confirmed the post-Sauchieburn regime in power? Why was Archibald, fifth earl of Angus, besieged in his castle of Tantallon in the autumn of 1491 by the royal forces, yet trusted with the highest secular office in the kingdom, the Chancellorship, little over a year later? Why did James IV call so few parliaments? How was he able to double, perhaps even treble, royal income without becoming highly unpopular in the process? How significant, in the short term, was the Treaty of Perpetual Peace of 1502? What role did James envisage for the royal navy, his greatest single item of expenditure from the early 1500s? Had the Scottish king any greater commitment to the crusading ideal than his European contemporaries?

Possible answers to all these questions are suggested below. Frequently the search for answers produces still more questions, and I cannot claim to have written anything like a 'definitive' biography of this perennially fascinating ruler. Given the nature of both 'official' and chronicle evidence, this would be impossible. But I hope to have demonstrated convincingly that those elusive skills necessary to the successful governing of medieval Scotland were possessed to a high degree by James IV.

NOTES

1. R. L. Mackie, *King James IV of Scotland: A Brief Survey of his Life and Times* (Edinburgh, 1958).

2. N.L.S. MS. 1746 (Adam Abell, 'The Roit or Quheill of Tyme'), ff. 112 r-v; Sir David Lindsay, 'Testament and Complaynt of the Papyngo', in David Laing (ed.), *The Poetical Works of Sir David Lindsay of the Mount* (Edin., 1879), i, 61–104, at 79–80; John Lesley, *The History of Scotland from the Death of King James I in the Year 1436 to the Year 1561* (Bannatyne Club, 1830), 59–96; Robert Lindesay of Pitscottie, *The Historie and Cronicles of Scotland* (Scottish Text Society, 1899), i, 213–278.

3. William Drummond of Hawthornden, *History of Scotland from the Year 1423 until the Year 1542* (London, 1681), 121–153; David Hume of Godscroft, *The History of the House and Race of Douglas and Angus* (4th edn., Edin., 1748), ii, 27–62.

4. Sir Walter Scott, *Tales of a Grandfather* (1828–9) (Edin., Adam and Charles Black, 1889), 78–87; 'Marmion' (1808), in *The Poetical Works of Sir Walter Scott* (London, Sands edn., 1899), 92–227.

5. Patrick Fraser Tytler, *The History of Scotland from the Accession of Alexander III to the Union* (Edin., 1868), ii, 244–295; Andrew Lang, *A History of Scotland from the Roman Occupation* (Edin., 1900), i, 361–391.

6. Peter Hume Brown, *History of Scotland to the Present Time* (Cambridge, 1911), i, 237–280; I. A. Taylor, *The Life of James IV* (London, 1913); John Herkless and Robert Kerr Hannay, *The Archbishops of St Andrews* (Edin., 1907), i, 165–214, 215–271.

7. *The Letters of James the Fourth, 1505–1513* [*James IV Letters*], ed. R. L. Mackie (S.H.S., 1953).

8. *T.A.*, i–iv, passim. The king's interest in medicine and dentistry is admirably summarised in John D. Comrie, *History of Scottish Medicine to 1860* (Wellcome Historical Medical Museum, Lond., 1927), 51–62, and in Douglas Guthrie, 'King James the Fourth of Scotland: His Influence on Medicine and Science', *Bulletin of the History of Medicine*, 21 (1947), 173–191.

9. Somerset Herald's account of Margaret Tudor's journey to Scotland and the marriage celebrations is in John Leland, *De Rebus Britannicis Collectanea* (Lond., 1770), iv, 265–300, 173–191.

10. A. L. Murray, 'Exchequer and Crown Revenue of Scotland, 1437–1542' (unpublished Ph.D. thesis, Edinburgh University, 1961); Craig Madden, 'Royal Treatment of Feudal Casualties in Late Medieval Scotland', *S.H.R.*, lv (2), (1976), 172–194.

11. T. M. Chalmers, 'The King's Council, Patronage, and the Governance of Scotland, 1460–1513' (unpublished Ph.D. thesis, Aberdeen University, 1982).

12. Leslie J. Macfarlane, *William Elphinstone and the Kingdom of Scotland 1431–1514* (Aberdeen, 1985).

13. *Acts of the Lords of the Isles 1336–1493*, edd. Jean Munro and R. W. Munro (Edin., S.H.S., 1986).

14. The revisionist view of late medieval Scottish government and society was heralded by a seminal article by Dr Wormald (then Brown): Jennifer M. Brown, 'Taming the Magnates?', in *The Scottish Nation*, ed. Gordon Menzies (BBC, 1972), 46–59. This was greatly expanded a few years later: Jennifer M. Brown, 'The Exercise of Power' in *Scottish Society in the Fifteenth Century*, ed. Jennifer M. Brown (London, 1977), 33–65; and a summary of the extensive research on which she based many of her views is to be found in Jenny Wormald, *Lords and Men in Scotland: Bonds of Manrent 1442–1603* (Edin., 1985). 'Taming the Magnates?', footnoted and updated, is more easily available in K. J. Stringer (ed.), *Essays on the Nobility of Medieval Scotland* (Edin., 1985), 270–280.

15. Alexander Grant, *Independence and Nationhood: Scotland 1306–1469* (Lond., 1984), esp. chapters 6 and 7.

16. Ranald Nicholson, *Scotland: The Later Middle Ages* (The Edinburgh History of Scotland volume 2: Edin., 1974), chapters 17 and 18. An important article by the same author, and highly relevant to James IV's money-making schemes, is Ranald Nicholson, 'Feudal Developments in Late Medieval Scotland', *Juridical Review*, 1973 (i), 1–19.

17. *Falcon: The Autobiography of His Grace James the 4, King of Scots*, presented by A. J. Stewart (London, 1970).

18. For a discussion of Ada Kay's claims, see Ian Wilson, *Reincarnation? The Claims Investigated* (Lond., 1982), 200–217.

Contents

Illustrations

1

A Family at War, 1473–88

On Friday 14 July 1486, Margaret of Denmark lay dying in Stirling Castle.[1] Thirty years of age, queen of Scots for seventeen of these, she had borne to her husband James III three sons, all of whom had survived infancy and generously fulfilled the queen's principal function of providing for the succession. On her deathbed, if her biographer is to be believed, Queen Margaret called her three boys to her and exhorted them to pursue virtuous lives. In particular, she singled out her eldest son, James, duke of Rothesay, heir to the throne, and said to him:

'James, my eldest boy, I am speeding towards death; I pray you, through your obedience as my son, to love and fear God, always doing good, because nothing achieved by violence, be certain, can endure'.[2]

This admonition may be little more than a conventional literary device by Sabadino, Margaret's Italian biographer, writing about five years after the queen's death; but it contains an element of grim prophetic irony. For within two years the Duke of Rothesay would have seized his father's throne by violence, James III would be dead at the hands of his own subjects, and Margaret of Denmark's memory would be abused even by her son, who would use the fabricated tale of her death by poison with her husband's compliance to justify to the Danes his successful rebellion in 1488.[3] And the new regime created by the violence of that rebellion, in spite of its assertive self-confidence and some striking successes, would not endure.

The eldest of the three sons of James III and Margaret of Denmark, Prince James, the future king, was born on 17 March 1473.[4] The absence of any major contemporary chronicle, and indeed of most of the Treasurer's accounts before 1488, makes it impossible to produce any more than a thumbnail sketch of the prince in his infancy and youth. He probably spent most of his time before 1488 at Stirling in the care of his mother, and latterly in the company of his two younger brothers, James and John. In 1478 Queen Margaret was officially entrusted with the custody and education of the heir to the throne for five years, though this was probably no more than the confirmation of an already existing situation following James III's general revocation of 1476.[5] From early infancy Prince James, already Duke of Rothesay, was used in his father's diplomacy. In October 1474 James III and Edward IV concluded the first firm Anglo-Scottish alliance of the 15th century, the foundation of which

was to be a marriage between the infant Rothesay and Edward IV's daughter
Cecilia when both should reach marriageable age — the prospective groom was
one year old in 1474, the bride-to-be was aged three. The immediate return for
the Scots king was a dowry of 20,000 marks sterling (approximately £40,000
Scots) which would be paid in advance, in annual instalments of 2,000 marks;[6]
in the longer term, the treaty marks the beginning of James III's obsessive
pursuit of friendship with England, a policy which was as unpopular as it was
innovatory. For the Duke of Rothesay, his father's Anglophile stance simply
meant a succession of marriage proposals — three prospective English brides
between 1474 and 1487[7] — none of which was realised.

The use of the heir to the throne in this high-powered if unsuccessful
diplomacy did not of course impinge on Rothesay's early life, and his motives
for suddenly emerging as the adolescent rebel of 1488 can only be guessed at.
The surviving Treasurer's account for James III's reign — a mere sixteen
months in 1473–4 — provides us with a few names of suppliers to the court
and members of Margaret of Denmark's household, together with a total of
£72 7/10d spent during part of this period on the infant Prince James;[8] but
this source, which would have been invaluable in indicating the motives of the
adolescent Rothesay in the 1480s, is lost to us until his accession as king in the
summer of 1488. From the exchequer records we learn only that Prince James
was taken — presumably from Stirling — on visits to Edinburgh in the summers
of 1474 and 1479, being lodged in the castle on both occasions. His nurse in
the 'seventies was Agnes Turing, wife of an Edinburgh burgess, she and her
husband being rewarded with half the farms of Drumcorse, Linlithgowshire,
which brought them in £10 per annum. The same source provides us with the
name of one servant of the prince, David Balfour, who received as payment
the lease of some royal lands in Menteith.[9]

Nor are chronicle accounts much more help. Bishop John Lesley, after
recording the prince's birth, described a marvellous comet which appeared
in the south for a month — 17 January to 18 February, anticipating James's
birth in March — and comments that this was 'ane signe of mony mervellus
changes in the warld.'[10] Lesley was writing about a century later, around 1570.
However, a contemporary chronicler interpreted the comet's appearance not as a
portent of marvels to come, but of disaster — the wrecking of Bishop Kennedy's
barge, the 'Salvator', at Bamburgh in the month of the prince's birth, and the
recent murder of King Henry VI of England in May 1471.[11] Giovanni Ferreri,
writing in the 1570s, confines himself to conventional praise of the young Duke
of Rothesay, remarking that while he and his younger brothers James and John
all showed a truly royal nature, the heir to the throne outshone the other two
by the beauty of his character and the brilliance of his talents.[12]

Neither such conventional praise nor the circumstantial detail of the
surviving exchequer and Treasurer's accounts takes us any further towards an
understanding of Rothesay's involvement in the successful rebellion of 1488. It
would appear that his life in infancy, youth, and early adolescence, spent mainly
at Stirling with the queen and the castle's keeper, James Shaw of Sauchie, was

uneventful — or at least that any dramatic events associated with the prince are lost to us together with the records which would reveal them.

There exists, however, one revealing glimpse of Prince James prior to 1488. Surprisingly, it is provided, almost in an aside, by Ferreri. In the late summer of 1482, the chronicler tells us, the prince and his mother were visited at Stirling by James III's brother Alexander, duke of Albany, who had come direct from Edinburgh accompanied by William Scheves, archbishop of St Andrews, Andrew Lord Avandale, the Chancellor, and Colin Campbell, earl of Argyll. While at Stirling, Albany spent some time discussing at length the proper education for the nine-year-old heir to the throne.[13] Superficially, this last statement does not appear of great interest; but the political events of 1482 raise it from the ordinary to the extremely remarkable. For the truth was that Albany was struggling for a dominant role in government, and that little over a month before his visit to Stirling, he had come to Scotland to try to overthrow his brother and make himself king as Alexander IV.

The prince's father, James III, was largely to blame for this state of affairs. We can never be certain exactly what caused him to attack his younger brother Albany in the spring of 1479, for the parliamentary indictment of the duke makes unconvincing reading and indeed failed to convince the estates that his offences were treasonable and that he should be forfeited. In fact, one of the principal charges brought against Albany — the defence of Dunbar castle against the king — simply begs the question, as Dunbar was only garrisoned against James III *after* his attack on Albany. As there is virtually no other evidence, we are forced to interpret the break between the two brothers in terms of the other main charge brought against Albany in parliament — the abuse of his office of March Warden, violating the peace with England by treasonable 'slauchteris reffis and hereschippis'.[14] As we have seen, maintenance of the English alliance of 1474 lay at the heart of James III's very personal foreign policy. It is clear that Albany, only two years the king's junior, did not share his opinion, that many southern Scots agreed with him, and that both as a royal Stewart and as a March Warden, he was a natural focus for their discontent. There may also have been an element of jealousy in the relationship between the two men. As Professor Donaldson has pointed out, James III was the first fifteenth century Scottish king to have to cope with the problem of having adult brothers;[15] and while the eminently quotable sixteenth century chronicler Lindsay of Pitscottie may have misinterpreted most of the events of this reign, his statements that James III 'desirit nevir to heir of weiris nor the fame theerof' while Albany (and his brother Mar) 'lovit nothing so weill as abill men and gud horss'[16] reflect surely the king's determination to preserve peace with England whatever the cost, his brother's opposition to such an attitude, and their respective popularity and unpopularity with sections of the political community as a result.

The crisis broke in the spring of 1479. Albany may have been arrested by the king, served a brief period of imprisonment in Edinburgh castle, and subsequently escaped, or more likely he anticipated arrest by taking refuge in

Dunbar castle, garrisoning it, and fleeing to France. A full-scale royal siege of Dunbar, possibly lasting as long as a month in April/May, followed, with artillery brought into play on both sides, the sound of the bombardment clearly audible to the twelve-year-old John Major, eight miles away at his home at Gleghornie near North Berwick.[17] The castle duly fell or was surrendered, but the sequel was much less satisfying to the king; for Albany had already escaped to France, and the parliament of October 1479, which might have been expected to accede to the king's wishes and forfeit the duke, simply continued the summons calling on him to appear to answer the charges[18] — and indeed did so again and again over the next two-and-a-half years. This public rebuff to the king probably reflects not only the unpopularity of his English peace — for the estates clearly did not regard as treason violations of the truce on the borders by Albany — but also a growing fear by prominent members of the political community that none of their number was safe from their overbearing and arbitrary ruler if they sought to take an independent line.

Yet the three years between Albany's flight in 1479 and his return in 1482 witnessed a remarkable diplomatic volte-face on the part of both James III and his brother. By the spring of 1480, the Anglo-Scottish alliance had collapsed, and the Scottish king was looking once more to Louis XI of France for support in resisting Edward IV of England. King James may of course have had no choice but to reopen serious negotiations for a French alliance; for his exiled brother Albany, welcomed by Louis XI and provided with a prestigious French marriage — in January 1480 he married Anne de la Tour, daughter of the Count of Auvergne and Bouillon — was a potential menace, the more so as the Scottish estates resolutely refused to forfeit him in absentia. Worse still, the belligerence of Edward IV, demanding both that the prospective Scots groom, Prince James, should be sent to England by 1 May 1480, and that Berwick should be ceded to the English, finally sealed the fate of the Anglo-Scottish alliance. War broke out between England and Scotland in April 1480; and James III, whose unpopularity at home was in large measure due to his intransigence in maintaining the 1474 alliance against the odds, found himself in the highly vulnerable position of seeking to raise the Scottish host to resist the inevitable invasion of his former ally.[19]

Albany's dramatic political shift from wronged Scots patriot in French exile to pretender to his brother's throne as a client of Edward IV was born of necessity. With James III and Louis XI proposing a renewal of the Franco-Scottish alliance, the duke could give up any hopes of French assistance to help him recover his position in Scotland. He determined therefore to take the enormous risk of seeking the aid of Edward IV, taking advantage of James III's growing embarrassment as the Anglo-Scottish war dragged on to his disadvantage. But the English price for military support was very high. By the treaty of Fotheringhay of 11 June, Albany, signing himself 'Alexander R.' and describing himself as King of Scotland by Edward IV's gift, accepted that the English king would aid his restoration in Scotland only if the duke took his brother's place on the Scottish throne as Edward IV's vassal. Significantly,

Albany was to attempt to secure an annulment of his recent French marriage and was thereafter to marry Edward IV's daughter Cecilia, the bride promised to the duke's nephew Rothesay, James III's heir. The treaty also required the cession to King Edward of Berwick, Liddesdale, Eskdale, Ewesdale, Annandale, and Lochmaben castle[20] — in fact the surrender of large areas of Albany's earldom of March and lordship of Annandale, to which the duke had hoped to be restored. It is difficult, if not impossible, to be sure whether Albany actively pursued an agreement which would win him his brother's crown, or whether Edward IV made that a precondition of his support, and the duke had no choice but to agree. It may be significant that Albany was already describing himself as King of Scotland within a fortnight of his arrival in England, and a full month before the treaty of Fotheringhay.[21] On the other hand, he must have realised that English military assistance, even if it resulted in the defeat and death — or removal — of James III, would hardly endear him to the Scottish political community, especially as King James and Margaret of Denmark had three sons, any one of whom had a better claim to the Scottish throne than Albany. So the duke's invasion of Scotland, in the company of a huge English army under the command of Richard, duke of Gloucester, in the summer of 1482, was a dangerous political gamble undertaken by a young man who may have reckoned that the alternative was to live out his life as an alien parasite in England. In any event, he must have known that only the total military defeat of James III gave him any chance at all of negotiating from strength.

So the summer of 1482 witnessed a remarkable exercise in political role reversal, with Albany, the former focus of opposition in southern Scotland to alliance with England, invading his own country at the head of a huge English army, and James III, from 1474 to 1480 a committed protagonist of friendship with England, mustering the Scottish host at Lauder to resist the formidable English threat. It seems unlikely that the Scottish response to military call-up by an unpopular king whose foreign policy had visibly collapsed was impressive; and a battle against the huge army of Albany and Gloucester would probably have ended in an overwhelming defeat for King James. But on 22 July, with the English army already entering the east March, James III was deprived of the opportunity to commit an act of suicidal — if patriotic — folly. He was seized at Lauder by a faction led by his own kin — his half-uncles John Stewart, earl of Atholl, and James Stewart, earl of Buchan — taken north to Edinburgh and lodged as a prisoner in the castle.[22]

This unprecedented seizure of an adult Stewart king instantly transformed the political situation. The vast army of Albany and Gloucester, entering the burgh of Edinburgh unopposed at the beginning of August, found the king whom they had intended to depose totally inaccessible. Gloucester had to resolve the situation quickly as he could only pay his army for a further ten days; and it must rapidly have become apparent to him that Albany was unacceptable to the Scots as Edward IV's vassal king. In fact, Gloucester's problem was to find anyone representing a powerful enough sector of the Scottish political community to make it worth negotiating with them. The

Stewart half-uncles, who had physical possession of James III and the royal seals, were inaccessible in the castle, and a siege was not a practical possibility. Likewise King James's queen, Margaret of Denmark, was thirty miles away in the powerful castle of Stirling with the heir to the throne and his two younger brothers.

The alternative — hardly a satisfactory one — was to negotiate with James III's displaced counsellors — Archbishop Scheves, a man close to the king throughout the 1470s, Andrew Lord Avandale, chancellor for 22 years, and Colin Campbell, earl of Argyll, the former Master of the Royal Household. These men, who had probably been on their way to the Lauder muster when King James was seized[23], now possessed little real authority. They did not have the royal seals; their failure to support James III in his hour of need was unlikely to endear them to their sovereign, incarcerated in Edinburgh castle and in fear of his life; and any agreement which they made in his name was unlikely to be honoured.

Thus the first of the peace settlements, concluded on 2 August between Scheves, Avandale, Argyll, and Bishop Livingston of Dunkeld on the one side, and Gloucester and Albany on the other, was optimistic to say the least. The Scots lords bound themselves to secure a grant from James III, ratified by parliament, restoring Albany to all lands and offices which he had held before his flight in 1479, together with a pardon for his treasonable dynastic aspirations.[24] This might have satisfied Albany if it had been possible to make the agreement effective at once; but there is some reason to believe that his English treasons had turned his head, and that he expected far more than a restoration to the earldom of March and lordship of Annandale, and his office of Admiral of Scotland. In any case, he must have realised that Scheves, Avandale, and Argyll did not possess the military muscle to free the king from his half-uncles, and that without James III's approval, internal Scottish political settlements were worthless. So there may be some truth in Edward Hall's statement that on 3 August, in spite of the restoration settlement of the previous day, Albany pledged himself secretly to Gloucester to abide by the terms of the treaty of Fotheringhay — that is, to make himself king with English aid.[25]

Such an agreement, if it was made, may simply reflect Albany's desire to keep his options open. He may also have felt that he should give Gloucester some assurance of his continuing loyalty to Edward IV in order to speed the departure of his embarrassing allies from Edinburgh. In practical terms, however, it was the city of Edinburgh which paid the price to see the back of Gloucester and his huge army. On 4 August the provost, Walter Bertram, together with the merchants, burgesses, and community of the burgh, promised that if the Rothesay — Cecilia marriage was no longer to take place, they would refund all the dowry money already paid to the Scots in yearly instalments — a staggering 8,000 marks sterling, the equivalent of about £16,000 Scots.[26] This agreement also left it to the English king to decide whether he wanted the marriage or the refund of the money. Not surprisingly, Edward IV opted for the latter. He wanted his money back; he had no further use for the marriage of Rothesay to his daughter; and he may still have had visions of fulfilling the terms of the treaty of Fotheringhay and making Albany his son-in-law.

The withdrawal of the English from Edinburgh, some time between 4 and 11 August, left Albany to resolve for himself the complex Scottish political crisis. He had negotiated a settlement with currently the least influential of the opposing parties, the triumvirate of Scheves, Avandale, and Argyll. But the real key to control of the government lay either in Edinburgh or Stirling castles. In the former, the Stewart half-uncles, possessing both the king and the royal seals, had no need of an accommodation with Albany. The attraction of Stirling lay partly in the fact that the exchequer audit had been transferred there from Edinburgh sometime between 20 June and 29 August,[26a] probably on account of the Lauder crisis; and partly — perhaps mostly — because in Stirling the duke could negotiate with Margaret of Denmark and her son Rothesay, the nine-year-old heir to James III's throne. So Albany went to Stirling, probably in late August or early September, lending some respectability to his position by taking his temporary allies, Scheves, Avandale, and Argyll, with him. It was in this context that the young Duke of Rothesay came face-to-face for the first time with the realities of Scottish politics from which he had so far been shielded.

Albany's association with the queen is described in three separate sources — Sabadino's eulogy of Queen Margaret, which was completed in 1492, and the much later histories of John Lesley and Giovanni Ferreri. Giovanni Sabadino, although much the nearest in time to the events which he is describing, makes the impossible statement that James III was seized 'with the consent of his brother and of the Queen' and subsequently that he was released 'through the agency of his brother, who had caused his imprisonment for the security of the Kingdom'. Sabadino's sources were probably a combination of expatriate Scots and Danes, his information hearsay; but his account reflects Albany's efforts to improve his lot in 1482 by negotiating with the queen.[27] Lesley's version of events, dating from 1568–70, contains a wealth of circumstantial detail. 'The Duik of Albany', we are told, 'the Archebischop of St Androis, the Chauncellar, the Erle of Argyle with certane utheris, passit to Striveling, and vissyit the Quene and Prince; quhare be the counsall of the Quene takin thair, the Duik returnit secretlye to Edinburgh and seiget the castell, quhill thay wer constraynit for want of victuallis to rander the same to the Duik, and sua put the King to libertie, and his servantis quha war haldin in ward.' Thereupon 'the Erle of Argyle, the Archebischop of St Androis, the Chancellar and utheris quha wer in Striveling, hereing thairof, throw gret feir fled into thair awin cuntreyis.'[28] Finally Ferreri, whose account of the reign was published in 1574 and who follows Lesley in many details, adds the information that Albany spent some of his time at Stirling discussing the proper education for the prince. When, on the queen's advice, he returned to Edinburgh to lay siege to the castle and free the king, Ferreri tells us that the castle was held by the Earl of Atholl, the eldest of the Stewart half-uncles.[29]

Fortunately we possess some contemporary evidence which corroborates the part played by Margaret of Denmark in her husband's eventual release, and which suggests that the chroniclers' tales of Albany's Stirling visit are broadly accurate.[30] However, the entire episode raises as many questions as it answers. Why did Albany and King James's displaced counsellors think that the queen might have any real influence in securing the release of James III from Edinburgh castle? In what capacity did Albany discuss his nephew's future education? Above all, why did Scheves, Avandale, and Argyll flee to their own estates on hearing of the king's release, as this was presumably their primary aim throughout the crisis?

Answers to these three questions must necessarily be speculative, but the evidence, slim though it is, would appear to point in one direction. First, Albany, Scheves, Avandale, and Argyll had already negotiated the duke's restoration to his estates and offices at the beginning of August; so their objective in visiting Stirling must have been to secure something more than this. On two issues they could all publicly agree, namely that the person of the heir to the throne must be secured in time of crisis, and that steps must be taken to free the king. The latter objective required the queen's support because Margaret of Denmark had been entrusted with the custody of Edinburgh castle more than five years before, and it was her salaried keeper, John Stewart, Lord Darnley, who appears to have had access to James III during his imprisonment by his half-uncles Atholl, Buchan, and the bishop-elect of Moray.[31] Privately, however, Albany can only have been interested in his brother's release in circumstances which would allow him control of the king, for a liberated James III restored to full power might be expected to react violently against the duke's very recent English treasons. On the other hand, Albany may have reasoned that the king might be deposed or murdered. In either case, his own safety and advancement lay in hedging his bets. So he renewed his acquaintance with his former steward in the earldom of March, Sir James Liddale of Halkerston, who was at the Stirling audit on 2 September as Ranger of Yarrow; and shortly afterwards despatched Liddale south to the court of the duke's patron Edward IV on an unspecified errand,[31a] but one which was surely connected with Albany's aspirations in Scotland. Meantime the duke himself would take the part of protector of Margaret of Denmark and her children.

Such a role would provide a plausible answer to the second question: young Rothesay's education was Albany's business as a potential lieutenant-general, the effective ruler of Scotland during his brother's imprisonment — or, if James III were done away with, lieutenant-general for the nine-year-old prince who would automatically become James IV. We know from Albany's behaviour later in the autumn that he aspired to be accepted in full parliament as lieutenant-general[32] — that is, as the individual exercising regal powers during the minority, incapacity, or absence of the king. Indeed, there were excellent precedents within the first century of Stewart government for such powers being assumed by those close in blood to the king. With the consent of the three estates, regal authority had been granted to, or taken by, John, earl of Carrick for the ageing

Robert II in 1384; Robert, earl of Fife for the infirm Carrick in 1388; David, duke of Rothesay for Robert III (the former Carrick) in 1399; Fife again, now Duke of Albany, for the absent James I in 1406; and Archibald, 5th earl of Douglas, for the eight-year-old James II in 1438.[33] Clearly Albany reckoned that if he had the right backing, the estates could be induced to appoint him lieutenant-general, with James III shorn of executive authority and — in Professor Duncan's memorable phrase about Robert II in similar circumstances — 'given statutory notice of redundancy.' In fact, Albany came very close to achieving this aim in the parliament of December 1482; and from the start, he had both an excellent pedigree for the job as the nearest adult male in blood to James III, and an appalling blot on his record, his abortive attempt to seize the throne with English aid.

It seems likely that Albany had private conversations with the queen about his future role in relation to both her husband and her eldest son, and that, in the course of these, he bargained for the office of lieutenant-general in return for freeing James III from Edinburgh castle. Then, on the queen's advice, he went to Edinburgh and laid siege to the castle with the assistance of John Dundas of that ilk, the new provost of Edinburgh, Patrick Baron, and 'the whole community' of the burgh.[34] Significantly, Scheves, Avandale, and Argyll do not seem to have been involved in the siege. According to Lesley, they were still in Stirling when they heard the news of James III's liberation.[35] If so, this would provide us with an answer to the third question, the reason for their flight at this point. They fled because Albany had abandoned them, had in fact done a deal with the Stewart half-uncles to share power with them; and there was no place for King James's displaced counsellors in the new government.

The exact nature of this deal is the great enigma of the 1482 crisis. We know that Edinburgh castle was besieged by Albany and the king was freed, probably on 29 September.[36] Considerably later, on 7 October, James III sent a letter to John Stewart, Lord Darnley, ordering him to hand over the castle to the eldest of the royal half-uncles, John Stewart, earl of Atholl; and a fortnight later still, he granted a remission to Darnley and the garrison of sixty-six in terms which make clear that James had feared for his life in the early days of his imprisonment. On 16 November, the king granted the city of Edinburgh two charters, one confirming its property, the other granting the burgh the privilege of holding its own sheriff courts, specifically for the community's assistance in his liberation.[37] Finally, the parliament which was intended to settle the crisis and legitimise the new government met on 2 December[38] — which means that, allowing 40 days' notice, it must have been summoned immediately after Lord Darnley had received a remission for himself and his Edinburgh garrison on 19 October.

This sequence of facts suggests strongly that the siege of Edinburgh castle at the end of September was neither a long-drawn-out nor dramatic affair; Albany arrived, made a show of strength, and the half-uncles, after bargaining for leading positions in the new administration, released James III to the duke. Probably they all then adjourned down the royal mile to Holyrood — with the exception of Lord Darnley, who may have feared that the new government might try to make him a scapegoat for the king's imprisonment, and refused to emerge with his garrison until he received a remission for all of them on 19 October. In all this, it is the role of Lord Darnley which requires explaining; for Darnley was Margaret of Denmark's man, charged with, and paid for, the keepership of Edinburgh castle throughout the period of the crisis.[39] We cannot be certain that he was personally present in the castle when James III was seized at Lauder on or about 22 July, for Darnley was Warden of the West Marches[40] and obviously had duties elsewhere. But at the latest he must have arrived in Edinburgh shortly after the crisis broke, and thereafter seems to have played the part of mediator between a terrified King James and his Stewart half-uncles. With Darnley in Edinburgh castle, Margaret of Denmark may already have opened negotiations through him with her husband's captors, to the extent that the siege of the castle and King James's liberation may have been a foregone conclusion, a formality for which Albany may have bargained to present himself in a better light to the Scottish political community.

Alternatively, the queen's collusion with the Stewart half-uncles may have been much closer than long-distance negotiation after the Lauder crisis. This is suggested by an isolated entry in the Exchequer Rolls concerning the keeper of Stirling castle, James Shaw of Sauchie, who had already spent more than a decade in royal administration, first as Comptroller (1471–6) and in the later 'seventies as Chamberlain of Crown lands near Stirling.[41] In February 1488 he would become notorious as the individual who allowed Prince James to leave Stirling castle and join the rebels against James III. Shaw's role in the crisis of 1482, though less dramatic, is no less suggestive; for he is named as one of those supplying Edinburgh castle with corn, cabbage, meal, and barley during the king's residence there from 24 July 1482[42] — that is, from two days after King James's seizure at Lauder. Taken together with the defence of Edinburgh castle by Lord Darnley, this association of Shaw, a man very close to Margaret of Denmark at Stirling, with the Stewart half-uncles from the very earliest stage of James III's imprisonment in Edinburgh castle strongly suggests the queen's vital political role from the outset, and strikingly anticipates Sabadino's remarks a decade later that King James was seized with the consent of the queen, and that after his release the king 'reposed more hatred than previously in the Queen, because of her consent to his arrest.'[43]

Sabadino does not appear to have had any knowledge of Scottish affairs beyond what he could understand of the information supplied by his Scottish and Danish sources, with the result that he makes some glaring errors.[44] However, his overall thesis — that the king was imprisoned so that he might mend his ways, that the queen required throughout the crisis that government should be carried on in her husband's name — which implies that she would not countenance his deposition — and that the king was ultimately released by Albany — fits the scanty official evidence of the events of the crisis very well. 1482, though complicated by a major English invasion, was essentially a royal Stewart crisis based on a combination of fear of, and resentment towards, the person of James III. That he survived at all was partly due to the fact that the major Stewart power group — the half-uncles and Albany — had very different ideas as to their respective roles in any new government. The half-uncles' combination of fear and ambition had gained them the royal seals and a claim to the primacy of the Scottish church; yet when James III had been released and the parliament of December 1482 should have put an end to the crisis, all that emerged from the estates was a lukewarm recommendation, soon withdrawn, that the king should 'speke to his bruthir the duke of albany to take apone him to be lieutennant generale of the Realme.'[45] The wily king was not slow to realise that support for his brother in such a key role was weak — apart from anything else the estates may not have relished paying Albany the lieutenant-general's fee — and his response to the parliamentary admonition was to do nothing, to wait until an upsurge of loyalty to himself as king made it possible to recover full power. Albany unintentionally speeded up this royalist recovery by engaging in an abortive coup early in January 1483; by the end of the same month King James was strong enough to bring back many royalists into government and summon a parliament to Edinburgh for 1 March. By this time Albany, a feckless conspirator, had reverted to his English treasons and lost the support of all but a few hard-liners, Buchan, Angus, and Gray; and his tenuous position in Scotland collapsed with the death of his principal supporter and potential overlord, Edward IV, on 9 April 1483. Long before July, when yet another parliament at Edinburgh at last pronounced sentence of forfeiture on the duke, the crisis of 1482–3 was over.[46]

Over — but not forgotten. To those who had been directly involved, life could not easily be the same again. James III emerged from the experience if anything more aloof and suspicious than before; of his three displaced counsellors of 1482, only Argyll wholly recovered favour, being made Chancellor in place of Avandale, who lost the office after an unbroken 22 years in it. William Scheves, the embattled archbishop of St Andrews, retained his see but lost much of the royal favour, some of which was transferred to Dr John Ireland, leaving Scheves to fight a rearguard action in support of the dignity of his office for the remaining fourteen years of his life. On the side of the opposition, its leader Albany had forfeited not only his lands — the earldom of March and lordship of Annandale — but also his credibility within these lands. His return to the West March with the long forfeited ninth earl of Douglas in the summer of 1484 produced only a violent reaction against him at Lochmaben, and his flight to France proved final, as he was killed in a tournament in Paris in 1485 by the future Louis XII, who a generation later was also to be indirectly responsible for the death of Albany's nephew James IV. Most of the other opponents of the king — the half-uncles, Angus, and Gray — suffered only modest punishment — Buchan was exiled for three years — or were not penalised at all;[47] but none of them can have felt optimistic about the future, for James III not only introduced an ominous Treasons Act in 1484, but showed no inclination to abandon his pursuit of former Albany supporters as the years went by — William, Lord Crichton, John Liddale, and David Purves, together with Crichton's younger brothers and the 35-strong garrison of Crichton castle were all forfeited in February 1484,[48] and as late as May 1485 James Gifford of Sheriffhall, who had taken part in Albany's attempted comeback the previous year, suffered the same fate.[49] Finally, in September 1485 Albany's messenger to England during the crisis, James Liddale of Halkerston, who had been forfeited together with the duke in July 1483, was captured, incarcerated in the Tolbooth of Edinburgh, and executed shortly afterwards.[50] He was the only prominent Albany supporter to pay with his life for his consistent loyalty to the duke; but his death can only have added to the alarm of those whose English treasons in 1482 were well known to the king, but who — like Angus and Gray — had been neither pardoned nor punished.

For the nine-year old heir to the throne, the crisis of 1482 had shattered the calm of his youthful existence at Stirling. Royal government had come to him with a vengeance in the person of his uncle Albany, his father's counsellors, and the displaced officials making their annual exchequer returns. He must have been aware that if James III were killed, he would have become king with Albany as lieutenant-general; and that even if his father survived, something for which Margaret of Denmark was clearly negotiating,[51] effective government would be in the hands of others headed by Albany. We cannot know Rothesay's reaction to the sudden prospect that he might replace his father sooner rather than later; but we cannot doubt that that prospect was brought forcibly to his attention at Stirling in the late summer of 1482, or that it was uppermost in his mind six years later.

Between early September 1482 and 2 February 1488, we again lose sight of Rothesay in official records. There appear to have been no further visits to Edinburgh for the prince and his mother, and though Sabadino's remark that James III was unwilling ever to see Margaret of Denmark again, because of her role in the events of 1482, is an exaggerated distortion of the facts, it does reflect the physical distance between the king in Edinburgh and Queen Margaret with her sons in Stirling for the remaining four years of her life. Yet if King James had become estranged from his wife on account of her association with Albany — by no means an unlikely supposition with one considers the king's appalling relations with other members of his family — he does not appear to have done anything practical about it. As far as we know, the queen retained control of her sons' education until she died in 1486, and the keeper of Stirling castle, James Shaw of Sauchie, remained unchanged even after her death. So if we are to find any overt hostility to his son and heir on the part of James III, we must look for it elsewhere, most probably his English diplomacy.

The rapid English political changes within the three years 1483–6, which saw the collapse of the Yorkist dynasty and the accession of the first Tudor, worked to the advantage of the Scottish king. A weak central government in England made it much easier for James III to revert to his policy of the 1470s, seeking peace and alliance with England while looking for the recovery of both Dunbar and Berwick, lost in 1482. Initially the Duke of Rothesay figured prominently in his father's plans, being named as the intended bridegroom in a marriage agreement following the conclusion of a three-year Anglo-Scottish truce at Nottingham in September 1484; the English bride was to be Anne de la Pole, niece of King Richard III, and as the marriage was to take place within the three years of the truce, it was clearly intended that it should form part of a longer and firmer peace to be concluded in the near future.[52] However, the truce had run for only eleven months when Richard III was killed at Bosworth and the Nottingham agreements were rendered obsolete. Yet the succession of Henry VII in 1485 gave James III a chance to make his foreign policy really effective; for in King Henry he was dealing with a usurper enjoying little security within his own country, acutely concerned about the possibility of Yorkist rebels finding a refuge in Scotland, and seeking a firm peace with the Scottish king as an important factor in ensuring his own survival.[53]

The advent of the Tudor dynasty was fortuitous for James III, who was able to recover Dunbar castle in the winter of 1485–6 without any protest from Henry VII,[54] and who could press ahead confidently with schemes for closer ties with England.[55] The first manifestation of the Scottish king's moves towards a new alliance with King Henry was however ominous for his son and heir. On 3 July 1486 a three year Anglo-Scottish truce was agreed by both sides as the forerunner of a projected long truce, and at the same time a marriage alliance was mooted between James III's second son, James, marquis of Ormonde, and Katharine, the fourth surviving daughter of Edward IV.[56] This agreement suggests that the Scottish king was deliberately slighting the heir to the throne in favour of his second son; for there survive no proposals to marry Rothesay elsewhere in Europe, in spite of the fact that he was already thirteen — three years older than Ormonde — and had already been the prospective bridegroom in the Anglo-Scottish peaces of 1474 and 1484. Worse still, in November 1487 a further agreement again emphasised the Ormonde-Katharine marriage as a means of extending the Anglo-Scottish truce; and further marriages were to be arranged between James III — now a widower — and Elizabeth Woodville, widow of Edward IV, and between Rothesay and an unspecified daughter of the same king.[57] These arrangements may have appeared ominous to the young heir to the throne because his brother's marriage assumed greater importance than his own in the negotiations — indeed, if Ormonde married Katharine, there remained no daughter of Edward IV available for Rothesay[58] — and because his father was contemplating remarriage in England, with all that that might mean for his future. His mother, Margaret of Denmark, had died within a fortnight of her husband's first truce with Henry VII; and the young Duke of Rothesay, continuing to live in Stirling without her guidance and without his father showing any interest in involving him in the business of government, may well have viewed James III's deliberate promotion of his younger brother — the 1486 and 1487 marriage proposals, followed by the conferring on Ormonde of the dukedom of Ross in January 1488 [59] — with growing apprehension. We cannot know why King James acted in this way. After all, his three sons had all been brought up at Stirling under the tutelage of their mother, so that even if the king had resented Queen Margaret's involvement in the 1482 crisis, there was no reason to prefer one of the boys to either of the others, for all three had fallen under her influence. Firm evidence is of course lacking; but it may be that James III's suspicion and distrust of his heir arose from the latter's association with Albany in 1482. However innocent that meeting may have been from the then nine-year-old prince's point of view, the fact that Rothesay had become aware so early in life of his father's obvious fallibility may have influenced the king against him. If so, then his position — isolated from government in Stirling as he entered adolescence — made him an obvious focus for widespread and growing discontent.

For the truth was that, although he had emerged as the victor of the crisis of 1482–3, James III had failed to resolve the problems which had provoked it. Worse still, he seemed to be unaware of the fact that his arbitrary behaviour was losing him support in many areas of the country. In some respects, therefore, Scottish politics of the 1480s is rather like a re-run of the 1470s. The king, rapidly recovering his confidence after 1483, seems to have believed that diplomatic successes abroad made secure his position at home. Thus he could congratulate himself on his negotiations with the new pope Innocent VIII, which produced not only a coveted symbol of papal favour, the Golden Rose, in 1486, but also the papal indult of April 1487, which when vacancies occurred in major Scottish benefices gave the king eight months to petition on behalf of candidates of his choice, and made the recent disputed elections at Glasgow and Dunkeld much less likely in the future.[60] Likewise the accession of Henry VII in England had made possible the peace negotiations of 1486 and 1487, the recapture of Dunbar castle, and the possibility of the recovery of Berwick.

But such ephemeral successes seem to have blinded James III to the fact that only the support of the majority of the Scottish political community was of any lasting value to him as King of Scots. Far from seeking this by endeavouring to distribute royal patronage in a more effective way, he seems to have gone out of his way to alienate a large number of powerful men. This is most clearly seen in what proved to be the last two parliaments of the reign, in October 1487 and January 1488.[61] In the first of these, the king launched what he clearly intended to be his final assault on the Humes, who had been intermittently opposing King James's schemes to suppress the priory of Coldingham and reallocate its revenues to the chapel royal for some fifteen years. Confident in his recent successes with Pope Innocent VIII, the king chose to ignore that the same pope had recently confirmed John Hume as prior of Coldingham, and therefore had adopted no consistent position in the dispute.[62] However, James III was determined to make an issue of it, and he moved swiftly from threats to parliamentary action. Thus in October he warned his lieges not to attempt to oppose his 'union and erection' of Coldingham to his chapel royal; if they did, they would be guilty of treason and forfeited. By the following January, he was summoning unspecified temporal persons to answer for committing the treasons he had warned against, and by the end of the month appointing a hopelessly cumbrous committee of fifty — almost two-thirds of the membership of the parliament — to proceed against those who had broken the Coldingham statute.[63] There was no need to name the principal offenders; the Humes — John, still tenaciously styling himself prior of Coldingham, his brothers George of Aytoun and Patrick of Fastcastle, and their nephew Alexander, Master of Hume — were all conspicuous by their absence from both parliaments. Their defiance of the king was not however ill-considered, for they had powerful kin and friends. As recently as 29 October 1486 the Master of Hume had made a bond of manrent with George, earl of Huntly, the most powerful north-eastern magnate.[64] The Humes were not only the neighbours of the Hepburns, Lords Hailes, but also closely related to them for almost forty years,[65] and from 8 August, Patrick, Lord Hailes, had been elected Lord Provost of Edinburgh.[66] The Hepburns in their turn had intermarried, with the Montgomeries of Ayrshire;[67] and Hugh, second Lord Montgomery, one of the principal western rebels of 1488, was married to Helen, third daughter of Colin Campbell, first earl of Argyll, James III's Chancellor, a magnate whose service to the Crown throughout the reign was unparalleled, but who would also turn against the king in 1488.[68] It is probably significant that James Shaw of Sauchie, Rothesay's keeper in Stirling castle, married his daughter Helen to Patrick Hume of Polwarth about this time,[69] and may well have felt that James III's assault on the Humes was a threat to himself, especially after his equivocal behaviour in 1482. In short, in attacking the Humes, the king was forcing their allies and kin — in the north-east, in the west, the south, in Edinburgh and Stirling — to make a stark choice: either they joined the crown in condemning the Humes, or they ran the risk of forfeiting their lives, lands, and goods.

In normal circumstances, the choice for all of them would have been easy. Conflicts between the crown and magnates who were regarded by their peers as having acquired too much power — the Livingstons in the 1440s, the Boyds in the late 1460s, and above all the Black Douglases in the 1450s — were all ultimately resolved by the king and the majority of the politically active nobility combining to attack the families concerned. As the ultimate source of the most lucrative patronage in Scotland, the monarch was obviously worth supporting; the hazards of rebellion were enormous; and underpinning such self-interest was the conservatism of the Scottish political community, which had ensured that the Stewart dynasty had survived and grown in strength in spite of royal incompetence, absence, or minority throughout much of its first hundred years.

Early in 1488, however, circumstances were far from normal. James III was not after all threatening an over-mighty family with the ultimate penalty. Indeed, he had reason to be grateful to the Humes for supporting him during the latter stages of the crisis of 1482–3;[70] and the intermittent contest with one of the Hume family over the future of Coldingham was something which the majority of the political community probably regarded as punishable by the warding of John Hume for a time, possibly fining him heavily for his misuse of royal letters at the Roman curia. But the royal response to this — after fifteen years of relative inaction — of threatening the entire family, their

kin and supporters, with forfeiture, was excessive; and the king was unwise
to attempt to proceed, in January 1488, beyond the threats he had made
three months before. For the truth was that the politically divisive events
of 1482 were still fresh in everyone's minds; an adult Stewart king *could*
be removed from government and imprisoned; the principal officers of state
and household *could* be changed without his consent. Faced with the choice
forced on them by an unsatisfactory ruler's sustained aggression, therefore,
the Hepburns, Montgomeries, and — eventually — the earl of Argyll threw
in their lot with the Humes; James Shaw of Sauchie released the heir to the
throne, who promptly joined them; and Huntly in the end remained neutral,
an attitude which in its own way was a serious indictment of James III.

The spectre of 1482 also plagued the king's efforts to build up a party
of effective royalists; for in some cases he had no alternative but to rely on
the men who had been found wanting during that crisis. Thus Andrew, Lord
Avandale, was replaced as Chancellor by Argyll; but Argyll's role in 1482–3
had been an equivocal one, and the king's suspicions of him may have led
to his removal from office in February 1488. Likewise Archbishop Scheves,
closer than anyone else to King James in the 1470s, had proved something of
a broken reed in 1482; indeed, the crisis of that year had been provoked in part
by a general desire to see Scheves deposed. But he was still James III's man,
and the king had no alternative but to support him in the mid-'eighties. Worse
still, Scheves' embassy to Rome in the winter of 1486–7 saw him transact not
only the king's business, but also his own: James III secured the indult from
Pope Innocent VIII, while the see of St Andrews was granted primatial status
— a move calculated to alienate not only Scheves' fellow ambassador and rival,
Robert Blacader, bishop of Glasgow, but also to upset other bishops within the
Scottish church hierarchy, including Brown of Dunkeld and Stewart of Moray.[71]
Forced by the Hume crisis of 1487–8 to declare their political allegiance, Blacader
and Brown opted for the rebel cause, while Moray, the king's half-uncle, who had
been on the wrong side in 1482, continued to lend cautious support to James
III. Events were soon to show that he had miscalculated again.

One prominent 'political' bishop who had not soiled his hands in the
more sordid events of 1482 and their aftermath was William Elphinstone
of Aberdeen.[72] To some extent he owed his advancement in the 'seventies
to Scheves' patronage; unquestionably his academic training — at Glasgow,
Louvain, Paris, and Orleans — had made him the most outstanding canon
and civil lawyer in Scotland; and his willingness to endure the drudgery of
acting successively as official of Glasgow and Lothian, serving as an auditor
or on the Lords of Council, eventually produced the medieval civil servant's
ultimate reward — a bishopric, though it was only that of Ross, hardly wealthy
or influential. Indeed, Ross was heavily encumbered with the debts owed to
the Apostolic Camera by Elphinstone's predecessor, John Wodman, and in his
two years (1481–3) as 'elect and confirmed' of Ross,[73] Elphinstone was never
consecrated as bishop. Further service to the crown, however, brought him
within reach of a far greater reward — the bishopric of Aberdeen, vacant on

the translation of Robert Blacader to Glasgow in March 1483. However, the same problem beset Elphinstone in Aberdeen as in Ross — his predecessor's debts to Rome, in this case Blacader's, had not been discharged, so that both bishops could not be consecrated for a further five years.

Elphinstone, already 52 when he was nominated to Aberdeen, was well treated by James in the years after 1483 — as was Blacader — for the king allowed both bishops to receive the temporalities of their sees even before their respective consecrations, although these should have fallen to the crown between 1483 and 1488, when both Aberdeen and Glasgow dioceses were technically vacant. Furthermore, James III wrote frequently and vigorously to Rome on behalf of both men, protecting them from the excommunication which they might incur for failure to pay their common services, though failing in the end to have the Apostolic Camera remit the payments.[74] Blacader might well have remained a royalist out of gratitude for the king's support had relations not become soured through Scheves' advancement to the primacy in 1487; but Elphinstone was a different case altogether. Throughout the complex diplomatic negotiations with England between 1483 and 1487, he had acted as ambassador for James III, and had represented the Scottish king at Henry VII's coronation;[75] when not abroad on diplomatic service, Elphinstone was consistently to be found witnessing royal charters, sitting on the Lords of Council, and acting as an auditor of exchequer. Like his fellow ambassador to England, John Ramsay, Lord Bothwell, a familiar of James III, Elphinstone appears to have been one of the very few who had the king's total trust in the 1480s. The early months of 1488 seemed to herald an annus mirabilis for him; in February, he was made Chancellor by the king, in March the dispute over undischarged payments to Rome were at last settled, and in April James III was personally present at Elphinstone's consecration as Bishop of Aberdeen in St Machar's Cathedral.[76]

Elphinstone and Bothwell were committed royalists whose careers eventually suffered a drastic setback by the course of events in 1488; but they were something of an exception to the rule that James III was heavily reliant on men whose attitudes to him were equivocal, and whose roles in 1482 had ranged from the questionable to the overtly treasonable. Prominent among these were his half-uncles, Atholl, Buchan, and Andrew, bishop of Moray, his Edinburgh gaolers in 1482. King James's recovery from that crisis seems to have given all three an exaggerated view of the strength of his position, for they all emerged as royalists in 1488. Their support was a mixed blessing for the king, for such evidence as there is suggests that he had to woo them to his side with an uncharacteristic distribution of money and favours.[77]

The Stewart half-uncles were northerners; it was however in the south that the king was most vulnerable, having few supporters of note, and many potential or real enemies, throughout the Marches; and perversely it was in this area that he launced his main offensive to show to his own subjects, and possibly also to foreign observers, that he intended to enforce his will on the localities. Thus it is no accident that the last two parliaments of the reign — in October 1487 and January 1488 — witnessed the attendance of a number of southern

lairds who had never come to parliament before, and would not come again —
Kilpatrick of Closeburn, Murray of Cockpool, Charteris of Amisfield, Dunbar
of Cumnock, Rutherford of that ilk, and Scott of Buccleuch, with Douglas of
Cavers making an isolated appearance in the latter parliament.[78] The south-west
was an area which lacked the presence of any dominant magnate to impose firm
rule and settle feuds, while in the middle and eastern Marches lairds were liable
to be influenced by the physical proximity of the greater magnates, above all the
Hepburns and Humes. So the presence in parliament of these families at this
time may be interpreted either as an effort to defend their own local interests
— they were afraid *not* to be there — or their response to coercion by the
king, or perhaps a combination of both. James III, having failed to show a
personal interest in the south for much of his adult rule, suddenly abandoned
his indolence and threatened to bring law and order to the country with a
vengeance. The first ten enactments of the October 1487 parliament and no
less than seven the following January, are concerned with the administration of
justice in the localities. They are of course expressed in very general terms; but
there is some reason to believe that they relate to specific problems of law and
order, and that in making them, the king was seeking to use parliament, rather
than the justice ayres which he had neglected throughout his personal rule, as
a means of settling feuds and making royal authority felt in the extremities of
his kingdom. It was a method liable not so much to bring disorder to an end as
to foment further trouble; for many of the feuds against which the estates had
fulminated in 1479 had been allowed to run their course without undue royal
interference — Lord Maxwell against Douglas of Drumlanrig in Nithsdale,
and against Murray of Cockpool in Annandale; the Rutherfords against the
Turnbulls in Teviotdale; and William Douglas of Cavers, sheriff of Teviotdale,
against James III's familiar, Crichton of Cranston, in the same area.[79] Now, in
a burst of energy, the king had determined to resolve his troubles in the south
— not by going there, but by insisting on his subjects' coming to parliament
in Edinburgh.

In the case of Cuthbert Murray of Cockpool, he may have been glad to
come; for he was unquestionably the underdog in the Maxwell-Murray feud,
and his rival John, Lord Maxwell, was present in the same parliament. On
the other hand, the king's ultimate support for Murray was bound to make
an enemy of Maxwell. In a rather different way, the experience of William
Douglas of Cavers sharply illustrates James III's inability to deal fairly or
even consistently with his more influential subjects.Thus on 13 October 1487
an act warned holders of regalities that they should not 'leif justice undone'
through showing favour to those who trespassed against royal justice.[80] This
act may have been directed against Douglas of Cavers, who made his solitary
parliamentary appearance on 29 January 1488, resigned his regality into the
king's hands, and did not immediately receive it back.[81] Clearly Douglas had
displeased King James, possibly through his association with 'trespassers' —
which could be a reference to his Hume neighbours — or perhaps because he
was related to Archibald, fifth earl of Angus, a prominent rebel in 1482–3. Yet

a few months later, on 24 May, the king, having reached a critical stage in the rebellion of 1488, made a conditional regrant of Douglas of Cavers' regality.[82] Such wilful and inconsistent behaviour was unlikely to produce enthusiastic supporters of the king in time of crisis.

The imminence of that crisis is apparent from the king's actions in the parliament of January 1488, which had as its principal business the extension of royal control over the administration of justice. Thus the legislation of October 1487 requiring litigants in civil cases to consult their judges ordinary, rather than appeal directly to the Lords of Council, was reversed, in order to avoid 'deferring of Justice to mony partiis'. This reversal of an act only three months old strongly suggests an effort by James III, faced by continuing defiance from the Humes and their allies, to win support in the localities; but his inconsistency is unlikely to have impressed potential supporters, while his interference probably alienated many holders of local jurisdictions. Likewise royal efforts in this parliament to improve the running of criminal justice must have come as an unwelcome shock. After eighteen years of personal indolence, James III proposed to drive the ayres as never before. He would not however go out on the ayres himself, but instead appoint Justiciars north and south of Forth, two in each region. Crawford and Huntly, earls with a good record of loyalty to the King, were appointed north of Forth; and parliament was invited to name candidates for the two posts south of Forth. Significantly the four names which they put forward were those of John Ramsay, Lord Bothwell, Robert, Lord Lyle, John Lyon, Lord Glamis, and John Drummond of Cargill,[84] the last about to be made a lord of parliament. In the months to come, these men would prove to be, respectively, a royalist, a rebel, a neutral, and a rebel. Their candidature, based as it was on parliamentary nomination, indicates that the king was becoming increasingly out of touch with large sections of the Scottish political community; and his announcement that he would send 'certane wise lordis and persons of his consale' out with the Justiciars to act as assessors[85] can hardly have been reassuring to that increasing number for whom the problem was their fear of the king himself.

Thus on the final day of the parliament — 29 January — we find James III publicly rewarding those who had been loyal in the past, and those whom he wished to conciliate for his earlier treatment of them. Four new lords of parliament were created — Crichton of Sanquhar, Drummond of Cargill, Hay of Yester, and Ruthven of that ilk — and three knights — David Kennedy, William Carlyle, and Robert Cunningham of Polmaise.[86] These devices to increase the number of committed royal supporters were only partially successful: the elevation of Crichton of Sanquhar alienated Lord Maxwell and helped to foster a major feud in the south-west, while that of Drummond of Cargill, undertaken no doubt to appease Drummond for the king's thrusting him out of the office of Steward of Strathearn in 1475, did not work, as Drummond became a rebel and a substantial beneficiary of the revolution of 1488.

In any event, the limited advantage which some of these creations might have given to the royalist party was far outweighed on the debit side by the results of James III's most important creation on 29 January. His second son James, already Marquis of Ormonde, Earl of Ross, and Lord of Brechin, was elevated to the dignities of Duke of Ross and Earl of Edirdale.[87] These new titles were no doubt intended to enhance Ross's status as the most important of the potential bridegrooms in the English alliance which the king had concluded just two months before; but they can only have been interpreted as a snub by the heir to the throne, now only a few weeks short of his fifteenth birthday. Four days after his younger brother's elevation, on 2 February 1488,[88] James, duke of Rothesay, left Stirling castle with its keeper, James Shaw of Sauchie, and without the king's knowledge or consent. Rothesay's first destination may have been Shaw's kinsmen, the rebel Humes; but in fact his movements over the next few months, until he is to be found back in Stirling late in May,[89] are uncertain. What is undeniable is that Rothesay's defection from Stirling on 2 February saw the start of a rebellion against his father far more serious than King James can have contemplated when he first moved to outlaw the Humes.

NOTES

1. *T.A.*, i, lxiv, n.2.
2. S.B. Chandler, 'An Italian Life of Margaret, Queen of James III', *S.H.R.*, xxxii (1952), 52–7, at p.56.
3. *Ibid.*, 57; Danske Rigsarkiv, T.K.U.A., Skotland, A.1, 1. The Danish reference is to a letter from King Hans of Denmark, Christian I's son and successor, to Prince James during the rebellion of 1488, in which the Danish king expresses great sorrow at the news he has received from Scotland, namely that his sister, Queen Margaret, has been poisoned by John Ramsay, and that in spite of the crime Ramsay is still retained as one of James III's closest advisers.
4. *T.A.*, i, xlv, n.1.
5. *R.M.S.*, ii, No. 1361. At the same time Queen Margaret was entrusted with the Castle of Edinburgh, though it seems unlikely that she lived there for any length of time.
6. *Rot. Scot.*, ii, 447. For a full discussion of the 1474 treaty and its aftermath, *see* Macdougall, *James III*, 115–118.
7. Cecilia, daughter of Edward IV, in 1474; Anne de la Pole, niece of Richard III, in 1484; and an unspecified younger daughter of Edward IV in 1487.
8. *T.A.*, i, 39–42.
9. *E.R.*, viii, 293, 403; ix, 55, 627.
10. Lesley, *History*, 39.
11. B.L. Royal MS. 17 Dxx, f.307v.
12. Ferreri, *Appendix to Boece*, f.397r.
13. *Ibid.*, f.396v.
14. For a full discussion of James III's attack on Albany, *see* Macdougall, *op. cit*, 128–130.
15. Donaldson, *Scottish Kings*, 111.
16. Pitscottie, *Historie*, i, 162.
17. *R.M.S.*, ii, No. 1426; Fraser, *Colquhoun*, ii, 197; *A.P.S.*, ii, 126 (for the dating

of the siege). J.H. Burns, 'New Light on John Major', *Innes Review*, v (1954), 83–100, at 84.

18. *A.P.S.*, ii, 128.

19. For the diplomatic background to the war of 1480–1482, *see* Macdougall, *op. cit*, 143–5.

20. P.R.O. Scots Doc. E 39/92 (38).

21. *Cal. Patent Rolls 1476–85*, 320.

22. The identities of those who seized King James at Lauder are discussed in Macdougall, *op. cit.*, 165–8. The king had certainly been lodged in Edinburgh castle by 24 July 1482: *E.R.*, ix, 436.

23. They may have been in command of that section of the Scottish host which Bishop Lesley locates at Haddington during the crisis: Lesley, *History*, 49.

24. Rymer, *Foedera*, xii, 160.

25. Hall, *Chronicle*, 334. It may be significant that some time after 2 September 1482, Albany sent his former steward, Sir James Liddale of Halkerston, as his ambassador to Edward IV of England, who paid Liddale £40 sterling. Liddale had returned to Albany at Dunbar castle by 30 December 1482: *E.R.*, ix, 187; *Cal. Docs. Scot.*, iv, No. 1478; *H.M.C. Rep. xii*, Pt. viii, App., 155–6.

26. Rymer, *Foedera*, xii, 161; Bain, *Cal. Docs. Scot.*, iv, No. 1480.

26a. *E.R.*, ix, 171, 180.

27. For Sabadino's text, and a discussion of his sources, *see* Chandler, op. cit., *S.H.R.*, xxxii (1952), 52–7.

28. Lesley, *History*, 50.

29. Ferreri, *Appendix to Boece*, f.396v.

30. NLS Dundas Chrs., B109 (a grant to John Dundas of that ilk for his services in liberating James III from Edinburgh Castle, made 'cum consensu et assensu carrissime consortis nostre Margarete Regine Scocie'); *E.R.*, ix, 213 (recording that Margaret of Denmark paid Lord Darnley £245 16/11d. for the custody of Edinburgh castle during exchequer year 1482-3).

31. *E.R.*, ix, 213 (for Darnley's payment as keeper); Fraser, *Lennox*, ii, 121–3 (a remission from James III to Lord Darnley and the Edinburgh garrison).

31a. *E.R.*, ix, 187 (for Liddale at Stirling in September 1482); *Cal. Docs. Scot.*, iv, No. 1478 (for Liddale's mission to England during Michaelmas Term 1482); Liddale was back in Scotland, at Albany's castle of Dunbar, by 30 December 1482: *H.M.C. Rep. xii*, Pt. viii, App., 155–6.

32. *A.P.S.*, ii, 143.

33. *A.P.S.*, i, 550, 555–6, 572; Bower, *Scotichronicon*, vol. 8, 64, 65; *A.P.S.*, ii, 31.

34. NLS Dundas Chrs., B 109; *Edinburgh City Chrs.*, 157.

35. Lesley, *History*, 50.

36. B.L. Royal MS. 17DXX f.308v. According to this contemporary account, the king was in the castle, 'fra the magdalyne day (22 July) quhill michaelmess' (29 September).

37. Lennox Chrs. No 80, printed in Fraser, *Lennox*, ii, 121; *ibid*, 121–3 (for the Darnley remission); *Edinburgh City Chrs.*, 157, 165.

38. *A.P.S.*, ii, 142.

39. *E.R.*, ix, 213.

40. *A.P.S.*, ii, 140.

41. *E.R.*, viii, ix, passim.

42. *Ibid.*, ix, 436.

43. *S.H.R.*, xxxii (1952), 52–7, at 55.

44. For example, he imagines that James III had been incarcerated in Edinburgh castle at the instance of Albany; and he suggests that the queen's third pregnancy was post-1482: *Ibid.*, 55.

45. *A.P.S.*, ii, 143.

46. For details of the crisis during the winter of 1482–3, see Macdougall, *James III*, 170–189.

47. *Ibid.*, 188–190, 198–199.

48. *A.P.S.*, ii, 161–4.

49. *Ibid.*, 173–4.

50. *Prot. Bk. Young.*, nos. 14, 15. Liddale was imprisoned in the Tolbooth on 7 September 1485. He was certainly dead by 12 July 1486 (*E.R.*, ix, 417).

51. Chandler, *op.cit.*, 55; Ferreri, *Appendix to Boece*, f.396v.

52. *Cal. Docs. Scot.*, iv, Nos. 1504, 1505.

53. Nicholson, *Later Middle Ages*, 518–9.

54. *E.R.*, ix, 433, 523. Dunbar was only covered by a six-months' truce in September 1484; but significantly a major assault on it does not appear to have been made by the Scots until after the accession of Henry VII.

55. An early manifestation of goodwill towards James III by Henry VII was the capture of the forfeited William Lord Crichton, early in October 1485, by Master (later Sir) Richard Nanfan; though by the following April, whether by accident or design, Crichton had escaped: *Nottingham Records*, iii (1485–1547), 262, 263–4.

56. *Rot, Scot.*, ii, 473–77.

57. *Rot. Scot.*, ii, 480.

58. For discussion of the various marriage options, see Macdougall, *James III*, 219–220.

59. *A.P.S.*, ii, 181.

60. *Cal. State Papers (Milan)*, i, 247; *C.P.L.*, xiv, 4. For the Glasgow and Dunkeld disputes, *see* Macdougall, *James III*, 222–5.

61. *A.P.S.*, ii, 175–184.

62. For a detailed discussion of the protracted Coldingham dispute, see Norman Macdougall, 'Crown Versus Nobility: The Struggle for the Priory of Coldingham, 1472–1488' in K.J. Stringer (ed.), *Essays on the Nobility of Medieval Scotland* (Edinburgh, 1985).

63. *A.P.S.*, ii, 179, 182, 184.

64. S.R.O. GD 44 13.9.23; *Spalding Miscellany*, iv, 184–5.

65. *Scots Peerage*, iv, 448.

66. *Edinburgh Burgh Records*, i, 52. Patrick, Lord Hailes, was to be the principal beneficiary of the revolution of 1488: *see below*, ch. 2.

67. *Scots Peerage*, iii, 432.

68. *Ibid.*, 435.

69. *E.R.*, x, 2–3; *Scots Peerage*, iv, 336.

70. Macdougall, *James III*, 178–9.

71. For details, see Macdougall, *op.cit.*, 227–230. Scheves had recently survived investigation for non-payment of annates to Rome by a papal legate, James Pasarella, bishop of Imola. Brown of Dunkeld had been elected against James III's wishes in 1483, and Stewart of Moray had attempted to replace Scheves in 1482.

72. Elphinstone has been fortunate in his biographers: his contemporary and first Principal of his University of Aberdeen, Hector Boece, wrote a eulogy of his patron in *Murchlacensium et Aberdonensium Episcoporum Vitae* (1522), ed. J. Moir (New Spalding Club, *Lives of the Bishops of Mortlach and Aberdeen*, Aberdeen, 1894); and much more recently, Leslie Macfarlane's magisterial study of the bishop and his times: L.J. Macfarlane, *William Elphinstone and the Kingdom of Scotland, 1431–1514* (Aberdeen, 1985).

73. Macfarlane, *Elphinstone*, 79.

74. *Ibid*, 131, 191–2.

75. *Rot. Scot*, ii, 461, 462, 464, 469, 480–1; *Bannatyne Miscellany*, ii, 37–40.

76. *R.M.S.*, ii, No. 1707; Macfarlane, *Elphinstone*, 192.

77. *See below*, Chapter 2.

78. *A.P.S.*, ii, 175, 181.

79. *A.P.S.*, ii, 122; Fraser, *Carlaverock*, i, 159–160 (for the Maxwell-Murray feud).
80. *A.P.S.*, ii, 176.
81. *Ibid.*, 181.
82. *H.M.C. Rep. vii*, App., 729.
83. *A.P.S.*, ii, 183.
84. *Ibid.*, 182.
85. *Ibid.*
86. *Ibid.*, 181.
87. *Ibid.*
88. *Ibid.*, 223.
89. S.R.O. RH 1/1/3.

2

The Reluctant Regicide

No contemporary evidence survives for Rothesay's motives in throwing in his lot with the rebels early in February 1488, but the sixteenth-century chroniclers provide a wealth of wisdom acquired through hindsight, the knowledge that the prince would not only become king but rule successfully for a quarter of a century. Thus there is unanimous praise for Rothesay. According to Bishop Lesley, the rebels were attempting to reform the government through the removal of wicked counsellors about the king, a highly conventional motive in medieval — and later — historical literature; in spite of these laudable aims, however, Lesley suggests that they had to compel the heir to the throne to side with them.[1] Ferreri follows a similar line, praising the prince's benign nature and his reluctance to rebel, and more plausibly remarks that Shaw of Sauchie was persuaded to hand him over to lend respectability to the revolt.[2] Buchanan makes the same points, adding that the rebels saw Rothesay as a suitable regent once James III had been defeated[3] — an unlikely attitude in view of the prince's youth, and one which probably reflects the political events of the chronicler's own day, when a series of regents ran the government following the deposition of Mary, Queen of Scots.

Surprisingly, it is the most fanciful of the sixteenth-century chroniclers, Robert Lindsay of Pitscottie, writing in the late 1570s, who probably comes closest to explaining Rothesay's motives for rebelling. As usual, Pitscottie provides a wealth of highly coloured detail on 1488, claiming as his source David, Lord Lindsay of Byres, who had fought at Sauchieburn on James III's side. Essentially his story is that the prince's defection from Stirling was a matter of self-preservation, as he had heard that his father was approaching with a large army to imprison him. The warning of King James's approach was brought to Shaw of Sauchie by a messenger from the (unspecified) rebels, who had some difficulty in persuading Shaw to release the prince to them and thereafter keep the castle in the prince's name against James III. Ultimately Shaw was moved not simply by argument but also by bribery, and the rebels took Rothesay to Linlithgow, where they issued proclamations justifying what they had done. The lieges were summoned to muster at Linlithgow to defend the prince against King James, who intended to deal with young Rothesay as he had dealt with his brother, the Duke of Albany.[4]

We can discount some of Pitscottie's detail as confused or fictional. It is highly unlikely that James III was aware of his son's defection from Stirling until weeks after it had happened, though Pitscottie's story that the king was approaching Stirling with an army to seize the prince would fit the final stages of the crisis, in early June. Likewise there must be considerable doubt as to the amount of pressure necessary to persuade Shaw of Sauchie to give up his young charge to the rebels — probably not very much. On the other hand, Linlithgow is quite a likely location for the rebel army in view of the speed with which they were able to reach Blackness later in the crisis. But the fascinating part of Pitscottie's story lies in his comment that the rebels issued proclamations following their removal of the prince to Linlithgow, for assuredly they must have done this. No written justification of their actions survives until October, long after James III's death, an event which in itself dictated the line they had to take in official propaganda. But in the early spring of 1488, with James III very much alive, they had to explain publicly why they had removed the heir to the throne beyond his father's control, and were themselves in rebellion in his defence — actions quite unprecedented in late medieval Scotland. Presumably part of their apologia stressed the need to remove bad royal counsellors, the perennial conventional complaint. But Pitscottie goes much further than this, for he makes the rebels accuse the king directly of threatening his heir with the fate of Albany — that is, forfeiture of lands and goods, if not his life.

Much of this has the ring of truth. The need to explain the abduction of the prince clearly lay at the centre of the rebel apologia, and is indeed reflected in the later proposals for a settlement between the rival parties signed by the king at Aberdeen in April.[5] But how could Rothesay's abduction be explained in public? Surely only by suggesting that his father was threatening him. Why, and with what? If Pitscottie is correct, the rebels claimed that James III was threatening his son with the fate of Albany, and, more importantly, that they believed the introduction of Albany's name into their propaganda would help them to raise support. This is possible, because James III's assault on his brother in 1479 had not been popular at the time — the estates had resisted his forfeiture for over three years — because even in 1482–3, there had been some support for Albany as lieutenant-general, and because the king had not been strong enough, or popular enough, to secure Albany's forfeiture as late as the spring of 1483, when his English treasons had clearly been renewed. The duke's flight following the death of his benefactor Edward IV, and the admission of an English garrison into Dunbar castle, had finally settled the issue in James III's favour in 1483;[6] but within a few years, with Albany dead in French exile and the king reverting to his Anglophile stance, it may have been possible to ignore Albany's English treasons and to start laying the foundations of the myth of Albany as a patriotic magnate who had consistently opposed his unpopular brother's foreign policy. Certainly this version of events had gained wide currency by the early sixteenth century,[7] and it may have been the acceptance of the Albany myth by a regime which came to power on James III's demise which assisted the restoration of the family in the person of the duke's son, John, duke of Albany, a governor of Scotland after James IV's death.

Some contemporary support for Pitscottie's view that the rebels of 1488 used Albany's fate as a justification for their defence of the prince against his father is to be found in subsequent rebel propaganda, which concentrates on James III's appalling relations with his close family. A letter from Hans, King of Denmark, to his nephew Rothesay, written in the spring or early summer of 1488, reveals that the Scottish rebels were accusing John Ramsay, Lord Bothwell, of poisoning Margaret of Denmark in 1486 and that in spite of the crime Ramsay was still retained as one of James III's closest advisors.[8] Although the conventional device of accusing evil counsellors is adopted, James III is being blamed — at the very least — for condoning the murder of his wife, the rebel prince's mother. It may also be significant that stories circulating in Europe during the next reign concentrate on King James's crimes against his family: by 1496 it was rumoured in the Empire that James III had had an incestuous relationship with his younger sister Margaret; while in France Philippe de Commynes reported that the Scottish king had been responsible for the death of his brother, John, earl of Mar.[9] These tales might be dismissed as pure fabrication devised after 1488 to justify the surprising outcome of the rebellion of that year, were it not for the fact that they are a lurid reflection of rebel propaganda *before* the event, as indicated positively by the Danish king's letter to the rebel prince, and — possibly — by Pitscottie's tale that James III planned to deal with his son as he had done with his brother. The conclusion must be that the rebels of February 1488 — or at least those of them immediately associated with the prince — sought to justify their cause by highlighting publicly King James's treatment of his family, and that they believed that such propaganda would win them popular support.

James III's response to the challenge presented by his son's defection suggests that though he had at last become aware of the threat to his kingship which it involved, he believed that he could win through simply by reshuffling the political pack. On 21 February, less than three weeks after Rothesay's departure from Stirling, King James abandoned the continuation of the January parliament to 5 May and dissolved the committee of fifty — hopelessly unwieldy and containing not a few potential or real enemies — which had been appointed to act against those who had opposed the king over the suppression of Coldingham.[10] The problem was apparently to be solved by summoning yet another parliament to Edinburgh for 12 May; if it had ever met, it would have been the third meeting of the estates within eight months, a reflection both of the extent of the political crisis and of James III's obsessive preoccupation with parliamentary settlements. He had taken action, he proclaimed, 'for certane reassonable and gret caus'; and it seems clear that he intended to pack the projected May parliament with his own supporters, something he had done successfully, for example, in March 1483. In the meantime, he found himself a new Chancellor. Bishop Elphinstone's years of loyal service were at last rewarded when on 21 February he is to be found for the first time occupying the most important office of state, replacing Colin Campbell, earl of Argyll.[11]

There is no question that Argyll, one of James III's most active and loyal servants, a man who had served the king for twenty years as Lord of Council, royal lieutenant in Argyll, Master of the Household, and latterly Chancellor, wished to be relieved of his post, for he recovered the Chancellorship as soon as the 1488 rebellion came to an end. Clearly he was dismissed by the king, for reasons which remain a mystery. Possibly King James had come to mistrust Argyll because of the earl's very extensive family connections, linked as he was through the marriages of his many daughters to an array of magnates who were potential or real enemies of the king — Hugh, Lord Montgomery, John, Lord Oliphant, William, Master of Drummond, even Angus Og Macdonald, natural son and heir of the forfeited Earl of Ross.[12] Whatever the king's motive, by dismissing Chancellor Argyll he had unleashed against himself powerful magnate groups who would now feel obliged to side with his enemies, the Humes and their allies. It is a commentary on the extent to which James III had abandoned political wisdom that in alienating Argyll, he had automatically lost two further royal councillors, Drummond and Oliphant, was forced to side with Cunningham against Montgomery in an unresolved Ayrshire feud, and lost any chance of restraining Argyll's son-in-law, Angus Og, in his assaults on the recently acquired earldom of Ross.

The month which followed Argyll's dismissal from the Chancellorship was one in which the king gradually became aware of the seriousness of his position, and his vulnerability in his chosen capital. Argyll remained at court, together with Bishops Blacader of Glasgow and Brown of Dunkeld — all of them soon to be prominent on the rebel side — for a full month, until 23 March.[13] This was a period of mutual suspicion and mistrust, with the new and displaced Chancellors both at court together with the rival incumbents of the sees of St Andrews and Glasgow, all of them dancing attendance on a king who looked to the upstart John Ramsay, Lord Bothwell, for guidance and whose continuing ability to repel rather than attract support in time of crisis must have become increasingly obvious to friend and enemy alike. In his search for allies, King James appears to have made an appeal for assistance even to Archibald, fifth earl of Angus, a committed — and as yet unpunished — rebel of 1482.[14] For Angus remained at court in Edinburgh until 7 March;[15] in spite of his recent bad record, his support for the Crown would be invaluable, for he was one of the most powerful magnates in southern Scotland, where King James had most to fear, and he had free tenants in many areas of the country. These included James III's most committed supporter, David Lindsay, earl of Crawford, his brother Sir Alexander Lindsay of Auchtermonzie, and John Lyon, Lord Glamis in Angus; Alexander, Lord Forbes, in Aberdeenshire; David Scott of Buccleuch, Angus's brother-in-law, and William Douglas of Cavers, sheriff of Roxburgh, both powerful men in the Middle March. In the event, Angus was not to be won over to the royal cause, for in the following month he appears as one of the commissioners appointed by the rebels to negotiate — at a safe distance — with the king in Aberdeen.[16] Probably Angus felt that there was already too much bad blood between James III and himself to make it possible for him to pursue any other course; but he attempted to hedge his bets to the end, for he was at best a lukewarm rebel. Thus his name is significantly absent from the list of ambassadors nominated by the rebels in May 1488 to put their case to Henry VII;[17] presumably his English treasons of 1482–3 were too recent for him to be regarded as presenting to King Henry the acceptable face of rebellion by men claiming to be acting in defence of the heir to the throne against an impossible king surrounded by evil advisors. When the end came at Sauchieburn, no contemporary record, no later chronicler even, mentions Angus's prowess at the battle, which suggests that he may not have played a major part, if indeed he was there; and it is a measure of his inability to command respect and support that many of his relatives and tenants did not join him in rebellion.[18]

This period of 'phoney war', with James III sitting in Edinburgh surrounded by bishops and magnates — Blacader, Brown, Argyll and Angus — who were about to defect, while his son's party had a free hand elsewhere in their efforts to raise support, came to an abrupt end on or about 24 March. On that date the king signed a privy seal letter in Edinburgh;[19] but thereafter, for the better part of two months, no royal business was transacted there. For the first time in his adult rule, James III was forced to leave the burgh which he had sought to make the only centre of royal government business. He was probably advised to move north to Aberdeen by Bishop Elphinstone and by the hereditary Constable, William Hay, earl of Erroll;[20] and he may eventually have realised that his position in Edinburgh was becoming extremely precarious. The heir to the throne with a rebel army was somewhere in the west, either at Linlithgow or Stirling; further south, with Angus gone and in spite of the existence of isolated groups of royalists, above all royal tenants in Ettrick forest,[22] the Crown had already lost the battle for support. A rebel advance on Edinburgh could hardly be long delayed; and if the burgh was lost, the king would rapidly find himself under siege in the castle with little or no chance of reaching Leith and the comparative safety of Fife.

In fact, King James seems to have left his departure for the north dangerously late. He may have been planning it for some time. On 11 March George Robison, the Comptroller, gave up his post of custumar of Edinburgh and left the city with more than £1,000 of the burgh customs, money which the new regime was still attempting to recover the following November.[23] He was probably sent north by the king with as much money as the burgh could provide to indicate that his royal master would display an unwonted generosity towards those who were prepared to support him in his hour of need. For there is no doubt that James III intended to use at least part of his hoard of treasure to buy support. Much or all of it appears to have been stored in the jewel house in Edinburgh castle, a fact which may explain the king's reluctance to leave the city until he was forced to do so. On 21 March, he confirmed to Sir Andrew Wood an earlier grant in feu-farm of the lands and town of Largo in Fife,[24] most likely as a means of confirming Sir Andrew's loyalty at a time when he needed his ships to cross to Fife; and a few days later, the king, accompanied by Elphinstone and Crawford, sailed across the Forth, probably in the 'Yellow Carvel', a ship with which both he and Wood were closely associated.[25] If Pitscottie is to be believed, the rebels were so close to cutting off the king's escape route that, pursuing him to Leith, they were able to seize some of his coffers, containing both money and clothing, and to use the money to hire 'fieit wageouris' — mercenaries — to fight for them.[26] An equally hasty departure from Edinburgh at about the same time must have been made by John Ramsay, Lord Bothwell, James III's familiar, sent to England — probably via Dunbar, of which castle he was keeper — to seek aid from Henry VII.[27] No such urgency attended the departure from Edinburgh of other prominent individuals at King James's rapidly dwindling court. The earl of Argyll, together with Bishops Blacader of Glasgow and Brown of Dunkeld, had only to go into the High Street to welcome the incoming rebels.

James III's route north took him through Fife to Perth, where he was joined by William Ruthven of that ilk, newly-created Lord Ruthven and no doubt anxious to show his loyalty, then through Angus to Aberdeen, which the king had probably reached by the end of March.[28] His principal purpose in visiting the city — apart from attending the belated consecration of Elphinstone as bishop of Aberdeen in St Machar's Cathedral[29] — was to raise support for the royal cause in the north. Certainly he was able to attract an impressive array of notables to Aberdeen: three bishops, Elphinstone, Andrew Stewart of Moray and Andrew Painter of Orkney; five earls, Huntly, Crawford, Erroll, Marischal, and Buchan; and four lords of parliament, Glamis, Forbes, Innermeath, and Ruthven. So a simple head count would suggest that in early April James III was in a stronger position than the rebels opposing him. But this is to assume that all the witnesses to royal charters granted at Aberdeen were committed James III men, and a simple analysis of those present immediately reveals that this was not the case. Erroll and Marischal had both been at court in Edinburgh in the early months of the year; but neither of them would join King James when he left Aberdeen the following month. Huntly and Glamis also refused to follow the king south, and the Bishop of Orkney, never a major figure in the political community, may only have turned up in Aberdeen to officiate at Elphinstone's consecration. So this imposing list was soon reduced to two men who had little option but to support the king, namely the new Chancellor, Bishop Elphinstone, and the loyalist Earl of Crawford, who was Chamberlain and was about to be made Master of the Royal Household; three lords of parliament, Innermeath, Forbes, and Ruthven; and the king's half-uncles, Buchan and the Bishop of Moray, both of whom had been his enemies in 1482–3.[30]

Why had James III failed to raise the majority of the supposedly conservative north in his defence? The answer surely lies in the fact that the northern lords thought he had gone too far, and felt that he should negotiate with the heir to the throne and his supporters. The king, much against his inclination as events were to show, was clearly advised in Aberdeen to attempt a negotiated settlement; and he chose the worst of both worlds by signing a preliminary list of nine articles for commissioners on both sides to discuss, and then promptly broke his word by leaving Aberdeen to settle the rebellion by force of arms. These nine Aberdeen articles — sometimes mistakenly referred to as the 'Pacification of Blackness'[31] — have been much quoted as proof that the rebel faction did not seek James III's deposition or death, that they sought simply to place some constraints on the king and to reconcile him with his son, at the same time seeking a general amnesty for all those prominently involved on both sides. If one takes this view, then James III threw away a golden opportunity and alienated an important group of potential supporters when he repudiated the articles and moved south. The articles are indeed, if taken at face value, full of sweet reasonableness. The king's 'hie honour, estate, riale autorite' is to be 'exaltit, conservit, and borne up'; he is to have wise counsellors, though it is not clear how these are to be chosen; he is to give a decent living to Prince James, and there is to be general forgiveness on both sides for hurts done in the past.[32] These were of course only preliminary points for discussion drawn up by royalists and rebels; but it is difficult to see how such pious hopes were to be transformed into political realities. For the truth is that the Aberdeen articles were the work of moderates on both sides, and that the northern lords with the king may have been more anxious for a negotiated settlement than the rebels in the south. Thus the six commissioners nominated for the Crown were all northerners — Elphinstone, Huntly, Erroll, Marischal, Glamis, and Sir Alexander Lindsay, Crawford's brother — and only two of them, Elphinstone and Lindsay, were prepared to support the king after his public repudiation of the articles. On the rebel side, the five commissioners were the Bishop of Glasgow, Argyll, Angus, and Lords Hailes and Lyle — the first three very recent defectors, while Hailes and Lyle both had excellent records of proven loyalty prior to 1488. Indeed Lyle would probably not have joined the rebel side at all but for his antagonism towards Buchan, on whom, in spite of his earlier treasons, the king was now lavishing favours; and the final clause of the Aberdeen articles rather optimistically pleads for peace amongst the king's lieges 'and specialy betuix the erle of Buchain and Lorde Lile.'[33]

It is clear, therefore, that the Aberdeen articles were a series of vague proposals — talks about talks — drawn up by men who were in no position to deliver the goods. On the royal side, most of the nominated commissioners were so lukewarm about James III that they would not even assist him in crushing the rebellion, while those named by the rebels, although they claimed to have 'full commissioune of my lord prince and of all the lordis being with him', were certainly not going to hand Rothesay over to any governing body in which the king's 'hie honour' was 'exaltit' in any meaningful way. This was the nub of the problem. Mistrust on both sides, often accumulated over years, had produced a situation in which it was too late for negotiation, and the 1488 rebellion could end only in two ways — with the capture and deposition, death, or flight into exile of James III, or with the total victory of the Crown and frightening consequences for those who had opposed the king. The very recent parallel of the events of 1482–3 must have concentrated the minds of those involved on both sides wonderfully.

The truth was, however, that the outright victory of King James was becoming an increasingly unlikely outcome of the struggle. In Aberdeen, surrounded by men encouraging him to negotiate rather than fight, the king's recorded efforts to attract individuals to his cause are indicative of his failing authority. Thus on 6 April he erected the town of Alyth in Perthshire into a burgh of barony in favour of Alexander, Master of Crawford, the Chamberlain's son and heir but very much the black sheep of the otherwise loyal Lindsay family.[34] This grant was obviously a calculated move to guarantee the Master's support for the Crown, but it failed. A rival bid was made by the rebels in May, with Prince James appointing as his commissioners George Brown, bishop of Dunkeld, Lords Gray, Oliphant, and Drummond to 'commoun, appoynt concord and bynd with our lovit cousing Alexander maister of Crawford' and any barons who might be prepared to come with him to join the prince.[35] The Master of Crawford chose the rebel cause, the right choice; by the following October he was appointed by the new regime to sit on the bench with Lords Gray and Glamis and exercise criminal justice throughout Angus,[36] while his father the earl paid for his loyal support for James III by being deprived of his sheriffship of Forfar.

The king's other recorded piece of business in Aberdeen was a charter of 16 April, confirming to his half-uncle Andrew Stewart, bishop of Moray, the 1452 charter of James II granting to the Bishop of Moray the cathedral church of Moray and the barony and burgh of Spynie in free regality.[37] Like the earlier grant to the Master of Crawford, this was an obvious bid for the bishop's support. Unlike the attempt to woo the Master, this grant succeeded to the extent that Andrew Stewart was prepared to follow his nephew south to attempt to crush the rebels by force; but it could be argued that the support of Andrew Stewart, and his elder brother Atholl and Buchan, was bought early at an exorbitant price by James III. Indeed, the king's heavy reliance in 1488 on the three men who had seized control of government from him in 1482 is in itself striking evidence of the weakness of his position.

In the event, the support of the Bishop of Moray probably did little to alter the outcome of the rebellion. If he was with King James at Sauchieburn — and there is no clear evidence that he was — he was sensible enough to make himself scarce thereafter. His elder brothers, however, were altogether more committed to their nephew's cause. Buchan, who had been received into favour following a period of exile, was anxious to justify the king's trust by acting as a hawk amongst his Aberdeen counsellors, advising James to break his word to negotiate and to move south. But the price of relying on the shifty, self-seeking Buchan, a man with a conspicuous political talent for choosing the wrong side in every crisis, was that he had many enemies, all of whom would either automatically align themselves with the king's enemies, or remain coldly aloof in his hour of need. To take only two examples, Robert, Lord Lyle, formerly a loyal supporter of the Crown, became a rebel because he both resented and feared Buchan's renewed favour with James III; for Lyle had acquired some of Buchan's Forfarshire lands during the latter's exile in 1485.[38] William Hay, earl of Erroll, had been at feud with Buchan in Angus at least since March 1479, when parliament had loudly complained about unresolved feuds all over the country; and Erroll's resentment at Buchan's return led him, with other northern earls, to withhold support from the king after April 1488.[39]

The eldest of the three half-uncles, John Stewart, earl of Atholl, was literally bought by the king. Atholl and his countess were the recipients of two boxes of James III's notorious treasure, of which an impressive total of 566 rose nobles, 1307 angel nobles, and 357 half crowns was recovered by the new regime after Sauchieburn.[40] As the purpose of sending money to Atholl was clearly to raise troops for the king, some of what he received — perhaps a great deal — must have been distributed to royalists in the last weeks of the reign; hence probably the complaints of the victorious rebels for years after 1488 that a large part of the royal treasure had not been recovered. In the short term, belated lavish distribution of his wealth was not a good investment for James III, far less effective in raising support in a crisis than even adequate rewarding of loyalty throughout the reign would have been.

As the 1488 crisis entered what proved to be its last phase, the king's strategy revealed both his growing concern at his deteriorating position, and his determination to bring the rebellion to a rapid end. Victory would be achieved partly through acquiring armed assistance from Henry VII of England; it was clearly the belief that such assistance would soon be forthcoming which made King James listen to Buchan's advice, repudiate the Aberdeen articles and move south to the Forth, probably late in April or at the beginning of May. Buchan was not alone in proferring such advice; his brother, the Bishop of Moray, the Lord Advocate John Ross of Montgrenan, Alexander Lord Forbes, and the lairds John Murray of Touchadam and Stephen Lockhart of Cleghorn were all involved in attempting to secure armed support from England, and even the royal tailor, James Hommyl, was pressed into service, presumably as a messenger.[41] However, the information on which all these men — and the king — were relying, was provided by King James's trusted ambassador, John Ramsay, Lord Bothwell, who had clearly announced his intention to return to Scotland in the near future — in fact he was back in Edinburgh by 28 May at the latest[42] — and it is probable that he promised to bring with him an expeditionary force raised in England to assist the king. He was then, and was to continue for the remaining twenty-five years of his life, an incurable optimist committed to a succession of lost causes. But with his extensive English ambassadorial experience in the 1480s, Ramsay was readily believed by James III and the rump of his supporters. To anticipate the arrival of the English force, the king came south to the Forth. With Dunbar and Leith lost to him, or at any rate too dangerous as embarkation points for English reinforcements, King James crossed the river to Blackness castle, held for the Crown by John Ross of Hawkhead, to await developments.[43]

It was a bad mistake which produced the king's first real confrontation with the rebels. The latter may not have had far to come, the prince and his supporters from Stirling, others probably no further than from Linlithgow, a mere seven miles away. Certainly they had soon mustered with a force superior to that of the king, and a battle — perhaps little more than a skirmish — took place in which the Earl of Crawford, Alexander, Lord Kilmaurs, William Douglas of Cavers, the Scotts of Branxholm, James Innes of Innes, James Dunbar of Cumnock, and Sir Thomas Turnbull of Greenwood, James III's standard bearer, all distinguished themselves on the royal side.[44] These names are significant, because with the exceptions of Crawford and Innes, they are southerners who had probably joined the king at Blackness. Also with King James were Chancellor Elphinstone, the Earl of Buchan, the Bishop of Moray, Lords Forbes, Ruthven, and (probably) Innermeath, John Ross of Montgrenan, the Lord Advocate, Sir William Murray of Tullibardine, Thomas Fotheringham of Powrie, and the castle's keeper, John Ross of Hawkhead.[45] The tally of names is impressive enough, and it is unfortunate that no information survives as to the size or composition of the rebel force at Blackness; it must have been imposing, for King James was rapidly forced into agreeing to negotiate. The king was understandably not trusted after the Aberdeen experience, and four hostages — Buchan, Ruthven, Murray of Tullibardine, and Fotheringham of Powrie — were handed over to the rebels as surety for James III's keeping his word. Buchan and Fotheringham of Powrie, together with Stephen Lockhart of Cleghorn, were later accused of helping to array the royal army at Blackness; but the evil counsellor who had taken Buchan's place was the Lord Advocate, John Ross of Montgrenan, who not only carried the chief responsibility for assembling James III's forces — he may indeed have encouraged those in his own county of Ayrshire such as Kilmaurs and Dunbar of Cumnock to turn up at Blackness — but apparently also gave the king the advice that he should abandon the hostages, repudiate even a verbal agreement to negotiate, and return to Edinburgh.[46] This was the course adopted by King James; presumably he left the beleagered castle of Blackness as he had entered it, by the sea gate, and by 16 May had regained the relative safety of Edinburgh castle.[47]

For the four hostages, the war was over. They would remain in rebel hands until after Sauchieburn, and in August charges of treason would be brought against two of them, Buchan and Fotheringham of Powrie, though only Buchan was in fact indicted in the first parliament of the new regime the following October. Viewed from a rebel standpoint, his crimes were obviously the most serious; since the outbreak of the rebellion, he had counselled King James to break his word in Aberdeen and helped array the royal army at Blackness. Also his dispute with Robert Lord Lyle over lands in Angus made him an obvious target for indictment. But what of the other three hostages, Ruthven, Murray of Tullibardine, and Fotheringham? Were they chosen at random as hostages by King James, or did the rebels specifically demand the surrender of these three? Some evidence exists to suggest that the latter may have been the case.

Late in May, we find the rebel heir to the throne at Stirling, appointing commissioners to negotiate with the Master of Crawford and other potential defectors in Angus. The commissioners were the men whom Rothesay had about him at Stirling — George Brown, bishop of Dunkeld and three lords of parliament — Lawrence Lord Oliphant, John, Lord Drummond, and Andrew,

Lord Gray.[48] These names at this stage in the rising strongly suggest a divided rebel command, with Prince James, one of the bishops and three lords at Stirling, while other leading negotiators — Argyll, Angus, Bishop Blacader, Lords Hailes and Lyle — were elsewhere, possibly negotiating for support or neutrality from other northern magnates. But in their efforts to neutralise or reduce royal support, the men about the prince — Oliphant, Drummond, and Gray — had good reason to require the surrender of the Blackness hostages Ruthven, Murray of Tullibardine, and Fotheringham of Powrie. Ruthven was Oliphant's principal — and recently ennobled — rival for the office of sheriff of Perth; in 1483 Murray of Tullibardine had been given the Stewartry of Strathearn by James III at Drummond's expense; and Fotheringham of Powrie, a supporter of the earl of Crawford in Angus, was an obvious target for the aspiring Lord Gray.[49] Thus the removal of all three — together with Buchan — from the conflict may be regarded as a combination of individual private enterprise and signal service to the rebel cause on the parts of Oliphant, Drummond, and Gray, sharply reducing royal control of Perthshire and Angus and shifting the political balance in these areas in their favour. The evidence is scanty and inconclusive; but as Oliphant, Drummond, and Gray were all close to the young prince, and as the latter two would reap very rich rewards following his accession in June, it is possible that the confrontation at Blackness was between James III and his son accompanied by his closest supporters. The individual ambitions of the lords with the prince would then explain the identities of the hostages. The king's cynicism in abandoning four of his most committed supporters amounted to his second public breach of faith within a month. He may, however, have felt that he had no choice but to play for time, sacrifice the hostages, and effect his escape. For it was highly unlikely that negotiations undertaken in siege conditions at Blackness would have left him with his freedom. So he returned to Edinburgh, very much on the defensive.

One ray of comfort for the king was the return from England of his ambassador and familiar, John Ramsay, Lord Bothwell, late in May.[50] So far as we know, Ramsay did not bring with him the much-needed English military assistance, and it is in any case highly unlikely that Henry VII would commit himself speedily and openly to James III's cause. Although King James enjoyed better relations with Henry VII than either of his two predecessors — mainly because, as Dr Nicholson has pointed out,[51] both kings were like-minded in their desire for peace — English armed intervention in Scottish affairs would be for Henry a costly and dangerous business, and not necessarily in the English king's best interests. Henry was after all a usurper, less than four years on the English throne and obsessed — justifiably — with the problem of his own security from the internal and external Yorkist threat. The previous June he had only just survived the Lambert Simnel rising by winning the battle of Stoke. So his situation at home may have dictated prudence in his dealings with James III. The Scottish issue was in any case complicated by a request for a safe-conduct, granted in May 1488, for a number of the rebel leaders — the Bishops of Glasgow and Dunkeld, Argyll, still styling himself Chancellor of Scotland,

Patrick Hepburn, Lord Hailes, Robert, Lord Lyle, Matthew Stewart, Master of Darnley, and Alexander Master of Hume, or any four of them — to come to England, presumably to put their case to King Henry.[52] The safe-conduct must have been requested shortly after the collapse of Scottish court life towards the end of March; circumstances prevented the rebels from using it, but the evidence of so many influential Scots — two of whom had attended his coronation in 1485 — in arms against their sovereign may well have helped to influence Henry VII's attitude to James III. A rebellion in Scotland was not necessarily bad news for the Tudor king; indeed a weak government north of the border might reduce the chances of an early Scottish siege of Berwick and alleviate the heavy cost of defending it. So King Henry probably settled for the cautious course of promising his support to Ramsay and James III in general terms without committing himself specifically; and he may well have done no more than concede Ramsay's request that the Scottish king should send commissioners to the Earl of Northumberland and Sir William Tyler, governor of Berwick, to ask both men to give pardons to all Scots refugees whom they might arrest — mainly fugitive criminals — if they expressed themselves willing to fight against King James's rebels.[53] This middle course, providing the possibility of limited assistance, yet essentially leaving the Scots to work out their own problems, may be regarded as a typical example of Henry VII's shrewdness. In fact the English king, failing to assist James III and thereby contributing to his ultimate collapse, was helping to bring to power in Scotland a government which would menace his own security within the decade.

In what were to prove the last few weeks of his life, James III exhibited an unwonted energy and generosity, the latter tinged with a neurotic suspicion which was perhaps a measure of his growing fear. Having safely reached Edinburgh castle and its jewel house — both preserved inviolate for him during his northern progress by part of his household[54] — by 16 May, he set about rewarding supporters, distributing cash and jewels in vast quantities to help recruitment, and mingling promises and threats in his appeals to those whose support he hoped to acquire. His most spectacular grant — at least in terms of prestige — was to David Lindsay, fifth earl of Crawford, on 18 May. For his services to the Crown throughout the reign, and especially for his defence of the king at Blackness, Crawford was made Duke of Montrose, the first non-royal duke in Scottish history.[55] It was a well-deserved reward; but it was also one calculated to incense Crawford's rivals in Angus, above all Andrew Lord Gray and Crawford's own son and heir Alexander, who within a few days would be subverted by the rebels.[56] Also on 18 May James III rewarded his standard bearer at Blackness, Sir Thomas Turnbull of Greenwood, with some Ayrshire lands; two days later, again for supporting the Crown at Blackness, the king granted in feu farm £44 worth of Morayshire lands to James Dunbar of Cumnock; and on 21 May he confirmed David Scott in his lands and barony of Branxholm, specifically mentioning the services to the Crown of Scott's son Robert and his followers at Blackness.[57]

Subsequent grants are rather less effusive in their praise of the recipients.

We have already seen that William Douglas of Cavers had been forced to resign his regality of Cavers into the king's hands four months before, in January 1488; now on 24 May King James regranted the regality to Douglas, but only on condition that the latter served him loyally throughout the crisis. If he did not, the charter was to have no force or effect.[58] On the same day, a rather less influential individual, James Innes of Innes, was granted £20 worth of land in Moray, and again the royal charter, while recognising Innes' loyalty at Blackness, required that he should continue to support the king 'pro toto tempore instantis discordie.'[59] On 28 May, James III committed himself firmly to one side in the Cunningham — Montgomery feud in northern Ayrshire. He made Alexander Cunningham, Lord Kilmaurs, Earl of Glencairn, and enhanced Cunningham's new dignity with some lands in the earldom of Lennox.[60] The new earl was required to assist the Crown until the rebellion was over. He did so, enjoying his new status until his death a fortnight later at Sauchieburn.

The other earl on whose support James III was counting in the final stages of the rebellion was, as we have seen, his half-uncle John Stewart, earl of Atholl.[61] Atholl was, however, only one of the recipients of royal treasure boxes which were probably distributed about this time. The others were David Lichtoun, abbot of Arbroath, the Treasurer, who received three boxes of French, Scottish, and English coins, gold and silver, together with gold jewellery;[62] Dean Robert Hog, a canon of Holyrood, who had charge of another box of assorted gold and silver coins;[63] Alan of the Avery, who received yet another box;[64] and William Cumming, who was entrusted with a box containing an unspecified amount of gold, silver, and jewels, and who — significantly — was closely associated with Alexander, Lord Gordon, Master of Huntly.[65]

Almost alone amongst the great magnates of the north, the Master of Huntly was at the end a committed James III man. He had good reason to be, for he clearly enjoyed the king's trust. Already confirmed as keeper of the castles of Inverness and Kildrummy as recently as 29 January 1488, lessee from the Crown of land in the earldom of Mar and the lordship of Strathdon, with Garioch, Petty, Brachly, and Strathern (all in Aberdeenshire),[66] the Master of Huntly successfully petitioned James III to grant him the authority to uplift the burgh mails of Inverness for the next nineteen years, and in the meantime to remit all arrears currently owed by the burgh to the Crown. The timing of this remission is significant. It was made on 17 May, almost immediately after King James' return to Edinburgh from Blackness; and in the letter of remission, the king refers to the fact that the burgesses and inhabitants of Inverness 'are so greatly impoverished, wasted, and failed, that they are not of power to pay to us the sums owing to us in our Exchequer Rolls of our burgh, mails of the same without utter poverty and hership of them.'[67] The wasting and impoverishing to which King James refers, presumably on information supplied by the Master of Huntly, would appear to be a sack of the burgh by the followers of Angus Og, the heir to the Macdonald lordship of the Isles and son-in-law of Argyll. Either taking advantage of, or anticipating, royal Stewart weakness following the outbreak of rebellion in the south in the early spring,

Angus Og launched the second of his major campaigns to recover Macdonald power, lost by his father, in the Earldom of Ross.[68] He attacked and sacked the burgh of Inverness, an obvious threat not only to Crown influence in Ross and Moray, but also to Huntly ambitions in the area.[69] It was essential for James III to ensure the continuance of both by rewarding the new keeper of Inverness castle, the only man with real power whom the king could trust in the north-east. So the Master of Huntly was rewarded — unconditionally — and he responded with unswerving loyalty to James III, even pleading James's cause after the king's death. This consistency would eventually pay off, for in the following reign, despite temporary setbacks, the irresistible rise of the Gordons and the earldom of Huntly would continue, surviving even Flodden. In the meantime, the Gordon family would hedge its bets, with George the earl remaining neutral in the final crisis of 1488, while Alexander the Master prepared to use the box of treasure delivered to him by William Cumming to raise armed support for the king.[70]

The crisis at Blackness, followed by the handing over of the four hostages, had removed one of the three northerners whom King James had planned to use, together with John Ramsay, in appealing for assistance from the Earl of Northumberland and Sir William Tyler, governor of Berwick.[71] With Buchan a captive in rebel hands, the king may still have gone ahead with the scheme. Certainly Ramsay did not go out with King James on his last campaign at the beginning of June, and it is likely that he had again been despatched to England, possibly with the Bishop of Moray and Lord Forbes, with the royal commission to enlist fugitive Scots in Northumberland for the Crown. It was too late. Although Ramsay's, later, indictment for treason, and the parliamentary apologia of October 1488, would seek to inflate Ramsay's missions into the inbringing of 'Inglismen . . . to the perpetuale subieccione of the realm'[72], in fact no English armed assistance had been given or promised in writing, before Sauchieburn was fought.

A rough estimate of the support available to James III in his last fortnight in Edinburgh may be made from witness lists to royal charters between 18 and 28 May. Elphinstone and Crawford, as Chancellor and Chamberlain respectively, were naturally present, as were the remaining Stewart half-uncles, Atholl and the Bishop of Moray; and Alexander Lord Forbes. Lord Kilmaurs, as his elevation to earl on 28 May shows, had been with the king since Blackness and would be with him to the end. James Douglas, earl of Morton, the king's uncle but a magnate who played little part in the political arena, managed the seven-mile trip from Dalkeith to join his nephew by 20 May; Robert Colquhoun, bishop of Argyll, brother of James's familiar, the late Sir John Colquhoun of Luss, and a committed royalist, had arrived by the following day; James Chisholm, bishop of Dunblane, made an isolated appearance on 28 May; and lords of parliament present in Edinburgh during this period included Lindsay of Byres, Maxwell, Graham, Borthwick, Carlyle, and Abernethy.[73]

It is not clear, however, that those who witnessed King James's last Edinburgh charters followed him to the battlefield of Sauchieburn. Some were so identified with his cause that they had no option but to do so, including the new Duke of Montrose and Earl of Glencairn; and Atholl had been well paid for his support. Some of the others, notably the Bishop of Argyll and Lords Carlyle and Lindsay of Byres, were royalists by conviction and probably joined James on his last campaign. But there must be, for a variety of reasons, some doubt about some of the others. The Bishop of Moray and Lord Forbes, as we have seen, may have gone south with Lord Bothwell; and in the case of Lord Maxwell, he must either have remained neutral or committed himself actively to the rebel side, as the following October he was given extensive powers by the new regime to exercise criminal justice in Dumfriesshire.[74] Maxwell probably deserted James III at the end because one of his principal rivals in the south-west, Cuthbert Murray of Cockpool, joined the king.[75] In the middle March, William Douglas of Cavers, as a very recent recipient of conditional royal favour, no doubt weighed up the odds and brought twenty-four of his kin, allies, and Roxburgh tenants to the support of King James; but it is not at all clear that Cavers' neighbour, James Rutherford of that ilk, did the same.[76]

A similar problem of loyalties faced the burgesses of Dumbarton. On 16 May, immediately on his return to Edinburgh from the confrontation at Blackness, the king sent a letter under the privy seal to the sheriff of Dumbarton and his deputies, ordering them not to compel the burgesses of Dumbarton to attend shrieval weaponshowings. Instead, the community might hold its own weaponshowings, in order more readily to be able to assist the king in 'our hoistingis and weris . . . now of late'.[77] The letter reflects James III's concern not to lose control of the principal strongpoint within the Lennox; for he must have been well aware that both John Stewart, Lord Darnley, who had laid claim to the title of earl of Lennox since 1473, and his son and heir Matthew, were prominent supporters of the rebel cause.[78] How the burgesses of Dumbarton responded to the royal letter of privilege which was, in fact, an appeal for support, presumably depended on their relations with, or fear of, Darnley. Probably, as in many other parts of the country, there was a mixed response in Dumbarton; and there is a certain irony that in little over a year, the burgh was again to become a focus for discontent, supporting Darnley — now officially recognised as earl of Lennox — in his condemnation of the new regime which he had helped to bring to power, and specifically complaining that no-one had been punished for the slaughter of James III.[79]

The Dumbarton burgesses' dilemma was one which had to be faced and resolved by prominent individuals throughout the country: how did one respond to the military demands made by an aggressive, vindictive king who in spite of his unpopularity had managed to survive a major threat to his kingship only six years before? Many, possibly most, hedged their bets and like the northern lords maintained a resolute neutrality throughout. Some, like the Humes and their allies, had been attacked by the king and had no option but to resist; others, including King James's displaced counsellors, Argyll, Oliphant, and Drummond, took the risk of coming out against him at least partly as a reaction against royal injustice and ingratitude towards themselves, while veterans of the 1482 crisis, such as Angus and Gray, were no doubt moved by fear of James's vindictiveness. Behind such specific motivation lay a general malaise born of unresolved feuds and royal partiality — Erroll against Buchan in Aberdeenshire; Gray against Crawford, Lyle against Buchan, in Angus; Drummond against Murray, Oliphant against Ruthven in Perthshire; Montgomery against Kilmaurs in Ayrshire; Maxwell against Murray of Cockpool, Rutherford against Turnbull, on the borders. In some sense, the violent events of 1488 can be explained as a temporary settlement of local feuds thrust on to the national stage by the king's interference and ineptitude. Thus the two bishops and two earls — Blacader, Brown, Argyll, and Angus — are no more than the tip of the rebel iceberg. In a country deeply divided locally as well as nationally, royal weakness added greatly to rebel strength, making possible acts of individual violence and revenge by those who chose the winning side.

By May of 1488 it was becoming increasingly likely that the winning side would be that of the rebels. In spite of the widely-ranging motives of their leaders, they had one inestimable advantage over their predecessors of 1482: the possession of the heir to the throne, which gave them both respectability and an ideal vehicle for propaganda. The rebellion could be represented, both at home and abroad, as an effort to protect Prince James against a vindictive father, surrounded by evil Anglophile counsellors. This theme naturally reappears in the parliamentary apologia of October 1488, when the rebellion was long over; but it is also to be found in a striking letter, already referred to, written by Prince James's uncle, King Hans of Denmark, in the spring or early summer of 1488, while the struggle between James III and the rebels was nearing its climax. Addressing the heir to the throne as 'illustrious prince and dearest nephew', the Danish king reports his sorrow on hearing th news that his sister and the prince's mother, Queen Margaret of Denmark, had been poisoned by John Ramsay. Not only had Ramsay not been punished for this crime, but he and other evil advisors were retained by King James, and they now sought to drive the prince and his brothers into exile, or even to have them killed, by attempting to bring in the English — the natural enemies of the Scots — to the destruction of the realm of Scotland.[80] As we have seen, the themes in this letter — in which King Hans is simply responding to information supplied by the Scottish rebels — were probably already well established in the initial propaganda put out by the prince's party: King James's assaults on his family and his evil counsellors. The 'inbringing of Englishmen' referred to in the Danish king's letter strikingly anticipates the apologia of the following October, and was probably a popular propaganda line at home and abroad during the rebellion itself. What is new, therefore, is the charge that John Ramsay, Lord Bothwell, had poisoned Margaret of Denmark. This was designed for Danish consumption only, and appears nowhere else in rebel propaganda, nor indeed in Ramsay's later indictment for treason. Its aim was probably to prevent Danish intervention on King James's side by discrediting him in the strongest terms, a necessary step as only the previous year James III had sought to provide evidence of Margaret of Denmark's sanctity for investigation by a papal commission.[81] In the end, the Scottish struggle would not be decided by Danish intervention on one side or the other; but King Hans's letter shows that the rebels had already won the propaganda war. One tangible result of Hans's concern may have been the arrival at Leith of a Danish fleet under the command of Count Gerhard of Oldenburg, the Danish king's uncle. It is not certain that the Danes had arrived in Scotland before Sauchieburn; but they were obviously in favour with the new regime as early as July 1488, and Count Gerhard would receive the sizeable sum of £500 from James IV in October, while the expense of lodging him in Edinburgh during the following winter cost the new king £386.7/-.[82]

The letter from King Hans of Denmark to Prince James casts a revealing light on the character of the Scottish heir to the throne at this time. Later chroniclers, followed by some modern writers, have sought to represent the prince as little more than a child, a pawn in the hands of determined and ruthless men. The evidence, slight though it is, hardly justifies such a conclusion. In the spring of 1488 Prince James was fifteen, only two years short of the age at which his father had taken effective control of government, a year less than his own son James V would be when he did the same thing. The prince can have seen little of his father during the 1480s, and it is possible that he was being deliberately excluded from taking any role in government — for example, by attending parliaments or going on justice ayres — because James III feared and mistrusted him after 1482, and after the death of Margaret of Denmark in 1486 sought to limit his heir's influence by showing conspicuous favour to his second son, also ominously named James, by using him as a potential bridegroom in his English marriage schemes and by making him a royal duke, Duke of Ross, in January 1488. With his mother dead and Ross the recipient of James III's patronage and trust, young Rothesay probably feared for his future, wondered indeed whether he had any future. His association with his uncle Albany and the late queen as a potential successor to James III in 1482 can have done him no good in his father's eyes, even though he was only nine at the time. Now Albany and many of his supporters were exiled or dead, and Queen Margaret was also dead. James III's vindictiveness towards the Albany faction might well extend as far as his son and heir; and from Rothesay's point of view, even the king's efforts in 1487 to achieve the canonisation of Margaret of Denmark may have seemed ominous. It was after all an effort to enhance royal prestige abroad, while at home it could be regarded as an attempt to paper over the cracks, to suggest a state of domestic harmony between King James and his wife which, if it had existed at all, had been shattered by the queen's political role in 1482. Small wonder that the prince, having left Stirling castle and thrown in his lot with the rebels, sought to expose his father's appalling relations with his close family, and the claim that Queen Margaret had in fact been poisoned and that James III had condoned the crime may be regarded as defensive propaganda which would justify the prince's rebellion in Danish eyes, at the same time setting the royal attempts to canonise Queen Margaret the previous year in the worst possible light. Rothesay may not have been the originator of the poisoning story, but he certainly accepted its use as propaganda for the Danes. It was a cynical act, for he and his supporters can hardly have believed the story for a moment; it does not appear, for example, where we should most expect it, in John Ramsay's indictment for treason in October 1488.[83]

It would seem, therefore, that the heir to the throne took up arms in his own defence. His presence on the rebel side gave its leaders an immense, indeed crucial, advantage; but he was there not as a pawn but because their cause was his — like many of them he feared for his safety if his father continued to rule. Not surprisingly, therefore, he made no attempt to meet or be reconciled with James III between February and June 1488; in April the Aberdeen articles, which were after all only moderates' points for preliminary negotiations, contain a demand by Rothesay for 'honorable sustentacioun' by his father and the hopeless plea for the reconciliation of irreconcilable enemies;[84] within a few weeks there followed the military confrontation at Blackness; and by late May Rothesay was not only styling himself 'Prince of Scotland' — a national title, implying his pretensions to head the government — but surrounding himself in Stirling with rebel hardliners, Lords Drummond, Oliphant, and Gray.[85] It would appear, therefore, that while Rothesay did not seek his father's death — there is contemporary as well as later evidence that he wished no harm to come to the king[86] — he certainly aimed at the removal of James III from government, and surrounded himself with men who not only looked to the same result but possessed the means and determination to bring it about.

When the end came, it was precipitated by King James. Early in June, having distributed his material wealth as far as possible amongst his supporters, he left Edinburgh castle and headed for Stirling, probably by way of Queensferry and the north side of the Forth. No contemporary record survives of his route, but his objective was clear enough — to put an end to the rebellion by seizing possession of his son. He may have journeyed as far north as Perth, where in Pitscottie's highly-coloured version of events he was joined by the chronicler's ancestor David, Lord Lindsay of Byres, who at this point presented the king with the fatal gift of a great grey horse. Pitscottie can hardly be right, however, in his statement that Lord Ruthven also brought a force to join the king at Perth,[87] for Ruthven had been a hostage in rebel hands since the confrontation at Blackness. If the king went to Perth at all, it must have been for strategic reasons — to drive a wedge between his enemies in Strathearn and Angus, to secure Perth for the royalists in Ruthven's absence, and perhaps also to join up with his one committed supporter of significance from the north-east who had not yet joined him — Alexander Gordon, Master of Huntly. There is evidence that the Master of Huntly, the recipient of extensive favours from James III since January, was indeed hurrying south to join the king, and that he fought on his behalf against a rebel force at Dunkeld.[88] The link-up between the two royalist armies was not, however, accomplished, and when James III appeared in the Stirling area in the second week of June — significantly arriving from the north — he did so with an army largely composed of those whose loyalty he had bought, those whose association with him was so close that they had no alternative but to join him, and those to whom he had made recent grants conditional on their support throughout the crisis. There were notable absentees on the royal side — John Ramsay, Lord Bothwell, in rebel propaganda the king's evil genius, and probably also the Bishop of Moray and Lord Forbes, sent to the north of England to raise support. The weakness of James III's military position is strikingly illustrated by the presence in his army of two bitter rivals from the south-west, John, Lord Carlyle and Cuthbert Murray of Cockpool, who had gone through a form of reconciliation in Edinbugh castle only weeks before Sauchieburn.[89]

It was the younger brother of the latter, Sir Adam Murray of Drumcrieff, who opened hostilities for the royalists by attacking and burning Sir William Stirling of Keir's estates between Stirling and Doune;[90] and when Prince James emerged from Stirling castle with a rebel force, probably in response to the attack on Keir, he was promptly put to flight by James III's Advocate, John Ross of Montgrenan, in the vicinity of Stirling Bridge.[91] This initial success, close to the site of Wallace's victory in 1297, may have encouraged James III to pursue his rebellious son south, and to put his trust in the success of his ancestor, the hero king Robert Bruce. On St Barnabas' Day, Thursday 11 June 1488, carrying Bruce's sword to the field, King James joined battle with the rebels on what contemporaries described as 'the field of Stirling', between the Sauchie and Bannock burns, and slightly to the south-west of Bruce's victory at Bannockburn. In the mid-seventeenth century Drummond of Hawthornden gave the name 'Sauchieburn' to the battle — perhaps to distinguish it from Bruce's victory of 1314 — and subsequent writers have followed Drummond in using this name.[92]

For an event which had such far-reaching significance, Sauchieburn has left remarkably little trace in contemporary records. We cannot be certain who was present on the royal side, or indeed in the rebel army, unless — as in the case of a few individuals — they were later arraigned for treason, or sought papal absolution for their presence on the field, or were killed in the battle itself. Certain salient facts are however suggestive. The first of these is the written oath made by many of the rebel leaders before the battle that they would not harm James III, which became enshrined in later tradition as an order by Rothesay that no-one should lay violent hands on his father.[93] The chroniclers from Abell onwards used this oath as an illustration of the prince's merciful nature; but surely what it tells us is that King James was at a disadvantage even before fighting started and that the rebels expected to win. Then there is the statement, admittedly not contemporary but made about 1530 by Sir David Lindsay of the Mount in his 'Testament and Complaynt of the Papyngo', that Rothesay brought the royal banner to the field with him.[94] If this is true, it complements his use of the title 'Prince of Scotland' as an illustration of his desire to replace his father rather than negotiate with him for a settlement. Finally there is the fact that no-one of note on the rebel side is known to have been killed, whereas in the royal army, apart from James III himself, the newly-created Earl of Glencairn and Sir Thomas Semple, sheriff of Renfrew, died in the battle.[95] This would be consistent with other evidence which suggests that the royalists fought at a disadvantage.

Using these facts — and the contemporary evidence of indictments and the eventual parliamentary debate about Sauchieburn some four months later — it is possible to produce a plausible reconstruction of the events of 11 June 1488. The royalists' surprise attack on the Keir estates and victory in the skirmish at Stirling Bridge forced Rothesay and his supporters to flee southwards. But James III's expedition from Edinburgh to Stirling can hardly have remained secret for long, and the main body of the rebel force — probably including the earls of Argyll and Angus, Lord Hailes, his Hume neighbours, Lord Lyle, Bishop Blacader of Glasgow and William Knollis, preceptor of Torphichen, and certainly including Hugh, Lord Montgomery, George Shaw, abbot of Paisley and the abbot and convent of Jedburgh[96] — hastened north-west from Linlithgow to reinforce the prince. Other lairds, including Shaw of Sauchie, Ker of Cessford, and Stirling of Keir, may have joined the rebels at this point; and Rothesay's own force included Lords Gray, Drummond, and Oliphant, and probably also Alexander, Master of Crawford, and the Bishop of Dunkeld, George Brown.[97] It was this army, led by one royal duke, two earls, two bishops, two abbots, and at least six lords of parliament, and drawn from the east and middle Marches, Ayrshire, Renfrewshire, Stirling, Perth, and Angus, which confronted James III on the field of Stirling. There was no question of further negotiation or a second Blackness with a surrender of hostages by the king, for his army was led by men whom he had bought, like his half-uncle Atholl, or very recently ennobled, like the new Duke of Montrose and Earl of Glencairn, or grudgingly patronised, like Douglas of Cavers and Scott of Buccleuch. The positions and careers of these men could only be maintained or advanced through fighting and winning. So the royal confessor, John Ireland, heard King James's confession,[98] the king's advocate, John Ross of Montgrenan, organised the arraying of the army,[99] and James III launched himself into his last battle.

Sauchieburn appears to have been fought without recourse on either side to new technology; there is no mention, even in the later chroniclers, of artillery being brought into play, and the battle may have been a fast-moving, unequal contest from the start, rapidly developing into a series of pursuits by the victorious rebels. Individuals used the occasion to settle old scores: the new Earl of Glencairn was killed, possibly by his Ayrshire enemy Hugh, Lord Montgomery, who used the rebel victory and his rival's death to go on to harry Glencairn's estates.[100] Less dramatically, but equally significantly in the long run, the royal defeat settled the regional power struggles which had brought many families to the field: Drummond prevailed over Murray in Strathearn, Oliphant over Ruthven in Perth, Gray over Crawford in Angus. None of this would have been possible had there not been one casualty of Sauchieburn which dwarfed all the others — James III, abandoning Robert Bruce's sword and a black box containing over £4,000 Scots in gold coin,[101] was pursued, overtaken and killed, at Bannockburn mill while in flight to the comparative safety of Sir Andrew Wood's ships in the river Forth.[102] The identity of his killer, or killers, was never discovered; perhaps no-one knew, though by the late sixteenth century Pitscottie had absorbed a rumour that James III had been slain by a servant of Lord Gray.[103] This is as likely an explanation as any; Gray was a rebel hard-liner who stood to gain substantially from the removal both of King James and of Crawford influence from Angus. Another late sixteenth-century chronicler, George Buchanan, even names Lord Gray himself as one of three assassins of the king.[104] This is however unlikely. As one of the rebel leaders, Gray probably gave his oath with the rest not to harm James III; he is never accused of the murder directly by contemporaries, not even by rebels of 1489 against the government in which he had acquired a prominent place; and the official version of the king's death, enshrined in the indictment for treason of John Ross of Montgrenan in July 1488, states that James was slain by unknown vile persons after leaving the field.[105] The eventual acceptance of this formula by the political community enabled the victorious rebel leaders at Sauchieburn to heave a collective sigh of relief. If a servant of Lord Gray had indeed divined his master's wishes and disposed of James III, he remained unrewarded and — probably fortunately for himself — undetected.

In the confusion surrounding the defeat and pursuit of James III's broken army, it may have been some time — possibly as much as a few days — before his body was positively identified.[106] But the victors lost no time in exploiting their success. On 12 June, only a day after Sauchieburn, Rothesay issued his first charter as King James IV. Significantly, the first recipient of royal bounty was a Hepburn.[107] It was the shape of things to come.

NOTES

1. Lesley, *History*, 56.
2. Ferreri, *Appendix to Boece*, f.399 r-v.
3. Buchanan, *History*, ii, 157.
4. Pitscottie, *Historie*, i, 203–4.
5. *A.P.S.*, ii, 210. For details of these proposals, see Macdougall, *James III*, 247–251, and 265 n.70.
6. For details of Albany's career in 1482–3, see Macdougall, *op.cit.*, 170–189.
7. See, for example, Adam Abell, 'The Roit or Quheill of Tyme' (1533–7), ff.110v–112r. (NLS MS 1746). The section on James III is little more than a hagiography of Albany.
8. Danske Rigsarkiv, T.K.U.A., Skotland, A.1, 1.
9. Philippe de Commynes, *Memoires*, ii, 161.
10. *A.P.S.*, ii, 184.
11. *R.M.S.*, ii, No. 1707.
12. *Scots Peerage*, i, 334–5.
13. *R.M.S.*, ii, Nos. 1709–1722.
14. This is my own interpretation of the stories which appear in the later histories of Ferreri, Lesley, and Buchanan, subsequently echoed in Hume of Godscroft and Drummond of Hawthornden, that the imprisoned and forfeited 9th Earl of Douglas

was approached and asked for assistance both by James III and by the rebels: Ferreri, *Appendix to Boece*, f.400r; Lesley, *History*, 57–8; Buchanan, *History*, ii, 156; Hume, *Douglas and Angus*, 206; Drummond, *History*, 169. In the context of the politics of 1488, these tales make no sense at all, because Douglas had been forfeited for 33 years and his support was of no value to anyone; but they *do* make sense if they are applied not to Douglas but to the Douglas earl of Angus, a magnate clearly uncommitted to either side in March 1488. Possibly the later tales of Douglas's involvement originated in oral evidence which came down to Buchanan, to the effect that the king invited Archibald, earl of Angus — whom Buchanan thereafter consistently calls Douglas — to Edinburgh castle, and there proposed an alliance against the rebels: Buchanan, *History*, ii, 156.

15. *R.M.S.*, ii, No. 1717.

16. *A.P.S.*, ii, 210.

17. *Cal. Docs. Scot.*, iv, No. 1539.

18. In some cases, this was because they were already, like Crawford, committed royalists. But the adherence of Scott of Buccleuch and Douglas of Cavers to the king rather than Angus (Fraser, *Buccleuch*, ii, 67–72; *H.M.C. 7th Rep.*, App. 228–9) in the latter stages of the rebellion may be a reflection of the unpopularity of Angus in the Middle March.

19. Fraser, *Wemyss*, ii, 111.

20. Erroll was at court in Edinburgh till 7 March; Elphinstone was a constant charter witness throughout the period to 23 March: *R.M.S.*, ii, Nos. 1707–1722.

21. The prince had returned to Stirling in May, if not before: S.R.O., RH 1/1/3.

22. John M. Gilbert, *Hunting and Hunting Reserves in Medieval Scotland*, 333.

23. *E.R.*, x, 57, 62.

24. *R.M.S.*, ii, No. 1720.

25. *E.R.*, viii, 293; *T.A.*, i, 54, 66, 68.

26. Pitscottie, *Historie*, i, 202, 204. Although Pitscottie is notoriously unreliable as to details, the gist of his story of James III's flight to the north seems acceptable. Contemporary evidence confirms the king's distribution of wealth amongst potential supporters both at this time and later in the rebellion; and as some of the most prominent future rebels — Argyll, Blacader and Brown — were still at court right up to the time of James's departure for the north, the king's plans can hardly have remained secret from his enemies. So a pursuit to Leith is quite likely.

27. Leland, *Collectanea*, iv, 240. Ramsay, as ambassador of James III, was with Henry VII at Windsor on 27 April.

28. He was certainly in Aberdeen by 6 April: S.R.O., Airlie Chrs., Section 12, 9. Ruthven was among the charter witnesses to both surviving grants made by James III in Aberdeen.

29. Macfarlane, *Elphinstone*, 192.

30. Those with the king in Aberdeen may be identified from two charter witness lists: S.R.O. Airlie Chrs., Section 12, 9; *Moray Registrum*, 234–6. Those who subsequently accompanied him to, or joined him in, Edinburgh are in *R.M.S.*, ii, Nos. 1723–1730.

31. For a discussion of this point, see Macdougall, *James III*, 265 n.70.

32. *A.P.S.*, ii, 210. The Aberdeen articles are discussed in full in Macdougall, *James III*, 248–250.

33. *A.P.S.*, ii, 210.

34. S.R.O., Airlie Chrs., Section 12, 9.

35. S.R.O., RH 1/1/3.

36. *A.P.S.*, ii, 208, c.9.

37. *Moray Registrum*, 234–6.

38. *R.M.S.*, ii, No. 1617; *A.P.S.*, ii, 210.

39. *A.P.S.*, ii, 210–11.

40. *T.A.*, i, 85–6.

41. *A.P.S.*, ii, 201, 202, 204.

42. S.R.O., Cunninghame-Grahame Muniments, GD 22/2/2.

43. *E.R.*, x, 33.

44. *R.M.S.*, ii, No. 1725 (for Crawford); S.R.O., Cunninghame-Grahame Muniments, GD 22/2/2 (for Kilmaurs); *H.M.C. Rep. vii*, App., 729 (for Douglas of Cavers); Fraser, *Buccleuch*, ii, 89 (for Scotts); *R.M.S.*, ii, No. 1730 (for Innes); *Ibid.*, No. 1727 (for Dunbar); *Ibid.*, No. 1724 (for Turnbull).

45. Buchan, Ruthven, Murray, and Fotheringham were all handed over as hostages at Blackness: *A.P.S.*, ii, 201, 204; Elphinstone, the Bishop of Moray, and Lord Forbes were all with the king in Aberdeen in April (*Moray Registrum*, 234–6) and still with him in Edinburgh on 18 May (*R.M.S.*, ii, No. 1724), so they were most likely also at Blackness. Thomas Lord Innermeath, also with the king in Aberdeen, was charged with treason in August (*T.A.*, i, 92), which suggests that he remained with James III to the end.

46. *A.P.S.*, ii, 204.

47. Dumbarton Burgh Records, No. 6.

48. S.R.O., RH 1/1/3. This commission is dated sometime after 21 May, but in the original the seal obscures the date: 'At Striveling the xxi . . . day of Maii' etc. Thus the date could be 22, 23, 24 or 29 May.

49. *A.P.S.*, ii, 208; Macdougall, *James III*, 109.

50. He had returned by 28 May: S.R.O., Cunninghame-Grahame Muniments, GD 22/2/2.

51. Nicholson, *Later Middle Ages*, 519.

52. *Cal. Docs. Scot.*, iv, No. 1539.

53. *A.P.S.*, ii, 201.

54. The castle was probably held for him by its keeper, Sir John Lundy of that ilk: *E.R.*, ix, 548; presumably part of the royal household — including the Privy Seal, David Livingstone, rector of Ayr, and the Secretary, Archibald Whitelaw, neither of whom accompanied the king on his northern progress — were also in the castle at this time.

55. *R.M.S.*, ii, No. 1725.

56. S.R.O., RH 1/1/3. For an earlier example of the Master of Crawford's wilfulness, see Macdougall, *James III*, 133.

57. *R.M.S.*, ii, Nos. 1724, 1727; Fraser, *Buccleuch*, ii, 89.

58. *H.M.C. Rep. vii*, App., 729.

59. *R.M.S.*, ii, No. 1730.

60. S.R.O., Cunninghame-Grahame Muniments, GD 22/2/2; *Laing Chrs.*, No. 198.

61. *T.A.*, i, 85, 87.

62. *Ibid.*, 86–7.

63. *Ibid.*, 79.

64. *T.A.*, i, 87.

65. *R.S.S.*, i, No. 1400.

66. *E.R.*, x, 7.

67. Fraser-Mackintosh, *Invernessiana*, 160.

68. The first campaign had been in 1481 or 1483, when Angus Og defeated Atholl at Lagebraad in Ross; Atholl being reinforced by George, earl of Huntly, Angus Og had partially burned Inverness before retreating to the west. For details, see the reconstruction of events in Evan Barron, *Inverness and the Macdonalds* (1930), 44–51.

69. *Highland Papers*, i, 51–2. Barron, *op.cit.*, 52–3, suggests that the assassination of Angus Og by the harper Art O'Carby (Diarmid O' Cairbre) occurred at this time, and that the sack of Inverness was his followers' response to Angus's assassination. But he cannot have died before 8 August 1488, on which date he is to be found granting land

in Mull to Hector MacLean: *Acts of the Lords of the Isles 1336–1493*, edd. Jean Munro and R.W. Munro (S.H.S., 1986), 193.

70. *R.S.S.*, i, Nos. 14, 1400.

71. *A.P.S.*, ii, 202. The only time in 1488 that Buchan, the Bishop of Moray, and Lord Forbes can be found together is between James III's departure from Aberdeen and the crisis at Blackness, when Buchan was abandoned as a hostage. John Ramsay, Lord Bothwell, did not arrive back in Scotland until after Blackness (*A.P.S.*, ii, 203), so all four men could never have acted together as James III's commissioners to Northumberland. It is likely, however, that the scheme originated before Ramsay's return in late May; and it may have been one of the possibilities which moved Buchan to encourage the king to come south.

72. *Ibid.*, 202, 210.

73. The charters from which these names are drawn are in *R.M.S.*, ii, Nos. 1724–1730 (18–24 May); Fraser, *Buccleuch*, ii, 89 (21 May); and S.R.O., Cunninghame-Grahame Muniments, GD 22/2/2 (28 May).

74. *A.P.S.*, ii, 208.

75. For the Maxwell-Murray feud, see Fraser, *Carlaeverock*, i, 159–160.

76. *H.M.C. 7th Rep.*, App., 729.

77. Dumbarton Burgh Records, No. 6.

78. *A.P.S.*, ii, 208; *Cal. Docs. Scot.*, iv, No. 1539.

79. Fraser, *Lennox*, ii, 127–131; and see below, Ch. 3.

80. Danske Rigsarkiv, T.K.U.A., Skotland, A.1., 1.

81. Vat. Reg. Supp. 870, f.121r; *Cal. Papal Letters*, xiv, 4.

82. *T.A.*, i, 89–90, 97, 106.

83. *A.P.S.*, ii, 202–3.

84. *A.P.S.*, ii, 210.

85. S.R.O., RH 1/1/3. The title 'Prince of Scotland' originates in 1404, when Robert III made his surviving son — the future James I — Steward of the royal family lands in Renfrewshire and Bute. These lands were subsequently referred to as the 'principality', and were conferred on the eldest son of the ruling king, who is sometimes described as 'princeps' — though this was not a territorial title, merely an acknowledgement of the status of successive heirs to the throne. The dukedom of Rothesay was the territorial title, and heirs to the throne are invariably described as dukes of Rothesay throughout the 15th century. The future James IV is also so described — *until* the revolution of 1488, when he first styles himself 'Prince of Scotland' — a significant change. For details, see W.C. Dickinson, 'An Inquiry into the origin of the title Prince of Scotland', *Economica*, iv, 212–220.

86. Fraser, *Lennox*, ii, 128–131; N.L.S. MS 1746, f.112r. (Abell); Lesley, *History*, 57; Ferreri, *Appendix to Boece*, f.400v.

87. Pitscottie, *Historie*, i, 204–5.

88. *R.S.S.*, i, Nos. 14, 32. Nicholson, *Later Middle Ages*, 538, places the fight at Dunkeld in the following year, during the rebellion of 1489. This is possible; but the Master of Huntly's presence at Dunkeld makes more sense as part of the civil war of 1488.

89. *Prot. Bk. Young*, No. 104.

90. *R.M.S.*, ii, No. 1811; *T.A.*, i, 96.

91. *A.P.S.*, ii, 204; Pitcairn, *Criminal Trials*, i, 8.

92. For the site of Sauchieburn, and an analysis of the king's movements in relation to the rebels before the battle, see Macdougall, *James III*, 255–7. For an alternative site, see Angus Graham, 'The Battle of 'Sauchieburn'', *S.H.R.*, xxxix (Oct. 1960), 95–6.

93. Fraser, *Lennox*, ii, 128–131. The written oath not to harm James III at Sauchieburn was recalled in the rebel apologia of 1489. The later chroniclers' statements that the prince ordered no-one to lay violent hands on his father are to

be found in N.L.S. MS 1746 f.112r. (Abell); Lesley, *History*, 57; Ferreri, *Appendix to Boece*, f.400v.

94. The relevant lines in Lindsay's poem are:
'Nou that the sone with baner bred displayit
Aganis the fader in battell come arreyit.'

95. *Scots Peerage*, iv, 234 (Glencairn); *Archaelogical Collections relating to the county of Renfrew*, ii, p. xiv; *A.D.A.*, 199 (Semple).

96. The presence on the rebel side at Sauchieburn of Argyll, Angus, Blacader, Hailes, Hume, Lyle and Knollis is inferred from their presence at Edinburgh a few days later making an inventory of the royal treasure: *T.A.*, i, 79–80. Montgomery was given a remission for his role at Sauchieburn by James IV (14 Oct. 1488, printed in Fraser, *Montgomeries*, ii, 48). George Shaw, abbot of Paisley, petitioned the pope on behalf of himself and William Crichton, one of his monks, for absolution for his presence at Sauchieburn: Vat. Reg. Supp., 947, f.95 r-v; for the Jedburgh convent's adherence to the rebels, see Wilkins, *Concilia*, iii, 634.

97. For a discussion of the likely rebel leaders at Sauchieburn, see Macdougall, *James III*, 256–7.

98. N.L.S. MS 1746, f.111r.

99. *A.P.S.*, ii, 204.

100. Fraser, *Montgomeries*, ii, 48.

101. *T.A.*, i, lxxi, 87; *E.R.*, x, xxxix, 82.

102. For a detailed analysis of James III's flight and death, see Macdougall, *James III*, 257–263.

103. Pitscottie, *Historie*, i, 209.

104. Buchanan, *History*, ii, 159, 161.

105. *A.P.S.*, ii, 204.

106. Pitscottie, *Historie*, i, 209, suggests that the assassin removed James III's body and that no-one discovered where he buried it, and that a month after Sauchieburn no information had been received by the new government as to the location of the body or the identity of the assassin. In fact, however, James III was buried in Cambuskenneth Abbey beside his queen, probably in the last week of June 1488: *T.A.*, i, lxxiv; *James IV Letters*, No. 542.

107. William Hepburn, who became clerk register in place of Alexander Scot: *R.M.S.*, ii, No. 1731.

3

1488-90: Rebels Without a Cause?

James III's defeat at Sauchieburn may have come as no great surprise, but his death was another matter. For the first time, a Stewart king had been killed in an armed struggle with his own subjects, and the beneficiaries of his death went on to form the government of his son. The victors of 1488 must have realised that they were playing with fire. For one thing, they were no more representative of the entire political community than the late king's narrowly-based group of supporters had been; for another, they had all taken an oath before Sauchieburn not to lay violent hands on James III, yet he had been pursued and slain. While a large number of important individuals — possibly a majority — had openly disliked, or been apathetic towards, the late king, and had remained neutral in the recent crisis, they must have been shocked by the manner of King James's removal and the effect which it might have on their futures.

Faced with this situation, the victors moved swiftly to consolidate their power and to assert their legitimacy as leaders of the new government. The late king's strongholds of Edinburgh and Stirling had to be secured together with his vast wealth in money and jewels; the young James IV had to be crowned as quickly as possible; the principal offices of state and household had to be divided amongst the rebel leaders and their sympathisers; and James III's erstwhile ally, Henry VII of England, had to be pacified without delay. Only when these steps had been taken, or at least initiated, would it be safe to call a parliament.

The early weeks of the new reign passed smoothly enough. Stirling castle was already in rebel hands, and having arranged for the late queen's jewellery to be sent after them, the victors of Sauchieburn conducted James IV to Edinburgh by way of Linlithgow and Leith. It was probably in these early days that they negotiated with Sir Andrew Wood, whose ships the 'Yellow Carvel' and 'Flower' had come down into the Firth of Forth from Stirling after the battle, possibly carrying royalist survivors of Sauchieburn to safety. Wood's ships had probably played a crucial role in James III's recent campaign, conveying the late king twice across the Forth in April, and the full length of the river to Stirling only a few days before. Wood's potential in 'the inbringing of Inglissmen', or for that matter, in aiding royalists to escape, was considerable; he may not have had James III on board, as Pitscottie has the fearful leaders of the new regime believe,[1] but it seems likely that the late

king's advocate, Sir John Ross of Montgrenan, who had helped array the royal
army at Sauchieburn,[2] used Wood's ships as his escape route to England and
the court of Henry VII. Pitscottie may well be right when he says that the
initial intention of those about the young king was to attack Wood as he lay
off Leith; but failing to find any local captains who would undertake the risk,
they wisely let him go, and came to an accommodation with him the following
month, whereby Wood's feu-charter of Largo, granted to him in 1483 by James
III, was confirmed.[3] He was perhaps the only prominent supporter of the late
king who did not initially suffer for being on the wrong side in 1488.

For the new regime, the most pressing business was the acquisition of James
III's treasure. Within a few days of Sauchieburn they had entered Edinburgh
and received from Dean Robert Hog, a canon of Holyrood, assorted gold and
silver coins in a tin box; and about the same time, on 17 June, a deputation
of magnates entered Edinburgh castle to examine the royal jewel house and
its contents. Both the rebel earls, Angus and Argyll, were there, with Bishop
Blacader of Glasgow, Lords Hailes and Hume, and William Knollis, preceptor
of Torphichen, who had already been appointed Treasurer in place of David
Lichtoun, abbot of Arbroath. The principal item recovered was the late king's
black kist, containing three coffers, a box, and a 'cageat', filled with a huge
quantity of jewellery, silver coin, and plate which included four macers of
Robert Bruce. Another relic of the hero king, Bruce's shirt, was discovered
in the nearby David's Tower. There was however much more to James III's
treasure than a tin box of gold and silver coin at Holyrood and a black kist
in Edinburgh castle; and the new regime set about recovering the remainder
— an impressive remainder — at once. Two rebel leaders — Patrick Hume
of Polwarth and George Touris, an Edinburgh burgess who would soon be
appointed custumar of Edinburgh — had captured John Stewart, earl of Atholl,
either at or after Sauchieburn, and forced his countess to deliver up two boxes
of the late king's money — though not before they had enriched themselves
by removing 320 Harry nobles from one of the boxes. These boxes were duly
examined in Edinburgh on 21 June by Argyll, John Hepburn, prior of St
Andrews, and Treasurer Knollis; Hume of Polwarth and Touris were forced
to give up their winnings and Hume accepted a much more modest reward
of forty Harry nobles. At about the same time the former Treasurer, David
Lichtoun, abbot of Arbroath, brought to Edinburgh a black coffer containing
further James III treasure, jewels and gold and silver coin, from the contents
of which the Earl of Angus was rewarded. Clearly, however, the rebel leaders
believed that Lichtoun was holding something back, and he was ordered to
produce a further black box and a white iron coffer at Perth — where the
court would be in residence after the coronation at Scone — on 26 June.[4]

Both before and after the coronation, the business of recovering James III's
money and jewels from his supporters continued apace. On 23 June at Scone,
Bishop Blacader, Lord Lyle, Prior Hepburn of St Andrews, Patrick Hume[5]
and Lord Drummond took time off from their preparations for the coronation
on the following day to draw up an inventory of yet another box of treasure,

'Avery's box', found 'in the myre' by James Avery, William Patonsone, and William Wallace.[6] The first of these men, James Avery, was the son of Alan of the Avery, James III's sheriff of Fife, who had clearly been entrusted by the late king with a box of gold coin, much of it loose; the'myre' in question may well be Sauchieburn. The most dramatic finds of all, however, were made by one Walter Simson, on the field of Sauchieburn itself — a box containing £4,000 in gold, and the sword of Robert Bruce,[7] the latter a pathetic reminder of James III's pretensions and inadequacy.

Thus only a fortnight after Sauchieburn, the new regime had forced the late king's supporters to disgorge an impressive hoard of treasure, eventually valued at over £24,000 Scots. Members of the new administration, however, remained unconvinced that they had received more than a fraction of what should have been there; and anyone who had any close dealings with the former Treasurer, David Lichtoun, abbot of Arbroath, might have been in a position to know the true extent of James III's treasure. It was an issue which would not go away, but return as a nightmare the following year, and subsequently rumble on well into the 'nineties.

Of more immediate concern, however, was the coronation itself. About 21 June, the young king and his supporters left Edinburgh for Scone, where they were to be found on 23 June. In order to impress on the Scots the legitimacy of the new king and his adherents, James IV was to be crowned at Scone, the first Stewart monarch to have his coronation there since his great-grandfather James I in 1424. The event itself took place on Wednesday 24 June,[8] the anniversary of Bruce's great victory at Bannockburn, a grim irony in view of recent events; and strenuous efforts were undertaken to make the ceremony as imposing as possible. Satin doublets — black, blue and crimson — were made for the king, who rode to his coronation sitting on a horse arrayed in velvet, attended by eight henchmen attired in black satin doublets and black velvet gowns, the procession preceded by a man bearing St Fillan's bell, renowned for its efficacy in curing the mentally afflicted.[9] The elaborate ceremony was attended by two bishops, Blacader of Glasgow and Brown of Dunkeld; Prior Hepburn of St Andrews, the new Keeper of the Privy Seal; Master Alexander Inglis, archdeacon of St Andrews, Keeper of the Rolls; Archibald Whitelaw, Subdean of Glasgow, the ubiquitous royal Secretary, completing his twenty-fifth year in the office, the perfect civil servant, no doubt relishing the prospect of serving yet another regime; Master William Hepburn, vicar of Linlithgow, the new Clerk Reigster; and Sir William Knollis, preceptor of Torphichen, the Treasurer. The laity were represented by two earls, Angus and Argyll, the latter already restored as Chancellor; Patrick Hepburn, Lord Hailes, styled Master of the Household; Robert, Lord Lyle, named as a justiciar; and that ominous trio of rebel hardliners, Lords Oliphant, Gray, and Drummond.[10] Conspicuous by their absence were William Hay, earl of Erroll, the hereditary Constable, and William Keith, earl Marischal, both of whom in other circumstances would have been expected to officiate during the coronation ceremony;[11] and the most significant absentee of all was the primate, William Scheves, archbishop of St Andrews, whose adherence to, and earlier intimacy with, James III made him persona non grata to the new regime. The crowning of the new king was probably carried out by Scheves' great rival, Robert Blacader of Glasgow, after which all the magnates present would come forward and touch the crown, each saying 'Sua mote God helpe me, as I sall supporte the'. The king would then take the royal oath, promising to be loyal and true to God and Holy Church, and to the three estates of his realm, and to govern according to the law and customs of the kingdom, making no changes in these without the consent of the three estates. The first two estates, clergy and magnates, would then respond with their respective oaths, promising loyalty and good counsels, and bringing the ceremony to an end.[12] A few days later, James IV rode south from Perth to Stirling to attend the burial of his father in Cambuskenneth Abbey, a scene later movingly if conventionally portrayed in James's Book of Hours.[13]

The events of the first fortnight of his reign must have given the young king much food for thought. His short life had been filled with intrigues, by himself and on his behalf, directed against his father; and while he had no cause to love James III, the latter's unexpected demise at Sauchieburn left him suddenly alone, a king without experience of, or preparation for, government, dominated by a faction of victorious rebels who first placed the crown on his head and then took him to bury his father, a salutory reminder to him of the mortality of unpopular kings. Yet what had happened in the early months of 1488 had largely been willed by himself. He had placed his trust in a number of rebel magnates who had made him king, and for the most part would continue to give them his support and patronage. However his acceptance of things as they were did not preclude remorse for his own involvement in regicide and patricide. All the chroniclers from Adam Abell onwards stress his sorrow and penances; and the contemporary Pedro de Ayala leaves us in no doubt as to James' piety, above all his favour to the Observantine friars.[14] So Pitscottie's famous story of the king's repentance for his part in his father's death, and his confession of guilt to the Dean of the Chapel Royal at Stirling,[15] certainly has a factual basis. The king was at Stirling castle from 29 June until 26 July; the main business of the month was the exchequer audit, which began on 7 July.[16] King James was no doubt present at the outset; but he probably played little part in exchequer business beyond authorising letters to be sent in his name to order the Earl of Crawford and John Ramsay of Corston to come to Stirling and render their accounts. Instead we find the king receiving £9 from the Treasurer to play in Stirling, presumably at cards; he offered 18/- at the soul mass of the late Lord Avandale in Stirling Blackfriars, and the same sum on 14 July at the soul mass of his mother, Margaret of Denmark, on the second anniversary of her death.[17]

This last doleful duty may well have contributed to feelings of repentance on the part of the young king. After all, he and his supporters had used his mother's name in their propaganda to Denmark, suggesting that the late queen was the victim of poison administered by John Ramsay, James III's familiar. The story he knew to be untrue;[18] but it had played its part in his father's removal and thus in making him king. In Pitscottie's story, James IV was brought to repentance in Stirling 'that he hapnit to be consallit to come aganis his father in battell quhairthrow he was murdrest and slaine.' So he consulted the Dean of the Chapel Royal — George Vaus, bishop of Galloway — who according to Pitscottie declined to tell the king his true opinion of the new regime for fear that it would get back to its leaders and 'that they murderaris wald be discontentit and utterlie displeisit at him gif he ha gevin the king his consall so far as his conscience dyttit him.' So the Dean kept his own counsel, 'quhill he saw the king farder in aige and uther consallouris about him.' In the meantime he spoke kindly to James IV, giving him hope of forgiveness, whereupon the king imposed his own penance on himself, the constant wearing of an iron belt to which he added weight every year throughout his life. Pitscottie's tale concludes with the reaction of the leaders of the new regime to all this; seeing the king 'dollourous and ewer mussing in his mynd, thinkand that he wald sum tyme be displeissit witht thair proceidingis', they began to fear that supporters of the late king would turn James IV's mind against them; and to forestall this they determined to call a parliament.[19]

This story is of course both oversimplified and highly coloured; but it contains elements of truth. As regards detail, it is significant that the famous iron belt is no figment of Pitscottie's imagination, for it is also mentioned in Lesley's vernacular history and, more pertinently, in the Treasurer's accounts for January 1507.[20] More generally, the passage reflects what contemporary records show to be true, namely that the new king was controlled by a small group of magnates whose power was based solely on victory at Sauchieburn, that they feared a reaction against their control of James IV, and that they were gradually applying themselves to the problem of retaining power which had to be exercised through an adolsecent ruler who would soon be of an age to make his own political decisions. Their response to this problem was eventually, as Pitscottie suggests, to summon a parliament to confirm their authority; and the chronicler has clearly grasped what again contemporary sources put beyond doubt — that the leaders of the new regime were in a dilemma: to call parliament meant to unleash the forces of political faction against themselves, to allow a public voice to the entire political community, whose most immediate business would inevitably be an inquest into the death of James III and the identities of those responsible for it. On the other hand, if parliament were not summoned soon, the country's new leaders could not justify their takeover, nor make effective charges of treason brought against their enemies, the men close to James III in the months before June 1488.

In the event, the leaders of the new regime showed some political good sense: that is, they delayed summoning parliament in the king's name until they had acquired the lion's share of power, and were therefore in a position effectively to resist the political backlash when it came. As the coronation had taken place on 24 June, and parliamentary summonses always gave forty days' notice, the three estates could have assembled as early as early August; instead, the first parliament of the reign met on 6 October. Long before its meeting, the post-Sauchieburn revolution in government had taken place; and it seems clear that the victors' main concern between Sauchieburn in June and parliament in October was to feather their own nests at the expense of the vanquished. What is important in relation to the late summer and early autumn of 1488, therefore, is not simply who benefited by the change of government, in terms of lands and offices bestowed, but exactly *when* they benefited.

Even a casual glance at early royal grants reveals that the family of Hepburn acquired formidable political strength at the very beginning. William Hepburn became Clerk Register the day after Sauchieburn; Alexander Hepburn was made sheriff of Fife four days later; John Hepburn, prior of St Andrews, not only became keeper of Falkland castle on 16 June, but by 25 June, the day after the coronation, he had acquired the office of Keeper of the Privy Seal, giving him effective control of crown patronage from the very start of the reign.[21] Most striking of all, however, were the honours heaped on the prior's nephew, Patrick Hepburn, Lord Hailes, who on 26 June was made keeper of Edinburgh castle and sheriff of Edinburgh;[22] by 10 September he already bore the title Earl of Bothwell, a dignity made up of the lordships of Crichton and Bothwell, and significantly conferred on Hailes before John Ramsay, Lord Bothwell, was forfeited in the October parliament. Hailes was the only earl created in this reign before 1503; and on 10 September he also acquired the post of Admiral of Scotland.[23] At the coronation in June, Hailes was already styling himself Master of the Royal Household,[24] and as keeper of Edinburgh castle he had effective custody of the king and his younger brother, the Duke of Ross, from the beginning. Thus the aftermath of Sauchieburn produced an immediate Hepburn takeover, strengthened as time passed by further Hepburn appointments to offices of state and household — Adam Hepburn of Ogston, the new earl's brother, becoming master of the King's Stable; John Hepburn of Rollandston, Steward of the royal household; Patrick Hepburn, Master of the Royal Larder and Cellar; and George Hepburn, Director of Chancery.[25] Although magnate families had dominated government during royal minorities in the past — the Livingstons and Douglases in James II's reign, the Boyds in that of James III — they had all been dramatically removed when the monarch took control. Nothing of the sort would happen to the Hepburns, partly because the political circumstances of 1488 were radically different — the family had helped to make James IV king — and partly because of the political skill and public service of the new Earl of Bothwell himself. Sheriff of Berwick, defender of Berwick Castle against Albany and Gloucester in 1482, Conservator of the English truce of September 1484, provost of Edinburgh in 1487, Bothwell as Lord Hailes had behind him a creditable career as a loyal border magnate, serving the Crown but not a member of the late king's council, a man who had come out against James III not primarily from a sense of personal grievance, but in defence of his Hume kinsmen: his mother was the daughter of Alexander, first Lord Hume.[26] Patrick Hepburn presented to the world the acceptable face of magnate protest in 1488; and the rewards for himself and his family were enormous.

Hepburn's kinsmen and neighbours, the Humes, likewise benefited substantially from the rebellion of 1488. In a sense the Hume achievement was the most striking, for there would have been no future for the family in south-east Scotland if James III had survived. As it was, Alexander Hume of that ilk, the future Lord Hume, was confirmed as Chamberlain for life in the parliament of October 1488;[27] the seemingly endless Coldingham dispute was at last settled in favour of John Hume as prior;[28] and royal grants to members of the family are scattered throughout the early years of the reign.[29] So the survival and continuing success of the Humes is remarkable. Nevertheless it is significant that their grants, unlike those of the Hepburns, came late rather than early. Although Alexander Hume of that ilk surfaces briefly in the records just after Sauchieburn, it is probably significant that his major offices — the wardenship of the East Marches for seven years, and the custody of Stirling castle and the king's brother, John, earl of Mar — were not acquired until 1489 and 1490 respectively, by which time the new regime had been severely shaken by rebellion and badly needed to be sure of Hume support. The Hume conspicuously favoured from the very start of the reign was Alexander's uncle Patrick Hume of Fastcastle, the recipient of two early grants of lands in Berwickshire and of the estates of the forfeited Lord Advocate, John Ross of Montgrenan, in October 1488.[30] The following year Patrick of Fastcastle was so closely identified with the new regime as to be named on a rebel hit-list, the only Hume to be singled out in this way.[31]

Having spent most of the month of July at Stirling, James IV emerged from his devotions to return briefly to Edinburgh, where his principal business at the beginning of August was to visit Leith to view the Danish ships — presumably those which had brought James's great-uncle, Gerhard of Oldenburg, to Scotland — and to authorise a payment of £47.4s.3d. to Alexander Hepburn to have the artillery house and burgh walls repaired.[32] The sum is not a large one, though of course the burgh may have been expected to find much of the cash for its own repairs; and it is tempting to connect the damage done with recent events, perhaps indeed with the new regime's initial efforts to negotiate with Sir Andrew Wood, whose feu-charter of Largo was not confirmed until 27th July, only 5 days before King James's visit to Leith. From the king's point of view, the visit marked the beginning of a fascination with ships which was to last to the very end of his life.

By 5 August, the king had moved west to Linlithgow, where he watched Patrick Johnson — later immortalised as one of William Dunbar's 'makars' — and the burgh players perform for him, gave alms to the friars, rewarded Jock Pringill, a trumpeter, and paid the royal gardener eighteen shillings. His keenest interest was in the forthcoming hunt; he bought hawking gloves from a Linlithgow skinner, and Sir William Knollis of Torphichen sent him a hawk. By 8 August King James had moved on to Stirling, and two days later he rode out to hunt in Glenfinglas. In the meantime, his new masters despatched summonses for treason against ten of the late king's supporters. Carrick Pursuivant was sent west on 6 August to summon John Ross of Montgrenan and John Ramsay, Lord

Bothwell, both of them already refugees in England; on 12 August, Montrose
Herald set off for the south-west with summonses against Cuthbert Murray
of Cockpool, Robert Charteris of Amisfield, 'and orderis'; on the same day,
a royal messenger named Scheto was sent to summon the Earl of Buchan,
Thomas Lord Innermeath, and Thomas Fotheringham of Powrie; and finally,
on 16 August, Ross Herald went north to summon Alexander Lord Forbes,
James Innes of Innes, and Sir Alexander Dunbar of Westfield.[33] The leaders
of the new regime had clearly determined to face the test of a parliament at the
start of October, and wanted, in Dr Nicholson's memorable phrase, 'to make
life miserable for members of the defeated party'[34] by using a parliamentary
tribunal to forfeit these ten former adherents of James III. The summonses are
however interesting as revealing the weaknesses as well as the strengths of the
new government. If not quite random, the list of those summoned for treason
contains some remarkable omissions, most notably the names of the Duke of
Montrose and the Earl of Atholl. The aim seems to have been to indict those
who were either already in exile — Ross of Montgrenan and Lord Bothwell
— or had been in ward since Blackness and could not avoid a summons —
Buchan, Fotheringham of Powrie, and probably Innermeath — together with
the late king's northern and southwestern supporters at the very end of the crisis.
Significantly, only four of the ten — Buchan, Ross, Lord Bothwell, and Murray
of Cockpool — were eventually indicted for treason, and their indictments make
unconvincing reading because the charges amount to little more than supporting
their late sovereign against his (then) rebels. The charges against Buchan, Ross,
and Lord Bothwell survive, and the leitmotif running through all of them is the
crime of 'inbringing of Inglissmen to the perpetuale subieccione of the realme'[35]
— in other words, negotiating with Henry VII of England on James III's behalf
during the recent crisis. On the whole, the ten August summonses, diminishing
to four October indictments, suggest an effort on the part of the victors to settle
old scores, tempered with caution when it became apparent that parliamentary
convictions were going to be difficult to secure.

A more practical way to ensure that what had been gained on the battlefield
was rapidly legalised was to make use of the new king. On returning from the
hunt, James IV was taken on his first justice ayre, to Lanark, arriving about
21 August, a fortnight after Carrick pursuivant had appeared at Lanark market
cross summoning John Ramsay, Lord Bothwell, to answer charges of treason.[36]
The device of taking the king on tour to legitimise the new regime's takeover — in
this case to underline the transfer of the lordship of Bothwell from John Ramsay
to Patrick Hepburn, Lord Hailes — was a shrewd political move, reinforced by
September visits by King James on ayre to Dundee and Perth, significantly both
places from which prominent James III supporters had just been displaced.[37] It
is surely in the context of these early ayres that the much-vaunted article eight
of the October 1488 parliament should be considered. This is the requirement
that the king go out personally on justice ayres,[38] and extravagant claims have
been made for this act as an illustration of James IV's determination to do his
job as king from the start in a way that his father had never done. In fact the act

was retrospective, because the king had already been out on the ayres in August — September, *before* the parliament, lending authority to the new regime's unpleasantness towards former James III men in the Clyde valley, Angus, and Perth; and he would be put on his horse again the following February, to do the same thing in the south-west.

A crucial factor in determining the survival and strength of the new regime was relations with England; for James III had worked assiduously, indeed obsessionally, in his last years for a firm peace with Henry VII, culminating in the projected triple marriage alliance of November 1487 and a final settlement of the contentious issue of Berwick, which was to have been the subject of talks by the two kings in person in July 1488. Sauchieburn not only put an end to such schemes of close alliance, but brought to power in Scotland a government committed to making hostile noises about Anglo-Scottish relations, if nothing worse. In the first week of the new reign, the Hepburn regime gave letters of safe-conduct in James IV's name to the Yorkist Francis, Viscount Lovel, together with his friends Sir Thomas Broughton, Sir Roger Hartilton, and Oliver Frank.[39] Lovel and Broughton were survivors of the battle of Stoke in June 1487, when Henry VII had been forced to confront head-on the threat presented by the pretender Lambert Simnel and John, earl of Lincoln. King Henry had duly won the battle and broken the rebellion; and while James III was alive in Scotland there can have been no place for Stoke's most distinguished Yorkist survivors.[40] In granting a safe-conduct to Lovel and his friends at the very outset of James IV's reign, the new Scottish government was clearly signalling a major diplomatic change. Henry VII could no longer rely on an obsequious James III pressing him for peace at almost any price; now Scotland must be regarded as a refuge for Yorkists and a potential ally of France — and this at precisely the time that the English king was becoming involved in schemes to preserve Breton independence in the face of a growing threat from France.[41] More specifically, the Scots' sheltering of Lovel and his Yorkist associates was an obvious diplomatic counterbalance to King Henry's harbouring of the Scottish fifth column, Ramsay and Ross of Montgrenan.

Behind these posturings lay the reality of the situation, which was that whatever ritual Anglophobic noises James IV's fledgling government might make, its leaders had an urgent need for foreign recognition of their status and that of the new Scottish king. Survival at home of a royal administration which did not as yet command widespread support in many areas of Scotland might well depend, if not on Henry VII's enthusiastic endorsement of the events of 1488, then at least on his grudging acceptance of them. Understandably the English king's initial response to the news of Sauchieburn had been to strengthen his border garrisons; on 19 July he ordered musters of hobelars and archers at Berwick, Norham, Newcastle, and Carlisle, together with proper supervision of artillery in all these places.[42] However, the expected Scottish assault on the borders never came; instead, on 8 September, commissioners were appointed to meet with their English counterparts at Coldstream on 23 September, to treat, as the English record optimistically puts it, for perpetual peace. What in fact was achieved on 5 October was a three year truce,[43] a far cry not only from perpetual peace but also from James III's recent ambitious alliance projects. It was however probably as far as the new Scots regime felt that it could credibly go; after all, within a few days its leaders would be asking the three estates to accept the recent 'inbringing of Inglissmen' by James III and his supporters as treasonable.

On 6 October, the day after the Coldstream truce had been agreed, the first parliament of the reign met in Edinburgh. The large attendance — a total of eighty-four, 34 clergy, 35 barons, and 15 burgh commissioners — reflects the importance of the business in hand, and the ten days that followed must have been regarded as a critical test by the leaders of the new regime; for present in parliament were not only those who had chosen to remain neutral in the recent conflict, but also active supporters of James III, such as William Elphinstone, the former Chancellor, William Scheves, archbishop of St Andrews, since 1487 primate of Scotland, William Keith, earl Marischal, and John Lord Carlyle, all men who were unlikely to give the new government an easy time in debate.[44] But the Hepburns and their allies had done their homework well, and ensured that the Committee of the Articles, which would draft legislation for consideration by the entire parliament, was largely composed of themselves and those favourably disposed towards them, a huge committee of twenty-eight in all, one-third of those present. Significantly Scheves, Elphinstone, Marischal, and Carlyle were not elected to the articles, though Marischal was thrown the sop of being allowed to sit with Elphinstone on the Lords Auditors. Other committed James III men, such as Crawford, the Bishop of Moray, and the Master of Huntly, prudently stayed away; Atholl sent a procurator, Buchan's appearance was at his trial for treason on 8 October, and Glencairn was dead. As for the treason trials themselves, it comes as no surprise to discover that those sitting in judgment had all been active against James III in the recent rebellion — Chancellor Argyll, Lords Gray, Drummond, Oliphant, Lyle, and Glamis.[45]

Despite the large attendance, therefore, the parliament of October 1488 was largely controlled by the Hepburns and their allies from the outset, because they had successfully packed the committees which really mattered. Their aim was not to try to bring James III irreconcilables back into the fold, but rather to convince the majority of the political community — above all committed neutrals like the Earl of Huntly — that they were a responsible government, here to stay. In this they were initially less than successful, probably because no public glossing over of recent events could conceal the one truth which must have been unpalatable to many, namely that one narrow faction had replaced another in power by means of armed rebellion. A broadly-based government seemed as far away as it had done in James III's 'crisis' parliaments of October 1487 and January 1488. For those outwith the charmed circle, nothing had changed but the name of the king.

Elected on 7 October, the committee of the articles spent much of the next ten days drafting legislation, though five of its number had first to sit, on 8

October, on the judicial tribunals to deal with those summoned for treason — Buchan, Ross of Montgrenan, John Ramsay, Lord Bothwell, and Cuthbert Murray of Cockpool. In the event, Buchan was present and given a remission — though not forgiven — while Ross and Ramsay, being out of the country, could be forfeited in absentia, and the case against Murray of Cockpool was continued.[46] This was a remarkably unconvincing result, particularly when one considers that both Ramsay and Ross were to be pardoned within a few years; for what in essence it meant was that having sounded off at great length about James III's 'perverse counsel', the new regime was only able to bring four of those responsible to judgment, and the results were one pardon, one continued case, and two forfeitures, both later rescinded.

This moderation, if moderation it was, on the part of the judicial tribunal may have been regarded as a matter or necessity in order to defuse an item of business on the parliamentary agenda which was potentially much more damaging to the regime — the debate on the causes of the field of Stirling and the death of James III. Either because they wished to lay the ghost of the late king once and for all, or because it was forced on them, the Hepburn regime allowed the reasons for the late king's demise to be debated by the entire parliament on its final day, 17 October. With such extremes of political opinion as Scheves and Blacader, Argyll and Elphinstone, Carlyle and Maxwell, present in the same chamber, the debate must have been acrimonious; but it was brought to an end by Lord Glamis — significantly one of the treason tribunal judges — flourishing a copy of the agreement which James III had made, at Aberdeen the previous April, to negotiate with the rebel lords, an agreement which he had signed and then promptly broken. The possession of a copy of this agreement was a godsend to the new regime, for it enabled them to advance the fiction that they had always been looking for a settlement with the intransigent James III, and that the late king, by using 'perverse counsel' — cautiously unspecified — had been responsible for the field of Stirling and his own death — at the hands, of course, of 'vile and obscure persons', which was probably the truth, though a necessary truth for magnates who had benefited so extensively from his death. Thus the official line was hammered out in familiar language — the late king used 'perverse counsel', was guilty of 'the inbringing of Inglissmen to the perpetuale subieccione of the realme', had 'happinit' to be slain.[47] The formula worked — up to a point. The estates dispersed on 17 October, with parliamentary power delegated to an impossibly large committee of sixty-one, the auditors ploughing on for another week through a backlog of civil cases,[48] and the real political power, as ever, in the hands of the privy council.

The parliament of October 1488 has been described by James IV's most recent biographer as displaying 'statesmanlike moderation';[49] another view is that 'reconciliation rather than revenge became the order of the day.'[50] But sweet reasonableness on the part of the new regime was surely limited to an act ordering the restoring of moveable goods seized from 'pure unlandit folkis' during the rebellion, together with an assurance that the heirs of those who had died fighting for James III at Sauchieburn would be able to buy brieves of service in their lands from the new king.[51] But in the vital areas of office-holding and the administration of criminal justice, no concessions were made at all. One act ordered the removal from office for a period of three years of all those holding heritable offices — wardens, justices, sheriffs, stewards, bailies, and lieutenants — under the late king; those whose offices were held only in liferent or for specified terms were to lose them for good.[52] Two big names immediately affected were David, earl of Crawford, whose sheriffship of Forfar went to Lord Gray; and Sir William Murray of Tullibardine, who lost the Stewartry of Strathearn to Lord Drummond. A further act, the second last of the parliament, confirmed the proclamation made at the Scone coronation in June, ordaining that all grants of lands and offices made by James III after 2 February 1488 were 'of nane effect nor force in ony tyme tocum.'[53] A number of magnates gave their oaths in parliament to seek out 'trespassouris' — a term covering many types of criminal, in this case thieves, reivers and those guilty of 'vtheris innormites' — and either punish them on the spot or send them to the king for punishment. With few exceptions, these very extensive powers went to the victors of Sauchieburn, the entire borders and most of the south-west being divided between Hepburn and Hume, Angus acting in the sheriffdoms of Roxburgh, Selkirk, Peebles, and Lanark, Angus and Maxwell dividing Dumfries between them, Lord Montgomery acting in Cunningham, and Lennox, Lyle, and Lennox's son Matthew Stewart in Renfrewshire, Monklands, Lenzie, Bothwell, Glasgow, Kilbride, and Avondale, though they had to divide their jurisdiction of Dumbarton, the Lennox, Bute, and Arran with Lord Montgomery. Not surprisingly, criminal jurisdiction in Angus went to Lord Gray, Lord Glamis, and Alexander, Master of Crawford, the appalling son of Earl David; while Lord Drummond received his rewards in Strathearn, Balquhidder, and Dunblane, and Lord Oliphant in the sheriffdom of Perth. These powers of criminal jurisdiction were conferred until the king should reach the age of twenty-one, that is, till the spring of 1494.[54] Such an act, if harshly applied, could lead to the continued pursuit by the new regime of their former enemies throughout much of Scotland, backed by parliamentary authority. Certainly it did little to help solve the basic problems which had caused the troubles of 1482 and 1488 — the failure of the Crown to distribute patronage with an even hand, together with the related inability to quell major feuds. Instead, one narrow clique had succeeded another at the top, a change liable to exacerbate existing feuds and to create new ones.

For it soon became clear that the new government had no intention of abandoning its pursuit of former James III men. The October 1488 parliament was continued to 14 January 1489, when the brief and incomplete record reveals that in spite of his remission the previous October, James, earl of Buchan, had done something to earn the government's further displeasure.[55] This is presumably a reference to the appearance of Buchan before the Lords Auditors — an unusually large body of 25 — three days after the start of the parliament, charged with his failure to pay to the king ten thousand marks Scots, in which sum he, Lord Erskine and Lord Gray had stood surety for the delivery of Buchan's brother, Andrew Stewart, bishop of Moray, to Lord Drummond, and thence to the king. Moray had not appeared, so Buchan and his associates were left with the problem of finding the surety money. What had clearly happened was that the new regime had called for Andrew Stewart, the last of James III's half-uncles and a man closely involved in his English negotiations in the late spring of 1488, to surrender, and he had not done so. Buchan, who had stood surety for his brother, was threatened with distraint of his lands and goods if he did not pay up.[56]

He did not suffer alone. Two days later, on 19 January, the same vast array of judges deprived John, Lord Carlyle, a prominent James III supporter at the end of the reign, of his lands of Drumcoll, which he claimed to hold in feu and heritage as a gift of the late king. The auditors found against Carlyle on the ground that James III had had no right to grant Drumcoll in the first place, as it was one of the lands already annexed to the principality and could not be alienated.[57] A similar case followed on 21 January, when David, earl of Crawford, who had already been deprived of his dukedom of Montrose and sheriffship of Forfar, was ordered to lose the lordships of Brechin and Navar because they had been annexed to the Crown as long before as 1455.[58]

None of these actions was illegal in the strict sense, and a fertile imagination might justify all of them by suggesting that the auditors were inspired by the most responsible of motives, the desire to preserve the king's patrimony, and to prevent its improper alienation, during his tender age. This would be a more convincing argument if the auditors had proceeded with equal vigour against those sympathetic to the new regime as well as its former enemies. But royal justice early in 1489 was closely related to the needs of the faction in power, and it is hardly surprising, in the later rebel complaints, to find the constantly recurring theme of 'parciall personis' about the king. In any case, the king's tender age had five years to run — far too long for those who had been singled out for judicial attacks, or even for those who feared they might be. Prominent among the former were William Lord Ruthven and Sir William Murray of Tullibardine, both James III men and both Blackness hostages. Both men were the subject of cases involving their ransoms — compositions of respectively £1,000 and 600 marks, presumably for their release after Blackness — at the time of, and shortly after, the January parliament of 1489;[59] and the exaction of ransoms would be another major grievance of the disaffected later in the year. Even Pitscottie's funny story of the trial for treason of his ancestor Lord Lindsay of Byres, with his brother appearing as his advocate and accidentally stamping on Lindsay's sore toe, may draw its relevance from the continuing vindictiveness of the new regime at this time.[60]

The sequel was rebellion on a scale unequalled even in 1488. Its organizer was Alexander Gordon, Master of Huntly, who took time off from the January 1489 parliament to retire to some quiet place and write to Henry VII of England, reminding the English king of 'the treasonable and cruel slaughter' of James III by a part of his (unspecified) 'fals and untrew liegis.' While appealing for English aid, the Master of Huntly makes it clear that he has enlisted the help of the late king's friends and kinsmen, and intends to launch an attack on the new Scottish government. As we have seen, Alexander, Master of Huntly, had been one of James III's few committed supporters, receiving grants — and probably some of the royal treasure — at the very end of the reign; and the royal kinsmen to whom he refers in his letter were presumably the late king's half-uncles, Atholl, Buchan, and the Bishop of Moray — indeed he mentions Buchan by name.[61] No direct response to this plea for assistance survives. Unquestionably Henry VII must have been attracted by the prospect of weakening — perhaps fatally weakening — a potentially hostile Scottish government which was already seeking foreign marriages for James IV, a renewal of the Franco-Scottish alliance,[62] and providing shelter for fugitive Yorkists. English armed intervention on behalf of the Master of Huntly's rebellion may therefore have been considered by King Henry, and most likely urged by his Scottish pensioners, Ramsay and Ross of Montgrenan; but Henry had problems other than the Scots. The month after the Master wrote his letter, the English king committed himself by the Treaty of Redon to aiding the Duchess Anne of Brittany against the French. In January, Parliament had voted a war tax of £100,000, but it proved difficult to collect, and its imposition provoked a savage uprising in Yorkshire and the murder on 28 April 1489 of Henry Percy, earl of Northumberland.[63] As warden-general of the East and Middle Marches towards Scotland and sheriff of Northumberland, Percy would have been a vital figure in any muster of northern levies to assist the Scots rebels. His death, and the English king's immediate problem of the ensuing rebellion in Yorkshire, removed the possibility of prompt or direct intervention in Scottish affairs. Instead, the Scottish fifth column — Sir John Ramsay, Sir Adam Forman, and John Liddale of Halkerston in a single ship laden with munitions — was reactivated, far too late, in an effort to reinforce the rebels in Dumbarton castle.[64]

In the early spring of 1489, blissfully unaware of the Master of Huntly's letter to Henry VII and the rebellion which it portended, James IV and members of his council set off on the southern circuit of justice ayres. This expedition, which travelled first to Jedburgh by 11 February, included Argyll, Bothwell, the Justiciar Lord Drummond, Treasurer Knollis, Alexander Inglis, serving as both comptroller and clerk register, and Master Richard Lawson, the Justice Clerk. After eleven days at Jedburgh, the ayre moved on to Selkirk, Peebles, and finally Dumfries by the end of the month. In early March the royal party passed by way of Tongland to Kirkcudbright and Wigtown, reaching Ayr about 21 March, staying five days, and returning via Glasgow to Edinburgh by 1 April.[65] The object of this lengthy ayre was clearly to impress on the south-west — an area notoriously difficult to govern — that a new and forceful government had replaced that of James III. This was undeniable; whether it was generally welcome is another matter, for even the scanty evidence which survives for this southern ayre reveals the bias of James IV's justices. Thus on 25 February at Dumfries, Thomas Huchinson and John Carruthers received remissions for their part in the burning of Thomas Maclellan of Bombie's manor of Cockfergus, while John Stewart, more remarkably, was granted a remission not only for arson but also for rape on the same occasion.[66] That remissions were granted for such serious crimes by a government attempting to enforce order in a difficult area may seem remarkable, but its casual pardoning of the criminals probably owes much to the fact that Maclellan of Bombie had been an adherent of James III at the end of the reign.[67] Very different was the treatment meted out on this ayre to Sir Adam Murray of Drumcrieff, Murray of Cockpool's brother, who had attacked and burned Sir William Stirling's house of Keir shortly before Sauchieburn. Stirling of Keir was a committed supporter of James IV, while Murray's act of arson at Keir had been carried out on behalf of the late king. So in spite of the general remission made at the time of James IV's accession for all goods stolen or damage inflicted before the field of Stirling, it was ignored to allow the justice ayre at Dumfries to pursue Sir Adam Murray for the huge sum of £1,000 as compensation for his destruction of Keir.[68] The message was clear; the new regime was continuing to use the established forms of executing criminal justice to attack its enemies and pardon or reward its friends. There is perhaps nothing very surprising in the misuse of judicial machinery to meet the needs of a faction in power; but in the case of this spring justice ayre, the obvious bias displayed by those serving on it is soon reflected in rebel complaints about 'parciall personis' about the king.

Hints of what was to come are revealed in isolated entries in the Treasurer's accounts early in April, shortly after James IV's return to Edinburgh from the southern ayre. On 3 April a messenger was sent to summon Chancellor Argyll, Lord Gray, and Lord Drummond, to join the king in Edinburgh. This may have been no more than an invitation to join the court at Easter. Such an invitation was sent to the 'Lordis of the Westlande' (unspecified) on 6 April; but only two days later, Bute pursuivant and Nisbet macer were sent with specific letters to Duchal and Dumbarton, respectively the strongholds of Robert Lord Lyle and John Stewart, Lord Darnley, the latter only recently recognised as earl of Lennox for his support of James IV in the rebellion of 1488. No record exists of the content of those royal letters to Lyle and Lennox, though the employment of Rothesay and Montrose Heralds to take further letters to Dumbarton on 16 April suggests that they must have been summonses of some kind. Good Friday in 1489 fell on 17 April, and we find the king on that day moving restlessly from Holyrood westwards to Linlithgow, giving drinking money to the masons working on the palace there, returning to Edinburgh by Easter Monday. There was no time for the king to withdraw during Holy Week into the Chapel Royal at Stirling, for apart from the growing concern at court about affairs in the west, messengers were being despatched throughout the Easter period to East Lothian, Perth, Dundee, Fife, Peebles, Selkirk, Jedburgh, Dumfries, Wigtown, and beyond the Mounth to bring in the tax of £5,000 levied on the estates in October 1488 for the expenses of ambassadors to proceed to France, Brittany, Spain 'and utheris placez'.[69] There had clearly been considerable resistance to the imposition of this tax; it should have been levied by the time of the parliament of

January 1489, and these Easter messengers indicate a further effort to overcome resistance. Clearly, however, many — perhaps most — regions did not pay up, for in the parliament of February 1490, an early enactment fulminates against the non-payment of the tax, and orders that sheriffs, bailies and other royal officers charged with its inbringing who fail either to do so or ignore repeated royal letters on the subject, should enter ward in Blackness castle within fifteen days or be put to the horn.[70] Resistance to taxation is not an uncommon form of regional protest; in the case of the 1488–9 tax, however, opposition was a serious matter because the new government was visibly weak, attempting to justify its existence by seeking foreign recognition of James IV in order to confer respectability on the magnate faction controlling him. The leaders of that faction — Bothwell, Argyll, Gray, and Drummond — must have spent a worrying Easter, lacking the authority to compel payment of the tax and unsure as to who their real friends were.

They were soon left in little doubt. The day before Easter, a messenger was sent with letters about the tax to the north-east, the area where the late king's support was strongest. Alexander, Lord Forbes, who had been so committed to James III that he was summoned for treason in August 1488, responded to this challenge, if Buchanan is to be believed, by carrying the late king's shirt, 'stained with blood and torn with the marks of his wounds, suspended on a spear, through Aberdeen and the chief towns of the adjacent counties, and by public proclamation called upon all men to avenge the horrid deed.'[71] Buchanan, writing in the late sixteenth century, is the only chronicler to have this story; but it may well be true, because he is the best informed of all writers on the reign about the events of the rising of 1489. His knowledge may be based on local information; for Buchanan was born in the Lennox, not far from the scene of the great crisis of 1489, and only seventeen years later. It is even possible that Lord Forbes' dramatic banner was intended to evoke comparison, shortly after Easter, between the fate of James III and Christ's passion, to underline the sacred character of monarchy, and that the 'bludy serk' may have inspired Robert Henryson's poem of that name.[72]

The government's immediate troubles lay much nearer home. On 23 April, messengers were once more sent into the regions, but this time with a summons to the lords of 'the Westlande', of Teviotdale, and of Galloway, to come to the host at Dumbarton.[73] These urgent summonses were the response to the frightening news that armed insurrection had begun, not among the late king's friends in the north-east, but in Renfrewshire and the Lennox, and that its leaders were men who had only recently benefited by the revolution of 1488 — Robert, Lord Lyle, John Stewart, earl of Lennox, and his son Matthew.

Why did these men rebel? During the October 1488 parliament, all of them had been granted extensive powers to execute criminal justice in the west; Lord Lyle had been made justiciar in Bute and Arran in July 1488, and is styled 'justiciar' in royal documents as early as 15 June 1488; Lennox had finally been recognized as earl after a long struggle against rival claimants and exclusion from the liferent of the earldom; and he and his son Matthew had also received joint keepership of Dumbarton castle, formerly enjoyed, like the liferent of the Lennox, by James III's recently deceased familiar Andrew Stewart, Lord Avandale.[74] At first sight, then, there seems no obvious reason for dissatisfaction by any of these western magnates; but the key to an understanding of their behaviour may lie in Bishop Lesley's much later statement that they were moved by envy 'that the king was mare governit be utheris of the factione nor be thame'.[75] Certainly they had been rewarded; but Lennox and his son Matthew had had to wait until four months after Sauchieburn for official recognition of their share of the spoils, in stark contrast to the Hepburn faction, who had started distributing lands and offices amongst themselves the day after the battle, and in the October parliament of 1488 had still been trumpeting about their successes, describing Hailes' elevation to the earldom of Bothwell as a reward intended to stimulate similar virtues in others who hoped to achieve high office.[76] Like Lennox and his son, Robert Lord Lyle may have felt himself excluded from this governmental clique, and resented it; but his position was rather different, as he had received a justiciarship immediately after Sauchieburn. Probably he was gradually elbowed out; it is likely, for example, that he was offended that Lord Drummond was chosen as royal justiciar, in preference to himself, in the south-western justice ayre in February and March 1489, especially as the ayre had passed through, or close by, his Renfrewshire lands towards the end of March. Also, Lyle can hardly have been enthusiastic about the pardon granted in the October 1488 parliament to his old rival Buchan. On top of all this, Lyle had seen James III's treasure as it came in to Edinburgh and Scone the previous June.[77] He may have known that it was not all accounted for, or that there was much more to come; and finding himself no longer of the Hepburn elect, he determined to make an issue of it, using a popular cause to mask his personal grievances.

Another loser in the distribution of patronage early in the reign was Archibald Douglas, fifth earl of Angus. Initially he had seemed to do quite well, being styled guardian of the young king in some early charters, serving regularly on the privy council, acting as Warden of all three Marches, and given extensive judicial powers in the sheriffdoms of Roxburgh, Selkirk, Peebles, and Lanark.[78] However in the summer of 1489, after the outbreak of the Lyle and Lennox rising in the west, Angus's position steadily deteriorated. He lost all his March Wardenships, with the West and Middle Marches going to Bothwell, and the East Marches to Alexander Hume, in parliament on 4 July 1489. His sheriffship of Lanark went to James, Lord Hamilton; on 26 November, at Dumbarton, the royal familiar John Hume of Whiterig, brother of Alexander Hume of that ilk, was granted Angus's Berwickshire lands of Earlston; and on 26 June 1490, at Falkland, Andrew Lord Gray, described as 'royal counsellor', received Angus's lands and castle of Broughty in the sheriffdom of Forfar.[79] This steady loss of lands and offices is paralleled by Angus's disappearance from the council and from parliament between the summer of 1489 and February 1492. This striking eclipse of one of the most prominent rebels of 1488 has led some writers, including Sir William Fraser,[80] to draw the obvious conclusion that

Angus, falling out with the new regime which he had helped bring to power, joined the insurrection of 1489, conducted intrigues with Henry VII, and was heavily penalised for his folly. However, the evidence of 1489 suggests no such sinister purpose. On 12 February 1489, Angus was granted a safe-conduct by Henry VII, for six months, to pass through England with eighty attendants, on pilgrimage to Amiens. Subsequently the fragment of a royal letter from James IV to Henry VII reveals that Angus had at least set out, his intention being to visit Amiens' most famous relic, the Head of St. John the Baptist, and that he had reached England en route.[81] The same fragment — bearing no date— describes Angus as 'our traist and weilbelovet cousing', and states that he made a report to the king on his return. The letter implies that Angus never reached his destination of Amiens; his journey might well have been cut short by news of the extent of the troubles in Scotland, or by the discovery that the Hepburn — Hume faction had decided to filch his March Wardenships while he was out of the country. It is however most unlikely that he was carrying on treasonable negotiations with Henry VII at this time. As we know from the Master of Huntly's letter to the English King the previous January, Buchan was the man to do that. A much more likely explanation of Angus's behaviour is that he was entrusted by the king with some innocuous charge while passing through England. The earl was after all more of a companion than a guardian of James IV in the early years, receiving letters from the king, presenting him with a very expensive hawk, and playing at dice and cards with the king in 1490 and 1491, the period of Angus's political eclipse.[82] Angus's absence from Scotland, sometime between May and November 1489,[83] deprived the regime of his assistance during much of the rebellion — something which he may have intended — but also allowed its leaders to divest him of his most valuable offices. His political comeback in 1492 would be spectacular.

The same could not be said of William, the former third Lord Crichton, who had so incensed James III not only by his rebellion in 1482-3, but also by his liaison with the king's younger sister Margaret, which had resulted in the birth of a daughter, also named Margaret, and in Crichton's forfeiture in the parliament of February 1484.[84] Crichton's subsequent career had been adventurous; he had been captured in October 1486 and brought to Nottingham, but had managed to escape the following April.[85] Both events, and Henry VII's keen interest in them, reflect the cooperation between James III and King Henry in dealing with each other's rebels as part of the elaborate peace proposals of 1486-7. With King James's death at Sauchieburn, however, Crichton might have expected to recover his lands and title from the new regime, but his lordship went at once to Hepburn as part of his new earldom of Bothwell. Crichton's response — the only one possible — was to join in the rebellion of 1489; he was duly condemned with the others in the July parliament, but unlike the others, he would not be restored, either to lands or title, and when he died, sometime before 23 October 1493, he was the only prominent rebel of 1489 not to benefit by coming out in that year.[86]

Some of the events of 1489 remain mysterious. We do not know at what point the Lennox/Lyle rebels in the south-west made common cause with the Master of Huntly and his north-eastern allies, though it may be significant that Bishop Lesley attributes the use of the 'bludy serk' banner to Lennox and Lyle.[87] This might suggest early collusion between the two rebel groups as to the line to be taken in winning support; alternatively the south-western lords may have imitated Lord Forbes' dramatic gesture in order to lend respectability to their cause. By the early autumn, both groups were clearly working closely together.

Another grey area is the period immediately after Easter, when the government became aware of dissent in the west. But its leaders would hardly have been troubled if Lennox, Matthew Stewart, and Lyle had simply retained possession of the castles — Duchal, Crookston, and Dumbarton — which they already possessed. What visible form, therefore, did their treasons take? One possibility is that they refused their contribution to the tax, already long overdue, or failed to ensure its proper collection in the west. However, as we have seen, resistance to payment of the tax had initially been widespread; only a much more heinous crime on the part of Lennox and Lyle would explain their rapid forfeiture. The key to this drastic action by the government lies in letters of fire and sword to Sir John Semple of Eliotstoun, dated 13 September 1489, against Matthew Stewart and Robert Lord Lyle. These letters make it clear that Lyle and Matthew Stewart were by this time in Dumbarton castle, and refer to 'gret hershippis byrnings, reffis, slauchters and injures' committed by them in the recent past, especially against John Semple, his familiars and tenants. The inference is clear: Matthew Stewart, Master of Lennox, and Lord Lyle had been blatantly abusing their shrieval jurisdiction over Renfrew to attack former James III men, amongst whom the Semples were prominent. They had to be resisted by force as soon as possible, for the government understood that if the rebels were allowed 'to comit sic hevy inuris upon our liegis it wald be occasion to diverse our liegis to assist to the perverst opynzean gif thai were not resistit be force and be our autorite'.[88] In other words, the Hepburn regime feared the spread of rebellion — with good reason in September 1489 — and the letter looks back to the initial crimes of Lyle and Matthew Stewart against the Semples in Renfrewshire.

Faced with this challenge, the regime moved boldly to attack its former supporters. Patrick Hepburn and his associates, however predatory their initial seizure of power for themselves, recognized as James III had never done the need to bring into government a broader geographical representation of important magnates. Failure to achieve this would mean that the tax could not be brought in, that income from Crown lands in many areas would simply be withheld, that rebellion, however modest, would be a great menace because few would be prepared actively to support the government in resisting it; and the example of 1488 must have been fresh in everyone's minds. So the first step was to bring some useful individuals into the privy council; Bishop Elphinstone, after a long slog on the Lords of Council throughout the winter, reappeared on 29 May, together with the Constable, William Hay, earl of Erroll,[89] both men inclined to support the regime from an early stage and both powerful representatives of the north-east. With Robert, Lord Lyle, in rebellion, the government sought to take advantage of the long-standing Lyle — Buchan feud by granting to James, earl of Buchan, some of Lyle's Forfarshire lands even before he was forfeited in July 1489 — though in this case without any lasting benefit.[90] Buchan's role remained equivocal throughout 1489 — he was certainly implicated in the Master of Huntly's English diplomacy — and his future career lay not with the government, but with the Scottish fifth column in England. Finally, as the crisis deepened in the autumn, an emergency meeting of the council at Stirling on 18 September extended the olive branch to David, earl of Crawford, by restoring his dukedom of Montrose for life.[91]

Much of the summer of 1489 was taken up with the government's response to the western rebellion. Another parliament — the third within nine months — was summoned to Edinburgh for 26 June, and its first business was to forfeit Lennox, Matthew Stewart, and Lord Lyle; shortly afterwards, on 4 July, a price was put on their heads, and on that of 'William, sumtyme lord Crechtoun'.[92] Not surprisingly, none of the rebel leaders appeared to answer the charges of treason brought against them; and in fact, their depredations had apparently gone on unchecked for some time. Efforts had been made to summon the host to lay siege to Dumbarton from late April, and it was clearly the regime's failure to make these summonses effective which forced it instead into the expedient of calling parliament at very short notice — three weeks instead of the customary forty days.[93] With the necessary forfeitures secured, parliament turned to organise the elaborate details of the forthcoming war: the king was to go out in person to lay siege to Crookston and Duchal castles, arriving in Renfrewshire on 19 July; as soon as he reached Glasgow, Chancellor Argyll was to move up the north bank of the Clyde to the siege of Dumbarton, taking with him the men of his own earldom of Argyll, with others from the Lennox, Menteith, and Strathearn, and to remain twenty days at Dumbarton. He would then be relieved on the last day but one by the men of Angus, Fife, Kinross, Clackmannan, the sheriffdom of Perth 'fra tay est', the Stormont, Atholl, Apnadull, and Rannoch for a further twenty days; and a third and final stint of twenty days would be undertaken by the Earls of Huntly, Marischal, Erroll, Lord Forbes, and all the men beyond the Mounth together with those raised in the sheriffdom of the Mearns.[94]

These provisions illustrate clearly the Hepburn regime's perception of the western threat. Duchal and Crookston were not expected to offer much resistance, but Dumbarton, a highly defensible stronghold on a great rock towering 240 feet above the river Clyde, was reckoned to merit a two months' siege conducted by sections of the host in rotation. The parliamentary timetable also reveals that the government were as yet unaware of the threat from the north-east, for when the Earl Marischal and Lord Forbes eventually turned up at Dumbarton, as they were required to do in early September, they would be fighting not for, but against, the regime.

Duchal and Crookston do not appear to have posed much of a threat;

indeed, although the king rode in person to Duchal, and was certainly there between 25 and 27 July, he seems to have been concerned more with the transaction of royal business — for example the despatch of Snowdon Herald to meet the Spanish ambassadors at Berwick — than with the siege itself.[95] The heavy work of reducing Duchal was probably left to Sir John Semple, sheriff of Renfrew, who had to provide oxen to pull the artillery, together with John Sandilands, laird of Hillhouse, who was sent to nearby Paisley to hire workmen with spades and shovels to clear and level the road for the guns.[96] Letters of fire and sword issued to Semple in September make it clear that he had already been responsible for 'birnings, herschips, and destruction' in Renfrewshire; and his attack on Duchal 'in tyme bygone' — presumably a reference to the siege in July — is specifically mentioned.[97] The huge artillery pieces supplied by the Crown — including Mons Meg and presumably also 'the gun callit Duchal' — made short work of the siege of Duchal, causing such damage that masons had to be employed to effect repairs early in September.[98] No similar record survives of the siege and surrender of Crookston; but it was all over by the end of July. Probably the rebel leaders, Matthew Stewart, Master of Lennox, and Robert, Lord Lyle, were not personally present, both having retired to Dumbarton by early September. The siege of Duchal had been a sideshow; Dumbarton was the main event.

For whatever reason — the strength of the castle, the time taken to bring up the guns, the probable reluctance of Chancellor Argyll to attack Lennox, whose eldest daughter Elizabeth was married to Argyll's son and successor Archibald[99] — Dumbarton castle did not fall to the Crown. August and early September passed innocuously enough, with the king receiving Spanish ambassadors at Linlithgow, watching another performance by Patrick Johnson and the burgh players, being entertained by 'Gentil Johne the Inglis fule', and moving on to Stirling by 6 September.[100] Only three days later, the first hints of trouble from the north-east reveal themselves in the records. On 9 September, Alexander Gordon, Master of Huntly, was already at Doune, only a few miles from the court at Stirling.[101] Having issued proclamations and called up his allies in the north, he had come south with an armed force to reinforce the rebels in Dumbarton. Together with William Keith, earl Marischal, the Master of Huntly had swept through Angus attacking Lord Gray's tenants, harrying Alexander Inglis' lands and barony of Dulbeth, and causing more than £1,000 damage in Lord Drummond's baronies of Cargill, Stobhall, and Kinloch.[102] Hence the sudden note of urgency at Stirling, as the privy council sent north to discover who their friends still were beyond the Mounth, and to urge them to meet the king at the siege of Dumbarton. In the meantime, the regime's fear of the new threat was reflected in the restoration of Crawford's dukedom of Montrose on 18 September[103] — an intelligent political act, given their shaky position in Angus, but one obviously related to the shock of realising that the rebellion had not been contained, but was spreading.

The motive for the rising in the north-east has puzzled many writers, and with justice; for while the most committed supporters of the late king might seek to air their grievances by using the 'bludy serk' as their banner, not even the Master of Huntly or Lord Forbes could get over the fact that James III was dead, so that they appear at first sight to be rebels without a cause. In fact, however, the cause is not far to seek; for there survive two remarkable documents — no doubt out of a welter of similar propaganda produced by the dissidents of 1489 — which leave no room for doubt as to their objectives.

The first of these is a resolution of Aberdeen burgh council on 12 September 1489,[104] only three days after the Master of Huntly had passed through Doune in Menteith. A rapid glance at the preamble to this makes it clear that although this is an item of burgh business, the initiative has already been taken by 'diverse lordis and baronis', who have produced a list of articles and opinions to which the burgh council is simply giving its assent. Thus what we have here is rebel propaganda, the apologia of the Master of Huntly, the Earl Marischal, and Lord Forbes before setting off for the south-west, echoed shortly after their departure by the Burgh of Aberdeen. Four points are made: that no punishment has been meted out to 'the treasonabile vile personis' who had killed James III; that the treasure left by the late king has been misappropriated, and should be put in the hands of reliable men, together with the royal artillery, so that the king and his brother (unspecified) might live in safety; that all ransoms taken by the new regime should be restored; and that justice should be administered to all the king's lieges equally. The panacea for all these ills was 'the advise and consal of the thre estatis' — the rebels wanted a proper settlement in parliament.

The second surviving rebel document, preserved in the Lennox charters, is the southwestern apologia, a list of articles bearing the legend 'The articles send to the King eftir the feild of the Mos' — that is, after the one battle of the rebellion, which took place on 11 October. Clearly, however, the gist of this Lennox apologia was produced long before that date, for it bears a remarkable resemblance to the Aberdeen burgh articles: all four complaints are the same, the language used in both documents is often identical, and the rebel articles are once again referred to the judgment of the three estates.[105] There can be no doubt, therefore, that by the autumn of 1489 the north-east and south-west had made common cause, at least in their public pronouncements. However, the Lennox apologia is much more detailed, and parts of it are framed to distance Lennox and Lyle from their involvement in the rebellion against James III the previous year, a necessary move if they were ever to unite with the late king's supporters. So they describe themselves as 'thir noble and weile avisit lordis' who had given written oaths before Sauchieburn that James III would not be harmed, that they intended only reformation of his council; while those who killed the king are unidentified and unpunished 'vile and tresonable personis'. Those who have assumed the government are throughout referred to as 'parciall personis' with the worst possible motives. The rebels stop short of accusing them of the murder of James III, but condemn them for failing to punish his killers; for 'the misgouernance and disposicioune of our souerane Lordis greit tresour and heritage', which together with royal 'strynthis and arsenallis' ought to be put 'in suyr and responsale mennis handis'; for the taking of ransoms; and for partiality in the execution of justice.

Thus the Lennox apologia, as Bishop Lesley was to suggest much later,[106] is at one level simply the complaint by a faction excluded from real power against those who had it. Its strength lies in the fact that the charges which it makes against the new regime are broadly justified: as we have seen, ransoms had been taken after Sauchieburn, the courts had been used to reward those in power and punish the vanquished, and the killers of James III had not been brought to justice. Such wide-ranging complaints must have made excellent propaganda; but the Lennox apologia does not confine itself simply to generalisations: the new regime is accused of 'maist vile tresoune', of acting 'vnder colour of our souerane Lordis autorite' to disinherit and destroy 'the trew barownis'; and recent assaults on Archbishop Scheves are cited to illustrate this claim. Furthermore, the present regime was working 'to distroy our souerane Lord his brothir and successioune' in order to rule in Scotland without impediment.[107]

Most interesting of all, the Lennox apologia includes a list of the 'parciall personis' against whom these charges are laid — Robert Blacader, bishop of Glasgow; George Vaus, bishop of Galloway; John Hepburn, prior of St Andrews; Patrick Hepburn, Lord Hailes, significantly denied his new title of earl of Bothwell; Andrew, Lord Gray; John, Lord Drummond; Sir William Knollis, preceptor of Torphichen; Master Alexander Inglis, archdeacon of St Andrews; and Patrick Hume of Fastcastle. Blacader's name tops the list not only as a prominent 1488 rebel, but as a beneficiary of the parliament of January 1489, in which it was proposed that Glasgow be made an archiepiscopal see.[108] George Vaus was not only bishop of Galloway but also dean of the chapel royal at Stirling, a man very close to the penitent James IV after Sauchieburn. The two Hepburns, Patrick, earl of Bothwell, and John, prior of St Andrews, are included as leaders of the regime in their respective roles as Master of the Royal Household and Privy Seal. Sir William Knollis, as Treasurer, was directly responsible for the inbringing of, and accounting for, the late king's treasure; while Patrick Hume of Fastcastle was not only a prominent courtier and active in the new administration, but also the recipient of the forfeited Ross of Montgrenan's Ayrshire lands. As for Lords Gray and Drummond, and Alexander Inglis, the estates of all three had recently been attacked by the Master of Huntly's forces in their journey south-west to Dumbarton. Gray and Drummond, as hardliners in 1488, had risen to prominence since, above all at the expense of James III's men, Crawford in Angus and Murray of Tullibardine in Strathearn; while Alexander Inglis had made the most remarkable volte-face of all those named. Only six years had elapsed since he had been James III's nominee for the vacant bishopric of Dunkeld, only to lose it following a two-year battle with George Brown, who had finally been accepted as bishop by King James through offering bribes both to the king and to his familiar, John Ramsay, Lord Bothwell.[109] Disgusted at James III's cupidity and deceit, Inglis had transferred his considerable talents to the service of the new regime in 1488, being named as Comptroller within four days of Sauchieburn, and until the late spring of 1489 holding the office of Clerk Register as well.[110] All these nine named men were therefore obvious targets for the rebels of 1489 as being among the most prominent beneficiaries of the rising of the previous year in terms of the acquisition of lands or offices, or both.

Equally significant are the omissions from their list. Chancellor Argyll was clearly not regarded as one of the 'parciall personis', in spite of his presence at court in the autumn of 1489 and his commission from the new regime to attack Dumbarton; and it may be that he was relatively lukewarm towards a government which had managed to alienate his western kinsmen so swiftly. Also omitted is the name of George Brown, bishop of Dunkeld, although like Argyll he was at court and had been a prominent James IV man from the start. Unlike Argyll, however, Brown held no public office. Likewise Laurence, Lord Oliphant, a regular member of the privy council since the beginning, is not on the list; and the same is true of Archibald, earl of Angus, prominent like the others at the very outset of the reign. The omission of Angus from the rebel hit-list probably reflects the speed with which he lost real influence with the new regime, and perhaps also the hope that, deprived of his March Wardenships, Angus might throw in his lot with the dissidents of 1489. In the cases of Brown, Oliphant, and Angus, therefore, their lack of, or removal from, office-holding under the new regime meant that they were not classed as 'parciall personis'.

At first sight, the most remarkable omission of all is the name of Alexander Hume of that ilk, soon to become second Lord Hume. Not only had he been made Chamberlain for life the previous October, but he had also received Angus's Wardenship of the East March as recently as August; and he was at court at Stirling with many of the 'parciall personis' in September.[111] The answer may lie partly in surviving Hume-Gordon bonds. On 29 October 1486, Alexander Hume of that ilk gave his bond of manrent to George, second earl of Huntly, father of Alexander Gordon, the rebel Master of Huntly; and after the crisis, on 8 August 1490, Hume, his kin, friends, and followers, gave a similar bond to the Master of Huntly himself, together with his kin, friends, and followers.[112] This Hume-Huntly collusion both before and after the crises of 1488–9 may partly explain why George, second earl of Huntly, refused to support James III's assault on the Humes in 1487–8, and why Alexander, Master of Huntly, did not regard Alexander Hume of that ilk as his enemy in 1489. Subsequent events would reveal further cooperation between these two magnate families.[113]

In the meantime, the rebels' demands in the Lennox apologia — the expulsion from the council of the nine 'parciall personis' — would have to be attempted by force. On 22 September the king wrote to Arbuthnott of that ilk from Stirling, warning him 'surely and sikkerly to ger observe and kepe his howsys and strenthis', because the Earl Marischal, the Master of Huntly, Lord Forbes, and others, were making certain leagues and bands at Dumbarton castle.[114] Clearly the north-eastern rebel force had joined up with Lennox, Matthew Stewart, and Lyle in Dumbarton — indeed, as the Master of Huntly had already reached Doune by 9 September, it seems likely that he and his allies had been in Dumbarton for at least a week before the king's letter to Arbuthnott. The nature of the leagues and bonds being made at Dumbarton is not revealed; presumably the rebels, like the Hepburn regime, were still casting about for support, and the Master of Huntly may have been attempting to renew contact with Henry VII — if indeed he had ever broken it off.[115] The rebel strategy appears to have been to entrust Dumbarton castle to Lyle and Matthew Stewart, Master of Lennox, while Lennox himself roved round his earldom mustering his vassals. By the end of September, the rebel leaders included the Earl of Lennox and the Earl Marischal; the Masters of Huntly and Lennox; and Lords Lyle, Crichton, and Forbes. Others, if not wholly committed to rebellion, would certainly not stir to assist the Hepburn regime; these included Atholl, his brother the Bishop of Moray, Lord Ruthven, Murray of Tullibardine, and Fotheringham of Powrie. Buchan continued to play his usual shifty role, supporting the regime briefly at Stirling late in September, but both before and after that date treasonably involved with Henry VII.

Early in October a large rebel force left Dumbarton and moved north-east towards Stirling. Clearly Lennox and his allies had determined to resolve the struggle in their favour by attacking the royalists and if possible securing the person of the king. For the second time in seventeen months, James found himself the leader of a faction at Stirling, waiting to be assailed in an armed struggle, the outcome of which was far from certain. He had an advantage now in that he was king; but his position, like that of the rebels, depended on the continuing loyalty of those about him. After brief visits to Perth and Edinburgh, James IV had returned to Stirling by 8 October.[116] Not all of his supporters were with him; John Hepburn, the Privy Seal, was probably in St Andrews, while Laurence, Lord Oliphant, had been left in Perth and was the subject of hasty letters from the king on 11 October.[117] The evidence, scanty as it is, suggests that the Hepburn regime feared that there would be a further rebel incursion from the northeast to reinforce the Master of Huntly, Marischal, and Forbes. This fear would explain the correspondence in late September between the king and George, earl of Huntly, the Master's father, playing his customary political role of masterly inactivity on his Aberdeenshire estates, hedging the family bets;[118] it would explain the royal letter to Arbuthnott, whose lands lay in the Mearns and who would be on the direct route south for rebel forces if Huntly or other northern lords were to change their minds; and it would explain the division of the royal command at this critical point in the regime's fortunes, with the loyal Lord Oliphant staying in Perth to prevent, or at least give warning of, the passage of rebel reinforcements across the Tay. In Stirling itself with James IV were — probably — Bishops Blacader, Brown, and Elphinstone, the Earls of Argyll, Bothwell, and Erroll, Lords Glamis, Drummond, Gray, and Alexander Hume of that ilk; Treasurer Knollis; Alexander Inglis, archdeacon of St Andrews; Richard Murehead, the Clerk Register; and Secretary Whitelaw.[119]

The opposing sides may have been fairly evenly matched when the king and his allies, who had moved north from Stirling to Dunblane, turned west across the Teith and rode towards the source of the river Forth. The battle itself, described in the Lennox apologia as 'the field of the Mos'[120] and by Bishop Lesley as taking place at 'the moss besyd Touche',[121] is a mysterious affair, because we have hardly any information as to who was present on either side. Clearly, however, the king's party became seriously alarmed on 11 October, the day of the battle, because they sent a messenger back to Stirling to bring culverins to the field.[122] This was a battle which they could not afford to lose if they were ever to make good their claim to be effective rulers of Scotland.

Short accounts of what happened are to be found in Lesley's and Buchanan's histories.[123] Lesley suggests the use of the 'bludy serk' of James III as the rebel banner, and Stirling as their objective, 'to invaid the King and his cumpany', briefly notes the defeat of Lennox and Lyle, the slaying of many of the Lennox men and the capture of some others, including the laird of 'Kilcrouicht' — Thomas Galbraith of Culcreuch — who were subsequently hanged. Buchanan names Lennox alone as the rebel leader, and like Lesley sees Stirling as his objective. He was thwarted in his advance because the royalists had possession of the town, and withdrew to the source of the river to await reinforcements. Here Lennox was betrayed by one of his own vassals, Alexander Macalpin, who informed Lord Drummond of the rebel whereabouts and strength. Drummond thereupon launched a surprise night attack, which was a total success, resulting in the death, capture or flight of many of the rebels. Those captured, according to Buchanan, were mostly very leniently treated; but he has no details as to who they were.

These late sixteenth-century accounts are not really at odds with the scanty contemporary evidence. The battle was probably fought over a wide area between the Touch Hills just west of Stirling and the Menteith Hills near Aberfoyle, a region widely covered by mossy ground on the upper reaches of the Forth and its tributaries. James IV himself rode to 'the felde of Gartalunane' — Gartloaning near Aberfoyle — and after the battle made an offering in Kippen Kirk.[124] Hostilities seem to have been spread over the two days 11–12 October, which suggests that Buchanan's night action is not improbable. And the records bear out Lesley's statement that the laird of Culcreuch was captured and executed; only five days after Gartloaning, Thomas Galbraith of Culcreuch's lands were granted by the privy council to Bothwell's brother Adam, for faithful service.[125] This last grant suggests that the battle was rather more than the small-scale affair described by Buchanan. James IV was present in person together with the leaders of the Hepburn faction, and summary justice seems to have been meted out to those captured; Galbraith of Culcreuch, sentenced to death for treason, was already dead by 16 October.

The king's party had had a close call, for Gartloaning cannot be construed as a victory for them; they had prevented the rebels from reaching Stirling, they had discouraged the spread of rebellion, and that was all. After the field of the Moss, as before it, the dissidents were able to spread propaganda pleading the justice of their cause; indeed, they went so far as to send an apologia to the king, warning him that the aim of those about him was to destroy him, his brother — presumably the Duke of Ross, like King James in Bothwell's care — and the succession, and urging the removal of all the 'parciall personis' on their list. The Lennox apologia is hardly the complaint of defeated and cowed rebels, but rather that of a powerful faction looking for a major role in government. Subsequent events showed that the Hepburn regime could not resist this pressure. Within a fortnight of Gartloaning they had started to make concessions. Thus on 24 October Sir John Ross of Montgrenan, forfeited for treason only the year before, was restored to his lands in the Perthshire lordship of Kinclaven;[126] and his remarkably swift recovery of lands and offices in the course of the next twelve months suggests not only that he was a useful man in government, but that he had the most powerful of friends — Henry VII of England, who had petitioned the Pope to press for his reinstatement as early as 15 January 1489.[127]

Above all, the Hepburn regime's weakness, and need to compromise, is revealed in the protracted siege of Dumbarton and its final outcome. The parliamentary timetable of July 1489 had envisaged the fall of the castle by September.[128] In fact, in spite of ample evidence of the renewal of the siege by the king's party immediately after Gartloaning in October, there is no evidence that the castle surrendered. This is hardly surprising, for the annual service of the Scottish host had already been exhausted, and nothing like a close siege of Dumbarton appears to have been possible. Indeed, the royal forces were encamped two miles upriver, at the Colquhoun castle of Dunglass, and wages had to be paid to the besiegers of Dumbarton. The king, with Bothwell in close attendance, flitted back and forth between Dumbarton, Edinburgh, Glasgow, and Linlithgow, receiving letters — but no assistance — from the Earl of Huntly, while Argyll, Hume, and Drummond carried the brunt of siege operations. At the end of October, the gun Duchal was floated across the Clyde on three boats and brought to the siege; and more boats were sent from as far afield as Grangemouth and Blackness. On 23 November James IV rode out of Linlithgow to return to the siege, stopping at Glasgow en route; and the final stage of the siege began about 4 December, when James reached Dumbarton. It lasted about a week; by 13 December the king was already at Linlithgow on his way home to Edinburgh for Christmas.[129]

The cost to the Crown of that final week was a staggering £537.14/-, which included not only wages for the besiegers supplied by Bothwell, Alexander Hume, Oliphant, Blacader, Privy Seal Hepburn, the Bishop of Galloway, Treasurer Knollis, and Patrick Hume of Fastcastle, but also the purchase of a ship by the king from Colquhoun of Luss.[130] Wisely, James IV's mentors decided that enough was enough. They had probably already applied to Henry VII for safe-conducts to pass through England and abroad, in case the worst should befall.[131] In the meantime, while they had no intention of relinquishing power in the manner demanded by the Lennox apologia, they decided to risk summoning a parliament — the fourth of the new reign —

thereby meeting the rebels' insistence, in the north-east and south-west alike, that political decisions should be made 'be avis and consail of his [the king's] avisit estatis'. Summoned around Christmas on the statutory forty days' notice, parliament met in Edinburgh on 3 February 1490.[132] The rebellion of 1489, like its more ambitious predecessor the year before, had succeeded.

NOTES

1. Pitscottie, *Historie*,i, 214.

2. *A.P.S.*, ii, 204.

3. *R.M.S.*, ii, No. 1758 (27 July). For a discussion of Pitscottie's sources, see below, Chapter 11.

4. The inventory of James III treasure recovered in the first two weeks of the reign is in *T.A.*, i, 79–87.

5. It is not clear whether this is Patrick Hume of Fastcastle or Patrick Hume of Polwarth — probably the latter, as he received a royal grant five days later, on 28 June: *R.M.S.*, ii, No. 1745.

6. *T.A.*, i, 87.

7. *E.R.*, x, 82.

8. NLS. Adv. MS. 34.7.3 (Gray MS.), f. 21r.

9. *T.A.*, i, lxxiii–lxxiv, 88; J.D. Comrie, *History of Scottish Medicine to 1860* (London, 1927), 18.

10. The presence of all these men at the coronation at Scone is inferred from their witnessing of a Great Seal charter at Perth on the following day, 25 June: *R.M.S.*, ii, No. 1739.

11. R.J. Lyall, 'The Medieval Scottish Coronation Service: some Seventeenth-Century Evidence', *Innes Review*, xxviii (1), 3–21, esp. 9.

12. *Ibid.*, 9–10.

13. Buchanan, *History*, ii, 223, says that the funeral took place on 25 June, only a day after the coronation. But royal grants were still being made at Perth on 26 June: *R.M.S.*, ii, Nos. 1740–1742. The court had moved to Stirling by 28 June, and it seems likely that the funeral took place about that date: *R.M.S.*, ii, No. 1743. For the James IV Book of Hours, *see* L.J. Macfarlane, 'The Book of Hours of James IV and Margaret Tudor', *Innes Review*, xi (1960), Plate VII.

14. Hume Brown, *Early Travellers*, 40.

15. Pitscottie, *Historie*, i, 218.

16. *R.M.S.*, ii, No. 1746; *T.A.*, i, 89; *E.R.*, x, 1.

17. *T.A.*, i, 89.

18. It was not part of Ramsay's indictment for treason in October 1488: *A.P.S.*, ii, 202–3.

19. Pitscottie, *Historie*, i, 218–9.

20. Lesley, *History*, 59; *T.A.*, iii, 250.

21. *R.M.S.*, ii, Nos. 1731, 1732, 1733, 1739.

22. *Ibid.*, Nos. 1741, 1742.

23. *Ibid.*, No. 1774.

24. *Ibid.*, No. 1739.

25. These appointments had all been made by 1491: *see E.R.*, x, passim.

26. *Scots Peerage*, ii, 148.

27. *R.M.S.*, ii, No. 1781.

28. For the Coldingham dispute, see N. Macdougall, 'Crown versus nobility: the

struggle for the priory of Coldingham, 1472–1488', in K.J. Stringer (ed.), *Essays on the Nobility of Medieval Scotland* (Edin., 1985), 254–269, esp. 265-6.

29. *T.A.*, i, lxx, n.1.

30. *R.M.S.*, ii, Nos. 1754, 1773, 1785.

31. Fraser, *Lennox*, ii, 128 -131.

32. *T.A.*, lxxvi–lxxvii, 90.

33. *Ibid.*, 91–93.

34. Nicholson, *Later Middle Ages*, 532.

35. The indicments and sentences are in *A.P.S.*, ii, 201–5.

36. *T.A.*, i, 93; *A.P.S.*, ii, 202.

37. Thomas Fotheringham of Powrie from Dundee, William Lord Ruthven, from Perth. Both men were Blackness hostages.

38. *A.P.S.*, ii, 208.

39. *R.M.S.*, ii, No. 1738.

40. The Scottish safe-conduct at least solves the problem of Lovel's fate at Stoke. Professor S.B. Chrimes, *Henry VII* (London, 1977) suggests that Lovel 'was either killed or fled and disappeared for ever.' Thomas Broughton figures in his list of slain at Stoke. (p. 77).

41. For details of Henry VII's Breton diplomacy at this time, *see* Chrimes, *op.cit.*, 280–2.

42. *Cal. Docs. Scot.*, iv. No. 1542.

43. *Ibid.*, No. 1545; *Rot. Scot.*, ii, 488. The Scottish commissioners at Coldstream were Alexander Hume of that ilk; Alexander Inglis, archdeacon of St Andrews; Walter Ker of Cessford; Master Richard Lawson; and Patrick Hume of Fastcastle. On 20 September, the Bishop of Galloway was ordered to join these men: *T.A.*, i, 95.

44. The sederunt list, taken on the second day of the parliament, 7 October, is in *A.P.S.*, ii, 199–200.

45. *A.P.S.*, ii, 201. Lord Glamis had been named as one of James III's commissioners to negotiate with the rebels in April 1488, but he presumably deserted the king shortly afterwards, as he is to be found on James IV's council as early as 28 June 1488, already styled Justiciar: *R.M.S.*, ii, No. 1745.

46. *A.P.S.*, ii, 199–205.

47. *Ibid.*, 210–11.

48. *Ibid.*, 211–12.

49. Mackie, *James IV*, 46. For a different view, see Nicholson, *Later Middle Ages*, 533.

50. Macfarlane, *Elphinstone*, 405.

51. *A.P.S.*, ii, 207, c.4; 207–8, c.7.

52. *Ibid.*, 207 c.6.

53. *Ibid.*, 211 c.19.

54. *Ibid.*, 208 c.9.

55. *Ibid.*, 213 c.5.

56. *A.D.A.*, 120.

57. *Ibid.*, 121.

58. *Ibid.*, 123.

59. *A.D.C.*, i, 100, 120–121.

60. Pitscottie, *Historie*, i, 219–222.

61. Pinkerton, *History*, ii, 437.

62. *A.P.S.*, ii, 207, c.2, 3.

63. For details of the Treaty of Redon, see S.B. Chrimes, *Henry VII*, 280; for the Yorkshire rising of 1489, *ibid.*, 80.

64. Agnes Conway, *Henry VII's Relations with Scotland and Ireland, 1485–1498* (Cambridge, 1932), 28–9.

65. *T.A.*, i, lxxxvi–lxxxvii, 104–6.

66. *R.S.S.*, i, Nos. 3, 4.

67. *Prot. Bk. Young.*, 22–3.

68. For the general remission, see *A.P.S.*, ii, 207, c.4; Murray was still being pursued by the Auditors on 3 July 1489: *A.D.A.*, 130.

69. *T.A.*, i, 106–7, for the events of spring 1489.

70. *A.P.S.*, ii, 218 c.4.

71. Buchanan, *History*, ii, 225.

72. H. Harvey Wood (ed.), *The Poems and Fables of Robert Henryson* (edn. New York, 1968), 171–6. I am grateful to Dr. R.J. Lyall for drawing to my attention Henryson's poem in this connection.

73. *T.A.*, i, 109.

74. *A.P.S.*, ii, 208, c.9; *R.M.S.*, ii, No. 1752; *E.R.*, x, 629–30; *R.M.S.*, ii, No. 1794.

75. Lesley, *History*, 59.

76. *A.P.S.*, ii, 206.

77. *T.A.*, i, 79, 86–7.

78. *R.M.S.*, ii, No. 1874; *A.P.S.*, ii, 214; *Ibid.*, 208 c.9.

79. *HMC 11th Rep.*, App., pt. vi, no. 24; *R.M.S.*, ii, No. 1907; *Ibid.*, No. 1959.

80. Fraser, *Douglas*, ii, 91.

81. *Cal. Docs. Scot.*, iv, No. 1547; George Neilson, "The Hede of Sant . . .': The Earl of Angus's Pilgrimage in 1489', *S.H.R.*, i (1904), 217–8.

82. *T.A.*, i, 91, 95, 99, 112, 133, 169, 170.

83. *T.A.*, i, 112; *R.M.S.*, ii, No. 1907.

84. *Scots Peerage*, iii, 64–6; *A.P.S.*, ii, 158.

85. *Nottingham Borough Records*, iii, 262, 263–4. I am grateful to Dr. Ian Arthurson for drawing these references to my attention.

86. *A.P.S.*, ii, 215; *A.D.C.*, i, 311 (for Crichton's death).

87. Lesley, *History*, 59.

88. S.R.O. Dalhousie Muniments GD 45/1/1. Sir John Semple's father Sir Thomas had probably been killed at Sauchieburn fighting for James III: *Archaelogical Collections relating to the County of Renfrew*, ii, p.xiv.

89. *R.M.S.*, ii, No. 1848.

90. *R.M.S.*, ii, No. 1857.

91. *A.P.S.*, ii, 215. The council, at which the king was present, consisted of Chancellor Argyll; the Earls of Bothwell and Buchan; Lords Oliphant, Drummond, St. Johns (Knollis); John Hepburn, prior of St. Andrews; Alexander Hume of that ilk, Chamberlain; Richard Murehead, Clerk Register; and Master Alexander Inglis, archdeacon of St. Andrews. Andrew, Lord Gray, Crawford's great rival in Angus, is conspicuous by his absence.

92. *A.P.S.*, ii, 215.

93. *T.A.*, i, 109–110, 113. On 1 June a messenger was sent to Fife and Angus to summon the lords to the parliament. Parliament met on 26 June.

94. *A.P.S.*, ii, 214–5.

95. *T.A.*, 116–7.

96. *Ibid.*, 116.

97. S.R.O. Dalhousie Muniments, GD 45/1/1.

98. *T.A.*, i, 119.

99. *Scots Peerage*, v, 350.

100. *T.A.*, i, 118–9.

101. *Ibid.*, 119.

102. *A.D.C.*, i, 265–6.

103. *T.A.*, i, 119; *A.P.S.*, ii, 215.

104. *Aberdeen Council Register*, 45–6.

105. Lennox Charters No. 85: printed in Fraser, *Lennox*, ii, 128–131.

106. Lesley, *History*, 59.

107. Fraser, *Lennox*, ii, 130.

108. *A.P.S.*, ii, 213.

109. Myln, *Vitae*, 28–9.

110. *E.R.*, x, 629; *R.M.S.*, ii, Nos. 1731–1841 passim.

111. *R.M.S.*, ii, Nos. 1781, 1893; *A.P.S.*, ii, 215.

112. Wormald, *Lords and Men*, 280.

113. *See below*, chapter 4.

114. Nisbet, *Heraldry*, ii, App., 83.

115. Henry VII's eventual response was to send John Ramsay, the former Lord Bothwell, Sir Adam Forman, and John Liddale with a boatload of munitions to Dumbarton, but it arrived only in February 1490, too late to influence events: Conway, *Henry VII's relations with Scotland and Ireland*, 28–30; *T.A.*, i, 129.

116. *R.M.S.*, ii, Nos. 1898, 1899; *T.A.* i, 121.

117. *T.A.*, i, 122.

118. *Ibid.*, 120.

119. These men witness a Great Seal Charter at Stirling on 13 October, two days after the battle of Gartloaning: *R.M.S.*, ii, No. 1900. I have omitted the names of Lord Oliphant and Privy Seal Hepburn, who are also supposed to have been present, as the *T.A.* shows them to have been elsewhere at the time of Gartloaning. It may be, therefore, that the 13 October witness list — and others at this time — are designed to give the impression of widespread commitment to the regime, and that the *R.M.S.* sederunt includes the names of other individuals who were not actually present at Stirling.

120. Fraser, *Lennox*, ii, 131.

121. Lesley, *History*, 60.

122. *T.A.*, i, 122.

123. Lesley, *History*, 59–60; Buchanan, *History*, ii, 225.

124. *T.A.*, i, 122.

125. *R.M.S.*, ii, No. 1901.

126. *Ibid.*, No. 1904.

127. *Cal. State Papers (Venice)*, i, No. 549.

128. *A.P.S.*, ii, 214–5.

129. *T.A.*, i, 123–6, for the two months between Gartloaning and the end of the siege of Dumbarton.

130. *Ibid.*, 125–6.

131. Safe-conducts were granted by Henry VII to Blacader, Bothwell, Argyll, Erroll, Morton, Drummond, Knollis, Patrick Hume of Fastcastle, and Richard Murehead the Clerk Register, on 8 February 1490: *Cal. Docs. Scot.*, iv, Nos. 1553–5.

132. *A.P.S.*, ii, 216.

4

Unholy Alliance: Bothwell, Angus, and Bishop Elphinstone, 1490–95

The extent to which the rebellion of 1489 had succeeded in its principal objectives is revealed not only in the acts of the parliament summoned to meet in Edinburgh in February 1490 to settle the problems which 1489 had posed, but also in the gradual broadening of the political spectrum to bring into high office at the same time former enemies of both the crises of the late 'eighties. Some such process was inevitable if any acceptable government were to be formed, for the king was still a minor; but creating a more representative privy council carried the risk of providing a forum for magnate rivalries. The early 1490s were fraught with such political struggles, including something remarkably like a coup d'état in 1492; but there would never be another Gartloaning, with the king, like his father before him, taking the field against his own subjects.

Parliament met on 3 February 1490. Though attendance was lower than in October 1488 — sixty-six names appear on the sederunt list on the second day[1] — the numbers elected to the lords of the articles remain proportionately the same as in 1488, exactly one third of the total attendance, a large committee of twenty-two. The composition of this group reveals the desire of the estates for a settlement following the chaos of 1488–9; present are not only the leaders of the Hepburn regime, including Bothwell, Blacader, Treasurer Knollis, and Lord Gray, but also committed James III men like Archbishop Scheves, the Duke of Montrose, and — astonishingly — John Ross of Montgrenan, with the balance maintained by the north-east's most ardent neutral, George, earl of Huntly, whose presence may partly be explained by the need to represent the Gordon interest in the prudent absence of his son, the rebel Master.[2] These were the men who would work out a political settlement in the course of ten days, 5 to 15 February, which would come close to bringing back to the Scottish political community the 'luf amite and frendschip' earnestly sought in one of the parliament's early articles.

The very first business of all, however, was the annulment of the forfeitures passed the previous summer against Lennox, his son Matthew Stewart, and Robert, Lord Lyle. On 5 February all three men were present to hear the king, in the presence of the assembled estates, declare the forfeitures null and void.[3] In keeping with the conciliatory theme of the parliament, the reason given for the annulment was that the original process of forfeiture 'was nocht lauchfully led nor deducit be Just and gudely ordour' — in short, the three men were reinstated on a legal technicality, with the invadings and slaughters of the lieges in the Clyde valley, the sieges of Duchal and Crookston, and the letters of fire and sword, all conveniently forgotten, and the original process against all three ordered to be removed from the records of parliament. It took a week longer to obtain a remission for those involved with Matthew Stewart in the defence of Dumbarton — some 130 individuals — but this too was achieved by 12 February and confirmed three days later,[4] the last day of the parliament.

The articles and statutes approved on this final day, 15 February, illustrate the extent to which the political community was determined to make a new beginning. All grants of any kind made by the Crown since the coronation were to be annulled; and there was to be no giving away of royal lands, rents, or farms before King James's twenty-first birthday — March 1494. Likewise the estates concerned themselves about the revenues due to the king's brothers, James, duke of Ross, and John, earl of Mar, minors like James IV; complaints were made that, in some of their estates, 'thare rentis, malez fermez and utheris dewiteis Ar withaldin and nocht brocht in' — a clear reference to the recent troubles in Ross and in the north-east. The solution provided for the 'honorable sustentacioun' of the king and his brothers in their minorities was the appointment of a committee to bring in the outstanding property and casualty of all three. The names of those appointed to this body make clear that the Hepburn regime had only partially relaxed its control; Bothwell, his uncle the prior of St Andrews, Hume, Drummond, Oliphant, Gray, Montgomery, and Knollis are all there. Clearly, however, they could not hope to bring in the rents of the king and his brothers without the support of 'lordis . . . of autorite and power in the partis quhare thare landis lyis', and this meant Lennox in Bute, George, earl of Huntly for Petty and Brachly in Aberdeenshire, and Alexander, Master of Huntly, for Mar and Garioch.[5] The cooperation of these enemies of the very recent past demonstrates that Scottish royal government was simply inoperable if controlled only by a narrow faction, no matter how justified the grievances which had brought its leaders to power might have been. It was a lesson which James IV was never to forget.

The appointment of committees in parliament as a panacea for all recent ills was repeated in the estates' election of auditors to investigate the accounts of the principal royal financial officers. Eighteen auditors were chosen to 'here and undirstand' the books of the Treasurer and Comptroller, including not only the leaders of the Hepburn regime but also the Duke of Montrose, the Earl of Huntly, Bishop Elphinstone of Aberdeen, and Robert, Lord Lyle.[6] This article is, however, more indicative of general concern over the administration of royal revenues than of a desire for change, and it seems unlikely that the auditors met at this time; certainly there was no audit of the Treasurer's accounts until February 1492.

The great healing acts of the 1490 parliament, much commented on since,

were the election of the privy council by the estates and the requirement laid
on the king that he should not make any grants of lands or goods, safe-conducts,
respites or remissions, without the council's consent.[7] These acts, however,
should not be torn out of context to illustrate earth-shattering constitutional
change;[8] they relate, surely, to the political traumas of the preceding two
years. The king was still a minor, and would be for another four years.
Others had to govern for him, and his privy council had to be chosen
from a broader spectrum of the political community than the narrow group
of magnates who had been feathering their own nests since 1488. In fact, the
new privy council was a judicious mixture of the Hepburn faction, the leaders
of the recent rebellion — Lennox, Marischal, and Lyle — and former James
III men, above all the Duke of Montrose, Elphinstone, and the indispensable
John Ross of Montgrenan. This elected council was to advise the king 'in all
materis concernyng his maieste' — principally the preservation of his lands and
goods and the administration of justice. Its powers were unlikely to be abused,
not only because its members had widely differing political opinions, but also
because they would hold office only until the next parliament.[9]

In the main, therefore, the demands of the rebels of 1489 had been
met. If the 'parciall personis' of the Lennox apologia had not been removed,
they had at least been prevented from exercising unlimited power. Substantial
concessions had been made to former rebels, with Lennox, his son Matthew,
and Lyle all being pardoned and brought into government, while the Master of
Huntly and Earl Marischal were pursued only for damages in the civil courts.
Some judicious changes were made at the top; in April 1490 Bothwell resigned
his Mastership of the Royal Household, which was assumed by Treasurer
Knollis;[10] and the keepership of Stirling, together with the guardianship of
James IV's youngest brother, the Earl of Mar, went to Alexander Hume of
that ilk[11] in a move probably calculated to allay the fears of those — including
Hume's northeastern friends, the Master of Huntly and his father[12] — who
believed that Bothwell already had more than enough control over members
of the royal family. Signs of further rapprochement between the Gordons and
Hepburns are to be seen in an indenture of friendship made at Perth between
George, earl of Huntly and his son Alexander, and Patrick, earl of Bothwell,
the following February.[13]

The peace established in the political community early in 1490 encouraged
the privy council to press ahead with outstanding affairs of state which had
been delayed by the rebellion. The tax of £5,000 already granted in 1488 for
an embassy to look for a foreign bride for the king was to be brought in as
quickly as possible; the French alliance was to be renewed, and treaties made
with Denmark and Spain; and parliament authorised a further tax of £300 for
an embassy of twenty persons to travel to Denmark.[14] However, there appears
to have been entrenched resistance to payment of this tax, possibly because the
young king had granted a number of letters of discharge, excusing his supporters
from payment, prior to February 1490; and even parliament's insistence that
these letters were invalid, and laying down of penalties for non-payment, had

little effect. Almost a year later, on 24 January 1491, royal messengers were being despatched all over the kingdom 'with letteris for the taxt.'[15] Payment of the matrimonial tax 'and uther dewiteis' must have been made, in whole or in part, sometime in 1491, enabling the French and Danish embassies to go abroad and complete their business in the spring and summer of 1492.

The real test for the reconstituted government lay nearer home. Parliamentary protestations of 'luf amite and frendschip' were useless unless translated into action of some kind, and the estates, recognising this, insisted that the king should 'put scharp Justice on the partiis quhilkis ar obstinate.'[16] Two widely differing cases, both in 1490, suggest that the government was determined to put the past behind it by replacing 'parciall' with even-handed justice. The first of these was the dramatic slaughter of twenty Murrays, by their local enemies the Drummonds, in Monzievaird church in Strathearn, an incident graphically if inaccurately described by Pitscottie.[17] The Drummond–Murray feud had dragged on throughout the reign of James III, with that king openly favouring the Murray interest by transferring the office of Steward of Strathearn from John Drummond of Cargill (later first Lord Drummond) to his rival Sir William Murray of Tullibardine.[18] Not surprisingly, Sauchieburn found the Drummonds and Murrays on opposite sides; and James IV's accession was swiftly followed by the elevation of Lord Drummond and his kinsmen within the new government. Indeed, at the field of the Moss in October 1489, Drummond's support may have been crucial to the survival of the new regime.

However, the advancement of the Drummonds simply ensured the continuation of the Drummond–Murray feud in Strathearn, with the Murrays as underdogs. The genesis of the Monzievaird conflict may be found in a case heard before the Lords of Council early in the new reign, on 22 October 1488. John Murray of Balloch and Trewin appeared and complained that David Drummond, Lord Drummond's second son, had seized the Isle of Monzievaird (also known as the Dry Isle, half way between Crieff and Comrie), which John Murray claimed he held in feu farm. David Drummond, on the other hand, stated that he had been granted a royal lease of Monzievaird. The case was continued for Murray to produce his proofs of tenancy; he failed to do so, and on 3 November the Lords of Council settled the matter of the possession of Monzievaird in favour of David Drummond. John Murray may well have declined to appear because Lord Drummond, the defendant's father, had been one of the Lords of Council judges on 22 October, and Murray may have reckoned that his chances of obtaining a favourable judgment were slim.[19]

The possession of Monzievaird by David Drummond, acquired by a judgment which the Murrays obviously regarded as loaded against them, led to further conflict. George Murray, abbot of the local abbey of Inchaffray, attempted to levy teinds from what had now become Drummond lands in Monzievaird parish; he was resisted by David Drummond and his ally Duncan Campbell of Dunstaffnage, a fight ensued, and the Murrays were driven for shelter into Monzievaird parish church. Later authorities suggest that the church was set on fire with the fugitive Murrays inside it as an act of revenge for the killing of one of the Campbells of Dunstaffnage.[20] Whatever the cause, contemporary sources make clear the fact of the burning and of the twenty deaths; and Pitscottie may well be right when he says that 'few escapit', though he is almost certainly wrong when he states that wives and children also died in the fire.[21]

A biased civil judgment in favour of David Drummond was one thing; but the atrocity perpetrated by the Drummonds against the Murrays at Monzievaird, and arguably made possible only by that judgment, was quite another. The government, to show off its new-found impartiality, had to invoke 'schairp justice' against Lord Drummond's son and his accomplices. A number of arrests had been made by 21 October, on which date the king himself was present in the Tolbooth of Edinburgh when 'Lord Drummondis folkis bayd the law.'[22] Probably they were executed; certainly David Drummond, the principal offender in the Monzievaird burning, was an outlaw at the horn by the following January; and Pitscottie says that he was afterwards beheaded at Stirling, a statement consistent with the fact that he was dead by May 1492.[23] Justice was done belatedly to John Murray of Trewin, who acquired some of David Drummond's lands in Strathearn.[24]

The condemnation and pursuit of those Drummonds involved in the Monzievaird burning by the government did not, of course, bring the Drummond–Murray feud in Strathearn to an end. But it made such an end possible by demonstrating that the Crown, after a shaky start, was determined to exercise rigorous criminal justice, even against a son of one of its most prominent supporters. This was the first step; the second was to summon both Lord Drummond and Sir William Murray of Tullibardine before the Lords of Council at Linlithgow in January 1491 and to order them, in the king's presence, to grant redress to the wives and children of those who had died at the Monzievaird fight, Drummonds as well as Murrays.[25] The subsequent failure of both rivals to comply, and their continuing support for their kin and friends involved in the 1490 struggle, led to both Lord Drummond and Murray of Tullibardine being summoned into ward in June 1491;[26] and it was not until a decade later, on 14 January 1501, that both men, together with their kin, friends, adherents, and servants, were given letters of remission for their support of those on both sides involved in 'the birnyng of the kirk of Moneward and the slachter of the kingis liegis at that tyme, revis, resettis and intercomoning with the persouns beand at the kingis horne for the saidis crimez'; forgiveness and 'hertlynes' was to be practised between Drummonds and Murrays in the future.[27]

Almost as striking as government intervention in the Strathearn feuds were royal efforts to restore peace and order in Renfrewshire, one of the major trouble spots of the 1489 rebellion. On 23 December 1490, the king visited Paisley Abbey at the end of a justice ayre circuit which had taken him as far afield as Peebles and Lochmaben. Paisley was King James's final port of call after a month in the saddle, his last business before retiring to Linlithgow for Christmas and New Year to indulge his passion for cards, in long sessions playing with Bishop Blacader, Bothwell, Hume, and Treasurer Knollis.[28] At the urging of George Schaw, abbot of Paisley, the king granted a letter under the privy seal in which he expressed his concern that the community and burgesses of nearby Renfrew 'and divers vther personis' refused to accept Paisley's new status as a burgh in barony, conferred on the town for its support of James IV in 1488, when Abbot Schaw had been present at Sauchieburn. The origin of the Paisley–Renfrew conflict lay in Renfrew's commitment to James III, with the sheriff of Renfrew, Sir Thomas Semple, losing his life in the late king's cause.[29] Renfrew's loss was Paisley's gain, with the burgh receiving a great seal charter as early as August 1488, granting the new burgh in barony the same privileges and freedoms as other royal burghs, including a weekly market day and a market cross. Abbot George Schaw and his successors were to have the right to elect the burgh's provost, bailies, and other officials.[30] Schaw's and Paisley's new dignity had however been challenged by 'evle avisit personis of the said toun of Renfrew' who had come under silence of night to Paisley and broken up the stones which were to be used to sculpt the new market cross, thereby challenging the burgh's new freedoms and privileges. The royal response was to order the king's 'traist and welebelouit cousingis and consalouris', John, earl of Lennox and his son Matthew Stewart, to make open proclamation at the market cross of Renfrew that Paisley's freedoms and privileges had to be respected under pain of royal displeasure; at the same time, both men were to try to identify the criminals who had destroyed Paisley's market cross 'and punys thaim with al rigour'.[31]

At first sight, this letter might seem to be concerned with a trivial local issue; but the personalities involved, and the solution proposed, cast a revealing light on the government's efforts to pacify a troubled area. Thus Lennox and his son, rebels at the king's horn the previous year, not only had their forfeitures annulled but became the king's trusted counsellors, charged by his justice ayre to uphold the rights of Abbot Schaw and his new burgh against the unspecified 'evil advised' inhabitants of Renfrew who had challenged Paisley's status. In 1489 the opposition to the Lennox–Lyle rebellion had been led by Sir John Semple, sheriff of Renfrew, the heir of the Sir Thomas killed at Sauchieburn; and as we have seen, he had been issued with letters of fire and sword against the Master of Lennox and Lord Lyle in September 1489.[32] So the paradox of the political situation in Renfrewshire was that the Hepburn regime, challenged by its allies of 1488, had had to rely on former James III men — Sir John Semple and his Renfrew adherents — for support in the autumn of 1489, and had therefore helped to stimulate the feud between Paisley and Renfrew, between Lennox and Semple. James IV's visit to Paisley at the end of the southern ayre in December 1490 may therefore be seen as an effort by the government to bring an end to unrest in Renfrewshire, with the physical presence of the king lending weight to the admonitions in his letter. Compromise was however the order of the day; Sir John Semple, who presumably felt aggrieved at the restoration of Lennox, was appeased with a lordship of parliament; the king again visited Renfrewshire in November 1491 following a pilgrimage to Whithorn;[33] and peace seems at last to have been restored by an agreement reached at Renfrew on 16 March 1492 between Lennox and his son Matthew Stewart on the one side, and John, now Lord Semple, his men, kin, and friends, on the other. The parties were to take each other 'in hartly kyndness and favoris, and to remit and forgeff rankour, hewenes, and all wnkyndnes done . . . in tymes bygane.'[34] The compositors 'ewynly chosyn' by both sides included prominent local men — Robert Lord Lyle, Sir John Ross of Hawkhead, Sir John Chawmir of Gatgyrth, Adam Muir of Caldwell, John Maxwell of Nether Pollok, Constantine Dunlop of that ilk, and Master Nicolas Ross, parson of Renfrew — whose involvement added weight to the Lennox–Semple compromise; but it seems unlikely that it would have been made at all had the royal government not demonstrated a direct interest in the area, showing favour to Semple as well as Lennox, and above all parading the king through Renfrewshire to underline the regime's determination to bring peace and order to the Clyde Valley.

By the end of 1490, as the Monzievaird and Paisley incidents show, the reconstituted government was well on the way to obtaining general acceptance from the Scottish political community. The new Earl of Bothwell and his associates had survived the crises of 1489 largely through an acceptance of political realities, the most important of which was that there was no future in attempting government by a narrow clique in the manner of James III. Their skill in attracting back influential neutrals and former enemies, through whom alone effective government in the localities could be carried on, vindicated their seizure of power in 1488. Even poor John Ireland, the late king's confessor, counsellor and diplomat in the 1480s, reckoned that he might find royal patronage in 1490. In that year he presented to James IV his newly-completed 'Meroure of Wyssdome', a treatise in the *speculum principis* tradition which had been intended for the edification of James III; much of it would no doubt have pleased that monarch, especially Ireland's frequent reiteration of the subject's duty to obey his king and eschew resistance.[35] Ireland, whose movements between 1488 and 1490 are unknown, may have felt that his highly derivative and conventional wisdom would bring him back into prominence at court; and in fact James IV wrote from Linlithgow to Pope Innocent VIII, on 26 September 1490, asking the pope to exempt Ireland from the jurisdiction of Archbishop Scheves.[36]

But this year of reconciliation and advancement of the worthy but disaffected saw no major change in Ireland's fortunes. For a minor cleric seeking royal support, he was perhaps too combative a personality to be comfortable to the courtiers surrounding James IV. His career had begun with his leaving St Andrews University without a degree in 1458, had continued with such unproductive enterprises as efforts, both scholarly and diplomatic, to reconcile James III and his brother Albany, and acting as royal confessor on the day of Sauchieburn; and it was to end with Ireland at odds with the two most powerful ecclesiastics of the day, Scheves and Blacader.[37] Ireland's mistake may ultimately have been bad timing. In the final, seventh, book of the 'Meroure', he remarks that when 'kingis and princis abusis thar power and dignite and causis the pepil to be evill and perwerst, than god . . . gevis that realme to ane vthir king and quhilis of ane vthir nacioun and causis him to conquest it.' Ireland had missed the boat. Such a sentiment, together with his later comment that in the case of 'miserable and unprofitable' kings, 'the pepil mycht put remeid be wis counsal and governyng of him and of the realme',[38] was unlikely to find favour in 1490; but both would have made wonderful rebel propaganda in 1488.

John Ireland was, of course, a political lightweight whose ultimate fate was unlikely to make or break governments. Very different was the case of the neglected heavyweight, Archibald Douglas, fifth earl of Angus. His equivocal role in 1489, together with the potential threat which he posed to the Hepburn–Hume regime on the borders, can hardly have endeared him to Bothwell and his kinsmen at court. As we have seen, his powerful position at the outset of the reign had been steadily eroded, especially on the borders, where he had lost his March wardenships to the Hepburns and Humes, together with lands in Berwickshire and Angus, and the sheriffship of Lanark, which was given to Lord Hamilton.[39] These losses were paralleled by Angus's absence from the council, and even from parliament, between 1489 and 1492, but not, significantly, from the court, where he is frequently to be found playing dice and cards with James IV.

Thus on 18 April 1490 we find the earl, the king, and Sir John Ross of Hawkhead having a game of dice with the royal stake money twenty unicorns, about £18 Scots. A rather more tense occasion was Sunday evening, 27 June, at Falkland, when the king played cards not only with Angus but also with the earl's implacable opponents on the borders, Bothwell and Chamberlain Hume, who may have been afraid to leave James IV alone with Angus for too long. However, late in November 1490, just before setting out on the southern ayre, the king had marathon sessions of cards with Angus, Ross of Hawkhead, and the royal henchman John Sinclair, stretching over three days, 26–28 November, with forty unicorns as his stake.[40] There can be no doubt that it was his intimacy with King James which not only helped to protect Angus when he was assailed by his political opponents in 1491, but also aided his remarkable comeback the following year.

1491 was not a good year for Angus. As in the previous year, he played no major political role, and he was not present at the fifth parliament of the reign, which met in Edinburgh for three weeks from 28 April to 18 May, after which it was continued to 2 August.[41] But it never met. On 29 July, Lyon Herald was sent from Linlithgow to the Earl of Angus at Perth ordering him to ward himself in his own castle of Tantallon in East Lothian.[42] No evidence survives as to the crime of which Angus was accused, but the timing of the order for his wardship is significant. For only a few days before Patrick, earl of Bothwell, had sailed from North Berwick to France in the 'Katharine', charged with the renewal of the Franco–Scottish alliance.[43] He and his colleagues may have been afraid to leave Angus at liberty for many reasons. Most important of these was probably the earl's equivocal relationship with Henry VII of England, whom Angus had visited in 1489, resulting in his loss of his March wardenships; and Angus's pro-English stance became much more pronounced in November 1491, when he entered into an agreement with Henry VII's commissioners, Sir John Cheyney and Sir William Tyler, about Anglo–Scottish relations and his place in furthering them.

This remarkable indenture, dated 16 November in the seventh year of King Henry VII — 1491 — survives only in very dilapidated condition;[44] but its purpose is clear. The English king can hardly have been unaware of the Scottish government's moves to renew the French alliance while he himself had only a three-year truce with the Scots, and that had expired on 5 October 1491. Not until 22 October did King Henry issue a safe-conduct for Scottish ambassadors to come south with a view to renewing the truce, in the teeth of protests by his own parliament that agreements with the King of Scots were worthless, as they were always broken by his subjects, and calls for open war.[45] King Henry, whose experience of war at home and abroad — at Bosworth, Stoke, and at one remove, in Brittany — must have convinced him what an uncertain business it was, had chosen rather to try to destabilise the Scottish government in time-honoured fashion by using the Scottish 'fifth column' — dispossessed magnates in his pay like John Ramsay — who acted regularly as spies. Thus on 16 April Henry VII had lent to James, earl of Buchan and Sir Thomas Tod the sum of £266 13/4d sterling (about £800 Scots), for which 'John Lord Bothwell' — that is, John Ramsay — and Tod guaranteed repayment. This was to be made before Michaelmas — 29 September 1491 — if Buchan and Tod failed in their objective, which was nothing less than to deliver into King Henry's hands the King of Scots and his brother the Duke of Ross.[46] This mysterious agreement did not apparently become known to King James, for Buchan was never punished and Tod was still in the Scottish king's service as a royal messenger in 1497.[47] But its timing — 16 April 1491 — makes good sense. The plot was clearly initiated by Buchan, who attended the Scottish parliament of April–May 1491[48] and was presumably aware that the embassy to France, headed by Patrick, earl of Bothwell, would be leaving Scotland some time during the summer. This in turn meant that James IV and the Duke of Ross, whose guardian Bothwell was, would be more vulnerable in his absence. However, for whatever reason, the scheme came to nothing, and King Henry turned instead to an unofficial agreement with the Earl of Angus to guarantee him some influence over Scottish affairs.

In its final form, the Angus indenture with Henry VII involved the earl in attempting 'to move the Kyng of Scottes . . . to take and kepe ferm [peace with the] said King [Henry].' If this failed, Angus and his son George, Master of Angus, were to attack those Scots who had opposed an agreement with England; and if they could not prevail, they would hand over to King Henry Hermitage castle and its lands, in return for a gift of lands of equal value in England. Henry VII for his part promised that he would conclude no peace or truce with the Scots commissioners — then in England — unless Angus agreed to it and was included in it, while Angus and his son and heir agreed that they and their friends would not reach any accommodation with the King of Scots — that is, with the government acting for James IV — without the counsel of the King of England.

This November 1491 agreement is interesting for a number of reasons. It shows Henry VII approaching Angus, presumably because he had been advised that the earl had some influence with James IV; and it shows the English king trying to stir up trouble between prominent members of the Scottish political community, above all Bothwell and Angus. As for the earl himself, it was by no means the first of his treasonable dealings with England. On 11 February 1483, during the Stewart governmental crisis of 1482–3, Angus had been one of Alexander, duke of Albany's commissioners making a convention at Westminster which involved Albany replacing his brother James III as King of Scots and Angus acquiring control of all the March wardenships; in a remarkable anticipation of the 1491 indenture, the Scots at Westminster in 1483 promised that even in the event of Albany's decease, they would continue to serve the English king — at that time Edward IV — as their liege lord, and keep their castles from the King of Scots. Perhaps most significant of all, James, the ninth and last earl of Douglas, an exile in England since his forfeiture in 1455, was to be restored, and the Westminster convention refers to an agreement already made between Douglas and Angus, of which unfortunately details do not survive.[49]

The Westminster convention did not bear fruit at the time due to the rapid recovery of James III, the death of Edward IV, and the subsequent collapse of Albany's position. But eight years later, having been elbowed out of his key position on the borders, Angus had a precedent for behaviour remarkably similar to that of 1483. He would in any event make himself indispensable to King Henry as a peacemaker in Scotland, a stance which involved him taking an anti-French and anti-Bothwell position in Scottish politics.

This was also a stance which threatened the minority government of James IV both at home and abroad, and required them to act. Angus's indenture of 16 November 1491 was probably only the final step in a long process of negotiation with Henry VII's commissioners, a process which may well have been in train during the previous summer, and on being revealed to the government, caused the earl's being ordered into ward at Tantallon. The regime may have had other worries about Angus in July 1491. Sometime shortly before that date, James, the ninth and last earl of Douglas, died at Lindores, where he had been confined since his capture at Lochmaben in 1484. He seems to have been generously treated after James IV's accession in 1488, with an annual pension of £200, a portion of which was paid, being awarded him out of the farms of Kinclaven in the exchequer accounts of 1489, 1490, and 1491. In the last of these, rendered in July 1491, he is described as 'quondam Jacobo Dowglas, militi'.[50] Clearly his death had occurred sometime in the first half of 1491, presumably at Lindores. In July 1491, Angus, who in extremis in 1483 had had dealings with Douglas and who was later to demand to be recognised as his heir, was probably either at Perth or on his estates at nearby Abernethy, only three miles from Lindores, when he was summoned to ward.[51] Angus's geographical proximity to the expiring ninth and last earl of Douglas may be pure coincidence, but it is tempting to see in his territorial ambitions both past and to come a desire to acquire for himself and his family part of the vanished Black Douglas empire. Frustrated in his efforts even to maintain his position at court or on the borders, he seems to have been attempting to take a short-cut, using his friendship with James IV to influence Henry VII in his favour as a magnate of some consequence in Scotland; but his negotiations with the English king were treasonable, and it is a reflection of the relative weakness of the Scottish government in the summer of 1491 that the earl's punishment was only warding in his own East Lothian stronghold.

It may be that the extent of Angus's treasons only leaked out later; certainly something must have reached the ears of James IV's counsellors in the late summer of 1491, for by 11 October, Angus's castle of Tantallon was under siege by the king. This assault may have been prompted by the threat which Tantallon posed to the nearby Hepburn strongholds of Hailes and Waughton — especially during Bothwell's absence in France — or perhaps by its position on the Firth of Forth close to the Bass Rock, a good landing place for English armed forces, and close to the scene of one Anglo–Scottish naval battle at the outset of the reign.[52] In any event, King James had reached Tantallon by 11 October, as on that day he sent Quarrier the gunner to Edinburgh 'to help furth with the gunnis.' At the same time a payment was made to the Laird of Dundas for the shipping of two more guns from Linlithgow and Blackness, while messengers were sent to Leith and Stirling for crossbows and culverins. By 13 October workmen had dug trenches round Tantallon, and on the same day six seamen were despatched in a boat across the Forth to Largo, presumably to enlist the help of the ubiquitous Sir Andrew Wood and 'the Kingis schip', either the 'Yellow Carvel' or the 'Flower', which could be used to block the sea-gate at Tantallon and prevent either the relief of the castle from the sea or the escape by sea of its defenders.[53]

The royal party does not seem to have remained long at the siege; by 16 October James IV was in Haddington, sending a messenger with letters to Bothwell in France, and by 24 October he had returned to Linlithgow.[54] We do not know the outcome of the siege of Tantallon, or even whether Angus was present in the castle with the defenders. Certainly he was not deterred from concluding his treasonable negotiations with Henry VII the following month, and it would be interesting to know the contents of the letters brought to James IV in Linlithgow, by 'Edwart Coke, Inglis man', from Henry VII on 26 October, just after the Tantallon siege.[55] In any extent, the final outcome was not the surrender and punishment of Angus, but a complex compromise. Bothwell's ship returned from France to the Firth of Forth on 29 November, and the king hurried from Perth to meet him.[56] The most pressing business was the French alliance; but the position of Angus must also have been discussed. The king may well have argued for a lenient approach towards a man whom he obviously liked; for he presented Angus with a Christmas present of a long gown.[57]

More serious dealings with the earl were deferred until after Christmas. On 29 December 1491, at Linlithgow, where the court was spending Christmas and New Year, Angus was given the lands and lordship of Kilmarnock in Ayrshire in exchange for his own border lordship of Liddesdale and castle of Hermitage. The exchange was to last for Angus's lifetime, and it was made, as the record reveals, by the king 'cum avisamento et matura deliberatione dominorum concilii sui' — in other words, by members of the privy council spending Christmas at Linlithgow: Elphinstone, Argyll, Bothwell (styling himself Admiral and Warden of the West and Middle Marches), his uncle the Prior of St Andrews and Privy Seal, Chamberlain Hume, Treasurer Knollis, and Richard Muirhead, Clerk Register.[58] Angus protested that Kilmarnock was an inalienable possession of the Crown, whereupon the king granted an assurance that when he reached the age of twenty-five he would confirm the Kilmarnock grant in open parliament. With this agreed, this oddly disparate group of magnates could give themselves over to the New Year festivities, listening to ballad singing, watching dancers, thrilling to the topical Anglophobe utterances of Blind Harry, admiring the king's new hawk and — no doubt — the Earl of Angus's new gown.[59]

In effect, the exchange of December 1491 substantially reduced Angus's power on the borders, and can hardly be understood as anything other than evidence of the government's — justifiable — lack of trust of the earl, especially in dealings with the English. It was a move clearly inspired by Bothwell and Hume, and the logical follow-up to it came on 6 March 1492, when King James gave Liddesdale and Hermitage to Bothwell in free regality.[60] This grant may be regarded as Bothwell rewarding himself for negotiating the Franco–Scottish treaty, which King James had ratified two days earlier, on 4 March. This treaty, like its immediate predecessor of 1484, was an offensive and defensive alliance directed against England;[61] but the normal corollary of such an agreement, a Franco–Scottish royal marriage, had not apparently been negotiated — Bothwell may well have curtailed his French visit on receiving news of Angus's depredations at home — and the parliament of February 1492 had to authorise a further matrimonial tax of £1,000.[62] For a number of reasons, not least the changing political situation at home and abroad, no French marriage was ever negotiated; but the treaty itself marks the closest that the minority government of James IV came to committing itself to France at the expense of any substantial Anglo–Scottish understanding. Thus when King James ratified the truce with England which his commissioners had negotiated at the end of 1491, he did so for a mere eight months, to 20 November 1492, not for the five years which had originally been proposed.[63]

The matrimonial tax was not the only item of business on the parliamentary agenda in February 1492. There were also curious echoes of the complaints of the rebels of 1489. After sitting for a fortnight from 6 to 20 February, the Lords of the Articles — an enormous committee of 23, half the attendance at the parliament, and including Angus for the first time since 1489[64] — complained that of James III's great hoard, only 'a small little parte thirof to little avale or quantite' had come into the hands of the new — that is, the post–1490–government. The solution was for sheriffs to hold secret inquisitions in Lothian, Fife, and other places where the late king had had 'maist residence' to try to recover the remainder from those who had stolen it.[65] Presumably it was only on such an undertaking being given in parliament that the auditors of the Treasurer's Accounts — who significantly included Lord Lyle, a man who had both seen the treasure as it came in in 1488 and protested that it had been misappropriated in 1489 — would sign the audit six days later, on 26 February.[66]

Even more striking was the next act of the same parliament. By command of the king and the Lords of the Articles, and for 'the eschewin and cessing of the hevy murmour and voce of the peple', a reward of a hundred marks of land was offered by the Crown for anyone who could provide information as to the identity of the killers of James III. In order to encourage those with such information to come forward, a promise was made that although James IV was still a minor, the gift would not be revoked when he came of age; and should the informant have been present at the slaying of James III, and be prepared to reveal to the king the names of 'the laif of his falowis that were committaris of the said deid with thare handis', he would duly receive a remission absolving him from any part in the affair.[67]

These two articles, resurrecting the complaints about the treasure and the death of the late king, leave little doubt that the settlement of 1490 had not brought magnate faction to an end, and that parliament remained a forum for dissent and its articulation through legislation. It is surely significant that little further business was transacted on 20 February 1492, which suggests strongly that the Lords of the Articles spent the better part of a fortnight raking up the past. That they should do so is hardly surprising in the case of James III's hoard, for of the £24,517 10/– recovered in 1488, less than £2,000 was left,[68] and the discovery of the remainder had become a matter of urgency for the government. Yet apart from one prosecution before the Lords of Council in June 1498,[69] no evidence exists for the success of the inquisitions in Fife, Lothian, and elsewhere. The complaint about the hoard may therefore reflect the fact that the 'parciall personis' of 1489 who had misappropriated the royal treasure – above all Treasurer Knollis, in office since the beginning of the reign — had not been removed; indeed, as the recent assault on Angus influence in the West March had shown, the power of the Hepburns and Humes to assail former allies of 1488 had not diminished at all. In spite of, or perhaps because of, the increase in numbers and opinions of those in government since 1490, therefore, the parliament of 1492 was clearly a very contentious body, with the Lords of the Articles including such recent enemies as the Earl of Erroll and the Earl Marischal, Treasurer Knollis and Lord Lyle, and the arch-rivals Bothwell and Angus.[70] Only an acrimonious debate amongst these men can have produced the resurrection of the issue which many members of James IV's government must have hoped was buried for ever, namely the identities of the late king's assassins; and the reward for information about this was clearly not to quell the 'hevy murmour' of the nation at large, but rather intended as a concession to those members of the Articles who had championed James III's cause both before and after his death. A gesture had to be made to silence complaints which otherwise could be levied against the regime at any time, on any pretext. In the event, no-one appears ever to have identified the killers or claimed the reward; and the raising of this issue, and that of the hoard, can best be understood as manifestations of wider discontent with the regime's policies by some of its newer members.

At first sight, Angus, with his recent dubious record, seems an unlikely leader of those who wished to oppose the continuing Bothwell hegemony in government. But 1492 was not 1488, and the rebel propaganda levelled against James III for his Anglophile stance had long since lost its potency. Indeed, there must have been many who were unhappy that Scottish foreign policy had been turned on its head through Bothwell's vigorous pursuit of the French alliance, already a costly venture which had failed to produce a bride for the king, and the rejection of English advances for a long truce which close adherence to France seemed to require. To those of this opinion, Angus's dealings with Henry VII in 1491 may have seemed much less than treasonable. He could easily be regarded as a powerful magnate who enjoyed intimacy with the king, and whose attitude to foreign affairs was more intelligent than that of Bothwell. Before the end of 1492, the flimsy Franco–Scottish treaty in which the Hepburn earl took such pride was rendered obsolete; on 3 November Henry VII made the peace of Etaples with Charles VIII of France, abandoning his expensive and unsuccessful support of Brittany and being paid handsomely by the French for doing so.[71] The Scots, as France's allies bound to her by an offensive and defensive treaty against England, were not even consulted.

Whatever the long-term merits of Angus's attitudes to foreign policy, he had obvious uses to the government much nearer home. His name appears on the list of those to whom the full power of parliament was committed at the close of the February session, a commission charged not only to bring in the matrimonial tax, and advance the matter of the royal marriage, but also to deal with other weighty affairs which might need attention before the next parliament. One of these is clearly indicated in the final article of the February parliament, a complaint by 'the kingis hienes and the lordis of the articlis' that the 'mony louable actis and statutis maid in the last parliament' concerning the execution of justice throughout the realm had been ignored or neglected through the negligence of sheriffs or other officers in making them generally known.[72] The most urgent of these acts of 1491 were those ordering the speedy pursuit and bringing to justice of murderers and the forbidding of 'convocacioun na Rising of commonis in the hendring of the commoun law.'[73] These acts refer, at least in part, to one of the most bitter and long-standing feuds in Scotland, one which the general settlement of 1490 had done nothing to resolve — the Montgomery — Kilmaurs struggle in northern Ayrshire.

The source of the dispute was the office of the bailiary of Cunningham, conferred on Hugh, Lord Montgomery's grandfather Alexander by James II as long before as 1448, and contested ever since by the Cunningham family.

The success of the Cunninghams had seemed assured when James III made the head of the family, Alexander Cunningham, Lord Kilmaurs, earl of Glencairn in May 1488; but the outcome was disastrous for the family, with the new earl being killed at Sauchieburn with his king, possibly by the hawkish Hugh, Lord Montgomery, who took part in the battle on the rebel side, and who clearly intended to destroy Cunningham influence in northern Ayrshire.[74] Montgomery was 'made' by Sauchieburn; he followed it up by destroying the Cunningham castle of Turnlaw in Lanarkshire, and not only received a remission for this assault,[75] but also received extensive Crown grants of lands in Arran and Bute, the offices of bailie of Cunningham and Chamberlain of Irvine — in June 1489 — and a commission to put down the crimes of theft, robbery and murder, in Carrick, Kyle, Ayr, and Cunningham.[76] These grants were nothing more than an invitation to Montgomery to pursue his feud with the Cunninghams with the authority of the government.

He did so with vigour and total ruthlessness. The position of Robert, Lord Kilmaurs, succeeding his father immediately after Sauchieburn, stripped of the title of earl and of recognised authority in northern Ayrshire, was difficult if not desperate. His response to the Montgomery challenge was armed resistance. Already on 2 May 1489 Robert, Lord Kilmaurs and Hugh, Lord Montgomery had been ordered to 'cess the cowrt of Cunnynghame'[77]; Kilmaurs was clearly determined to prevent Montgomery enjoying his new status by bringing an armed following to Irvine, the venue of the court of the bailiary, to disrupt the court. Montgomery retaliated before the end of the year by taking the law into his own hands and personally killing Kilmaurs.[78] This brought the tally of deaths of rivals for which he was directly or indirectly responsible, within five years, to three. In 1484 he had killed the young James, second Lord Boyd,[79] possibly hoping for a share of Boyd's Kilmarnock lands, which however had reverted to the Crown; and he had seen off two generations of Cunninghams, Alexander the father and Robert the son. His new-found authority was enhanced by his close relationship with Colin, earl of Argyll — he was the Chancellor's son-in-law[80] — and he clearly intended to use his power to dominate the whole of northern Ayrshire, at the expense of Boyd and Cunningham alike.

Montgomery's ambitions, however, went further than the government would or could allow. He might protest that he was being impeded by the Cunninghams in his exercise of judicial powers conferred on him by that government; but the truth was that the recent killing had all been perpetrated by Montgomery himself, and if nothing were done, there was a danger that a serious political imbalance might be created in a sensitive area. The regime's solution — perhaps the only solution in the circumstances — was to provide an effective counterbalance to Montgomery power in Ayrshire, in the person of Archibald, earl of Angus.

Angus was an obvious choice to deal with unrest in Ayrshire. For one thing, he had been married to Elizabeth Boyd, the daughter of Robert, first Lord Boyd, for twenty-five years, so that the grant to him of the lordship of Kilmarnock made good sense. For another, Ayrshire was a county which the

Hepburns and Humes would find difficult if not impossible to control directly, and establishing Angus there effectively removed much of his influence from the borders. Making a virtue of necessity, therefore, the regime added to Angus's grant of Kilmarnock; on 4 July 1492, a royal charter conferred on Angus the lands and castle of Bothwell in free regality, following on the resignation of both by Patrick Hepburn, earl of Bothwell.[81] This grant is significant in that it reveals a further loosening of the tight Hepburn control of royal government; and it added substantially to Angus's authority in the south-west.

The earl made no secret of his ambitions. Already married to a Boyd, in June 1492 he pursued links with the new head of the Cunningham family, and on the 24th of that month contracted his daughter Marion to marry Cuthbert Lord Kilmaurs.[82] His furthering of the Boyd–Cunningham connection hardly boded well for these families' arch-rival, Hugh Lord Montgomery; and on 10 August 1492 Ormond pursuivant was sent by the king to Irvine 'to gar cess the gaderin betwiss the Lord Kilmawris and the Lord Mongumre'.[83] This might at first seem merely to be a repetition of the trouble seen at the Cunningham bailiary court the previous year and in 1489; but the new-found power of Angus produced a dramatic follow-up. On 7 August Angus himself was in his own castle of Dean at Kilmarnock, only a few miles from Irvine, receiving a discharge from Cuthbert Lord Kilmaurs, for the dowry of his daughter, Marion Douglas. With him were not only Andrew Forman, apostolic protonotary and Angus's former servant, and Lord Hume, the Chamberlain, but also an array of Ayrshire lairds and knights — John Wallace of Craigie and his brother Hugh, Sir Alexander Boyd and Sir John Sinclair, Robert Mure of Polkellie, George Campbell of Cessnock, and Angus's brother-in-law Archibald Boyd of Naristoun.[84] These individuals — a combination of royal officers and anti-Montgomery locals — had assembled at Kilmarnock not only to witness Angus — Kilmaurs family business, but also to enlist the support of the king and court, who had arrived at Dean castle only five days later, on 12 August.[85] James IV had come directly from Stirling, where he had not only dispatched his herald to Irvine but also issued a charter on 10 August; its witnesses included Angus and Hume.[86] Thus between 7 and 10 August, Angus, Hume, and — probably — Forman, informed by the pro-Cunningham locals of an armed struggle with Lord Montgomery at Irvine, hastened to Stirling to fetch the king to Kilmarnock to lend authority to the Angus — Kilmaurs faction in northern Ayrshire.

It soon emerged, however, that much more was at stake than an Ayrshire feud, however serious. For 12 August saw the beginning not only of royal support for the Cunninghams in northern Ayrshire, but of a remarkable change, stretching over some four–five months, in government personnel. Sir William Knollis, preceptor of Torphichen, who held the offices of Treasurer and Master of the Royal Household, was removed from both, which went respectively to Henry Arnot, abbot of Cambuskenneth, and Andrew Lord Gray; Richard Muirhead, dean of Glasgow, who had been Clerk Register since 1489, was removed from office and replaced by John Fresell, dean of Restalrig, a man close to Angus; by December 1492 John Hepburn, Bothwell's uncle, had resigned the Keepership of the Privy Seal, which passed to William Elphinstone, bishop of Aberdeen, who was to hold it for a remarkable twenty-two years. Most significant of all, about the end of the year or early in 1493, Colin Campbell, first earl of Argyll and Chancellor for both James IV and his father, died; and Angus was enjoying the Chancellorship by 15 January 1493.[87] These changes amount to little less than a coup d'état by Angus and his supporters. How had this been achieved?

It seems likely that the post-1488 government, in spite of its dogged struggle to survive the initial bad years and its efforts to enhance the king's, and its own, reputation through firm enforcement of criminal justice, was neither very successful nor popular in the eyes of many of the political community in the summer of 1492. In foreign policy, a French alliance which did not even produce a bride for the king was of little value if it precluded an enduring settlement with Henry VII of England. At home, pious noises had been made in the parliament of April 1491 about the breaking of the king's peace in the Isles; but nothing had been done to punish Alexander of Lochalsh, nephew of the last Lord of the Isles, who had invaded Ross — now technically a royal dukedom — sacked Inverness, and seemed set to revitalise the Macdonald lordship.[88] Above all, there was the matter of the money, the James III inheritance of £24,500 recovered in 1488 and almost totally expended in the first four years of the new reign; furthermore, as the estates made clear in February 1492, large portions of the late king's treasure had not been recovered, or at least had not been paid into the Treasury. These were the sort of complaints which could not be answered simply by a further broadening of government personnel. Changes had to be made.

Not surprisingly, Treasurer Knollis was the first to be dismissed. As the individual directly responsible for the casual income of the Crown since Sauchieburn, he was the easiest to accuse of any irregularity. His removal from the Treasurership and Mastership of the Royal Household seems to have taken place on or about 12 August 1492, and for some time afterwards he is to be found fighting a desperate rearguard action against claims made against him for undischarged debts to the Crown, including an enormous £518 15/6d which he had received from Sir Alexander McCulloch, sheriff of Wigtown.[89] It is unlikely that Knollis was guilty of abusing his office to make illegal profits for himself; more probably he was a scapegoat for those who had seen the royal income shrink alarmingly since 1488. As only £2,000 of James III's hoard was left in February 1492, by August it was probably all gone;[90] and the unfortunate Knollis was dismissed at a time when he had no chance to recoup the heavy debts which he had incurred through his office. A long career in the royal service, stretching back twenty-three years to 1469, when Knollis had first been appointed Treasurer, had effectively come to an end. Knollis would continue to be employed on embassies to the border and into England for about a year; but he had lost his offices of state for good. The new Treasurer, Henry Arnot, abbot of Cambuskenneth, was — unlike Knollis — a man who had served the late king loyally, both as his procurator in Rome in 1471 and as one of those who rallied to James III after the crisis of 1482–3. As a former James III man, Arnot may have been more acceptable than Knollis in a year when the political community was agonising about the supposed disappearance of the bulk of the late king's treasure; and it may be significant that shortly after Knollis' dismissal, Duncan Forster, the comptroller, took possession of a hoard, probably found in Fife — one of the places in which the parliament of February 1492 had specifically ordered secret inquests to be made — for which the finder, John Mercer, was paid £13 6/8d.[91]

Knollis' other office, that of Master of the Household, went to Andrew Lord Gray, a bitter opponent of the late king and of James III's most loyal earl, David, earl of Crawford. Gray had obtained rewards immediately after Sauchieburn, including Crawford's sheriffship of Forfar; but in spite of having an almost constant record of attendance on the council throughout the first four years of the new reign, he had not been entrusted with any of the major offices of state. His appointment to the Mastership of the Royal Household on or shortly after 12 August 1492 may have been due to Angus's new-found influence at court; for the earl and Gray had a long history of cooperation, including treasonable dealings with the English on behalf of the Duke of Albany in the crisis of 1482–3, and both men were the most notable survivors of James III's retaliation after that event.[92] Ten years on, a pro-English stance had acquired far greater respectability; and Gray's career in the royal service would go from strength to strength as the reign went on.

The individual who conferred much of the respectability on the new Scottish foreign policy was William Elphinstone, bishop of Aberdeen, who became Privy Seal, some time before 12 December 1492,[93] in place of Bothwell's uncle John Hepburn, and who was pro-English by conviction, the architect of James III's projected alliances with Henry VII in 1486 and 1487. As we have seen, Elphinstone had taken some time to ingratiate himself with the new regime after Sauchieburn; he had been taken back on to the privy council during the rebellion of 1489, and had worked hard as a council judge and on the lords auditors ever since; and he had an excellent record of attendance on the council. But the autumn of 1492 saw the bishop's real breakthrough to power, for the office of Privy Seal gave him effective control of royal patronage. It remained an open question whether he would be able to retain power, for the king's minority would soon end, and the changeover to James's personal rule might be expected to produce further changes in personnel in household and state offices.

The last and most dramatic change was one which could hardly have been planned in advance: some time between 12 December 1492 and early January 1493, Colin Campbell, earl of Argyll, died, and the Chancellorship went to Angus, who is first described as Chancellor in a charter of 15 January 1493.[94] As Argyll had been nominated to a commission to let Crown lands as recently as 12 December, it seems likely that his death was unexpected, a shock both to his son and successor Archibald and to the political community in which he had played a prominent part for over thirty years. It seems likely, however, that in spite of his continuing attendance on the privy council, Argyll's influence was

on the wane after 1488 — certainly after the rebellion of 1489, when he played
a curiously equivocal role and was not even among those condemned by the
rebels. The summer of 1492 displays Argyll's influence slipping still further;
for in the Cunningham–Montgomery feud in Ayrshire, if he backed anyone
at all it would be his son-in-law Hugh, Lord Montgomery. But Montgomery
was the loser in that contest, while Angus, with his Boyd and Cunningham
relatives and allies and the vital ingredient of royal support, was the clear
winner. Politically, therefore, the latter half of 1492 may be seen as a period of
growing Angus ascendancy, underlined by the earl's reappearance, on a regular
basis, on the council, and confirmed by Argyll's death and Angus's assumption
of the Chancellorship by January 1493.

Royal support was vital to Angus's success from the beginning. Without
it, he could be regarded at best as a magnate of dubious reputation, at
worst a traitor. But Angus's intimacy with the young king went much
further than playing the occasional game of cards or dice with James.
On 12 August 1492, at the height of the Cunningham–Montgomery crisis,
James IV was in Kilmarnock confirming a grant of some Lanarkshire lands
to Archibald Boyd of Naristoun and his wife Christina Mure.[95] Archibald
Boyd was not only Angus's brother-in-law, but also the father of Marion
Boyd, who sometime the following year[96] was to produce the first of two
illegitimate children — Alexander Stewart, later archbishop of St Andrews
— by James IV. Significantly, no business appears to have been transacted
by the king, or in his name, for about a month after his visit to Kilmarnock
on 12 August 1492; and it is likely that his liaison with Marion Boyd began
at this time. It was a lengthy affair, with the two children — Alexander and
Catherine — being born, probably, in 1493 and 1494 respectively. There seems
no doubt that the Earl of Angus owed much of his advancement, possibly even
his Chancellorship, to his Boyd niece's long association with the king. This is
indeed suggested by the Spanish ambassador Pedro de Ayala, writing in 1498
and looking back over the royal minority on the basis of information supplied
to him when he spent a year in Scotland in 1496–7. When the king was a
minor, remarks Ayala, 'he was instigated by those who held the government
to do some dishonourable things. They favoured his love intrigues with their
relatives, in order to keep him in their subjection.'[97] This comment, although
rather exaggerated, clearly indicates that the basis of Angus's power was his
ability to provide a mistress for the king out of his Ayrshire kin. For James
IV, still a minor as Ayala notes, was less than two years short of his twenty-first
birthday and his wishes had to be taken seriously by his counsellors. Thus the
Hepburn faction, headed by Bothwell and his uncle, the Prior of St Andrews,
showed considerable political astuteness when they relinquished control of major
offices — above all the Privy Seal in 1492 — to others acceptable to Angus. Both
Bothwell and his uncle continued to serve regularly on the privy council; but
they avoided the trap of being caught with a monopoly of offices of state and
household, which would have made the newly-elevated Hepburns an obvious
target when the king came of age. Instead, Angus was left to assume the most

important office of state during an awkward transition period, and to rely on his niece's continuing association with James IV to keep him in power.

Up to a point, he succeeded; but it is unlikely that he would have done so if James IV, like his father and grandfather, had been eager to take control of government himself. Clearly, however, he was happy to let Angus and Elphinstone take charge for him, with the ever-present Bothwell keeping a watchful eye on his family's gains since 1488. In many ways, the combination in the two most important offices of state of the rebel earl and defeated Bishop-Chancellor of 1488 was an unholy alliance; but Angus and Elphinstone could at least agree on altering the emphasis of Scottish foreign policy from Bothwell's over-enthusiastic and unproductive commitment to France to develop a closer association with Henry VII of England. On 17 October 1492 six Scottish ambassadors, headed by Elphinstone himself, were commissioned to negotiate an extension of the feeble eight-month truce with England. The ambassadors on both sides duly met at Coldstream on 3 November and agreed to extend the truce to April 1494;[98] and this proved only the prelude to intensive negotiations for a much longer Anglo–Scottish peace. Time and experience had taught Henry VII that the government of James IV had survived its initial trials and could not be overcome simply by reactivating the Scottish fifth column; and in his own quest for security against pretenders, the English king was anxious to deny potentially the most dangerous of these, Perkin Warbeck, a base from which to launch an assault into England. In 1493, therefore, both Scotland and England were governed by men who saw the advantages of a longer and firmer peace.

The initiative lay with Henry VII, who on 28 May authorised commissioners not only to treat for peace with the King of Scots, but also to propose a marriage alliance between King James and Katherine, daughter of Eleanor, countess of Wiltshire and daughter of the late Edmund, duke of Somerset, Henry's uncle. The Scots do not appear to have been impressed with the status of the proposed bride — after all both James II and James III had married foreign princesses — but Elphinstone received Henry's ambassadors at Edinburgh, and on 25 June agreed on a huge extension of the truce, to last a further seven years beyond 1494, ending only on 30 April 1501. Significantly, the Scottish ambassadors were all committed Anglophiles — apart from Elphinstone himself, they included Sir John Ross of Montgrenan who owed his swift restoration in 1490 largely to the good offices of Henry VII, and Master John Fresell, dean of Restalrig, the clerk register, an associate and — no doubt — nominee of Angus.[99] The obvious wisdom of furthering peace with England was underlined by one immediate result of it; as part of the new seven years' truce, Henry VII promised to pay 1,000 marks sterling to the King of Scots as compensation for damages done by Englishmen to the Scots prior to the treaty. The promise was honoured in less than a month.[100]

Although James IV went along with the English truce negotiated by his new administration, it is unlikely that it represents his own policy in any meaningful sense. He was still a minor; there appeared — as yet — to be no English bride of suitable status to make a firm alliance with England a worthwhile proposition; and most significant of all, within three years King James would show beyond doubt that his minority was at an end by breaking the truce and invading England on behalf of the pretender whom Henry VII most feared. In the meantime, he would continue to entrust the running of his government to the varied talents of Angus, Elphinstone, Bothwell, and their associates. He himself would do his duty as expected of him, attending the northern and southern ayres, going on pilgrimage to Whithorn and — probably for the first time in October 1493 — to the shrine of St Duthac at Tain. He took time off to hunt at Falkland and in Glenartney; and it seems likely that he visited Marion Boyd to see his new son, in the late spring of 1493.[101] Most important of all, he played an active part in helping to further his government's policies in attempting to solve the long-standing problems in the Western Highlands and Isles, and in Ross, a Herculean task rather inadequately described in a later parliament as the 'danting of the Ilis.'[102]

The source of the problem lay in the survival without real authority of John, the last Macdonald Lord of the Isles, who had been stripped of his earldom of Ross as long before as 1476, and compensated — if that is the correct word — with having his Lordship of the Isles converted into a lordship of parliament. His position in the Isles, as we have seen, was at once challenged by members of his immediate family — first by his bastard son and designated heir Angus Og, who had taken the war to the Crown and its vassals by his raids on Ross and Inverness in the 1480s; and after Angus's assassination, Macdonald leadership had passed to his cousins Donald Gorme of Sleat and Alexander of Lochalsh, who like Angus ignored John Macdonald as a feeble vassal of the Stewart Crown — a Crown, moreover, in minority and therefore more open to attack in areas outwith its direct control.

The threat to Crown territory in Ross, however, was mitigated by divisions amongst those who sought to control the earldom. Alexander of Lochalsh, after a devastating raid on Inverness in 1491, was heavily defeated, some time in the same year, by the Mackenzies at Park near Strathpeffer,[103] and his reputation in Ross dwindled as a result. He continued, however, to grant charters within the lordship in 1492 — from Colonsay, Oronsay, and Iona, two of them with the consent of the council of the Isles, and one of these in association with John Macdonald.[104] Clearly, therefore, whatever the attitude of James IV's government, Alexander of Lochalsh was accepted by the council of the Isles as effective Lord of the Isles, with the power to grant lands and offices within the lordship. By contrast John, lord of the Isles, made no independent grants in the Isles between 1486 and his last charter, made at Aros on 6 December 1492 — perhaps significantly giving the patronage of the church of Kilberry in Knapdale to Robert Colquhoun, bishop of Argyll.[105] So the charter evidence of 1492 shows the last Lord of the Isles dithering between collaboration with his hawkish nephew, Alexander of Lochalsh, and granting church patronage to the local bishop. Hugh Macdonald, writing admittedly in the seventeenth century, probably sums up the situation in the Isles in the early 'nineties quite accurately when he remarks that 'the Islanders were let loose and began to shed one another's blood.'[106] Divisions amongst the chief men of the Isles, together with the disintegrating authority of John Macdonald, may well have suggested to those in charge of James IV's government that the time had come to launch a full-scale assault in the West; and Dr Jean Munro argues convincingly that those loyal to the Crown within the lordship expected firm intervention by the king.[107] The result, in the parliament of May–June 1493, was the forfeiture of the Lordship of the Isles to the Crown, followed by a series of royal naval expeditions to the west to make that forfeiture effective.

It is probably no accident that the forfeiture of the lordship occurred in the first parliament after Angus's assumption of the Chancellorship. Indeed, the earl may well have instigated the forfeiture to improve his position in a number of ways. With Argyll dead and his son Archibald, the new second earl, lacking friends at court, the forfeiture would help to damage the interests of the Campbells both in royal government and in the Western Isles. For both Campbell earls, Colin and Archibald, in turn exhibited a close interest in the fate of the lordship; Angus Og had been Earl Colin's son-in-law, and after Angus's death, his son Donald Dubh — an infant born about 1490 — was incarcerated in Argyll's castle of Inchconnell on Loch Awe.[108] Thus the Campbell earls of Argyll held the key to the future of the Macdonald lordship; for the child in Inchconnell was not only Earl Colin's grandson, but the heir to the Lordship of the Isles. The forfeiture of that lordship to the Crown would not only help to undermine the power of the new earl of Argyll, but would also assist Chancellor Angus in his efforts to establish himself, his kin, and his allies, in the west of Scotland. Certainly Archibald, second earl of Argyll, suffered a political eclipse from 1493 to 1495. He turned up at the 1493 parliament and was elected to the Lords Auditors,[109] but he did not become a member of the privy council, far less an officer of state or household, for almost two years.

Furthermore, the eclipse of Argyll meant that one of Hugh, Lord Montgomery's most powerful backers in the Cunningham–Montgomery feud in Ayrshire was unable to assist him, which worked — at least temporarily — to the advantage of Angus, the Boyds, and Cuthbert Cunningham, Lord Kilmaurs. It is also significant that the very first royal grant from the forfeited lordship, that of the lands of Greenan in Ayrshire, went to Angus's second son William, displacing the Davidson family who had held the lands for a generation and who were to protest the change right down to Flodden.[110] The most likely conclusion to be drawn from this mass of evidence is that the first six months of 1493 saw an enormous increase in the power of Chancellor Angus and his allies, an increase which was tolerated by the young king at least partly because of his continuing involvement with Marion Boyd, which would produce a further child, a daughter Catherine, probably in 1494.

This new-found power was forcefully demonstrated, not only in the forfeiture of the Lordship of the Isles, but in the royal act of revocation made at the end of the same parliament, on 26 June 1493.[111] Dr Nicholson describes it as 'a sweeping act',[112] and so it is in the sense that it claims not only to annul all heritable jurisdictions granted by James IV and his father, but also requires the restoration of all lands which had been Crown property in the reign of James II. But to regard it as a turning point in the reign, the point at which James IV took control of government for himself, is surely to misinterpret its significance. The king was only twenty, almost five years short of the legal age of majority. The 1493 act was not the first of its kind, but the third, preceded by the revocations of 1488 and 1490; furthermore, it would not be the last. On 16 March 1498, the day before his twenty-fifth birthday, James IV issued a further act of revocation;[113] and remarkably, at the outset of the 1504 parliament, at the age of 31, he would issue yet another, an act which significantly ordered all donations, gifts, acts, and statutes done 'in tymis bigane othir hurtand his saule his crovne or halikirk' to be 'put furtht of the bukis and writingis'.[114] This order of 1504 was apparently carried out, for there is no record of the statutes of 1493 in the original books of parliament; and there is no surviving record of any kind of the forfeiture of the Lordship of the Isles. The conclusion is inescapable that the 1493 forfeiture and act of revocation were statutes made in the king's name, but not by an adult king decisively asserting his authority for the first time. When James IV finally had that authority, he annulled the 1493 acts.

A glance at the leadership of the political community in 1493 confirms the continuing royal minority. There was no dramatic change of royal councillors, with Angus continuing as Chancellor, Elphinstone as Privy Seal, Gray as Master of the Household, and Henry Arnot as Treasurer throughout. The dominance of this group is reflected in the fact that Patrick Hepburn, earl of Bothwell, and John Ross of Montgrenan — the major beneficiaries of 1488 and 1490 respectively — took the trouble to record that they were not to be affected by the 1493 revocation.[115] For the act was surely Angus's inspiration, closely linked to the forfeiture of the Lordship of the Isles which immediately preceded it. The latter would allow the new Chancellor legitimate expansion in the west, while the former, by ending the king's legal minority, would avoid the danger of gains made by Angus being revoked later by the Crown — or so, no doubt, the earl hoped.

The sequel to this energetic parliamentary activity was the first of King James's expeditions to the Western Isles, in August 1493. On 18 August James IV, accompanied by Chancellor Angus, Elphinstone, Bothwell, both justiciars, Lyle and Glamis, Chamberlain Hume, Andrew Lord Gray, Treasurer Arnot, Secretary Whitelaw, and John Fresell, the Clerk Register, had reached the ancient fortress of Dunstaffnage on the Firth of Lorne.[116] The visit was brief — only 11 days later the king was already at Durisdeer on his way south to Whithorn — and there is no reliable account of what happened at Dunstaffnage. Most likely those chiefs in the area who feared for their futures given the greatly weakened and divided Macdonald leadership and the recent forfeiture of the lordship came in to declare their loyalty to the Crown. Certainly by the following year John MacLean of Lochbuie and John MacIan of Ardnamurchan had been confirmed in lands and offices — the bailiaries of southern Tiree and of Islay respectively

— which they had formerly held from John, Lord of the Isles.[117] It is possible to envisage an impressive scene at Dunstaffnage, with the royal fleet anchored offshore, and the galleys of MacLean and MacIan emerging from the Sound of Mull into the Firth of Lorne bringing the local chiefs to offer their service to the young king and his assembled council. But there was one notable absentee. In the heart of his lordship of Lorne, Archibald Campbell, earl of Argyll, was nowhere to be seen. His absence from Dunstaffnage — and Chancellor Angus's very prominent presence — can only have made public divisions and rivalries among James IV's magnates, and cast doubt on the effective power of the Crown and its officers in the Highland west.

No-one, however, could fault Angus and his colleagues in government for lack of energy. All of them accompanied the young king on his pilgrimage to Whithorn in late August — early September, immediately after the journey to Dunstaffnage and without any time to recover from the sea voyage back to Ayr. The following month the entire court had moved from the extreme south-west to the far north-east, parading James IV as far as Dingwall, at the heart of the Stewart dukedom of Ross and so recently the scene of Alexander of Lochalsh's depredations. King James was then hurried south to catch up with the southern justice ayre at Jedburgh late in November; and it is not until a fortnight before Christmas that he is to be found in Glen Artney, taking a break from most of the duties imposed on him by hunting with his exhausted councillors.[118]

These rapid royal tours of troubled, or potentially troublesome, areas during the final stages of the minority show a sensible political awareness on the part of the Angus government. However, they would not of themselves solve the problems posed by the collapse of Macdonald authority in the Isles and Ross. The government's problem in the west lay in knowing with whom to deal. In the event, there were too many chiefs, all of them possessing some influence but lacking overall authority. At one extreme was John, the recently forfeited Lord of the Isles, in 1494 brought into the royal household and given an annual pension of £133 6/8d,[119] perhaps as a security measure, to prevent him being used by those who wished to restore the lordship. At the other extreme was John's grandson and — to many — successor as Lord of the Isles, Donald Dubh, a youth languishing in Argyll's custody in Inchconnell castle on Loch Awe. In the uncertain political climate of 1493–1494, it may have appeared likely to Angus and his colleagues in government that Argyll, slighted by being excluded from high office, would use his possession of Donald Dubh to attempt to reunite the divided lordship. To avoid this danger, the government must woo other Macdonald leaders, men prepared to accept that their best chance of dominating part, if not all, of the old lordship lay in actively supporting the Crown.

The two most prominent of these individuals were Alexander of Lochalsh, after Donald Dubh the obvious heir to the lordship and, as we have seen, capable of issuing charters with the support of John of the Isles and the council of the lordship as recently as 1492; and John Macdonald of Dunivaig, sometimes described as John of Islay, the leader of the Macdonalds in the south of the lordship. Both men may have professed their loyalty to the Crown as early as the royal visit to Dunstaffnage in August 1493; certainly both were knighted, and Alexander of Lochalsh appears to have received a royal promise that all freeholders in the former lordship would be infeft in their lands.[120] Why this conciliatory policy failed is not clear. Possibly Alexander of Lochalsh could not abandon his former aggression without losing credibility amongst his own supporters; and he appears to have been involved in an abortive raid on Ross in 1494. But a more likely explanation for the continuing troubles is to be found in the ambitions of John MacIan of Ardnamurchan, who as the representative of a junior branch of the Macdonald kin could hardly aspire to dominate a revived lordship, and who therefore looked for advancement by destroying its leaders and accepting substantial rewards from a grateful government. Some time in 1494 MacIan put an end to the career of Alexander of Lochalsh by killing him on the Isle of Oronsay.[121] The circumstances surrounding the murder are obscure, though the seventeenth-century historian of the Macdonalds may be correct when he says that MacIan feared the consequences for himself if Alexander of Lochalsh were permitted to repossess the ancient heritage of the Macdonalds.[122] What is not in doubt is that on 14 June 1494 MacIan of Ardnamurchan, for 'obedience and good service', received a royal grant not only of extensive lands on Islay, but also the office of crown bailie on the island;[123] and it is tempting to see this substantial reward as a response by the government to MacIan's timely elimination of Alexander of Lochalsh. Failing to win the trust of either Alexander of Lochalsh or Sir John of Islay, Angus and his colleagues may well have looked to MacIan as their most promising hatchet-man in the Isles. It was a role which he was to fill admirably for many years.

The demise of Alexander of Lochalsh, together with MacIan's Islay rewards, may well explain the rebellion of Sir John of Islay in 1494, and James IV's two visits to the west in that year. John of Islay probably felt — with some justification — that the government could not be trusted, and that the intrusion of MacIan into Islay with royal backing was a clear threat to himself. The king had briefly visited the Isles in May, though we have no evidence as to where he went;[124] but in July, after the MacIan rewards, he summoned part of the host — the lords of the east, south, and west — to meet him at Tarbert castle on Loch Fyne. James IV was at Tarbert on 24 July, having sailed there from Dumbarton on board the 'Christopher', well supplied with victuals, gunners, and gunpowder.[125] The castle, which had originally been built by Robert I, was repaired at considerable cost, after which the king sailed south to take control of Dunaverty castle at the southern tip of the Kintyre peninsula. Here again he had repairs carried out, at one point sending across to Ayr for a ship to bring victuals to Dunaverty.[126] By 20 August, after perhaps a month in and around Kintyre, James IV was already at Stirling;[127] and the autumn would be given up to the northern ayres, which would take the king as far north as Inverness before returning to Edinburgh for Christmas.[128]

In fact, the July–August visit to Tarbert and Dunaverty could hardly be described as a success. It may indeed have been intended as no more than a defensive measure, to strengthen fortresses which guarded the western approaches to the Firth of Clyde and the Stewart — and Angus — lands in the area. But its immediate result was to make an implacable enemy of Sir John of Islay, who according to a much later tale stormed Dunaverty and killed King James's keeper, displaying the corpse outside the castle wall in view of the departing royal fleet.[129] What is certain is that by 8 September 'Schir Johnne of the Iles' had been summoned for treason committed in Kintyre, that there was some difficulty in executing the summons,[130] and that — once again — the man who appears to have solved the government's problems was MacIan of Ardnamurchan. Either in 1494 or 1499 — the evidence is inconclusive — MacIan surprised and captured Sir John and three of his sons at Finlaggan on Islay. According to the Book of Clanranald, all four were brought to Edinburgh and hanged on the same gallows on the Borough-muir.

From the point of view of the government, therefore, the bold stroke of 1493, carrying through the forfeiture of the lordship and a royal act of revocation in the same parliament, had brought only partial success in the Isles by the end of 1494. Much remained to be done before the Crown could hope to place its own men in, and raise substantial rents from, the former lordship; the Angus government understood this, and responded to the challenge not only by making a court pensioner out of the former lord of the Isles, but also by paying for extensive shipbuilding and repairing operations at Dumbarton throughout the winter of 1494–5.[133] The king would indeed return to the Isles in the late spring of 1495; but when he did so, it would be as his own master.

On 17 March 1494 James IV reached his twenty-first birthday, the date at which he officially emerged from the tutelage of Patrick, earl of Bothwell, and on which he acquired — in theory at least — the power to cancel the extensive grants of criminal jurisdiction made in the parliament of October 1488. In the event, little changed, with the officers of state and household remaining the same men, the only exception being caused by the retiral around the previous Christmas of Archibald Whitelaw, Secretary for over thirty years and the survivor of more political crises than any other royal servant. Whitelaw was in his early 'seventies,[134] and his final year in office, embracing sea voyages to Dunstaffnage and pilgrimages to Whithorn and Tain, would have tried the constitution of a much younger man. So it was probably with relief that he relinquished the Secretary's office to Richard Murehead, Dean of Glasgow, and retired to spend his few remaining years perusing the works of Lucan, Horace, Sallust, and Albertus Magnus,[135] carrying his political secrets to the grave in 1498.

If James IV did not change his counsellors in March 1494, he at once showed that he was prepared to act against, as well as with, their advice. In an enigmatic and intriguing story told by John Knox in his 'History of the Reformation in Scotland', King James was present at a trial of thirty

persons from Ayrshire, summoned by Archbishop Blacader before the Lords
of Council during a visit of king and council to Glasgow. Knox dates the trial of
these 'Lollards of Kyle', as he calls them, to the sixth year of James IV's reign,
and the twenty-second of his age — that is, some time between 17 March and
10 June 1494. This is quite plausible. The king and court can be shown to be
in Glasgow between 15 and 17 May, and to be transacting judicial business on
the latter date, though no contemporary record of the case described by Knox
exists.[136]

Knox's garbled tale of the trial of the 'Lollards of Kyle' is interesting
not so much for the heresies with which his accused were indicted – a vast,
and in places contradictory, list of thirty-four articles — as for the names of
those involved. There are six of these, including not only the hero of the
episode, Adam Reid of Barskimming, who apparently acted as spokesman for
the rest in answering the archbishop's charges, but also George Campbell of
Cessnock, John Campbell of Newmilns — possibly George's son — Andrew
Shaw of Polkemmet — probably related to Campbell of Cessnock through his
father's marriage — Helen Chalmers, Lady Polkellie, and Marion (or Mariota)
Chalmers, Lady Stair.[137] Many years ago, Dr Easson demonstrated that Adam
Reid makes an unlikely heretic, as he is later to be found appointing a chaplain
to say mass on behalf of souls in Purgatory, applying for a royal respite to go
on pilgrimage to Canterbury and Amiens, and referring an appeal case to the
Roman curia.[138] So Knox's information about heresy in this trial is probably
based on the *later* experience of John Campbell of Cessnock, who had the New
Testament read in the vernacular in his household. It is however quite possible
that Knox's named 'Lollards' were all found guilty of heresy in the court of the
diocesan Official of Glasgow, that they refused to recant, and that Blacader was
invoking the aid of the secular arm, in terms of the parliamentary act of 1425
against heresy, 'in suppowale and helping of halykirk'.[139] If so, presumably
he was simply invoking secular aid to carry out sentence on heretics already
condemned in his own diocesan court. Instead, in Knox's account, there was a
trial before king and council, after which 'the greattest part of the accusatioun
was turned to lawchter.'

But why should the king have resisted his archbishop's obvious wishes in
relation to this tight-knit group of heretics from Kyle and Cunningham? One
answer is provided by Knox himself, who says that some of the accused were
the king's 'great familiaris.' It is true that in 1498 and 1499 Adam Reid — who
may have recanted when required to do so by the king himself — is to be found
receiving lands in North Kintyre from the Crown, that he is described therein as
the king's 'familiar servitor', and that the grants are made 'for good service.'[140]
Likewise George Campbell of Cessnock would greatly improve his position as
the reign advanced, and was Sheriff of Ayr by 1511.[141] But this hardly proves
the king's interest in these individuals at the much earlier date of 1494.

There is, however, one important sense in which the leader of those accused
in 1494 — George Campbell of Cessnock — may be described as a royal familiar.
On 7 August 1492, just before the Earl of Angus's Kilmarnock coup, Campbell

of Cessnock is to be found witnessing a discharge by Cuthbert Cunningham, Lord Kilmaurs, to Archibald, earl of Angus, for the dowry of Cunningham's wife, Angus's daughter Marion. Campbell's appearance on this list places him firmly in the Angus–Cunningham–Boyd camp, and also in very distinguished company; for other witnesses included Andrew Forman, the prothonotary, Lord Hume, the Chamberlain, and — perhaps most significant of all — Archibald Boyd of Naristoun, the father of Marion Boyd, James IV's mistress. On the same list we find the name of Robert Mure of Polkellie, probably the husband of Helen Chalmers, 'Lady' Polkellie, another of Knox's 'Lollards'.[142] This witness list places beyond doubt the very close association of some of the leaders of the 'Lollards of Kyle' with Archibald, earl of Angus, his Boyd and Cunningham kinsmen, and the royal mistress drawn from their ranks. Thus while it is impossible to be certain as to the reasons for Archbishop Blacader's attack on Campbell of Cessnock, Reid, and the rest — his motivation may have been political, arising from jealousy of Angus and his Ayrshire friends rather than a concern about heresy — it is easy to understand why James IV — and Angus, who was with the king in Glasgow — sprang to their defence. Some time in 1494, King James had a second child, a daughter Catherine, by Marion Boyd; and his long-standing affair with Marion probably served as protection for her Boyd kinsmen and their Ayrshire friends, even against a determined assault on them by a powerful archbishop, the man who had crowned the king.

The end of James's minority was clearly in sight. In theory, if not in practice, he had been in control of his government since 1493. By March of 1494 he had emerged from tutelage, and could move to assert himself at any time. Two apparently unrelated events in the winter of 1494–5 suggest that changes were at last on the way. About that time the king arranged for the marriage of Marion Boyd to John Mure of Rowallan, providing her with a generous annuity in money and Ayrshire lands;[142] and from the time of her marriage, if not before, Marion clearly ceased to be the royal mistress, with all that that implied for the Angus hegemony in government. Secondly, and probably of greater immediate importance, on 24 March 1495 the deliberate neglect of Archibald, second earl of Argyll, came to an end when he was appointed Master of the Royal Household.[144] He would retain the post until he died with James IV at Flodden.

NOTES

1. *A.P.S.*, ii, 216.
2. *Ibid.*, 217.
3. *Ibid.*, 217–8.
4. Fraser, *Lennox*, ii, 132–4; *A.P.S.*, ii, 223. Among the 130 defenders of Dumbarton were Matthew Stewart's brothers Alexander and Robert, and George Weir, Montrose Herald. The last-named had been used by the Hepburn regime on

16 April 1489 'to pass with letteris to Dumbartane' (*T.A.*, i, 108). Clearly he not only delivered the royal summons to the rebels but also decided to join them.

5. *A.P.S.*, ii, 219–220, c. 7, 8.

6. *Ibid.*, 220, c. 10.

7. *Ibid.*, 220–221, c. 11, 12.

8. *See*, for example, Rait, *Parliaments of Scotland*, 38–9.

9. *A.P.S.*, ii, 220–221, c. 11, 12.

10. *R.M.S.*, ii, Nos. 1944, 1945.

11. *Ibid.*, Nos. 1919, 1946.

12. *Spalding Miscellany*, iv, 184–5, 186–7.

13. *Ibid.*, 187–8.

14. *A.P.S.*, ii, 218–9.

15. *T.A.*, i, 175.

16. *A.P.S.*, ii, 218, c. 3.

17. Pitscottie, *Historie*, i, 237. Pitscottie gives the number of the Murray dead as six score. But *see* NLS Adv. MS. 34. 7. 3 (MS. of James Gray), f. 36v., where all twenty slain are named in a memorandum at the foot of the page; and note by George Neilson in *S.H.R.*, i (1904), 218–9.

18. Atholl Royal Letters no. 2. (Blair Castle).

19. *A.D.C.*, i, 90, 99.

20. *T.A.*, i, cii–ciii.

21. Pitscottie, *Historie*, i, 237; NLS., Adv. MS. 34. 7. 3., f. 36v.

22. *T.A.*, i, 170.

23. *A.D.C.*, i, 167; Pitscottie, *Historie*, i, 237; *E.R.* x, 708, 709.

24. *E.R.*, x, 708.

25. *A.D.C.*, i, 167–8.

26. *T.A.*, i, 178.

27. *R.S.S.*, i, No. 613.

28. *T.A.*, i, 171.

29. *Archaeological Collections relating to the County of Renfrew*, ii, p.xiv.

30. *R.M.S.*, ii, No. 1768.

31. Fraser, *Lennox*, ii, 140–142.

32. S.R.O. Dalhousie Muniments GD 45/1/1.

33. *T.A.*, i, 182–3. James IV was in Paisley on 21 November.

34. Fraser, *Lennox*, ii, 142–4.

35. Ireland's career and works are described in the introduction to the Scottish Text Society of the *Meroure*: Johannes de Irlandia, *The Meroure of Wyssdome* (ed. Charles Macpherson, S.T.S., 1926), vol. i, pp. xiv–xxxviii; more detail, and a more scholarly analysis, is to be found in J.H. Burns, 'John Ireland and 'The Meroure of Wyssdome'', *Innes Review*, vi (1955), 77–98. The most recent analysis of Ireland's political thought is Roger Mason, 'Kingship, Tyranny and the Right to Resist in Fifteenth-Century Scotland', *S.H.R.*, lxvi (2) (1987), 125–151. The final — seventh — volume of the 'Meroure' (NLS MS. 18. 2. 8) forms part of the forthcoming Scottish Text Society publication, edited by Dr. Craig Macdonald.

36. Ireland, *Meroure*, i, pp. xxviii–xxx.

37. Burns, 'Ireland and 'The Meroure''. passim. On 21 May 1491 Ireland was present — presumably as Rector of Ettrick — at the meeting of the Glasgow chapter which opposed Bishop Blacader's pretensions to archiepiscopal rank: Burns, *op.cit.*, 94–5; *Glasgow Registrum*, ii, 478.

38. Both these statements are cited in Mason, 'Kingship, Tyranny and the Right to Resist', 140 n.2.

39. *See above*, chapter 3; for the sheriffship of Lanark, *see HMC. 11th Rep.*, *App.*, pt. vi, no. 24.

40. *T.A.*, i, 133, 169, 170–171.

41. *A.P.S.*, ii, 223–228.
42. *T.A.*, i, 180.
43. *Ibid.*, 179.
44. It is printed in full in *Cal. Docs. Scot.*, iv, App. I., No. 32, pp. 416–7.
45. *Cal. Docs. Scot.*, iv, No. 1577; *Statutes of the Realm*, ii, 553.
46. *Cal. Docs. Scot.*, iv, No. 1571.
47. *T.A.*, i, 314.
48. *A.P.S.*, ii, 223.
49. Rymer, *Foedera*, xii, 172–176.
50. *E.R.*, x, lxvii.
51. *T.A.*, i, 180.
52. Pitscottie, *Historie*, i, 226–7.
53. *T.A.*, i, 181.
54. *Ibid.*, 182.
55. *Ibid.*
56. *Ibid.*, 183.
57. *Ibid.*, 188.
58. *R.M.S.*, ii, Nos. 2072, 2073.
59. *T.A.*, i, 184, 188.
60. Fraser, *Douglas*, iii, 130–131.
61. S.R.O. MS. Treaties with France, no. 20.
62. *A.P.S.*, ii, 230.
63. *Cal. Docs. Scot.*, iv, No. 1580; Rymer, *Foedera*, xii, 473.
64. *A.P.S.*, ii, 229.
65. *Ibid.*, 230 c. 2.
66. *T.A.*, i, 196.
67. *A.P.S.*, ii, 230 c. 3.
68. *T.A.*, i, 167, 196.
69. *A.D.C.*, ii, 233. The case involved Sir Oliver Sinclair of Roslin, who was accused of withholding from James IV treasure to the value of about £1,000 which had belonged to the king's father; Sinclair was ordered to pay 400 marks to the Treasurer.
70. *A.P.S.*, ii, 229.
71. Chrimes, *Henry VII*, 281–2.
72. *A.P.S.*, ii, 230 c. 4.
73. *Ibid.*, 225 c. 9; 226–7 c. 17.
74. Fraser, *Eglinton*, i, 27.
75. *Ibid.*, ii, 48.
76. *Ibid.*, i, 28.
77. *T.A.*, i, 110.
78. S.R.O., CS 5/19, f. 131v; *E.R.*, xi, 373. I am indebted for these references to Steve Boardman.
79. *Scots Peerage*, v, 150.
80. *Ibid.*, i, 335.
81. *R.M.S.*, ii, No. 2106; Fraser, *Douglas*, iii, 134–5.
82. Fraser, *Douglas*, iii, 131–4.
83. *T.A.*, i, 201.
84. Fraser, *Douglas*, iii, 135–6.
85. *R.M.S.*, ii, No. 2111.
86. *Ibid.*, No. 2110.
87. The above changes in government personnel are calculated mainly from the printed *R.M.S.* witness lists: *R.M.S.*, ii, Nos. 2110–2122. Caution is necessary in using these, as the clerks entering royal grants in the register frequently apply the same witness list indiscriminately to a bundle of charters of widely differing dates, which can give a misleading impression of when individuals held and renounced specific offices;

for example Angus's tenure of the Chancellorship might seem, at a casual glance, to date from 12 August 1492: *R.M.S.*, ii, No. 2111; but Argyll is still Chancellor on 20 September and 8 October of the same year: *R.M.S.*, ii, Nos. 2112, 2113. Reference to the MS. register (S.R.O. C2/13/35) explains the confusion, as the Kilmarnock charter of 12 August 1492 has been engrossed in the register together with a bundle of charters dated 15 January 1493, and erroneously given the same witness list by the scribe. For Argyll as Chancellor and commissioner to let Crown lands, with Elphinstone as Privy Seal, Gray as Master of the Royal Household, and Henry Arnot as Treasurer, as late as 12 December 1492, see *E.R.*, x, 710–11; for John Fresell as an associate of Angus, see Fraser, *Douglas*, iii, 134.

88. *A.P.S.*, ii, 228; Gregory, *History of the Western Highlands and Isles of Scotland*, 56–7.

89. *T.A.*, i, 208.

90. The problems of securing adequate Crown income at this time and later are dealt with at length in A.L. Murray, 'Exchequer and Crown Revenue of Scotland, 1437–1542' (unpublished Ph.D. thesis, Edinburgh 1961), chap xiii, esp. pp. 342–3.

91. *T.A.*, i, 207. For Arnot's earlier career, see Macdougall, *James III*, 105, 185.

92. For the details of the Angus/Gray collusion in 1482–3, see Macdougall, *James III*, 155, 175, 180.

93. *E.R.*, x, 710–11.

94. *Ibid.* (for Argyll as Chancellor, 12 December 1492); *R.M.S.*, ii, No. 2121 (for Angus as Chancellor, 15 January 1493).

95. *R.M.S.*, ii, No. 2111.

96. There is some doubt as to the precise date of Alexander Stewart's birth. Erasmus describes him as 20 in 1513, yet 18 in 1509, which would place the birth either in 1491 or 1493. The situation is further confused by a papal dispensation of October 1497, allowing Alexander to hold benefices despite his illegitimacy, and stating that he was then in his sixth year, giving a likely birthdate of 1492. However, the information on which the dispensation was based was provided by the Scots, and Alexander's age may well have been exaggerated to make his subsequent appointments seem more acceptable. In 1505, James IV described his son to pope Julius II as below the age of puberty. This, together with James IV's association with the Boyd family from the summer of 1492, makes the 1493 date the most likely: M. Mann Phillips, *The Adages of Erasmus: a study with translations* (Cambridge, 1964), 307; John Dowden, *The Bishops of Scotland*, 37; James IV letters, 16–17.

97. *Cal. State Papers (Spanish)*, i, p. 170.

98. *Cal. Docs. Scot.*, iv, Nos. 1585, 1586.

99. *Ibid.*, Nos. 1588, 1590, 1592.

100. *Ibid.*, Nos. 1591, 1596, 1597.

101. Pitcairn, *Criminal Trials*, i; *T.A.*, i, passim (for the ayres); *R.M.S.*, ii, Nos. 2173, 2181 (for pilgrimages); *Ibid.*, Nos. 2146–8, 2185 (for hunting trips). There is no record of a visit to Ayrshire to see Marion Boyd; but it could easily have occurred as part of the final stage of the southern ayre of 1493, or during the gap in recorded Great Seal and Privy Seal business between 11 April and 11 May, or between 11 and 30 May.

102. *A.P.S.*, ii, 240.

103. *Highland Papers*, i, 55.

104. *Acts of the Lords of the Isles 1336–1493* (edd. Jean and R.W. Munro) (S.H.S., Edinburgh 1986), Nos. 122–4.

105. *Ibid.*, No. 125.

106. *Highland Papers*, i, 55.

107. Jean Munro, 'Lordship of the Isles', in *The Middle Ages in the Highlands* (Inverness Field Club, 1981), 33.

108. For the career of Donald Dubh, see *Acts of the Lords of the Isles*, 313–4.

109. *A.P.S.*, ii, 231.

110. *R.M.S.*, ii, No. 2171; *Acts of the Lords of the Isles*, 222, 235.
111. *A.P.S.*, ii, 236–7 c. 22.
112. Nicholson, *Later Middle Ages*, 541.
113. *T.A.*, i, 383.
114. *A.P.S.*, ii, 240.
115. *Ibid.*, 237.
116. *R.M.S.*, ii, No. 2171.
117. *Ibid.*, Nos. 2700, 2201, 2202, 2216. For details and comment, see *Acts of the Lords of the Isles*, 223–226.
118. *R.M.S.*, ii, Nos. 2172, 2173, 2181, 2185; Pitcairn, *Criminal Trials*, i, 14.
119. *E.R.*, x, 534; *T.A.*, i, 233, 234.
120. *R.M.S.*, ii, No. 2438.
121. *Highland Papers*, i, 56.
122. *Ibid.*, 60.
123. *R.M.S.*, ii, No. 2216.
124. *E.R.*, xi, 181.
125. *T.A.*, i, 217, 237, 244, 253, 254.
126. *Ibid.*, 244.
127. *Ibid.*, 238.
128. *Ibid.*, 238–9. James IV was accompanied on the northern ayre by Chancellor Angus; Chamberlain Hume; John, Lord Glamis, justiciar; Andrew, Lord Gray, Master of the Royal Household; George, abbot of Dunfermline; George Schaw, abbot of Paisley, Treasurer; Richard Murehead, dean of Glasgow, Secretary; and Master John Fresell, dean of Restalrig, Clerk Register: *R.M.S.*, ii, No. 2224.
129. Gregory, *History of the Western Highlands and Isles*, 89.
130. *T.A.*, i, 238. At the end of November 1494 the summons against Sir John of Islay had only recently been executed in Bute: *Ibid.*, 239.
131. Gregory, *op. cit.*, 89–90, for the capture and execution of Sir John and his sons. The execution is placed in 1494 by Gregory; but the contemporary — and normally highly accurate — Ulster annalist places it in 1499: *Annals of Ulster*, iii (1379–1541), ed. B. MacCarthy (Dublin, 1895), 443. 1499 is the year in which MacIan of Ardnamurchan received extensive rewards from the crown, specifically for the capture of Sir John and one of his sons: *Acts of the Lords of the Isles*, 230–231.
Dr Jean Munro has kindly suggested to me that the capture *and* execution of John of Islay and his sons may have occurred very rapidly in 1499; see the Clanranald account: *Reliquae Celticae*, edd. A. MacBain and J. Kennedy (Inverness, 1894), ii, 163.
132. *Ibid.*
133. *T.A.*, i, 245–254.
134. Whitelaw graduated M.A. at St Andrews in 1439: *Bannatyne Misc.*. ii, 41–48.
135. Ross, 'Early Scottish Libraries', *Innes Review*, ix (1), 1958. Whitelaw's library is listed on p. 159.
136. John Knox, *History of the Reformation in Scotland*, ed. W.C. Dickinson (Edinburgh, 1949), 7–11; *R.M.S.*, ii, Nos. 2211–2214: *A.D.C.*, i, 319.
137. Knox, *History*, i, 177.
138. D.E. Easson, 'The Lollards of Kyle', *Juridical Review*, xlviii (1936), 123–8.
139. *A.P.S.*, ii, 7. c. 3.
140. *R.M.S.*, ii, Nos. 2454, 2500.
141. Easson, *op. cit.*, 125.
142. Fraser, *Douglas*, iii, 136.
143. *R.M.S.*, ii, Nos. 2471, 2472.
144. *Ibid.*, No. 2240.

5

1495–97: The Watershed

Judged by the standards set by his two predecessors, James IV was a late developer. James II had taken personal control of his government in 1449 shortly before his nineteenth birthday; and when James III emerged from his minority in November 1469 he was only seventeen. In both these cases, however, there was an obvious and pressing need for the king to assert his authority against those who were constraining it — in James II's case, the Livingston–Douglas combination, in that of James III, the Boyds of Kilmarnock. In each case, the king used his foreign marriage to end a long period of tutelage in the most dramatic fashion, striking out at those families who had dominated the latter stages of the minority and rewarding magnates who had assisted the Crown in bringing them down.

No such violent change accompanied the coming to power of James IV. This was partly the result of 1488 itself, when James had played an active part in the overthrow of his father, and was thereby committed to support those magnates who had made him king; and his reliance on these men was increased rather than diminished by the immediate challenge to the new regime by the rebels of 1489. Thereafter the minority government enjoyed a much easier existence, largely because — contrary to the norm during minorities — more and more influential magnates were admitted to it. A government which by 1493 could include in its ranks men with such widely contrasting political backgrounds as Angus, Bothwell, Hume, Elphinstone, Blacader, Ross of Montgrenan, Lyle and Gray — to name only some of the most important examples — was bound to command wide support, because at least one prominent magnate from most areas of Scotland was to be found on the royal council. By the mid-1490s, in sharp contrast to the situation a decade before, most of the localities had a powerful representative at court.

By 1495, however, contentious issues had arisen which required the attention of an adult king in full control of his kingdom. Above all there was the problem of evolving a coherent foreign policy, a task closely linked to the king's marriage and the diplomatic possibilities associated with it. The need to find a foreign bride for James IV had been recognised as early as the parliament of October 1488, but efforts to negotiate firm alliances with France and England had been disappointing. No bride of any standing appeared to be forthcoming from either country, and the Scots were left with a rather

112

unsatisfactory French treaty, negotiated by Bothwell in 1491–2, and an uneasy seven years' truce with Henry VII of England, the brainchild of the Angus government. Nearer home, there was the continuing problem of the Isles, above all the consequences of the forfeiture of 1493. Perhaps most of all, the Crown urgently needed to tackle the problem of royal finance, for the great windfall of James III's treasure was long since gone, and about this time the king is to be found pawning his French saddle, his gold locket, and his copy of Gower's *Confessio Amantis*.[1] Thus there was an obvious need by 1495 for James IV to assert himself, not in assailing the leaders of the minority government in the manner of his predecessors, but in making clear at home and abroad that the minority was at an end. Within a year, neither the inhabitants of the former lordship of the Isles, nor Henry VII of England, can have had any doubts that the policies of the Scottish government were those of James IV in person.

The transition from minority to personal rule is most clearly reflected in changes in the privy council in 1495–6. Apart from the appearance of Archibald, earl of Argyll, as Master of the Household for the first time on 24 March 1495, John Lord Drummond, a magnate under something of a cloud since 1492 in spite of his earlier service to the Crown at Gartloaning in 1489, is named as justiciar from 18 February 1495, and is the only individual to be so described until 1501.[2] Drummond's advancement may have owed something to the growing influence of Argyll, whose sister Isabel was Drummond's daughter-in-law;[3] and this link may also be reflected in the replacement, in the autumn of 1497, of John Fresell, an adherent of Angus, with Drummond's kinsman Walter Drummond, dean of Dunblane, in the office of Clerk Register.[4]

The advancement of both Drummonds in royal service at this time may also be connected with the fact that James IV's new mistress, Margaret Drummond, was Lord Drummond's daughter.[5] It is difficult to date the beginning of Margaret's liaison with the king. The first reference to her in royal accounts comes on 3 June 1496, when James had her installed in Stirling castle and so made public the association; but it is likely that he had known Margaret for some time, at least since his visit to Drummond Castle on 25 April 1496,[6] and possibly since 1495, when his affair with Marion Boyd appears to have come to an end. The wealth of speculation which later surrounded the king's liaison with Margaret Drummond — that James had known her since 1488, that he wished to marry her, and that she and her sisters were poisoned in 1502 by those who feared that the king would never marry as long as she was alive — rests on not a shred of contemporary evidence, but is mainly the work of Viscount Strathallan (William Drummond), writing a eulogistic history of his family in the late seventeenth century.[7] The official records tell rather a different story: Margaret Drummond occupied the king's attentions for about a year after June 1496, and the affair resulted in the birth of a daughter, Margaret. From June to October 1496 Margaret Drummond lived in Stirling castle under the care of the keeper, Sir John Lundy, and his wife; on 30 October she was transferred to Linlithgow, where she spent the winter of 1496–7, finally being sent home to Drummond castle at the end of March 1497.[8] Her career is probably best summed up by

Don Pedro de Ayala, the Spanish ambassador who arrived in Scotland in the same month that King James installed Margaret Drummond in Stirling castle. 'When I arrived', remarks Ayala, 'he [the King] was keeping a lady with great state in a castle. He visited her from time to time. Afterwards he sent her to the house of her father, who is a knight, and married her.'[9] In fact, no husband can be traced for Margaret Drummond after the king had sent her home, though on 23 January 1498 she received a nine years crown lease of lands in the earldom of Strathearn, possibly to provide a living for herself and a husband not identified in the Privy Seal record.[10] Although James IV had begun his long-standing affair with Janet Kennedy in 1498, he made a payment of £21 to Margaret Drummond, and 41/– for her daughter's nurse, as late as June of 1502;[11] and following Margaret's death later in the year, the king had his daughter by her brought from Drummond castle to Stirling,[12] and paid a quarterly fee — at least until 1508 — to two priests in Dunblane cathedral to sing masses for the soul of his dead mistress.[13] These few facts do not provide much of a foundation for the towering superstructure of legend which the Drummond family was later to build on Margaret's career. Her relationship with the king was similar to that of her predecessor Marion Boyd and probably less remarkable than that of her successor Janet Kennedy; and the most that we can say with assurance is that her intimacy with James IV helped the career in royal service of her father and kinsman Walter Drummond in the first few years of the king's personal rule.

For William Elphinstone, bishop of Aberdeen and Privy Seal, James IV's assumption of control also marked a new beginning. Between November 1493 and August 1495 there is no trace of Elphinstone at court or on the Lords of Council.[14] Perhaps fortunately for himself, he was abroad for much if not all of the time, on the king's business and his own. His own business, reinforced by a royal supplication, was to seek permission from Pope Alexander VI to erect a university in his own diocese, at Old Aberdeen; and following an interview with the pope on 6 February 1495, Elphinstone had the satisfaction of obtaining the Bull of Foundation, which he not only paid for but carried back to Aberdeen in the summer.[15] In the winter of 1494–5, however, Alexander VI had more on his mind, to put it mildly, than the creation of a studium generale in Old Aberdeen. On the last day of 1494 Charles VIII of France, with a huge army, had appeared at Rome's northern entrance, the Porta Flaminia, the pope had prudently fled from the Vatican along the fortified wall connecting it with his stronghold on the Tiber, Castel Sant' Angelo, and from his position of relative safety within its walls he had negotiated a treaty with the French king which would save Rome from being sacked. What Charles VIII wanted, and what Alexander VI was finally — and temporarily — prepared to concede, was papal confirmation of his title to the Kingship of Naples. To gain time, and after nearly a month's negotiation, the pope made an elaborate treaty of perpetual friendship with Charles VIII, accepted his claim to Naples, and saw the back of the French army on its way south by 28 January 1495.[16]

When Elphinstone had his audience with the pope little over a week later,

Alexander VI was therefore in the process of emerging from the greatest crisis of his career, and no doubt already preparing for the role which he was to assume later in the year, that of leader of Italian and European opposition to Charles VIII. The pope had before him not simply a provincial bishop, but the Privy Seal of the King of Scots, an ally of France since 1492; and Dr Macfarlane is surely right to suggest that Alexander VI, committed to breaking any alliance which other nations had with France, may well have given his swift approval to Elphinstone's supplication for the founding of a university at Old Aberdeen to help achieve a specific political end — the wrecking of the Franco–Scottish treaty of March 1492.[17] There can be no doubt that James IV himself was rapidly aware of the diplomatic possibilities which his alliance with the French king now presented, that is, of the advantages which he might hope to gain for his kingdom from the pope and other European princes if he were to abandon Charles VIII. He was probably counselled in this sense by Elphinstone, following the bishop's interview with Alexander VI and his growing understanding of the realities of Italian politics. It would appear, therefore, that Elphinstone did not return home to Scotland immediately, as might have been expected. He had reached Bruges by Easter 1495, where we find him taking over the ceremonial duties of the Bishop of Tournai;[18] but his king had further diplomatic work for him in the Empire, and so Elphinstone, no doubt still bearing his Bull of Foundation, had to turn east rather than sail north, and to accept a further delay in the provision of higher education for the 'uncultured' and 'barbarous' inhabitants of the North of Scotland.

If Elphinstone was exercised by the need to train the minds of James IV's subjects in the remoter regions of the kingdom, King James himself was primarily concerned with securing their loyalty. Shortly after Easter 1495, as the bishop toiled off from Bruges on his imperial embassy, James IV moved from Stirling to Glasgow to meet 'the lordis of the Westland, Estland, and Southland' whom he had summoned to take part in his forthcoming expedition to the Isles.[19] The policy was similar to that of the previous two years — to find and reward supporters of the Crown within the forfeited lordship — but the new faces about the king, together with the intensive preparations for the journey, alike indicate James IV's guiding hand. The Treasurer's accounts reveal in minute detail the king's earliest naval building programme, at Dumbarton in the winter of 1494–5 — the construction of a large rowbarge, mainly from timber brought from the woods about Loch Lomond, and involving more than six months' work; the repair of the 'Christopher'; and the building of two further ships, at a total cost of £517 9/11d.[20] By Easter the fleet was ready; and on 5 May James IV embarked at Dumbarton, probably in the 'Flower', commanded by the ubiquitous Sir Andrew Wood. After putting in briefly at Newark castle on the south side of the river Clyde, he sailed to Bute and thence to Kintyre and out into the Isles.[21]

His objective was Mingary castle on the Ardnamurchan peninsula, at the head of the Sound of Mull, the seat of the most committed of all royalists in the Isles, John MacIan of Ardnamurchan. James IV had reached Mingary by 18 May, accompanied not only by Archbishop Blacader, Chancellor Angus, and Chamberlain Hume, but by the new Master of the Household, Archibald, second earl of Argyll, who as bailie of Cowal had contributed to the provisions required for the expedition; by John, Lord Drummond, the justiciar; and by the new Treasurer, George Schaw, abbot of Paisley, a committed supporter of James IV at Sauchieburn.[22] The king's presence at Mingary was a public demonstration of his trust in the castle's keeper, MacIan of Ardnamurchan, who had rendered signal service to the Crown the previous year by killing Alexander of Lochalsh and capturing John Macdonald of Islay. It seems likely that other prominent chiefs, reluctantly recognising which way the political wind was blowing, came in to Mingary to submit and offer their allegiance to James IV in person. The king responded by confirming them in lordship lands and offices; before the end of the year Hector MacLean of Duart had received a royal grant of confirmation of his constableship of Cairn-na-Burgh castle in the Treshnish Isles; Alan, captain of Clan Cameron, was similarly confirmed in his keepership of Strome castle, on Loch Carron in Wester Ross; and MacNeill of Barra, not surprisingly, was given a charter of confirmation of the lands of the entire island of Barra.[23]

The royal visit to the west was short; by 7 June, little more than a month after his departure, the king was back in Dumbarton en route for Glasgow.[24] He had secured a temporary peace in the Isles, based on showing favour to those who were loyal enough, and powerful enough, to do the Crown's work in the west — principally Argyll and MacIan of Ardnamurchan. If these men, and their associates, could bring in royal rents from the forfeited lordship, they would have earned the trust imposed in them by the king; for beyond a healthy interest in ensuring that he received what was due to him, there is no evidence that King James had any deep personal interest in the Isles. The expedition to Mingary in 1495 was simply a re-run of the visit to Dunstaffnage in 1493, this time with a more effective cast. The king would not return to the Isles; indeed he did not even revisit the Firth of Clyde until 1498, and then only to spend some time at his newly constructed castle at Loch Kilkerran near Campbeltown, a more useful site than Dunaverty for protecting the approaches to the Clyde. The building of Kilkerran may have been started in 1495; Tarbert, at the northern end of the Kintyre peninsula, had already been reconstructed; and as for the problems of the Hebridean west, James IV was initially happy to leave their solution to others. After all, the forfeited Lord of the Isles was a court pensioner; his grandson and potential successor, Donald Dubh, was a prisoner in the hands of the Master of the Household; and those who had attempted to revive the lordship, principally Alexander of Lochalsh and John Macdonald of Islay, were either dead or in prison. The king could confidently turn to other matters.

James IV had returned to Glasgow by 30 June, if not before, and he remained there for at least a fortnight.[25] His principal purpose was to receive the individual described in the accounts as 'Gret Adoneill'[26] — Hugh O'Donnell of Tyrconnell in Ulster, the most powerful northern Irish magnate and a committed enemy of Henry VII's government in Ireland. No record of James IV's Glasgow meeting with O'Donnell survives; but clearly the two men made an offensive and defensive alliance of some kind, for the Scottish king referred to it eighteen years later, in the summer of 1513.[27] There can however be little doubt as to the main subject of their discussions at Glasgow; for O'Donnell, together with Maurice Fitzgerald, earl of Desmond, had for years been a major supporter of the individual whom Henry VII feared more than anyone else in Europe, the Yorkist pretender Perkin Warbeck.[28]

Viewed with benefit of hindsight, Perkin Warbeck appears a rather pathetic, almost comic, figure, a pretender who could not decide from the outset whom he was supposed to be impersonating — he started as a bastard son of Richard III, then became Edward, earl of Warwick, before finally taking on the character of Richard, duke of York, the younger of Edward IV's sons — and who flitted unhappily about Europe in the early 'nineties, obtaining at various times some recognition, but little effective support, from his 'aunt', Margaret of Burgundy, various groups of Irish lords, Charles VIII of France, Isabella of Spain, Albert, duke of Saxony, and Maximilian, the Emperor-designate. His fortunes at the hands of all these rulers waxed and waned according to their current relationships with Henry VII of England, and it is clear that none of them — with the possible exception of Margaret of Burgundy, the most committed Yorkist in Europe and an implacable foe of Henry VII — believed for long, if at all, in Perkin's claim to be the Duke of York. He was simply a useful diplomatic pawn in the European game, to be brought into play to bring various kinds of pressure to bear on Henry VII.[29]

Denied benefit of hindsight, King Henry took Perkin's pretensions very seriously indeed. Henry had, after all, won his throne by conquest from the Yorkist Richard III in 1485, arriving by sea with some limited French assistance. Two years later he had been forced to defend his conquest in battle at Stoke against the pretender Lambert Simnel, whose support included not only disaffected Yorkists headed by the Earl of Lincoln, but also a combination of Irish and German mercenaries. By the 1490s, therefore, Henry VII was only too aware — his own experience proved it — that any pretender with a plausible background and the prospect of armed assistance from Europe or Ireland, or both, represented a serious threat to the fledgling Tudor dynasty. In the case of Perkin Warbeck, King Henry attempted to nip trouble in the bud before it occurred. Thus he denied Perkin any further support from France by making the Peace of Etaples with Charles VIII in November 1492; he made clear that he was aware of Perkin's lowly origins by the summer of 1493; and he tried to prevent the pretender from receiving armed support from the Low Countries by sending a high-powered embassy to Archduke Philip of Burgundy, eventually employing an early form of economic sanctions to convince him that he and his father Maximilian ought to abandon any thoughts of backing Warbeck against him. Closer to home, he was constantly preoccupied with the Irish problem, for Perkin had received some lukewarm assistance from the Earl of Desmond at Cork as early as 1491, and he was to receive a warmer reception in 1495.

Indeed, in the latter year Henry VII demonstrated his increasing obsession with security by having his step-uncle and Chamberlain, Sir William Stanley, tried and beheaded for treason; Stanley's treason was that he had been in communication with Warbeck since the summer of 1493, attempting to hedge his family bets in the event of a possible Yorkist comeback.[30] When the real crisis came, however, it would surface not in England, the Low Countries nor Ireland, but in Scotland.

The minority governments of James IV had flirted with displaced Yorkists since the very beginning of the reign, offering shelter to Lord Lovel in 1488 and receiving envoys from Margaret of Burgundy in 1489 and 1490.[31] Then on 2 March 1492, a messenger named Edward Ormond had arrived at the Scottish court bearing letters from 'King Edwartis son' — Perkin Warbeck – and his Irish backer Maurice Fitzgerald, earl of Desmond.[32] No record of what ensued has survived, but it may be that the pretender was looking for no more than a recommendation from the Scots to the court of Charles VIII; certainly Bothwell's Franco–Scottish treaty was ratified two days later, on 4 March, and Perkin had arrived at the French court before the end of the month, receiving from King Charles a bodyguard of a hundred men commanded by the expatriate Scot, William Monypenny, Lord of Concressault.

All this diplomatic activity had had a salutory effect on Henry VII. Certainly he was moved to make peace with France before the end of 1492 partly, if not mainly, by the need to deny an obvious refuge to Warbeck. The pretender's subsequent departure from France into the open arms of Margaret of Burgundy meant that King Henry could not lay hands on him; but he must also have been alerted to the danger of Perkin receiving assistance from the Scots, and his hard work in negotiating the truces of 1493 and 1494 with James IV's government is a reflection of his concern to avert an obvious threat. For all that, he miscalculated — perhaps as a result of neutralising the French in November 1492 he had become complacent — by offering the Scots government no more than Katherine, daughter of the Countess of Wiltshire, as an appropriate bride for James IV.[33] Not surprisingly, the offer was not taken up, and the Anglo–Scottish truce fell considerably short of the peace and marriage alliance which might have been negotiated. Denied suitable brides in both France and England, the Scots were liable to look elsewhere. This was the background to Warbeck's reception in Scotland late in 1495.

To James IV, taking over the running of his government for the first time, the attraction of Warbeck lay in his affiliations with major Continental rulers — Maximilian, King of the Romans, Ferdinand and Isabella of Spain, Archduke Philip, and Margaret of Burgundy. His support of Warbeck, or even the threat of it, would give the Scottish king the chance to play a much greater part on the European stage than his country's size and importance would seem to merit, and could bring about a striking enhancement of the prestige of his dynasty in Europe. Embracing Warbeck's cause would enable King James to seek European alliances which offered more than the eternal triangle of Scotland, England, and France, with the disappointing results which Scottish association with both these major powers had already brought during James's minority. At the very least, threatening Henry VII with Warbeck would surely produce a much more attractive offer of alliance from the English king. Nearer home, James IV could demonstrate to the Scottish political community that the minority was definitely at an end, could steer a diplomatic course somewhere between Bothwell's committed pro-French stance and the Angus government's inclination towards England, and could — if war with England were the outcome — indulge in a popular plunder campaign on the borders, for which the loss of Berwick as long before as 1482 always provided an excuse. At a personal level, there can be no doubt that the 22-year-old James IV was attracted by the prospect of military glory, and that, as events were to show, he wanted to gain a reputation for himself as a warrior king in an area where he would be noticed. Accompanying the fleet to the Isles each year would hardly win him a European military reputation; but the invasion of England was another matter.

For all that, his attitude to Warbeck was cautious and calculating. In July 1495, when James received O'Donnell of Tyrconnell at Glasgow,[34] he may have been considering an alliance to assist Warbeck's abortive landing in England, which occurred at Deal in Kent on 3 July.[35] The Scottish king had already despatched four ambassadors, headed by Bishop Elphinstone, to Warbeck's patron of the moment, the Emperor-elect Maximilian, at Worms. They arrived on 3 June,[36] faced with the difficult task of associating their king with Warbeck's cause by hinting that James IV was already actively assisting 'the Duke of York' with ships and troops. Warbeck was reported to be attacking England with 1500 men, and Maximilian had offered to provide only a paltry reinforcement of a further eight hundred. There is an element of comedy in the assurances given by the Scots that victory for 'the Duke of York' was confidently expected;[37] then, in a private meeting with the King of the Romans on 9 June, they got down to the real business of their embassy, which was to seek a treaty of friendship and alliance between James IV and Maximilian's daughter Margaret. In their address to Maximilian, the Scots remarked that their king had 'not . . . hitherto busied himself with state affairs', but had 'now arrived at a becoming age', thereby placing the timing of James IV's takeover of power in Scotland beyond any doubt;[38] and they went on to seek Maximilian's assistance in a league against England, promising to favour his protégé 'the Duke of York', and 'hoping thus to recover Berwick and certain other places belonging to their king, which have been held by England for many years.'[39]

In the event, the projected imperial alliance failed, and in little over a year Maximilian would have aligned himself with Pope Alexander VI's 'Holy League', directed against Scotland's ally France. However, Elphinstone's embassy to Worms does reveal James IV's view of foreign affairs in the summer of 1495. He was prepared to offer token support to Warbeck in his expedition to England in the hope that it might win him the huge prize of an imperial alliance; but failing that, he was already keenly interested in acquiring Berwick and other strongholds on the borders, at this stage by negotiation rather than force. A recent writer has described James IV's diplomatic flirtation with Maximilian as displaying vain hopes;[40] but James was, in fact, simply following through a policy which had been recommended as early as the first parliament of his reign, in October 1488, that of finding a suitable European bride. The French had failed to provide one, and as Elphinstone had no doubt impressed on King James after his visit to Rome early in the year, Charles VIII was not the most useful of European allies in 1495–6. If James IV was exhibiting delusions of grandeur in hoping, as Boece puts it, to increase his dignity by an alliance with the blood of the Caesars,[41] it must also be said that in all ages, perhaps in this one more than most, diplomatic dreams always far outstrip practical possibilities. In any case, if there had been a prize awarded for crackpot European diplomacy in 1495, it would surely have gone not to James IV, but to Maximilian himself, who spent the first half of the year believing that a small force would be sufficient to place Perkin Warbeck on the throne of England, after which he would show his immediate gratitude by invading France.[42]

Perkin's odyssey in fact came to grief at an early stage. Part of his force landed at Deal in Kent on 3 July, but received little or no support, and those involved were rapidly killed, captured, or executed. The pretender sailed on to Ireland, where he appeared with a fleet of eleven ships off Munster, hoping no doubt to be welcomed there with greater enthusiasm than had been displayed in 1491. The Earl of Desmond was prepared to assist Perkin in the siege of Waterford, the most formidable English stronghold in southern Ireland, and there followed a siege lasting eleven days from 23 July. But the siege was raised on 3 August by an expeditionary force from Dublin, led by Sir Edward Poynings, and Warbeck became a fugitive, protected in his flight through Connaught and Donegal by John de Burgh of Galway and Hugh O'Donnell of Tyrconnell. The latter had returned to Ireland from James IV's court by 7 August, and it was probably O'Donnell who advised Warbeck that his best chance — perhaps his only chance — of succour lay with the Scottish king.[43]

King James was in no hurry to receive Warbeck within his kingdom. In August he was already preoccupied with an alternative foreign strategy, the possibility of an alliance with Spain. This was probably the main purpose of the meeting of a greatly enlarged Council — twenty-eight members representing all three estates — at Stirling on 25 August, after which Archbishop Blacader of Glasgow, James's ambassador, must have left almost immediately on his mission, for he had reached the court of Ferdinand and Isabella at Tarazona before 12 September.[44] He received a sympathetic reception from the Spanish rulers, though he had presumably been instructed to employ polite blackmail — the prospect of Warbeck's being received in Scotland and the Anglo–Scottish truce being broken — in order to make Ferdinand and Isabella take seriously the proposal of an alliance with the Scots. Blacader also seems to have proposed that in return for such an alliance, James IV would break with his ally Charles VIII of France.[45]

The Spanish sovereigns were placed in something of a dilemma by Blacader's embassy. For the only interest which Ferdinand and Isabella had in Scotland, at this time and subsequently, was as the ally of France and the potential enemy of England. They required Henry VII to be free of problems on his northern border so that he could join the Holy League against France; and they had begun the long process of negotiating an alliance with the English king based on the marriage of his son and heir Arthur to their daughter, the Infanta Katharine. To find the Scots looking for a similar alliance on the strength of their ability to make trouble for Henry VII if their advances were rejected outright posed an awkward diplomatic problem for the Spanish sovereigns. In the short term they solved it by throwing up red herrings, including proposals that the Scots might wish to enter the Holy League and efforts to have Blacader made a cardinal.[46] They could also play for time; on 23 September the Archbishop of Glasgow was already on his way home, accompanied by two Spanish ambassadors — the royal chaplain, archdeacon Don Martin de Torre, and Garcia de Herera — with instructions to procure a long truce between Scotland and England, so that Henry VII could invade France without trouble from his northern neighbour.[47]

In the event, the whole business was badly bungled by the Spaniards. Blacader had returned to Scotland by 14 October;[48] but Don Martin and Garcia de Herera took much longer to arrive, presumably because they visited England en route, with the result that a series of written instructions to them from Ferdinand and Isabella arrived in Scotland before they did and were opened by James IV.[49] Thus before negotiations even began at the Scottish end, King James learned what he probably already suspected — that the Spanish sovereigns had no interest in a Scottish alliance for its own sake, but sought simply to string the Scots along with false promises in order to free Henry VII from the danger of a Scottish invasion. James's response was rapid and deliberately provocative. On 16 October 1495, within a few days of Blacader's return from Spain, the king sat in council in Edinburgh. There was a remarkable turnout of forty — in effect the size of a parliamentary sederunt, though in this case drawn only from the first two estates. The king's younger brother, James, duke of Ross, was present, together with all the politically active clergy and magnates in the kingdom, of whatever shade of opinion — Scheves, Elphinstone, Blacader, Brown of Dunkeld, Argyll, Angus, Bothwell, Hume, Erroll, Marischal, and the Master of Huntly.[50] Beyond the record of a single judicial decision, the council's business has not been preserved; but the sheer size of the meeting, the political eminence of those who were present, and the presence of the king and heir presumptive to the throne, indicate a highly important — and urgent — matter of state policy. This can only have been the Spanish business and the decision whether or not to receive Perkin Warbeck.

Polydore Vergil, the contemporary Italian historian who spent much of his life in England from 1502 onwards, includes in his *Anglica Historia* — which was first published in 1534 — an account of the debate in the Scots council on the subject of Perkin Warbeck. He names no names; but in essence the arguments advanced on both sides seem likely enough. According to Vergil, the more prudent magnates argued that the whole affair was nothing but a deceit prepared by Margaret of Burgundy, and that Perkin should not be trusted. Others, however, sought any excuse to fight the English, and although, as Vergil puts it, 'they judged the facts of the case to be uncertain' — presumably Perkin's claim to be the Duke of York is referred to here — they urged that he should be accepted as heir to the English throne so that the Scots might have a legitimate excuse for waging war on England.[51] This latter view probably reflects the attitude of James IV himself; Warbeck was to be used to enhance the Scottish king's reputation at home and abroad.

On 8 November, King James wrote from Edinburgh to Ferdinand and Isabella, again urging them to consider an alliance with Scotland;[52] but he had already decided on the method necessary to convince them that he meant business. Less than a fortnight later, on 20 November, Perkin Warbeck rode into Stirling with his followers, was received by James IV as 'Prince Richard of England', and was given a lodging in the town.[53] Within days of Warbeck's arrival, couriers were sent to Strathearn, Atholl, the Mearns, and Angus, ordering the lords and barons in these areas to meet the king and 'Prince Richard' at Perth; and sheriffs at the extremities of the kingdom were ordered to hold immediate wappinschawings.[54] To reinforce this impression of active commitment to Warbeck's cause, James IV at last consented to give an audience to the two wretched Spanish ambassadors, Martin de Torre and Garcia de Herera, at Stirling on 23 December.[55] As James had already opened their mail from Spain and formed his own conclusions, their task was a hopeless one. They had come to argue the case for James abandoning Warbeck and allying with Henry VII of England; deprived even of their written instructions, which were in the hands of the man they were trying to convince, they were faced by a king who believed — with some justification — that they were little more than agents of Henry VII; and it is likely that the pretender, who was resident in Stirling and who tended to be in James IV's company during the early months of his stay in Scotland, was present to witness their discomfiture. Not surprisingly, nothing was achieved; indeed both ambassadors were probably now forced to listen to round abuse of Henry VII by James IV and Warbeck. Certainly James's behaviour was unusual enough for the Spanish ambassador in England, De Puebla, to remark on it to Ferdinand and Isabella, who responded cryptically that 'we are very sorry for what the King of Scotland did in the garden of the Castle, especially as our ambassadors were present.'[56] Having indulged himself in this piece of theatre, James IV departed to spend Christmas at Linlithgow.[57] However, he did not as yet dismiss Don Martin and De Herera, no doubt because he wanted to impress them at close quarters with his commitment to Warbeck's cause.

Superficially, at least, that commitment was impressive. Early in January 1496 the court moved from Linlithgow to Edinburgh, and there, on or about 13 January, Warbeck was married to Lady Catherine Gordon, daughter of George, second earl of Huntly. For the occasion, the pretender appeared in a 'spousing goune' of white damask presented to him by the king, and there followed a tournament to celebrate the marriage, the first of many such events during James IV's personal rule. The king took part in the jousting together with Sir Robert Ker, Patrick Hume, Patrick Haliburton, and William Sinclair, in the course of which James appears to have been wounded in the hand, which was duly bandaged in silk and provided with a sling. Warbeck was also present at the tournament, attired probably in another of King James's gifts, a suit of armour covered with purple damask, and accompanied by six servants, two trumpeters, and Laurence the French armourer; but it is not recorded that he took part in the jousting.[58]

Still more impressive was James IV's willingness to finance Warbeck's cosmopolitan gang of followers and hangers-on as they made their way into Scotland in the wake of their provider. In the first half of 1496 they landed at Leith and Ayr in considerable numbers, and their costs were duly defrayed by payments from the Treasurer. The king also contributed a ship to the enterprise, purchased from two Bretons and intended for the use of Roderic de Lalain, the Burgundian agent who maintained close links with Warbeck's 'aunt', Margaret of Burgundy.[59] The greatest cost of all, however, was Warbeck's personal annual allowance of £1344, paid monthly and financed by a contribution which fell at least partly on the royal burghs north of the Forth.[60]

By the early summer of 1496, then, James IV had invested a great deal of his time, and his own and his subjects' money, in Warbeck and his cause. It is however highly unlikely that he believed for a moment that Warbeck was Richard, Duke of York. For one thing, almost every other European ruler had become cynical about the pretender's claims, a fact which must have been known by James; for another, the wedding which the Scottish king had arranged for Warbeck was hardly a convincing match for a man who was supposed to be the rightful King of England. Catherine Gordon, though distantly related to King James because her father, George, earl of Huntly, had once been married to the king's great-aunt Annabella, was in fact no more than the earl's third daughter by a subsequent marriage.[61] At this time, and indeed for the remainder of his stay in Scotland, Warbeck existed simply to serve the needs of King James's diplomacy. Thus although wappinschawings had been ordered before the end of 1495, no invasion of England in support of the pretender occurred until September of the following year; and much happened in the intervening nine months.

The truth is that James IV appears to have been much more interested in his Spanish diplomacy than he was in Perkin Warbeck, and that, having Warbeck physically in Scotland, he was keen to see whether he could achieve a better deal from Ferdinand and Isabella as the price of his leaving Henry VII in peace. Sometime before Easter 1496, therefore, King James sent Archbishop Blacader off to Spain in the company of Garcia de Herera, with orders to insist on the marriage of the King of Scots with a princess of Spain, in return promising perpetual peace with England, and 'perfect safety to Henry from him of York'.[62] In short, within a few months of taking up Warbeck, James IV was quite prepared to ditch him if he got the correct answer from Spain. This put Ferdinand and Isabella on the spot, for as Queen Isabella candidly admitted in a letter to her ambassador in England in August 1496, there was no available Infanta to marry to the Scots king even if the Spanish sovereigns had wanted this: Dona Isabella, the eldest of their daughters, would in fact be married in Portugal the following year; but in 1496 she was a widow refusing to remarry, so that a Portuguese marriage had been arranged for her younger sister, Dona Maria; and the only remaining Infanta, Dona Katharine, was already the subject of negotiations for an Anglo–Spanish alliance.[63]

The Scots had no place in all this, and so, quite simply, they must be deceived. Blacader and De Herera were already in Spain, at Soria, on 14 April, waiting for an audience with Ferdinand and Isabella. On that day, writing to their ambassador De Puebla in England, the Spanish sovereigns described their policy towards the Scots in a few sentences, saying that 'we have no other purpose in our negotiations with Scotland than to win over the King of Scots, and to make him friends with the King of England, so that he may no longer show favour to *him of York*, or enter into an alliance with France. At all events, we intend to put him off some time longer with vain hopes, in order that he may not begin war with England or join the King of France. Whatever negotiations we have with him are only for this purpose.'[64] So Blacader was first kept waiting — Ferdinand did not report the details of a meeting with him until 21 June — and subsequently efforts were made to deceive him with evasive answers about the projected alliance. He was not deceived, and indeed it would have been surprising if he had been, given the Scots' experience of Ferdinand's diplomacy the previous year; furthermore, as De Puebla shrewdly advised his sovereigns, they must be very careful, for the Scots 'are astute in the highest degree.'[65] In fact, James IV's patience appears to have been wearing thin, for despite his promise not to undertake anything against England before the return of his embassy from Spain, shortly after Whitsunday he sent couriers as far afield as Aberdeen, Banff, Elgin, Inverness, Caithness and the Isles, summoning the host to meet him at Lauder.[66] No date is specified for the meeting, but the summons is significant in demonstrating that James IV was prepared to use the threat of force up to the last possible deadline to bring pressure to bear on Spain or England. In the case of Ferdinand and Isabella, their course was already set. The King of Scots must not be told that there was no available Infanta for him to marry; instead, yet another ambassador was to be sent to him 'to keep him in suspense' over the matter of a marriage alliance.[67] This was Don Pedro de Ayala, who came to Scotland at the end of June or beginning of July 1496,[68] probably preceded, a few weeks earlier, by Archbishop Blacader. De Ayala would fail in his initial mission, to deceive James IV; but his obvious liking for the king and country would produce a remarkable letter to Ferdinand and Isabella, written two years later,[69] describing Scotland and King James — for the most part — in glowing terms, and providing countless generations of later historians with the chance, eagerly seized upon, to tear his remarks about James IV out of context. In July

1496, De Ayala's influence with the Scottish king still lay in the future; James was probably much more interested in Blacader's report, and he responded to it by continuing his preparations for war. A tax of spears, or 'spear silver', was to be levied from all three estates to help finance the forthcoming campaign, and the Treasurer's accounts reveal the actual payment of £1027. 17/10d over the next two years.[70] A final meeting of the Council on 2 September saw agreement reached between James IV and Warbeck as to the price of James's support; and the muster point for the Scottish host was re-located at Ellem Kirk, ten miles from the border, on 15 September.[71]

For Henry VII, the ruler on the receiving end of these unwelcome attentions, the crisis which he had sought to avert was at last upon him. Yet things might have been much worse had it not been for his own diplomatic successes in Europe. He had striven throughout the 'nineties to cut the ground from under Warbeck's feet by denying him refuge wherever he could in northern Europe. Thus France had abandoned the pretender in 1492; Maximilian's assistance to Warbeck had been lukewarm in the extreme; and even the Earl of Desmond, who had supported Warbeck's siege of Waterford in the summer of 1495, had come to terms with Henry by March 1496.[72] The threat to the English king's position was therefore limited to what James IV and Margaret of Burgundy might achieve between them to revive Warbeck's very tarnished reputation.

The situation was however complicated by Henry's diplomatic aims in Europe. Above all, as we have seen, he wanted to conclude a marriage alliance between his son and heir Arthur and a daughter of Ferdinand and Isabella; but the Spanish monarchs were fighting shy of a definite commitment so long as Henry's position was under threat from a pretender. Furthermore, they wanted to ensure that the English king joined the Holy League, and if possible, took up arms against Charles VIII of France; and Henry was concerned that the marriage alliance with Spain might depend on whole-hearted commitment on his part to this, the major purpose of the League. By the summer of 1496 he was also aware that Ferdinand and Isabella had sent a new ambassador to Scotland, and that James IV had also been seeking a Spanish marriage alliance since the previous year; so the continuing evasiveness of the Spanish monarchs on the subject of an English alliance, while at the same time they professed to be acting purely in Henry's interests in Scotland, presented the Tudor king with a major diplomatic headache. In the end he solved it with some skill so far as the major European powers were concerned. He would join the Holy League — it was proclaimed in Rome on 18 July 1496[73] — and would even make some threatening noises against France. But he was quite adamant that he would not make war on Charles VIII, Scotland's ally, as long as his relationship with the Scots was not 'satisfactorily arranged'[74] — a euphemism for Henry's concern that breaking the Peace of Etaples with Charles VIII might induce the French king, as well as James IV, to welcome Warbeck, as he had done before in the spring of 1492.

King Henry's entry into the Holy League on his own terms greatly simplified his diplomatic difficulties. He was left with the immediate problem of war with the Scots, with Warbeck, and with such disaffected elements of the English north as might join the pretender against him. He was inclined to take this last threat very seriously indeed, partly because a gloomy letter, written on 4 June, from the loyal Sir Henry Wyatt, Captain of Carlisle, a veteran of Henry VII's Scottish policies, suggested that the king could not wholly trust his lieutenants on the borders. Indeed Wyatt named as inefficient, or worse, Sir Richard Salkeld, keeper of Carlisle castle; Sir John Musgrave, keeper of Bewcastle, charged with the defence of the West March against the Scots of Liddesdale; and as for Henry, Lord Clifford, the hereditary sheriff of Westmorland, Wyatt claimed that he was 'guided by simple and undiscreete persons, and to his greate hurte.'[75] All this must have seemed extremely ominous to King Henry, as the Scots might well launch an attack on the West March.

Up to the last weeks before the invasion, Henry VII strove hard to solve the problem of Warbeck by diplomatic means. In spite of the Anglo–Scottish truce, which was not due to expire until 1501, he had feared that the Scots would break it and invade as soon as James IV became master within his own kingdom. Thus there had been a war scare as early as 22 March 1495, when the English king had commissioned Thomas, earl of Surrey, the vice-warden of the West and Middle Marches, to array all defensible men between the rivers Trent and Tweed, to resist the Scots 'and other enemies' who were threatening to attack the north of England immediately in force. In the east, a similar commission was given to Richard Fox, bishop of Durham, for the county of Northumberland, his bishopric and his lordships of Tynedale and Redesdale. Six days later, Henry Martyn was appointed by the English king to provide for the conveying of artillery to Berwick for its defence.[76] In the same month of March 1495, King Henry issued some suggestive secret instructions to Richmond Herald, travelling on embassy to France. He was to tell Guillaume Briçonnet, Cardinal of St Malo and a confidant of Charles VIII, that Henry VII had information suggesting that James IV of Scotland intended to move against England that year. He was therefore to request that, in the event of a Scottish invasion, the French might hand over to Henry the son of Alexander, duke of Albany. Albany had died in France, in an accident at a tournament in Paris in 1485, and his son John, the child of the duke's French marriage, had been brought up entirely in France. Richmond was instructed to say that no prince could so well help the Duke of Albany to recover his rights in Scotland ('a Recouvrer ce que par droit luy appartient en escosse') as Henry himself.[77] In the event, nothing came of this suggestion, possibly because Charles VIII had no wish to alienate either of his allies, England or Scotland; but it is clear that King Henry, faced with a hostile Scottish government known to be negotiating with Perkin Warbeck, was looking for a diplomatic response by attempting to secure a suitable pretender to the throne of Scotland. The son of Alexander, duke of Albany, whom King Henry's two predecessors had supported as an alternative King of Scots, would have been an excellent choice.[78]

By the end of 1495, however, with Warbeck in Scotland and James IV recognising him as 'Prince Richard of England', King Henry needed a more positive initiative to try to solve his diplomatic problems. He found it, no doubt with some reluctance, in a commission issued on 5 May 1496 to his Privy Seal, Richard Fox, bishop of Durham, together with the Bishop of Carlisle and the earl of Surrey, to open negotiations with a view to a marriage between the Scottish king and his daughter Margaret.[79] Over seven years later, this marriage would eventually take place as part of the terms of the Anglo–Scottish treaty of perpetual peace concluded the previous year. Yet in 1496, in spite of the fact that Bishop Fox, a skilled diplomat, made the trip to Berwick to open negotiations on the subject with James IV's commissioners, the only effect of the meeting seems to have been to confirm the Scottish king in his determination to make war on Henry VII.[80] King James's intransigent attitude undoubtedly reflects the fact that he did not trust the English king to keep his promises; his daughter Margaret — admittedly a substantial improvement as a prospective bride on Henry's previous offer of Katherine, the Countess of Wiltshire's daughter — was only six years old and could not therefore be married for some years. In the meantime James had his recent experience of the abortive Spanish match to make him wary, not to mention his own father's endless English marriage treaties, none of which had ever been fulfilled. He probably believed, therefore, that Henry VII was prepared to promise Margaret Tudor in marriage simply to save himself from the threat of Scottish invasion and a northern rising on behalf of Warbeck, and that, once the danger had been averted, the offer would be withdrawn. This was a realistic analysis of Henry's attitude to the Scots; and James IV was after all not the only candidate for his daughter's hand. An alternative, and to Henry for a time more attractive, possibility was the twelve-year-old Christian, son and heir of King Hans of Denmark.[81] A Scottish invasion, therefore, might help to concentrate Henry VII's mind wonderfully over the matter of the marriage, and in the last analysis it is clear that by the late summer of 1496, James IV's preparations for war were too far advanced for him to call it off. Nor, probably, did he want to call it off. If Polydore Vergil is to be believed, James did not attach much trust to Warbeck's assurances of support in northern England, and was moved primarily by the desire to fight a popular war — a war in which his followers envisaged no battle or major siege, but rather only the prospect of booty on a vast scale.[82] If Warbeck had some success, so much the better; but his claim to the throne of England provided the occasion, not the cause, of the Scottish invasion of September 1496.

Unable to avoid war with the Scots, and unsure of some of his commanders on the borders, Henry VII relied heavily on the Scottish fifth column — those Scots who had found themselves on the wrong side in 1488 and had never become fully reconciled to the various minority regimes of James IV's reign — to provide him with information about the Scottish king's intentions. The most prominent of these men were James Stewart, earl of Buchan, and John Ramsay, formerly Lord Bothwell, the latter in receipt of an annual pension of 100 marks from Henry VII since 1489. In 1491 both men, together with Sir Thomas Todd of Sheriffhall, had been employed in an obscure plot to kidnap James IV and his brother James, duke of Ross, and hand them over to Henry VII.[83] By

1496 both were involved in another abortive scheme, this time to kidnap or assassinate Perkin Warbeck before the Scottish campaign got properly under way.[84] These projected treasons apparently remained undetected by James IV, for Buchan was trusted occasionally as a member of the royal judicial council on sessions,[85] while Ramsay clearly had access to court and council in 1496, if not before. The grievances of both men no doubt lay in the fact that neither of them — understandably in view of their records both before and since 1488 – had benefitted greatly from royal patronage during James IV's minority.

Two remarkable letters written by Ramsay to Henry VII in September 1496, just before the invasion, provide us with a clear picture of the final decisions of the Scots, and the hollowness of the relationship between James IV and Warbeck.[86] Writing from Berwick on 8 September, Ramsay informed King Henry that the Scottish king planned to muster his host at Ellem kirk exactly a week later, 15 September; that Perkin's followers, numbering some 1400 men 'of all maner of nations', would be there as well; and that the combined army would enter England two days later, 17 September. On 2 September, Ramsay continued, the king had summoned his council, who agreed that the price of Scottish support for Warbeck was 100,000 marks within five years, and the delivery of the town and castle of Berwick. These terms had been put to the pretender, who asked for a day to consider them; and on 3 September, 'after lang commonyng', the final deal — 50,000 marks in two years, together with Berwick — was reached, and a written agreement drawn up to that effect.

Following the council, Ramsay had gone with James IV to St Andrews to receive Sir William Monypenny, Lord of Concressault, arriving direct from France as the ambassador of Charles VIII. It seems that, even at this late stage, Monypenny had been sent to mediate between James and Henry, and that the French king had authorised him to offer James 100,000 crowns for the delivery of Warbeck into his hands. James would have none of it, and pointed out to Monypenny that he had suffered greatly at the English king's hands, losing many ships and an abundance of cattle on the borders. He was, he claimed, the injured party in the dispute with England — though he omitted to mention that three years earlier, when the eight-year truce with Henry VII was being negotiated, he had accepted — or rather his counsellors had accepted for him — the sum of 1000 marks English money — about £2000 Scots — in full satisfaction of all injuries done by the English king's subjects on land or sea.[87] Monypenny, however, seems to have been very ready to believe James's version of events, and he remained quite unmoved by Ramsay's efforts to convince him of Warbeck's low birth. Monypenny was, after all, Charles VIII's ambassador, and the French king had no desire to see King James married to Margaret Tudor; so, as Ramsay noted, the ambassador and 'the boye' — Warbeck — 'ar everie day in counsaill'.

It is when he passes from hard fact to his own opinions that Ramsay becomes a much more dubious source. Thus he is correct in saying that James IV was short of money for the 1496 campaign, and that he had coined his silver plate and chains to help pay for it;[88] but he is certainly carrying wishful thinking to its limits when he claims that 'thar was nevir pepill wors content of the kings guvernans than thai ar now', that the projected war was widely unpopular, and that many Scots looked to Henry to punish James 'for the cruell consent of the mourdir of his fadyr.'[89] This last statement might have had some validity for a small minority of Scots in 1488–9, but was an absurd claim in 1496. As for the unpopularity of either James or the war, there is no evidence to support Ramsay's view, and indeed much to contradict it. No Scottish king could hope to muster even an adequate host if his war aims were unpopular; James IV not only gathered together a sizeable army but was able to impose a levy on the whole country to help finance the 1496 campaign.[90] The unpopularity to which Ramsay refers may well draw its relevance from the cost to the Scots of maintaining Warbeck and his 1,400 men during their protracted stay in Scotland. Aberdeen was presumably not the only major burgh which had to provide financial support for Warbeck's followers;[91] and the attitude shared by many of King James's lieges may well have been that the sooner the war came, the better, as it would serve the double purpose of ridding them of any further financial obligation to the pretender's motley collection of supporters while allowing them to indulge in a profitable plunder raid into northern England.

In fact, Ramsay is at his least convincing when he tries, in a second letter to Henry VII, to put names to those disaffected Scottish magnates whom he claims would not support James IV's invasion.[92] Apart from the Earl of Buchan, a compulsive conspirator since the late 1470s, Ramsay can name only Buchan's younger brother, Andrew Stewart, bishop of Moray, who like Buchan had lost out heavily in 1488. The two brothers had different tasks to perform for Henry VII. Buchan was to kidnap or assassinate Perkin Warbeck at the outset of the campaign; Ramsay is quite specific that the business was to be accomplished at night, in Warbeck's tent, because 'he has na wach bot the Kings apoinctit to be about him.' Moray's task was to persuade James, duke of Ross, heir-presumptive to the throne, not to come to his elder brother's host; and to this end Ramsay had laid the ground at St Andrews by presenting Ross with the gift of a crossbow from Henry VII. According to Ramsay, the young duke's response was favourable; he said that he intended to do Henry VII service in spite of the wishes of his brother James IV, and Ramsay reckoned that Ross was ready for 'softening up' by the Bishop of Moray.[93]

In the event, Warbeck was neither kidnapped nor assassinated; and there is no direct evidence that Moray was responsible for further turning the Duke of Ross's head. Ramsay's comments about Ross are however significant in that they reflect a possible antagonism between the duke and James IV. In 1486–7, and during the early stages of the crisis of 1488, such feelings had surfaced briefly when Ross, the second son, had emerged as his father's favourite in place of the heir to the throne; and some ill-will may have persisted after Sauchieburn, when Ross as heir-presumptive could be regarded as an obvious focus of discontent for all those — including Buchan, Moray, and Ramsay — who had suffered for their support of James III. It may also be significant that during his very rare appearances as a Lord of Council between 1493 and 1495,[94] Ross is frequently to be found in the company of Archbishop Scheves, James III's old familiar. On 17 October 1493 they left the council together during the afternoon sitting; on the 19th and 21st of the same month they came in together; and on 10 June 1494, both were again present.[95] On 16 October 1495, at a greatly enlarged council meeting — a sederunt of 40 – with Warbeck probably on the agenda, Ross was once more present in spite of the fact that he had apparently taken little interest in affairs of state up to this time.[96] Ramsay's letter to Henry VII, therefore, would appear to confirm what the official records show to be true, namely that by 1496 the Duke of Ross, who was no mere youth but already twenty years of age, had had a modest but significant public career for the past three years, much of it in the company of James III's archbishop and prominent familiar. His absence from James IV's host in 1496 is therefore suggestive, as is the king's instruction to George Brown, bishop of Dunkeld, Lord Glamis, and others, 'to remain in Edinburgh wyth the Duke of Ros.'[97] Clearly James was taking no chances that his brother might fall into the bad company of the Bishop of Moray during his absence on campaign.

Thus when Ramsay, in his two letters to Henry VII in September 1496, suggests that James IV is undertaking the war contrary to the wishes of his barons and his whole people, he is wildly inaccurate. The real or potential opposition was limited to a very few individuals who could not forget 1488 — two of the Stewart half-uncles, possibly the king's brother, and Ramsay himself. Only such men can have thought it worthwhile harking back to the death of James III; and this leitmotif of one of Ramsay's letters can hardly have made convincing reading to Henry VII.

Ramsay's factual information, rather than his political ramblings, was what the English king wanted; and he must have been particularly interested in Ramsay's report of a meeting at Edinburgh on 28 August between Warbeck and a messenger from Carlisle who had come from Randall of Dacre, brother of Thomas, Lord Dacre, Warden of the English West Marches.[98] This information, together with what Henry VII had already heard about the wavering loyalties of the keepers of Carlisle and Bewcastle and the sheriff of Westmorland,[99] must have made it clear to the English king that he had much to fear from a Scottish invasion of the West Marches. But Ramsay had also revealed that the Scottish host was to muster at Ellem, which meant that the invasion would come in the east, not in the west.[100] This fact alone strongly suggests that this was James IV's war, not Perkin's, that the Scottish king was concerned to fight where he could display what Ramsay calls his 'young adventurousness' and win easy victories, and that the pretender's potential support on the English West March was of little interest to him.

On 12 September James IV assembled his artillery in Restalrig meadow, placing the big guns under the command of John Sandilands of Hillhouse, a veteran of the siege of Duchal in 1489. The king's gunners from the Low Countries, Henric and Hans, and a French gunner named Guyane, were reinforced by some skilled craftsmen — smiths, carpenters, and quarrymen

— and a host of workmen. On 13 September the bellman was sent three times through the city of Edinburgh 'for werkmen to tak wagis' — 143 carters with 196 horses hired for fourteen days' service at a shilling a day for each man or horse, paid in advance, a total bill of £237 6/–. A further seventy-six men with spades and mattocks were hired on the same day, once again for a fortnight, to clear a passage for the artillery en route, at an overall cost of £53 4/–.[101] Warbeck's entourage had been enlarged by the inclusion in it of the prothonotary Andrew Forman,[102] and by the arrival from Flanders of his long-suffering Burgundian lieutenant, Roderic de Lalain, with two ships and 60 German mercenaries.[103] On 14 September, judiciously waiting until the heads of the powder barrels in the abbey had been closed and the barrels removed, James IV and Warbeck made offerings of 18/– and 14/– respectively in Holyrood, ordered masses for the success of the enterprise at Restalrig,[104] and began the journey south to Ellem.

The campaign was short — it had to be, owing to the lateness of the season and because James's 219 workmen had only been paid for a fortnight — and the Scottish king had begun his homeward journey by the early morning of 26 September, having been in the field for a total of twelve days. Five of these had been spent reaching the muster point at Ellem, travelling by way of Haddington over the Lammermuir Hills to Johnscleuch, then south to Duns and Langton, which some of the artillery had reached by 17 September. Langton lies about eight miles south of Ellem, where we find the king and two of his foreign gunners, Henric and Guyane, by 19 September.[105] This relatively slow progress south may be accounted for partly by the difficulties of dragging the big guns over the Lammermuirs to the Merse, and James IV's reluctance to cross the Tweed ahead of them. Another factor may have been James's caution; in Polydore Vergil's account of the campaign, the king 'sent forward some cavalry to find out whether or not the English were prepared for war. When the cavalry who had been sent forward found that all was quiet, they returned to the king and reported the time to be ripe for an attack.'[106] This caution, combined perhaps with the late arrival of parts of the host at Ellem and a delay to allow those Northumbrians who would acknowledge Warbeck as Duke of York to come in to the muster point, meant that James was running four days behind his initial schedule.

However, on 20 September the king, having spent the previous night in a house in Ellem — whose occupants he rewarded with a gift of £5 — rode south to the Tweed, presumably crossing the river into England near Coldstream on the same day. On the following day the artillery was ferried across, aided by 'the cobill men of Tweid', who received 18/– for their pains.[107] Once across, James IV 'laid waste the fields, pillaged and then burnt the houses and villages. The natives who resisted he cruelly killed . . . having widely devastated the countryside of Northumberland, he would have gone even further but for his troops being so laden with spoils that they refused to follow him.'[108] This is Polydore Vergil's version of the 1496 campaign; though perhaps rather exaggerated, it probably captures the spirit of the occasion much more accurately than Henry VII's dismissive remarks about the campaign later the same year.[109] But by then the English king was less concerned about the menace to his own position which Warbeck had posed.

For in September 1496 Warbeck's entry into the country he hoped to inherit lasted little more than twenty-four hours. He crossed the Tweed with James IV on 20 September, witnessed the beginnings of the Scots plunder raid in the Tweed and Till valleys, and made an immediate protest to the king, memorably recorded by Polydore Vergil. Warbeck, terrified that no English had moved to support him — though allowing for the circumstances of his arrival in Northumberland this was hardly surprising — appealed to King James not to harry his people and his native land any further, whereupon the Scottish king retorted that it seemed Warbeck was meddling in other people's business and not his own; for though he had called England his country and the English his countrymen, none of them had hurried forward to assist him. 'Thus' remarks Vergil, 'the king exposed the man's foolish impudence.'[110] Whether or not the chronicler is correct in his description of the quarrel between king and pretender, the records show beyond any doubt that Warbeck recrossed the Tweed into Scotland after little more than a day's campaigning. On 21 September he moved north from Coldstream accompanied by Andrew Forman, who had been given £69 8/– from the king for Warbeck's expenses.[111]

James IV was probably neither surprised nor sorry to see Warbeck leave the host. Certainly his departure allowed the Scottish king to intensify his attack on Northumberland in the few days remaining to him. The host attacked and destroyed no less than five tower houses in the Tweed and Till valleys, after which James himself laid siege to Heton castle on the Till; on 24 September he had his masons drive a mine under the wall, and gave them 18/– 'drinksilver' as a reward for mining all night. On the following day, he brought his artillery, under the command of his master-gunner Hans, into play against Heton; and on the evening of the 25th, the Scottish masons prepared for a second night's mining.[112] However, about midnight, James, having received word that an English army had left Newcastle during the day, raised the siege and recrossed the Tweed into Scotland with his entire army in eight hours.[113] The 1496 campaign, the ultimate Scottish response to years of tortuous diplomacy, was at an end.

The campaign has been described by one recent writer as 'an utter failure',[114] and this is certainly the case if one views it from Warbeck's point of view. His failure to achieve any English assistance, his early return to Scotland, and James IV's increasing coolness to him — he kept Warbeck in Scotland for a further ten months, but not apparently with him at court — added another dismal chapter to his career and no doubt immensely comforted King Henry VII. But it may be doubted whether James IV had ever expected much of the pretender. Certainly he might have been able to screw some money out of Warbeck if the latter had achieved any success in the English north; but the acquisition of Berwick, by negotiation rather than assault, was never even a remote possibility. James showed no interest in helping Warbeck in the English West March, where he might have fared rather better. The entire campaign was designed by the Scottish king as a fortnight's plunder raid into Northumberland; and viewed in this light, it was a success. James's army had not only made a profit, but had destroyed the towers of Twizel, Tillmouth, Duddo, Branxton, and Howtel, thereby isolating Heton castle and making it vulnerable to James's full-scale siege. The advance of an English relieving army from Newcastle induced James, who in terms of overall strategy had acted cautiously and sensibly throughout, to withdraw at once.

The campaign appears to have involved considerable personal danger for the king, danger which he probably relished. Don Pedro de Ayala, after only a few weeks in Scotland as Spanish ambassador, found himself acting as a kind of unofficial war correspondent in a struggle which his embassy to Scotland had been designed to prevent. Of his first journey into Northumberland, struggling along in the wake of James IV and losing four of his servants dead and three wounded,[115] De Ayala was later to remark that James was 'courageous, even more so than a King should be. I am a good witness of it. I have seen him often undertake most dangerous things in the last wars. I sometimes clung to his skirts, and succeeded in keeping him back. On such occasions he does not take the least care of himself.' But Ayala went on to remark that the king had told him that as his subjects were bound to serve him 'in just and unjust quarrels, exactly as he likes', he felt it right to be first in danger in any war. James IV, in Ayala's view, loved war, and with good reason; it was profitable to him and to his country.[116] Given James's sizeable outlay on hiring workmen, carts, and horses, not to mention paying his gunners and craftsmen and Warbeck's monthly pension, the material rewards to himself must have been huge — a matter of more than £1000 Scots — if he was to break even on the 1496 campaign. There were, however, other considerations. Showing Henry VII that he could not adequately defend the north-east of his kingdom was probably one of these; another was James's wish to display his martial prowess at home and abroad; and a third may have been a desire to try out his artillery. For James IV, having softened up the valleys of the Tweed and Till, was to return there the following year, on his own account, to attack a more substantial target than Heton castle.

Henry VII's response to the Scottish campaign of September 1496 was excessive. The following month he proclaimed that the seven-year truce had been broken by the King of Scots, who had invaded his country and done great cruelty to man, woman and child. His subjects should therefore ignore the truce with the Scots and make war on them wherever they could, on land and sea.[117] He followed this up by holding a council of war at Sheen and by summoning a Great Council which met at Westminster between 24 October and 6 November, discussed the further threat of invasion by the Scots, and granted Henry VII £120,000 sterling, a grant ratified in the parliament of January 1497.[118] This staggering sum — the equivalent of more than twenty times the Scottish king's annual revenue from normal sources — was mainly to be used to supply, equip and pay an enormous army, commanded by the Lord Chamberlain, Giles Daubeney, and a sizeable fleet — twenty armed merchantmen, twenty-six transports, Henry's flagship the 'Regent', together with two new warships, the 'Mary Fortune' and the 'Sweepstake' — in the charge of Lord Willoughby de Broke, steward of the household, these huge land and amphibious forces to be used in the invasion of Scotland. The researches of Dr Ian Arthurson[119] leave no room for doubt as to Henry VII's commitment to the organisation of this massive enterprise during the early months of 1497; nor can there be much doubt as to what its outcome would have been.

James IV, returning to Edinburgh by the beginning of October 1496, set about the immediate dispersal of Warbeck's travelling circus. On 7 October Roderic De Lalain, the pretender's long-suffering Burgundian supporter, received payment of 100 marks; on the 15th Warbeck's agent, Rolland Robysone, was given a further £200, promised in an earlier indenture between king and pretender, to ship some of Warbeck's followers out of the country. Four days later Lord Monypenny, the French ambassador, sailed home from Leith, having been paid £90, while two French heralds who had come with him received £14 each. A servant of O'Donnell of Tyrconnell, who had no doubt acted as an observer for his master throughout the campaign, departed with a payment of £7 4/–.[120] By late October they had all gone, taking the news of Warbeck's continuing failure to the Low Countries, France, and Ireland. But the pretender did not leave with them; the Scottish king was presumably still aware of Warbeck's diplomatic value to him, even though he had proved useless in the field. So he kept him in Scotland, probably for much of the time at the Blackfriars in Edinburgh, and paid his pension monthly until the following June.[121]

For the remainder of October and the first week of November, while Henry VII and his Great Council at Westminster were concocting a massive war of revenge on the Scots, James IV was hunting in Fife, Perthshire and Angus. He spent some time boating on the River Isla in the company of the new Earl of Crawford, made modest payments to children who set up wild duck for his hawks, and gave a gift of 3/6d. to a Coupar Angus man who had recently endured an operation for the removal of a stone. These innocent pursuits were rudely interrupted on 5 November by the arrival of the king's 'Maister Spyour', presumably with news of Henry VII's proclamation of war against the Scots. King James at once broke off his hunting holiday, was ferried back over the Isla at Kinclaven, and hurried south-west to the royal castle of Methven, six miles from Perth.[122] Four days later he had reached Linlithgow, to which he rapidly summoned his officers of state. By 18 November they had all come in — Privy Seal Elphinstone; Chancellor Angus; Argyll, the Master of the Household; Bothwell; Chamberlain Hume; Justiciar Drummond; George Schaw, abbot of Paisley, the Treasurer; Secretary Murehead; and John Fresell, the Clerk Register.[123] On the following day the king took most of these men south to the Chamberlain's castle of Hume in the Merse, seven miles north-west of the border at Coldstream on the Tweed.

The royal visit to Hume castle, and King James's subsequent movements, make it clear that the king had been alerted as to the danger of his position. He spent no less than ten days — 21 November to 1 December — at Hume, to which he rapidly summoned Drummond, Schaw, Murehead, Fresell and his host, Lord Hume, in what was probably a council of war.[124] Whatever plans were laid, caution initially prevailed; the Scots' first concern had to be that of defence of the borders. In the middle of December, therefore, the king inspected the strength of Dunglas castle, a Hume stronghold on the boundary of the Merse and an obvious target for an English army taking the eastern coastal route into Scotland.[125] By the new year, the lack of foresight shown by his counsellors in ordering the destruction of Dunbar castle in 1488 had been fully realised by the king; Sir Andrew Wood was appointed the castle's governor, and the long work of reconstruction began early in March 1497.[126]

James IV's understandable obsession with the war throughout the winter is reflected in the fact that at Christmas and New Year, he deserted his usual haunts of Stirling, Linlithgow, or Edinburgh and celebrated both festivals at Melrose Abbey, less than ten miles from the border.[127] In fact, it appears that the king was unprepared to stay on the defensive, waiting for an English retaliatory raid somewhere on the borders. By the end of January 1497, he had determined on a preemptive strike led by himself, supported by the Humes — 'the raid of Hume' which took place about 12 February.[128] No details survive as to the destination of this brief expedition, though it must certainly have intensified the anger of Henry VII, who only a day later, and obviously before he had heard about the raid, issued a commission to Sir Thomas Dacre, his lieutenant on the West March, ordering him to make an array against the Scots, 'since our enemy of Scotland, with a great array of our rebels and traitors, has hostilely invaded our kingdom of England . . . and intends further mischief.'[129]

This was no less than the truth. For though James IV, returning from the raid of Hume, left his armour and some coffers at Hume castle and rode north in March on his annual pilgrimage to the shrine of St Duthac at Tain,[130] the preparations for renewal of the war on the borders which he had initiated were pushed inexorably forward in his absence. From 14 February, when a muster of the king's lieges was ordered for 6 April, right through to the summer, the Treasurer's accounts are full of details of the measures taken to prepare for war. The letters sent out to the sheriffs on 14 February reveal that this was a call-up of the entire host, following on wappinschawings ordered throughout the country earlier in the month, and for the maximum period of forty days.[131] The master gunner Hans was stationed at Coldingham, and his subordinate of 1496, the Scottish gunner Robert Herwort, was ordered to remain on the border. Between the beginning of February and Easter, there were, off and on, a maximum of fifteen gunners in Coldingham alone, clearly to prevent the passage of any English force from Berwick, ten miles to the south. As in 1496, the woods of Irneside and Melrose were raided to 'wale tymmyr for the artailyeri' — indeed, timber for the making of gun-carts, wheels, and gunstocks had to be brought from as far afield as Clydesdale.

By early April the artillery was being prepared to move, with new wooden wheels being supplied 'to the bombardis and Mons'.[132] The renovation of the carriage of the great gun Mons Meg, idle since 1489, indicates the kind of war King James intended to fight; for Mons was the heaviest piece of artillery in the British Isles till the eighteenth century, capable of firing an 18-inch stone ball more than a mile and a half.[133] Thus she was designed not for defence, but to bombard a worthwhile enemy stronghold from a considerable distance. In spite of the formidable odds against him, or perhaps because he was not fully aware of them, King James was clearly planning to attack. No wonder Pedro de Ayala later remarked that 'the Scots spend all their time in wars.' During his — highly untypical — year in Scotland, he saw virtually nothing else.

The war was however delayed, partly perhaps because the April call-up was too soon for James IV's preparations, certainly because a further Spanish embassy arrived at the Scottish court at Stirling in April, and spent ten days there.[134] Their mission was probably similar to that of the Spanish ambassador in London, De Puebla, namely to secure peace between England and Scotland so that Henry VII might be free to honour his obligations — as the Spanish saw it — to the Holy League. On 28 March, De Puebla reported to Ferdinand and Isabella that as James IV had virtually abandoned Perkin Warbeck, the reasons for war between Scotland and England had largely been removed.[135]

The normally shrewd De Puebla had miscalculated. Certainly the main obstacle to peace on Henry VII's side was the presence in Scotland of Warbeck; but Warbeck was no longer a factor in Scottish calculations because James IV was keen to wage war on his own account. If he was shaken by the discovery, some time after Easter, of the extent of the English king's war preparations,[136] he gave no sign of it — though he did send Angus and Hume as his commissioners, probably in May, to an abortive peace conference at Jenynhaugh.[137] The English demand for the surrender of Warbeck proved the stumbling block, as might have been expected, and the war was on in earnest.

On 1 and 6 June royal letters were sent out to summon the host south of Forth and in the Westland to 'the first diet' — the muster — on the borders. King James, as usual mixing business with pleasure, spent late May slowly moving around the south and south-east, inspecting the repair work at Dunbar castle, shooting at the butts and playing cards while he was there, taking a trip to the Bass Rock, ordering masses to be said for the success of his enterprise at Whitekirk, where he also distributed alms to the poor and lepers. His falconers, left behind in Stirling, were ordered to meet the king at Peebles.[138] James's studied calm as he approached the crisis of his career impressed De Ayala. 'He esteems himself', said the ambassador about the king, 'as much as though he were Lord of the world.'[139] War was a sport; the king would ride to it in a new green coat, attended by his falconers and musicians.[140]

Most successful rulers owe a great deal to luck. James IV was no exception. Towards the end of May, he was saved from the probable consequences of his own audacity by a sudden crisis in England. Apparently moved by anger against the counsellors who had advised Henry VII to impose the taxation voted for the Scottish war in the parliament of January 1497, perhaps also concerned that, in the words of the Venetian ambassador, 'under the pretence of war the King amassed much money', the Cornishmen and Devonshire men rose in revolt, and in their thousands made their way with considerable speed towards London. Henry VII's normally efficient intelligence service had failed him. Part of his army was already en route for Scotland; part was on its way to the muster point at Newcastle; and part had not yet been called up. Such was the chaos that the rebels, led by an intransigent blacksmith named Michael Joseph, had reached Surrey before they were challenged; almost exactly ten years after the battle of Stoke, King Henry had to take the field again, this time to defend his capital. The crucial battle was fought and won for him by part of the army destined for Scotland under its leader, Lord Daubeney, at Blackheath, near Guildford in Surrey, only 20 miles from London, on 17 June; and though Henry was immediately able to order masses in honour of the Virgin Mary in celebration of his victory, the rebellion rumbled on in the south and west for much of the rest of the year, and there was good reason for the king to cut his very considerable losses and come to terms with the Scots.[141]

He attempted to do so within three weeks of the battle of Blackheath. On 5 July he commissioned Richard Fox, bishop of Durham, to offer peace to James IV if he would surrender Warbeck and send Angus, Hume, and Andrew Stewart, bishop of Moray, south as his ambassadors. Reckoning that James was unlikely to agree to hand over the pretender, Henry suggested as an alternative that the ambassadors should in any case be sent, and that the two kings should meet, with hostages given for the proper observance of any peace. But in any event, Fox was to get the best deal with the Scots that he could.[142]

Fox's brief was an impossible one, because the King of Scots was not looking for peace. James had spent the month of June conducting a 'phoney war' on the borders, the perfect example of a Scottish king fulfilling the most crucial of his duties, that of war leader, and well supported by his lords. He rode on the first raid from Melrose on 12 June, taking with him artillery brought from Edinburgh by Sir Robert Ker of Ferniehirst, an expedition which lasted some five days. On 26 June James was at Lauder for the second 'diet', and there followed a raid lasting about a week. No information survives as to the destination of either of these expeditions; but an English attack on the Scottish East March, on or about 8 June, was defeated by the Humes in a skirmish at Duns, and on 19 June Patrick Hume of Polwarth — 'Lang Patrik of Pollart' — was duly rewarded for his services to James IV in that fight.[143]

The main event of the war, however, was reserved for the month of July. Before it could be undertaken, and about the same time as Henry VII's commission to Bishop Fox to make overtures for peace, James IV had determined to rid himself of the cost and — by this time — embarrassment of maintaining Warbeck. Early in the month he set him on his way from Ayr to Cork in southern Ireland, accompanied by his wife Catherine, Huntly's daughter, in a 'see goune' gifted by the king. The pretender fleeced his former provider right to the end, the provisions for his fortnight's sea voyage costing King James over £150, much more than Warbeck's monthly pension. He set sail in the Breton ship, the 'Cuckoo', whose owners may have been forced to sell her to the Scottish king, and which for this voyage was commanded by two of the Bartons, Robert and Andrew. One of Warbeck's final acts in Scotland was to leave his brown horse in pledge for debts contracted in Ayr while waiting to sail; but by the second week of July he was gone, with the long-suffering Andrew Forman, who had been detailed to act as Warbeck's 'minder' for much of his visit,[144] no doubt heaving an enormous sigh of relief as he watched the 'Cuckoo' vanish over the horizon to the south-west. King James was well rid of Warbeck; the Irish were unfriendly; and landing in Cornwall too late for the rebellion, the pretender was taken prisoner on 5 October and conveyed to London, where he would remain Henry VII's prisoner until he was hanged two years later.[145]

With Warbeck out of the diplomatic reckoning, and no doubt with full knowledge of King Henry's domestic difficulties, James IV summoned his host south of Forth on 9 July, the muster being called for 20 July.[146] To help pay for the greatly increased artillery park and the craftsmen and workmen to maintain it, the king coined part of his great gold chain, producing £571 in the process. Further 'spear silver' was levied, and various well-disposed persons made contributions — £30 from Elizabeth, countess of Ross; £100 from the Abbot of Holyrood; £333 6/8d. from the Abbot of Arbroath; and even £236 17/– from the king's brother, James, duke of Ross, who two months before had been postulated with James IV's backing for the archbishopric of St Andrews, vacant since January by the death of William Scheves. Further financial support came from burghs which offered compositions for non-attendance on 'the great raid': Perth gave £150, Dundee £225.[147] Leaving aside the tax, these contributions produced a total of £1,646 3/8d. for the expedition.

The object of the raid was Norham castle, the great stronghold of King Henry's erstwhile peacemaker, Bishop Fox of Durham, towering over the south bank of the river Tweed some six miles inland from Berwick, and right on the border with Scotland. As in the case of the first June raid, the army was to muster at Melrose, where the king had already arrived on 20 July.[148] The huge artillery train — the guns dragged by oxen, together with no less than 187 horses, 110 drivers, 221 workmen with spades and mattocks, 61 quarrymen and masons, carpenters, gunners, and no less than 100 workmen and five carpenters for Mons Meg alone — lumbered out of Edinburgh on the following day, with minstrels playing Mons Meg 'doune the gait' from the castle. The great gun broke down on the outskirts of Edinburgh, it took two-and-a-half days to make a new carriage for her, and she does not seem to have reached the border until early August, together with some of the other artillery from Holyrood Abbey.[149] The king, joined by artillery already laid up at Coldingham and Hume, had reached the Tweed long before the Edinburgh guns, and made his camp at Upsettlington, just on the north side of the river and less than two miles from Norham. On 4 August he was already receiving a new consignment of gunstones from Edinburgh.[150] On the 5th, he made a further grant to Patrick Hume of Polwarth, a solitary item of business amidst wine drinking and card playing with De Ayala and the other Spanish ambassadors.[151] None of them had far to go to admire Mons Meg and the other artillery pieces pounding Norham castle from the Scottish side of the Tweed, while sections of the host crossed the river and ravaged the surrounding countryside, probably at this time destroying the nearby towers of Thornton and Shoreswood.[152]

But Norham was not taken, either because of a spirited defence or because the siege was not pressed home by the Scots; or perhaps a combination of both. An overriding factor with King James may have been that he had only paid his hundreds of workmen for a week; the raid had already lasted a fortnight, and further payments had had to be made. Then there was the problem that he could not keep the host in the field for ever; parts of it, or the whole, had already been involved in the June raids from Melrose and Lauder; and while these may have been well supported as quick plunder raids bringing an immediate return, an assault on Norham castle was a very different matter. So about 10 August King James bowed to the inevitable and returned to Edinburgh, reaching the city by the 12th.[153]

He had no sooner arrived in the city than he started to receive 'tithingis . . . of the Inglismennis cummyng' from messengers in the East March. Thomas, earl of Surrey, hastening north from Yorkshire hoping to raise the siege of Norham, had missed the Scots;[154] nonetheless, he crossed the Tweed and laid siege to the Hume castle of Ayton in the Merse, about five miles north of Berwick. James IV responded immediately, calling up parts of his dispersed host and seeking support for a new raid from as far north as Angus. By 16 August, only four days after his return to Edinburgh, he was already at Haddington on his way south again, taking as many guns and supporters as he could muster to 'the raid of Aytoun'. The entire affair was very short-lived. Avoiding the coast, James struck inland from Haddington across the Lammermuirs and spent three nights — the 17th to the 19th — in a house at Cattleshiel, a few miles from Duns.[155] He could not save Ayton from Surrey, and spent his few days on the borders exchanging threats with the English earl, which were ultimately reported in a letter from Henry VII to the Lord Mayor of London at the end of the month. James, reported the English king, had challenged Surrey to a battle, or a hand-to-hand fight, to decide the fate of Berwick, which was not even in contention at the time. Surrey had accepted, though it is not clear from Henry's letter exactly *what* he accepted, whereupon James suddenly, and in Henry's view shamefully, withdrew.[156] By 21 August, James IV was already sending letters round much of the country announcing 'the scaling of the Inglismen' and stopping any further call-up of the host. The king had set off for home on the 19th, and by the evening of that day we find him drinking wine in Haddington. On the following day he had an interview with Sir William Tyler, the governor of Berwick, at Dunbar castle, though what was discussed is a mystery. It is possible that James promised not to attack Berwick under certain conditions, and that there is a correlation between his interview with Tyler and the withdrawal of Surrey's host, which began on the following day.[157] But the Scots, so far as we know, had never threatened Berwick.

The war was over for both sides. King Henry's description of events on 28 August should probably be taken with a pinch of salt, for he was in fact extremely disappointed with the entire campaign, and raged at what he regarded as Surrey's failure. The weather was blamed; sickness in the army was blamed; the Scots' refusal to play the game was blamed. As for the reported fight to settle the fate of Berwick, it must be said that if Surrey, a man in his 'fifties, had really agreed to settle such an issue in single combat with James IV, who was twenty-four, he would have been singularly lacking in the sound military intelligence which we know him to have possessed; likewise, King James would have been a fool to take on Surrey's army with only a fraction of the Scottish host in the field.

The truth was that James IV and Henry VII had fought each other to a standstill. Henry badly needed peace to deal with continuing trouble in the south-west, and his outlay on the projected Scottish war was somewhere between £60,000 and £90,000 sterling.[158] King James had used war as a forceful extension of his diplomacy, taking audacious risks which were vindicated by a combination of luck and good judgment. He could have come to grief very rapidly in the spring of 1497; but, as Dr Arthurson perceptively remarks, 'the war [against Scotland] that Henry VII planned collapsed under its own weight.'[159] Without this planned overkill and the taxation required to support it, there would probably have been no Cornish rising. The entire affair reflects Henry's misjudgment as much as James's audacity. But it is also true that King James had used parts of the host to the limit, and probably beyond, in the raid of Ellem in 1496, and those of Hume, Melrose, Lauder, Norham, and Ayton in 1497. It may not simply have been the sudden call-up and short time-span of the last of these raids, but rather a general feeling of war-weariness, which caused a fair number of those summoned to Ayton to fail to appear.[160]

On 5 September, less than three weeks after the end of the Ayton campaign, Henry VII took the prudent course and commissioned William, bishop of Carlisle, Sir Thomas Dacre, William Warham, and Henry Wyatt — or any two of them, Warham, who was Keeper of the Rolls, always being one — to treat for peace with James IV or his commissioners.[161] The peace process which was eventually to culminate in the Treaty of 1502 and King James's marriage to Henry's daughter the following year was under way. It began modestly enough at the end of September 1497 when Bishop Fox, Warham, and John Cartington met Elphinstone, the ubiquitous Andrew Forman, Sir Patrick Hume of Fastcastle, and Master Richard Lawson at Ayton — the scene of the previous month's hostilities — and agreed on a seven years' truce.[162] However, as it was exactly such an undertaking which James IV had broken in 1495–6, something more durable was clearly welcomed by the English; and Pedro de Ayala ended his stormy fifteen-month visit to Scotland by going south as King James's ambassador in October 1497, with authority to negotiate a revision of the September truce, altering its duration to one year after the death of the survivor of the two kings. By February of the following year, both sovereigns had ratified the amended treaty, and had agreed to accept Ferdinand and Isabella as arbitrators in any future disputes.[163]

Henry VII had found an opponent worthy of him north of the border. The Scots had come a long way from James III's obsequious pursuit of any English marriage treaty he could obtain, and it may be that James IV's wars against King Henry in 1496–7 helped to exorcise a sense of collective shame which had oppressed many Scots during the last years of the previous reign. Certainly, as Pedro de Ayala noted, King James's wars were popular with his countrymen. Conducted as they were without reference to France, they carried no risk of censure from Pope Alexander VI; and there is no doubt that they greatly enhanced James IV's prestige with his own subjects. This prestige was well deserved, for the king had distinguished himself not only on the field of battle, but in his own area of European diplomacy. He was the king of a small and relatively poor country; in so far as the rulers of the enormously wealthy and powerful monarchies of Spain and England had any interest in him at all in 1495–6, it was their objective, by whatever means possible, to prevent James IV from invading England in support of Perkin Warbeck. Ferdinand and Isabella, and Henry VII of England, are all — rightly — regarded by historians as subtle and highly successful diplomats. But on this occasion their diplomacy achieved precisely the opposite of what they intended: James IV invaded England again and again, and got away with it. He was clearly a man to be treated with caution and respect — a man, in fact, whom Henry Tudor might allow to marry his daughter.

NOTES

1. *T.A.*, i, 330, 367; *E.R.*, xi, 123. These items were all redeemed by James IV some time in 1497.

2. *R.M.S.*, ii, passim.

3. *Scots Peerage*, i, 335.

4. *R.M.S.*, ii, Nos. 2373–2380; and see comment by Chalmers, 'Council, Patronage and Governance', 431.

5. Margaret was the eldest of Lord Drummond's six daughters: *Scots Peerage*, vii, 44–45.

6. *T.A.*, i, 273, 276.

7. Hon. William Drummond (Viscount Strathallan), *The Genealogy of the most noble and ancient house of Drummond* (1681), publ. Edin., 1831, pp.138–9.

8. *T.A.*., i, cxxxii–cxxxiii, 277, 280, 288, 293, 304, 309, 310.

9. *Cal. State Papers (Spain)*, i, No. 210.

10. *R.S.S.*, i, No. 326.

11. *T.A.*, ii, 152.

12. *Ibid.*, 376.

13. *Ibid.*, 248, 358, 372, 388, 410, 418, 436; iii, 56, 59, 346, 357, 367, 391; iv, 75, 83, 101, 115.

14. Elphinstone is absent from court and government between 22 November 1493 and 18 August 1495: *R.M.S.*, ii, Nos. 2184, 2270.

15. Macfarlane, *Elphinstone*, 293–5.

16. *Ibid.*, 295–6.

17. *Ibid.*, 296.

18. *Ibid.*, 232.

19. *T.A.*, i, 241–2.

20. *Ibid.*, 245–254.

21. *Ibid.*, cxix–cxx; *R.M.S.*, ii, Nos. 2251, 2252.

22. *R.M.S.*, ii, No. 2253.

23. *Ibid.*, Nos. 2264, 2281, 2287.

24. *Ibid.*, No. 2256.

25. *Ibid.*, Nos. 2257–2265.

26. *T.A.*, i, 242.

27. *R.M.S.*, ii, No. 3856.

28. For details of Perkin Warbeck's Irish visits, see Agnes Conway, *Henry VII's Relations with Scotland and Ireland, 1485–1498* (Cambridge, 1932), esp. chapters II, V, and VI.

29. There is an extensive Perkin Warbeck bibliography, much of which is summarised in S.B. Chrimes, *Henry VII* (London, 1977), 81–92. In some ways, the best account of Perkin's career is to be found in J. Gairdner, *History of the Life and Reign of Richard III* (1893), Appendix. Conway, *op. cit.*, is invaluable for details of Perkin's travels in Ireland in 1495, and for details of Anglo–Scottish and Anglo–Irish diplomacy in the 1490s, though in places her version of events needs to be treated with caution. But to understand Warbeck as an international figure and a menace to Henry VII over many years, one should really look at the Venetian and Spanish calendars, especially for the period 1495–7.

30. Chrimes, *Henry VII*, 79–88.

31. *R.M.S.*, ii, Nos. 1738, 1798; *T.A.*, i, 99, 120, 130.

32. *T.A.*, i, 199.

33. *Cal. Docs. Scot.*, iv, No. 1588.

34. *T.A.*, i, 242.

35. Chrimes, *Henry VII*, 85.

36. *Cal. State Papers (Venice)*, i, No. 643.

37. *Ibid.*, No. 644.

38. *Ibid.*, No. 645.

39. *Ibid.*, No. 647.

40. Nicholson, *Later Middle Ages*, 550–1.

41. Boece, *Vitae*, 80.

42. *Cal. State Papers (Venice)*, i, Nos. 649, 650.

43. For details of the Deal and Waterford expeditions, see Chrimes, *Henry VII*, 85–6; Conway, *op. cit.*, 84–6.

44. *A.D.C.*, i, 385; *Cal. State Papers (Spain)*, i, Nos. 104, 105. Another Scottish ambassador preceded Blacader and had reached Tarazona by 24 August: *Ibid.*, i, No. 103.

45. *Ibid.*, i, No. 132.

46. *Ibid.*, i, Nos. 103, 104, 105.

47. *Ibid.*, i, No. 107.

48. *A.D.C.*, i, 386.

49. *Cal. State Papers (Spain)*, i, No. 132.

50. *A.D.C.*, i, 390.

51. Polydore Vergil, *Anglica Historia*, 87.

52. *Cal. State Papers (Spain)*, i, No. 112.

53. *T.A.*, i, 267.

54. *Ibid.*
55. *E.R.*, x, 580.
56. *Cal. State Papers (Spain)*, i, No. 130.
57. *T.A.*, i, 257.
58. *Ibid.*, i, 257, 262–4.
59. *Ibid.*, i, 274, 276, 277, 280.
60. *Ibid.*, i, 335, 340, 342. The last monthly payment of £112 Scots was made in July 1497. Evidence survives of Aberdeen being amongst those burghs required to contribute to Warbeck's subsidy: *E.R.*, xi, 49.
61. *Scots Peerage*, iv, 528–531.
62. *Cal. State Papers (Spain)*, i, No. 137.
63. *Ibid.*, i, No. 150.
64. *Ibid.*, i, No. 130.
65. *Ibid.*, i, No. 136.
66. *T.A.*, i, 269.
67. *Cal. State Papers (Spain)*, i, No. 150.
68. *Ibid.*, No. 137. Blacader seems to have arrived in Scotland in time for the parliament of 13 June 1496: *A.D.C.*, ii, 1.
69. *Cal. State Papers (Spain)*, i, No. 210.
70. *T.A.*, i, 312–3.
71. Letter from John Ramsay, formerly Lord Bothwell, to Henry VII, 8 September 1496: printed in full in A.F. Pollard, *The Reign of Henry VII from Contemporary Sources* (London, 1913), i, No. 101.
72. Conway, *op. cit.*, 104 n.1.
73. *Cal. State Papers (Venice)*, i, No. 714.
74. *Cal. State Papers (Spain)*, i, No. 143.
75. Conway, *op. cit.*, 236–9.
76. *Cal. Docs. Scot.*, iv, Nos. 1608, 1610.
77. Conway, *op. cit.*, 82–3, 220. Henry's instructions to Richmond Herald are dated 5 March 1495.
78. John was the issue of Alexander, duke of Albany's second marriage, in 1480, to Anne de la Tour, daughter of the Count of Auvergne and Bouillon. His first marriage, to Lady Catherine Sinclair, from whom he was divorced in March 1478, produced three sons and — probably — a daughter, all of whom were being brought up in Scotland, at least partly at James IV's expense: *T.A.*, i, cxlviii–cxlix; iii, lxxxvii–lxxxviii.
79. *Cal. Docs. Scot.*, iv, No. 1622; *Rot. Scot.*, ii, 520. The commission was twice renewed during the summer: *Ibid.*, ii, 521, 522.
80. Ramsay to Henry VII, September 1496, in Pollard, *op. cit.*, No. 100.
81. Henry was still interested in a Danish marriage for Margaret Tudor as late as November 1498: *Cal. State Papers (Milan)*, i, No. 594.
82. Polydore Vergil, *Anglica Historia*, 87.
83. *Cal. Docs. Scot.*, iv, No. 1571.
84. Pollard, *op. cit.*, No. 100.
85. Chalmers, 'Council, Patronage and Governance', 459.
86. Pollard, *op. cit.*, Nos. 100, 101.
87. *Cal. Docs. Scot.*, iv, No. 1597.
88. *T.A.*, i, 313.
89. Pollard, *op. cit.*, No. 101.
90. *T.A.*, i, 312–3.
91. *Ibid.*, i, cxxviii, n.1.
92. This letter from Ramsay to Henry VII deals inter alia with events which occurred at the end of August 1496; but it may not have been written until the invasion was underway in mid-September, as there is a specific reference to Perkin Warbeck's tent, implying that the royal party had already taken the field: Pollard, *op. cit.*, No. 100.

93. *Ibid.*
94. His name is to be found on only 12 sederunts of council during these years, i.e. 7% of the total number of council meetings held: Chalmers, *op. cit.*, 459.
95. *A.D.C.*, i, 304, 305, 306, 321.
96. *Ibid.*, i, 390.
97. *T.A.*, i, 269.
98. Pollard, *op. cit.*, No. 100.
99. Conway, *op. cit.*, 236–9.
100. Pollard, *op. cit.*, No. 101.
101. *T.A.*, i, 295–7.
102. *Ibid.*, i, 299.
103. Pollard, *op. cit.*, No. 101.
104. *T.A.*, i, 296.
105. *Ibid.*, i. 298–9.
106. Polydore Vergil, *Anglica Historia*, 87.
107. *T.A.*, i, 299.
108. Polydore Vergil, *Anglica Historia*, 89.
109. *Cal. Docs. Scot.*, iv, App., No. 35.
110. Polydore Vergil, *Anglica Historia*, 89.
111. *T.A.*, i, 299, 300.
112. *Ibid.* (for the siege of Heton). For the destruction of English tower houses, see D.H. Caldwell, 'English Campaigns of James IV and Governor Albany', in Scottish Historical Atlas II (forthcoming).
113. *Cal. Docs. Scot.*, iv, App., No. 35; Pollard, *op. cit.*, No. 102.
114. Chrimes, *Henry VII*, 89.
115. *Cal. State Papers (Spain)*, i, No. 211.
116. *Ibid.*, i, No. 210.
117. *Cal. Docs. Scot.*, iv, App., No. 35.
118. Chrimes, *Henry VII*, 144.
119. I. Arthurson, '1497 and the Western Rising', unpublished Ph.D. dissertation, Keele, 1981. Dr Arthurson's findings in relation to the projected Scottish war are neatly summarised in I. Arthurson, 'The King's Voyage into Scotland: The War that never was', in *England in the Fifteenth Century: Proceedings of the 1986 Harlaxton Symposium*, ed. Daniel Williams (Bury St Edmunds, 1987), 1–22.
120. *T.A.*, i, 301, 303.
121. *E.R.*, xi, 153–4; *T.A.*, i, 342.
122. *T.A.*, i, 304–5.
123. *R.M.S.*, ii, No. 2333.
124. *Ibid.*, ii, No. 2334; *T.A.*, i, 306.
125. *T.A.*, i, 308.
126. *Ibid.*, i, 323, 328, 331, 334, 335, 338, 342, 351. Repairs to Dunbar were still being made in 1501.
127. *T.A.*, i, 308.
128. *Ibid.*, i, 310, 320. The king's presence on the raid is inferred from the fact that his armour was left in Hume castle and had to be sent for on 1 April: *Ibid.*, i, 328.
129. Rymer, *Foedera*, xii, 647.
130. The king was at Tain on 18 March: *T.A.*, i, 324–5.
131. *Ibid.*, i, 320.
132. *Ibid.*, 320, 326, 328.
133. R.B.K. Stevenson, 'The Return of Mons Meg from London, 1828–1829', in D.H. Caldwell (ed.), *Scottish Weapons and Fortifications 1100–1800* (Edin., 1981), 419–436, at 419.
134. *E.R.*, xi, 87.

135. *Cal. State Papers (Spain)*, i, No. 175.

136. Henry VII sent out letters to 27 captains to serve in the army against Scotland in the second week of April: Arthurson, *op. cit.*, 9–10.

137. Gairdner, *Letters and Papers Richard III and Henry VII*, i, 104–8, at 104. For an alternative dating of this conference, see Mackie, *James IV*, 86.

138. *T.A.*, i, 337–8.

139. *Cal. State Papers (Spain)*, i, No. 210.

140. *T.A.*, i, 340.

141. For the crisis in England briefly described here, I owe a great deal to the thesis of Dr Ian Arthurson, '1497 and the Western Rising'; and *see above*, n. 119. Other sources are Chrimes, *Henry VII*, 89–90; *Cal. State Papers (Venice)*, i, No. 743; Pollard, *op. cit.*, Nos. 106, 107.

142. Gairdner, *op. cit.*, 104–8.

143. *T.A.*, i, 341–2; *R.M.S.*, ii, No. 2365.

144. Warbeck's departure from Ayr is covered in great detail in *T.A.*, i, 342–5. For the 'Cuckoo', see *ibid.*, i, clii, n. 1.

145. Chrimes, *Henry VII*, 91–2.

146. *T.A.*, i, 344–5.

147. *Ibid.*, i, 313–4. At least three of the contributors to the raid of Norham had also given financial support to James earlier in the year, two of them to the raid of Melrose in June.

148. *T.A.*, i, 347.

149. *Ibid.*, i, 346–9.

150. *Ibid.*, i, 350.

151. *R.M.S.*, ii, No. 2370. Present at Upsettlington on 5 August were Elphinstone; Argyll; Bothwell; Lord Hume; Lord Drummond; the Abbots of Dunfermline and Paisley, respectively former Treasurer and Treasurer; Secretary Murehead; and Clerk Register Fresell. Also in the camp were Andrew Forman and Sir John Ramsay, the traitor of the previous September: *T.A.*, i, 350.

152. John Hodgson, *History of Northumberland*, pt. iii, vol. ii (Newcastle, 1828), 190. The destruction of towers in the Tweed and Till valleys in 1496–7 is noted by the English March Commissioners, Bowes and Elleker, on 2 Dec, 1542: *Ibid.*, 178, 186, 190–2.

153. *T.A.*, i, 351; *R.M.S.*, ii, No. 2371.

154. *T.A.*, i, 351–2; Polydore Vergil, *Anglica Historia*, 101.

155. *T.A.*, i, 352–3.

156. Henry VII to J. Tate, Lord Mayor of London, 28 August 1497, in Guildhall MS Great Chronicle of London, ff. 258v–259r: cited in Mackie, *James IV*, 87–8.

157. *T.A.*, i, 353.

158. Arthurson, *op. cit.*, 11.

159. *Ibid.*

160. There are nine surviving remissions for absence from the host at Ayton, some of them covering a number of people: *R.S.S.*, i, Nos. 1955, 1956, 1957, 1958, 1961, 1962, 2100, 2189, 2330.

161. *Cal. Docs. Scot.*, iv, No. 1636.

162. *Rot. Scot.*, ii, 532.

163. *Cal. State Papers (Spain)*, i, No. 186; *Rot. Scot.*, ii, 535; *Cal. Docs. Scot.*, iv, No. 1644.

6

Money and Power

The wars of 1496–7 had enhanced James IV's prestige at home and abroad, but it is unlikely that they had improved his financial position. The coining of fifty-four links of his great gold chain, for example, had brought in £571; but this was more than offset by the payment of a fortnight's wages to those working, moving, and repairing the artillery on a single campaign, the raid of Norham, at a total cost of £743 11/6d.[1] As we have seen, the Treasurer's accounts show that the tax of spears had realised a little over £1000,[2] and this may only have been part of a larger sum raised during 1496–8. Whatever the total sum, however, it cannot have been anything like adequate as the only contribution by James's subjects to a war which had lasted more than a year and involved, in addition to six armed raids on Northumberland, a major reconstruction programme at Dunbar castle, the maintenance of Warbeck and some of his supporters at court, and the making and renovating of the artillery which Pedro de Ayala so much admired.[3] It is of course impossible to assess how much the king might have acquired in plunder from his border raids, sums which would not necessarily appear in official accounts; and it may be added that no Treasurer's accounts survive for the period between May 1498 and February 1501. The evidence which we have, however, is quite sufficient to reveal that the king, if he wished to continue to pursue his interests in foreign diplomacy and war, either offensive or defensive, would have to be able to raise much more money on a regular basis.

Events were to show that James IV cherished schemes — undoubtedly nurtured in the period 1495–7 — of acquiring further prestige in Europe, of the creation of a royal navy at huge expense, of major additions to the royal artillery park, and of continuing and expanding the building programmes already under way at many royal castles and palaces. Royal prestige also required an ostentatious display of liberality, most clearly seen on the part of James IV in the huge sums he expended on the celebration of his wedding to Margaret Tudor in 1503; and there was the overriding problem of maintaining royal authority at home through the distribution of patronage, the judicious rewarding of committed supporters of the Crown with lands, offices, or other gifts. Only a king with greater wealth than James possessed in 1497 could realise the ambitions which he nurtured in that year, and which De Ayala commented on so perceptively. The problem for the king and his counsellors lay in finding a means of generating more money for the Crown without offending too many people in the process.

In late medieval Scotland, this was a major problem because there was relatively little that could be done to increase royal income from normal sources – that is, revenue from royal lands and from burgh customs and mails, collected respectively by the *ballivi ad extra*, burgh custumars, and bailies of burghs. The gross annual income from these sources remained roughly the same until the very end of the reign, in the region of £5000 – £6000, with a drop to about £4,300 in 1512.[4] Nor did the king benefit from more than a fraction of the gross income generated in this way, largely because burgh customs and mails had been very extensively alienated to provide annuities for those whom the Crown regarded as deserving of rewards. Thus David, fifth earl of Crawford, the magnate with the highest gross income in Scotland, had received annuities totalling £224 6/8d. from the customs and mails of the burghs of Aberdeen, Dundee, Montrose, Banff, Forfar, and Crail; and after David's death in 1495 his successors in the earldom appear to have continued to claim, and often to receive, many of these.[5] On a much more modest scale, we find John Reid, or Stobo, one of the makars of William Dunbar's 'Lament', continuing to receive a few pounds' annuity from the vast customs of Edinburgh for his work in the Secretary's office, writing royal letters to foreign princes and the pope since the days of James II.[6] These ongoing payments, great and small, from the revenues of royal burghs help to explain why, in the period 1497–1501, when there was a gross annual average yield from customs of £3,106, in fact the net return to the Comptroller from this source in 1501 was only £654.[7] In spite of a modest improvement in the overall return from the burghs over the next few years, probably due to the increasing practice of letting the customs, no major increase in that part of royal income for which the *ballivi ad extra*, custumars, and bailies of burghs were responsible was possible, or at any rate politically desirable. The rental of Crown lands was another matter, as we shall see.

The area of Crown income which seemed to offer greater opportunities was that of casualty, above all casualty in its most direct form of extraordinary taxation. Between 1488 and 1497, taxation had become almost an annual event, regularly voted by the three estates during the minority and the 1496–7 wars with England, to support Stewart diplomacy and war. Thus in 1488, parliament had voted a tax of £5,000 for an embassy to France and elsewhere to seek a bride for the king; in 1490 and 1491, the rather more modest sums of £300 and 400 marks respectively were to be levied for embassies to Denmark for the same purpose; in February 1492 an embassy to France was to receive a further £1,000 to add to the original £5,000 granted in 1488; and in May 1493, another £1,000 was voted by the estates for yet another embassy to France.[8] In less than five years, then, taxation in the quest for an alliance and a foreign bride for James IV had totalled £7,566 13/4d., and no bride had been found. The cost of embassies to the Crown, and probably therefore the estates, was further increased by Elphinstone's visit to Worms in 1495 and Blacader's two journeys to Spain in 1495–6. No record of taxation levied for these embassies survives; but it may be noted that the principal object of both, the finding of a bride for the king, was not achieved.

Taxation to support James IV's wars in the Isles and with England appears frequently in the royal accounts between 1494 and 1497. Though information is fragmentary, we know that the Bishop of Dunblane and the Abbot of Newbattle paid £40 — probably as part of a tax levied on the clergy — towards the repair of Tarbert castle in 1494–5; that the burgh of Wigtown's contributions to the 'taxt of the Ilis' in 1496 was £20, while that of Adam Gordon, chanter of Moray, for the same purpose early in 1498 was £33 6/8d.[9] Taken together, these fragments would suggest a tax to support royal campaigns in the forfeited lordship, levied at least on clergy and on some burghs, and amounting overall to a few thousand pounds. How much of the total was paid is another matter, for the tax was probably levied in 1493–4, and details as to the sum involved and the identities of the individuals and communities who had to pay are almost completely lost, together with the Treasurer's accounts for 1492–4. It is also possible that payment of the original 'tax of the Isles' was delayed through the natural reluctance of taxpayers in any age to contribute, and that it became subsumed within the 'tax of spears' for the greater war against England in 1496–7, a levy which produced at least £1,000 and probably considerably more.[10] In any event, the 'tax of spears' was paid with greater alacrity than the levy north of Forth for the expenses of 'the Duke of York' — a total of £500 for which the collector, Andrew Wood of Fettercairn, did not receive an acquittance from the Comptroller until July 1499.[11]

In the first nine years of James IV's reign, therefore, taxation had been imposed in almost every year, and it would have been surprising if the king had totally abandoned such a profitable source of extraordinary revenue. Clearly, however, he came to recognise its limitations. He could not continue to impose levies on the estates because his English wars were over and because, in the diplomatic field, the search for a European bride was at an end. In fact, evidence of resistance to taxation, even for the legitimate purpose of sending an embassy to England to settle the royal marriage once and for all, is provided by a letter written by King James on 7 September 1501 to royal officials north of the Forth. The king recalled that in a recent council meeting, a 'taxt and contribucioun' of 5000 marks and 500 crowns had been 'devisit and ordanit be us and the lordis of our consale', to be paid by all three estates, for the expenses of an embassy to travel to England 'for the completing of our mariage.' The clergy's two-fifths appears to have been paid by the appointed day, but neither of the receivers for the remainder — Lyon King-of-Arms for the barons, and Alexander Lauder, provost of Edinburgh, for the burghs — had been paid. As a result the embassy, which was ready to depart for England, had been delayed, awaiting the inbringing of the remaining three-fifths from the secular estates north of Forth. The defaulting sheriffs, stewards, provosts, aldermen, and bailies were to be warded in Dumbarton castle, while inhabitants of the burghs which had failed to contribute to the tax would lose their burghal privileges until their contributions to the levy were duly made.[12]

King James's anger is easier to explain than the reasons for the extensive resistance to his tax north of Forth. His embassy was indeed waiting for its expenses — in fact, his ambassadors had been chosen at least as long before as December 1499.[13] Since then, the necessary papal dispensation to enable the marriage to take place had duly arrived — James and Margaret Tudor were both descended from a common great-great-grandfather John Beaufort, marquis of Dorset, and were therefore within the forbidden degrees of consanguinity — James had accepted that he would have to wait till Margaret was of marriageable age — she was eleven at the end of 1500 — and he had become anxious to reach a firm agreement with Henry VII, above all on the matter of the dowry which his daughter would bring with her as part of the treaty. A safe-conduct for the Scots ambassadors had been issued by the English king as early as 9 May 1501,[14] since when the entire summer had gone by without more than part of the ambassadorial tax having come in. James's threats in September appear to have had the desired effect; only a month later, on 8 October, he was able to commission his ambassadors, Blacader, Bothwell, and Andrew Forman, now postulate of the See of Moray, to go south to treat for marriage and perpetual peace between England and Scotland.[15] On this occasion they were able to proceed, and the Anglo-Scottish treaty was concluded a few months later, on 24 January 1502.[16]

It may be that the widespread resistance north of Forth to payment of the 1501 tax indicates no more than a general reluctance to contribute to yet another embassy seeking a royal marriage; after all, thousands had already been expended to no purpose at all during the minority, and what was being demanded in 1501 must have seemed a high sum for the expenses of only three men travelling no further than England for a few months. However, another possibility is that the projected alliance with Henry VII may have been widely unpopular in Scotland. This had certainly been the case with James III's treaty of 1474 and the Anglophile policy which had followed it; as recently as 1496–7, James IV's wars with England had to some extent harnessed a popular reaction to pre-1488 diplomacy; and Pedro de Ayala was in no doubt that King James had made the Peace of Ayton in 1497 'against the wishes of the majority in his kingdom.'[17]

There would obviously be no further need for a matrimonial tax; and the treaty of 1502, renewed after the accession of Henry VIII in 1509, seemed to remove the likelihood of a 'tax of spears' for many years to come. Yet only a year after meeting with resistance to payment of the tax of 1501, James IV attempted to raise the astonishing sum of £12,000 from the estates, to supply and pay ships and men — a small army of 2000 — bound for Denmark to assist the Scottish king's uncle, King Hans, against rebellious Norwegian and Swedish subjects. Very little is known about the levying of this huge sum; indeed, the figure of £12,000 is drawn from Sir John Skene's early seventeenth-century records of exchequer accounts, in which it is mentioned only on passing under the dates

1502–4.[18] It seems, however, that a very large tax for the Danish expedition was imposed at this time, and that there was some resistance to it; for the Treasurer, David Beaton of Creich, was charging for arrears of £171 14/4d. 'in partem solutionis arreragii et reste taxe navium missarum in Denmark' in his treasury account of 1504.[19] Certainly King James was disappointed in the outcome of the expedition; contemporary evidence suggests that he planned to send a much larger force to Denmark,[20] and his failure to do so may well reflect his difficulties in bringing in the tax.

The king appears to have learned the obvious lesson, namely that taxing the whole body of the estates was an uncertain business, likely to provoke resistance while not bringing in anything like the sums originally stipulated. No further taxation was imposed until July 1512, and then the levy was to be drawn from the clergy alone. As it was anticipated that the Scottish king would make war on England in the summer of 1512, following on the renewal of the Franco-Scottish alliance of the previous March, messengers were sent out on 1 July to order the collection of 'the spirituall taxt' from Fife, Strathearn, Angus, Argyll, Galloway, Lothian, the Merse, Teviotdale, Ewesdale, 'and diverse uthiris placis'.[21] This 'spirituall taxt' is surely to be identified with the contributions recorded in the Treasurer's accounts later in the same year, with the dioceses of St Andrews, Glasgow, Dunkeld, Aberdeen, Moray, Galloway, Ross, and Caithness delivering a grand total of £6,581 10/- by 29 October.[22] A further contribution was laid on parts of Glasgow, St Andrews, Galloway, Dunkeld, Aberdeen, Brechin, and Dunblane dioceses in the final account of the reign, 29 October 1512 — 8 August 1513, with a total yield to the Crown of about £2,300.[23] Thus in rather less than a year, James IV had acquired little short of £9,000 from taxation laid on the most amenable of the three estates. War was deferred until August 1513, and indeed much if not all of the clerical tax may have been used to offset James's runaway expenses, above all the cost of artillery and the navy. Clearly the king had touched on a very rich vein, one which he might have exploited further had he lived. However, when war had become inevitable in the summer of 1513, King James reverted to the old device of imposing a 'tax of spears' on the burghs. On 2 August 1513, Aberdeen burgh council authorised the collection of some £400 to provide for the sending of twenty spearmen and three mounted men 'to pas with our souerane lord in his weres in Ingland, for the space of xl dais efter thair cuming to his grace.'[24]

On the whole, however, we may say that between the end of James IV's English wars of 1496–7 and their projected renewal in 1512–13, there is little sign that the Crown used taxation extensively as a means of generating revenue, and some evidence of resistance to its efforts, in 1501 and 1502, to impose taxes to support the costs of diplomacy and war. How then did the king increase his annual income so remarkably between 1497 and the end of the reign?

Part of the answer lies in the fact that he was lucky. In 1497 and 1498, when he most needed them, James IV had two substantial windfalls, one unexpected, the other anticipated but very timely. The first was the sudden death of Archbishop Scheves on 28 January 1497, while James was preparing for a second season of campaigning on the borders. The king pounced on the opportunity which the demise of James III's recalcitrant archbishop presented to him, and by May of 1497, if not before, he had nominated his brother, James, duke of Ross, the heir apparent and a layman aged around twenty, to fill the vacant see of St Andrews. This nomination, rightly described by Dr Macfarlane as 'a master stroke', both removed possible difficulties from King James's path and helped to generate income for the Crown. As archbishop, the Duke of Ross would cease to be an obvious focus for dissent, or even rebellion, within Scotland, or a target, like James III's younger brother Albany, for the intrigues of the English king. More important, when Ross became archbishop, James IV would be able to resume the lands of his dukedom; and most important of all, as the new archbishop would not reach the canonical age of consecration – twenty-seven — for about seven years, King James was assured of control of the archiepiscopal revenues of St Andrews for that length of time.[25]

The king's second windfall came as a direct result of his age. On 16 March 1498, James IV had completed his twenty-fifth year and was therefore entitled to make a formal act of revocation of all grants made by him during his legal minority. This he did in Duchal castle, where he happened to be, having just returned from a short visit to his new castle of Kilkerran and the restored fortress of Tarbert in Kintyre. On 17 March, his birthday, having paid a notary 4/- for witnessing his revocation, the king was ferried across the Clyde to Dumbarton, where he spent a few days distributing alms and rewarding the local piper.[26] He could well afford to; for despite the casual way in which he executed his act of revocation, King James and his subjects alike knew that it could have far-reaching financial consequences. The minority had, after all, been a stormy period politically, with acts of revocation made by the victorious rebels of 1488, by the peacemakers of 1490, and by the Angus government of 1493. In March of 1498 it was technically possible for James IV to cancel at a stroke all grants of lands and offices which had been made since his accession, on the ground that they had been made without his consent during his tender age.

In practice, it would have been impossible — and political madness — for King James to revoke all minority grants, and the object of the revocation was not only to assert royal authority by regranting lands and offices surrendered to the Crown, but to make money through doing so. Thus those who felt that their position as land — or office-holders were in some doubt now that the minority was at an end, hastened to pay compositions — lump sums — to the Treasurer to receive royal confirmations of their holdings. Some of these sums were huge: £500 by Sir James Dunbar of Cumnock for a confirmation of the office of sheriff of Elgin and Forres, with the castle hill of Forres given to him in heritage; £1,666 13/4d. from Hugh, Lord Montgomery to be confirmed in the offices which had caused more friction than any others during the minority, the bailiary of Cunningham and chamberlainship of the burgh of Irvine.[27]

The loss of the Treasurer's accounts from the summer of 1498 — only a few months after King James's revocation at Duchal — until February 1501 makes it impossible to work out how much the king obtained from compositions for charter confirmations; clearly the total figure must have been a high one, running into many thousands. The act of revocation also gave King James the chance to reward familiars of the Crown by giving them rapid confirmations, a form of patronage which did not cost the king anything and which ensured continuing loyalty from the parties involved. Thus Sir Andrew Wood had a confirmation of his feu-charter of Largo; Sir Patrick Hume of Polwarth, for his services in war, resisting the king's old enemies, the English — clearly a reference to the fight at Duns in June 1497 — was confirmed in lands within the lordship of Menteith; Sir Alexander McCulloch of Myreton, one of the few trusted servants of the Crown in the south-west, and his wife Marjory Sinclair, were confirmed in lands within the lordship of Galloway, first granted to them by James III. Nor did the king forget old servants: on 13 February 1500 John Ballone, the brother of David, prior of Inchmahome, and described as 'oure lovit familiar squear and servitieur', was regranted the tack of the lands of Old Lindores in Fife, and at the same time absolved of further service to the Crown, 'becaus we undirstande wele . . . that the said Johne our servitur is waik and ageit in his person.'[28]

The revocation of 1498, therefore, underlined the king's direct control of royal patronage, enabled him to reward familiars cheaply, and brought in much needed revenue to the Crown. In one spectacular development, all these three facets were combined. As we have already seen, Hugh, Lord Montgomery, was prepared to pay a very large sum to ensure his tenure of the offices of bailie of Cunningham and chamberlain of Irvine after the royal act of revocation. Montgomery's payment of £1,666 13/4d. is however less remarkable than the king's willingness to grant the offices to him at all; for during the previous six years, since Angus's rise to power in the summer of 1492, James IV had consistently backed Angus — Kilmaurs — Boyd control of the bailiary of Cunningham against Montgomery's violent efforts to recover the office for his family; and Chancellor Angus himself was described as bailie of Cunningham in June 1493.[29] So the grant of the bailiary in 1498 to Montgomery, the principal enemy of Cuthbert, Lord Kilmaurs, and his father-in-law Angus, was a remarkable volte-face by the king. Why did he do it?

Part of the answer lies in the fact that Angus was no longer the powerful protector of Lord Kilmaurs and his supporters. We have already seen that the earl's political success in 1492–3 had been based on his niece's liaison with James IV. But Marion Boyd had ceased to be the king's mistress by 1495, and two years later, about a month after the end of the Ayton campaign of August 1497, Angus was removed from the Chancellorship and replaced by George Gordon, second earl of Huntly. No specific reason for Angus's dismissal survives; but there were probably a number of contributory factors. One of these was the earl's efforts throughout his Chancellorship to have himself recognised as heir-at-law to the last earls of Douglas — James, the forfeited ninth earl, had died in 1491 – an enterprise which can have won him few friends amongst other border or north-eastern magnates, or for that matter much favour with the king.[30] Also

Angus's pro-English stance, an asset to him in 1492–3, worked against him when James IV and Henry VII went to war in 1496–7. There may even be some doubt as to Angus's commitment to that war; Henry VII's suggestion in July 1497 that Angus should act as a Scottish ambassador in company with Lord Hume and Andrew Stewart, bishop of Moray — the latter a man of very doubtful loyalty — may not have endeared the earl to James IV; and Angus does not appear to have been present in the Scottish host at Upsettlington.[31] By the autumn, the king had clearly determined to remove Angus, and sometime between 22 September and 12 November, he was dismissed.[32]

His departure from the court and government circle left his Cunningham and Boyd relatives in Ayrshire dangerously exposed. Not only had Cuthbert, Lord Kilmaurs, lost his powerful ally, the earl strong enough to support the Boyds against the Ayrshire Campbells by 'fixing' royal courts,[33] the Chancellor who would champion Kilmaurs' control of northern Ayrshire; he had also acquired a powerful adversary in Archibald, second earl of Argyll, the Master of the Royal Household, Lord Montgomery's brother-in-law. In the circumstances, Kilmaurs and his allies had clearly become the underdogs in the Cunningham-Montgomery feud.

The decisive factor was the intervention of the king. At some point during the 1496–7 wars, Kilmaurs and Montgomery, turning up in the Scottish host, were required by James IV to shake hands and swear 'amite and concorde' in the future[34] — an interesting example of the king using a very public occasion to attempt to compose feuds, as well as a convincing illustration of the royal power; for Kilmaurs and Montgomery were probably both present in the host because each was afraid to let the other go alone to win King James's favour. In the early summer of 1498, however, the king had concerns other than the settlement of the Cunningham-Montgomery feud. He had clearly already been influenced in Montgomery's favour — perhaps by Argyll — when he approved a marriage contract between Hugh, Lord Montgomery, and a royal familiar, Sir Archibald Edmonstone of Duntreath, on 1 June 1498. John Montgomery, Hugh's son and heir, was to marry Elizabeth Edmonstone, Sir Archibald's daughter; the father of the bride was to pay a dowry of 1,300 marks, and Montgomery was to respond by giving lands in conjunct infeftment to his son and new daughter-in-law under the supervision of the earls of Argyll and Lennox, George Schaw, abbot of Paisley, and Lord Ross of Hawkhead, all of them committed king's men. The marriage, however, was conditional on Lord Montgomery being accepted as bailie of Cunningham by the king.[35] Thus King James's desire to arrange a good marriage for the daughter of one of his familiars — Edmonstone had been a household servant in 1490, and subsequently became keeper of Doune castle and steward of Menteith[36] — led him to confirm Montgomery in what was after all a royal office, the bailiary of Cunningham. It was a profitable piece of post-revocation business: Edmonstone was prepared to pay a substantial dowry for an influential marriage for his daughter, while Montgomery was euphemistically described in his charter of the bailiary as the heir of his grandfather, Alexander, Master of Montgomery, who had died in 1452.[37] This version of events conveniently ignored the recent history of the bailiary, which Montgomery had twice attempted to seize by killing the father and grandfather of Cuthbert Cunningham, Lord Kilmaurs. King James's straightforward view of the situation in 1498 was no doubt that Montgomery was related to Argyll, not to Angus, and that he was prepared to pay handsomely for the bailiary. Thus the business was arranged very quickly, with the marriage contract on 1 June, the royal grant of the bailiary of Cunningham and chamberlainship of Irvine three days later, and Montgomery's payment of £1,666 13/4d. two days after that, on 6 June. On the same day James IV, no doubt anticipating further trouble in Ayrshire, issued letters ordering all his lieges in Cunningham to obey Lord Montgomery and his deputes, and expressly forbidding any convocations to impede him in the execution of his office.[38]

The king was right to anticipate a fierce reaction from the Kilmaurs faction. As soon as Hugh, Lord Montgomery, arrived in Irvine — probably in August 1498 — to try to hold the bailiary court, he was attacked by Cuthbert, Lord Kilmaurs, and a small army of his 'name and surname', numbering no less than 515, who seized the tolbooth of Irvine[39] and effectively prevented Montgomery from entering to perform his office. It was, in effect, a repeat, probably on a much larger scale, of the Kilmaurs — Montgomery clashes in Irvine in 1489, 1491, and 1492. The difference in 1498 was that the minority was long over, and that the Cunninghams were directly challenging the authority of an adult Stewart king. The royal response was firm: the entire Cunningham faction was ordered to appear to answer for their crimes in the spring justice ayre at Ayr in 1499.[40] Cuthbert, Lord Kilmaurs, and four other defendants, duly appeared, were found guilty of forethought felony on Hugh Lord Montgomery at Irvine, and were fined. Significantly the royal justiciar who tried them was the new Chancellor, George, earl of Huntly — a salutory reminder to the Cunninghams that the days when they might expect protection for their actions from Chancellor Angus were now over.[41] At about the same time, Kilmaurs and twenty others received remissions for other crimes, including 'the violent hurting of Downald Robison cummand fra the kingis hoist'.[42] Presumably Robison was a Montgomery man, and an attack on him by a gang of Cunninghams led by the head of their family while Robison was in the king's service cannot have helped the Cunningham cause in the eyes of the king. In fact, the Kilmaurs–Montgomery feud would rumble on for much of the rest of the reign before coming to arbitration before the Lords of Council. But in 1498–9, James IV was the overall gainer from the Ayrshire conflict. He had made his choice in northern Ayrshire; he had enhanced his authority by coming down hard on those who resisted his decision; and he had made substantial profits in the process.

The Kilmaurs–Montgomery feud, and the royal reaction to it in 1498, is of course an extraordinary case; but in its financial aspect it typifies the unremitting pursuit of wealth by James and his counsellors both at this time and later. In the same month of June 1498, there was a final feeble echo of the issue which had stirred enormous political passions between 1488 and 1492, namely the fate of James III's hoard of treasure. On 26 June Sir Oliver Sinclair of Roslin appeared before the Lords of Council charged with wrongously withholding from the king 'gold and depois to the availe of a thousand crounis or thereby that pertenit til umquhile our soverane lordis fader'; and he was ordered to pay 400 marks to Sir Robert Lundy of Balgonie, the Treasurer.[43] This was hardly a princely sum, given the fulminations of the estates in 1492 about the total treasure recovered by that time — £24,517 10/- — being only a small part of the whole;[44] and it may be that other beneficiaries, more fortunate than Sinclair of Roslin, secretly enjoyed portions of the remainder of James III's hoard throughout the reign. Certainly there were no more cases of this kind heard before the Lords of Council; if the king's counsellors hoped that they had uncovered a new seam of untapped Crown income, they must have been disappointed.

However, the greatest single financial windfall of the reign was still to come. As part of the Treaty of Perpetual Peace with England concluded in January 1502, James IV was to marry Henry VII's daughter Margaret Tudor in the summer of 1503. The bride's dowry would be 30,000 angel nobles — £10,000 sterling, about £35,000 Scots — and would be paid in three yearly instalments, starting in 1503.[45] This was not a large dowry — in 1500 King James had been looking for double the amount finally agreed upon[46] — and compares unfavourably with the sums received by James's successor for each of his two French marriages in 1537 and 1538; indeed it does not even equal the amount promised to James III in 1474 as the dowry of Edward IV's daughter Cecilia.[47] Furthermore the acquisition of Margaret Tudor was not all gain for James IV; as part of the treaty he was required to maintain his bride's household of twenty-four attendants, to grant her lands and castles with an annual rental of £6,000 Scots, and to give her an annual allowance of £1,000 Scots.[48] There was, of course, much more to the 1502 treaty than immediate material gain for King James; it gave him both added security and a certain flexibility in his future foreign policy. And Henry VII was a prompt paymaster. The first instalment of Margaret Tudor's dowry was duly paid in Edinburgh on 10 August 1503, two days after the wedding, the second at Coldingham on 28 July 1504, and the last, also at Coldingham, on 13 August 1505.[49]

Thus in the years 1503–5 James IV's annual income was swollen by more than £10,000 Scots. But the king, increasingly committed to his naval programmes, to meeting the costs of war in the Isles in 1504–6, and to the renovation or rebuilding of royal castles and palaces — not to mention the 'one-off' expense of a lavish wedding, a total of £6,125 4/6d.[50] — began to treat this huge annual boost to his income as normal revenue. After 1505, when the English dowry payments ceased, James IV required urgently to find further sources of income to take their place, for all the dowry money had gone by August 1508.[51] To some extent the problem had been foreseen by the king, or at any rate by his counsellors. The only satisfactory methods of generating the huge sums required by the Crown were the systematic exploitation of feudal casualties, the raising of rentals on Crown lands, and further tapping of the wealth of the Church.

The last of these methods had been undertaken with some success, as we have seen, as early as 1497, when James, duke of Ross, became archbishop of St Andrews, and the king acquired control of the revenues of the archbishopric. To these were added the rich prizes of Holyrood (December 1497), Dunfermline (June 1500) and Arbroath (July 1503) abbeys, granted in commendam to the unconsecrated archbishop, their revenues diverted to continuing and increasing royal financial needs.[52] It is probable that King James never sought permanent control of St Andrews, viewing 1497 and the subsequent chance to make his brother commendator of the richest abbeys in the country as a short-term windfall; and it seems that in February 1503, the young archbishop had already reached, or shortly expected to reach, the canonical age of twenty-seven and was applying for permission to be consecrated.[53] In material terms, however, the king's luck held; for on 13 January 1504, still unconsecrated, James, archbishop of St Andrews, suddenly died.[54] With great speed, the king nominated his eleven-year-old illegitimate son, Alexander Stewart — already archdeacon of St Andrews — to the archbishopric, and the boy was provided on 10 May 1504.[55] Like his uncle before him, Alexander would remain only administrator of the archdiocese until he reached the canonical age for consecration, twenty-seven, in his case some sixteen years, during which time his father could continue to draw on St Andrews' revenues.

How much all this was worth to the king is impossible to say exactly. After his brother's death in 1504, James received a total of £3,791 19/- from the archiepiscopal revenues; this appears in the Treasurer's account for 1502–4 and seems to be a payment for a number of years.[56] Rather more substantial evidence is provided by later accounts: in 1505–6 James IV drew £1,098 10/1d. from the archbishopric,[57] and in 1507–8 his takings from the same source had risen to £1,865 19/1d.[58] It seems unlikely that, prior to 1504, he took much less from Arbroath and Dunfermline, both of which abbeys enjoyed annual revenues on a par with those of St Andrews; and Holyrood's annual yield was probably rather more than half of each of these. On these figures, King James's annual takings from the ecclesiastical wealth which came to him by way of his brother might have been £2,000 — £2,500, though this is probably a substantial underestimate. Certainly the accounts show that he took more from St Andrews as the reign progressed; possibly he had to, for following his brother's death in 1504, it was not until 1509 that James was able to acquire the commends of Dunfermline and Coldingham for his archbishop son.

From 1497 onwards, then, we see James IV acquiring considerably more wealth — initially fluctuating, but latterly rising steeply — from the richest benefices within the Scottish church. A similar trend can be detected in his efforts to improve his revenues from rentals of Crown lands. Here the main development, eventually yielding spectacular financial returns for the Crown, was the conversion of large areas of the royal demesne from lease-hold to feu-farm tenure. Feu-farm grants were not of course a novelty introduced by James IV; the

Crown had begun to feu royal lands at the end of his grandfather's reign, and his father had continued the development on a modest scale, while royal grants of feus to the communities of major burghs, and some feuing of church lands, had been going on since the fourteenth century.[59] A feu-farm grant brought the obvious advantage of security of tenure to the feu-holder; so long as he and his heirs paid a fixed annual feu-duty, either in cash or victuals, or occasionally both, his tenure was secure. And there was normally the additional advantage that the holder of a feu was not liable to the feudal casualties of wardship and relief. For the Crown, the motive for feuing was material profit; in addition to the annual feu-duty being considerably higher than the former annual rent of the land, the feu-holder had to pay a lump sum — the grassum — before receiving his feu-charter. In most cases the grassum was a single payment on entry, though occasionally it was levied every fifth or seventh year; and it could be as large a sum as the annual feu-duty. Thus for feuing to satisfy both parties to the agreement, Crown and feu-holder, it was obviously necessary to have available and interested sitting tenants or outsiders of sufficient wealth to pay the grassums and higher feu-duties.

James III, a king not noted for missing opportunities to amass money, used the device of feuing Crown lands only sparingly, with a recorded total of thirteen confirmations and twenty-two new feu-grants.[60] This may reflect a government view that there were at the time an insufficient number of sitting Crown tenants wealthy enough to make extensive feuing a worthwhile investment for the king; and eviction of sitting tenants when their leases expired to make way for those who *could* afford to feu was a risky business which might lead to social unrest or rebellion. If this was indeed the official attitude to feuing, it persisted through the difficult early years of James IV's minority; down to the end of the century, feuing of Crown lands was a relatively rare device, though there were a number of confirmations of earlier feu-grants.

The beginning of the new century produced a different government attitude; the king's continuing need for money led his advisers to look about for irregularities in tenancies on royal lands. They had not far to look. At the eastern end of Loch Tay, Neil Stewart of Fortingall had been enjoying possession of Crown lands — £30 worth of the lordship of Apnadull between Fortingall and Weem — without paying any rents since early in the previous reign. Only a few miles further north, Stewart was entrenched in the royal lands of Rannoch, again without apparently paying rent for them. In September 1502 the government decided that Stewart would have to go, and as their instrument in this process they chose his near-neighbour, Robert Menzies of Weem, a man who, whatever his other qualifications, had proved the previous year that he had sufficient money to pay triple rent for the feu-grant of the barony of 'Cammysarnay' — Camserney, a few miles west of Weem — in Apnadull.[61] On 1 September Menzies received two further Crown grants — the barony of Rannoch in feu-farm, and a five-year lease on the £30 land of Apnadull, for which Menzies would pay double rent of £60 annually, obtaining at the same time the bailiary of all the lands of the lordship of Apnadull.[62] Recognising that the intrusion of Menzies, an individual with few friends in Perthshire, into Rannoch and Apnadull might be regarded as a challenge to the incumbent, Stewart of Fortingall, the government took the precaution, on 7 September, of making a further feu-farm grant, of the barony of Glen Lyon, just west of Fortingall, to Sir Duncan Campbell of Glenorchy, no doubt expecting Campbell's support if Menzies' possession of Rannoch or Apnadull were resisted.[63]

The royal scheme misfired spectacularly. Menzies barely had time to take possession of his new lands before he was attacked by the displaced Stewart of Fortingall and Sir Duncan Campbell of Glenorchy, the latter clearly unmoved by his recent government feu-grant of Glen Lyon. In October 1502, with the assistance of Alexander Robertson of Struan and the backing of their powerful kinsman John Stewart, earl of Atholl, Stewart of Fortingall and Campbell of Glenorchy assailed Castle Menzies, captured Menzies himself and threw him into prison. This open defiance of the king is at first sight surprising, for the sums of money involved were small — £30 in Rannoch, £60 for Apnadull — and certainly not worth committing treason for. The issue, however, involved not only money but also authority; Menzies had been given the bailiary of the lordship of Apnadull,[64] and his neighbours clearly found the prospect of his sitting in judgment in the bailiary court, a royal official imposed on the locality, quite unacceptable. So they removed him by force.

James IV had been directly challenged by a combination of Perthshire knights and lairds supported by his great-uncle, the Earl of Atholl; and not only his authority, but his ability to make feu-grants of royal lands in the future, was in question. He responded at once. On 11–12 January 1503, during a flying visit to Perth,[65] the king ordered Menzies' immediate release; the following June he was present at a high-powered justice ayre in Perth, bringing with him the entire court, who included the justices — Lord Gray, Matthew Stewart, earl of Lennox, and Master Richard Lawson — who had only just completed the ayres of Kirkcudbright, Wigtown, and Ayr.[66] The Perth summer ayre, to which the offenders of the previous autumn were summoned, lasted a fortnight from 17 June; but the defendants did not appear, and they were eventually summoned for treason to an assize of the 1504 parliament, the first to be held for almost eight years. Not until 8 June 1504 did John, earl of Atholl, and Neil Stewart of Fortingall appear before an assize headed by Alexander, Lord Hume, the Chamberlain, declaring themselves ready to 'undirly the lawis' — in other words, to pay for a remission for their attack on Castle Menzies. The case against Campbell of Glenorchy and Robertson of Struan, who did not appear, was continued to 3 October, but before the end of the summer the case had been resolved before the Lords of Council and Menzies restored to his rather tenuous occupation of Rannoch and Apnadull.[67]

Vigorous royal action, sustained over two years, had won the struggle in the Menzies-Stewart contest. The king's victory in Perthshire was reinforced by an act of parliament in March 1504, laying down that the king might grant any royal lands, both annexed and unannexed, in feu-farm 'to ony persone or persones he pless . . . and sett with sic clauss as our souerane thinkis expedient.'[68] This act would help to discourage a repetition of events like the raid on Castle Menzies in other areas of the country. Prudently, it was made for the lifetime of James IV only, and on condition that feu-farm grants·'be nocht in diminution of his Rentale, grassoums, not all uthir dewitez' — a most unlikely eventuality.

In fact, the act of 1504 opened the floodgates to a spate of royal feuing in the last years of the reign. Crown lands on Bute were granted in feu in 1506, but it is not until 1510-11, with the feuing of Fife, that a dramatic increase in rents becomes clearly visible. Thus in 1508 the rentals from the five 'quarters' or districts of Fife – Eden, Largo, Auchtermuchty, Falkland, and Lindores — had totalled £733 11/-; in 1510–11, following feuing, the same rents had more than doubled to £1,529 10/-.[69] The years 1510–11 also saw extensive feuing in the lordship of Methven and in Stirlingshire; and the feuing of royal property within Ettrick Forest from 1510 onwards produced an astonishing rise in Crown annual rents from £525 13/4d. to £2,672 13/4d., an increase overall of more than 500% not counting the entry fine or grassum for most of the new holdings, amounting in 1510 to at least £1,611, with a further rise of £312 by 1512. Thus, on Dr Madden's figures, in the two years following 1510 the Crown's gross income from Ettrick forest property was around £7,269.[70]

The effect of all this on Crown tenants is difficult to estimate, and undoubtedly varied sharply on different royal estates. Certainly some rents had remained more or less unchanged since the middle of the fifteenth century, and were therefore quite unrealistically low by 1510. The enormous increase imposed by James IV in Ettrick Forest argues in favour of the ability and willingness of many people to pay the new rents and grassums, and indeed there is evidence of competition for Crown feus in the Forest. There was, of course, a danger to the sitting tenant who could not afford the sudden huge increases and who faced eviction as a result; but conversion to feuing seems to have been resisted successfully by some Forest tenants, for example the Pringles in Galashiels, who remained under the old leasehold system until at least 1541.[71] It is doubtful, however, whether many Crown tenants could afford to view feuing as the blessing which, only a few years later, John Major believed it to be, as an inducement to improvement of houses and estates. Security of tenure brought about by feuing, Major argued, would inevitably lead to better living conditions;[72] but a more accurate social comment on the process may have been that of Sir David Lindsay, a young man at court in James IV's last years, who much later, in 'Ane Satyre of the Thrie Estatis', would condemn the high rents which were the inevitable result of feuing, and which led to evictions:

> 'And now begins ane plague among them new,
> That gentillmen thair steadings taks in few,
> Thus maun they pay great ferme or lay their stead.'[73]

Lindsay was describing conditions a generation after 1510, and bemoaning the lot of impoverished 'gentillmen'. In 1510 itself royal tenants in general unwilling or unable to take feus appear to have received short shrift from Crown officials; on 21 January of that year Master James Henryson, the king's advocate, appeared before the Lords of Council and protested that 'sen the tennentis of the erledome of Marche war summoned to this day to tak thair fewis an na man com to tak thaim, that thairfor the lordis mycht sett the saidis landis to other tennentis.'[74] On the other hand, the royal rental books of Menteith, of Stirlingshire, and of Fife contain some examples of rather more humane policies in operation. When George Schaw was granted the lands of Branquhalzie in Menteith in feu-farm in February 1510, it was on condition that he should not remove the poor occupiers from their steadings during their lifetimes; in April 1511 Robert Colville of Ochiltree had to accept similar conditions to obtain the feu of the barony of Tillicoultry in Stirlingshire; and there is even the remarkable case, between March 1510 and July 1511, of the tenants of Kingsbarns in Fife successfully competing with the new feuars, having the original feu-grant cancelled, and then taking their holdings in feu themselves.[75] Crown profits from feuing, therefore, were not invariably attended by tales of human suffering; suffering was reserved, in two of the three cases mentioned above, for the next generation.

In general, however, feu-grants were a means whereby the king might confer a favour on the well-to-do, combining a reward for good service with a monetary return to himself. Dr Nicholson's analysis of royal grants of feu-farm (around 100) during James IV's personal rule reveals what one would expect: between one third and a half of the grants were to royal familiars or their sons; two earls, Argyll and Bothwell, and one bishop, Caithness, received feus, as did seven lords of parliament; of the remainder, almost all of them went to untitled landholders — untitled but not necessarily unknown, for some of them turn up in minor household or government posts.[76]

Feuing escaped widespread contemporary censure partly because of the benefits which it conferred — not only freedom from the feudal casualties of wardship and relief, but also, in terms of an act of 1504 (immediately following the royal feu-farm act) encouraging freeholders to follow the king's example and feu their lands, exemption from the most disliked of all feudal casualties: recognition. In the case of crown finances, recognition, or repossession, might occur when more than half of an estate held by service of ward and relief was alienated without consent of the Crown; the lands in question could then be 'recognosced' – repossessed – by the king. This device, little employed by James III, was to be used 149 times during the adult rule of his son;[77] and it was the subject of sharp criticism by all the sixteenth-century chroniclers. Thus Adam Abell, writing in the 1530s and in general praising James IV to the skies, commented that he had two vices: sins of the flesh and recognition. In the case of the latter, clearly what Abell objected to was the 'knock-on' effect; 'be prewat consall', he says, 'he (the king) maid a recognitioun of his baronis landis and the baronis for that taxat the pure lauboraris'.[78] He was right; recognition, like the other highly unpopular casualty of the reign, non-entry, affected not only the tenant-in-chief but also his vassals. Free tenants had to assist their lords by producing contributions — according to the extent of their individual holdings — to help pay for the recovery of an estate which had fallen under recognition. For in the cases of recognition and non-entry, the object of the exercise was not to ruin those who had fallen into technical error, but to subject them to polite blackmail which would produce large financial returns for the Crown. Thus the personal rule of James IV is filled with extravagant royal demands, followed eventually by the payment of compositions by landholders who wanted to retain their heritages intact and could not resist Crown pressure indefinitely. All that was possible was delay in paying compositions, and this was soon followed by Crown letters to the relevant sheriffs ordering them to distrain either the moveable goods or part of the landed property of defaulters. Normally the threat of distraint — the appalling prospect of losing part of one's heritage temporarily or, at worst, permanently — was enough to bring recalcitrant Crown debtors into line.[79]

There were however some exceptions, most notably the wretched George Leslie, second earl of Rothes, who fell foul of the government almost from the outset of the reign, trapped by the feudal casualty of non-entry. This was simply a technicality which allowed the Crown to fine its tenants-in-chief for failure to obtain legal title to certain estates in the past — sometimes the distant past. It was, of course, sharp practice. By resurrecting a feudal device the Crown was able to threaten with total ruin tenants who had been no more than careless in the past, and then to accept a composition, in money or kind, for not pursuing the matter any further. In the case of Rothes, his problem was that he fell out at an early stage with the wrong man. On 22 October 1490 the Lords of Council judged that the earl would have to pay to Patrick Hepburn, earl of Bothwell — at that time guardian of the king and his brother — a total of £869 3/4d. and forty-six and a half chalders of victual for the mails and farms of the barony of Ballinbreich and other Fife lands, which had been discovered to be in non-entry and had therefore fallen into Crown hands, after which the relief and non-entry of all the lands had been given as a royal gift to Bothwell. Rothes had no chance in this case, for Bothwell himself was one of the Lords of Council trying it; Rothes failed to appear, and his Fife lands were ordered to be distrained.[80]

This early case before the Lords of Council cannot be dismissed simply as an example of Hepburn greed or vindictiveness, or both, during the early stages of the minority, for Rothes was pursued for non-entry on a grander scale later in the reign. In March 1508 the Lords of Council found that his barony of Balmain in Kincardineshire had been in non-entry for no less than twenty-six years; Rothes would not, or could not, compound with the Treasurer for the huge sum of £2,210 held to be due as the accumulated farms of the barony, which fell to the Crown and was regranted, in May 1510, to Sir John Ramsay of Terringzeane.[81] Rothes' resistance, therefore, was very heavily punished, and not only in his pocket, for the loss of part of his inheritance meant that his tenants in Fife and in the barony of Balmain found themselves with new legal superiors — the king and Ramsay respectively — with the result that they had to compound on their own account for fresh infeftments in the lands which they had formerly held of Rothes. The earl's failure to protect his tenants can hardly have enhanced his authority in their eyes; and when he died in March 1513, his son and heir William Leslie, third earl of Rothes, hurried to make a deal with the Treasurer to recover some of the family's Fife lands.[82] No doubt in an effort to ingratiate himself with James IV, the third earl also went with his sovereign to Flodden; this was his first and last mistake.

Throughout the Rothes non-entry cases, the Crown had been the gainer in terms both of resources and authority. The king acquired further sources of patronage with which to reward his supporters; in the case of Balmain, he received a composition for Ramsay for legal entry into the barony; and in the dismemberment of the Rothes inheritance, he showed that the Crown would not hesitate to deal severely with all those — even earls — who resisted its pursuit of its rights through rigorous imposition of legal technicalities.

One man who got the message very clearly was Archibald, fifth earl of Angus, whose fortunes had taken a turn for the worse after his dismissal from the Chancellorship in the autumn of 1497. Elizabeth Boyd, his wife for thirty years, died in 1498; and perhaps in an effort to recover some of his lost influence in Ayrshire, Angus made substantial grants of land — the baronies of Braidwood and Crawford-Lindsay in Lanarkshire — to his mistress Janet Kennedy, daughter of John, Lord Kennedy.[83] He was unlucky; within a year[84] Janet had ceased to be Angus's mistress and was instead performing the same services for the king, who was quite happy to confirm the earl's Lanarkshire grants to Janet and — eventually — to instal her as the third, and most durable, of his mistresses.[85] At about the same time Angus seems to have begun to fight a losing battle to preserve the grants which had been made to him before the revocation of 1498; in particular the ward of the lands of the deceased John Auchinleck, originally given to Angus's son William in 1492, was reassigned by the king to John Hepburn, prior of St Andrews, the eminence grise of the Hepburn faction at court, in March 1501.[86] The dispute which followed may have had something to do with Angus's being ordered into ward in Dumbarton castle late in 1501. Freed from Dumbarton, apparently through the good offices of his former servant Andrew Forman,[87] Angus was almost immediately warded once more, this time for the remarkable period of seven years, 1502–9, on the island of Bute.[88] Although the reasons for his second confinement are uncertain, they may again have been connected with antagonism between Angus and the Hepburns; certainly the former's wardship on Bute did not end until after the death of Patrick Hepburn, earl of Bothwell, in 1508.

There may, however, have been another reason for the warding of Earl Archibald on Bute. Hume of Godscroft, the seventeenth-century historian of the families of Douglas and Angus, tells the curious tale that Angus was sent to the Isle of Arran because of James IV's infatuation with the earl's second wife Janet Kennedy.[89] The details are inaccurate — Angus was sent to Bute rather than Arran, and Janet was his mistress rather than his wife — but it is clear that Godscroft had absorbed some source which explained the wardship of the earl in terms of his contest with James IV over Janet Kennedy. The true nature of this struggle, if it existed, was probably territorial rather than sexual;

Angus may have wished to recover his Lanarkshire lands. If so, he eventually succeeded only at a price; for on 7 February 1510, with a few months of his release from confinement on Bute, Angus confirmed Janet Kennedy in his former lordship of Bothwell in order to recover Braidwood and Crawford-Lindsay, an arrangement which was ratified on the same day by James IV and may indeed have been one of the conditions of the earl's release.[90] He emerged a chastened sixty-year-old, relieved to be entrusted with some public duties, an earl running scared of his king.

Almost at once he was pursued — savagely — for non-entry to his lands of Kirriemuir in Angus and his border lordship of Eskdale, the latter resigned into the king's hands in March 1502.[91] In the case of Kirriemuir, on 17 June 1510 the lands were held by the Lords of Council to have been in non-entry for forty-five years, since the death of George, fourth earl of Angus, in 1465. Earl Archibald had retained actual possession of Kirriemuir since that time, but the Crown now asserted its right to the total rent of the property, which at £1,000 annually produced an appalling bill of £45,000. Probably mindful of what had happened to Rothes the previous month, Angus hastened to make a settlement, and by August had promised to pay a composition of 5000 marks in return for a new infeftment in Kirriemuir.[92] In 1512, about half of this sum — £1,446 — was still outstanding; Angus made a part payment of £649 and a further £510 was remitted by the king.[93] No doubt a similar composition — a fraction of the original total demanded — was made by Angus in the case of Eskdale, assessed at 66,000 marks — £44,000 — for past farms.[94]

Even yet, the earl's troubles were not at an end. Within only a few months of his recovery of the barony of Crawford-Lindsay, and in spite of the king's confirmation of this, he had lost the barony to the Crown. As he had alienated it without the royal consent — presumably to Janet Kennedy, a nice irony in the circumstances — it fell into the king's hands through recognition. In this case, Angus's free tenants within the barony, fearing that they would lose their Martinmas rents, petitioned the Crown at the end of October 1510 to restore the earl to Crawford-Lindsay; and on 20 January 1511, Angus was duly restored to the barony, no doubt in return for a further sizeable composition.[95] It may have been less a sense of his increasing age than a concern for the preservation of the Angus inheritance in the face of relentless and cynical royal demands which made the earl resign much of his property to his sons George and William in 1511.[96]

Rothes and Angus were merely the most spectacular sufferers in the Crown's exaction of feudal casualties; for Dr Nicholson shows that recognition alone affected no less than eleven earls, sixteen lords, sixteen knights, two clergy, and one royal burgh, during James IV's personal rule; and he is surely right to draw the conclusion that 'the rosy picture of an easy-going king is scarcely credible.'[97] Recognition, non-entry, extensive feu-farm grants, compositions for charters after the 1498 revocation, income from profits of justice, above all from remissions — all those helped to swell the royal income without for the most part causing the kind of offence which would lead to armed resistance.

In some areas, for example in his liberal distribution of remissions, sometimes for serious crimes, James IV seems to be pursuing a policy very similar to his father, who was condemned in parliament for making money in this way. But there is a difference. James III had largely failed to make an impact on the localities because he had not personally attended the justice ayres; by contrast, James IV had gone out on ayre every year since his accession — frequently in both spring and autumn — levying fines, 'justifying' criminals, composing feuds. From Wigtown to Aberdeen — and occasionally Inverness — he could be seen to be doing his job as it was expected of him. Thus even the parliament of 1504, seeking to condemn the royal granting of remissions 'for slauchtir to be committit upon forthocht fellony' — premeditated murder — took a very different tone to that of the estates of James's father. The statute ordering an end to remissions of this kind was made 'be his (the king's) awin aviss', and was to remain in force only 'unto the tyme our said souerane lord mak speceale revocatioun of the samyne.'[98] Even in implied criticism of him there is here a note of respect for a successful king; and the king's ability to recoup any losses which the act might cause is demonstrated by a statute of the same parliament, condemning those who in the past had sought to obtain remissions cheaply through attempting to comprehend, within a general clause, greater crimes than those cited in the special clause upon which the cost of the remission was based. In future, according to the act, 'if he (the criminal) expremys nocht the greitest cryme in speceale, the generale clauss sall nocht saif him for ane greit cryme.'[99]

Whether or not the king followed his promise of March 1504 not to give remissions for premeditated murder, the granting of remissions in general continued apace. Indeed, a royal proclamation such as that made at Inverness in 1501 that after the forthcoming ayre the king would no longer accept compositions for 'commone gret crimes' may, as Dr Nicholson suggests, have been intended to stimulate a demand for remissions. The same author's analysis of these shows 522 grants of remission over the entire reign, 182 of these being for manslaughter, 88 for 'forthocht fellony', and 71 for support of rebels and outlaws.[100] In some of this last category, there is an element of cynicism in the government's concern to pursue individuals for ancient — and often obscure — crimes. Thus between 1493 and 1510 there are no less than eleven remissions granted to different men for 'treasonably being with the Duke of Albany' — James III's brother, whose last treasons had occurred in the years 1482–4.[101] Then there is the belated penalising of sins of omission, the nine remissions to individuals who had failed to turn up to the host at Ayton in August 1497;[102] not only are these granted very late in the reign, but also the reason for imposing them, beyond the obvious financial return to be gained by the Crown, is difficult to see. From beginning to end, the Ayton crisis had lasted exactly a week, 14–21 August 1497, hardly time for James's lieges to receive summonses to the host, far less respond to them. In both the Albany and Ayton remissions, it is difficult to escape the conclusion that Crown officials were using these serious charges — treason and absence from the host in time of war — to screw as much as possible out of individuals who may have been guilty of lesser crimes — in some of the Albany remissions these are actually specified — but who felt it safest to cover themselves by paying sizeable compositions to secure their futures.

In spite of all this high-powered royal fiscal activity, steadily increasing as the reign advanced, the popularity of James IV with his subjects probably remained unimpaired. Bishop Lesley suggests as much when he lays the blame for recognitions on unspecified members of the royal council rather than on the king himself; indeed, 'the noble and gentle Prince, persevand his subjects to gruge thairwith as ane new inventit maner to truble the estate of the cuntrey, did easely and gentlie aggre with the auld possessouris and awnaris, for the quhilk he conqueist gret favour of his people.'[103] One may doubt whether compositions to avoid recognition of one's lands were ever paid 'easely and gentlie'; but Lesley is probably right to suggest that King James was not blamed. George Buchanan, who takes a very dim view of the king's prodigal expenditure, nevertheless remarks, in the case of recognition, that it was believed that Bishop Elphinstone was responsible for its introduction.[104] So the unpopularity which attached itself to the Crown's relentless enforcement of its rights may not have been directed at the king at all — for the measures employed were unquestionably legal — but rather at those who actually pursued defaulters and fixed the levels of composition which they would have to pay — civil servants like Privy Seal Elphinstone, who probably advised the king as to his feudal rights, and the royal advocate Master James Henryson, who pursued them before the Lords of Council. In most cases, except where his rights were directly challenged as they were by the Perthshire lairds in 1502–4, James IV remained aloof from, and above, the implementation of these measures. And unlike his three predecessors, he did not make extensive use of the ultimate royal weapon — forfeiture of life, lands, and goods. The two forfeitures of 1488 — Ramsay and Ross — had been rescinded before the end of the minority; those of the rebels of 1489 (with the solitary exception of Lord Crichton) were cancelled within a few months; the forfeiture of the Lordship of the Isles in 1493 was not the work of the adult king, though the results of it remained an albatross round his neck for more than a decade; and of all those accused of treason and threatened with forfeiture during King James's personal rule, only the intransigent Torquil MacLeod of Lewis was actually forfeited. The king's aim was not to deprive his subjects of their inheritances, but simply to extract larger returns from all available sources of revenue.

By the end of the reign, he had certainly achieved this objective. The Treasurer's annual receipts had shot up from around £4,500 in 1496–7 to a staggering £28,000 by 1512. When this total is added to James's (probable) income from ecclesiastical properties and from the revenues paid to the Comptroller, including the new rents on Crown Lands, James IV may have received a total income of as much as £44,500 by the last years of the reign. His problem was that in 1513 expenditure was outrunning income, possibly by more than £7,000 per annum.[105] The only ways of coping with this difficulty were severe retrenchment — not an option which James IV is likely to have considered — or the regular acquisition of still more money for the Crown. It seems probable that, had he lived, the king would have further exploited what was possibly the most fruitful source of extraordinary revenue generated throughout the entire reign, the 'spirituall taxt', those massive contributions from the Scottish clergy which had brought in almost £7,000 in 1512 alone. As events were to show, James's successor was not slow to recognise the clergy as his most promising fiscal target.

NOTES

1. *T.A.*, i, cliv–clv; 345–350.
2. *Ibid.*, i, 312–3.
3. *Cal. State Papers (Spain)*, i, No. 210.
4. *E.R.*, x, xi, xii, xiii, passim.
5. Charles A. Kelham, 'Bases of Magnatial Power in Later Fifteenth-Century Scotland': unpublished Ph.D. thesis, Edinburgh 1986, 337–8.
6. *E.R.*, xi, preface, xxix–xxx.
7. *Ibid.*, xi, preface, xxviii; 364–384, passim.
8. *A.P.S.*, ii, 219, 224, 230, 233–4.
9. *T.A.*, i, 215, 312, 315.
10. *Ibid.*, i, 312–3.
11. *E.R.*, xi, 49; *R.S.S.*, i, 405.
12. Supplementary Register House Charters, cited in A.L. Murray, 'Exchequer and Crown Revenue, 1437–1542', unpublished Ph.D. thesis, Edinburgh, 1961, Appendix, 85–6.
13. *Cal. Docs. Scot.*, iv, No. 1660.
14. *Ibid.*, iv, No. 1670.
15. *Ibid.*, iv, Nos. 1675, 1676.
16. *Ibid.*, iv, No. 1680.
17. *Cal. State Papers (Spain)*, i, No. 210.
18. S.R.O. 1/2: Sir John Skene, 'Tabill and repertour of the Cheker rollis', 104.
19. *T.A.*, ii, 196.
20. *James IV Letters*, No. 37; and *see below*, Chapter 9.
21. *T.A.*, iv, 351.
22. *Ibid.*, iv, 360–365.
23. *Ibid.*, iv, 391–396.
24. *Aberdeen Council Register*, 85.
25. For the details of Ross's elevation to the archbishopric, *see* Leslie J. Macfarlane, 'The Primacy of the Scottish Church, 1472–1521', in *Innes Review*, xx (1969), 111–129, at 119–21; and the same author's *Elphinstone*, 313–4. On assuming control of the archbishopric, Ross retained only the principal messuage of each of his secular possessions: Herkless and Hannay, *Archbishops of St. Andrews*, i, 213–4.
26. *T.A.*, i, 383, 388, 389.
27. *Ibid.*, i, 316.
28. *E.R.*, xi, 78–9, 161–3, 191, 296. Other confirmations following on King James's 1498 revocation are in *Ibid.*, xi, 81, 165–9, 171–2, 176, 184, and 301–2.
29. *See above*, Chapter 4.
30. Fraser, *Douglas*, iii, Nos. 133, 147. For a full discussion of Angus's political manoeuvres during his Chancellorship, see M.G. Kelley, 'The Douglas Earls of Angus:

A Study in the Social and Political Bases of Power of a Scottish Family from 1389 until 1557': Edinburgh Ph.D. thesis, 1973, pp. 107–111, 223–4.

31. *Cal. Docs. Scot.*, iv, No. 1635; *R.M.S.*, ii, No. 2370.
32. *R.M.S.*, ii, Nos. 2374, 2382.
33. For details, see *A.D.A.*, 196–7.
34. S.R.O., A.D.C., xix, f.131. I am indebted to Steve Boardman, who is working on Scottish politics and the feud for a Ph.D. thesis, for much information on the Kilmaurs-Montgomery feud.
35. Fraser, *Eglinton*, ii, No. 65.
36. *E.R.*, x, 185; *T.A.*, ii, 113.
37. S.R.O. Eglinton collection, GD 3/1/116; Fraser, *Eglinton*, ii, 54–6.
38. *R.S.S.*, i, No. 215; S.R.O. Eglinton collection, GD 3/1/120.
39. *R.S.S.*, i, No. 360.
40. S.R.O. Eglinton collection, GD 3/10/2028 (temporary number): Document dated 7 February 1499.
41. S.R.O. Glencairn Muniments, GD 39/1/24.
42. *R.S.S.*, i, No. 360.
43. *A.D.C.*, ii, 233.
44. *A.P.S.*, ii, 230 c.2.
45. *Cal. Docs. Scot.*, iv, No. 1680.
46. *Cal. State Papers (Spain)*, i, Nos. 249, 268.
47. By the terms of the marriage alliance of 1474, James III was to receive a dowry of 20,000 marks sterling — about £40,000 Scots — for the marriage of his son and heir (James IV) to Edward IV's daughter Cecilia: *Cal. Docs. Scot.*, iv, No. 1437. The dowries of James V were 100,000 livres — about £45,000 Scots — for the king's first wife Madeleine, daughter of Francis I of France; and 150,000 livres — £67,500 Scots — for his second marriage, a year later, to Mary of Guise-Lorraine: Donaldson, *James V — James VII*, 48–9.
48. *Cal. Docs. Scot.*, iv, No. 1680.
49. *R.M.S.*, ii, Nos. 2740, 2798, 2868.
50. *E.R.*, xii, liv.
51. *T.A.*, iv, 141.
52. Macfarlane, 'Primacy', 119–121.
53. *T.A.*, ii, 241–2.
54. He witnessed a royal charter at Edinburgh, as archbishop and chancellor, on 4 January 1504: *R.M.S.*, ii, No. 2765; on 13 or 14 January arrangements were being made for his funeral: *T.A.*, ii, 415.
55. Macfarlane, 'Primacy', 121.
56. *T.A.*, ii, 196.
57. *Ibid.*, iii, 29.
58. *Ibid.*, iii, 243; iv, 11–12.
59. For feuing in general, *see* R.G. Nicholson, 'Feudal Developments in Late Medieval Scotland', *Juridical Review* (1973, pt. 1.), 1–21, at 3–8. For one specific application of feuing on Crown lands, *see* Craig Madden, 'The Feuing of Ettrick Forest', *Innes Review*, xxvii (1), (1976), 70–84.
60. Nicholson, 'Feudal Developments', 4.
61. *R.M.S.*, ii, No. 2566.
62. *Ibid.*, ii, No. 2664; *R.S.S.*, i, No. 866.
63. *R.M.S.*, ii, No. 2668.
64. *R.S.S.*, i, No. 866.
65. *T.A.*, ii, 354.
66. *Ibid.*, ii, 299.
67. *A.P.S.*, ii, 255–6.
68. *A.P.S.*, ii, 244 c.30.

69. *E.R.*, xiii, 617–625.

70. Craig Madden, 'The Feuing of Ettrick Forest', 72–5.

71. *Ibid.*, 72–3.

72. Major, *History*, 31.

73. *Works of Sir David Lyndsay* (Ed. D. Hamer, S.T.S., 1931), ii, 224.

74. *E.R.*, xiii, 656.

75. *Ibid.*, xiii, 634, 643, 618–9.

76. Nicholson, 'Feudal Developments', 5.

77. *Ibid.*, 17.

78. Adam Abell, 'The Roit or Quheill of Tyme', f.112v. (NLS., Adv. MS. 1746).

79. See, in general, Craig Madden, 'Royal treatment of feudal casualties in late medieval Scotland', *S.H.R.*, lv (1976), 172–194, esp. 187–191. This is in part a distillation of the wisdom contained in the same writer's Ph.D. thesis: Craig Madden, 'The Finances of the Scottish Crown in the later Middle Ages'. (Glasgow University, 1978).

80. *A.D.C.*, i, 152–3.

81. S.R.O., ADC., xix, ff.198, 238; *R.M.S.*, ii, No. 3460.

82. Madden, op.cit., *S.H.R.*, lv (1976), 191.

83. *R.M.S.*, ii, Nos. 2434, 2457.

84. Janet Kennedy bore a son to James IV about 1500: *E.R.*, xii, xliv.

85. Janet Kennedy is described in the exchequer accounts of Moray as 'domina de Boithvile' in 1501, suggesting that in addition to Angus's grants to her of Braidwood and Crawford-Lindsay, he also conferred on her the lordship of Bothwell, or at least its title. The lands of the lordship were in the hands of Angus's son William from 30 May 1504: Fraser, *Douglas*, iii, No. 159.

86. Fraser, *Douglas*, iii, 136; *R.S.S.*, i, No. 646.

87. Angus was in Dumbarton castle before 10 December 1501, and was still there on 28 March 1502: Fraser, *Douglas*, iii, Nos. 156, 157. For Forman's role in Angus's release, see Fraser, *Douglas*, ii, 100.

88. For Angus on Bute, see *Prot. Bk. Foular*, 182–3; Fraser, *Douglas*, iii, No. 159; *E.R.*, xii, 428–9; xiii, 139; *T.A.*, iv, 73, 77. Kelley, 'The Douglas Earls of Angus', 225, notes that Angus was on Bute from 1502 to 1509 without apparently realising that he was not there of his own volition. For Angus in ward, see S.R.O., A.D.C., xvi, f.284v. (24 April 1505).

89. David Hume of Godscroft, *The History of the Houses of Douglas and Angus* (Edinburgh, 1644), 232.

90. *R.M.S.*, ii, No. 3413.

91. Fraser, *Douglas*, ii, 100 n.l; iii, No. 157.

92. *Ibid.*, iii, Nos. 172, 173.

93. *T.A.*, iv, 155–6.

94. S.R.O., A.D.C., xxi, f.196.

95. Fraser, *Douglas*, iii, Nos. 174, 176.

96. *Ibid.*, iii, Nos. 175, 177.

97. Nicholson, 'Feudal Developments', 17–18.

98. *A.P.S.*, ii, 250 c.7.

99. *Ibid.*, c.6.

100. Nicholson, *Scotland: The Later Middle Ages*, 569; *A.D.C.P.*, lix.

101. Pitcairn, *Criminal Trials*, i, 16, 17, 18, 29–30, 40, 71; *R.S.S.*, i, Nos. 121, 571, 1280, 1740.

102. *Ibid.*, i, Nos. 1955, 1956, 1957, 1958, 1961, 1962, 2100, 2189, 2330.

103. Lesley, *History*, 73.

104. Buchanan, *History*, ii, 241.

105. Madden, op.cit., *S.H.R.*, lv (1976), 194; *T.A.*, i, ii, iii, iv, passim.
It should be emphasised that totals of overall royal income are imprecise, because

the Exchequer and Treasurer's accounts are incomplete, because the exact value of ecclesiastical properties is unknown, and because royal income may have been considerably augmented by sums which were diverted away from royal officials to the king's private use.

7

The Demise of Parliament

On Monday 29 June 1488, five days after the coronation of James IV at Scone, James Monynet completed the early chapters of a 400-folio manuscript of ancient Scots laws and statutes.[1] Amongst the miscellanea which it contains is a short section on coronation oaths, including that allegedly made by James II, not at his coronation in 1437 but eight years later, in the summer following his fourteenth birthday. The king was made to swear that he would neither interfere with the statutes of the realm nor do anything 'tuoching the comon profitt of the realme bot (without) consent of the three estaitts.'[2] In June 1488 this part of Monynet's manuscript was — probably coincidentally — highly appropriate to the contemporary Scottish political scene, for the circumstances in 1445 and 1488 were remarkably similar. In each case a civil war had brought to power a group of magnates who sought both to legitimise their rule and impose their wills on an adolescent king. If the royal oath to govern only with the consent of the estates was indeed made by James IV at his coronation, then it is one of the ironies of the reign that the magnates who heard him take the oath were, as we have seen, initially reluctant to call a parliament at all, while the king himself would finally settle the matter by dispensing with parliaments altogether.

A glance at the table of James IV parliaments on page 171 reveals at once that although ten meetings of the estates occur between 1488 and 1496, there are only three during the remaining seventeen years of the reign. Furthermore, sederunt lists indicate a substantial dropping off in numbers attending parliaments as the reign progresses, from eighty-four in 1488 to less than half that number in 1506, the last recorded parliamentary sederunts for the reign. Again, during individual sessions of parliament, numbers might drop after the first few days; there is evidence of this occurring in 1504 and 1506. Thus the overall pattern of meetings of the estates in parliament throughout this reign is of annual and initially well-attended sessions during the royal minority, followed by long gaps — in one case of eight years, 1496–1504 — and diminishing attendances during the king's personal rule. Why should this be so?

The simple answer might be that no explanation is really necessary, that James IV was merely following the lead of the more powerful contemporary English and European monarchies in playing down the role of representative assemblies and placing heavy reliance on conciliar government. In England, the Yorkist Edward IV's mere six parliaments in twenty-three years were parallelled

THE PARLIAMENTS OF JAMES IV

All held at Edinburgh

			Lords of Articles	*Total Present*	
1.	1488	October 6–17 thereafter powers delegated to a commission numbering 61.	28	84	
2.	1489	January 14–26	/	/	
3.	1489	June 26 - July 4 [18 Sept: Royal council at Stirling to restore Crawford's dukedom.]	/	/	
4.	1490	February 3–15	22	66	
5.	1491	April 28–May 18 thereafter powers delegated to a commission of 33 - continuation to 2 August 1491 - but no parliament recorded then.	/	52	
6.	1492	February 6–20	23	44	
7.	1492	May 7	/	/	
8.	1493	May 8-31, June 26	/	/	
9.	1494	November 27	/	/	
10.	1496	June 13–30	/	/	
11.	1504	March 11–20 with continuations for judicial purposes to 4 June, 7 June, 8 June, 3 Oct., 31 Dec. 1504; 7 Jan., 3 July, 12 July, 4 Nov., 18 Nov., 20 Nov., 21 Nov., 23 Nov., 26 Nov., 1 Dec., 15 Dec. 1505; 20 Jan. 1506.	19	61 (approx) 38	(13Mar) (18 Mar)
12.	1506	February 3–16	/	41 (3 Feb.) 24 (16 Feb.)	
13.	1509	May 8	/	/	

by the Tudor Henry VII's seven in twenty-four; indeed, at his last parliament in 1504, five years before the end of the reign, King Henry expressly stated that he was not inclined to summon another unless there were 'great and necessary and urgent causes' for it.[3] And in France by the late fifteenth century the Estates-General had so convinced the Crown that it was virtually useless as a source of taxation that it was not summoned at all for seventy-six years after 1484.[4] However, these examples, interesting though they are in illustrating a European trend of which James IV was no doubt aware, cannot provide an adequate explanation for the dearth of Scottish parliaments in the latter years of his reign — for with very few gaps, meetings of the three estates in parliament had become an annual event in late fifteenth-century Scottish politics, and in the case of James III, two parliaments had been held in each of the years 1479 and 1482, while no less than four had met in the sixteen months between March 1482 and July 1483. This is not, of course, to exaggerate the importance of the Scottish parliament; it was and remained an occasional body summoned when required by the king, and the table shows that parliamentary sessions lasted a fortnight, sometimes three weeks, often much less. But it is nonetheless true that in the personal rule of James IV, the well-established mould was broken, that the practice of summoning the estates to parliament at some time virtually every year was abandoned.

Some explanations have already been advanced to make sense of this. In 1980, Dr Irene O'Brien drew attention to the estates' function as providers of extraordinary revenue for the Crown.[5] As we have seen, five of the ten parliaments between 1488 and 1496 can be shown to have granted taxes ranging from £300 to £5,000 for embassies to France, Denmark, and elsewhere, the primary objective in each case being to look for a bride for the king; and although the printed parliamentary record does not reveal this, it is likely that the estates were responsible for voting the tax for the expeditions to the Isles in 1494–5, and perhaps also the 'tax of spears' for James's English wars of 1496–7.[6] With the ending of these wars, an English treaty and the choice of an English bride by King James it could be argued that taxation was no longer necessary or appropriate, and that parliament, having thereby lost one of its principal functions, ceased to be summoned with anything like the same regularity by the king.

This view is attractive in the sense that it neatly fits the facts so far as the surviving parliamentary record is concerned; for none of the later parliaments — 1504, 1506, and 1509 — appears to have voted taxes, not even the parliament of March 1504, when the main business was responding to a major rebellion in the Isles, for which a contribution from the estates might have been expected. However, parliament was clearly not the only body which might authorise taxation, for as we have seen taxes were raised without its authority — for the expenses of an embassy to England in 1501,[7] for the Danish expedition of 1502,[8] and for the war with England in 1512–13.[9] During this reign, therefore, we must look further than parliament's fiscal role to explain the reasons for its demise.

Probably the date at which parliaments ceased to be held on a regular basis — 1496 — is significant, for it more or less coincides with the emergence of James IV from his minority and his assumption of a leading role in government. Up to that point, parliament's principal functions — apart from its grudging assent to ambassadorial taxes — had been political and judicial, consisting of efforts to establish a regime acceptable to the majority within the political community, at the same time seeking to condemn that regime's enemies, as publicly as possible, before judicial assizes of the estates. As we have seen,[10] the birth pangs of the minority government had been difficult. The parliament of October 1488 had been one of victors seeking to punish the vanquished, that of January 1489 a continuation of the same process. In June-July 1489 parliament met to concert measures against those who had rebelled as a result of the government's earlier intransigence, and in February 1490 met again to annul the forfeitures which it had recently proclaimed. In February 1492 the related issues of James III's death and his hoard troubled the estates, and in June 1493 parliament was used by a new group in power to forfeit the lordship of the Isles and to issue a premature act of revocation on behalf of the twenty-year-old king. The various embassies sanctioned and grudgingly paid for by the estates had failed in their principal task of finding a bride for James IV; the early forfeitures of Ramsay, Ross, Lennox, Matthew Stewart, and Lyle had been rescinded; the forfeiture of the lordship had intensified, rather than solved, the problems of the Isles; and the unseemly bickering of the two archbishops, Scheves and Blacader, condemned by parliament in June 1493, continued unabated throughout the minority years.[11] When he took control of government in 1495, therefore, James IV's experience of parliaments — his own and the last two summoned by his father — had hardly been happy. Parliaments in the late 1480s and early 'nineties were either forums for the expression of political dissent, or unrepresentative bodies struggling none too successfully to cope with violent responses to the policies they themselves had initiated. Indeed, in the decade before 1495, successive Scottish parliaments had presided over, sanctioned, or helped to stimulate, one regicide, three major rebellions — one of them unresolved — six failed embassies and a coup d'état. It was not a good model for future government.

The king learned his lesson quickly. In the year of his takeover, 1495, he summoned no parliaments at all; pressing affairs of state, such as the decision to receive Perkin Warbeck in the autumn of that year, appear to have been the business of greatly enlarged sessions of the royal council, of which there were at least four between late August and early November.[12] Before King James abandoned the practice of calling frequent parliaments, however, there was one meeting of the estates at Edinburgh on 13 June 1496.

If we were to judge the 1496 parliament solely by the surviving record,[13] we would certainly receive a false impression of the main items of business which it had been summoned to discuss. A parliament meeting in mid-June must have been summoned at the beginning of May — that is, at the time that Henry VII, recognising that an invasion of northern England by the Scots on behalf of Perkin Warbeck was imminent, commissioned Bishop Fox of Durham to treat for peace with James IV on the basis of the Scottish king's marriage to Henry's daughter Margaret.[14] It is inconceivable that the impending invasion was not one of parliament's main concerns when it met in June, together perhaps with the English king's marriage proposals; indeed, it is likely that there was a debate on the extent of Scottish military support to be given to Warbeck, perhaps even on whether the host should assist him at all.[15] The Scots were after all planning the first major invasion of England since the summer of 1463, when Mary of Gueldres and Bishop Kennedy had made an abortive raid on Norham castle with the young James III.

None of these concerns is apparent in the fragmentary record of the June parliament of 1496, which is not even preceded by a list of names of those who attended. However, on a fly-leaf at the beginning of a volume of acts of the Lords of Council in which the first recorded business occurred on 14 June 1496 — the day after parliament assembled — the clerk has inscribed some fifty names; and this looks very much like the sederunt list for the entire parliament. Present are both archbishops, three bishops including Elphinstone of Aberdeen, thirteen other members of the clergy, the Duke of Ross, eight earls, nine lords of parliament, and fourteen other laymen. Parliament sat from 13 to 30 June, making it one of the longest sessions of the entire reign.[16]

It is doubtful if many of those present — most of the 'political' earls, the warring archbishops, the heir to the throne and Andrew Stewart, bishop of Moray, who was charged with the task of ensuring Ross's defection from the host — had much interest in the recorded legislation of the 1496 parliament. Only six 'articles' survive, including the traditional first clause guaranteeing the liberty and defence of the church, another repeating earlier legislation forbidding the sending of petitions for church benefices to Rome without royal licence, yet another ordering the appointment of a competent Master of the Mint, and an unconvincing effort to fix prices for 'all maner of stuffe' made by craftsmen and workmen.[17] But by far the most famous enactment of this parliament is the so-called 'education act', which in the five centuries since James IV's time has acquired almost legendary status as the bedrock on which Scottish state education was eventually to be based. In fact, the act was intended to have very limited application, and was probably a failure. It required the eldest sons of barons and freeholders 'that ar of substance' to be sent to grammar school from the age of eight or nine, and to remain there until they acquired a basic education and had 'perfite latyne'. They would then spend three years 'at the sculis of art and Jure' so that they might acquire knowledge and understanding of the law. As a result, those of them who became sheriffs or local judges would be properly equipped to do their jobs, the desired end of all this being 'that the pure pepill suld haue na neid to seik our souerane lordis principale auditoris for ilk small Iniure'. In short, the purpose of the act was to relieve royal judicial committees of the growing pressure of appeals from the localities. A fine of £20, payable to the king, was laid down as the penalty for those who ignored the act.[18]

The 'education act' has traditionally been ascribed to Bishop Elphinstone — probably rightly, for he was present in parliament in 1496, and his concern to provide education in general, and knowledge of the law in particular, for those in the remoter regions of the kingdom had only recently found practical expression in the bishop's foundation of the university of Aberdeen. But the 1496 act, like so many other late medieval parliamentary statutes and articles, seems in the short term to have been no more than an expression of pious hopes. It is true that no evidence survives of the £20 fine being imposed, and this in a period when the king's financial officers were increasingly concerned to make money from casualties might suggest that barons and freeholders rushed to comply with the act. But likewise there is no evidence that the principal object of the act — the improvement of local justice to reduce continual appeals beyond it to the council — was rapidly achieved; in fact, eight years later, the first parliamentary statute of 1504 after the traditional defence of 'halykirk' recalled that there had been so much confusion to summonses to the Lords of Session that there had been no time for session judges to get through the cases referred to them, 'And thirthrou pure folkis hes bene delayit and deferrit fra yeir to yeir throw the quhilk thay wantit Justice'. The solution in 1504 was simply to increase the workload of the Lords of Council; parliament laid down that there was to be a council chosen by the king sitting continually — which meant daily — in Edinburgh 'or quhare the king makis residence or quhare It plesis him' to decide 'all maner of summondis' in civil matters.[19] Education act or no education act, the pressure on the royal, rather than franchisal, courts continued to increase.

From the end of June 1496 to 11 March 1504 — close on eight years — James IV called no parliaments. He had discovered more effective ways of raising revenue, and he probably disliked meetings of the estates as providing a forum for dissent. Why then did he summon any further parliaments? One answer is that the administration of civil and criminal justice needed improvement, and there is ample testimony to the efforts of James's professional civil servants to deal with the law's delays, the inter-relation between franchisal and central courts, and — as we have seen — pressure on the session judges, in the legislation of the parliament of March 1504.[20] This legislation certainly demonstrates that, given a parliamentary session, royal councillors with formal qualifications in law would take advantage of it to conduct what Dr Macfarlane rightly calls 'a serious attempt to reappraise the whole area of civil and criminal law.'[21] But what happened once parliament was in session does not necessarily explain why the king summoned it in the first place; and it is surely significant that the last three parliaments of the reign — 1504, 1506, and 1509 — had as their principal political business the settling of the widespread risings in the Isles which James's personal policy had helped to provoke. Would James have summoned parliament at all in 1504, one wonders, if he had not required sentences of forfeiture against Highland rebels which only a parliament could pronounce?

For the truth was that King James had not succeeded in the Highlands and Islands. Certainly he had inherited a problem from the minority government which in 1493 had sought to solve its difficulties by forfeiting the lordship and maintaining the former Lord of the Isles as a court pensioner. As we have seen, the success or failure of such a policy depended on the government obtaining sufficient support from influential chiefs within the former lordship to make Crown control a reality — and to ensure the payment of royal rents from the king's new territories. A start had been made with a Crown assessment of Islay and Tiree in 1495–6,[22] no doubt a follow-up to James IV's voyage to Mingary in May 1495. But the real problem from the government's point of view was that of establishing law and order over a vast area in which the Crown could not possibly exercise direct control. The king had begun well by attempting to appease the major chiefs, not only the obsequious MacIan of Ardnamurchan but also MacLean of Duart, Alan, captain of Clan Cameron, and MacNeill of Barra.[23] However, James's early work in the Isles was rapidly undone by his councillors. On the afternoon of 3 October 1496, shortly after the return of the host from the raid of Ellem, the Lords of Council ordered that any royal summons issued against any person dwelling in the Lordship of the Isles before 26 April 1497 was to be executed by the chief of his clan; any failure on the chief's part to do so would lead to proceedings being taken against him as though he were the defendant in the case.[24]

The perpetrators of this act were six in number, including Duncan Forester, George, abbot of Dunfermline, Henry, abbot of Cambuskenneth, and James, abbot of Scone. By far the most influential of the six, however, were Elphinstone, the Privy Seal, and Archibald, earl of Argyll, Master of the Household. Between them they had abandoned appeasement and turned to a policy of coercion. Arguably they had also made the position of chiefs who were as yet uncommitted difficult if not impossible with their clansmen, undermining their authority in an effort to drive them along the road towards acceptance of Crown control of the lordship. Probably the main instigator of this insensitive act was Argyll; on the same afternoon he had it set on record that five of the principal chiefs — MacLean, MacIan, MacRuari of Moidart, Ewen Allanson, and Donald Angus, son of Keppoch — had promised to refrain from attacking each other under a penalty of five hundred pounds.[25]

Argyll's hawkish attitude towards the chieftains of the Isles was reinforced by personal intervention on the part of the king. This was delayed until 1498, almost certainly because war with England occupied King James for most of the 1497 campaigning season; but with characteristic energy, in March, May and June 1498 the king sailed to Kintyre, paying at least two, and probably three, visits to his new castle at Loch Kilkerran. The first two of these were brief — a week in March, visiting Arran and Tarbert castle en route, and a short sea voyage from Dumbarton to Kintyre in May — but on his third visit to Kintyre, King James spent no less than six weeks at Kilkerran, arriving there some time before 28 June and departing after 5 August.[26] These three voyages to Kintyre reveal the extent of James IV's personal interest in the Isles. He would travel no further than Kilkerran and Tarbert, his fortresses at either end of Kilbrannan Sound on the Clyde; he would use his act of revocation, significantly made at Duchal in Renfrewshire on 16 March 1498 at the end of his first visit to Kintyre, to coerce the Highland chiefs into submission; he would spend a considerable time — the third visit — at Kilkerran receiving submissions and making grants and confirmations of lordship lands and offices; and he would then regard his problems in the Highlands and Islands as settled.

He was wrong. In fact the year 1498, far from seeing an end to troubles in the Isles, witnessed the beginnings of fierce resistance to Crown policies from end to end of the lordship. The news of the royal act of revocation, swiftly borne to the Isles from Stirling on 20 March — only four days after it was made — by a servant of Alexander, Lord Gordon, the future earl of Huntly,[27] must have upset the king's supporters, especially MacLean of Duart, Alan, captain of Clan Cameron, and MacNeill of Barra, all of them men who had only three years before been confirmed in their lands and offices within the lordship. Now they were being informed, by the same adult king, that their charters were invalid and would have to be renewed at a price. Other chiefs must simply have resented direct Crown intervention in the affairs of the lordship, undermining their authority with extravagant demands for compositions for new charters, backed by threats to convert them to mere tenants-at-will of the king if they failed to pay up.

Not surprisingly, the response from the Island chiefs to the new royal demands was unimpressive. James IV sat in his new castle of Kilkerran in Campbeltown Loch for much of the summer, together with Elphinstone, Argyll, Chancellor Huntly, Bothwell, Hume, Drummond, and the Treasurer, Robert Lundy of Balgonie, waiting to receive the galleys bearing the lordship chiefs to submit and pay their compositions.[28] The results were disappointing in the extreme. Only Torquil MacLeod of Lewis, Argyll's brother-in-law, Ranald MacLean of Uist and Eigg, and Angus MacRanald of Eigg, Arisaig and Morar were granted charters of confirmation while the king was at Kilkerran.[29] Furthermore, on 28 June, Torquil MacLeod of Lewis was granted the same office in Skye — the bailiary of Trotternish — as had been conferred on Alexander MacLeod of Dunvegan at Stirling only a fortnight before, thus guaranteeing continued disorder in the Outer Hebrides.[30] The Trotternish grant to Torquil MacLeod may well have been a cynical device, inspired by Argyll, to put a strong man in charge of the royal bailiary in northern Skye, ousting MacLeod of Dunvegan, whose lands lay nearby, in the process. Certainly the grants of the bailiary to two separate individuals within a fortnight suggest that the king was not much interested in the details of what was being done in his name in the Isles. Shortly after 5 August 1498, he sailed away from Kilkerran. He would not visit Kintyre, far less the Isles, again during the remaining fifteen years of the reign; and the direction of royal business in the west would be delegated to others.

The most obvious beneficiary of the king's declining interest was Archibald, earl of Argyll; indeed Argyll had probably counselled the king in 1496 to abandon appeasement and to take a hard line in the lordship. The first signs of this policy being carried beyond threats are apparent in the summer of 1499. According to the contemporary — and normally highly accurate — Ulster annalist, a

month before Lammas 'a great deed was done. . .by the king of Scotland';
John MacDonald of Islay, described as 'king of Insi-Gall' (the Hebrides), and
his sons John Cattanach, Ragnall the Red, and Domnall the Freckled were all
hanged on one gallows.[31] Their execution in July 1499, which may rapidly have
followed their capture at Finlaggan by MacIan of Ardnamurchan, may have been
inspired by fear in government circles that they could provide a focus for
rebellions with the aim of restoring a MacDonald lordship; hanging them all also
served as a warning to Islesmen who continued to defy the Crown in the west
that even the heads of the MacDonald kingroup were not immune from the full
rigour of royal Stewart justice. Little more than a month after the hangings, Argyll
was given custody of Tarbert castle, together with the bailiary of all royal lands
in Knapdale; on 22 April 1500 he received a royal commission with five others,
including his kinsmen Lords Montgomery, Drummond, and Duncan Campbell
of Glenorchy, to 'set' all royal lands within the lordship for three years, with the
exception of Kintyre and Islay; and this commission was simply the prelude to
Argyll's appointment, three days later, as royal lieutenant within the old lordship,
again excepting Kintyre and Islay, with the power to make statutes in the king's
name, to seize and execute rebels, to lay siege to their castles and homes, and
where necessary to grant remissions. The appointment was for three years, and
the message was clear: within that time, Argyll was expected to use the royal
powers delegated to him to bring order to the lordship of the Isles.[32]

He failed spectacularly. Perhaps the task was impossible in any case,
for what he had been given was a royal commission which, in the eyes of
many within the lordship, simply legalised further Campbell aggrandisement.
It was to be expected that Argyll, as by far the most powerful single magnate
in the west, would to some extent use his commission to feather his own, and
his kinsmens', nests; but MacLean of Duart, MacNeill of Barra, and above all
the unfortunate MacLeod of Dunvegan, had every reason to resist royal policies
which not only failed to reward, but actively punished, their loyalty, and which
had been subject to bewildering changes since 1493. The king may have had
his doubts about Argyll's ability, or willingness, to exercise his commission
effectively, and solved his immediate problem in this respect by issuing a
further commission of lieutenancy to Alexander, Lord Gordon, who became
third earl of Huntly when his father, the Chancellor, died early in June 1501. On
11 August 1501, about two months after Alexander's succession to the earldom,
he received royal authorisation to receive all 'bandis and oblissingis' of magnates
north of the Mounth, if necessary by force; he was also to collect royal rents
in Lochaber and to use force against anyone who resisted payment.[33] Huntly's
commission, unlike that of Argyll, was not subject to a time limit; his remit
— anywhere north of the Mounth — was geographically vast and imprecise,
including large areas of the former lordship of the Isles and the earldom of Ross;
and his opportunities for family aggrandisement were clearly greater than those
of Argyll. Nor can there be much doubt that Alexander, third earl of Huntly,
was hungry for power in the north and west. He had spent the early 'nineties
fighting for royal acceptance following his committed support for James III in

1488 and his masterminding of the rebellion of 1489. When his father George had replaced Angus as Chancellor in 1497, Alexander's opportunity had come; the necessary long absences of Earl George in royal service left him in charge of the Gordon family lands in the north-east; and his close involvement with James IV's 1498 act of revocation and its circulation to the Islands chiefs[34] underlines his desire to increase the already extensive Gordon empire by expansion into the west. This could most effectively be achieved through service to the Crown in Lochaber, in Wester Ross, even in the Outer Hebrides; and in the five years following his commission, it was Huntly rather than Argyll who would take the lead in bringing order to the principal trouble-spots in the Highlands and Islands.

Argyll was further embarrassed by the attitude of his brother-in-law Torquil MacLeod of Lewis, who was soon to emerge as the most committed opponent of Crown policies in the lordship of the Isles. His motives are not clear, for as recently as 1498 he had been given, or received a royal confirmation of, the office of bailie of Trotternish in Skye. He had however used this office as a sinecure, pocketing the 100 marks acquired annually from the royal rents of the bailiary;[35] and he probably feared and resented the proposed royal intervention in the Isles which following Huntly's lieutenancy seemed likely to be pursued more vigorously than by his kinsman Argyll. Effective resistance to the Crown in the Isles required a cause, and Torquil MacLeod found it in the restoration of the lordship. Probably some time in the autumn of 1501, within a few months of Huntly's commission, the MacIans of Glencoe released from captivity in Argyll's castle of Inchconnell on Loch Awe, Donald Dubh, grandson of John MacDonald, the forfeited Lord of the Isles, an eleven-year-old youth whom many in the west believed to be the rightful heir to the lordship.[36] It is not clear whether he was given up by the keeper of Inchconnell, escaped on his own, or found himself at the centre of a successful rescue attempt, but what is certain is that by October 1501 he had been transferred to the keeping of Torquil MacLeod.[37]

The government was quick to read the danger signs, and royal messengers were sent to Torquil demanding that he hand over Donald Dubh, described as 'Angus of the Ylis bastard son' to the king in person at Inverness during the north-eastern ayre in late autumn 1501.[38] James IV duly arrived at Inverness by 4 November, and stayed in the burgh for a fortnight,[39] but neither Torquil MacLeod nor his new protégé appeared. Further summonses were issued, and when these were ignored the king determined to use the courts to outlaw Torquil. On 15 March 1502 the Lords of Council — including Torquil's brother-in-law Argyll — ordained that MacLeod was guilty of rebellion and was to be put to the horn, while his goods were to be escheated to the Crown. To put real pressure on Torquil, on the same day the Lords brought an action against him, at James IV's instance, for wrongous withholding of the mails, profits, and duties of Trotternish in Skye for no less than nine years — that is, since the forfeiture of the lordship in 1493 — and required payment of 900 marks.[40] When this demand alike produced no results, the Lords of Council met once more, on 13 August 1502, declared that Torquil MacLeod had failed to show any title to his lands in Lewis, Skye, and Wester Ross, and ordained that Torquil's estates now belonged to the king.[41] Argyll, having sat on the Lords of Council in March, was not present to condemn his brother-in-law in August. His reaction to the release of Donald Dubh was probably one of frustrated fury. He had been challenged successfully within his own territories; he had been made to look foolish and unreliable to other members of the royal council; and it was becoming clear that if he could not control his own kinsmen, then James IV would employ someone else who could.

The magnate already cast in the role was Huntly. On 21 March 1502, only six days after Torquil MacLeod had been declared a rebel by the Lords of Council, Huntly, together with Lord Fraser of Lovat and William Munro of Fowlis, was given a commission authorising him to let the royal lands in Lochaber and Mamore for a period of five years to reliable men who would both enhance the value of the lands and also expel from them all 'trespassouris and brokin men'; in addition Huntly and his two allies were empowered to let Torquil's lands of Assynt and Cogeach in Wester Ross to 'gud trew men, being afald in our souerance lordis opinion', an indication that the Gordon earl was already in the field and had much support from those seeking to acquire Torquil's estates.[42] Nor were Torquil MacLeod and Donald Dubh the only leaders of resistance; in March 1502 Kenneth Mackenzie of Kintail and Farquhar MacIntosh, captain of Clan Chattan, escaped from prison in Edinburgh castle, where both had been imprisoned since about the time of the Duchal revocation of 1498.[43] The former had been an opponent of MacDonald control of Ross, and had offered similar opposition to the Crown's efforts to secure allegiance from the earldom; the latter's father Duncan had taken part in Alexander MacDonald of Lochalsh's violent efforts to recover Ross in 1491, while Farquhar MacIntosh himself had laid hold on the lands of Durris in Invernessshire, claimed by the Dunbars of Westfield with the backing of their powerful ally Chancellor Huntly.[44] The danger to Crown interests in Ross — and to effective control of the royal estates in Moray — presented by these two men had been removed by their imprisonment, probably following the January 1498 ayre at Inverness, at which the king himself was present.[45] Their escape in March 1502 was a matter of grave concern to James IV; they were pursued, Mackenzie seems to have been killed, possibly in the Torwood in Stirlingshire, and MacIntosh was recaptured early in April by Quentin Focart and William Spicehouse, both of whom were rewarded by the king.[46] King James's relief at MacIntosh's capture is clearly indicated by his despatch of a messenger to Moray, bearing the news to Janet Kennedy, his mistress and mother of the two-year-old James Stewart, earl of Moray, at Darnaway castle.[47] He had reason to be relieved, for the royal estates in Moray were vulnerable to attack from the west, given the general state of unrest in the lordship of the Isles and Ross and the kind of leadership which MacKenzie and MacIntosh might have provided.

By 1503, however, there was clearly open warfare in many parts of the

1. James IV, attended by St James, from the Book of Hours of James IV and Margaret Tudor. A contemporary likeness of the King and probably the most accurate representation of his features. Original in the Austrian National Library.

2. James IV (late sixteenth century, anonymous). (*Reproduced by permission of the Scottish National Portrait Gallery*)

3. James IV (Jacques le Boucq, 1559). A less flattering image of the Renaissance prince than that portrayed by Mytens (see cover).

4. Dirge for a King of Scots. One of the nineteen plates in the Book of Hours of James IV and Margaret Tudor, which was probably commissioned at the time of the royal wedding of 1503. The royal dirge may be intended to represent the funeral obsequies of James III. If so, this is a striking illustration of James IV's continuing penance for his part in his father's death. It is a stylised representation, bearing a close resemblance to a similar dirge in the contemporary Grimani Breviary, with the added trappings of the Scottish saltire, lion and unicorn flags.

(18)
James the fourt
Began his Rayne
1489 He maried
Margaret eldest dochter
of Henry the sebinth

5. James IV and Margaret Tudor. One of the seventeen royal portraits in the Seton Armorial (1591). The artist has managed to make a feature of the king's penitential iron belt, worn over James's tunic rather than next to his skin.

6. Ladykirk church, Berwickshire, on the north bank of the Tweed and within sight of Norham castle, besieged by James IV in 1497 and 1513. Construction of Ladykirk may have begun shortly after the royal host's encampment at Upsettlington in August 1497. (*Crown copyright: Royal Commission on the Ancient and Historical Monuments of Scotland*)

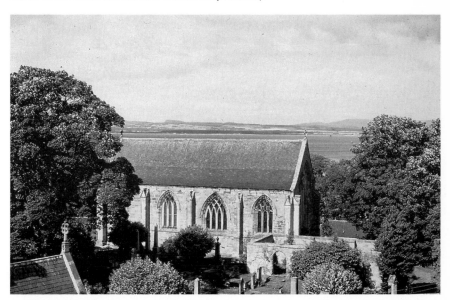

7. The collegiate church of St. Duthac at Tain, Easter Ross, which the King visited annually on pilgrimage from the 1490s to the very end of the reign. (*Crown copyright: Royal Commission on the Ancient and Historical Monuments of Scotland*)

8. The gatehouse, Whithorn cathedral priory. The shrine of St. Ninian at Whithorn was the objective of annual pilgrimages by James IV, including his remarkable journey on foot from Edinburgh in March 1507. (*Crown copyright: Royal Commission on the Ancient and Historical Monuments of Scotland*)

9. Tantallon castle, East Lothian, stronghold of the great political maverick of the period, Archibald Douglas, 5th earl of Angus. Though besieged in Tantallon by royal forces in the autumn of 1491, the earl made a spectacular comeback to become Chancellor a few months later.

10. Mingary castle, Ardnamurchan, stronghold of James IV's most ruthless supporter within the lordship of the Isles, John MacIan of Ardnamurchan. The King visited Mingary on 18 May 1495, at the outset of the personal rule.

11. The Usurper. Henry VII of England, by Pietro Torrigiano.

12. The Pretender. Perkin Warbeck, by Jacques le Boucq (1559).

13. Model of James IV's *Great Michael*, launched at Newhaven in October 1511, and for a short time the largest warship in Northern Europe.

14. Mons Meg, the heaviest piece of artillery in the British Isles until the eighteenth century. Originally a gift from Philip, duke of Burgundy, to James II in 1457, the gun was used by James IV during the rebellion of 1489, and again at the siege of Norham in 1497. (*Crown copyright: Royal Commission on the Ancient and Historical Monuments of Scotland*)

15. William Elphinstone (*c.* 1431–1514), bishop of Aberdeen, briefly Chancellor for James III (1488), and Keeper of the Privy Seal for 22 years (1492–1514). The outstanding clerical statesman of the reign, Elphinstone was a strong supporter of James IV's 'liturgical nationalism'.

16. The Ally. Louis XII of France, by Jean Perréal. The French king's practical assistance, from 1502 onwards, in the construction of the Scottish navy provided a strong inducement to James IV to renew the Franco-Scottish alliance in 1512.

17. The Enemy. Henry VIII of England, James IV's brother-in-law, in early manhood. Henry's obsessive desire to renew the Hundred Years' War made him blind to the realities of European politics.

18. The Target. Norham castle, Northumberland, on the south bank of the river Tweed. Isolated in 1496 and besieged in 1497, this great fortress was taken by storm by the Scots at the end of August 1513, only twelve days before the battle of Flodden. (*Crown copyright: Royal Commission on the Ancient and Historical Monuments of Scotland*)

Highlands and Islands, much of it provoked by the very wide powers given to Alexander, third earl of Huntly, by the king. Huntly needed no second bidding to raise a royal army in Lochaber to attack all those who resisted payment of the king's rents 'without ony cryme to be imputt to him thairfor'; and it is likely that he undertook a wholesale removal of sitting tenants from Lochaber in 1501–2, replacing them with his own supporters, the 'gud trew men, being afald (afield) in our souerane lordis opinion', men who were not only loyal but would pay rents to the Crown.[48] This intrusion of Huntly with armed support into the Highland west provoked a furious response; using Donald Dubh as a figurehead — 'bastard sone to angus of the Ilis bastard', as the royal government described him — Torquil MacLeod and Lachlan MacLean of Duart swept into Huntly's lordship of Badenoch at Christmas 1503, burning and looting.[49] In the south-west, the royal lands on Bute were assailed by Islesmen between 1502 and 1504, and so much damage was done that royal tenants on Bute were excused payment of rents for three years;[50] Archibald, earl of Angus, settling into his long confinement in Rothesay castle, must have viewed the flames rising from the nearby royal estates with mixed feelings. But the message was clear; neither the renovated fortress at Tarbert, in Argyll's keeping, nor the new castle of Kilkerran, had so far proved of much value in protecting the Stewart lands in the Clyde estuary.

It was the events of 1503 which made necessary the summoning of parliament early in the following year. Not only had royal lands been attacked, royal lieutenants defied, and the loyalty of those in the Highlands who wished to support the Crown put to a severe test, but also the freeing of Donald Dubh from Inchconnell in 1501, an obvious threat at the time, became a much greater menace in 1503. For in January of that year John MacDonald, the forfeited Lord of the Isles, died at Dundee. His last years had been spent as a court pensioner, a pathetic end for the man who in 1449 had inherited a huge semi-independent seaborne empire in the west. In September and October 1502 preparations had been made for him to travel to the Isles and to Lochaber,[51] presumably as part of a Crown propaganda exercise in areas where the king was faced with open rebellion. Producing John of the Isles, Donald Dubh's grandfather, in the Highlands might well help to nip unrest in the bud. Probably John MacDonald never made the journey; James IV was present at Dundee when he fell ill, and by 5 February payments were remitted from the Treasury for his 'furthbringing and berying.'[52] His death not only deprived the king of a useful propaganda weapon, but also enabled those in rebellion to claim with more conviction that they sought a restoration of the lordship with Donald Dubh as the rightful heir of his grandfather. Hence the government's repeated claim that Donald was the illegitimate son of an illegitimate son; but their efforts to discredit him appear to have had little effect in the Isles.

On 18 December 1503, messengers were despatched to various parts of the country bearing summonses to parliament; and only a week later the devastation of Badenoch by Torquil MacLeod and Maclean of Duart added urgency to the situation.[53] In the Isles, in the Firth of Clyde, in Wester Ross,

Lochaber, and Badenoch, even in Perthshire, James IV was now being openly defied by a disquieting number of his subjects. In none of these areas had he totally lost support, but his policy of granting commissions of lieutenancy to Argyll and Huntly had clearly not been a success, especially in the case of the former. The king now needed moral — not financial — support from the three estates to back up his Highland policies; above all he had to have recourse to one judicial function unique to parliament, that of pronouncing sentence of forfeiture on rebels.

Parliament met at Edinburgh on 11 March 1504, but business was slow to get underway. Only on the third day, 13 March, was a sederunt list recorded — a total of fifty-one excluding the burgess estate, who numbered about ten — and the committees of the articles and for 'discussing of Dumyss' elected. The last day of the parliament was 20 March, and by the 18th a second sederunt list reveals that the total attendance had already dropped to thirty-eight. This was therefore a parliament which met for only a week, with enthusiasm for its business visibly declining as the days passed. Much of the legislation, especially that affecting the administration of civil justice, had presumably been drafted a long time in advance by James's long-suffering civil servants, who must occasionally have wondered whether the king would ever call a parliament again; only advance preparation explains the estates' ability to get through no less than fifty-one statutes and articles by the fifth day of the parliament, 15 March.[54]

It was political, rather than administrative, business which first concerned the king. On 13 March — that is at the earliest possible opportunity — James IV issued yet another act of revocation. With consent of the estates, he revoked all donations, gifts, acts, statutes of parliament or general council 'and all vthir thingis done be him in tymis bigane othir hurtand his saule, his crovne or halikirk' — an enormous brief, open to any interpretation the king cared to place on it. Furthermore, the act went on to state that all donations, gifts, acts, statutes and the like revoked in this way were to be 'put furtht of the bukis and writingis'.[55] This probably explains why the original books of parliament contain no entries for the parliaments of 1493 and 1496, fragments of which had to be gathered together later for the first printed edition of parliamentary acts in 1566. The acts of these parliaments were missing because James IV ordered their removal from the original records; he had no wish to be saddled forever with the Angus government's decisions with regard to the Isles in 1493, or indeed some of his own later schemes, which had been less than happy. For the king, especially with regard to his policies in the Highlands and Isles, 1504 was intended to be a new beginning; and the act of revocation made it possible for him to confirm the cancellation of grants made to former supporters now in rebellion, of whom MacLean of Duart and MacLeod of Lewis were the prime examples.

After a perfunctory nod in the direction of the freedom of 'halykirk', parliament turned on the same 13 March to the most urgent business of the week, namely, the arrangements for restoring royal authority in the Highlands and Islands. The original parliamentary record is incomplete at this point; but from what remains it is clear that the leading role in the north was given to

Huntly. The Gordon earl undertook to lay siege to the castles of Strome and Eilean Donan in Wester Ross, and to be responsible for garrisoning both when they were taken; James IV would assist him with a ship and artillery. Together with Crawford, the Earl Marischal, and Lord Lovat, Huntly appears to have been entrusted with the overall command of the royal forces sent to subdue 'the northt ylis'; tantalisingly, the tasks assigned to Argyll at the same time have not been preserved.[56]

It remained to identify the guilty parties. On the afternoon of the following day, 14 March, James Henryson, the royal advocate, presented to parliament summonses of treason against John MacLean of Lochbuie, Lachlan MacLean of Duart, and Ewen Alanson.[57] Some debate must have followed, for the publication of the summonses was delayed for five days; and on 19 March only MacLean of Duart and Ewen Alanson were summoned 'for the vsurpin of our souerane lordis autorite and othir tressonabill crimez'.[58] Remarkably, those who were to be entrusted with the harrying of the rebels' lands and, if possible, the capture of those forfeited included not only MacLeod of Dunvegan, Ranald Alanson, the ubiquitous MacIan of Ardnamurchan, MacNeil of Barra, MacKinnon, MacQuarrie, and MacLean of Lochbuie, the last apparently exonerated of blame for recent events, but also Torquil MacLeod of Lewis. It seems that at this stage, the government was unaware of his involvement in the Badenoch raid; they cannot, however, have been unaware of Torquil's earlier custody of Donald Dubh, or of his failure to hand him over when charged to do so at Inverness. In 1504, however, Donald Dubh was in the hands of MacLean of Duart, who was therefore identified as the main target in the Isles. MacLean's great crime was fully described in his forfeiture on 18 March; he had committed treason in maintaining, fortifying, and supplying Donald, bastard and unlawful son of the late Angus of the Isles, bastard son to the late John of the Isles; Maclean had further caused Donald to usurp royal authority by claiming 'that the said donald suld be lord of the ylis. . .and for the causation of our souerane lordis liegis to obey to the said donald as lord of ylis quhilk Is our souerane lordis propirte.' The government's philosophy seems to have been to give influential Highland chiefs of either undoubted or dubious loyalty the chance to perform a service to the Crown by attacking and capturing MacLean and Ewen Alanson; their reward would be half of the forfeited men's lands.[59] It was an obvious attempt to divide and rule in the west by a government uncertain as to whom its friends and enemies were, but who had undoubtedly identified the main threat as the general acceptance by the Islesmen of Donald Dubh as rightful heir to the entire lordship of the Isles.

It remained to be seen whether the eight chiefs who were to receive royal letters encouraging them to assail the rebels would in fact respond to the invitation to do so. In the meantime the king prepared for war. Parliament recommended that he entrust to Huntly the building of a castle at Inverlochy on Loch Linnhe, while Argyll was to be consulted about the strengthening of Dunaverty and Loch Kilkerran in Kintyre. Ship-owners in all parts of the realm 'quhare our souerane lord thinkis expedient' were to make ready their ships to sail to the Isles when they received open proclamation from the king to that effect; and the royal artillery, dispersed throughout the country, was to be gathered in for early use.[60]

The 1504 parliament sought not only to lay plans for the winning of the war, but also to look, in the long term, to the bringing of effective justice to the Highlands and Islands. What was needed, according to the government, were justices and sheriffs who did their jobs in more manageable areas; the vast size of the sheriffdom of Inverness was identified as part of the problem, because failure to hold justice ayres in many areas of the sheriffdom had led to a breakdown of law and order. 'For lak and falt of Justice Airis', lamented the estates, 'the pepill ar almaist gane wild.' The solution adopted lay partly in the creation of new sheriffdoms in Ross and Caithness, with the sheriff in the former holding his court in Tain or Dingwall, in the latter in Dornoch or Wick; partly in a division of the Isles into two areas, north and south, with the south Isles served by a justice and a sheriff based at Tarbert or Loch Kilkerran, the north Isles similarly served from Inverness or Dingwall.[61] The inadequacy of this last provision is obvious: if Torquil MacLeod would not come from the Isles even to meet his king at Inverness, he and his clansmen, and any of his allies in the west, were unlikely to respond to the demands of a royal official based on the same burgh, or at Dingwall in Easter Ross. Behind these elaborate schemes lay the reality of the situation, which was that the king's only hope of winning any real control in the Isles was through force and subsequent delegation of authority to chiefs whom he could trust. The difficulty lay in identifying the men, for shifts of allegiance on the part of prominent Highland chiefs since 1493 seem to have been about as frequent as changes in royal policy.

There is even some evidence that James IV could not wholly trust his own Master of the Household, Archibald, earl of Argyll. In an early clause of the 1504 parliament, subsequently erased, the Lords of the Articles laid down that though the earl of Argyll was hereditary sheriff of Lorne and Argyll, and his justice ayre was therefore normally held within the bounds of Argyll and Lorne, this practice was only to continue 'als lang as the said lord kepis gude Reule and dois Justice.' If however the king was to be 'sikkerly aduertist' that justice in Argyll and Lorne was failing and that the earl was to blame, he would command Argyll to transfer his justice ayre to Perth 'sa that the king and the lordis of consale may consider and se that Justice be ministrate.'[62] This remarkably explicit indictment of Argyll may reflect a widespread fear that the earl could not control, or did not wish to control, his own clansmen and tenants, perhaps even that he sympathised with the cause of Donald Dubh. This is unlikely to have been the case; but it must have been easy for the Committee of the Articles to point the finger at Argyll in 1504. His three years' lieutenancy had been a failure and was not immediately renewed; and his close kinship with both Torquil MacLeod and MacLean of Duart can hardly have endeared him to other members of the royal council. Argyll was present as a member of the articles to defend his position; and this may explain why there is no reference in the published clause on the subject to the earl's control, or lack of it, of Argyll and Lorne. In its place is a bland statement that the justice ayre for the lordship of Argyll and its bounds should be held at Perth at the king's pleasure.[63]

In any event, the decisions of the 1504 parliament would have to be implemented by force. The Earl of Huntly was probably quickest off the mark; as early as January 1504, within a month of the Badenoch raid, he had received three stones of gunpowder from the king.[64] On 14 April James IV despatched a messenger from Edinburgh with letters to the loyalist MacIan of Ardnamurchan, no doubt to endeavour to discover the strength of the opposition which his forces would have to face; and on the following day the king rode with the Scottish gunner Robert Herwort to visit the fleet at Dumbarton. Two days later he had arrived in the burgh, and had himself rowed out to visit the ships, which were ready to sail under the command of the veteran Sir Andrew Wood. A Frenchman named Martin was the supplier of victuals to the royal fleet, and it appears from the Treasurer's accounts that by mid-April he had already made a number of visits to the Isles — perhaps a euphemism for Kilkerran or Tarbert — to victual ships there. His task on 18 April, the transport of ten tuns of wine to the royal ships in the Isles for a payment of £70, must have made him widely popular. On or about 20 April the fleet sailed, calling at Ayr — and presumably Kilkerran — before rounding the Mull of Kintyre and heading north towards its main objective, the remote castle of Cairn-na-Burgh in the Treshnish Isles to the west of Mull, a MacLean stronghold in which MacLean of Duart may have placed Donald Dubh for his own safety.[65]

James IV did not sail with the fleet. Instead he rode from Dumbarton to Stirling, where on his arrival on 22 April he received letters from MacIan of Ardnamurchan, presumably in response to his own of eight days before. A week later he received a report from the Earl of Huntly, no doubt campaigning in Wester Ross; and on the same 29 April King James ordered the sending of more gunpowder to the siege of Cairn-na-Burgh.[66] We have no eye-witness accounts of this event, which must have been extremely difficult to organise, with the small ships of the royal fleet lurching about in an uncertain sea, trying to bring their artillery pieces to bear on a forbidding stronghold perched on the rock of Cairn-na-Burgh More. By 6 May the king had decided that the besiegers needed stiffening, and he ordered his principal gunner Hans to sail to Cairn-na-Burgh in Robert Barton's ship. The following day King James received a messenger with letters from John Campbell, the loyal bishop of the Isles; clearly the news cannot have been good, for on 11 May the king sent Garioch pursuivant to Edinburgh with 'commissionis for the Ilis' for his kinsman James Hamilton, created Earl of Arran following the royal wedding the previous August, and the commander of the fleet on the Danish expedition of summer 1502. King James probably paid another flying visit to Dumbarton in mid-May to see Arran depart, his ship piped away down the Clyde by the pipers of Dumbarton, and laden not only with bread, chickens, and capons, but also with more artillery and gun-stones.[67]

By late June the fleet had returned, part of it having spent at least a fortnight longer in the Isles than had been anticipated.[68] What had been achieved? Cairn-na-Burgh was either taken or surrendered, and its custody was transferred to the Earl of Argyll.[69] But Donald Dubh had not been captured, and a commission of parliament meeting at Edinburgh on 7 June had already identified three more rebel Islesmen who were to be summoned for treason — MacLean of Lochbuie, MacQuarrie of Ulva, and MacNeill of Barra, three of the eight who had been offered royal bribes in March to attack MacLean of Duart and Ewen Alanson.[70] Clearly 'the danting of the Ilis' was going to take some time.

In fact, the Crown's limited success in the Highlands and Islands following the parliament of March 1504 largely explains why the estates were called together again in February 1506. From June 1504 to January 1506 summonses of treason were repeated again and again by parliamentary commissions specially summoned for the purpose; but it was not until December 1505 that Torquil MacLeod of Lewis was added to the list of those to be indicted.[71] It took time for the royal government to realise who its irreconcilable enemies were; but as 1504 and 1505 went by, the king's policy began to pay off. The threat of forfeiture proved to be a sufficient deterrent for those who, like MacQuarrie and MacNeill, began to see that their best hope lay in an early submission. Even the MacLeans — of Duart and Lochbuie — eventually recognised that they could not prevail against the Crown when it was actively backed by Argyll and his aggressive lieutenant MacIan of Ardnamurchan.

For by 1506 Argyll, regardless of his poor showing in the initial crisis of 1503–4, was clearly back in favour. His lieutenancy in the west was restored, and he had been the first to benefit from the surrender of Cairn-na-Burgh, the custody of which was transferred to him from MacLean of Duart. Really there was no alternative for the Crown but to trust Argyll in the Western Isles; and his unconvincing performance during his first three years of lieutenancy probably made the earl anxious to prove himself by furthering royal policy in the Isles as scrupulously as possible. That policy had of necessity become what it had originally been in 1493 — that is, to reward obvious loyalists like MacIan while not making life impossible for those like MacLean of Duart who had adopted rebellious stances but could be induced to submit. MacLean had certainly had a bad fright in the late spring of 1504 when he discovered that even the Treshnish Isles were not immune from royal attack, as one after another the king's best naval commanders sailed against him; wisely he cut his losses and at an early stage — possibly by June 1504 — he had abandoned Donald Dubh and accepted the loss of Cairn-na-Burgh to Argyll.[72]

MacLean of Duart was a loser — on a modest scale — in the western conflict of 1504–6. An obvious gainer was MacIan of Ardnamurchan, whose consistent support for the Crown for more than a decade — killing and capturing the king's enemies, and providing a wealth of written information about rebel dispositions in the Isles — earned him a royal audience, the gift of a new wardrobe, and — rather more substantially — the confirmation of his lands in Islay and Jura, of

Ardnamurchan and Sunart with his castle of Mingary, and the bailiary of the Crown lands on Islay.[73] Rewards to MacIan were not, however, carried too far, for he was clearly feared and disliked by other Highland chiefs in the vicinity of Mull; indeed the adherence of MacLean of Duart and MacLean of Lochbuie to the cause of Donald Dubh may have been largely inspired by their desire to check MacIan's growing power, and it took Argyll himself, in June 1506, to reconcile the parties by obtaining a promise from MacIan that both MacLeans would remain unharmed by him in their persons and goods for a year, and that in the meantime disputes between MacIan and MacLean of Lochbuie would be submitted for arbitration to the King and Council.[74]

We should not, however, exaggerate the threat posed to James IV's authority by the problem of Donald Dubh and his supporters in the Isles. The king responded firmly and confidently to the challenge by delegating responsibility for the suppression of the rebellion to men whom he could trust; but he did not become directly involved, possibly because he was not particularly interested in the Isles beyond their potential as providers of revenue and as a proving ground for his ships and artillery. Even in the late spring of 1504, with the rebellion at its height, he had other more pressing interests. One was the search for a better harbour for his fleet than that provided by Leith; in May 1504 the king was rowed west from Leith 'to seik the New Havin', from which seven years later he would launch the largest warship in northern Europe.[75] Another, more pressing, duty was the raid of Eskdale in the West March, a punitive expedition together with the English warden Thomas, Lord Dacre, which lasted from 14 to 25 August and was immediately followed by three weeks' hawking at Lochmaben.[76] Altogether it cannot be said that James IV spent the spring and summer of 1504 in a sweat of fear about the rebellion of Donald Dubh.

By the end of 1505, however, King James had identified Torquil MacLeod as his main enemy in the Isles, an irreconcilable harbouring Donald Dubh in his castle of Stornoway in Lewis, defying the king and relying on distance and the Minch to protect him. His defiance led the king to summon parliament around Christmas of 1505, and the estates met at Edinburgh on 3 February 1506.[77] Even more clearly than in 1504, the record of this parliament reveals that the main business was judicial and political. Thus on 3 February there was a total attendance of forty-one; but by 16 February, following the serious judicial business but preceding the legislation, the number present had dropped to twenty-four, less even than the size of the committee of the articles in 1488.[78]

3 February, the first day of the parliament, proved to be a busy day. The main business was the forfeiture of Torquil MacLeod; but on the same day, and the following one, more than half those present — one archbishop, four bishops, seven earls, four lords of parliament, five abbots, and the Prior of St Andrews — met as Lords of Council to pronounce on the longest-running dispute of the reign, the Cunningham-Montgomery feud in northern Ayrshire.[79] Since 1498 Cuthbert Cunningham, Lord Kilmaurs, had

been fighting a rearguard action over the consequences of the Crown's grant of the bailiary of Cunningham to Kilmaurs' bitter rival Hugh, Lord Montgomery. Initially he seemed to be fighting a lost cause against the powerful combination of the Earl of Argyll and Lord Montgomery, the earl's brother-in-law. However, Argyll's temporary lapse from grace sometime before 1504, followed by a more serious lapse by John, Master of Montgomery, in 1505 — he had attacked and wounded William Cunningham, coroner of Renfrew[80] — made it politically possible for Cuthbert, Lord Kilmaurs, to recover some of his family's lost authority in Ayrshire. His aim was to obtain exemption from Montgomery's jurisdiction, and he brought his case to parliament because during its sitting he was guaranteed a large — and therefore less obviously biased — number of judges on the Lords of Council; to have made the same plea before half-a-dozen judges including Argyll would probably have been a waste of time. In the event, the twenty-two Lords of Council granted Lord Kilmaurs exemption from Montgomery's jurisdiction on 3–4 February 1506.[81] This did not end the Cunningham-Montgomery feud, which rumbled on — in this reign alone — to 1510;[82] but the case is interesting as illustrating the interaction of matters political and judicial in parliament, and the enormous flexibility in the size and personnel of the Lords of Council throughout the reign. It also highlights the very specific reasons which might bring individuals, eagerly or reluctantly, to parliament at Edinburgh; for having obtained judgment in their case at the outset, Kilmaurs and Montgomery both went home and were nowhere to be seen later in the parliament.

The parliamentary trial of Torquil MacLeod of Lewis, also on 3 February, was something of a foregone conclusion. MacLeod did not appear; John Ogilvy, sheriff-depute of Inverness, the royal messenger who had been sent to summon him, was a cautious man. 'Becaus I cuth nocht apprehend him personaly', he told the estates, 'nor thir vas na sure passage to me till his duelling place', he had gone to the market cross of the burgh of Inverness at eleven o'clock on the morning of Christmas Eve 1505, and there by open proclamation he had summoned Torquil to appear to answer the charge of treason before the king and his justices in the Tolbooth of Edinburgh on the following 3 February. Torquil MacLeod, no doubt enjoying Christmas with Donald Dubh in Stornoway castle, more than a hundred miles and a good sea journey from Inverness, may perhaps be forgiven for not having heard, far less responded, to Ogilvy's summons. On 3 February 1506, not surprisingly, he was found guilty of treasons stretching back to the 1503 Christmas raid on Huntly's lordship of Badenoch; but his most heinous crime was to have attacked royal lieges in the Isles 'to the effect that the said Donald [Dubh] suld be lord of the Ilis'; and for this and the rest he was sentenced to forfeit life, lands, and goods.[83]

Torquil MacLeod had sinned not only against the king, but more directly against the Earl of Huntly; and it was appropriate that Huntly was given the task of bringing the rebellion to an end. The king would of course assist him with ships, gunners, and artillery, vessels on this occasion sailing not only from Dumbarton but also from Newhaven, King James's new port a mile west of Leith. One of the royal gunners, Robert Herwort, was paid two months' wages 'to pas in the Ilis' on 24 June — an indication of how long the campaign against Torquil was estimated to last — and the master gunner Hans supervised the carriage of two cannon, powder, and gunstones from Edinburgh castle down to Newhaven, where they were loaded on board a ship belonging to William Brownhill, one of James IV's most trusted captains. It may have been Brownhill's ship which was sent to carry the Earl of Huntly to the Isles, while at the same time another vessel was ordered out of Dumbarton to meet Brownhill's ship in the Isles.[84]

As in 1504, so also in 1506, James IV was not directly involved in the campaign in the Isles. The king spent much of July 1506 in and off Fife, sailing to the Isle of May in his newly-launched warship, the 'Margaret', visiting Crail and Kinghorn, and even being supplied with two golf clubs on 23 July for a game which may have taken place at St Andrews.[85] August found James on pilgrimage to Whithorn, his devotions followed by a hunting trip to Menteith, Balquhidder, and Aberlednoch, and visits to Strathfillan and Inchcailloch, a small island near Balmaha, on the east side of Loch Lomond, at the end of the month.[86] The king was not, however, behaving frivolously towards his responsibilities in the Isles. He could trust Huntly, the newly-reconciled MacLean of Lochbuie, MacIan, and Mackay of Strathnaver in Sutherland, to do the Crown's work effectively, since all of them stood to gain by its success; and as we have seen, he reckoned on a two-month campaign. That campaign was clearly underway in July and August, and reports of its progress filtered through to King James as he moved about the country. On 2 August some prisoners — 'Erschmen' — taken by the Earl of Huntly were brought from Stirling to Edinburgh; on 29 August, while hunting in Balquhidder, the king gave a reward 'to ane man. . .with tithingis of the Lewis'; and on 9 September James provided money for the transport to Inverness of nine Spaniards who had been taken on Lewis.[87] They may well have been victims of shipwreck rather than supporters of Torquil MacLeod, for they were generously treated by King James; but the fact that they had fallen into royal hands at all suggests that Huntly's forces had already landed on the Isle of Lewis by late August, or early September at the latest.

Thus there is some strategic significance in the king's pilgrimage to Tain in September. He travelled north through Badenoch to Inverness and Dingwall, and so to Tain for 11 and 12 September; while at Dingwall on the evening of 9 September, King James made a further payment to his gunner Robert Herwort, who had presumably returned from the Lewis campaign and whose pay was certainly in arrears. The following day the king paid £30 to Thomas Hathowy for the hire of his ship, the 'Raven', to be sent to Lewis, presumably to bring off members of Huntly's expeditionary force.[88] Although no account survives of the siege of Torquil MacLeod's castle of Stornoway, it seems likely therefore that it was all over by early September.[89] Donald Dubh was captured and imprisoned, either in Stirling or Edinburgh castle, for most of the remainder of his life, while Torquil MacLeod fled and remained a forfeited rebel until his death in 1511.[90]

The king had done what was expected of him, and probably rather more than that. Having provided and paid for ships, some artillery and gunners, he had delegated authority to Huntly and his associates in the north; then, with the campaign over, he had reinforced his lieutenant's authority by appearing personally in many of the unsettled areas from Badenoch to Ross. The price which King James had to pay, and was prepared to pay, for the successful summer campaign in the Isles was a huge extension of the power already devolved to Alexander, earl of Huntly. The earl's subordinates in the assault on Torquil MacLeod, above all Hugh MacKay of Strathnaver, were also well rewarded for their loyalty; MacKay, who had probably seized Torquil's lands of Assynt and Cogeach in Wester Ross at the outset of the rebellion, had them granted to him for life by a seemingly grateful king in March 1508.[91] But MacKay's case illustrates on a small scale what was true of the Highlands as a whole; that is, the king made retrospective grants of land to powerful individuals prepared to support him simply because he had no alternative. He might receive some rents from parts of the former lordship of the Isles — from Islay by 1507, and from Kintyre, Morvern, Mull, and Tiree by 1509;[92] but he relied in these areas on MacIan and Argyll screwing money out of Crown tenants. Further north, in Skye and the Outer Hebrides, unrest continued in spite of the ending of the rebellion in 1506. As late as 1510, a full seventeen years after the forfeiture of the lordship, King James was still ordering his tenants in Trotternish to pay their rents;[93] the two MacLeans — of Duart and Lochbuie — fell out again over control of lands assigned to them in Morvern and Tiree;[94] and Torquil MacLeod remained at large, and in rebellion, until 1511.[95] In the circumstances, and dealing as he was with a king who had lost interest in the Highlands and Isles, the Earl of Huntly was in a position to name his terms for his loyalty in the north.

In the autumn of 1507, royal grants began to pour in. On 8 September, Huntly received lands formerly held by Alexander of Lochalsh's sister, who had unwisely become involved with one of Torquil MacLeod's allies; five days later he was empowered to set the royal lands of Glengarry and Invergarry for five years; and on 13 December he received a similar commission for the lands of Knoydart.[96] But the most striking grant of all, confirming powers which Huntly already exercised, came on 16 January 1509, when he was made hereditary sheriff of Inverness, with the power to appoint his deputies to the sheriff courts of Caithness, Ross, and Lochaber. The same grant confirmed his keepership of Inverness castle and its lands.[97] By the early months of 1509, Huntly and his associates controlled almost the whole of Scotland north of the Great Glen, the lordships of Lochaber and Badenoch, and the huge tracts of Aberdeenshire territory which formed the centre of the earldom.

The enormous power of Huntly in the north explains, if anything can, the final parliament of the reign, held at Edinburgh on 8 May 1509. We possess only a fragment of the record of this meeting of the estates — no sederunt lists, no names of those appointed to parliamentary committees, only two surviving clauses.[98] The first of these, about the maintenance of the freedom of 'halikirk', is the traditional first business of all parliaments; but the second is interesting in that it goes some way towards cancelling the elaborate arrangements for the division of sheriffdoms made by the parliament of 1504. Only the justice ayres created at that time were to remain in force; sheriff and other courts were to return to the status quo 'befoir the making of the said act of Parliament.' Thus the new sheriffdoms of 1504 were abandoned, perhaps because in the north Huntly had only recently been empowered to put his own men into Ross and Caithness. It may be added that he should not have been granted Inverness castle and its lands, since these were annexed lands, not to be alienated without consent of parliament. In May 1509 parliament dutifully gave its consent to Huntly's fait accompli of the previous January.[99] So far as we can judge, therefore, the last parliament of James IV's reign, like its two predecessors, was summoned to deal with the problems created by rebellions in the Highlands and Islands. 1509 was a kind of postscript to the other two, an acceptance of the power of royal lieutenants and an end to innovation; and the king would call no more parliaments.

How then did King James govern effectively for the eighteen years of his personal rule? Part of the answer may lie in his use of General Councils, bodies of a size similar to parliaments, involving the principal members of the political community but often summoned at shorter notice and to deal with specific business.[100] Unfortunately evidence of such meetings during the reign is slight, consisting only of passing references to General Councils in the Treasurer's accounts and — possibly — in the published and unpublished acts of the Lords of Council; and in almost every case we have to guess what business General Councils were summoned to discuss. In the autumn of 1495, that is in the year of James IV's assumption of full power, there are four large Lords of Council sederunts, ranging in number from 24 to 37 instead of the normal maximum of 12 – 15, and with the king present with the most prominent members of the political community on three of the four occasions.[101] Clearly these bodies, if not General Councils in name, are at least considerably enlarged sessions of the royal council, doing some judicial business certainly, which is why they find their way into the judicial records at all, but surely summoned by King James to deal primarily with affairs of state — in the case of autumn 1495 almost certainly the Council's attitude to, and preparations for the reception of, Perkin Warbeck.

Significantly, occasional General Councils — or greatly enlarged royal councils — are to be found meeting in the eight-year gap between the parliaments of 1496 and 1504. There was a General Council in 1497, summoned on 4 October on twenty days' notice, and it was clearly in session by 28 October, though no record of its business has been preserved;[102] and it is likely that two more followed in June 1498 and early March 1502.[103] The latter date is particularly interesting, because summer 1502 was the time of the Scottish naval expedition to Denmark, in response to a plea from King Hans, for which preparations were made in April and May; and it seems likely that taxation to finance that venture was part of the business of a General Council meeting in March. This might in turn explain clause 39 of the 1504 parliament which insists 'that the commissionars and hedismen of burrowis be warnit quhen taxtis or contributions ar gevin to haif thir votis as ane of the thre estatis of the Realme.'[104] This clause may reflect alarm on the part of members of the third estate that they had not been consulted over the Danish taxation of 1502, and also, as Rait suggested over sixty years ago,[105] that the king was summoning General Councils which did not include the burgess estate. However, no major constitutional principle surfaced in 1504, and the estates in general simply adhered to the practical — and usual — solution of resisting the Danish tax as long and as forcefully as they could.[106]

By inference, therefore, we may understand the regular workings of James IV's government. Throughout the personal rule he summoned occasional meetings of bodies larger than the normal 'daily' council charged with the day-to-day running of the royal administration, assemblies of the most active members of the political community, either in General Council or as part of a specially summoned, and greatly enlarged, royal council. In addition to the examples cited above, two General Councils were summoned — on the last day of 1511 and at the end of February 1512[107] — whose business must have been the renewal of the Franco-Scottish alliance in March 1512 and its likely consequences. As for large sederunts of the Lords of Council, indicating the presence of an enlarged council whose main purpose in meeting was urgent political business, these occur in February 1508, March 1511, and April 1513;[108] the list is probably incomplete because there are gaps in the Lords of Council records.

All this evidence seems to point in one direction, namely that with the solitary exception of the third estate's — unrepeated — call for consultation on taxation in March 1504, there appears to have been no great enthusiasm for parliaments on the part of the estates in general during the adult rule of James IV. The king's professional civil servants certainly thought differently, and rushed to legislate given virtually their only chance in 1504. But King James was probably at one with most of his lieges on the subject of parliaments. He could — and did — summon the estates in General Council, or take the views of a wide cross-section of magnate opinion in enlarged council meetings, if urgent business required him to do so. But parliaments, as the post-1488 years showed, frequently meant political trouble; and on the whole, after his real coming of age in 1495, James IV neither needed them nor wanted them.

NOTES

1. N.L.S., MS. Adv. 25.5.6.

2. *Ibid.*, ff.203r – 205v. A full discussion of the authenticity of these oaths, and their application to the fifteenth century, is to be found in R.J. Lyall, 'The Medieval Scottish Coronation Service: Some Seventeenth-Century Evidence', *Innes Review* xxviii (1), 3–21, at 9–11, 14–16.

3. Ross, *Edward IV*, 346–7; Chrimes, *Henry VII*, 135.

4. Briggs, *Early Modern France*, 6.

5. Irene O'Brien, 'The Scottish Parliament in the 15th and 16th centuries', unpublished Ph.D. thesis, Glasgow, 1980. For details of extraordinary taxation authorised by parliament, see Ibid., Appendix O, pp. 404–405. The list is however not quite complete, and the sources cited need to be checked.

6. *T.A.*, i, 304, 312–3. The original parliamentary record is incomplete, totally lacking the sessions of 1493, 1496, and 1509, for which information has had to be supplied from other manuscripts and incorporated into the printed edition of *A.P.S.* edited by Thomas Thomson. Also it is clear that much has been lost from the records; for example, much of the business of the parliaments of January 1489, May 1492, and May 1509 has clearly been lost, and we know nothing at all about the parliament of November 1494 beyond the names of the Lords Auditors and the fact that it met at Edinburgh on the 27th of that month. On the other hand, Thomas Thomson's printed *A.P.S.* is probably complete in the sense that it lists all the parliaments of the reign, however briefly. Had there been other meetings, references to them would certainly have appeared in *T.A.*, *E.R.*, or the published or unpublished *A.D.C.*; but nothing in any of these sources adds anything to Thomson's list.

7. Murray, 'Exchequer and Crown Revenue', Appendix, 85–6.

8. Skene, 'Tabill': S.R.O. 1/2, 104; *T.A.*, ii, 196.

9. *T.A.*, iv, 351, 360–365, 391–396; and *see above*, chapter 6.

10. For a detailed analysis of the James IV minority parliaments, *see above*, chapters 3 and 4, passim.

11. *A.P.S.*, ii, 232–3, c.7.

12. *A.D.C.*, i, 385, 390, 398, 421.

13. *A.P.S.*, ii, 237–9.

14. *Cal. Docs. Scot.*, iv, No. 1622.

15. Polydore Vergil, *Anglica Historia*, 87.

16. *A.D.C.*, ii, 1. Although the printed volume deals almost exclusively with acts of the Lords of Council, it opens with the acts of the Lords Auditors who sat during the 1496 parliament. This enables us to determine the length of the parliamentary session: *Ibid.*, ii, 1–28.

17. *A.P.S.*, ii, 237–9.

18. *Ibid.*, ii, 238, c.3.

19. *Ibid.*, ii, 249, c.2.

20. *Ibid.*, ii, 249–254.

21. Macfarlane, *Elphinstone*, 423; and for a perceptive analysis of specific acts, *Ibid.*, 423–5.

22. *E.R.*, x, 550.

23. *R.M.S.*, ii, Nos. 2264, 2281, 2287.

24. *A.D.C.*, ii, 41.

25. *Ibid.*

26. *T.A.*, i, 382, 389–90; *R.M.S.*, ii, Nos. 2424–2440.

27. *T.A.*, i, 383.

28. *R.M.S.*, ii, Nos. 2436, 2440.

29. *Ibid.*, ii, Nos. 2424, 2437, 2438, 2439.

30. *Ibid.*, ii, Nos. 2420, 2424.

31. *Annals of Ulster*, iii, 443, and see above, p.105 and p.111, n.131.

32. *R.S.S.*, i, Nos. 413, 513, 520.

33. *Ibid.*, i, Nos. 722, 723.

34. *T.A.*, i, 383.

35. *A.D.C.*, iii, 174.

36. *Acts of the Lords of the Isles*, lxxii–lxxiii, 313–4.

37. By late October 1501 the king had already set out on the north-eastern

ayre, and reached Inverness by 4 November, having earlier proposed that he receive custody of Donald Dubh from Torquil MacLeod while he was in the burgh: *R.M.S.*, ii, No. 2162; *A.D.C.*, iii, 174–5.

38. *A.D.C.*, iii, 174–5.
39. *R.M.S.*, ii, Nos. 2612–4.
40. *A.D.C.*, iii, 174–5.
41. *Ibid.*, iii, 187.
42. *R.S.S.*, i, No. 792.
43. *T.A.*, ii, xcii.
44. *A.D.C.*, ii, 94–7.
45. *R.M.S.*, ii, No. 2386.
46. *T.A.*, ii, 141, 145. The story that Mackenzie was killed in the Torwood is in Gregory, *History of the Western Highlands and Islands*, 93.
47. *T.A.*, ii, 143.
48. *R.S.S.*, i, Nos. 723, 792.
49. *A.P.S.*, ii, 263.
50. *E.R.*, xii, 247–8.
51. *T.A.*, ii, 301, 344.
52. *Ibid.*, ii, 354, 357.
53. *Ibid.*, ii, 410; *A.P.S.*, ii, 263.
54. The 1504 parliament receives very full treatment in Thomas Thomson's printed version of the acts: *A.P.S.*, ii, 239–254. Note however that in his anxiety to make *A.P.S.* as full a record as possible, Thomson adds material which might give the erroneous impression that the statutes of the parliament were enacted twice, on 15 and again on 20 March. The original record is a safer guide to what went on, and the order in which business was dealt with: S.R.O., PA 7.
55. *A.P.S.*, ii, 240.
56. *Ibid.*
57. *Ibid.*, ii, 241.
58. *Ibid.*, ii, 248.
59. *Ibid.*, ii, 247–8. Ewen Alanson's forfeiture was for the crimes of seizing and imprisoning a royal messenger.
60. *A.P.S.*, ii, 248.
61. *Ibid.*, ii, 249.
62. *Ibid.*, ii, 241.
63. *Ibid.*, ii, 249.
64. *T.A.*, ii, 416.
65. *Ibid.*, ii, 428–9, 430.
66. *Ibid.*, ii, 429–30.
67. *Ibid.*, ii, 431, 433–4.
68. *Ibid.*, ii, 442.
69. *E.R.*, xiii, 224.
70. *A.P.S.*, ii, 255.
71. *Ibid.*, ii, 255–262.
72. MacLean of Duart's name is not among those of chiefs summoned for treason from June 1504 onwards.
73. *T.A.*, iii, 103; *R.M.S.*, ii, No. 2895.
74. Mackie, *James IV*, 195–6.
75. *T.A.*, ii, 432.
76. *Ibid.*, ii, 453–8.
77. *A.P.S.*, ii, 261–3.
78. *Ibid.*, ii, 262–3, 266.
79. S.R.O., A.D.C., xviii, f.33.
80. *A.P.S.*, ii, 258; *R.S.S.*, i, Nos. 1192–4.

81. S.R.O., A.D.C., xviii, f.33.
82. S.R.O., A.D.C., xix, f. 132 r–v (1508); xxi, f. 97v (1510).
83. *A.P.S.*, ii, 263–4.
84. *T.A.*, iii, 200.
85. *Ibid.*, iii, 202–208. The king paid 2/- for two golf clubs on 23 July. No venue is specified, but King James made a payment on the same day to James Watson 'for the barnis expens in Sanctandrois'; the bairns in question were James's illegitimate son James, earl of Moray, aged 5 or 6 by this time, and the son of Robert, Lord Lyle, both of whom were being brought up and tutored by Watson in St Andrews. The payment to Watson for the two boys may indicate James's presence in St Andrews; on 20 and 26 July he also made payments to 'the potingair of Sanctandrois': *T.A.*, iii, Pref., lxxxiii–lxxxv, 206–7.
86. *T.A.*, iii, 280, 281, 336–8.
87. *Ibid.*, iii, 209, 338, 340, 343.
88. *Ibid.*, iii, 340, 342.
89. For an alternative view, *see* Mackie, *James IV*, 196.
90. *Acts of the Lords of the Isles*, lxxiii, 313–4; *R.S.S.*, i, No. 1690.
91. *R.M.S.*, ii, No. 3202.
92. *E.R.*, xiii, Pref., xliv–xlv.
93. *R.S.S.*, i, No. 2094.
94. *E.R.*, xii, Pref., lxvi–lxvii.
95. *R.S.S.*, i, No. 1690; *R.M.S.*, ii, No. 3990.
96. *R.S.S.*, i, Nos. 1532, 1543, 1582.
97. *R.M.S.*, ii, No. 3286.
98. *A.P.S.*, ii, 267–8.
99. *R.M.S.*, ii, No. 3286 *note*.
100. For General Councils see R.S. Rait, *The Parliaments of Scotland* (Glasgow, 1924), 132–142.
101. *A.D.C.*, i, 385 (25 August); 390 (16 October); 398 (22 October); 421 (6 November).
102. *A.D.C.*, ii, 81.
103. *Ibid.*, ii, 222 (21 June 1498); iii, 152 (3 March 1502).
104. *A.P.S.*, ii, 245.
105. Rait, *Parliaments*, 39, 162.
106. *T.A.*, iii, 138.
107. *Ibid.*, iv, 323, 333.
108. S.R.O., A.D.C., xix, f.132 r–v; xxii, f.95r; xxv, f.22r.

8

Piety and Politics

On the morning of Easter Sunday, 4 April 1507, during the celebration of solemn High Mass in the abbey church of Holyrood, James IV, surrounded by a large assembly of Scottish clergy and nobility, and in the presence of Antonio Inviziati, special emissary of Pope Julius II, received from the hands of James Beaton, abbot of Dunfermline, two costly and symbolic papal gifts, the blessed Sword and Hat, the former still to be seen in the Crown room of Edinburgh castle. King James had every reason to be pleased; he was the first Scottish king to receive these honours since William the Lion in 1202; and the Sword and Hat undoubtedly helped to increase his prestige as a defender of the rights and liberties of the Church and of the Apostolic See. James could afford to be generous, and celebrations of his new honours were as public and as lavish as possible, involving drummers, harpers, heralds, six trumpeters and thirty-seven minstrels. On their departure from Scotland about the middle of April, the papal emissaries were showered with royal gifts, including the enormous sum of one thousand French crowns — about £700 Scots — for Antonio Inviziati alone.[1] To European princes in general, and to his own subjects in particular, James IV displayed on that Easter Sunday his public face, the face of a powerful ruler, a benefactor of the Church, favoured by the pope, beloved of God.

There was however another, more private, face. Only a few weeks before that same Easter, the king, according to Bishop Lesley's much later account, had been inconsolable because of the queen's illness at the time of the birth of James's first legitimate child, a son James, born on 21 February 1507.[2] Fearing for the life of Queen Margaret — and probably also for his infant son and heir — King James 'grevit him sa sair that he wald not be comforted: nouther of man wald receive ony consolatione'.[3] In his search for spiritual comfort, James IV set off, on foot, to make a pilgrimage to the shrine of St Ninian at Whithorn, a full 120 miles from Edinburgh. On the first evening, 10 March, he had reached Dolphinton, where he gave a poor man eighteen shillings for the loss of his cow; the second night took him to Lamington, the third to Crawford. The king's small party then crossed from Leadhills to Durisdeer, where the night of 13 March was spent. The following day saw King James cover only about seven miles, probably because he had to cross the river Nith, and when he reached Penpont he stopped for two nights, possibly to recover from his exertions, certainly to have his shoes soled at a cost of 16d. By 16 March he was on

196

his way again, travelling south-west to Dalry, where he spent that night; and then pushing on to Penningham, a few miles north of Newton-Stewart, and turning south, the king reached Wigtown on the 17th. But James did not rest overnight in the burgh; instead fourteen shillings were given to a guide to take him the final ten miles south to Whithorn before daybreak on 18 March, and he arrived in time for the first mass in the outer kirk. Eight days after leaving Edinburgh, James IV, a footsore penitent, knelt before the relics of St Ninian at Whithorn.[4]

Only twelve days elapsed between the king's return to Edinburgh from this pilgrimage and his ostentatious public display on Easter Sunday. The latter occasion, showing King James to the world as a proud and confident ruler, suits the popular vision of him as a powerful secular prince in full control of the national church. But it is the Whithorn pilgrimage which brings us much closer to James the man, wracked with fears for his queen and his heir, dreading God's judgment on his house as a response to his sins, above all his role in the appalling crime which had opened the reign. His prayers for the queen's recovery were answered, and in July Margaret Tudor, judging her restored health to be the result of 'the pietie and devocions of her housband throuch the help of S. Ninian under God',[5] accompanied James IV to Whithorn to give thanks to the saint and to God.[6] God did not however save the infant heir to the throne, James, Prince of Scotland and the Isles, who died, only one year old, in February 1508.[7]

The Whithorn pilgrimages of 1507 are not untypical. Indeed, if one judges James IV's piety by his addiction to pilgrimage, then he was far more than a conventionally pious ruler going through the motions for the sake of his soul and the benefit of the monastic chroniclers. A glance at the records reveals that royal pilgrimages to Whithorn began as early as the autumn of 1491 and were, at the least, annual events; from October of 1493 the shrine of St Duthac at Tain in Ross became part of James's annual itinerary; and there were also more modest pilgrimages to the shrine of St Mary at Whitekirk in East Lothian and that of St Adrian on the Isle of May in the Forth.[8]

These journeys were not of course devoid of entertainment en route; in the early 1500s a pilgrimage to Tain generally involved a visit to Janet Kennedy at Darnaway, including one made in the autumn following the king's wedding; and Janet was moved to Bothwell to entertain King James on his way to Whithorn in April 1503.[9] Even when the king reached his destination, he occasionally managed to combine pleasure with piety. Thus in the last seven years of the reign, he paid a number of visits to the Isle of May, and initially his devotions seem to have been rigorous and unrelieved: on 3 June 1504 he was rowed across to the May with the clerks of the Chapel Royal who sang mass on the island; the following day, having been rowed back to Anstruther, the king heard mass in Crail and St Monans.[10] In the summer of 1506, James IV returned to the Isle of May, but this time on board the pride of his fleet, the newly-launched 600-ton warship 'Margaret';[11] in March 1508 he paid fourteen shillings to the island's hermit who brought him a seal, though what he did with it is not recorded. By the end of June he had returned with another fourteen shillings for the hermit, but appears to have spent little time with him, as the main object of the visit seems to have been a boating trip round the island with local lairds and canons of Pittenweem, shooting at seabirds with culverins.[12] In February 1512, the hermit managed to improve the amount of alms bestowed on him by King James by abandoning his island retreat and bringing coneys to the king in Edinburgh. 'Our impression of this hermit', remarks Monsignor McRoberts, 'is as a sort of Friar Tuck.'[13]

It seems clear, therefore, that apart from the penitential and devotional aspects of the pilgrimages which he undertook, James IV enjoyed them as occasions when he was free of the court and its intrigues, and when travelling the length and breadth of Scotland with only a small company of retainers, he came closer to his people than at any other time. There was probably an element of ostentation in all this, as no-one in the wilds of Kirkcudbright or the Grampians can have failed to realise that the pilgrim passing by was the king, clearly identifiable by his travelling circus of Italian minstrels. This is not to deny the validity of King James's piety on his arrival at the shrines which he visited, when, as at Whithorn, the minstrels were dismissed to the abbey of Tongland and the king spent long hours on his knees; but it requires little imagination to understand that James preferred being serenaded on the banks of the Nith while the local cobbler in Penpont mended his shoes, to staying in Edinburgh and enduring homilies from Bishop Elphinstone on the need to overhaul the entire fabric of civil and criminal law.

In the same month of March 1507 that James IV made his pilgrimage on foot to Whithorn, he was already considering a much longer and more arduous journey. On 13 March, the day that the Scottish king and his company trudged down from Leadhills to Durisdeer, Hugh O'Donnell of Tyrone, styling himself Prince of Ulster, wrote a letter to King James from Donegal in which, amongst other matters, he mentioned a report which had been circulating amongst his Irish enemies, that James had for some time been considering leaving Scotland on pilgrimage — presumably to the Holy Land, though no destination is specified. O'Donnell begged the king not to do so, on account of the dangers involved. On 22 April James IV replied thanking O'Donnell for his advice, and assuring him that he would under no circumstances leave Scotland unless the realm were safe in his absence.[14]

Behind this friendly exchange of letters lies the reality of the situation. O'Donnell, son and heir of the Hugh O'Donnell who had allied himself with James IV in support of Perkin Warbeck in 1495, was writing to the Scottish king primarily to ask him for armed support — four thousand armed clansmen led by MacIan of Ardnamurchan — to assist him against unspecified Irish enemies by 1 May. The timing is significant, for in March 1507 the news of James's final victory over Donald Dubh and Torquil MacLeod was still very recent; and O'Donnell, attempting to embroil James in Irish feuds, seems to have been concerned that if the Scottish king left his own country, not only would he be unable to assist O'Donnell with loyal Highlanders, but a fresh rising of MacDonalds in the Isles, which might result from James's absence, could be used by rival Irish lords against him. James's reply was friendly but unhelpful; he could not possibly send four thousand men to Ireland by 1 May, but would be glad to assist O'Donnell out of respect for the memory of his father, provided that his cause was just. He therefore asked to know who O'Donnell's Irish enemies were — a reasonable request — and what was at stake. O'Donnell seems to have realised that his 'try-on' had failed, and wrote back to the Scottish king on 16 April with no more than conventional expressions of goodwill.[15]

O'Donnell's Irish enemies were correct: King James was indeed planning to go on pilgrimage to the Holy Land. In this he was following a well-established fifteenth-century tradition; as Dr Macquarrie puts it, 'as the aggressive crusade became more and more impracticable, the peaceful pilgrimage became increasingly fashionable.'[16] The first Scot of note to undertake such a journey was the soldier of fortune, Sir John Stewart of Darnley, who had gone on pilgrimage to Jerusalem in the 1420s; in the later fifteenth century the voyage from Venice to Jaffa was undertaken by a number of Scottish clergy; and in James IV's own day, Sir Cuthbert Hume of Fastcastle returned from a long stay in Egypt and the Holy Land in 1509, arriving home in the company of the king's illegitimate son Alexander Stewart, archbishop of St Andrews, who had been travelling in Europe.[17] James's father, that most static of kings, had been moved, probably by his Burgundian familiar Anselm Adornes,[18] to consider foreign pilgrimages, at least as far as the shrines of St Peter and Paul in Rome and St John at Amiens; indeed James III had struck a medallion in anticipation of his journey to Amiens, though in the event it never took place.[19] But James IV was probably moved most of all by the prospect of being the first Scottish king to succeed in making a pilgrimage to Jerusalem. It had been the dying wish of his ancestor Robert Bruce, whose heart was carried part of the way; and the heart of James's great-grandfather James I had been taken to the Holy Sepulchre some time after the king's death in 1437, being returned some time before 1444 for burial in the Charterhouse of Perth by an unnamed knight of St John of Jerusalem, returning from Rhodes.[20] At the beginning of the sixteenth century, then, James IV stood squarely within a well-established tradition of Scottish pilgrimages to foreign shrines, above all to the Holy Sepulchre at Jerusalem.

James's approach to the subject was cautious and calculating. The first indication of his interest is to be found in the appearance of an envoy of the King of Scots, Marco Alvise, before the Signory of Venice, just before Christmas 1506, bearing letters of credence from James IV and requesting that, as the Scottish king wished to go to Jerusalem, the Signory would provide him with galleys, or the artificers to build them.[21] The Venetians responded favourably; but in fact King James may at this stage have been doing little more than seeking to attract Venetian shipbuilders to add to the Normans and Bretons already working in Scotland. It was probably news of this embassy which leaked indirectly to O'Donnell and caused him to attempt to drag James IV into wars in Ulster the following spring; and the Scottish king's uncle, Hans of Denmark, likewise protested against James's contemplated pilgrimage in a letter written to Robert Blacader, archbishop of Glasgow, on 20 July 1507. James, remarks King Hans, should think first of his young wife and his country.[22] It should be added that Hans, like O'Donnell, had an ulterior motive; for the departure of the Scottish king to the Holy Land would deprive Hans of his North Sea ally against his enemies, the Swedes and men of Lübeck.

In 1507, therefore, it appears that James's pilgrimage, if it were to occur at all, would involve a journey to Venice and the traditional sea voyage from the Republic to Jaffa, sailing in a Venetian ship. Early in 1508, Archbishop Blacader, a man clearly in the king's confidence concerning James's projected journey, set out on pilgrimage to the Holy Land by this route; and it is probable that his journey was undertaken as a preliminary reconnaissance, to inform James of conditions in the east in preparation for the royal pilgrimage. Blacader left Scotland shortly after 5 February 1508, probably visiting Orleans and certainly spending Easter (23 April) in Rome before finally reaching Venice by 16 May. On that day, clad in purple silk, the archbishop entered the College of the Republic and was received by the Doge, to whom he made a Latin oration in praise of the Venetian state, at the same time presenting letters of credence and recommendation from James IV and Louis XII of France. The courtesies observed, the Venetians later got down to business about what transport the archbishop intended to use — either the Jaffa galley, hired out by the State to rich pilgrims, or another, cheaper, sailing ship. In spite of the fact that the Venetians later described him as 'that rich Scots bishop', Blacader opted to sail on a ship belonging to the Marconi rather than on the Jaffa galley. He stayed in Venice for more than a month, sailing out with the Doge and other members of the Signory to the traditional espousal and blessing of the sea on 1 June; prudently he also made his will on 13 June, and deposited it with the Florentine bankers, the Nerli. Some time after the feast of Corpus Christi, 22 June, Blacader sailed for Jaffa with 35 other pilgrims, possibly all members of his suite. On 28 July, somewhere on the voyage, together with 26 others, Blacader died, presumably of an infectious illness which had become an epidemic on board ship.[23] He should have taken the Jaffa galley.

The death of the man who had crowned him may have helped to concentrate King James's mind about the advisability of sailing from Venice to Jaffa; and in any case the League of Cambrai, formed in December 1508 by James's ally Louis XII, Emperor Maximilian, Ferdinand of Spain, and Pope Julius II to dismember portions of the Venetian republic, made it diplomatically unwise to consider a visit to Venice for the time being. James did not however abandon his plans to go on pilgrimage to Jerusalem, as he reckoned he could find assistance elsewhere in Europe. For in 1507–8 Louis XII was actively endeavouring to have the Scottish king renew the Franco-Scottish alliance, and James, while politely receiving the French king's ambassadors, was in the meantime unprepared to commit himself, probably because he could use his value as a potential ally of the French to attempt to secure diplomatic concessions for himself. One of these was the possibility of Louis XII's assistance in furthering James's pilgrimage to Jerusalem, the subject of letters from James to Louis and the Cardinal of Amboise in the last months of 1507; King James's enthusiasm had been fired by a visit to Scotland of Charles de Tocque, Seigneur de la Mothe, just returned to Europe from Jerusalem and Alexandria, and in the final months of 1507 the Scottish king appears to have been trying to interest Louis XII in a joint Franco-Scottish venture — a crusade rather than a pilgrimage — to the Holy Land.[24]

We should pause here to consider what James IV was trying to achieve; for his crusading diplomacy has dealt his reputation a blow from which it has never really recovered. James's biographer, R L Mackie, in a chapter amazingly entitled 'The Road to Flodden', remarks that 'the middle-aged monarch was no wary, disillusioned statesman, but a moonstruck romantic, whose eyes were ever at the ends of the earth'. He justifies this by asserting that a crusade, 'to every other sovereign in Europe, to the Pope himself, a useful phrase in the jargon of diplomacy, was to James something far different: he saw himself in the near future, leading a great fleet to the shores of Palestine, and then, at the head of the united forces of Christendom, advancing, sword in hand, against the Turk.'[25] This broadly accepted view of James's naivety in relation to contemporary European rulers is to be envied for the author's ability to see into the innermost recesses of the Scottish king's mind; but how far does it accord with the known facts?

It is of course true that King James professed himself interested, first in the concept of a pilgrimage to the Holy Land, and later in the idea of a European crusade; but to suggest that either scheme, particularly the latter, obsessed him, or was treated by him as a matter of grave urgency, is surely to misunderstand the evidence. Had it not been for James's defeat and death at Flodden in 1513, it seems highly unlikely that later writers — not, significantly, the sixteenth-century chroniclers — would have viewed the king as a quixotic fool, for there would have been nothing which needed explaining away. But the carnage at the battle of Flodden — the origins of which had only the most tenuous links with James's earlier European diplomacy — required to be explained, and could best be justified in terms of the Scottish king's naivety and romanticism in the face of cynical and much more powerful European rulers, whose treatment of James pushed him inexorably towards his doom. But trying to explain the events of James IV's reign by continually anticipating the battle of Flodden — Mackie is at it as early as 1496[26] — hardly displays sound historical judgment, and we do well to consider Dr Nicholson's alternative view of James's character late in the reign: 'Never blind to his own interests, he had a longer experience of statecraft than most rulers and could rival all of them in deviousness.'[27]

Thus the evidence is not always what it seems. Some time between February 1507 and December 1508, for example, King James received a gift from George Brown, bishop of Dunkeld, of forty chalders and seven bolls of oats towards the financing of his pilgrimage to the Holy Land.[28] On the face of it, this would seem to suggest that the king's journey was imminent; but the context is interesting, for in letters to Hans of Denmark and Louis XII in April 1508, James IV commented that the previous year's harvest had been very poor because of the continuous rain. In particular the wheat crop had been ruined, so that the royal household lacked leavened bread. James was therefore appealing to his allies for a licence to import their surplus wheat or flour, either for direct payment, or in exchange for Scottish merchandise.[29] Thus it seems likely that Brown's gift of oats in 1507–8, made from the Dunkeld lands in Lothian and transmitted to the king by certain Edinburgh merchants, was partly inspired by James's need, not to finance a journey to Jerusalem, but to find the wherewithal to offset the effects of a bad harvest. Bishop Brown's other motive was probably that of fear, for as early as August 1506, the king had suggested to the pope that as Brown was 'labouring under the burden of years', he ought to resign his bishopric in favour of the king's nominee, James Beaton, abbot of Dunfermline. In his letters on the subject to the Holy See, King James was looking for a declaration from the pope that there was nothing illegal in the reservation of a benefice not yet vacant, especially when this was at the Crown's request and with the consent of the incumbent.[30] It is, however, abundantly clear that George Brown, the incumbent in this case, was determined to retain possession of Dunkeld. By 1508 he made his gift to the king, tactfully allocating it to the projected pilgrimage, no doubt in the hope that James would abandon his efforts to have him resign his see on the pretext of his old age. In fact, Brown managed to retain his bishopric in spite of royal pressure, and James Beaton was eventually the indirect beneficiary of the king's pilgrimage plans; for Archbishop Blacader's death en route to the Holy Land left the see of Glasgow vacant, and Beaton was translated to Glasgow on King James's recommendation. As for Bishop Brown, if his gift of oats, or their equivalent in cash, had been intended to appease the king, he does not seem to have been successful, for by 1512 relations between the two men were very bad. The king had attempted to obtain the archdeaconry of Dunkeld for his wife's former chaplain, and was opposed by Brown, who wanted the office for his cousin. The case went to Rome, evidently to King James's great annoyance, for as he candidly admitted in a letter to Henry VIII, Bishop Brown was old, did not come to court, and if James dealt with him according to the law he would be accused of causing his death, even though he really died of old age.[31] Given the background of this running fight between king and bishop from 1506 to the end of the reign, Brown's gift of 1507–8 probably tells us something about Scottish ecclesiastical politics, but not much about King James's plans for an early visit to Jerusalem.

In any event, by 1509 those plans had been superseded by James IV's apparent interest in the possibility of a European crusade. The outworn crusading ideal had acquired new relevance in European diplomacy following the seizure of Constantinople by the Turks in 1453; and Pope Pius II had died at Ancona in the summer of 1464 when about to lead a crusade against them. The Turkish menace to eastern Europe was a real one, preoccupying Emperor

Maximilian as one of those most obviously threatened, and from time to time he appears to have had crusading ambitions. The French aim, if it was ever seriously entertained by either Charles VIII or Louis XII, was the rather different one of using the invasion and successful conquest of parts of Italy as a base from which to liberate the Holy Land; and Ferdinand of Aragon had actually conducted a crusade of sorts in Spain, by driving the Moors from Granada in 1492. These widely differing concepts of crusading, springing more from territorial ambitions and political necessities than anything else, were sustained in the early sixteenth century, as Dr Macquarrie has shown, by a sizeable crusading literature, of which the example most likely to have influenced James IV, if he ever read it, was a French romance entitled 'Livre des trois filz de Roys', published in Paris in 1504. In this work the sons of the kings of France, England, and Scotland wear disguises and join together in a series of adventures against the Turks.[32] King James, then, was simply following fashion in the Europe of his day in talking and writing about the possibility of crusades. Did he believe in them any more than his contemporaries?

Late in 1509 the Scottish king's crusading diplomacy got underway, for in a letter written to Pope Julius II at that time James assured the pope that he would gladly shed his last drop of blood in the cause of Christendom. Again, however, the context of the letter is of interest, for James reports that he had been informed by Louis XII that the pope himself intended to lead an expedition against the Turk, and that he was currently making preparations for a crusade. Louis and Julius II, though still technically allies against Venice in terms of the League of Cambrai, were already regarding each other's designs on northern Italy with mutual suspicion; and the French king was certainly trying to make trouble for the pope by suggesting to James IV that Julius's crusade was imminent, adding that he himself was prevented from going in person because he was suffering from gout. The Scottish king and his advisers, while showing an enthusiasm for the projected crusade, did so with a purpose. If the pope planned to depart the following summer, James would have to prepare his fleet quickly, and provide it with masts and arms; at the moment, James claimed, the work was going slowly and negligently, largely because the pope himself had so far delayed the Scottish king's pilgrimage to the Holy Sepulchre. In any case, as the pope well knew, the undertaking would be difficult because James had to come from the uttermost ends of the earth, a euphemism for Scotland already familiar in northern Italy.[33]

This letter from King James to Pope Julius may well be the letter of a man ready to shed the last drop of his blood in the crusading cause; but it also reads remarkably like the letter of a man looking for money. The Scottish king ends by commending to the pope his servant and ambassador Thomas Halkerston, provost of Crichton, who would acquaint Julius with James's difficulties. Unfortunately Halkerston's instructions do not appear to have survived, but there can be little doubt that James IV was looking for a large sum of money, ostensibly at least to complete the building and arming of his fleet in time for an early crusade. Julius II, whose crusades never ranged beyond those parts of Italy which he wished to seize, seems to have got the message, for he neatly side-stepped the pressure which James was attempting to apply; on 24 February 1510 he wrote to the Scottish king announcing that he had given pardon and absolution to the Venetians, and commended to James the position and maritime strength of Venice as the state best placed to render valuable service to the cause of Christendom.[34]

In its European perspective, Julius II's volte-face over Venice, soon to be followed by the opening of hostilities against his former ally Louis XII of France, stands out as a bold and totally cynical diplomatic coup. The Scottish perspective, not surprisingly, was rather different. There the clergy were attempting to come to terms with a king who had moved swiftly from the concept of a pilgrimage to that of a crusade, and who was likely to receive papal blessing for his enterprise, together with the authority to raise a clerical tax in Scotland in order to pursue it. By 1509–10, there was no real chance that such a tax could be resisted, for James IV had acquired greater control over the regular and secular clergy than any of his predecessors, and all Scottish 'political' churchmen of importance — for example Alexander Stewart, archbishop of St Andrews, the king's bastard son, James Beaton, archbishop of Glasgow, Andrew Forman, bishop of Moray, the ageing but perennially active Elphinstone, and Patrick Paniter, the influential Secretary — were king's men, owing their advancement entirely to King James. This combination of an obedient church and a ruler making enthusiastic noises about crusades may well explain the vast sums contributed by the clergy to the Treasury in the last two years of the reign, a total little short of £9,000.[35] These payments may perhaps have their origins in a composition by the Scottish clergy to the Crown in order to obtain exemption from a general tax for a crusade, though by 1512–13 the enemy was not the Turk but the English. In 1509–10, however, there must have been some cynics in Scotland who wondered if there was any enemy at all, or whether James's enthusiasm for crusades could really be understood in terms of finding more money to finance the building of his navy, his most cherished project and by far his most expensive outlay in the latter years of the reign.

By the early months of 1510, rumours about James IV's crusading intentions became strongly linked to the prospects apparently presented by Venice, now declared respectable once more by the pope. On 20 April Andrea Badoer, Venetian ambassador in London, reported to the Signory that for the past week a Scots priest, a former royal ambassador to England, had been staying in London, and that he had had several conversations with him. The Scot had apparently asked Badoer about the recent death of the Signory's commander-in-chief, the Count of Pitigliano, and had enquired what stipend he had received. He then made the remarkable statement that James IV would make a good general of the Venetian forces, and wished to come and see Venice. Badoer not only communicated this tale to the Signory, but followed it ten days later with a fantastic development which he can only have acquired from the same source. The King of Scots, according to Badoer, wished to be the Signory's captain-general, and he could bring with him ten thousand fighting men, who would arrive in 150 vessels on pretence of going on a pilgrimage; on completion of his undertaking to the Venetians, James IV would then attack the infidels, free of cost to the Republic. On 11 May Badoer championed James's cause yet again, praising the Scottish king as a man of valour anxious to do himself honour; and in June he wrote once more to the Signory along the same lines.[36]

These amazing propositions no doubt have their origins in the Scottish king's enthusiasm for pilgrimage, via Venice, to the Holy Land, an enthusiasm that was probably communicated to the Signory by Archbishop Blacader in the summer of 1508; and they may have been further stimulated by James's letter to Julius II late in 1509, about the prospect of a crusade led by the pope in person. But it is difficult to believe that King James was actively seeking the Signory's captain-generalship. The story, as related by ambassador Badoer, is incredible. In 1510 James IV would have been lucky to muster fifteen vessels, far less 150; and the suggestion that he would, or could, conduct a seaborne crusade against the Turks free of charge passes belief. It must also be said that Badoer and his unidentified Scots priest are hardly unimpeachable sources. The Scot does not appear to have been an official ambassador of James IV; and as for Badoer, his reputation as Venetian ambassador in London was steadily sinking. He complained constantly that he was desperately short of money; and as early as 11 September 1510 a motion to remove him from his London post was debated in the Signory, his embassy being described as both costly and unnecessary. Only the fear that Badoer's recall might offend Henry VIII kept the ambassador in London.[37] His salary was further reduced; before the end of 1510 he was attempting to defend himself against charges that he was asleep on the job, that he spent his time with ladies or prostitutes, or at the tavern; and by 1512 his reports to the Signory were described as 'stale' and 'rancid'. He was also apparently a compulsive talker; in one of his letters he describes himself as having talked to Henry VIII so much that he went away with a pain in his side.[38] The Signory were not impressed; and it seems likely that Badoer was looking for some sensational information to transmit to Venice to bolster up his reputation and improve his salary. Hence his insistent letters about James IV as a prospective Venetian captain-general are little more than tavern gossip — probably literally so in this case, with Badoer and his Scots friend dreaming impossible, alcohol-induced dreams, not of King James as a Venetian commander, but of their own promotions by their respective masters.

Another ambassador in hot pursuit of advancement — in his case a cardinal's hat — was Christopher Bainbridge, archbishop of York, King Henry VIII's ambassador to Julius II in Rome in November 1510. In the course of the main business of his embassy, the negotiation of King Henry's entry into a league with the pope and the Venetians against France, Bainbridge remarked that the King of Scots, a valiant man, would be a suitable Venetian commander-in-chief.[39] This curious aside was already irrelevant, because by September the Signory had already chosen a new commander-in-chief, Francesco Gonzago, marquis of Mantua.[40] Probably Bainbridge, a bellicose and violently anti-French cleric, was simply trying to stir up trouble between France and Scotland; for the Venetians, not surprisingly in view of their recent experiences, loathed the French.

In short, the view that James IV cherished naive and grandiose crusading dreams rests on the authority of a zealous English ambassador seeking to break the Franco-Scottish alliance, together with the gossip of an unidentified Scottish priest as reported by a discredited and possibly inebriated Venetian ambassador. How different all this is from King James's actual diplomatic activities in the autumn of 1510. The ruler of a small kingdom, he was suddenly faced with the problem of his most powerful European friends, Julius II and Louis XII, moving inexorably towards war. For in the summer of 1510 the pope had made his first move against France, bribing ten thousand Swiss mercenaries, formerly employed by the French, to enter papal service and attack the pro-French Duke of Ferrara. King Louis responded by calling a synod of the French clergy to Tours, having them accept that war against the pope was justified, and urging a meeting of a General Council of the Church at Pisa the following year. By October 1510 the French were very much on the offensive, laying siege to the city of Bologna, in which Julius II himself had taken refuge.

In these circumstances, the only possible diplomatic role for James IV was that of mediator. On 22 October 1510 he wrote to the Marquis of Mantua, the new Venetian commander-in-chief, announcing that he had sent Andrew Forman, bishop of Moray, to Italy, to attempt to reconcile the French king and the Venetians, so that a combined attack might be made on the enemies of the Christian faith.[41] Forman's first task, however, was to speak to Louis XII at Blois, and to urge the French king to make peace with the pope. Louis prevaricated, saying that he could not act without his ally Maximilian; but he was sufficiently impressed by Forman's diplomatic abilities to employ him when the bishop went on to Rome, early in 1511.[42] The first five months of the year were taken up with efforts on the part of James IV to promote peace between irreconcilables. After all, the pliable Julius II had given King James the authority to dominate, and in financial terms to exploit, the Scottish clergy, while Louis XII was the European ally who had supplied artificers, timber, and in the last analysis money, towards the building and running of the Scottish fleet, at least since August 1506, and probably earlier.[43] Thus James's efforts to reconcile Julius and Louis were conducted with vigour, employing not only Andrew Forman but also his cousin John, duke of Albany, who had been brought up in France. In a burst of frenetic activity early in February 1511, James wrote to Albany, to Pope Julius, to the Cardinal of St Mark's, to the Marquis of Mantua, to the Duke of Savoy, to the Emperor-elect Maximilian, to the King of Hungary, and to the College of Cardinals.[44] To all of them he reported that his ambassadors were attempting to secure peace between the Pope and Louis XII, and asked for their support so that Christian arms might be turned, not against other Christians, but against the foes of Christ. Thus by 1511 James IV was describing crusades in conventional diplomatic language; that is, they were desirable, but would have to wait for the conclusion of peace among European princes, the real object of the diplomacy.

The truth seems to be that the Scottish king was unfortunate rather than naive. In the course of 1511 the indomitable Julius II, who had remarkable powers of recovery both from his enemies and from dangerous illnesses, not only survived the perils which he had largely brought upon himself the previous year, but also pre-empted the General Council of the Church which Louis XII proposed to summon to Pisa by calling his own Council to meet at the Lateran in the spring of 1512. On 4 October 1511 the Pope made a treaty with Spain and the Venetians, euphemistically described as a Holy League; and worst of all from the point of view of James IV, on 17 November Henry VIII, young and ambitious, naively believing that he could recover Aquitaine with the support of Ferdinand of Aragon, joined the League.[45] His admission to the alliance composed of Julius II, Ferdinand, and the Venetians — soon to be joined by Maximilian — seems to have remained secret for a few months; for in January 1512 Louis XII was still unaware of it. He was, however, acutely concerned about the formation of the Holy League against him; and his alarm produced the flurry of diplomatic activity which finally led to the renewal of the Franco-Scottish alliance in September 1512 after months of hard bargaining. In his hour of need King Louis evidently feared that even James IV might join the League; and when, in January 1512, the French king despatched to Scotland Bishop Forman, who had come to him at Blois with demands from King James as to how much Louis would contribute to a crusade, and even — surely a wry jest — what its destination should be, Alexandria or Constantinople, Louis was prepared to promise the earth.[46] In return for James IV's assistance against the League, the French king promised that within a year after peace had been restored, he would grant a tithe from his lands in France and Italy to James, together with cavalry, infantry, cannon, ammunition, and ships for the crusade.[47] As events were to show, the Scots were determined to make the most of these promises before the event, for they managed to extort ships, gunners, and artillery from Louis XII during the war of 1512–13. But for the Scots that war was no crusade, rather a renewal after sixteen years of something much more familiar, a struggle against England, the auld enemy.

This prospect concentrated Scottish minds very rapidly. Henry VIII's entry into the League was probably suspected by them at the very end of 1511, and on the last day of February 1512 a General Council was summoned to Edinburgh.[48] If its business was the renewal of the Franco-Scottish alliance — and it is hard to see what else it could have been — then its decision must have been reached very quickly, for on 6 March 1512 James IV decided to offer to renew the alliance with France.[49] Thus twenty years after the Earl of Bothwell had saddled the youthful king with a French treaty, James reverted to the foreign policy of his minority. But there was a difference. The treaty of 1492 had been of little practical value to the Scots; King James intended that its renewal in 1512 should bring pressure to bear on Henry VIII not to invade France, and to screw as much out of King Louis as he possibly could as the price of his support. The extent of that support had not yet been decided, and was the subject of negotiation for the remainder of the year and well into 1513. James did not rush into war with England in the expectation of receiving French aid for a crusade; indeed, his approach to Anglo-French diplomacy throughout 1512 and for much of 1513 was cautious, calculating, and skilful.

The decline of the crusading ideal in the mind of James IV during the last years of the reign is most clearly illustrated by the fate of the preceptory of the Knights Hospitallers at Torphichen in West Lothian. In the late fifteenth and early sixteenth centuries the Hospitallers were a curious survival of a bygone age, maintaining a crusading outpost at Rhodes in the front line of the struggle to defend Christendom from the Turk. In Scotland the order had declined to the point of collapse, though the revival of interest in crusading produced by the fall of Constantinople in 1453 took a number of Scottish laymen and brothers of the Hospitaller order to the Eastern Mediterranean, to spend some years at Rhodes in active defence of the Christian faith.[50] The preceptory of Torphichen was thus something of an anomaly amongst Scottish religious houses, above all because promotion to the office of preceptor had to be obtained through at least five years' membership of the Hospitaller Order and three years' residence at Rhodes; and only the Grand Master of the order, at Rhodes, could legitimately confer the preceptory on the appropriate Scot.

By the mid-1460s, however, these rules had been abandoned to allow William Knollis to acquire the preceptory of Torphichen. Knollis, whose career as a royal civil servant distinguished him from his predecessors, was a secular individual, a well-to-do merchant and diplomat, Treasurer to James III and James IV, sometimes sitting in parliament with the clergy, but more often with the second estate under the title Lord of St Johns. He paid regular taxes to the convent at Rhodes throughout his long tenure of Torphichen; but he does not appear to have done much for the Knights of St John of Jerusalem in Scotland.[51] Three years after his death in 1510, Hospitaller services in Scotland, according to one — admittedly biased — report, had been 'extinct for so many years', and the Order's churches were 'half-buried.'[52]

Whatever his faults, Knollis seems to have been concerned to provide an able successor to himself at Torphichen. In 1504 brother George Dundas, a Hospitaller knight, visited Rhodes and secured the right of expectation to succeed to Torphichen on Knollis' death or resignation. The grant of a right of expectation was a favoured method of succession within the Hospitaller order because it avoided the problems which might arise in a vacancy; and Dundas duly received this right at Rhodes on 1 July 1504, being presented, probably on Knollis' nomination, by the corporation of English knights and accepted by the lieutenant Grand Master. He seemed to be a good choice, a Scot who clearly satisfied the rules, a preceptor who might be expected to attempt to revive the Hospitaller Order in Scotland. He came home from Rhodes in March 1508 with letters from the Grand Master to James IV. The king enthused over the defence of Christendom by the knights of the Order, their conduct of ceaseless war against the Turks, and Dundas's worthy role in this; and by November 1508 he ordered that Dundas should be admitted to the temporalities of Torphichen, as he had already been provided to the preceptory by the grand master.[53] On 24 July 1510, following Knollis' death after no less than forty-four years as preceptor, King James issued a respite for Dundas, already described as 'Lord of St Johns', to journey abroad to Rome and Rhodes, taking twenty-four of his household with him. Dundas appears still to have been in Scotland on 20 September 1510, when James IV wrote to Henry VIII asking for a safe-conduct for the Lord of St Johns and his retinue, and he presumably departed shortly after that date.[54]

With astonishing speed Patrick Paniter, the ambitious royal Secretary, totally ignoring Dundas's very recent provision to Torphichen and its acceptance within Scotland, had himself provided to the preceptory by Julius II, on the ground that it was vacant through the death of William Knollis. The pope's letter to James IV commending Paniter is dated 30 January 1511,[55] which means that Dundas can barely have reached Rome before he discovered that his provision had been undermined by the king who had only recently praised his virtues as a worthy defender of Christendom in the east. This volte-face probably had more to do with the ambition of Paniter than with duplicity on the part of James IV; for the Secretary's influence with the king had become very strong, and within a fortnight of the pope's letter commending Paniter to Torphichen, King James was writing to Rome requesting that no royal letters from Scotland nominating individuals to vacant benefices should be accepted as genuine unless they were countersigned by the Secretary.[56] Paniter's ambition since his days as a scholar in Paris — a contemporary of Erasmus, John Major, and Hector Boece — had been rewarded by James IV's appointment of him as tutor to his illegitimate son Alexander Stewart, the future archbishop of St Andrews, and subsequently in 1507 Paniter began to perform the same service for the king's son by Janet Kennedy, James, earl of Moray. Royal Secretary since 1505, as a loyal Crown servant he expected — and received — ecclesiastical preferment in spite of the fact that he does not ever seem to have taken priest's orders. In 1508 he had become archdeacon, and later Chancellor of Dunkeld, and in 1509 archdeacon of Moray (which office however he resigned in 1510).[57] Paniter's influence with the king was however far greater than the relative modesty of his ecclesiastical sinecures would suggest. As the tutor who had trained Alexander Stewart, the archbishop-chancellor, the diplomat who enjoyed the complete trust of James IV, and the royal familiar who in April 1513 was described by a frustrated English ambassador as the individual who 'doothe all with his maister',[58] Paniter could expect more; and the Torphichen vacancy was not to be missed as a useful source of income to add to his other incompatible benefices.

However, George Dundas, a former fellow-student of Paniter's in his Paris days, was determined to make a fight of it, and in the summer of 1511 he managed to obtain from the Roman curia a sentence against Paniter and an acknowledgment of his right to Torphichen. The struggle which followed, and which was not resolved before the end of the reign, seems quite out of proportion to the actual value of the preceptory. However, the issue may have been seen as one of royal authority; James had promised Torphichen to his most trusted servant, and finding Dundas appealing from this judgment to Rome, regardless of the justice of his case, the king responded by writing strong letters to the curia in support of Paniter. Essentially the royal case was that Sir William Knollis had died in office as preceptor of Torphichen; he had not resigned, nor had a coadjutor been appointed.[59]

This was a distortion of the facts, and it was certainly a reversal of the king's earlier position on the subject. The real issue, apart from James's determination to appoint whom he pleased to major Scottish benefices, was probably the nature of George Dundas's provision to the preceptory in 1508; he had been promoted, as King James later protested in a letter to the Grand Master of Rhodes, 'with the consent of the English' — meaning on the recommendation of the English knights of the Order at Rhodes. This, James announced in June 1513, was an insult to Scotland. No-one, even though a Scottish subject by birth, should be installed as preceptor in Scotland if he recognised the Hospitaller Prior in England as his superior and lord. Authority and resources were at stake. The king had woken up to the fact that Scottish members of the Knights of St John had to take legal cases affecting the preceptory to the Prior of England, and that payments on vacancies were made from Scottish funds to the treasurer of the Hospitallers in England. The spectre of English ecclesiastical overlordship reared its head again. As James pointed out to Guy de Blanchefort, the Grand Master at Rhodes, Scotland had often had wars with England, and such bitter strife that Englishmen were looked on as intruders in his realm, while even Scotsmen promoted by English influence were objects of suspicion to him. The Scottish king claimed that he deserved better of the Order, because he had instituted one of his councillors — Patrick Paniter — as a brother of the Order and preceptor of Torphichen, admitting no English superiority, in imitation of his ancestors, who had always kept the English out of their kingdom.[60] By the summer of 1513, then, Paniter's main qualification for provision to Torphichen was that he was an anti-English councillor of James IV. Only as an afterthought was it suggested that he would seek to rescue the Order in Scotland from the neglect into which it had fallen.

The Torphichen case is revealing. It shows James IV, up to the last months of the reign, seeking to confer further ecclesiastical rewards on his ambitious Secretary. In the process he was totally disregarding the needs of an order which, with its tenuous hold on Rhodes, ought to have been supported as a spearhead in any crusade against the Turks. George Dundas, whom the king had initially commended, would have helped to answer those needs. But he was tainted by English associations — with the English knights at Rhodes, even with the appalling Christopher Bainbridge, archbishop of York, whose hatred of the French and advocacy of the Holy League in England had recently won him a cardinal's hat from Julius II.[61] With the threat of war with England looming, James undoubtedly saw his stance over the Torphichen case as a defence of the integrity of the Scottish church against English encroachment, a belated reform of a kind. The fact that he was also seeking to promote a cynical pluralist who was not even a member of the Order, and certainly no crusader, does not appear to have been a consideration.

Had James IV lived, it is likely that he would have succeeded in the Torphichen dispute as he had succeeded almost everywhere else in appointments to high office within the Scottish church. It is easy — too easy — simply to dismiss his choice of nominees to the great benefices as unattractive illustrations of political jobbery or insatiable greed, and sometimes both. For James had inherited a powerful weapon to use in his dealings with the papacy — the indult of April 1487 granted to his father by Pope Innocent VIII, conceding that when vacancies occurred in Scottish cathedral churches or in monasteries valued at more than two hundred florins a year, the pope would make no provisions to them for eight months, while waiting for the king to nominate suitable candidates.[62] This practical measure, which was almost certainly bound up with James III's failure to secure the see of Dunkeld for his nominee Alexander Inglis in the years 1483–5,[63] had political connotations; for in May 1485 the Scottish parliament, no doubt inspired by the king and his advisers, had put to the pope the case for royal nomination to important vacancies forcefully and succinctly. Those promoted were to be 'personis as is thankfull to his hienes', the object being 'that thir be na personis promovit to prelaciis nor digniteis without avise of his hienes sen all the prelatis of his Realme has the first vote in his parlment and of his Secrete counsale.'[64]

This plea for papal recognition of the vital role of the clergy in government and politics was echoed more than a decade later by Don Pedro de Ayala when he remarked: 'The prelates are very much revered; they have the larger share in the government.'[65] But De Ayala was writing in 1498, commenting on what he had seen in Scotland in 1496–7. If he had come to Scotland at the end of James III's reign, he would have found a king distracted by the struggle between his two most powerful ecclesiastics, Scheves and Blacader, defied by a powerful border family over the revenues of the wealthy priory of Coldingham, and finally — in spite of papal injunctions to his subjects to obey him — opposed on the battlefield where he met his death by large numbers of the Scottish clergy, including the bishops of Glasgow and Dunkeld and the abbots of Paisley and Jedburgh.[66] No clearer warning could have been given to James IV of the need to secure the appointment of 'personis as is thankfull to his hienes' within the Scottish church.

James III had failed to achieve what the indult of 1487 might have secured for him, given time: a loyal, obedient, and united church whose principal office-holders were men nominated by himself. Divisions continued during the minority of his son, especially the protracted struggle between the archbishop of St Andrews and the bishop of Glasgow, a contest which was easily won by Blacader. That he succeeded so spectacularly was largely due to his having backed the right side in 1488; but the fight with Scheves, by the mid-1480s a discarded familiar of James III, would have happened anyway, and just before the end of the reign Blacader had already been granted personal exemption from Scheves' jurisdiction.[67] Under the post-1488 regime his gains were rapid and impressive: a royal counsellor from the very start, his loyalty was swiftly rewarded by petitions to the pope in James IV's name, which were finally answered, following a visit to Rome in November 1491 by Blacader himself, by the creation of a second Scottish archbishopric. On 9 January 1492 Glasgow was erected into an independent archbishopric for Blacader. Although Scheves remained primate, Blacader had his Glasgow province exempted from St Andrews' jurisdiction for the duration of his life, and his new dignity was to be sustained by the assignment to his archiepiscopal jurisdiction of the bishoprics of Dunkeld, Dunblane, Galloway, and Argyll.[68] Within only five years of St Andrews becoming a primatial see with Scheves as primate, thus placing him unequivocally at the head of the Scottish church hierarchy, Innocent VIII had removed almost half of the province from the primate's authority, and in Dr Macfarlane's words, 'undermined the whole concept of the primacy itself.'[69] Scheves reacted furiously, and the subsequent pleading and counter-pleading at the Roman curia by both archbishops aroused the ire of the Lords of the Articles in the parliament of 1493. The cost of the pleas was causing 'vnestimable dampnage to the Realme'; the king's authority was to be invoked to put an end to it; and the estates agreed that if the dispute continued, subjects of the rival archbishops should be forbidden to pay them rents to support their legal costs in the court of Rome.[70]

Political necessity was therefore one of the motives which dictated James IV's ecclesiastical policy when he assumed control of government in 1495. The entire Scottish church province could be fatally weakened if the two archbishops continued to squander the resources of their sees indulging their grievances in Rome. King James's response was swift. In 1495 and 1496, he despatched Blacader on two diplomatic missions to Ferdinand and Isabella in pursuit of a Spanish Infanta as a prospective royal bride.[71] When the archbishop finally returned empty-handed in the summer of 1496, it is significant that he immediately ceased to serve on the royal council in which he had been a prominent member since the start of the reign; indeed, he would make very few further appearances on the council between 1495 and his death in 1508. His work as a judge on the Lords of Council also declined sharply, and although he attended the parliaments of 1504 and 1506, it is clear that his role in royal government was much less important after 1495. This cannot have been due to ill-health, otherwise Blacader would surely never have undertaken a pilgrimage to the Holy Land in 1508. It follows that the king was responsible, and it is possible that James not only resented Blacader's dispute with Scheves being dragged before the Roman curia, but also the archbishop of Glasgow's efforts, backed by Ferdinand and Isabella and the Spanish ambassador in Rome, to obtain a cardinal's hat. James IV may have regarded this as a suitable reward for Blacader if his mission had succeeded; as early as 12 September 1495, Ferdinand and Isabella stated that the scheme to make Blacader a cardinal had the full support of the King of Scots, 'and the Archbishop has rendered signal services.'[72] Signal services to whom? As we have seen,[73] the principal object of the Spanish sovereigns was to dupe the Scots with false promises, and by

1496 James may well have felt that Blacader was playing a double game in the hope of being made a cardinal. The archbishop may not have been so subtle, or disloyal; but his diplomatic mission had certainly failed, and he had to wait three years before he was entrusted with another.

James IV was lucky. Blacader's political eclipse was swiftly followed by the death, in January 1497, of the primate William Scheves. Political, financial, and possibly also dynastic needs were swiftly met by the promotion of James, duke of Ross, the king's brother, to the archbishopric of St Andrews.[74] Obviously this was a cynical act, for Ross was a twenty-year-old layman who could not be consecrated for at least seven years. Leaving aside financial issues, however, it may be relevant to ask whether James could have made a better appointment. Of the senior bishops, Blacader was a non-starter as Scheves' recent rival and a forceful careerist. George Brown of Dunkeld had played a diminishing role in government since about 1490, and within a decade King James would be seeking to replace him. William Elphinstone of Aberdeen was the most experienced administrator of all of them, but also James III's Chancellor in 1488; in any case he had a strong interest in the affairs of Aberdeen diocese and had only recently founded the university there. Andrew Stewart, bishop of Moray, might have been rejected on the grounds of age — though he was younger than Elphinstone — but more probably because he was a potential menace, the individual entrusted during the recent war with the task of winning over the Duke of Ross to the side of Henry VII.[75] In all these circumstances, James IV's choice of his brother as archbishop may be criticised for its cynicism and lack of any commitment to the spiritual requirements of the office, but it made excellent political sense.

Having established his brother at St Andrews, James IV pressed ahead with his refurbishing of the Scottish episcopate, taking advantage of every vacancy to nominate men who had distinguished themselves in royal service. Promotion to a bishopric for these individuals could be regarded partly as a reward for good service, but continuing loyalty to the Crown was expected and received, particularly in the encouraging response from the localities to clerical taxation. Thus John Fresell, archdeacon of Aberdeen and clerk register between 1492 and 1497, was rewarded with the bishopric of Ross in the latter year; George Hepburn, abbot of Arbroath, and uncle of Patrick, earl of Bothwell, served as Treasurer in 1509–10 and was made bishop of the Isles in 1510; while Andrew Stewart, who had become bishop of Caithness in 1501, served for a short time in 1511–12 as the royal financial officer par excellence, for he was both Treasurer and Comptroller at the same time, a remarkable achievement given that the latter office was normally the exclusive preserve of laymen. His service to the Crown as Treasurer eventually brought the rich prize of Blacader's archbishopric to James Beaton, abbot of Dunfermline; and the irresistible rise of Andrew Forman, in royal service from 1489, if not before, apostolic protonotary, nursemaid and guardian of Perkin Warbeck, ambassador to England, was confirmed by his acquisition of the bishopric of Moray in 1501.[76]

All these episcopal appointments follow an established pattern — already familiar in Henry VII's England — of promoting faithful civil servants or supporters in anticipation of further service. By contrast, James's nomination to the archbishopric of St Andrews of his illegitimate eleven-year-old son Alexander Stewart, in the spring of 1504, comes into a quite different category. Inevitably this provision has been widely condemned as the classic example of nepotism, financial corruption, and spiritual degradation within the late medieval Scottish church.[77] In fact it was nothing of the kind. Long before the unexpected death of the incumbent archbishop, James's brother, created the St Andrews vacancy in January 1504, Alexander Stewart had been groomed for a career in the church; dispensed from illegitimacy by Julius II at the age of four so that he might receive a benefice in due course, the boy was already archdeacon of St Andrews by September 1502.[78] He received a superb education, initially from James Watson, later Dean of the Arts Faculty at St Andrews, and latterly from Patrick Paniter, the royal Secretary, for whom he showed a warm affection. After his provision to the archbishopric, his education continued with a lengthy journey to the Low Countries, France, and Italy in 1507. In Padua he studied rhetoric and Greek under Erasmus, who was to write a moving obituary of his able pupil; and letters from Paniter in Scotland encouraged him to concentrate on becoming a man and a scholar, so that he might return to be the father of his country and the ruler of his see.[79]

Until Alexander Stewart's return to Scotland in 1510, aged about seventeen, the see of St Andrews was under the control of vicars-general; as James IV anxiously assured both the pope and the Cardinal of St Mark's, protector of Scottish royal interests at the curia, St Andrews would be administered with care and prudence until the archbishop could assume responsibility himself.[80] While there is no doubt that the Scottish king's initial enthusiasm for Alexander's provision was prompted by the prospect of acquiring the archiepiscopal revenues for at least sixteen years, other issues were also at stake.

One of these was the need to establish a clear pecking order between the archbishoprics of St Andrews and Glasgow. The opportunity to achieve this was provided by Blacader's death in the summer of 1508; although James Beaton was rewarded for his services to the Crown with Blacader's see, it was soon apparent that he was not going to be allowed to wield anything like as much power as his formidable predecessor. Thus Beaton, as a condition of his nomination to Glasgow, was compelled to surrender the abbey of Dunfermline and priory of Coldingham to Alexander Stewart; and he was not exempt, as Blacader had been, from the primatial and legatine authority of the archbishop of St Andrews. A further concentration of power at St Andrews resulted from the transfer of Galloway diocese from the jurisdiction of Beaton's Glasgow province, which by the end of the reign was confined to the archdiocese of Glasgow and the bishopric of the Isles.[81]

A further outstanding need was to fill the office of Chancellor, vacant since the death of the duke-archbishop in 1504. During the vacancy, and indeed for some time before it, the duties of the office had probably been discharged by Bishop Elphinstone, the Privy Seal. On 23 May 1503, when James Stewart was at least nominally Chancellor, the Treasurer's accounts record a payment 'to ane man to pas to Abirdene and brocht the keyis of the grete sele fra the Beschop of Abirdene'.[82] The great seal should have been in the possession of the Chancellor; clearly Elphinstone, on one of his visits to his diocese, had taken it home with him, which in turn suggests that he was the real incumbent of the office, doubling as Chancellor and Privy Seal. Presumably he continued to do so until 1510.

In 1510, however, Elphinstone entered his eightieth year, and despite his formidable record of service to the Crown, James IV must have realised that the bishop could not go on for ever and that an alternative arrangement was necessary. In the late spring or early summer of 1510, therefore, he conferred the Chancellorship on Alexander Stewart.[83] By the age of seventeen, the king's son had fallen heir to the most important of the secular offices of state to add to his primacy of the Scottish church.

How much power he wielded in either office for the remainder of his brief life is uncertain. Presumably the answer, as Dr Macfarlane suggests,[84] is that he had as much authority as his father was prepared to give him. Certainly he turned up assiduously to meetings of the royal council, he took his duties as Chancellor of St Andrews University seriously, and he took part — together with Prior Hepburn — in the foundation of St Leonard's College at St Andrews in 1512. There is also some evidence that he was his own man. In 1508, while abroad, he aroused Elphinstone's ire by attempting to secure the archdeaconry of Aberdeen for his guardian Sir Thomas Halkerston, provost of Crichton; and his response to his father's attempt to exempt the Chapel Royal from his jurisdiction was forthright.[85] All in all, he might have made an excellent archbishop-Chancellor — a primate capable of laying the ghosts of 1488 which had created schism in the episcopal hierarchy for so many years, a secular officer of state close enough in blood to the king to be able to dominate meetings of the council. His only disqualification for the primacy was his age; but he was not a child. In fact, seventeen was the age at which his father's father had taken control of the government of Scotland.

Towards the end of the reign, therefore, James IV had largely succeeded in creating an episcopate composed of his own men — no saints perhaps, but capable administrators, loyal servants of the Crown, able diplomats; and he had brought a unity to the Scottish church hierarchy which deserves praise rather than blame. The same cannot be said of his ruthless exploitation of the regular clergy. While the king no doubt genuinely regretted the decline in the austerity of monastic life — something which was hardly new at the end of the fifteenth century — it enabled him to pursue an ambivalent policy of demanding reform with the backing of parliamentary utterances on the subject stretching back to 1425,[86] while at the same time using the indult of 1487 to exploit and cripple the religious orders. Some of the richest abbeys — for example, Arbroath, Holyrood, and Inchaffray — were almost continually held in commendam, while the employment of the abbots of Dunfermline, Cambuskenneth, Paisley, Jedburgh, Scone, and Glenluce as financial officers of the Crown served only to

increase the secularisation of the monasteries. And there were other commends —
Coldingham as well as Dunfermline for Alexander Stewart, Kelso and Dryburgh
for Andrew Forman, and — later — Kelso and Fearn for Andrew Stewart, bishop
of Caithness.[87] On 7 April 1513 James IV assured the new pope, Leo X, that the
abbey of Cambuskenneth was dearer to him than any other religious house in his
dominions, because his father and mother were buried there. No doubt he meant
it; but the context of the remark was a letter nominating his Secretary, Patrick
Paniter, a layman who would certainly be an absentee, to the Cambuskenneth
vacancy.[88]

Such a pragmatic attitude, only partially obscured by the king's apparent
reforming zeal, was bad news for the incumbents of many religious houses.
The long and complex struggle for control of the great Cistercian abbey of
Melrose, in which the monks, with James III's support, had tenaciously
defied the consistory's choice of David Brown as abbot, is a case in
point. On one of the very few occasions on which he criticised his father
in writing, James IV described the rejection of Brown by James III and the
Melrose chapter as a serious offence to ecclesiastical liberty perpetrated by his
deceased parent. Waxing lyrical on the decline at Melrose — buildings falling
or already in ruins, the abbey unable to house the brethren — the king asked
for intervention from Rome to effect 'reform' at Melrose;[89] but what he really
wanted, as his correspondence to the pope and the curia reveals from October
1506 onwards, was not to restore the victimised David Brown, but to secure
Melrose for Robert Beaton, abbot of Glenluce, postulate to the less wealthy
house of Coupar Angus.[90] As with Melrose, a great Cistercian house, so also
with Saddell in Kintyre, one of the smallest of the order, James IV used the
language of reform to justify a proposal to add to the endowment of a favoured
servant of the Crown in a sensitive area, in this case David Hamilton, bishop of
Lismore (Argyll). Commenting that the abbey of Saddell had seen no monastic
life within living memory — a dubious statement — that it had fallen to the
use of laymen, and that there was no hope of reviving monastic life, in 1507
the king requested that a papal commission should investigate a proposal to
unite Saddell with the bishopric of Lismore.[91] This request was successful,
and in 1508 the abbey was suppressed, its endowments were confirmed by
royal charter to the bishop and his successors, and incorporated in a free
barony of Saddell.[92] It is not at all clear that monastic life had ceased to
exist at Saddell; but the bishop of Argyll, David Hamilton, was young, active
in the royal interest, and well-connected — he was the half-brother of James
Hamilton, first earl of Arran — and the king was apparently concerned to
reward a loyal supporter with rights and lands on the Kintyre peninsula, a
troubled area since the forfeiture of the MacDonald lordship in the previous
decade.[93]

If the suppression of Saddell could be disguised as a reforming measure,
no such justification can explain the outright gift, about March 1504, of the
revenues of the abbey of Tongland in Galloway to the alchemist John Damian.[94]
On 19 March 1507, when four footsore and hoarse Italian minstrels staggered into

Tongland at the end of the royal pilgrimage from Edinburgh to Whithorn,[95] they would not have found their compatriot, the abbot, there to offer them hospitality. For Damian was in his laboratory at Stirling castle, seeking the quintessence — the elixir of life — consuming large quantities of 'acqua vitae' supplied by the Crown for his experiments, and no doubt preparing for his most celebrated exploit, his attempt to fly from the battlements of Stirling castle to France in September of that year.[96]

Contemporaries, however, did not judge the king harshly for his distribution of monastic wealth among friends, supporters, or court hangers-on. Even the great poet William Dunbar, who viciously satirised Damian in two poems, was not objecting to the principle of church benefices being used as royal patronage; quite the reverse, in fact, for the complaint which runs like a leitmotif through his work is his failure to obtain a benefice which would enable him to live well on the proceeds.[97] And appearances counted for a lot. As Don Pedro de Ayala noted, the king 'fears God, and observes all the precepts of the Church. He does not eat meat on Wednesdays and Fridays. . .He says all his prayers. Before transacting any business he hears two masses. . .he has a great predilection for priests, and receives advice from them, especially from the Friars Observant, with whom he confesses.'[98]

Ayala's comment on James IV's patronage of the Observants is interesting, for it reveals that in 1496–7, the period of the Spanish ambassador's stay at the Scottish court, the king was already displaying conspicuous generosity towards one of the strictest orders of the day, introduced to Scotland by his grandmother Mary of Gueldres and well established in four houses — Edinburgh, Aberdeen, Glasgow, and St Andrews — by 1479. To these Observant friaries five more were added in James IV's reign, Perth and Elgin during the minority, Ayr, Jedburgh, and Stirling after the king's assumption of power in 1495.[99] Of these, the last was undoubtedly a royal foundation, highly favoured by the king as a place of retreat during Easter week, as the frustrated English ambassador Nicholas West discovered to his cost when he could gain no access to James IV at Stirling in April 1513.[100] In a letter to Julius II in February 1507, the Scottish king described the virtues of the Observants. They stood, he said, for the salvation of souls; they had remedied neglect by others, they ministered the sacraments, and faithfully proclaimed Christ's word. James himself had completed and furnished for them house after house (implying that at least some of the other foundations were royal ones), and in the friaries of the Observants he found cleansing for his conscience. As a devoted son and defender of the order, he was totally opposed to any union of the Observants and the Conventual Grey Friars, for the latter represented 'a less strict manner of living'.[101] A generation later Adam Abell, an Observant friar of Jedburgh, would look back on James's reign and praise the king for peacefully guiding the kingdom through use of the wise counsel of members of his order; and though he commented that James had endowed 'outhir halie places', it was the Observantine friary at Stirling which he mentioned first.[102] If James IV is to be remembered as a reformer in any sense, it must be for his generosity towards, and defence of, the Observant Franciscans.

Viewed overall, his ecclesiastical policies bear a striking similarity to those of his father-in-law Henry VII. Both men displayed an ostentatious piety; both received not only the Golden Rose, but also the Sword and Hat, from the pope; both exerted so much control over their respective churches that cathedral chapters were removed from any real part in the election of bishops during their reigns; both founded Observantine friaries, though Henry was less committed in his support for the order than James, as he also actively supported the conventuals; and both paid lip-service to the papal call for a crusade against the Turks, Henry rather more than James, for he allowed £4,000 to be contributed to a crusading levy in 1501.[103] The attitude of both to crusades is probably best summed up in a royal letter written to the pope in 1502, in which the king remarked that although his Kingdom was geographically much further from the Holy Land than France or Spain, nevertheless he would personally undertake a crusade at his own expense 'if the Pope will personally go against the said Turk.' The writer was not James IV, but Henry VII.[104]

There was, however, an added dimension to the ecclesiastical policies of the Scottish king. James IV was influenced not simply by a desire to display his piety, reward his friends and supporters, make money for the Crown, or by adherence to the Bartolist theory that the king is emperor in all things in his own realm, but by a very practical consideration, the need to defend the Scottish church against external assaults on its independence. Of its thirteen bishoprics, two had technically been Norse, one English, until the late fifteenth century; and internal Scottish disputes as to the jurisdiction of the archbishops cannot have helped to present a united front to the outside world. As king, James IV had to deal with two determined and predatory popes, Alexander VI and Julius II, whose efforts to form European alliances to suit their own secular purposes carried the danger that the English might be drawn in and revive claims to overlordship of all or part of the Ecclesia Scoticana. As recently as the 1470s Richard Neville, archbishop of York, had protested against the archiepiscopal status awarded to St Andrews; and shortly after Flodden, Henry VIII was to reassert York's claims to superiority.[105] For James IV, therefore, it was not enough to try to extract occasional concessions from successive popes. He had to dominate his clergy in order to protect the church. In addition he had to give the Scottish church a clear identity; hence partly James's injunction to Chepman and Myllar, when he licensed Scotland's first printing press in 1507, to print 'mess bukis and portuus (breviaries), efter the use of our realme, with additiouns and legendis of Scottis sanctis now gaderit to be ekit thairto.'[106] The man who had done much of the 'gadering', Bishop Elphinstone of Aberdeen, did perhaps his greatest service to his church and king by giving Scotland a national liturgy, by supplanting the English Sarum Use in Scotland, and by immortalising over seventy Scottish saints, all of them assigned to feast days, in the Aberdeen Breviary of 1509–10.[107] The clergy responded to this 'liturgical nationalism' by lending broad support to the king against the English in 1513, in a war which they construed as a struggle not only for the defence of national, but also of ecclesiastical, independence. When James IV, an excommunicated king, died at Flodden, there died with him a large number of Scottish clergy, including even a contingent from the diocese of his ageing enemy, George Brown of Dunkeld;[108] and amongst the church's leaders, there fell Alexander Stewart, archbishop of St Andrews, George Hepburn, bishop of the Isles, Laurence Oliphant, abbot of Inchaffray, and William Bunch, abbot of Kilwinning.[109]

Perhaps, therefore, the most moving memorial to James IV is not to be found in the Chapel Royal, nor the Observantine friary at Stirling, nor in any of the other friaries which he endowed, but rather in the 'kirk of steill', the beautiful little church of Ladykirk in Berwickshire, in the parish of Upsettlington on the north bank of the river Tweed, about seven miles north-east of Coldstream. Traditionally founded by James IV and dedicated to the Virgin Mary in thanks for the king's deliverance from drowning when the Tweed was in spate — perhaps in September 1496 or when the royal army was encamped at Upsettlington in August 1497 — the church is undoubtedly a royal foundation under construction early in the sixteenth century.[110] A simple structure, cruciform but aisleless, Ladykirk stands today, as it stood in 1513, looking out over the Tweed towards the great English fortress of Norham, only a mile to the south-east, the principal objective of two — and possibly all three — of James IV's invasions of England. A few miles to the south, King James and many of the first estate stood and fell together at Flodden; but Ladykirk remains as a memorial to a unity of purpose, and a sense of aggressive independence, shared by King and clergy alike.

NOTES

1. *T.A.*, iii, 289, 378–9. For the history of papal gifts and their conferral on Scottish kings, see Rev. Charles Burns, 'Papal Gifts to Scottish Monarchs: The Golden Rose and the Blessed Sword', *Innes Review* xx (2), 1969, 150–194.

2. *T.A.*, iii, 287.
3. Lesley, *De Origine*, ii, 123.
4. *T.A.*, iii, 287–8, 372–4.
5. Lesley, *De Origine*, ii, 123.
6. *T.A.*, iii, 399–400.
7. Lesley, *History*, 76; *E.R.*, xiii, Pref., lxxxiv–lxxxv.
8. *T.A.*, i, ii, iii, iv, passim.
9. *Ibid.*, ii, 366, 401, 402–3.
10. *Ibid.*, ii, 437.
11. *Ibid.*, iii, Pref., xxvii.
12. *Ibid.*, iv, 130.
13. David McRoberts, 'Hermits in Medieval Scotland', *Innes Review* xvi (2), 1965, 199–216, at 206.
14. *James IV Letters*, Nos. 89, 104.
15. *Ibid.*, 106.
16. Alan Macquarrie, *Scotland and the Crusades, 1095–1560* (Edinburgh, 1985), 92.

17. Macquarrie, *op. cit.*, 92, 105; David McRoberts, 'Scottish Pilgrims to the Holy Land,' *Innes Review* xx (1), 1969, 80–106, at 91.

18. Macquarrie, *op. cit.*, 97, 99–100.

19. Macdougall, *James III*, 114, 143.

20. *E.R.*, v, 156, 179; Macquarrie, *op. cit.*, 92–3.

21. *James IV Letters*, Nos. 65, 66.

22. *Ibid.*, No. 122.

23. For the details of Blacader's pilgrimage, see McRoberts, 'Pilgrims', 92–4; John Durkan, 'Archbishop Robert Blackadder's Will', *Innes Review* xxiii (2), 1972, 138–148.

24. *James IV Letters*, Nos. 142–144.

25. Mackie, *James IV*, 201–2.

26. *Ibid.*, 83, 84.

27. Nicholson, *Later Middle Ages*, 594.

28. *Rentale Dunkeldense 1505–1517*, ed. R.K. Hannay (S.H.S., 1915), 247.

29. *James IV Letters*, Nos. 166–168.

30. *Ibid.*, Nos. 45, 62, 67.

31. *Ibid.*, No. 462.

32. Macquarrie, *op. cit.*, 31, 107–8.

33. *James IV Letters*, No. 294. On 27 September 1474 the Milanese ambassador at the French court had written to his master, Galeazzo Maria Sforza, duke of Milan, describing Scotland as lying 'in finibus orbis': *Cal. State Papers (Milan)*, i, 186–8.

34. *James IV Letters*, No. 300.

35. *T.A.*, iv, 360–365, 391–396.

36. *Cal. State Papers (Venice)*, ii, Nos. 63, 66, 73.

37. *Ibid.*, ii, Nos. 82, 83, 84.

38. *Ibid.*, ii, Nos. 64, 92, 147, 191.

39. *Ibid.*, ii, No. 90.

40. *Ibid.*, ii, No. 81.

41. *James IV Letters*, No. 332.

42. *Letters and Papers Henry VIII*, i, pt. 1, Nos. 649, 708.

43. *James IV Letters*, No. 42.

44. *Ibid.*, Nos. 347, 349, 350, 351, 352, 353, 354, 355, 356, 359.

45. Scarisbrick, *Henry VIII*, 27–29.

46. *Flodden Papers*, 6–19. The editor has tentatively dated James's requirements for a crusade to December 1510, when Forman was at Blois. But such a request seems inappropriate to Forman's *first* mission; and the statement that the King of Spain was already making war on Louis suggests a date after the formation of the Holy League in the autumn of 1511, when Forman was again in France.

47. *Flodden Papers*, 19–26.

48. *T.A.*, iv, 323, 333. On 31 December 1511 royal letters were sent to members of the spiritual estate summoning a General Council 'concernyng the Paip and the King of Francis materis'. On 28 February 1512 a messenger was sent to notify unspecified lords to come to a General Council — possibly the same one — though there is no indication as to its business.

49. *Letters and Papers Henry VIII*, i, pt. i, No. 1089.

50. For extensive treatment of the decline of the Hospitaller Order in Scotland, and the dispute over the preceptory of Torphichen, *see* Macquarrie, *op. cit.*, 101–2, 114–116; and *The Knights of St. John of Jerusalem in Scotland*, edd. I.B. Cowan, P.H.R. Mackay, and A. Macquarrie (S.H.S., 1983), xlvii–xlix, 199–200.

51. Macquarrie, *op. cit.*, 101–2, 114; for Knollis' public career during James IV's minority, see chapters 3 and 4.

52. *James IV Letters*, Nos. 553, 554.

53. *Ibid.*, No. 159; *R.S.S.*, i, Nos. 1771, 1772.

54. *James IV Letters*, Nos. 317, 323.

55. *Ibid.*, No. 346.

56. *Ibid.*, No. 360.

57. For Paniter's career, see R.L. Mackie's short biography: *James IV Letters*, Pref., xxviii–xxxiv.

58. *James IV Letters*, Appendix II.

59. *Ibid.*, No. 395.

60. *Ibid.*, No. 553.

61. *Letters and Papers Henry VIII*, i, pt. i, No. 1566.

62. *Cal. Pap. Reg.*, xiv, 4.

63. For the Dunkeld dispute, see J.A.F. Thomson, 'Innocent VIII and the Scottish Church', *Innes Review* xix (1), 1968, 23–31, at 23–26.

64. *A.P.S.*, ii, 171.

65. *Cal. State Papers (Spain)*, i, No. 210.

66. Macdougall, *James III*, chapter 11, passim.

67. *Cal. Pap. Reg.*, xiv, 220–1. Andrew Stewart, bishop of Moray, was similarly exempted from Scheves' jurisdiction: Macfarlane, 'Primacy', 117.

68. *Ibid.*, xiv, 289.

69. Macfarlane, 'Primacy', 116, 118.

70. *A.P.S.*, ii, 232–233, c.7.

71. *See above*, chapter 5.

72. *Cal. State Papers (Spain)*, i, Nos. 104, 105.

73. *See above*, chapter 5.

74. Macfarlane, 'Primacy', 119–120.

75. *See above*, chapter 5.

76. *H.B.C.*, 172–192, 281–301, passim; Nicholson, *Later Middle Ages*, 558–9. Biographies of Forman and Beaton are to be found in Herkless and Hannay, *Archbishops*, vols. ii, iii. These should be treated with caution.

77. Typical of this attitude is the first paragraph of Herkless and Hannay's chapter on Alexander Stewart: *Archbishops*, i, 215–6.

78. Macfarlane, 'Primacy', 121; *T.A.*, ii, 300.

79. Macfarlane, 'Primacy', 121–2; *James IV Letters*, No. 145.

80. For the likely date of Alexander Stewart's return, see Chalmers, 'Crown Patronage', 433; Macfarlane, 'Primacy', 122. For the administration of St. Andrews in his absence, see *James IV Letters*, No. 20.

81. *James IV Letters*, Pref., xxxvi–xxxvii.

82. *T.A.*, ii, 373.

83. By 19 June 1510: *R.M.S.*, ii, No. 3480.

84. Macfarlane, 'Primacy', 122.

85. *James IV Letters*, Nos. 161, 191, 211.

86. *A.P.S.*, ii, 7.

87. *H.B.C.*, passim; Nicholson, *Later Middle Ages*, 558–9.

88. *James IV Letters*, No. 542.

89. *Ibid.*, No. 50.

90. *Ibid.*, Nos. 51, 91. Other royal letters on the subject of the Melrose dispute are in *Ibid.*, Nos. 48, 49, 93, 94, 95, 311, 335.

91. *Ibid.*, No. 149.

92. *R.M.S.*, ii, No. 3170.

93. For a full discussion of the context of the Saddell suppression, *see* A.L. Brown, 'The Cistercian Abbey of Saddell, Kintyre', *Innes Review* xx (2), 1969, 130–137, at 135–7.

94. *T.A.*, ii, 423.

95. *Ibid.*, iii, 375.

96. John Read, 'A Flying Alchemist', in *Humour and Humanism in Chemistry*

(London, 1947), 16–36, esp. 30–31; Lesley, *History*, 76; *T.A.*, iii, Pref., lxxxvi–lxxxvii; *T.A.*, iv, passim.

97. Dunbar's poems about Damian are 'The Fenyeit Freir of Tungland' and 'The Birth of Antichrist' in *The Poems of William Dunbar*, ed. J. Small (S.T.S., 1884–93), ii, 139–43. A good example of his complaints about his failure to obtain a benefice is in the poem 'Of the warldis instabilite', in *Ibid.*, ii, 227. See also, in general, R.J. Lyall, 'Politics and Poetry in Fifteenth and Sixteenth Century Scotland', *Scottish Literary Journal* 3 (2), (1976), 5–29.

98. *Cal. State Papers (Spain)*, i, No. 210.

99. Cowan and Easson, *Medieval Religious Houses: Scotland*, 129–133.

100. *James IV Letters*, No. 539.

101. *Ibid.*, No. 76.

102. N.L.S. Adv. MS. 1746, f.112r.

103. Chrimes, *Henry VII*, 240–244, 304–5.

104. J.O. Halliwell, *Letters of the Kings of England* (Lond., 1846), i, 185–194, at 192.

105. Theiner, *Vetera Monumenta*, 512.

106. *R.S.S.*, i, No. 1546.

107. David McRoberts, 'The Scottish Church and Nationalism in the Fifteenth Century', *Innes Review* xix (1), 1968, 3–14, esp. 8–9.

108. *Rentale Dunkeldense*, 315.

109. The most accurate Flodden death roll is to be found in W.K. Emond, 'The minority of King James V, 1513–1528' (unpublished PhD. thesis, St. Andrews, 1988), Appendix A.

110. See, in general, John R. Baldwin, *Exploring Scotland's Heritage: Lothian and the Borders* (H.M.S.O., 1985), 102; *T.A.*, ii, Pref., lxxxiii–lxxxiv, 85; *E.R.*, xi, 276. (for building operations at Ladykirk, 1500–1504).

9

Royal Obsession: The Navy

In the middle of August 1506 James IV wrote to Louis XII of France reporting that the building of a fleet to defend Scotland was a project of long standing which he was bent on realising.[1] This was no less than the truth. In the course of the reign King James built, purchased, hired, received as gifts or seized as prizes a total of at least thirty-eight ships.[2] His naval building programme was large by any standards, quite remarkably so for the ruler of a small kingdom; and his expenditure on ships, their supplying and maintenance, was by far the greatest single item of royal expenditure in the latter years of the reign.

The origins of this striking development are to be found in the mid-fifteenth century, and may perhaps be traced to James II's vision of himself as a European ruler of some importance, a belief to some extent justified by the marriage alliances obtained for his sisters in France, Brittany, Veere, and Austria, and culminating in his own marriage to Mary of Gueldres, niece of Philip the Good of Burgundy, in the summer of 1449.[3] Before the end of the reign, the king was able to employ a fleet — of sorts — to carry an invasion force from Kirkcudbright to the Isle of Man, though the raid was unsuccessful and indeed provoked English retaliation in Galloway.[4] Most likely the ships used as troop transports on this occasion, and in the sending of Scottish expeditionary forces to France in the reign of James I, were merchantmen, hired by the Crown and suitably armed for a specific occasion, rather than ships owned by James II. We should not, however, underestimate the number, or size, of Scottish vessels available to the king at this time. In 1457, on the orders of Philip the Good of Burgundy, the water bailiff of the port of Sluys in Flanders made a list of ships using the harbour. Apart from a large number of Scots, Breton, and Spanish small ships — most of them of less than 50 tons — there were about forty fishing boats, twelve 'ungainly and poorly regarded' Hanseatic ships, and a Portuguese hulk of 150 tons. But the striking part of the water bailiff's list is his description of the big ships — not only a Scots carvel of 140 tons belonging to Ingeram Lindsay, bishop of Aberdeen, and a Scots barge of 150 tons whose master was one Bartholomew Buton, but also a larger Scots barge of 350 tons captained by Robert Barton. Towering over all of these was the ship which Hector Boece was later to describe as 'the biggest [ship] that had been seen to sail upon the ocean', Bishop Kennedy of St Andrews' famous barge, the 'Salvator', listed by the water bailiff as 'a very fine vessel' of 500 tons.[5] Boece was exaggerating and Sluys is not perhaps a typical Low Countries port; but the list gives no mean idea of Scottish maritime enterprise in the mid-fifteenth century, and consequently of the available pool of large merchantmen upon which the king might draw in time of war.

There was at this time no royal navy in the sense of ships designed solely for war and maintained at Crown expense. This was not because there was no need for proper defence of the Firth of Clyde or the east coast — especially the latter, as the early fourteenth-century campaigns of Edward I and III, with their skilful interplay between land forces and ships bearing supplies and reinforcements, had repeatedly shown. The problem was partly one of resources. If no fifteenth-century English king — with the brief exception of Henry V — could sustain the expense of long-term naval activity,[6] even given the English Crown's vast income in comparison with that of the King of Scots, it was hardly likely that the Stewarts would be able to do so. Besides, for much of the fifteenth century there were relatively few Anglo-Scottish crises which might have justified the huge expense. There was, after all, no major English invasion of Scotland between 1400 and 1482. During that period the Scottish kings had other, more mundane, problems to cope with at sea — the protection of merchants, especially on the North Sea crossing to the Low Countries or the Baltic, making safe coastal waters for fishermen, and — if possible — organising the hunting down of pirates. Apart from its recognised duty of defending the realm, the Crown had a personal interest in this because, together with some of the nobility, clergy, and the third estate, the king himself engaged in overseas trading ventures. Yet if we judge by the available evidence, admittedly scanty, the protection of Scottish coastal waters and the North Sea passage proved too much for the government during the reign of James III. That king, who seems to have had an interest in the late Bishop Kennedy's barge, the 'Salvator', spent eighteen months obtaining compensation for the seizure and spoliation of the great ship by James Ker, an Englishman, following her shipwreck, laden with merchandise, near Bamburgh in March 1473.[7] Around the same time the 'Yellow Carvel', later immortalised by Pitscottie as Sir Andrew Wood's ship, a vessel probably owned or part-owned by the king, was captured by the Duke of Gloucester's 'Mayflower', and a ship of Sir John Colquhoun of Luss was seized by a vessel belonging to Lord Grey.[8] Even the favoured port of Sluys in Flanders was not safe for the Scots; in the mid-1470s, discovering that one of John Barton's ships was carrying a valuable cargo, a Portuguese piratical fleet had followed it out of Sluys harbour, seized the Scots vessel, slain some merchants and sailors, and made off with the best of the merchandise and fittings.[9]

As the Treasurer's accounts are lacking for almost all of James III's reign, these examples may not give a fair balance. What they show clearly, however, is that the principal menace to Scots shipping in the North Sea was the hostility of the English. For sea warfare, even in time of truce, tended to form a category of its own, and it is extremely unlikely that any English compensation would have been paid for the seizures of the 'Salvator', the 'Yellow Carvel', and Colquhoun's ship had it not been for the Anglo-Scottish alliance of October 1474.

It was however the collapse of that brittle alliance, and the war of 1480–82 which followed, which most clearly revealed the inability of the Scots to meet a major English naval threat. In the early summer of 1481 John Lord Howard raided the coast of the Firth of Forth with a naval squadron composed of his own vessels and some royal ships. According to Bishop Lesley, he took as prizes eight Scottish ships — presumably quite small ones — lying at Leith, Kinghorn, and Pittenweem, landed at Blackness, burned the town, and seized a large ship which was in the harbour.[10] Howard appears to have been attacked at sea by Sir Andrew Wood of Largo, and from Wood's later reward from James III — a feu-charter of Largo in 1483 — we learn that he inflicted extensive damage on the English at sea, though not without loss to himself.[11]

Worse was to follow. In the summer of 1482, the huge English army led by Gloucester and Albany entered south-east Scotland supported by a sizeable fleet under the command of Sir Robert Radcliff. The Scots, wracked by their own internal political upheavals, had no response to this, and the English fleet — probably, as in 1481, including the huge 'Grace Dieu' — sailed without opposition into Leith.[12] This combination of army and fleet made the burgh and castle of Berwick indefensible, and in spite of James III's efforts to retain it through paying mercenaries out of his own pocket, Berwick fell to the English for the last time in 1482.[13] The following year Albany admitted an English garrison to the sea-girt fortress of Dunbar, which was not recovered by the Scots until 1485–6.[14] The message was clear. Faced with full-scale English invasion by land and sea for the first time in over eighty years, the Scottish political community had rediscovered the vulnerability of their east-coast ports and castles. In spite of the personal valour of Sir Andrew Wood with his few — possibly only two — ships, in 1481–2 the Scots had no adequate response to the English fleet, ably organised and maintained on the orders of Thomas Rogers, Clerk of the King's Ships from 1480.[15] In fact there could be no adequate Scottish response without a vast capital investment in ships; and this was presumably considered to be out of the question financially in the early 1480s.

Luck was with the Scots. The sudden death of Edward IV in April 1483, followed by the English usurpation crisis and the turbulent two-year reign of Richard III, meant that there would be no early repetition of the traumas of 1481–2. Furthermore the accession of Henry VII of England in August 1485 marked the beginning of the end for the Yorkist navy which he inherited. Henry's seven royal ships of 1485 had diminished to five three years later; and though there was some replacement of older vessels — for example the 'Grace Dieu' was broken up in 1486 to supply timber for the new 800-ton 'Sovereign' — by 1504 English royal ships numbered only five and had only increased to seven by Henry's death in 1509.[16] Yet even within this context of cutbacks, in 1497 King Henry, as we have seen, had been able to threaten the Scots with a frightening repetition of 1482, based on a combination of land and sea forces, the latter consisting of three royal ships as the nucleus of a fleet of hired transports and armed merchantmen.[17] The invasion never came because

Henry VII was suddenly threatened by the Cornish rising; but 1497, like 1482, was a salutory reminder to the Scots of the vulnerability to attack — by sea as well as by land — of the capital of the Scottish kingdom, and of the need for adequate defence of the Firths of Forth and Clyde, and the south-eastern coastline. Indeed, this need had been underlined since the outset of James IV's reign, when his father's Anglophile policies went into reverse, 'the inbringing of Inglismen' was something to be feared, and Henry VII's support — such as it was — for the rebels of 1489 consisted of the rather tardy despatch of three ships commanded by Stephen Bull to prey on Scottish fishing vessels in the Firth of Forth and the appearance in the Clyde of another ship laden with supplies and munitions for the defenders of Dumbarton.[18]

There is in fact ample evidence in the early years of the new reign to show that, in spite of the three years' truce concluded with England in October 1488, the war at sea continued as though the truce had never been made. Indeed, the early chapters of Pitscottie's colourful chronicle which deal with this reign read almost like a naval history, with Sir Andrew Wood cast in the role of victorious hero, winning two seafights, in the summers of 1489 and 1490, against superior English forces.[19] We do not have to believe everything which Pitscottie says; it is likely, for example, that he has made one seafight into two, and his dates cannot be verified. However, he does cite Sir Andrew Wood as one of his sources — not a direct source, though Sir Andrew's son and namesake may have been, for he died only in 1579, the year in which Pitscottie completed his chronicle.[20] It seems likely that in his descriptions of the exploits of the elder Wood, Pitscottie was using a written rather than an oral source, for George Buchanan's history, completed without reference to Pitscottie a few years later, echoes much of what Pitscottie says about naval affairs.[21] The two chroniclers would therefore appear to have used a common written source, possibly a Wood family chronicle completed some time in the mid-sixteenth century.

Pitscottie's seafights have a factual basis. Sir Andrew Wood was heavily involved in resisting English and piratical attacks in the Firth of Forth; and Stephen Bull was undoubtedly an English commander employed in some capacity by Henry VII and rewarded — admittedly with only the paltry sum of £6 sterling — in Michaelmas Term 1490, for his expenses at sea.[22] So there may be some truth in Pitscottie's description of the seafight which he dates as occurring on 10 August 1490, when Stephen Bull, with three heavily-armed English vessels, lay in wait off the Isle of May for Sir Andrew Wood's two ships, the 'Yellow Carvel' and the 'Flower', returning from Flanders. Bull had captured some Scottish fishermen whom he asked to identify Wood's returning ships; and there followed a furious fight which went on all day, and during which the weapons used included not only artillery and crossbows, but also lime pots and two-handed swords. In short, the fight took place at very close quarters following Wood's successful manoeuvring to grapple with Bull's vessels; and it came to an end only the following morning, when the English ships had drifted into the Tay and Bull had no option but to surrender. His three vessels, according to Pitscottie, were then towed into Dundee as prizes. Stephen Bull and the survivors amongst his seamen were well treated; indeed, Pitscottie remarks that they were given gifts by James IV, restored to their ships, and sent back to Henry VII 'doand him to vnderstand that [James] had allis manfull men baitht be sie and be land in Scotland as he had in Ingland' — and warning Henry that anyone attempting to follow Bull's example in the future would not be so well treated.[23]

The record evidence corroborates Pitscottie's tale up to a point, and — not surprisingly — reduces the scale of the heroism and chivalrous behaviour on both sides. On 18 May 1491, during the first parliament to be held since the Wood — Bull seafight according to Pitscottie's dating of it, Sir Andrew Wood was given a royal licence, confirming the approval of the king and estates for building operations which he had already undertaken within his burgh and lands of Largo. Using English captives, Wood had built not only houses but also a fortalice to defend Largo against attack from pirates or other invaders. A grateful parliament, recognising Wood's services in inflicting damage on the king's enemies at sea and his losses in the process, also confirmed his feu-charter of Largo, first granted by James III, and stated that it would not be affected by any future royal revocation.[24] Reading between the lines, one sees James IV's minority government anxious to retain the services of a skilled seaman who had formerly served James III, and hurrying to confirm Wood's private enterprise at Largo by licencing his fortalice long after it had been built. The confirmation and licence, granted as they were in parliament, obviously received the widest publicity; and both give the impression that in the 1490s, Wood could do very much as he liked.

Four days earlier, on 14 May 1491, the same parliament made further provision for the defence of the Forth. Deploring the many instances of spoliation, harrying, and rape which his subjects had suffered at the hands of the English and other pirates in the vicinity of the Firth of Forth, James IV, with the advice of his parliament and council, granted to John Dundas of that ilk and his heirs the island and rock of 'Inchgard' (Inchgarvie) sited in the Forth at the narrows by the Queensferry, with the power to erect on the rock a castle or fortalice with which to defend the firth from hostile attacks. As in the case of Wood, the grant to Dundas was not to be affected by any future revocation.[25] This intelligent defensive measure placed a fortress on a rock only a few hundred yards long, stategically sited in the middle of narrows less than two miles wide, with a commanding view of all shipping entering the Forth, and gave the responsibility for its maintenance to a loyal local laird. On the other hand, parliament had effectively recognised as early as October 1488 that the East Lothian coast could not be defended, and had ordered that Dunbar castle should be 'cassyne doune and aluterly distroyit', the reason given being that the castle 'hes done gret scaith in tyme bygane' — presumably a reference to Albany's recent surrender of Dunbar to the English — 'and war gret danger to the realm and It wer necligently kepit'.[26] Interestingly the view that Dunbar was indefensible was rejected by James IV when he took control of government, and the castle underwent extensive and costly repairs between 1497 and 1501, with the ubiquitous Sir Andrew Wood appointed as the castle's new keeper.[27]

Thus the experience of the Scots on the coastline of the Firth of Forth during the latter years of James III's reign and the seven years' minority of his son was of intermittent official and unofficial war conducted against them by English fleets, smaller squadrons, or by pirates. Clearly a spirited response was made to these attacks — for example the ship of the Danish pirate Lutkyn Mere, which had committed 'heavy Iniuris' in Scottish waters, was speedily captured in the summer of 1489, thirty-six of the Danes were executed and a further nine volunteered for the siege of Duchal[28] — but the real and continuing problem for the government was the threat represented by the English. Cautious defensive measures like the building of the fortalices at Largo and on Inchgarvie, and the part-time employment by the Crown of skilled seamen like Wood and the Bartons of Leith would help to prevent raids such as that made by Lord Howard on Blackness in 1481, but they would do little to make safe the more exposed coasts, far less the sea routes to the Low Countries and the Baltic. And local private enterprise was unlikely to be able to stop an English invasion or supply fleet acting in conjunction with a land force, as had happened in 1482 and almost happened in 1497.

It was in this context — the need to protect Scots merchantmen at sea and to defend Scotland from English seaborne attacks — that James IV made the construction of a royal navy a principal policy objective shortly after the turn of the century. His growing interest in ships is reflected in spiraling costs. For the first ten years of the reign, the Treasurer's accounts reveal a total royal expenditure of £1,482 12. 10d. for the building, buying, repairing, and victualling of ships — an annual average of only about £140, and boosted to that figure by including in the total the single huge cost of £500 for a rowbarge built at Dumbarton. However, in the period 1501–4, expenditure on ships had shot up to an annual average of approximately £600; and in the following two years, 1505–7, the real 'take-off' occurred, with the annual average expenditure reaching £5,000. In 1507–8 the total expenditure for the year was £7,279, and by 1511–13 the average spent annually on the fleet was £8,710 10/-.[29] This last figure is certainly an underestimate, as it excludes many victualling, building, and wages costs which cannot be exactly calculated. Allowance also needs to be made for the fact that there are missing Treasurer's accounts — 1492–4, 1498–1501, and 1508–10 — so that overall royal expenditure throughout is clearly greater than the records show. What the figures do show is that over the twenty-five years of a reign during which royal income approximately tripled, expenditure on ships and their maintenance increased more than sixty times, with the huge rise in costs coming in the second half of the reign. This vast outlay reflects a close personal interest in the development of a royal navy by the king himself, and taken together with other record evidence it suggests that James IV saw the possession of a fleet, including some vessels of considerable size, as a means of conferring international prestige on himself and his dynasty.

As we have seen, King James had spent much of the minority being toured around the west. The rebellion of 1489, centred on Dumbarton, probably explains the royal purchase of a ship from Colquhoun of Luss at a cost of £130, to which more than double that figure had to be added for outfitting and sailors' wages; and the forfeiture of the lordship of the Isles in 1493 was followed by James's sea trips in 1493–5 to Dunstaffnage in Lorne, Mingary in the Sound of Mull, but above all to Kintyre, ordering the building of one new castle at Loch Kilkerran and the repairing of those at Tarbert and Dunaverty. These expeditions, which began in the minority but spread over into the period of James's personal rule, came to an end as far as the king was concerned with the three trips to Kintyre in 1498.[31] It remained necessary to retain royal ships at Dumbarton — probably the 'Christopher' was bought and maintained by the king, and a large row-barge was built for King James at Dumbarton in the winter of 1494–5, together with two smaller ships[32] — and to augment their numbers by hiring others in times of need; for example, Sir Andrew Wood's 'Flower' to sail to Mingary in 1495, and possibly also Cairn-na-Burgh in the Treshnish Isles in 1504, and the merchantman 'Raven' to bear Huntly's expedition to the siege of Stornoway in 1506.[33] Nor does shipbuilding at Dumbarton appear to have been abandoned during James's personal rule, for an unnamed royal vessel was under construction in a priest's yard, or garden, probably between Dumbarton collegiate church and the confluence of the rivers Leven and Clyde, in the years 1505–7. Despite payments to the provost of Dumbarton and others for the building and outfitting of the ship — including an intriguing 42/- 'drinksilver' to a shipwright named Goherrall, probably Portuguese — and a visit to the yard by the king in July 1507,[34] royal shipbuilding on the Clyde is not noted in the Treasurer's accounts during the final years of the reign.

For the most striking change of all in King James's development of a royal fleet was geographical, a shift from west to east, from building or repairing vessels at Dumbarton for service in the Isles to creating two new naval dockyards in the Forth capable of accommodating the largest ships. The main stimulus to this may have been the failure of James's Danish expedition in the summer of 1502, something which troubled the Scottish king for at least four years. The expedition was James's response to an appeal from King Hans of Denmark in terms of the Scoto-Danish treaty of 1492. A rising against Hans by the Swedes and members of the Norwegian aristocracy during the winter of 1501–2 resulted in the capture of a number of key castles from the Danes, including Akershus near Oslo.[35] Following a meeting of what was probably a General Council at the beginning of March 1502,[36] James IV called out a levy in Fife, Forfar and Perth on 18 April, at about the same time despatching Robert Herwort, one of his gunners, to Kinghorn for artillery. At the end of the month the king sent 'new lettrez for Denmark' to the earls of Atholl and Crawford and the Earl Marischal, together with 'lordis in tha boundis'; by 7 May he was distributing 'drinksilver' to the workmen at Leith preparing the 'Eagle' and the 'Towaich' for the sea voyage to Denmark; and on 22 May the 'Trinity' returned to Leith from Denmark, presumably bringing James up-to-date news of the rebellion in King Hans's dominions. Also present at Leith were the 'Douglas' and the 'Christopher', the latter a veteran of James's expedition to Kintyre in 1494, and both probably formed part of the small fleet bound for Denmark. James was certainly taking the matter seriously. On 20 May he ordered his 'cote of gold' — presumably a surcoat with the royal arms emblazoned on it — to be brought from Stirling to Edinburgh, so that he might send it to King Hans; and the expedition was to be financed by an enormous tax of £12,000 levied on all three estates.[37]

Writing almost seventy years later, Bishop Lesley made the most he could of the Danish expedition, wildly exaggerating King Hans's plight, suggesting even that Hans came to Scotland in person looking for assistance, and remarking that James IV was moved to support his Danish kinsman 'be advyse and persuatione of the King of Fraunce.' In Lesley's account, the Scottish king 'prepared ane army of ten thousand men, and appointit the Erle of Arrane thair liuetenaunt, and send thame in Denmark with the King (Hans), quhairby he wes restorit to his kingdome'; and the Scottish fleet 'returned in Scotland with greit honour to the King of Scotland and his cuntrey, for his princely support gevin to this afflicted King. . .and in doing thairof shew himself a mirrour in geving guide exampill to all uther Princis in the like case'.[38]

Quite apart from his exaggeration of King Hans's troubles — the Danish King did not flee to Scotland — and his placing of the event under the date 1503, Lesley was doubtless moved to give a good press to the Danish expedition in order to enhance the virtues of the man whom he claimed to be its commander, James Lord Hamilton; for in Lesley's own day the Hamiltons had shown themselves active supporters of his patroness Mary, Queen of Scots. Thus in Lesley's account Hamilton becomes James, earl of Arran, a title he received only at the wedding of James IV and Margaret Tudor, and the expedition is placed *after* the royal wedding of August 1503 rather than a year before it in order simply to accord Hamilton his new status. In any event, the gist of the story is that King Hans was restored to his kingdom with the aid of ten thousand Scots.

In fact, the Danish expedition was a fiasco, and the fleet did not return 'with greit honour'. Indeed, a relevant question is how much of it sailed in the first place. One major defaulter was George Lord Seton, who had been paid £400 by the Treasurer to have his ship, the 'Eagle', ready for sea by 8 May 1502, to ferry 'men of weyre', at the king's command, to Denmark. Seton sent the king his minstrel to entertain, and perhaps to mollify him; but 8 May came and went, and the 'Eagle' was not ready. On 19 May King James crossed the Queensferry to Inverkeithing to see the ship; and he paid a second visit to the 'Eagle' on 27 May. It is not clear that the 'Eagle' ever sailed to Denmark with James's small fleet, and the picture we have of the Scottish king in the last fortnight of May is of James hastening about the Firth of Forth visiting ships, liberally throwing 'drinksilver' to his workmen, endeavouring to make up for lost time.[39] On 9 September 1502, after it was all over, Seton was called to account before the Lords of Council for his failure to prepare the 'Eagle' for sea within the prescribed time, and was ordered to repay his advance of £400, together with £526 16/11. which the king had subsequently spent on the ship, and double these sums as a penalty for defaulting on his agreement — in all, a staggering £1,853 13/10d, and Seton was also to forfeit his ship.[40] As so often in Lords of Council cases in which the king was the pursuer, however, the Crown's aim was to reach a settlement based on payment of a composition by the defendant — in this case £952, a large enough sum, which Seton agreed to pay on 17 September 1502, and in return for which he would have the 'Eagle' restored to him.[41]

Seton's failure to prepare the 'Eagle' for use as a royal troop transport in early May not only delayed the start of the expedition, but probably considerably reduced its scale. Lesley's figure of ten thousand troops could never have been realised in any event; the number of two thousand cited in one Danish source[42] seems much nearer the mark, and may indeed be rather high. It is clear from the Lords of Council records that there had been some response to the royal levy from the eastern counties; on 23 May a proclamation was made to the effect that litigants had been 'occupyit and put to gret charges and expensis cummand to Edinburgh for the furnising furth of our soverane lordis armey to pas to Denmark', and that many respites had been granted.[43] However, these respites also reveal that the prospect of service in Denmark was not greeted with any great enthusiasm. In one action, at the king's instance, against William Weir, his brother John Weir, and Andrew Myllar, for violence against a tenant of the abbot and convent of Kelso, all three defendants — who did not appear to answer the charges — were found guilty and ordered into ward at Blackness within eight days under pain of being denounced as rebels; however, they had an alternative: 'gif of thir persons that this decret is gevin aganis passis in our soverane lordis service to Denmark, that the execucione of the sade decret be suspendit to thare hamecummyn of the sade land of Denmark.'[44] We do not know what choice the Weirs and Myllar finally made — flight as rebels, warding in Blackness, or service in Denmark in order to obtain — at least — a respite from further royal pursuit. But their case, displaying a government seeking to employ convicted criminals in the army, strongly suggests what we would also expect, namely, that service in the army of Denmark was unpopular, and that the initial levy had fallen below King James's expectations.

In the end, the fleet which sailed from the Firth of Forth about the end of May 1502 probably consisted of the 'Towaich', the 'Douglas', the 'Christopher', and possibly the 'Jacat' and 'Trinity', all ships of modest size and all of them, with the possible exception of the 'Christopher', hired by the Crown for the occasion. James, Lord Hamilton, future earl of Arran and the king's cousin, was probably with the fleet as Lesley suggests, for he was to serve in seaborne expeditions again in 1504–5 and in 1513. However, the royal commander was probably Alexander, Lord Hume, the Chamberlain, a councillor who had survived every political change since 1488 and who was clearly trusted by the king.[45] The fleet was abroad for approximately two months, returning some time between 21 and 30 July; and on 16 August 'the gunnys and powdir that wes in Denmark' were dragged from Leith up to Edinburgh castle in four carts.[46]

Little had been achieved at considerable cost. A contemporary Norwegian report claims that a large number of Scots were killed in the Danish attack on Akershus castle; others, together with Danes and Germans under the command of King Hans's son, Prince Christian, had besieged Bahus in Norway and Elvsborg in Sweden; and many Scots were reported, as early as August 1502, to have fled home by sea.[47] It comes as little surprise to discover that James IV had little success in the ingathering of the Denmark tax, and that efforts to collect it throughout the country were being made as late as May 1505.[48] The Scottish king indicated his frustration with the whole affair in a letter to Hans's queen, Christina, in July 1506, when he remarked that the fleet which he had sent to Copenhagen 'achieved less than it should have done and returned sooner than was expected.'[49]

The failure of the Danish expedition, the reported cowardly flight of the Scots, the reluctance at home to provide the money or levies to support it, and the inadequacy of a system whereby the Crown had to rely almost exclusively on hired vessels, all seem to have concentrated James IV's mind. He found the solution within four months of the return of the Scottish ships from Denmark. He had able captains — Wood, John Barton and his three sons Robert, John, and Andrew, William Brownhill, David Falconer, William Merrymouth — but lacked native shipwrights. If James's reputation amongst his own subjects, far less European rulers, were to be enhanced, he would require to have constructed a fleet which would be owned and maintained by the Crown, and in which the largest ships would be designed primarily for war. The first necessity was to import skilled foreign shipwrights. As the editor of the Treasurer's accounts cautiously puts it, 'England was naturally a country from which there might be some delicacy in importing labour of this sort, so resort was had to France.'[50] On 20 November 1502 'John Lorans, the French wricht, that com first for the schip bigging', was installed at Leith and given a gift of £10 from the king. More to the point, King James ordered Robert Barton to give Lorans a month's wages — ten French crowns, the equivalent of £7 Scots — in advance.[51] The genesis of the royal navy of James IV may be traced to this payment.

The Treasurer's accounts for the next few months are full of entries relating to royal shipbuilding. Under John Barton's supervision, woodcutters were employed to go with Lorans to Cambusnethan wood in Lanarkshire, where trees were felled and sawn up over a period of two months from mid-January 1503. Early in May 1503 Lorans was joined by a second French wright, Jennen Diew, who the month after his arrival had gone 'in the Hieland to cheis tymir for the schip', with Robert Barton acting once more as royal paymaster and hirer of workmen to fell the timber.[52] However, shortage of hard wood necessary for shipbuilding within Scotland meant that, as early as 1503, wooden keels for two ships to be built on the Forth were being imported from France. Indeed, Jennen Diew was employed in choosing wood for a keel in France two months before his arrival in Scotland, assisted by Robert Barton; and a third French wright, Jacques

Terrell, who also arrived in Scotland in 1503, procured a second wooden keel from a forest near Dieppe, from which, with a large quantity of oak planks, it was shipped to Scotland by Robert Barton in July. The first keel had already arrived at Leith; on 26 May 1503 'drinksilver' was paid to 'the men of James Makysonis schip, that brocht hame the keill of the Kingis schip.'[53]

One of these keels was to be used for the building of the 'Margaret', the pride of James's fleet, completed at Leith in 1505 and, following outfitting, floated out onto the Forth in June 1506. Named after the king's young wife, the 'Margaret' was — for Scotland — a vessel of unusual size, her armaments and her four masts suggesting possibly as much as 600 or 700 tons, on a par with, and anticipating, the English 'Mary Rose' of 1509. A special dock had to be built at Leith in the spring of 1504 before the 'Margaret's' construction could begin, so that from beginning to end, her building and outfitting took over two years and cost the king an estimated £8,000. Small wonder that the annual expenditure on royal shipbuilding rocketed in the years 1505–7. Not surprisingly, King James took great interest in the vessel which had cost him more than a quarter of his annual income.[54] At each stage in the 'Margaret's' construction — the taking of the ship off the stocks in the dry dock in January 1505, the raising of the mainmast in November of that year, and the floating of the ship in June 1506 — there was a celebration with trumpeters and minstrelsy; and long before the 'Margaret' had been floated, on 27 May 1505 the king came down to Leith and dined on board, with tapestries hung for the occasion and silver plate for the dinner table carried down from Edinburgh.[55] Two months later the ship received her main armament — four falcons (small cannons) and a cannon, the latter being tested on 9 July by Hans, the royal gunner, on Leith sands in the presence of the king. The remainder of the 'Margaret's' armament consisted of twenty-one guns of unspecified size, but as their total cost was a mere £20, they can hardly have been more than hand-guns. More impressive was the traditional weaponry of all warships of the period — axes, spears, and crossbows.[56]

James IV, clearly delighted with the 'Margaret', had already provided himself with the insignia of the office of Admiral, a whistle and a chain of gold. On 10 September 1505 he sent a servant, John Francis, to France with a gold chain valued at £106 13/4d. 'to the Kingis quhissil making.'[57] In his interest in the navy, its guns, the details of ship design, above all in his identification of himself as admiral-in-chief, King James strikingly anticipates his younger contemporary and rival Henry VIII of England. But in spite of the gold whistle, James knew better than to act as his own admiral in time of war, and his experience of sailing from 1498 to the end of the reign was largely confined to visits to the Isle of May in the Forth, or dining at anchor off Blackness — or even in dry dock at Leith. His personal horizons do not seem to have included voyages in his own ships to Alexandria or Constantinople.

The 'Margaret', built at Leith by foreign shipwrights using wood from Strathearn, Kincardine, Alloa, possibly from Caithness, and certainly from France and Norway,[58] was not King James's only acquisition in the years

1502–6. In July 1504 James bought a ship from Michel Denis, a Breton merchant of Le Conquet near Brest. The vessel cannot have been very large, for she cost only £100; but James went on to commission a much larger ship from the shipwright Martin Le Nault, also of Le Conquet, paying a total of £1,085 Scots between 1504 and 1506 for a vessel brought from Brest to Scotland by Robert Barton, and named the 'Treasurer'.[59] In July 1504 the king bought or hired a French barque, the 'Colomb', from Robert Barton at a cost of £108 17/6d. Her duties were very varied; already in June King James and the clerks of the Chapel Royal had used her to visit the Isle of May; in July she was sent up the Forth to collect timber from Alloa; in early August she was sent from Leith to reinforce the western fleet at Dumbarton; and in October John Merchamestone, one of the king's ablest seamen, was sent to the west as captain of the 'Colomb.' The following summer the 'Colomb' was despatched from Dumbarton to Arran with the royal gunner Robert Herwort on board, to obtain the surrender of 'Lord Hammiltons hous' — James, earl of Arran's castle of Brodick — which had been seized by one Walter Stewart.[60]

The varied tasks assigned to the 'Colomb', in both the Forth and Clyde, underline the fact that before the launching of the 'Margaret' and the 'Treasurer' in 1506, King James was hard pressed to find vessels adequate to his needs, and that these were small barques rather than capital ships. In a revealing letter to Hans of Denmark, written on 3 April 1505, the Scottish king explained that he could not send assistance to his uncle in the shape of the two ships asked for by Hans, because the larger ships of the Scottish navy were still in the builders' hands, while others were being rebuilt after wreck and collision. James went on to say that some of the 'large swift ships' sent to Denmark in the past — a reference to 1502 — he had hoped to use to quell a rebellion of the Islesmen, but they had been detained in Brittany with their masters, following a dispute with the Bretons. Such servicable ships as remained were at sea with merchandise, some sailing to Flanders, others to Normandy; and even the vessel in which the Scottish king's envoy, Lyon Herald, had sailed to Denmark had only been obtained with difficulty.[61] We must make allowances for the fact that King James, no doubt with memories of his expensive fiasco in Denmark in 1502, was reluctant to repeat the experience by sending more ships to Hans, preferring the safer and cheaper role of mediator between the Danish king and his Swedish enemies. Nonetheless the letter makes it clear that royal ships were in very short supply, and that James IV relied heavily, like other European rulers, on the hire of vessels owned and often captained by his most able and aggressive merchant seamen. Thus the trading ventures of the Bartons and others in Flanders and Normandy were reckoned a sufficient reason for the Scottish king's inability to assist his Danish uncle; the fleet was simply not available.

Not surprisingly, therefore, royal hire, or part-ownership, of merchant ships which could be used in a wide variety of roles continued to be a feature of Crown policy throughout the reign. Thus Robert Barton was paid £150 in November 1505 for 'half the schip callit Jacat'; the 'Unicorn', a French vessel originally bought for £441.10/-, was used to travel up the Forth to Alloa, presumably, like the 'Colomb', to transport timber; the 'Raven', apart from her duties as troop transport to the Isles in 1506, was also hired by the king from her owner, Thomas Hathowy, to fetch timber 'in the Northland'; and in 1507 the same ship was used by the Crown to transport merchandise from Flanders.[62] More famous than any of these, because of her ultimate fate, was the 'Lion', yet another Barton ship, on which the king travelled to the Isle of May in 1506.[63] The 'Lion' was a ship of 120 tons, crewed by forty mariners,[64] and probably considerably larger than most of the other vessels hired by King James; yet beside her the newly-launched royal ship, the 'Margaret', was a monster.

The king's fascination with ships and their construction on the Forth soon led him to find fault with Leith, probably because of the sandbanks at the mouth of the Water of Leith, which had made the floating out of the 'Margaret' something of a problem.[65] As early as May 1504 King James had had himself rowed west from Leith 'to seik the New Havin';[66] he found it about a mile to the west, a natural haven with deeper water, and set about the construction of a new dockyard, the New Haven of Leith, using a vast array of craftsmen from France, Flanders, Denmark and Spain, as well as local artificers and labour. In 1507 a chapel, dedicated to the Virgin and St James, was completed in the centre of the small village of Newhaven which served the dockyard; and so successful was the entire royal enterprise that in March 1511, the city of Edinburgh, probably fearing Newhaven as a rival to its own port of Leith, got a grant of it from the king.[67]

Although Newhaven was a more satisfactory location for a naval dockyard involved in the construction of large ships than Leith, both ports lay some miles to the east of the fortalice on Inchgarvie at the Queensferry narrows, and therefore exposed to attack, especially if the Bartons were absent from Leith and Wood from Largo. It was probably with a view to finding a completely safe haven for his fleet that James IV ordered the construction of yet another naval dockyard on the Forth, this time at the Pool of Airth, eight miles south-east of Stirling and about twelve miles west of the Queensferry narrows. This dockyard is first mentioned in the accounts in October 1506, by which time it was clearly already in use for fitting out and repairs.[68] The docks at Airth were clearly of considerable size, for the 'Margaret' wintered there in 1507–8, was newly tarred in the spring, received a visit from the French wright Jacques Terrell in July, and returned at least once more, to have a new mainmast fitted, in 1512.[69] Also, it is certain that the waters of the Forth at Pool of Airth were deep enough to permit the passage to the dockyard of a ship even larger than the 'Margaret' — the 'greit schip' of the accounts, the thousand-ton 'Michael', or 'Great Michael', as she is popularly described; for on 22 March 1512, some five months after the launch of the 'Michael', and while the great ship was lying at the Queensferry, a pilot was sent up-river 'to seik the depis and passage to the Pollertht'.[70] His soundings were clearly satisfactory, for within a fortnight a contribution of £10 was made by the Dean of Glasgow towards 'the making of ane dok to the gret schip' at Airth.[71] The royal docks at Pool of Airth were by this time in the charge of Robert Callendar, Constable of Stirling castle, who by the autumn of 1511 had been paid £240 for the construction of three docks and the erection of stabling for fifty horses.[72]

Callendar received further royal payments for the custody of unspecified royal ships at Pool of Airth in 1512 and 1513, and £37 9/4d. for work on the ship 'James' 'quhen sho lay in the powis of Arth' at the end of October 1512.[73] Together with the 'Michael' and 'Margaret', the 'James' is the only named ship which appears in the late sixteenth-century chroniclers' descriptions of James IV's fleet; Buchanan indicates that James had 'three vessels of very large bulk', while Lesley and Pitscottie name all three ships.[74] The identification of the 'James' as part of this trinity of capital ships is curious, for although at the time of her purchase in October 1511 she was described as 'ane greit boit', she cost only £65 and carried a crew of fifty-six.[75] These details suggest that while the king may have bought her at a greatly reduced price — she had to be repaired and refitted — the 'James' was a vessel not much larger than Barton's 'Lion', and certainly dwarfed by the 'Michael' and 'Margaret.'[76] The explanation may lie in the use of a common source by all three chroniclers, someone close to Wood or the Bartons. An eye-witness could certainly have seen the 'Michael', the 'Margaret', and the 'James' in dock at Pool of Airth in the spring and early summer of 1512; and the frequent visits to Airth by the king and his master shipwright Jacques Terrell, the presence there of James's most valued ships, and the large sums paid to Callendar for their custody, leave in no doubt the dockyard's importance to the Crown, if not as a building yard, then certainly as a safe haven for refitting and repairs. It was presumably to add further protection to the upper reaches of the Forth, and Pool of Airth in particular, that King James took over the defence of the narrows at the Queensferry, adding a tower to Dundas's fortalice on Inchgarvie and a stone house at either side of the ferry. In February 1513 the English ambassador Thomas Lord Dacre saw these defence works as James IV's means of protecting his ships, which he intended should lie above the ferry.[77]

It was however six miles below the ferry, at Newhaven, that the main shipbuilding event of the reign occurred. On 12 August 1506, within two months of the floating out of the 'Margaret' at Leith, James Wilson of Dieppe — presumably an expatriate Scot in France — was paid £42 for the freight of an unidentified vessel bringing to Scotland 'plankis and treis to the gret schip'.[78] This is the first reference in the accounts to the building of the ship which the chronicler Pitscottie would later describe as 'the greattest scheip. . .that ewer saillit in Ingland or France',[79] and whose construction would become Newhaven's raison d'être over the next five years.

Pitscottie, writing in the 1570s, was exaggerating — but not by much. For example, he states that the 'Michael' had a crew of three hundred, and the records show this to be exactly correct; he claims that the ship 'was of so greit statur and tuik so mekill timber that scho waistit all the wodis in Fyfe except Falkland wode, by (besides) all the tymmer that was gottin out of Noraway.' This, remarkably for Pitscottie, is an understatement, as Scottish oak for shipbuilding was also supplied from Rossshire, from Darnaway in Moray, Cambuskenneth, Cawdor, Kincardine and Tulliallan, while foreign timber came not only from Norway but also from Denmark and France — from France perhaps most of all.[80] The chronicler also cites the overall cost of the 'Michael' to the king as being a staggering £30,000 Scots; while there is no way of being positive, because the Treasurer's accounts for 1508–10 do not survive, we know that in 1514, after James IV's death, the 'Michael' was sold to the French for 40,000 francs — approximately £18,000 Scots.[81] As the sale was made by a Scottish government in difficult political and financial straits, it seems likely that the French got the 'Michael' cheap in 1514; thus Pitscottie's total of £30,000 for her building and outfitting seems not unlikely.

Pitscottie's exaggerations concerning the 'Michael' relate to her length and — probably — to her artillery. He states that she was 'xij scoir of futtis of length' — 240 feet, which is hardly credible given what we know of ship design in the fifteenth and early sixteenth centuries. Even Henry V's huge troop-carrier, the 'Grace Dieu' of at least 1400 tons, measured only 129 feet along the keel and about 184 feet along the deck.[82] The 'Michael', a ship of perhaps 1,000 tons, cannot have been longer, and probably 150 — 180 feet from end to end of her deck would be nearer the mark than Pitscottie's 240 feet.

As regards the 'Michael's' artillery, the chronicler is not implausible when he suggests that her big guns — twelve bronze cannon on each side, and three great 'basilisks', one forrard and two aft — were few in number, twenty-seven in all. This makes a sensible comparison with the twenty-one bronze cannon on Henry VIII's 'Great Harry', the 'Henri Grace a Dieu', launched a year after the 'Michael' and possibly built in imitation of her. On the other hand, it is more difficult to accept Pitscottie's figure of 300 small cannon on the 'Michael', as compared with the 39 iron guns on the 'Great Harry'. Possibly, however, his list includes all the smaller artillery pieces right down to culverins — hand-guns — and perhaps even crossbows and long bows. Only such a wide interpretation of artillery would explain Pitscottie's figure of 120 gunners.[83] In any event, in an age when fighting at sea, even by the largest ships, was still conducted at very close quarters — in August 1512 the French 'Cordelière' and English 'Regent', both huge capital ships, were destroyed by fire while grappling together[84] — it is likely that the most effective artillery pieces on the 'Michael' were the hand-guns, crossbows, and longbows.

On 12 October 1511, the 'Michael' was launched at Newhaven, with music playing and fanfares provided by three trumpeters. There followed a lengthy period of outfitting, including the erection of her masts, and it was not until 18 February 1512 that she was towed out into the Forth. Three days later the king dined on board, and the following month he sailed in the 'Michael' as far as Queensferry. The great ship then sailed, or was towed, up the Forth to Pool of Airth, presumably for further outfitting, with the king going up-river from Bo'ness to visit her in June and July 1512. When the 'Michael' came back down river at the beginning of August, tapestries were brought on board from Falkland, and the king and queen dined on the ship.[85] King James had good reason to show off the 'Michael'; if she was not 'the greattest scheip that ewer saillit', she was probably — and briefly — the largest and most powerful in her own day. Henry VIII's building of the 'Henri Grace a Dieu' to roughly the same specifications was a form of flattery.[86]

Thus the navy of James IV, in the strict sense of ships built, bought, or wholly owned by the king, appears to have consisted of some four large vessels — the 'Michael', 'Margaret', 'Treasurer', and 'James' — together with a few smaller craft such as the Cardross ship, the 'Christopher' and 'Colomb', and ships for special tasks, the Dumbarton rowbarge of 1494–5 and a further rowbarge which acted as a tender to the 'Michael' on the Forth. Equally or more important, and certainly more successful as warships, were the privately owned vessels of the three Bartons, Wood, Brownhill, Chalmers, Falconer, and the rest, ships which the king hired when he needed them; and it was undoubtedly these vessels and their captains, encouraged and supported, both officially and unofficially, by James IV, which gave the Scots their European reputation as formidable opponents at sea, and as pirates. No king ever worked more closely with his seamen and shipowners, nor had such an aggressive interpretation of the defence of Scottish merchantmen at sea.

The main instruments of Scottish aggression at sea were the three Barton brothers, Robert, John, and Andrew, all of them shipowners and captains, the sons of a seafaring merchant father John Barton. As we have seen, Robert was used time and again by James IV to bring timber for shipbuilding, and skilled craftsmen to work at Leith, Newhaven, and Pool of Airth. On 2 July 1508, returning from a visit to Fife via the island of Inchcolm, the king was rowed across the Forth to Leith and spent the evening at Robert Barton's house, being entertained by musicians and distributing alms to the poor on the Leith shore. Barton had only recently returned from Spain, where at the shrine of St James at Compostella he had made an offering on King James's behalf of a ship of silver and given gifts to the priests at the shrine; Barton had arrived home early in May 1508, and the royal visit to his house in July may be regarded as a mark of favour to a man close to the king.[87] This intimacy and trust James extended to the other Barton brothers. It was John Barton who was entrusted with the safe carriage of James's son, Alexander Stewart, archbishop of St Andrews, to France in September 1507, using the royal ship, the 'Treasurer', for the purpose, and vainly and briefly pursued by the flying alchemist, John Damian, later in the month.[88] By May 1512, if not before, John Barton had been given command of the 'Margaret'; and Bishop Lesley may have been confusing Andrew Barton with his brother John when he described the 'Margaret's' exploits under his command, attacking 'Holanderis' — probably Flemish pirates — taking many of their ships, filling a number of barrels with their heads and sending them to King James.[89]

It was, however, the third of the Barton brothers, Andrew, who caught the headlines. On 16 October 1510, for services which are not specified in the grant, James IV conferred some of the Fife lands of the hapless Earl of Rothes, with the considerable annual value of 222 marks, on Andrew Barton and his son Alexander.[90] Valuable though these lands were, they were of small account compared with an earlier royal gift to all three Barton brothers, namely the renewal in their favour, shortly after July 1507,[91] of letters of marque against the Portuguese, letters which had been granted to their father John Barton by James III some thirty years earlier, but had subsequently been suspended. Armed with these letters, the Bartons were authorised to attack any Portuguese vessel which they encountered, and to take both ship and cargo by way of reprisal for a Portuguese crime of the mid-1470s. It is difficult to escape the conclusion that, in renewing these letters of marque, James IV was seeking to reward the Bartons for their services past and to come, providing them, at no cost to himself, with a legitimate means of furthering their already considerable seaborne enterprises. The returns to the Bartons were likely to be enormous, for James IV estimated the losses suffered by their father John at 50,000 French crowns — approximately £45,000 Scots.[92]

If the returns were huge, so also were the dangers. In 1508 Robert Barton, having used his letters of marque to capture a Portuguese ship, was arrested at Veere, and only James IV's protests secured his release.[93] A year later John Barton, putting to sea in his brother Robert's 'Lion', seized another Portuguese vessel carrying not only native goods but also those of an English merchant, and two others who claimed to be Flemish and French respectively. On 17 December 1509 John Barton, having been sued by the merchants whose goods he had seized, appeared before the Lords of Council, who continued the case until they should have heard evidence from England, from Bruges and Middelburg, from Rouen, Honfleur and Harfleur.[94] Barton does not appear to have suffered as a result; but in June 1510 James IV, following complaints from King Emanuel of Portugal, suspended the letters of marque for a year.[95]

These ground rules appear to have had little effect on the activities of Andrew Barton, whose aggressive reputation soon came to the notice of King Hans of Denmark; for by the end of 1509, in the course of repeated appeals to his nephew King James for ships to support him against the Swedes and Lübeck, Hans was asking for Andrew and Robert Barton by name. The Scottish captains would attack the Lübeckers in their own ships, not with the 'Margaret' and other royal vessels requested by Hans, and which James, as ever, prudently withheld.[96] By the autumn of 1510 the Bartons' depredations seem to have been so extensive that James IV was having to defend his support for Hans of Denmark against complaints from Maximilian, the Emperor-elect; for Lübeck was an imperial city.[97] Some time in the early spring of 1511 Hans wrote yet again to King James, sending Robert Barton with his letter, and informing the Scottish king that his struggle with the Swedes and Lübeckers was still continuing; to help him in this war, he made an urgent request for the services of Andrew Barton with his own ship and any others which could be despatched speedily to Copenhagen. In the same letter Hans advised James against his projected pilgrimage (peregrinatio), the Scottish king's perennial excuse for avoiding too close involvement in Hans's affairs, and as bait to secure Barton informed James that the masts for his ships had been provided from Norway and would be shipped to Scotland as soon as possible.[98]

In fact, Andrew Barton was delighted to quit Scotland in a hurry. In March 1511 he had been summoned before the Lords of Council to answer the charge brought against him by Aloysius Bonciannus, an envoy of Margaret, duchess of Savoy, Governor of the Netherlands, that he had seized a Breton ship and taken from it goods belonging to some merchants of Antwerp. The Lords of Council made a good show of bringing Andrew Barton to justice; understanding that he was about to leave the realm by sea, they summoned him to appear within sixteen days, that is by 1 April 1511.[99] Barton, who was after all a royal familiar who played cards with the king,[100] was probably secretly instructed to leave for Denmark at once, and when 1 April came and he could not be found, the Lords of Council simply told Bonciannus that if he or any other complainant could capture Barton, justice would be done.[101]

Soon it was not only the merchants of Antwerp who were in pursuit of Andrew Barton. King Hans of Denmark, who had asked for his services more than once, must have regretted that Barton ever came to Copenhagen, for when he did he took Hans's pay and then sailed off, without licence, in the 'Lion' — a ship which had by this time been used by all three Barton brothers — taking with him another ship, the 'Jennet of Purwyn', which had earlier been presented to Hans by James IV.[102]

By this stage Barton had probably gone beyond what even James IV was prepared to countenance, and was threatening to become an international embarrassment. Worse was to follow. According to the later — and not unnaturally biased — English chronicler Edward Hall, Barton, with his two ships, sailed south and 'saiying that the kyng of Scottes had warre with the Portingales', attacked every ship he met and claimed that any goods he took were Portuguese. Hall also accused Barton of attacking and plundering harbours on the English east coast.[103] Even allowing for some exaggeration, there seems no doubt that Andrew Barton had turned more openly than before to piracy as a profitable enterprise. If indeed he claimed the authority of letters of marque for his seizures at sea, he soon lost any such authority, for on 30 July 1511 James IV refused to renew the letters following an appeal from the King of Portugal's procurator at Antwerp, made on 24 June.[104] Barton may therefore have been taking advantage of a brief period, June – July 1511, during which time James IV's forbidding of reprisals against the Portuguese had technically lapsed. In any event, Barton's interpretation of his king's wishes had always been over-generous to himself. Certainly he could not claim royal authority or protection for attacks on the English; but equally certainly, these would be privately commended if he could get away with it.

But he did not get away with it. In June, July, and August 1511 Sir Edward Howard was paid a total of £617 9/9d. sterling by the English Crown for the fitting out, victualling, and taking to sea of two or three hired ships, their task being to give a safe convoy to the vessels of the Merchant

Adventurers on their way to Zealand, and to defend the merchants against 'the rovers of the see.'[105] Howard's original commission, therefore, was not to attack Sir Andrew Barton but to protect a convoy. However, when lying in the Downs late in June, Howard and his brother, Lord Thomas Howard, son and heir of the Earl of Surrey, encountered Barton — probably by chance — with his two ships, the 'Lion' and the purloined 'Jennet of Purwyn', and gave chase in two hired vessels, probably the 'Barbara' and the 'Mary Barking.' The 'Barbara' was a vessel of 140 tons, slightly larger than the 'Lion' and twice the size of the 'Jennet.'[106]

What happened next is uncertain. The patriotic Bishop Lesley, attempting to put the best possible interpretation on Andrew Barton's behaviour and courage, claims that Barton was 'on the sey in weirfair contrar the Portingallis'; that he was sailing peacefully towards Scotland with 'bot one schipe and ane barke'; that the Howards set upon him at the instance of Henry VIII, bringing with them 'certane of his best schippis'; and that Barton believed up to the last moment that he had nothing to fear from the English because there was peace between England and Scotland.[107] Not surprisingly, the English version of the battle, by Edward Hall, is rather different. In it the two Howards, with two ships, became separated by the weather, and it was only Lord Thomas Howard in a single vessel who caught up with Barton. A bloody fight ensued, with Andrew Barton blowing his whistle to encourage his men, and the end came when the English boarded the 'Lion', Barton was mortally wounded and his surviving crew were made prisoner. At this point Sir Edward Howard comes back into Hall's story, in pursuit of the easier Scottish target, the 'Jennet', which he boarded in person, killing or taking prisoner the entire crew. On 2 August, the two captured Scottish vessels were brought to Blackwall.[108]

There is, of course, no doubt as to the eventual outcome of the seafight; Barton was killed, his ships were taken, and his crews were made prisoner. Hall's highly coloured version of events, though inaccurate in some details — for example, Sir Edward Howard was not made Lord Admiral until over a year after his fight with Barton's ships — seems to be substantially correct. What is uncertain is the nature of James IV's response to Barton's death. Both Lesley and Hall are at one in stating that the Scottish king was furious, and that he sent a herald to Henry VIII with letters demanding redress for the slaughter of Andrew Barton, and the restoration of the captured ships, otherwise he might consider the Treaty of Perpetual Peace as no longer binding. Hall goes further than Lesley, and states that James IV invoked the treaty in 1502 (renewed in 1509), and summoned both Howards before the next Scottish Warden Court for the slaughter of a Scottish subject within the English Marches. Henry VIII, who significantly freed the Scottish captives, replied to James's threats that they were unjust, that he had simply done justice on a pirate, and that he had shown mercy to Barton's crew, who were as guilty as Barton himself.[109]

Hall is here embroidering a good story. There can be little doubt that James IV protested about Barton's death and sought to have his crews released; but that he meant to break the English treaty over this one incident seems highly unlikely. Significantly claims for redress for losses suffered in this seafight are not a feature of James's diplomatic correspondence in late 1511 and 1512. Writing to the pope on 5 December 1511, James condemns Henry VIII's actions in the most general terms; the English king, though sworn to his father's treaty, had attacked the Scots 'by land and sea'.[110] Subsequent correspondence with Henry VIII himself, in July 1512, mentions a Barton — but it is the live Robert, not the dead Andrew, Barton to whom James IV refers. Indeed, Andrew receives only the briefest, almost apologetic, mention in a letter from James IV to Hans of Denmark written towards the end of 1512.[111] Probably Edward Hall, who like the Scottish chroniclers was seeking, with benefit of hindsight, to find reasons for the Anglo-Scottish enmity which led to Flodden, makes far too much of the affair of Andrew Barton. There were other problems; and the English safe-conducts issued on 26 July to Scottish commissioners — including the Earl of Argyll and John Lord Drummond — to enter England to confer with Lord Dacre and Sir William Drury had nothing to do with Barton, but were concerned with settling breaches of the treaty on the borders.[112] In fact, James IV may have been much more philosophical about Andrew Barton's death than the later accounts suggest. He had lost an able but insubordinate seaman, and may have felt the loss of Barton as a friend with whom he occasionally played cards. But the ships lost were not royal ships, nor even particularly significant ones; the 'Lion' of 120 tons was the Bartons' collective loss, and the 70-ton 'Jennet' had been filched from the King of Denmark. James could console himself with the continuing services of John Barton, captain of the 'Margaret', Robert Barton, who rapidly replaced the captured 'Lion' with a 300-ton vessel of the same name,[113] and with the launch, in October 1511, of the 'Great Michael'.

In the last analysis, we may ask the purpose of James IV's huge expenditure on ships between 1502 and 1513. If they were simply for the defence of Scotland, as James remarked in a letter to Louix XII in 1506,[114] he could probably have fared as well using hired ships under his experienced commanders, protected by the forts at the narrows of the Forth. Furthermore, while it is true that the Danish expedition of 1502 revealed the inadequacy of hiring as a means of conducting an aggressive war at sea, it was clearly not James's intention to spend vast sums of money on a fleet simply to assist his uncle Hans against the Swedes and Lübeck; it was the Bartons and other 'unofficial' Scottish privateers who performed this service, and did so largely at their own expense in anticipation of huge profits.

There was undoubtedly an element of ostentatious display in the creation of warships of the size of the 'Margaret' and 'Michael', vessels which allowed the king to indulge his growing interest in artillery. However, beyond James IV's undoubted desire to impress, both at home and abroad, there lay a serious purpose. For running like a leitmotif through all James's naval plans, ship construction, outfitting, and projected use of his growing fleet, is the king's close relationship with France and its king, Louis XII. The Scottish fleet was largely built by French shipwrights, using large quantities of French timber, and ultimately financed by French money. Thus when James, in August 1506, promised the French king that the Scots fleet would go anywhere Louis wished in his service,[115] this may have been more than mere diplomatic rhetoric. It is surely significant that the building of a Scottish royal fleet began in the autumn of 1502, the year of the Treaty of Perpetual Peace with England. King James was bound by the most solemn oaths to the alliance with the English; but the treaty gave him a loophole to the effect that, as long as he did not invade England, the Scottish king might help to defend the territories of any princes who were at war with England without breaking the alliance.[116] In the case of the Scots, this was likely to mean France; and James's construction of a fleet with French aid may be seen as providing him with an outlet to pursue an alternative foreign policy, to maintain a useful connection with the French while not becoming too heavily involved in France's affairs. In the end, with the adherence of England to the Holy League in 1511 and the ensuing Anglo-French war, the Scottish king opted for a closer alliance with France in 1512. But that he did so is not surprising, for it was to Louis XII that James looked for ships, for munitions, for money to victual his own ships and pay his seamen.[117] In the last analysis, the French king offered James IV a better deal than Henry VIII ever could, or would. The problem was whether King Louis could be trusted.

On 30 November 1512 Charles de Tocque, Seigneur de la Mothe, Louis XII's ambassador to Scotland, arrived in the Firth of Forth during a great storm. First he anchored at Leith and fired off cannon to announce his arrival, alarming the citizens of Edinburgh, who believing themselves under attack, rang the common bell for three hours and prepared to defend the burgh. Driven further up river by the weather, De la Mothe finally anchored at Blackness, where both the 'Michael' and 'Margaret' were lying. James IV had himself rowed out to the 'Michael' and received the French ambassador on board.[118] This was not simply ostentation. De la Mothe had been in Scotland before, but he had probably not seen the great ship;[119] the Scottish king clearly wanted the ambassador to be able to report on its size to King Louis, to impress the French king with his worth as an ally at sea. Louis was duly impressed: on 5 March 1513 he described the 'Michael' according to De la Mothe's reports, as a ship 'laquelle. . .est si puissante qui ne s'en treuve une telle en chrestiente.'[120] By the spring of 1513 it was clear — if indeed there had ever been any doubt — that the Scottish fleet of James IV would find its true métier not in the defence of Scotland, but as part of a French crusade against the English.

NOTES

1. *James IV Letters*, No. 42.
2. *T.A.*, i–iv, passim.
3. Nicholson, *Later Middle Ages*, 347–8.
4. *E.R.*, vi, 204, 349; Dunlop, *Bishop Kennedy*, 176–7.
5. A.W.K. Stevenson, 'Trade between Scotland and the Low Countries in the Later Middle Ages' (Aberdeen University unpublished Ph.D. thesis, 1982), 171.

6. See, in general, C.F. Richmond, 'English Naval Power in the Fifteenth Century', *History*, lii (1967), 1–15.

7. Rymer, *Foedera*, xi, 820–1; *Cal. Docs. Scot.*, iv, Nos. 1416, 1424; Lesley, *History*, 39.

8. B.L. Cotton, MS. Vespasian Cxvi, ff. 118–120 (Edward IV's instructions to his almoner, Alexander Legh.).

9. *James IV Letters*, Nos. 125, 206.

10. Lesley, *History*, 44; Richmond, 'English Naval Power', 10.

11. *R.M.S.*, ii, No. 1563.

12. Richmond, 'English Naval Power', 10; R.C. Anderson, 'The Grace Dieu of 1446–86', *E.H.R.*, xxxiv (1919), 584–6.

13. *Cal. State Papers (Venice)*, i, 145–6.

14. Macdougall, *James III*, 188, 217.

15. Richmond, 'English Naval Power', 10–11.

16. *Ibid.*, 11–12; Scarisbrick, *Henry VIII*, 499–500.

17. *See above*, Chapter 5.

18. Conway, *op. cit.*, 29–31.

19. Pitscottie, *Historie*, i, 226–231.

20. *Ibid.*, Pref., cix–cxii.

21. Buchanan, *History*, ii, 223–4, 225–7.

22. *Cal. Docs. Scot.*, iv, No. 1566.

23. Pitscottie, *Historie*, i, 227–231.

24. *R.M.S.*, ii, No. 2040; *A.P.S.*, ii, 227–8.

25. *A.P.S.*, ii, 270.

26. *Ibid.*, ii, 211 c. 18.

27. *T.A.*, i, 323–389 passim; ii, 82, 86, 115.

28. *A.P.S.*, ii, 214 c. 4; *T.A.*, i, 118.

29. *T.A.*, i, ii, iii, iv, passim. The Prefaces to *T.A.*, i, ii, iii, and iv contain sections on naval building and expenditure, and there is a fascinating and very detailed series of shipbuilding accounts for 1512–13: *T.A.*, iv, 451–507.

30. *T.A.*, i, 125–6.

31. *See above*, chapters 4, 5 and 6, passim.

32. *T.A.*, i, 245–254.

33. *E.R.*, x, 571; *T.A.*, ii, 433; iii, 340.

34. *T.A.*, iii, 296–9, 382, 405.

35. See, in general, Barbara E. Crawford, 'Scotland's Foreign Relations: Scandinavia', in J.M. Brown (ed.), *Scottish Society in the Fifteenth Century* (London, 1977), 90–93.

36. Deduced from the unusually large A.D.C. sederunts at this time; and *see above*, chapter 7.

37. *T.A.*, ii, 144–149; S.R.O., RH/1/2: Sir John Skene, 'Tabill and repertour of the Cheker rollis', 104.

38. Lesley, *History*, 72–3.

39. *T.A.*, ii, 145–8.

40. *A.D.C.*, iii, No. 717.

41. *Ibid.*, iii, No. 721; *T.A.*, ii, Pref., lxxxvi.

42. Crawford, op. cit., 91n.

43. *A.D.C.*, iii, No. 682.

44. *Ibid.*, iii, No. 681.

45. Hume was in Denmark on the king's service on 21 July 1502: *A.D.C.*, iii, No. 689. He was probably accompanied by his kinsman Sir John Hume: *T.A.*, ii, 149.

46. On 21 July, Alexander Lord Hume is described as being abroad in Denmark in royal service; on 30 July he is to be found pursuing a case before the Lords of Council: *A.D.C.*, iii, Nos. 689, 698; *T.A.*, ii, 157.

47. Crawford, op. cit., 92 and n.

48. *T.A.*, iii, 138.
49. *James IV Letters*, No. 37.
50. *T.A.*, ii, Pref., lxxxvi.
51. *Ibid.*, ii, 281.
52. *Ibid.*, ii, 282–3.
53. *Ibid.*, ii, 283–4, 373.
54. *Ibid.*, iii, Pref., lix–lxv; ii, 476; iii, 135, 171, 189, 195, 199.
55. *Ibid.*, iii, 143.
56. *Ibid.*, iii, 90, 203–5.
57. *Ibid.*, iii, 41.
58. *Ibid.*, iii, 132, 134, 190, 295.
59. *Ibid.*, ii, 445; iii, Pref., lxvi–lxvii, 157, 347.
60. *Ibid.*, ii, 437, 448, 449, 452, 461; iii, 145.
61. *James IV Letters*, No. 8.
62. *T.A.*, iii, 173, 206–7, 341–2, 378.
63. *Ibid.*, iii, 342.
64. Alfred Spont, *Letters and Papers relating to the War with France, 1512–1513* (Navy Records Society, x, 1897), 8.
65. *T.A.*, iii, Pref., lxiii–lxiv, 199.
66. *Ibid.*, ii, 432.
67. *Ibid.*, iii, iv, passim.; *R.M.S.*, ii, No. 3551.
68. *T.A.*, iii, 296.
69. *Ibid.*, iv, 68, 114, 131, 396.
70. *Ibid.*, iv, 336.
71. *Ibid.*, iv, 280.
72. *Ibid.*
73. *Ibid.*, iv, 444.
74. Buchanan, *History*, ii, 241; Lesley, *History*, 86–7; Pitscottie, *Historie*, i, 255–6.
75. *T.A.*, iv, 287, 506.
76. Though in February 1513 Thomas Lord Dacre, writing to Henry VIII from Carlisle following a recent visit to Newhaven, described the 'Margaret' *and* the 'James' as 'two great ships': *James IV Letters*, No. 527.
77. *James IV Letters*, No. 527.
78. *T.A.*, iii, 295.
79. Pitscottie, *Historie*, i, 251.
80. *Ibid.*; *T.A.*, iii, 132, 134, 190; iv, 45–7, 502–5.
81. *Flodden Papers*, 113 n.l; *A.D.C.P.*, 39.
82. Pitscottie, *Historie*, i, 251; Frank Howard, *Sailing Ships of War 1400–1800* (Lond., 1979), 18.
83. Pitscottie, *Historie*, i, 251–2.
84. Spont, *op. cit.*, xxv–xxvi.
85. *T.A.*, iv, 313, 331, 351, 355–6.
86. For the 'Michael', see *T.A.*, iv, passim; Norman Macdougall, "The greattest scheip that ewer saillit in Ingland or France': James IV's 'Great Michael' ", in Norman Macdougall (ed.), *Scotland and War* (Edinburgh, 1991) 36–60.
87. *T.A.*, iv, 40–1, 131.
88. *Ibid.*, iv, 72; Lesley, *History*, 76.
89. *T.A.*, iv, 346; Lesley, *History*, 74.
90. *R.M.S.*, ii, No. 3511.
91. *James IV Letters*, No. 125.
92. *Ibid.*, No. 208.
93. *Ibid.*, Nos. 206–8.
94. S.R.O., A.D.C., xxii, f. 67r; *A.D.C.P.*, App., lxiv.
95. *James IV Letters*, nos, 271, 315.

96. *Ibid.*, No. 286.

97. *Ibid.*, No. 318.

98. *Ibid.*, No. 387.

99. S.R.O., A.D.C., xxii, 78r.

100. *T.A.*, iv, 316.

101. S.R.O., A.D.C., xxii, 112r.

102. *James IV Letters*, No. 412; Spont, *op. cit.*, viii, n. 3.

103. Edward Hall, *Chronicle*, ed. Sir H. Ellis (Lond., 1809), 525.

104. *James IV Letters*, No. 381; *Letters and Papers Henry VIII*, i, pt. i, No. 828. Citing the latter source, R.L. Mackie claims that 'with incredible levity, James renewed the letters of marque': Mackie, *James IV*, 209. In fact, the reverse is true. James had revoked the letters for a year in 1510; when the year expired, on appeal from the Portuguese he renewed *his revocation*.

105. Spont, *op. cit*, ix, n. 1.

106. *Ibid.*, ix–x, xiv. The late June date for the seafight in the Downs is inferred from the transfer of a Scottish prisoner taken in the Downs to London in early July: *Letters and Papers Henry VIII*, i, pt. i, No. 855.

107. Lesley, *History*, 82.

108. Hall, *Chronicle*, 525.

109. *Ibid.*

110. *James IV Letters*, No. 394.

111. *Letters and Papers Henry VIII*, i, pt. i, No. 1314; *James IV Letters*, Nos. 467, 494.

112. *Letters and Papers Henry VIII*, i, pt. 1, No. 833 (65).

113. *James IV Letters*, No. 565.

114. *Ibid.*, No. 42.

115. *Ibid.*

116. Rymer, *Foedera*, xii, 793.

117. *See*, for example, *James IV Letters*, Nos. 497, 498, 565.

118. *Ibid.*, No. 498.

119. De la Mothe's previous visit to Scotland had been in June–July 1512, during the negotiations as to the final details of the Franco-Scottish treaty: *Flodden Papers*, 44–7. Thus the ambassador had missed seeing the 'Michael', which was fitting out — probably — at Pool of Airth.

120. *Flodden Papers*, 68–72, at 70.

10

The Four Horsemen

'Swme sayis thair come foure men wpoun foure horse
rydand to the feild witht foure speris and ane wyspe
wpoun ewerie speir heid to be ane signe and wittar to
thame that ewerie ane of them sould knawe ane wther.
They raide in the feild and horssed the King and brocht
him fourtht of the feild on ane dune haiknay. Bot soume
sayis they had him in the Merse betuix Dunce and Kelso.
Quhat they did witht him thair I can not tell. . .'[1]

Robert Lindsay of Pitscottie's tale of the enigmatic four horsemen who
appeared on the battlefield of Flodden and took King James IV away to an
uncertain fate shows the chronicler attempting, more than sixty years after the
event, to come to terms with the mass of conflicting evidence circulating about
the disaster of 1513. Rumours of James IV's survival were current by the early
1530s, and probably earlier; and a variety of apparently well-informed sources
was drawn on to add authenticity to the king's escape.[2] James was seen riding
back across the Tweed; he had dressed others in his coat-armour, so that the
English had recovered the wrong body; he had gone on pilgrimage to Jerusalem.
These stories, arising out of the refusal of the Scots to come to terms with
the awfulness of Flodden, constitute a remarkable exercise in collective wish
fulfilment. Pitscottie was not deceived. Though he hedged his bets by insisting
that the English could not have removed the body of the king because the
corpse which they claimed as James IV had no penitential iron belt around
the waist,[3] Pitscottie seems to have had little doubt that the four horsemen
were sinister figures, bearing James to his death. The harbinger of James
III's death, according to John Major, had been a comet at Sauchieburn;[4] and
Pitscottie, looking for a similar prophetic manifestation of the death of princes a
generation later, may have had in mind neither Hume horsemen from the Merse,
nor English horsemen from Surrey's army, but rather the riders from the Book
of Revelations — the four horsemen of the apocalypse. After the conquest of
Norham, the war carried into Northumberland, and the famine caused by the
depredations of two marauding armies, came death in the field.

For Pitscottie, James IV's dramatic end was a necessity, giving point to
his claim that the king had brought his fate on himself, not only through
wasting time in 'stinkand adullterie and fornicatioun' with the Lady of Ford,
but — much more seriously — through his rejection of the good counsel of his

nobility before the battle. These two themes allowed Pitscottie to construct a convincing moral tale, explaining James's defeat and death in terms of the classic vices which generations of writers in the *speculum principis* tradition urged kings to avoid. Thus James IV 'wald vse no counsall for defence of his honour and preserving of his airme bot wssit himself to his awin sensuall plesouris quhilk was the cause of his rwen.'[5]

More recent writers have understandably rejected King James's indulgence in the pleasures of the flesh as a major factor in his defeat at Flodden, but have tended to follow the Pitscottie line on the king's rejection of good advice, both before the campaign and before the battle itself. There are, however, wide differences of opinion as to James's behaviour, not only as a commander on the 1513 campaign, but as a diplomat in the years leading up to it. Although R L Mackie's forcefully argued view that James IV was out of his depth in the European diplomacy of his day has been convincingly challenged by Dr Ranald Nicholson, it is still widely held, and has most recently been resurrected in print by Dr Leslie Macfarlane in a perceptive analysis of worsening Anglo-Scottish relations and the machinations of Pope Julius II.[6] We are thus faced with the challenging spectacle of scholars using essentially the same body of evidence to arrive at radically different conclusions. It would seem, therefore, that no consensus is likely to be achieved as to James IV's diplomatic skill, or lack of it, during the years leading up to Flodden, nor as to his military ability, or even his objectives, on the campaign itself.

Yet the effort must be made; and we must be wary of falling into the trap of basing our judgements on hindsight, on the knowledge that Flodden was an appalling disaster. Likewise presuming that James IV was motivated in everything he did by the desire to lead, or at least play a major role in, a European crusade is an unprofitable exercise, for it assumes that James's diplomatic utterances about crusades are all to be taken at their face value, while those of every other European prince are to be rejected as the conventional rhetoric of the times. We would do better, perhaps, to look at the causes of friction between Scotland and England in the eleven years of the Treaty of Perpetual Peace, and to seek to analyse the king's motives for the 1513 invasion, the popularity — or lack of it — of the war, and James's conduct of the three-week campaign.

1. *Diplomatic Manoeuvres 1502–13*

The Treaty of Perpetual Peace of 1502 has been much praised as the beginning of a new and more realistic Anglo-Scottish relationship, mainly, perhaps, because it led a century later to the union of the crowns. But at the time it could hardly have been regarded by either side as a major turning point. It was not after all the first such alliance. A generation earlier, in 1474, James III had initiated a major change in Scottish foreign policy with a treaty which, had it been followed through, would have provided the future James

IV with an English Yorkist wife some time in the 1480s. But the 1474 alliance had been unpopular and collapsed within six years, being succeeded by palace revolutions and a devastating English invasion in the summer of 1482. In the nineties Scottish Anglophobia had been channelled by James IV into the invasions of 1496 and 1497, and the Peace of Ayton and the subsequent years of negotiations to achieve the treaty of 1502 involved hard and frequently frustrating ambassadorial work on both sides. Henry VII had had to be moved from a position of seeking to chastise the Scots with a huge army and fleet in 1497, to a sudden frightening realisation of his own insecurity, and of the need to offer his daughter in marriage as part of a full-scale Anglo-Scottish alliance.[7] This necessity did not endear the Scots to King Henry or his subjects; indeed, in England Don Pedro de Ayala was looked upon as remarkable not simply because he had spent a year in Scotland, but because he could hear the word 'Scotland' pronounced without losing his temper.[8] English dislike of the Scots was heartily reciprocated. Ayala remarked in 1498 that it was only King James who had really looked for peace with England, which was made against the wishes of the majority of his subjects; and a skirmish near Norham castle in the early summer of 1498, in the course of which some Scots were killed by members of the English garrison, brought an immediate threat from James himself that he would not consider himself bound by the peace if redress were not immediately made.[9] All in all, it cannot be said that the treaty of 1502 was occasioned by any spontaneous outburst of Anglo-Scottish amity. Both kings arrived at it faut de mieux, after the investigation of other possibilities and an expensive and inconclusive war; and the high praise lavished upon King Henry and on London by the poet William Dunbar, attached to the Scottish embassy which went south to negotiate the treaty in 1501–2,[10] should probably be viewed in the context of Dunbar's continuing struggle to obtain a benefice as a living. His studied obsequiousness towards the English king was duly rewarded with a gift of money; but the benefice — the rectory of Cottingham in Yorkshire — had already gone not to Dunbar but to James IV's familiar Andrew Forman, probably the main architect of the peace on the Scottish side.[11] The ambivalence of the Scottish king towards the English treaty is reflected in the variety of tasks which he assigned to Forman, a man close to him throughout his personal rule, using him first as watchdog to Perkin Warbeck, then as ambassador to England, and finally as the diplomat who more than anyone else was responsible for the Franco-Scottish alliance of 1512.

The English treaty of 1502 was an improvement on its predecessor of 1474 in the sense that the marriage on which it was based actually took place; on 8 August 1503 the wedding of James IV and Margaret Tudor was duly celebrated at Holyrood. Furthermore, elaborate rules were laid down to cope with the inevitable breaches of the peace on land or sea, as and when they occurred. Thus a Scot, if attacked by an Englishman on the borders or at sea, had first to complain to the English Warden of the Marches; likewise an offended Englishman would take his case to the Scottish March Warden. If the Wardens took no action, further appeal could be made to the king concerned, who would write to his ally demanding redress; if none were granted, he would then be entitled, on behalf of his injured subjects, to issue letters of reprisal within six months. The treaty was to be further protected and solemnised by the stipulations that all future English and Scottish kings would renew it within six months of their accession, and that papal approval and confirmation of the peace was to be sought, together with a declaration that should either prince break the treaty, or allow it to be broken, he would be excommunicated.[12]

All this appears very impressive; but from the beginning there were doubts and undercurrents of mistrust on both sides. According to Polydore Vergil, followed exactly by Bishop Lesley, the Scottish marriage proposals had been debated at length by Henry VII and his councillors, presumably in 1500 or 1501. Some of those present had argued against the marriage on the ground that it might eventually happen that the heritage and succession of England would fall to Henry's daughter Margaret, and therefore through her to a Scot; so they had urged the alternative of a foreign marriage. At the time, Henry had made the reply that if such things did happen — which God forbid — nonetheless the realm of England would not be damaged, for 'in that caise Ingland wald not accress unto Scotland, bot Scotland wald accress unto Ingland, as to the most noble heid of the hole yle' — in other words, the greater would draw the less, just as Normandy had come into the hands of Henry's English ancestors.[13] Normandy was not perhaps the most convincing historical example which Henry could have chosen to make his point; but his famous remark, if it was made at all, was made with all the confidence of a king who had already provided more than adequately for the succession, with two surviving sons Arthur and Henry, the former already betrothed to Catherine of Aragon. But on 2 April 1502, within five months of the marriage of Arthur and Catherine, Arthur died;[14] and his father, committed for some six weeks to the Anglo-Scottish treaty, suddenly found the prospect of a Scottish succession in England a more immediate possibility than he could have imagined. The Tudor king's anxiety about the succession can only have increased when, early in 1503, he suffered a double calamity; a child christened Catherine died after only a few days, and — far worse — her mother, Queen Elizabeth, died nine days later, on 11 February.[15] Henry's growing insecurity may account for his letter to James IV on 27 June 1503 asking the Scottish king to repudiate, or at least not to renew, the Franco-Scottish alliance. King James replied on 12 July to the effect that although 'we and oure predecessouris has bene always accustumyt thareto', he would not confirm the league with France until he had spoken to King Henry.[16] When a month later, James IV married Henry's daughter Margaret, only Henry's surviving son — the future Henry VIII — stood between the Scottish king and the English succession. Faced with this alarming prospect, the councillors of Henry VII who had advised against the Scottish match can hardly have enjoyed the pageantry of Margaret Tudor's progress north, and the festivities surrounding her wedding to James IV in August 1503, vividly described in the narrative of John Young, Somerset Herald.[17] According to Edward Hall, the English guests were unimpressed by

King James's deliberate prodigality, and returned home sneering at the rude hospitality of the Scots.[18] Such an attitude may have been prompted partly by jealousy; for in August 1503 James IV's problems seemed to be behind him, while those of Henry VII, in spite of his long and skilful struggle to secure his dynasty, persisted until his death in 1509.

In spite of the marriage of James IV and Margaret Tudor, the alliance of 1502 was in many ways even more brittle than its predecessor of 1474, which at least had had the enthusiasm of James III for closer relations with England to sustain it. James IV had however no intention of repeating his father's obsequiousness towards the English king, which he may well have felt ultimately contributed to the invasion of Scotland in 1482 by giving Edward IV of England the impression that the Scottish political community was divided and ripe for attack. James IV was not prepared to be bound by a single policy of alliance with England, and by pursuing French and Danish connections after 1502 as before it, he was able to satisfy his own countrymen and to present a united front to the only ruler who, as even James III had recognised, made war on Scotland. A casual glance at James IV's published correspondence with foreign governments and individuals associated with them reveals that he sent three times as much diplomatic mail to France and Denmark as to England. And the available evidence does not really show that the Anglo-Scottish treaty worked for any length of time in reducing tension and conflict in areas where friction was always to be expected, that is, on the borders and at sea.

It is true that in August and early September of 1504 James IV in person rode to the West March with a sizeable force — the records call it a host — to cooperate with the English West March Warden, Thomas Lord Dacre, in a punitive raid on Eskdale.[19] King James was first in the field, hanging thieves near Dumfries before meeting the English Warden at Canonbie in Eskdale. There followed a few days of cooperation between James and Dacre, hawking, playing cards, and hanging another batch of thieves, this time at Canonbie. On the face of it, this would appear to be a striking example of Anglo-Scottish cooperation to reduce violent crime on the borders, a vindication of the value of the treaty of 1502. But James IV may have had another motive in undertaking the raid of Eskdale. Canonbie, where he met Dacre, and surrounding large tracts of land between the rivers Esk and Sark, fell into the category of 'debateable land' — that is, territory in which the Anglo-Scottish border was unclear, and possession of which was disputed by both countries. By appearing in person and punishing the criminal elements in the debateable land of the West March, James IV was effectively claiming jurisdiction over it, and securing an acceptance of his claim by having the English March Warden join him on his raid.

In the large and sensitive Middle March, on the Scottish side the shires of Roxburgh, Selkirk, and Peebles, Anglo-Scottish cooperation does not seem to have endured longer than a few years. The basis of such cooperation was frequent meetings between wardens on opposite sides of the border, at recognised meeting places either on the frontier or a short distance from it, to enforce the international law, built up over centuries and based on custom and negotiation. Such meetings were known as 'days of truce', and they were, in effect, international courts in which the English and Scottish wardens would deal with frontier offences, such as the taking of prisoners in time of peace and the protection in one realm of fugitives and rebels from the other, together with the basic crimes of murder, robbery, wounding, and arson.[20] On one such day of truce, probably a meeting on Reddenburn, a tributary of the Tweed near Carham, the Scottish Warden of the Middle March, Sir Robert Ker of Ferniehurst, was slain by the bastard John Heron. The murder of a Scottish warden by an Englishmen on the solemn occasion of an international court was a grave crime which required immediate redress. But James was unable to obtain this; Bastard Heron was allowed to go free in England, and by April 1508 the Scottish king had apparently been complaining for some time about Ker's murder, remarking that injuries done to his subjects were to be counted as injuries done to his own person, and claiming that he had suffered by the alliance.[21] Though he obtained some satisfaction for other grievances, not enough was done on the English side to make redress for the slaying of James's warden. Significantly Ker's death still headed the list of the Scottish king's grievances in July 1513;[22] and he may have justified his assault on Ford castle in Northumberland a month later by the fact that it was a Heron stronghold.

King James had other substantial grievances. In September 1507 the 'Treasurer', a royal ship, sailed to France carrying not only the young Archbishop of St Andrews abroad for his studies, but also James IV's kinsman, James Hamilton, earl of Arran. Early the following year, on his return journey, Arran was detained in England on the ground that he did not have a safe-conduct.[23] His arrest provoked a furious response from King James, and by the spring of 1508 there were fears at the English court that the Scots were about to renew the alliance with France.

These fears were not unfounded; for Arran's business in France in the winter of 1507–8 was described by King James as 'certane chargeis and erandis of ouris', clearly revealed in a subsequent letter to Louis XII. The background to Arran's visit was a request made by the French king in July 1507 for four thousand Scottish troops, to be sent by sea to Genoa or Savona, to assist the French in the defence of the Duchy of Milan, at the time under threat from Maximilian, the Emperor-elect.[24] The Scottish king clearly had no intention of becoming embroiled in Louis XII's Italian wars; and it is significant that James responded to the French king's appeal for military aid in August by indicating his sympathy towards the French cause, but adding that longer notice should have been given. King Louis replied on 23 August, indicating that Scottish troops would no longer be necessary, but asking that they should be kept in readiness in case of need.[25] On 20 September James responded by exuding both warmth and reserve, stating that he and his subjects were prepared to come to Louis' defence at any time, but asking that the French king should in future give him greater notice of his needs. In a separate letter, written at the same time, James IV told Louis that he was sending the Earl of Arran to France with a full answer to the recent request for Scottish foot soldiers. About three weeks later, on 10 October, James sent instructions along the same lines to Robert Cockburn, postulate of the bishopric of Ross and chaplain to Louis XII. Cockburn was to tell Louis that James, given sufficient notice, would supply the French king with troops, and if Louis' need were great, James would send every available man and go to France himself. The Scottish king added that if God advanced him to greater fortune — presumably a reference to the English throne — he would still continue to send troops to Louis whenever he was asked for them.[26]

This diplomatic exchange reveals that James IV — and Secretary Paniter, who drafted the king's letters and had increasing influence in making the policies outlined in them — was quite as adept at making promises as Louis XII was later to become. The French king was obviously pushing for a renewal of the Franco-Scottish alliance, and seeking a definite commitment from James IV which would tie him closely to French interests in Europe. In response, James was neatly side-stepping such a commitment while professing continuing friendship and offering indefinite promises of armed support, at the same time inviting Louis to recognise his position as second in line to the English throne. It would be interesting to know what King James's private instructions to Arran and Cockburn were, especially those given to the latter to pass on to Louis by word of mouth because the Scottish king did not wish to trust them to writing; but it is surely significant that on 14 October, only four days after giving Cockburn his private instructions to communicate to the French king, James wrote to Louis enthusing over the Sieur de la Mothe's recent pilgrimage to Jerusalem, and commending the idea of crusade.[27] The intention was presumably to do what he could to divert Louis from his increasingly unsuccessful ventures in northern Italy, at the same time attempting to impress upon him the value of Scotland as an ally. At this stage James cautiously avoided a formal renewal of the Franco-Scottish treaty of 1492; but there is no doubt that he recognised the worth of the French connection, especially perhaps of France as a source of skilled craftsmen and timber for the construction of the Scottish fleet, and that a renewal was always a likely option.

This was certainly the English view. In spite of the treaty of 1502, Henry VII and his advisers remained deeply suspicious of James IV's possible designs on northern England. As early as 25 August 1505 — that is, little more than a month after the third and final payment of Margaret Tudor's dowry to James IV — the English king issued a commission to his Warden-General of the East Marches, Sir Thomas Darcy, to array the men of Northumberland in anticipation of a Scottish siege of Berwick.[28] Although this war scare came to nothing, and although 'days of truce' continued to be held on the marches in 1506 and 1507,[29] Henry remained concerned by the close links between Scotland and France, and was clearly well aware of Louis XII's efforts to have James IV formally renew the treaty of 1492. So the English king resorted to the device of arresting James's ambassador and kinsman, Arran, on a technicality — in the circumstances an unwise move, for it almost achieved what Henry was trying to prevent, a renewal of the Franco-Scottish alliance.

Probably fearing the imminent arrival in Scotland of the expatriate Bernard Stewart, Lord of Aubigny, as Louis XII's ambassador, Henry VII sent north his young and able almoner Thomas Wolsey, a royal servant in the early stages of what was to develop into a spectacular career, to try to forestall the making of a Franco-Scottish treaty.[30]

Wolsey's report to King Henry, following his visit to the Scottish court in late March and early April 1508, provides a fascinating insight into James IV's domination of his council and his devious diplomatic technique. Arriving in Berwick on 22 March, Wolsey had to wait five days for a safe-conduct to enter Scotland, King James being at Whithorn. When he finally arrived in Edinburgh on 28 March, Wolsey enlisted the support of the queen to obtain him an early audience; but James would not see him until 2 April because, as he explained, he was busy shooting and making gunpowder. When he was finally admitted to the royal presence, Wolsey had short audiences with King James every day for over a week, in the course of which he encountered both inconstancy and some hostility towards Henry VII. Henry's complaint that many Scottish subjects were passing through England without safe-conducts was immediately challenged by the Scottish king, who retaliated by complaining that some of his subjects, trusting to the alliance, had suffered great harm; and he cited the case of the slaying of Ker by Bastard Heron. When king and ambassador moved on to the topic of breaches of the truce on the borders in more general terms, Wolsey asserted that, in terms of raids, murders, and robberies, the English had suffered four hurts to the Scots' one, and commented in his report to Henry VII that Lord Hume, the Scottish warden on the East March, was 'somewhat abashed' when he made this claim.

The serious business of Wolsey's embassy was the prevention of a renewal of the Franco-Scottish alliance. Clearly James IV wanted to impress on him that such a renewal was not only imminent, but the collective wish of his council and his subjects. Thus Wolsey reported that when he arrived in Scotland, King James had already decided to renew the French treaty, and that all his subjects, with the exception of the queen and Andrew Forman, bishop of Moray, were calling on him daily to do so. Forman told Wolsey that no-one was ever less welcome in Scotland, because it was generally believed that he had come to prevent a renewal of the French league. In an aside Wolsey remarked that the Scots 'keep their matters so secret. . .that the wives in the market knoweth every cause of my coming.'

Yet this seeming openness, coupled with an enlistment of anti-English sentiment, had the desired effect. Wolsey went away with the impression that only the release of the Earl of Arran would keep James from renewing the French league; and he must also have been impressed by the unanimity of opinion among the Scottish king's councillors. Present in Edinburgh when he was received by James IV were Elphinstone, the Privy Seal; Argyll, the Master of the Household; Patrick Hepburn, earl of Bothwell, one of the chief negotiaters of the 1502 treaty; Matthew Stewart, earl of Lennox; Alexander, third Lord Hume, who had succeeded his father as Chamberlain in 1506; Andrew, Lord Gray, the Justiciar; James Beaton, abbot of Dunfermline, the Treasurer; and Gavin Dunbar, Clerk Register.[31] This wide spectrum of Scottish political opinion was firmly united behind the king, and the only concession which certain individuals on the council had been prepared to make in private conversations with Wolsey was to suggest that the two alliances, English and French, could stand together. Ultimately the affair was settled by Andrew Forman, who seems to have been employed as James's 'fixer' throughout, asking Wolsey to write to Henry VII for the release of the Earl of Arran. At the same time, the Scottish king left the diplomatic door open by making soothing noises: as long as King Henry treated him kindly, he said, he would never break with him, nor renew the French league; but he felt that so far Henry had not treated him like a son.[32] Henry VII got the message, acted like a wise father and duly released the Earl of Arran.

This concession did nothing to improve Anglo-Scottish relations, nor to break the Franco-Scottish connection. Although there was no formal renewal of the league, James received a French embassy only a few weeks after Wolsey's departure. This consisted of Bernard Stewart, Lord of Aubigny, James's kinsman, and Jean Sellat, president of the Parlement of Paris; and their reception in Scotland provides a marked contrast to that of Wolsey. Gifts were showered on Bernard Stewart, an elaborate tournament was arranged in honour of the French, and James IV wrote to Louis XII asking permission to retain the Lord of Aubigny in Scotland long enough to allow him to join James on a pilgrimage to Whithorn, during which Stewart might inform him thoroughly about his commission from King Louis.[33] The pilgrimage, however, never took place, for Stewart died at Corstorphine on 11 June, prompting William Dunbar to extol his chivalric virtues in a eulogistic poem, and King James to grieve his death in letters to Louis XII and Queen Anne of France.[34]

Grief did not long interfere with business. On 18 June, a week after Stewart of Aubigny's death, James sent his Clerk Register, Gavin Dunbar, archdeacon of St Andrews, as his ambassador to France, accompanied by Antoine d'Arces, Lord of La Bastie, 'who speaks French'. Both men travelled in the royal ship, the 'Treasurer', bearing from James to Louis expressions of goodwill, promises of service, assurances that the treaty of 1492 would not only be maintained but also strengthened — but not, apparently, any commitment to a formal renewal.[35] Nonetheless, Franco-Scottish cordiality aroused Henry VII's suspicions; and when Gavin Dunbar was on his homeward journey to Scotland in the 'Treasurer', the ship was wrecked somewhere on the east coast of England, and Dunbar and his fellow travellers — three hundred in number if Bishop Lesley is to be believed — were taken to be interviewed by King Henry.[36] They were soon released, possibly through the intercession of Jean de Ganay, Chancellor of France, and an anonymous friend to whom King James wrote at the beginning of the following February, and had apparently returned to Edinburgh by November 1508.[37] The 'Treasurer' seems to have been a total wreck, for she does not reappear in the records for the remainder of the reign. James IV had lost one of his own ships, and though King Henry was not personally responsible, his temporary arrest of Gavin Dunbar and his companions must have seemed to the Scottish king like a repeat performance of the seizure of the Earl of Arran at the beginning of the year. His response may have been more threatening than the records reveal, for on 12 December 1508 Henry VII appointed Sir William Conyers captain of Berwick, his appointment to take effect from 16 February next. If besieged by the Scots or others, he was to hold out for two months, and thereafter to the uttermost of his power. He was to be supplied with a regular garrison of 230, to be increased by 400 if the Scots threatened invasion or siege; and provision was made for twenty-five masons, and the same number of labourers, to repair the town and castle in peace time, and also to direct the inhabitants of Berwick to dig ditches and fortify the burgh.[38] All in all, it can hardly be said that the Treaty of Perpetual Peace, less than seven years after its creation, was proving a resounding success.

Part of the problem, of course, was the perennial difficulty of keeping the peace on the borders, where violent infringements of the treaty were part of life, and part also of the normal give-and-take of Anglo-Scottish diplomacy. But much more serious — and damaging — were the ailing Henry VII's neurotic suspicions about a renewal of the Franco-Scottish alliance; for such an alliance, if it were to be formally concluded, was not after all incompatible with the Anglo-Scottish treaty of 1502. Perhaps, however, King Henry's precautions for defence of the north against his Scottish ally are understandable. He had, after all, witnessed two damaging invasions of Northumberland by the same king in 1496 and 1497, and he was certainly aware that the shifting pattern of European alliances could play a major role in Anglo-Scottish relations. James IV's earlier invasions of England had been made with little outside assistance. With the active support of the French fleet, the Scots might well think it possible to jettison the 1502 treaty and to attempt to recover Berwick in a combined operation by land and sea. If this was indeed the way King Henry's mind was working, it may still be questioned whether his earlier seizures of Arran and Dunbar were not in fact likely to drive the Scots further towards a firm treaty with France, the reverse of what Henry intended. In any event, when Henry VII died on 21 April 1509,[39] Anglo-Scottish relations were hardly cordial; and the Franco-Scottish alliance of 1492, although it had not been renewed by James IV, seemed to be bearing greater fruits for the Scottish king than the 1502 treaty with England.

The accession of Henry VIII temporarily arrested the growing rift between Scotland and England. On 29 June 1509, that is well within the six months allowed following the death of one or other of the original signatories, King James renewed the Treaty of Perpetual Peace of 1502. He did so following receipt, some time before 11 June, of what he described as 'loving letters' from the new English king, written in Henry's own hand.[40] This brief period of cordiality continued until at least 28 November 1509, when James IV swore by the gospels and the canon of the mass, and in the presence of a large number of his clergy and magnates, that he would observe every article of the 1502 treaty, and to the best of his ability cause it to be observed by his subjects.[41]

Before long, however, the brittle Anglo-Scottish peace was subjected to strains which it could not withstand. One of these was the character of the new English king, Henry VIII, aged eighteen on his accession in 1509. Dr Nicholson describes him as 'an egocentric teenager whose tantrums and petulance bespoke an inferiority complex',[42] though to R.L. Mackie Henry was 'the realist. . .who sat on the English throne'.[43] Whatever his personal attributes or failings, it is clear that Henry VIII intended from an early stage to be a very different king from his father, and that European war figured in his ambitions almost from the beginning. France was to be his battleground; as Dr Scarisbrick points out, 'it is damaging historical surgery that cuts (Henry) off from his ancestry — Edward I, Edward III, Henry V — for they, surely, were his models.'[44] Shortly after his coronation, Henry VIII swore publicly that he would soon attack the king of France;[45] and the English campaigns of 1512 and 1513 are perhaps most realistically seen as a renewal of the Hundred Years' War. The only reason that King Henry delayed as long as he did in attacking France was that he needed allies, that members of his council were opposed to English intervention in European affairs and had even made a treaty with France — against Henry's wishes — in March 1510.[46] This faction did not however remain dominant for long. By the autumn of 1511 Henry had easily been weaned away from the French alliance through the agency of the indefatigable Francophobe, the Cardinal of York, and Pope Julius II himself, who secured the young English king's adherence to the Holy League with the gift of the Golden Rose, some barrels of wine, and a hundred Parmesan cheeses.[47] By the winter of 1511–12 it was only a matter of time before Henry VIII launched an attack on France, with the approval and backing of the pope and the dubious support of the two least constant allies in Europe, Maximilian and Ferdinand of Spain.

The English king's pugnacious attitude carried advantages and disadvantages for the Scots. Obviously King James gained from the fact that Henry's ambitious eyes were turned away from Scotland towards Europe. On the other hand, the ultimate object of his warlike attentions was France, Scotland's ally in terms of a treaty much older than the English peace of 1502, and a country of considerable importance to James IV. Wolsey's report of April 1508 makes clear beyond any doubt that the French connection was valued not only by the Scottish king, but also by his council; it was a link hallowed not only by tradition, but by practical considerations, above all trade, the import of skilled shipwrights, the purchase of timber, the development of shipbuilding in the Forth. Thus by 1511, with Henry VIII's entry into the Holy League, James IV was faced with a dilemma, for the two alliances rapidly became incompatible. Failing James's own entry into the League, thereby abandoning France, the only remaining question was whether the Scottish king would lend active assistance to his French ally when Henry VIII went to war.

In the event, and hardly surprisingly given the history of Anglo-Scottish and Franco-Scottish relations since 1502, James IV opted to renew the Franco-Scottish alliance, and did so following extensive negotiations with the French in 1512. This was no quixotic decision, the mad act of a dreamer seeking alliance with the only ruler who professed an active interest in crusading, but a carefully considered political decision, arrived at following consultation in General Council, and based on the advice of some of the most experienced European statesmen of the day. So long as there had appeared any hope of reconciling Julius II and Louis XII, James IV had employed Andrew Forman on what Dr Kaufman has aptly termed 'a prototype of shuttle diplomacy',[48] seeking to influence European affairs in the only way possible to the ruler of a small nation, that is by mediation between the major powers. When that proved to be a vain hope, the offensive and defensive alliance with France was renewed because the existence of a new Franco-Scottish treaty might give Henry VIII pause before he committed himself to the invasion of France.

There were, of course, other reasons for reverting to the old alliance rather than adhering to the new. As we have seen, the long-standing Scottish grievance about the slaughter of Sir Robert Ker had never been settled; and in the summer of 1511 the death of Andrew Barton increased the growing Anglo-Scottish rift. More important than either of these issues was the delicate matter of the succession to the English throne. Since James's marriage to Henry's elder sister Margaret in 1503, it had become possible that he or one of his successors might succeed in England if the Tudor line failed. On 20 October 1509, shortly after the renewal of the 1502 treaty and about the time of James IV's solemn oaths to defend it, Margaret Tudor had a son who was christened Arthur — not a Scottish name, but one recalling — probably consciously — Henry VIII's elder brother. The infant died the following year, and on New Year's Day 1511 Henry VIII's queen, Catherine of Aragon, produced the apparent answer to the Scottish challenge in the shape of a son, Henry, Prince of Wales. However, the see-saw of natal upsets continued when the boy died within seven weeks[49] and Margaret Tudor — and through her, her Scottish husband — once more became heir presumptive to the English throne. Even at this early stage in his reign, Henry VIII responded to his initial failure to secure the succession in his own family with a venom and ruthlessness which were already hallmarks of the Tudors. Thus he withheld payment of Henry VII's legacy to Margaret Tudor, a piece of spite which drew a sharp response from Margaret herself in April 1513;[50] he tried to convince James IV, without success, that the renewed French alliance would never bring him the succession to England because Louis XII had already recognised the exiled Yorkist, Richard de la Pole, younger brother of Edmund, duke of Suffolk;[51] and before he left England to invade France in the early summer of 1513, he had Suffolk brought out of the Tower and beheaded,[52] thereby removing any possibility of a Yorkist comeback supported by the Scots.

Throughout, Henry VIII seems to have been much more concerned about the English succession than his brother-in-law. In 1512, after all, James IV was already thirty-nine, Henry only twenty-one. Catherine of Aragon's catalogue of miscarriages and stillbirths lay, for the most part, in the future, and there was every reason to hope that she would give her husband the heir that he wanted. As for King James, following the deaths in infancy of two sons and a daughter, on 10 April 1512 he was at last provided with an heir who would survive to become James V.[53] But the child's survival must still have been a matter of some doubt in 1513, and his existence can hardly be counted a factor in Henry VIII's increasing irritation with the Scots. What seems to have exercised him most was that James IV was using the Franco-Scottish alliance to draw from Louis XII an acceptance of his claim to the English throne.

There was an element of comedy about this. In the spring of 1513 James IV assured Louis XII that he had already declared war on the English, having first turned down offers made by English ambassadors on behalf of Henry VIII, declaring James heir to the English throne if Henry died childless, on condition that he kept the peace.[54] Neither statement was true; but in so far as both provided Louis with a firm commitment by James to war with England, they were what the French king wanted to hear. So Louis responded in kind, asking James what he wanted done with the Yorkist Richard de la Pole, and offering to send him to Scotland if this was James's wish.[55] Neither ally was being honest with the other, and both probably knew it. Louis would not surrender to the Scots a valuable diplomatic pawn like Richard de la Pole, and James was never likely to be recognised in England as King Henry's heir. But he had registered his claim, rather like one of the competitors in the Great Cause; and his ultimatum to Henry VIII, delivered by Lyon Herald to the English king's camp at Thérouanne on 11 August 1513, provoked Henry to drape himself figuratively in the mantle of Edward III and declare that he was 'the very owner' of Scotland and that the Scottish king was his vassal.[56] In that struggle of summer 1513, therefore, James IV was claiming to be, and in terms of strict legitimacy was, Henry VIII's heir; King Henry, rather less modestly, was demanding the throne of France and the overlordship of Scotland.

Breaches of the peace on the borders and at sea, the withholding of Queen Margaret's legacy, the arrogant assertion of overlordship — any one of these unresolved grievances might have provided James IV with a legitimate motive for war. However, the main attraction for the Scottish king was that Louis XII was making a practical material offer; by 8 May 1513 he promised to equip and victual the Scottish fleet and to deliver 50,000 francs — about £22,500 Scots — to King James, together with seven galleys commanded by the most formidable of all the French admirals, Prégent de Bidoux, to serve the Scottish king. James's part of the bargain was to invade England as soon as Henry had embarked for France, and to send the Scottish fleet to France at the same time, if possible adding ships from Denmark to his own navy.[57] In the context of the political situation in 1513, there was much in Louis' offer to attract James IV; for there was no question that James could afford to equip and victual his fleet for a lengthy war, and a sizeable pension from King Louis would help him to clear his annual deficit on current expenditure. In the face of such practical incentives Henry VIII had really nothing to offer — except thinly veiled threats, conveyed to James by the unpleasant Nicholas West, dean of Windsor, the English ambassador.

In one sense, it is difficult not to sympathise with West. His Scottish embassy was hopeless from the start, for it is clear that James IV and his council had no

intention of giving him a firm answer — and certainly not a written answer —
to the one assurance which he had come to seek, namely an undertaking by the
Scottish king to keep the peace while Henry VIII invaded France. Judging by
his letters,[58] West spent a miserable three weeks in Scotland, complaining that
the people were proud and ungracious, and that he would have preferred to be
sent to Turkey. He appears to have been trying to impress his king with his
diligence — one of his letters concludes not only with the date, 1 April, but
also the time, 'at xij of the clok in the nyht' — and used his spare time to spy
on the Scottish fleet. His visits to Leith and Newhaven left him unimpressed
with the strength of James's navy; but he should have visited the Forth above
the Queensferry, or even journeyed to Pool of Airth.

West's official business could not be undertaken immediately because James
IV had vanished into the Observantine friary at Stirling during Easter week.
So he turned first to the queen, asking her to keep her husband out of the
war, whereupon Queen Margaret demanded to know why her father's legacy
had been withheld from her. When the king finally emerged and consented to
receive West, he did so in a series of interviews conducted over the course of
a fortnight, at both Stirling and Edinburgh. The unhappy ambassador, whose
treatment by the Scots strongly recalls that of Wolsey five years earlier, could
obtain no satisfaction from either King James or those members of the privy
council with whom he spoke — Archbishop James Beaton, Argyll, Paniter,
and Sir John Ramsay. Throughout West's embassy, the Scottish king and his
councillors appear to have been stalling him with promises — Scotland would
keep the peace if England would do the same, James would not break with Henry
if the English king did him justice, and so on. But whenever West attempted to
be specific and ask for either a written undertaking or the sending of a Scottish
ambassador to England, James excused himself on the ground that he did not
want to lose the support of the French king, who alone could provide him with
the means to undertake a crusade. West was shrewd enough not to believe that
this was James's true motive for refusing to break with France, and within a
fortnight Henry VIII himself, in a letter to Cardinal Bainbridge, commented
that James 'would rather help the King of France than further the cause of
Christendom, or prepare an expedition against the Infidel, which he neither can
nor will do.'[59] At length, on 13 April, West saw no further point in pursuing his
embassy; he could extract no definite answer from King James, and had spent a
frustrating time wondering whether to laugh at the heavy royal jokes — that the
'Michael' carried more heavy artillery than the French king had ever had at any
siege, and that if Julius II had lived — he had died in February 1513 — and only
three bishops had kept a council, James would have been with them against the
pope. West left Scotland convinced that James IV was going to commit himself
firmly to France — he had twice refused to lend the 'Michael' to Henry VIII
on the ground that he had already promised her to Louis XII — and impressed
with the influence of the royal Secretary, Patrick Paniter.

West was certainly correct about King James's intentions. Little more
than three weeks after his departure from Scotland, there arrived from France

Master James Ogilvy, bearing from Louis XII the offer of support that James found impossible to refuse — not philosophical ramblings about crusades, but firm promises about supplies, victuals, a large pension, and the service of his best admiral in the forthcoming war.[60] It is fascinating, if not in the end very useful, to speculate on how James IV might have responded to Henry VIII's embassy if the English king had offered him a high price for his neutrality. But James probably rated his ability to influence Henry's actions too highly, and for his part Henry did not reckon that the military threat from Scotland was a matter of great concern. West's commission shows the English king to have been more worried about the Scottish fleet, and his mind may have been set at ease by West's — inaccurate — report on the subject of Scottish naval strength. But whatever he thought, Henry would not be deterred by the Scots from his projected invasion of France. As West roundly told James IV, King Henry would be able both to invade France and to resist him; a war with Scotland might delay, but would not stop, an invasion of France.[61]

Viewed with hindsight, that is with the knowledge that the battle of Flodden was to end in disaster for the Scots, James IV's entry into the war of 1513 on the side of France has been widely viewed, as we have seen at the beginning of this chapter, as an act of almost criminal folly, his death its inevitable outcome and, by implication at least, his just reward. Such a view is usually sustained by reference to the fact that James, in breaking the Anglo-Scottish treaty of 1502 — which he himself had renewed in 1509 — was inevitably inviting immediate excommunication, and doing so moreover to support an ally encircled by powerful European enemies. Thus James IV is seen as embarking on a desperate adventure, unnecessarily abandoning a long-standing English treaty and substituting in its place a dubious alliance with the hard-pressed Louis XII in a war which could not possibly benefit the Scots. These views merit closer examination.

It is of course true that James entered the war of 1513 as an excommunicated king. Shortly before his death on 21 February 1513, Pope Julius II had issued letters monitory and a bull executorial, denouncing excommunication against the King of Scots; and despite King James's efforts to persuade the new pope, Leo X, not to confirm the sentence — sending the ubiquitous Andrew Forman abroad as his ambassador, for what proved to be the last time, on 31 March — nothing was achieved, for the pope responded only with a letter, brought very belatedly to Scotland in August by the papal envoy Octavian Olarius, accusing the Scottish king of dividing Christendom, ordering James to keep the peace with Henry VIII and assuring him that excommunication would inevitably follow his breaking of the English treaty.[62] All this is fact; what is arguable is the effect which papal censures had on James IV, and on the support which he might hope to receive within Scotland for war against England.

As early as 5 December 1511, in a letter to Julius II, James IV had summed up the Anglo-Scottish treaty by remarking that, as a result of — unspecified — attacks by the English on his subjects by land and sea, peace had become even worse than war, and that, as there was no sign of redress on the part of Henry

VIII, James presumed that the pope had freed both English and Scottish kings from their oaths to defend the treaty, and from the sanctions which would follow the breaking of it by either party. He was compelled, he wrote, by necessity to infer that the treaty was dissolved.[63] There was no response from Julius II; but as he had only just drawn Henry VIII into his Holy League, it was clear what his response would be.

A more immediate and threatening response came only a month later, not from the pope but from England. In January 1512 the English parliament not only voted a subsidy of two-fifteenths to finance Henry VIII's invasion of France, but also declared that the King of Scots was 'very homager and obediencer of right to your Highness'[64] — in short, they resurrected the English king's claim to overlordship over Scotland, last advanced at the time of Albany's abortive invasion of 1482. The justification for this incredibly inept and arrogant claim was the generalised complaint that James was not observing the peace, indeed, was preparing for war;[65] but if Henry VIII and his councillors had truly been seeking peace with Scotland, the subsidy act of January 1512 and the English claim of suzerainty was calculated to achieve the opposite of what they intended. At the end of the following month, James IV summoned a Scottish General Council, decided to renew the French alliance, and drew up proposals for a new treaty with Louis XII within a week.[66] Although what followed was what Dr Head rightly calls 'a year of frenzied diplomacy'[67] during which the Scots neither accepted French pleas for aid nor gave in to English demands for neutrality, there was really little doubt from the start that when Louix XII offered acceptable terms, as he did by May 1513, James IV would commit himself to the French side; for England, as West's mission shows, was offering nothing in return for Scots neutrality. Scotland, of course, was peripheral to Henry VIII's interests; and the intelligent advice of the English March Warden, Thomas Lord Dacre, that a gesture towards the Scots, such as the payment of Margaret Tudor's legacy, might help to avoid war,[68] was totally ignored by King Henry, who sailed to France and left Dacre to do the best he could in the north of England, charged with the defence of an area in which the towers razed by the Scots in 1496–7 had not even been rebuilt.

In Scots minds, English arrogance and papal threats were probably inextricably linked; for the individual charged to deliver the papal ban of excommunication against James IV was Christopher Bainbridge, Cardinal of York, whose combination of aggressive patriotism and hatred of the French was to extend in 1513 to a demand that the pope should be ready to come to Rheims in order to crown Henry VIII as King of France.[69] As the totally committed servant of an English king whose parliament had already proclaimed him overlord of Scotland, Bainbridge represented a potential menace to the Scottish church and nation alike; for as archbishop of York, he might use his influence at Rome to resurrect York's claim to act as metropolitan over the Scottish church. For James IV, who had lent his support to the Aberdeen Breviary and the discovery of seventy new Scottish saints, the combination of the neurotic and bellicose Henry VIII and the xenophobic Bainbridge was one which had to be resisted. The leaders of the Scottish clergy agreed with him. The Secretary, Patrick Paniter, tutor to Alexander Stewart, archbishop of St Andrews, had been frustrated in his claim to the preceptory of Torphichen by the personal intervention of Bainbridge against him in Rome;[70] and by 1512–13 the incumbents of most major Scottish benefices owed their positions to James IV. Indeed, it was probably the Scottish clergy's perception of a Holy League dominated by a hostile pope and arrogant English king which produced some generous contributions, in 1512 and 1513, towards the cost of King James's war. It is true that the danger was potential rather than immediate, for there were no plans in England for an invasion of Scotland; and the overlordship issue had only been touched upon in 1512, and was not thereafter insisted upon in English official documents. But years of growing tension with England, and a series of what he regarded as slights for which no redress had been made, clearly persuaded James IV that the time had come to take the offensive. In terms of up-to-date weaponry, he was better prepared to do so than any previous Scottish king; and there can be little doubt that the Scottish political community was, for the most part, in favour of war.

He may also have been encouraged by the fact that Henry VIII, in spite of his impressive resources, was visibly out of his depth in the business of European diplomacy and war which so fully engaged his attention in the first few years of his reign. In May 1511 he had sent Lord Darcy to Cadiz with a thousand men to assist Ferdinand of Spain on an expedition to North Africa against the Moors — a crusade of sorts. When the English force arrived, they were told that Ferdinand had abandoned the idea and were ordered home. They went, but only after they had run amok in a drunken brawl, destroying Spanish property and killing a number of Ferdinand's subjects. In the following year, with Henry a committed member of the Holy League, the military objective was the reconquest of Aquitaine, which was to be accomplished by a combined Anglo-Spanish army, the English under the command of the Marquis of Dorset. At immense expense, Henry despatched his army of six thousand by sea, his fleet commanded by Sir Edward Howard; but when the English expeditionary force landed at San Sebastian and made for the agreed muster point at Fuentarrabia, they discovered that they had again been deserted by the Spanish. Ferdinand intended to use the English only as cover for his own seizure of the kingdom of Navarre, and had no interest in entering Aquitaine. In the autumn of 1512, racked by illness, desertion, and mutiny for lack of pay, Dorset's expeditionary force returned to England pursued by abuse from Ferdinand.[72] The only English to come to grips with the French in 1512 were aboard Sir Edward Howard's fleet; and a hard fought naval action off Brest on 10 August, following which both sides claimed victory, resulted in the destruction by fire of the 'Regent', one of the two largest capital ships in Henry VIII's navy.[73]

Worse was to follow in the early months of 1513. Although King Henry became part of the four-power alliance — the pope, Ferdinand, Maximilian, and England — to attack France in April, this imposing league soon started to fall apart. On 23 March the Venetians, unable to stomach being party to an alliance which included Emperor Maximilian, had withdrawn from the Holy League and made a treaty with France;[74] and, as Henry VIII was to discover, Maximilian was a shifty ally. Even shiftier was Ferdinand of Spain, who in April, at the same time as he committed himself to war against France on behalf of the League, concluded a one-year truce with Louis XII.[75] At sea, an uncertain struggle continued, with the French king's Norman and Breton fleets substantially strengthened by the appearance in the Channel of his famous Mediterranean admiral, Gaston Prégent de Bidoux, with his six war galleys. On 25 April the manic English Admiral Sir Edward Howard, short of victuals and desperate to bring the French to action, personally boarded Prégent's galley in a struggle off Brest, was trapped aboard, and thrown into the sea to his death.[76] Writing to Henry VIII a month later, by which time he had committed himself to the French side, James IV commented, probably with grim satisfaction, that Howard's services would have been better employed against the enemies of Christ.[77] Henry did not reply.

In the late spring of 1513, then, King James turned from diplomacy to war. His long delay in committing himself to active support of Louis XII had produced material benefits in the shape of munitions, artillery, and money. At the same time he had managed to stand aloof from the Church Council which the French king had summoned to Pisa in 1511, and which the pope had immediately denounced as schismatic; in spite of his jokes to Nicholas West about supporting the Council against the pope even if only three bishops attended,[78] James cautiously sent no Scottish representatives to Pisa. A neutral stance on that issue would no doubt aid his reconciliation with Leo X when the league against France broke up and the ban of excommunication, which James saw as little more than an English political device, was lifted.

2. The War of August–September 1513

Scottish preparations for war had long been underway. The Treasurer's accounts from 1507 onwards are full of entries relating to the manufacture of artillery, at Stirling and Edinburgh, on an increasingly imposing scale. In 1511 a group of French gunners arrived in Scotland and were set to work in Edinburgh castle, probably under the direction of a Scot, Robert Borthwick, who had charge of the royal cannon foundry and who by 1512 was described as 'master meltar' of the king's guns.[79] Much of the material used in the forging of the artillery — iron, brass, and bronze — was imported from France and Flanders, and the huge costs incurred by the Crown in the manufacture, manning and transport of the guns are revealed in a fascinating series of accounts relating to royal expenditure on artillery between March and August 1513.[80] Some of the guns were intended for the fleet rather than the army, with the 'Michael' and 'Margaret' each carrying a complement of gunners, Flemish, French, and Scots, including the redoubtable Henrik 'Cutlug' and Jacob, the Flemish 'Maister gunner'.[81]

Wise after the event, the late sixteenth-century chroniclers described portents of disaster immediately prior to the departure of the king from Edinburgh in August 1513. According to Pitscottie, citing as his authority Richard Lawson, a prominent member of the Lords of Council and former provost of Edinburgh, on the night that the artillery were being taken out of the castle, a voice was heard at the market cross at midnight, summoning 'all men to compeir baitht earle, lord, barone and gentillmen and all honest burgessis' before Plotcok — Pluto, or the Devil — within forty days. Lawson promptly appealed from the summons, calling on the mercy of God and his son Jesus Christ; and according to an anonymous landed gentleman, who in Pitscottie's account was twenty years of age in 1513 and who heard the midnight summons, only Lawson amongst all those named by the mysterious voice escaped death at Flodden. Pitscottie is honest enough to admit, in spite of his sources, that the 'summons' may have been no more than a disturbance created at the market cross, by 'dronkin men for thair pastyme'.[82] Rather more convincing is his statement that Queen Margaret protested to the king that he should not make war, at great danger to himself, while the succession rested on the life of an infant boy whose survival was still in doubt. All her children except the second James — James, Arthur, a daughter who died shortly after birth in 1508, and a second daughter who had only recently died, probably early in 1513 — had failed to survive; and in the summer of 1513 — probably in July — the queen conceived the child who was to be born seven months after his father's death and live for only two years as Alexander, duke of Ross.[83]

The most famous of all Pitscottie's portents, and one described also by Buchanan, is the tale of the man in the blue gown. According to Pitscottie, after the host had been summoned, and while James IV was in Linlithgow — presumably St Michael's church is indicated — praying for the success of his expedition, a yellow-haired, balding man, fifty-two years of age, wearing a blue gown and carrying 'ane great pyk staff' in his hand, demanded to see the king. On being admitted, he gave James two pieces of advice — not to lead his army to war, as neither he nor anyone who went with him would fare well; and not to use female counsel 'nor lat them. . .tuitch thy body nor thow thairs'. Having delivered this message, the man in the blue gown disappeared without anyone present seeing him go. Pitscottie — and Buchanan following him — claims that his source for this incident was Sir David Lindsay, later Lyon Herald, at that time a young man in James IV's service, who together with the Marshal of the Household, John Inglis, had tried to seize the stranger.[84] Mackie's ingenious suggestion that the mysterious individual was in fact an actor got up to resemble St James by those opposed to the war may well be correct;[85] and we may believe this without believing Pitscottie's story of his advice to the king, telling James not to 'mell' with women — which in Pitscottie's tale is precisely what the king, and his bastard son, go on to do, to the ruin of them both.

It is rather more difficult to identify a party at court which might have wished to oppose the war. Queen Margaret, although English, stood firmly by her husband in 1513, though she may have resented his earlier recourse to mistresses, and this in turn may have provided the origin of Pitscottie's tale. Of more substance is Hector Boece's statement, made only a few years after Flodden, that when Bishop Elphinstone had spoken in the council against war with England, 'there arose. . .a tumult of opposition', and Bishop William 'was taunted that, like a dotard, he had spoken foolishly and thoughtlessly against the public interest, against their sacred league, and in a spirit contrary to the nation's ancestral honour'.[86] In 1513 Elphinstone was eighty-two, and his middle age in Crown service had been spent attempting to make or patch up treaties with England. His colleague in this enterprise, Archibald Douglas, earl of Angus, a man of sixty-four, is praised by Buchanan for making a speech in council, once the campaign was underway, opposing the war; though Buchanan's suggestion that, when the king would not take his advice, Angus burst into tears, carries less conviction.[87] The story may in fact be no more than a reflection of Buchanan's bias in favour of his own erstwhile Douglas patron, the Regent Morton; in the context of the latter years of James IV, it draws its relevance from the fact that Angus, though released from wardship on Bute in 1509 and to some extent rehabilitated within the political community, did not apparently fight at Flodden. He was, however, one of the very few earls who did not; and indeed, the chroniclers are in no doubt that the queen, Elphinstone, and Angus represented only a minority opinion. As Pitscottie himself says, in spite of the portents, 'nothing wald be hard bot 'fordwart'.'[88] Although there was some resistance to the general call-up for service in the army to be carried in the fleet to France,[89] the invasion of northern England appears to have been generally popular.

There was nothing rash or ill-considered about King James's entry into the war in 1513, either at sea or on land. He had, after all, been expected to invade England on behalf of the French in the previous summer, and had cautiously waited until Louis XII's terms for Scottish assistance had substantially improved. Now, in the summer of 1513, it was time to enter into a seaborne alliance, consisting of the French, Scottish, and — if possible — Danish fleets, with the objective of gaining control of the Channel and preventing Henry VIII, who sailed to France on 30 June, from returning home in safety.[90] To assist the alliance, James and Louis also hoped for the support of the Scottish king's cousin Charles, duke of Gueldres, against whom Henry VIII had sent an expeditionary force in 1511,[91] and Hugh O'Donnell of Ulster, with whom King James made an alliance on 25 June, an agreement witnessed by no less than nineteen Scots including both archbishops and six earls.[92]

Like most Grand Designs, this one proved more impressive in conception than in execution. Naval assistance from the Danes had rarely been forthcoming; indeed, as we have seen, from 1502 onwards the Danish king had looked for Scottish seaborne support. Any hopes that King Hans might honour the Scoto-Danish treaty and send his newly-built fleet to assist his Scottish nephew were dashed when Hans died on 21 February 1513.[93] As for O'Donnell, his forging of an alliance with King James in June 1513 was probably an effort, similar to that of spring 1507, to involve the Scottish king in Ulster politics. Certainly James promised to assist O'Donnell with ships and men when they were asked for, though in return he expected armed assistance, for which he provided artillery, ammunition, workmen, and quarriers 'for undirmynding of wallis'.[94] It may be that O'Donnell had undertaken to assist in the Scottish attack on the English stronghold of Carrickfergus, which followed in August; the payment by James of a month's wages in advance to his workmen and quarriers suggests a definite objective. However, for whatever reason, O'Donnell sailed back to Ulster without the artillery, which had to be dragged back from Glasgow to Edinburgh in mid-August, too late to join the royal army on its invasion of Northumberland.[95] According to the contemporary annals of Ulster, O'Donnell had spent three months in Scotland at King James's invitation, and had 'changed the king of Scotland's intent as to going to Ireland'; only long after the alliance had collapsed, in January 1514, would he write to Henry VIII claiming that he had had no sinister design in visiting James IV. On his homeward voyage, according to the Ulster annalist, O'Donnell encountered great peril at sea. Perhaps he should have taken King James's artillery with him; but if the annalist is correct, he had had a profitable visit, with a promise of support from a powerful ally.[96]

Even allowing for Danish and Irish defections, however, there was much which the combined Franco-Scottish fleets might have achieved against the English in the summer of 1513. Between 16 and 20 June, James IV sent messengers beyond the Mounth, to the west, to Galloway, Stirlingshire, Clydesdale, East Lothian, the Merse, and Teviotdale 'for the furnesing of men to the schippis'. They were to be ready by 1 July, a date soon changed to 8 July,[97] and finally to 19 July.[98] The delay may have been caused by lack of enthusiasm for service with the fleet, a reluctance which drew forth at least one exasperated letter from the king to William, Lord Livingstone, on 13 July, complaining that although Livingstone had been requested to furnish 'certane abill yong men weill abilyeit to pas in our schippis with our armee', his tenants had refused to obey, even though time was short and the expedition ready to depart.[99] The reluctance of Livingstone's tenants — and possibly others — to serve is understandable, for they were being asked to form part of an expeditionary force which would certainly require them to perform more than forty days' service, and which depended on the King of France for supplies and victuals. Far safer and more profitable to join the host in a plunder raid into Northumberland — or so it seemed.

However, at least one Scottish captain was eager to benefit from Louis XII's bounty. On 24 August 1513, weeks in advance of the Scottish fleet, Robert Barton, with his fine new three-hundred-ton 'Lion', had already reached Honfleur at the mouth of the Seine, where together with the ships of the Norman and Breton fleets, he received two months' victuals for two hundred and sixty men. Probably about sixty of these were seamen, the remainder soldiers serving with the fleet.[100] The victualling of the 'Lion' came towards the end of French naval preparations during the summer. Already in July the galleys of Prégent de

Bidoux had been supplied with rowers and crossbowmen; four hundred extra mariners were levied in Normandy; and as early as 12 August, Louis XII, having learned from James IV that the Scottish fleet had sailed, was eagerly awaiting its arrival in Brest. It would then join with Queen Anne of Brittany's ships and sail to Honfleur, where the entire Franco-Scottish fleet would be placed under the command of Louis de Rouville. As a further inducement to Scots in French service, Louis XII granted them the right to dispose of their goods by will, to inherit estates, and to hold benefices in France, without requiring letters of naturalisation.[101]

King Louis had not been misinformed; the Scottish fleet had indeed sailed. On 25 July the royal ships, accompanied by privately owned vessels of John Barton, William Brownhill, and Thomas Chalmers, by newly acquired foreign ships, the Spanish barque, the huge 'Barque Mytoune', and the barque of Abbéville, and by at least two smaller vessels, the 'Mary' and the 'Crown', sailed out into the Forth under the command of James's cousin, James Hamilton, earl of Arran.[102] The fleet's route lay north rather than south, where the English were waiting for the Scots in the Downs, and only after the Scottish ships had joined up with Prégent and the Norman and Breton fleets at Brest and Honfleur would a concerted attack be made on Henry VIII's lifeline to England. Perhaps in optimistic expectation of great things, King James ordered the striking of a new gold coin, similar in style to the English rose noble, bearing on the obverse the dragon being slain by the archangel Michael, on the reverse a three-masted ship with the Scottish arms attached, and carrying the legend 'Salvator in Hoc Signo Vicisti' ('Saviour in this sign hast thou conquered').[103] The striking of an English-style gold coin may well reflect James's claim to be Henry VIII's heir; and Michael, the dragon-slayer of the obverse, is perhaps complemented on the reverse by Michael the warship, which would conquer for the Lord. If James IV was interested in crusades, their destination was surely the English Channel rather than Constantinople or Alexandria.

In the last week of July, then, the Scottish fleet sailed north, the king himself on board the 'Michael' as far as the Isle of May;[104] presumably the ships then passed through the Pentland Firth before turning south into the Hebrides and following the west coast route to France. Yet the voyage took far longer than expected, with the fleet arriving in Normandy only in mid-September. For Arran had apparently broken his journey en route to sail into Belfast Lough and bombard Carrickfergus, the principal English stronghold in Ulster. It was the 'Michael's' only action in Scottish service, graphically described by Pitscottie and Buchanan, though not mentioned by the contemporary Ulster annalist, in spite of his knowledge both of the Irish treaty of the previous month and of Flodden in September.[105] We may perhaps give Pitscottie some credit for his description of events at this point; though hearsay and understandably garbled in transmission, it was based on information passed on through the family of Sir Andrew Wood.[106] Essentially Pitscottie sees the Carrickfergus raid as a piece of private enterprise by Arran, very much against James IV's wishes. According to the chronicler, the admiral 'keipit no derectioun of the king his maister bott passit to the wast sie wpoun the cost of Ireland and thair landit and brunt Carag-forgus witht wther willagis', subsequently returning to Ayr where the Scots 'repossit and playit' for forty days.[107] The furious king sent Sir Andrew Wood 'witht wther gentill men' to relieve Arran of his command — according to Buchanan, Wood was accompanied by Archibald, earl of Angus, who was to take Arran's place as admiral[108] — whereupon Arran, learning of their coming to Ayr, prudently sailed before he could be arrested. En route to France, he encountered a heavy storm which battered his ships and further delayed his arrival. Pitscottie concludes by stating that James IV, realising that the fleet would bring no early succour to France, summoned the host to the burgh muir of Edinburgh.[109]

These tales are a mixture of half-truth and misconception. There is no reason to doubt the fact of a bombardment of Carrickfergus or the fleet's return to Ayr. The reported fury of James IV is less certain, for Arran's attack on Carrickfergus may well have been a logical follow-up to the O'Donnell treaty of 25 June, planned in advance and arguably as good a way of bringing pressure to bear on the English as any other. Alternatively Arran may have been obeying the spirit rather than the letter of his master's instructions, and the king's anger might then have been caused by the fleet's apparent failure in Ulster, followed by a return to Ayr which was presumably to take on more victuals and ammunition. So long as the royal ships were still in Scottish waters, they were a charge on King James's already over-expended income; and there was of course the fact that King Louis had been expecting the Scots since mid-August. It is highly unlikely, however, that James IV intended to replace Arran with the maverick Angus, who probably became admiral only after Flodden, in the last few weeks of his life;[110] there is no doubt that the host was summoned for the invasion of England on 24 July, the day before the fleet sailed,[111] and not, as Pitscottie suggests, only as a consequence of delays by Arran on his voyage to France; and the storm to which the chronicler refers, while it may have delayed the Scottish fleet on its way to France, was only one of many, a later storm scattering the combined Franco-Scottish navy after its assembly in Normandy in September.[112] It may therefore have been the weather more than any other factor which prevented the Norman, Breton, and Scottish fleets, together with the war galleys of Gaston Prégent de Bidoux, attacking Henry VIII in strength on his return from Picardy to England in October 1513. The 'Michael' ran aground, the enterprise was abandoned, and according to a report which had reached Lord Dacre by mid-November 1513, the Scottish soldiers returning home from the fleet complained of ill-treatment by the French.[113] Nonetheless, the summer and early autumn of 1513 must have been a worrying time for Henry VIII's almoner Thomas Wolsey; for his career in royal service depended on making a success of King Henry's expedition, following the English fiascos of 1511 at Cadiz and 1512 at Fuentarrabia, the near-mutinous state of English seamen,[114] and the death of Admiral Sir Edward Howard, in the spring of 1513.

James IV's mistake was perhaps to overestimate the effect which these diversionary tactics — the sending of the fleet, the Irish treaty, the potential intervention of the Danes, even the Scottish invasion of Northumberland — would have on King Henry. The truth was that the English king was not to be deterred by any threats from disporting himself as a great war leader in northern France. Rejoicing in the fact that the late Pope Julius II had stripped Louis XII not only of his title of Most Christian King but also of his kingdom of France, both of which dignities he had bestowed on Henry, the youthful English king looked to the total defeat of French arms and his promised coronation in Paris, at the hands of the pope, as King of France. His ally, Emperor Maximilian, was quite happy to encourage Henry in his wild dreams, to place himself under Henry's banner, and to let him fritter away his father's legacy and English lives in the capture of Thérouanne, a former Habsburg stronghold in Artois, currently held by the French.[115] Even the English king's quest for glory on the battlefield was denied him, for he missed the one dramatic engagement of the campaign, the so-called 'Battle of the Spurs' at Enguingattes, near Thérouanne, on 16 August, when a French relieving force was pursued at the gallop by English and Burgundian horse. Henry made the best of it, describing his and Maximilian's martial exploits against superior odds in a letter to Margaret of Savoy the day after the battle;[116] and à week later Henry and the Emperor entered Thérouanne in triumph.[117] In the midst of the excitement, and flattered by the presence of Maximilian in his own army, Henry VIII paid little attention to what amounted to an ultimation from James IV, delivered by Lyon Herald at Thérouanne on 11 August. Dismissing both Lyon and King James's demands that he should desist from attacking Louis, Henry remarked that the Scottish king was 'no competent judge of so high authoritie to require us in that behalfe'.[118] He then went on to lay siege to the more substantial target of Tournai, which he captured in eight days and retained in English hands as a useful forward base to launch future attacks on Louis XII. In spite of all the ostentation, however, Henry's enormously expensive campaign had achieved little. Certainly he returned home in one piece, though that was as much attributable to luck as anything else; he had two conquests, Thérouanne — which he handed over to Maximilian — and Tournai; and that was all. Within a year all his allies — Pope Leo X, Maximilian, and Ferdinand of Spain — would have deserted him and he would be forced into marrying his younger sister Mary to the man whose kingdom he had claimed in 1513, Louis XII.[119]

He would also have missed the main event of the 1513 war, which occurred not on the Continent, but in Northumberland. For in three days — 24–26 July 1513 — James IV saw his fleet sail to assist the French king, despatched Lyon Herald with his ultimatum to Henry at Thérouanne, and summoned the Scottish host to Ellem in Berwickshire, the muster point of 1496.[120] Freed from constraints at last, the Scots prepared for war. Indeed, the Chamberlain, Alexander, third Lord Hume, did not wait for the host; about a week after James's summons, Hume rode into Northumberland, at the head of a large force of borderers, on a plunder raid. He was unlucky; during his withdrawal on 13 August, he was ambushed at Milfield, four miles north-west of Wooler, by Sir William Bulmer with a force of about one thousand, including two hundred archers. Hume's losses were heavy, and he had to abandon his plunder — and his banner — to the English. With his customary bias, Bishop Lesley describes Hume's raid — the 'Ill Raid' — as retaliation for an English incursion into Scotland; but it seems more likely that Hume, seeking to emulate his predecessor of 1497, was indulging in some private enterprise which went badly wrong.[121] James IV was not present or even in the vicinity of the borders; on 8 August he was on his way to the shrine of St Duthac at Tain, paying his annual, and as it happened his last, visit to the saint.[122]

Hume's discomfiture at Milfield did little to cheer those entrusted with the defence of Northumberland against the Scots. Only four days later, on 17 August, Lord Dacre wrote to Thomas Ruthal, bishop of Durham, urgently recommending that Henry's government should buy off the Scots to delay invasion until it became too late in the season for King James to contemplate a major offensive. A rapid payment to the Scots, Dacre had been assured, was all that was necessary.[123] Dacre's urgency was certainly prompted by the knowledge that, though Henry VIII had appointed Queen Katharine as Regent during his absence in France and — more to the point — Thomas Howard, earl of Surrey, as his lieutenant in the north of England, Surrey's headquarters were at Pontefract in south Yorkshire, far too far away to offer any immediate protection to the Tweed and Till valleys. Worse still, the towers destroyed by the Scots in 1496–7 — Duddo, Tilmouth, Twizel, Howtel, Lanton, Shoreswood, Thornton, Branxton — had not been rebuilt. When the King of Scots rose from his devotions at the shrine of St Duthac and came south, there appeared to be little to stop him ravaging the far north-east of England.

The lack of Scottish official records for the period of the 1513 campaign — understandable in view of the absence from Edinburgh not only of the king but of most of the political community — makes certainty about the host's movements impossible. It is clear, however, that James IV had assembled one of the largest armies — possibly the largest — ever to enter England, well supported by a sizeable artillery park — at least seventeen guns, five of them 'great curtals', throwing shot weighing up to sixty pounds, dragged south by a total of four hundred oxen.[124] On this occasion Mons Meg does not appear to have been employed; probably both her size and age were against her, and King James was eager to try out his new guns, both those recently made in Edinburgh castle by Robert Borthwick, and those imported from Flanders and France since 1510.[125] It is difficult to identify amongst the seventeen Scottish guns the 'Seven Sisters', large cannon of equal size forged by Borthwick and immortalised by Pitscottie; but they seem to have been present on the campaign, as they are mentioned in a contemporary report of Flodden sent from England to Venice in late October.[126]

James IV's target on the 1513 campaign was Norham castle, Bishop Ruthal's great stronghold just south of the Tweed and a long-standing Scottish military objective. Bishop Kennedy, Mary of Gueldres, and the young James III had failed to take the castle fifty years before, in the summer of 1463. James IV himself had isolated it in 1496 and laid siege to it unsuccessfully in 1497. In 1513 he intended to do the job properly, and to do it, moreover, in about three weeks. Thus we find that those in charge of the guns — both drivers and pioneers — were paid fourteen days' wages at a shilling a day for service in Scotland, with a further eight days payment for service in England at the higher rate of sixteen pence a day. These payments, made on 18 August in Edinburgh at the outset of the campaign, would guarantee service with the artillery until 9 September.[127] There was therefore no question that the king had in mind any military objectives beyond the Tweed and Till valleys; and the statement that he would be in York by Michaelmas,[128] if he ever made it, may have been intended as a taunt to the Cardinal of York, Christopher Bainbridge, to encourage him to abandon his manic efforts to have Henry VIII crowned King of France by the pope and instead return to protect his diocese.

At first the Scottish campaign was spectacularly successful. The portion of the host which had assembled on the burgh muir of Edinburgh moved south over the Lammermuirs to the muster point of Ellem between 19 and 22 August, closely followed by the guns. Sometime between 22 and 24 August, the entire host forded the Tweed, probably at or close to Coldstream, and advanced eastwards up the south bank of the Tweed to Twizelhaugh, about three miles from Norham. There, on 24 August, an ordinance was made laying down that the heirs of any man killed, mortally wounded, or even dying of disease while with the army, should come into their inheritances exempt from payment of the feudal casualties of wardship, relief, or marriage.[129] This was a sensible measure designed to hold the army together during an important siege, and employed not only before great occasions such as this one, Harlaw, and Pinkie, but also to lend greater legitimacy to minor occasions such as the government raid on the Merse in the summer of 1518 and the Edinburgh street fight known as 'Cleanse the Causeway' in the spring of 1520. There is no reason at all to conclude that the 'Act of Twizelhaugh' was made in August 1513 because 'a foreknowledge of approaching death seems to have weighed upon the nobles'.[130]

In fact, Norham castle fell to the Scots in five days. John Anislow, the English Constable of Norham, may have counted on a relieving force coming to his assistance; but none appeared, and on 28 or 29 August, a stormy night, the Scottish king assaulted, scaled and won Norham, parts of which he destroyed at once. Thomas Ruthal, bishop of Durham, was appalled at the rapid loss of his episcopal castle, remarking in a letter to Wolsey that he would never forget it nor recover from grief.[131] James IV had accomplished his principal objective; the campaign had been underway for only eleven days; and it was clearly now his purpose to defend his early conquest until the end of the campaigning season. There was no point in returning to Scotland and leaving Norham to be recaptured by the Earl of Surrey. So King James despatched Treasurer Hepburn to Edinburgh on 29 August to bring up more ammunition, oxen, and wheels for the gun carriages;[132] and at the start of September, he moved south up the Till valley, rapidly taking the smaller castles of Etal and Ford.[133] The latter was surrendered by Lady Heron; the English pardon given to John Heron, the bastard, as recently as 18 August,[134] had not apparently induced him to return to defend his family's estates against the Scots. By early September the Scottish army had taken up a strong defensive position on Flodden Hill on the edge of the Cheviots.

At this time also desertions from the host, probably on quite a large scale, began; certainly Edinburgh burgh council was fulminating against returning deserters by 5 September.[135] There was however nothing surprising in this; the campaign had been fought and Norham won, and to many of the rank-and-file, all that remained was to remove as much plunder as they could carry and return home. Unlike the gunners, drivers, and pioneers, they were not being paid — on the contrary, they had to bring their own provisions — and the experience of 1496 and 1497 had shown that it was difficult, if not impossible, to keep the host in the field for much longer than a week to ten days, a fortnight at the very most, in spite of the theoretical forty days' service.[136] Yet no contemporary, or near-contemporary, Scots account suggests that desertions from the host meant that King James's army at Flodden was inferior in numbers to that of the Earl of Surrey. In the event, the battle of Flodden happened because both sides wanted it to happen. Thomas, earl of Surrey, the English commander, was late in the field because his headquarters were so far south, at Pontefract; but he made swift progress north, in spite of appalling weather, as soon as he learned, on 25 August, that the Scots were in the field. By 30 August he was at Newcastle, having borrowed the banner of St Cuthbert from the prior of Durham; and at Newcastle he was joined by Lord Dacre, who was no doubt able to supply him with first-hand information as to the dispositions of the Scots. On 4 September, in spite of the storms, Surrey's son, Lord Thomas Howard, the new Admiral, arrived safely from France with a contingent of about a thousand, and joined Surrey at Alnwick.[137] Thus James IV had at least partially achieved one aim in waging war: a portion of Henry VIII's army had been detached from the conquest of northern France to assist in the defence of the borders.

Flodden was preceded by a week of challenges and counter-challenges as Surrey hurried north to prevent the escape of the Scots. He need not have worried, except perhaps about the outcome of the battle; for James IV was determined to fight, at least until Friday 9 September, the limit of his payments to those manning his guns. He had, after all, a large army in spite of desertions, containing no less than twelve earls and perhaps twenty lords of parliament; he had a superior position, and probably — in spite of statements by the later Scottish chroniclers — more victuals; and he was not inclined to answer Surrey's challenge and come down on to the plain of Milfield, where Lord Hume had been badly mauled by Sir William Bulmer less than a month before.[138]

Surrey was therefore left with the problem of forcing James IV to fight on ground less advantageous than Flodden Edge, which the earl complained was 'like a fortress'. On Thursday 8 September he moved his men north past James's position, arriving by evening close to the fords of Twizel and Heton on the river Till.[139] His manoeuvre had been visible through the mist and rain to the Scots on Flodden Hill, and it may have been at this point that a council of war, much elaborated on by the later chroniclers, took place, with advice being given to the king to attack Surrey while he was vulnerable, or alternatively to retire to Scotland as swiftly as possible. Whatever counsel was given to James IV — and the chroniclers' reports are made with benefit of hindsight — the decision which prevailed, and with which James's name is closely associated, was not to attack Surrey at this stage, possibly in a mistaken belief that he was heading for the Merse rather than continuing to seek battle. But on the morning of Friday 9 September, after a miserable night in the wind and rain, Surrey moved his army and guns west and south across the Till at Twizel and Heton, and by the middle of the day had reached the foot of Branxton Hill, a few miles north of King James, and barring any Scottish retreat north. The Scottish king had no option but to strike camp on Flodden Hill and hurry his entire force and artillery across the two miles of intervening high ground to the top of Branxton Hill before Surrey gained possession of its summit.[140] That afternoon, Friday 9 September, on the slopes of Branxton Hill, the battle of Flodden was fought.

Two large armies of roughly equal size were matched against each other; and much ink has been spilt in an effort to explain why the result was not either a drawn battle, with both sides drawing off and claiming victory, or a moderate defeat for one or the other.[141] Instead, after a hard struggle, there followed spectacular carnage on the Scottish side. The answer lies perhaps partly in James IV's 'wilful misgovernance', much commented on by later chroniclers, that is his failure to take good advice and his apparent ignorance of the need to give proper direction to his forces once they were engaged. Equally serious may have been the position of his handsome artillery park, hastily dragged to the summit of Branxton Hill and badly sited if it was to play any effective role in the battle that followed. Worst of all, and commented on by Bishop Ruthal shortly after the battle, was the Scots' use of pikes, eighteen to twenty-two feet in length and formidable weapons so long as the phalanx of troops bearing them was able to advance in tight formation, repelling any efforts by cavalry to break them up by projecting five rows of spearheads beyond the front rank of the phalanx and making penetration impossible. Advancing phalanxes of Swiss pikemen had defeated and killed Charles the Bold of Burgundy at Nancy in January 1477; the Swiss had become the most feared and respected tacticians during the Italian wars from 1494 onwards; and it was undoubtedly Swiss or 'Almayn' tactics which James IV was endeavouring to employ at Flodden.[142]

But the rough ground of Branxton Hill was not suitable for a rapid tight formation advance of pikemen; and the windy and rainy weather, producing soft, even marshy, ground at the foot of the hill must have helped to break up the phalanxes, making individuals within them, weighed down in many cases by heavy armour, appallingly vulnerable as they floundered about with their enormous pikes, totally useless for fighting at close quarters. Against these, and the swords which the Scots were forced to rely on when their pikes were broken or smashed, the English brought to bear a fearsome weapon, the brown bill or halberd, an eight foot spear-axe which could cleave heavy armour and smash swords and pikes. Writing to Wolsey on 20 September, Bishop Ruthal remarked that 'the bills disappointed the Scots of their long spears, on which they relied'.[143]

James IV had attempted to turn the new technology of the Swiss to his advantage in unfavourable conditions. His five huge phalanxes, each directed by eight French captains, would advance on foot rapidly down Branxton Hill, overrun the English artillery and put Surrey to flight. He himself would lead the main battle to give an example to others. Beyond this King James appears to have given no real direction to his troops. In the wind and rain, the five hedgehog-like phalanxes started grimly down the hill,[144] only to lose their close formation as they advanced over uneven or soft ground, to suffer penetration by the English halberdiers in the hollow at the foot of the hill, and to find themselves fighting at a terrible disadvantage. The rest of the battle was a grim slogging match in which neither artillery on either side, nor even English longbowmen, played any major part. The only successful Scots were commanded by Lord Hume, who together with Alexander, earl of Huntly, defeated the Cheshire detachment of Edmund Howard, the English Admiral's younger brother; but the victorious Hume and Huntly could not exploit their success, as they were prevented from assisting other Scottish formations by the appearance of Lord Dacre and fifteen hundred horse; and in any case they appear to have had no directions as to what to do when they had won their own battle. So Hume's cynicism, as reported by Pitscottie, when he refused to launch a second attack, saying 'he dois weill that dois for himself', may have a factual basis.[145] The Chamberlain had after all been fighting since early August, had been badly mauled in the 'Ill Raid', and he lost many kinsmen at Flodden. He and Huntly were amongst the few peers of note who survived.

Somewhere in the carnage in the centre of the field, the Scots suffered their worst casualty. Late in the battle, Sir Edward Stanley managed to reach the top of Branxton Hill, coming up to the side and rear of the phalanx commanded by the Earls of Lennox and Argyll, catching them at a disadvantage, and pursuing them across the hill through the area already fought over by the main battles of Surrey and James IV. Stanley's men, attracted more by the prospect of plunder than that of further pursuit, began to strip the bodies of the Scottish dead. Although they did not apparently recognise the fact at the time, one of the dead, struck by an arrow and gashed by a halberd within a spear's length of Surrey himself, was James IV.[146] Writing to Wolsey on 20 September, Bishop Ruthal remarked that the Scottish king fell near his banner; and he paid tribute to the courage and strength of the Scots, who were 'such large and strong men, they would not fall when four or five bills struck one of them'. The Scottish guns, Ruthal reported, were taken — though it proved later that the men in charge of them, Robert Borthwick and Secretary Paniter, had both escaped. The remainder of the bishop's letter makes dismal reading. The English, according to Ruthal, 'did not trouble themselves with prisoners, but slew and stripped King, bishop, lords, and nobles, and left them naked on the field. There might be seen a number of goodly men, well fed and fat, amongst which number was the King of Scots' body found, having many wounds, and naked'.[147]

Together with his son, the Archbishop-Chancellor, George Hepburn, bishop of the Isles, two abbots, nine earls, fourteen lords of parliament,[148] and thousands of others, the most successful of all late medieval Scottish kings had suffered the death which had always been an occupational risk for a ruler who habitually led his armies from the front. James IV's death strikingly recalls that of Charles the Bold of Burgundy, who like the Scottish king died in battle, in Charles's case against the Swiss and the Duke of Lorraine at Nancy in January 1477, his corpse being discovered only two days after the battle, naked, frozen to the ice of a pond, the head split to the chin with a halberd and the body pierced many times with pikes.[149] The comparison between the fates of Charles the Bold and James IV was indeed made, many years later, by Bishop Lesley.[150] But there was a difference. The great Burgundian duke's fate was perhaps foreseeable, given that he had been twice beaten, at Grandson and Morat, by the Swiss, and that, in his last battle at Nancy, he was heavily outnumbered. At Flodden, James IV had suffered from no earlier defeats and does not appear to have been at a numerical disadvantage; ironically, when he fell, he fell attempting to use the Swiss techniques which had been such a success at Nancy and in the Italian wars, but which had no place on the uneven terrain of Branxton Hill. Fascination with new technology, but lack of skill in using it — a Stewart failing if ever there was one — killed James IV in the end. There were, in all probability, no significant portents, no apocalyptic visions, no four horsemen. James IV's first — and fatal — mistake in 1513 was made on the afternoon of 9 September, when the five Scottish phalanxes started down Branxton Hill.

To the English, Flodden was little short of a miracle. Bishop Ruthal ascribed the great victory to the intercession of St Cuthbert, who never suffered injury to be done to his Church unrequited. 'The Scots', he remarked, 'might have done much more injury if they had not attacked St Cuthbert'.[151] But in his more prosaic moments, Ruthal knew that it had been the halberd, rather than the Saint, which had destroyed the great Scottish field army.

NOTES

1. Pitscottie, *Historie*, i, 272.

2. For the battle of Flodden, Pitscottie claims the authority of an eye-witness account by a 'landit gentillman' who at the time was twenty years of age: Pitscottie, *Historie*, i, 260–1. Buchanan cites Lawrence Telfer, who was in James IV's service, for his statement that after Flodden King James was seen crossing the Tweed into Scotland: Buchanan, *History*, ii, 259–60. Lesley is more cautious, remarking only the 'sundry' persons affirmed that the king had been seen, the night after the battle, at

Kelso, and had later gone on pilgrimage to Jerusalem: Lesley, *History*, 95–6; while Adam Abell's authority for the king's survival is a relative of his at Jedburgh, who had picked up the local rumours: N.L.S. MS. 1746, f. 112v.

3. Pitscottie, *Historie*, i, 273.

4. J.H. Burns, 'New Light on John Major', *Innes Review* v (2), 1954, 83–100, at 85.

5. Pitscottie, *Historie*, i, 276.

6. Mackie, *James IV*, 200–203; Nicholson, *Later Middle Ages*, 594–600; Macfarlane, *Elphinstone*, 427–430.

7. *See above*, chapter 5.

8. *Cal. State Papers (Spain)*, i, No. 204.

9. *Ibid.*, i, Nos. 210, 221; Polydore Vergil, *Anglica Historia*, 111, 113.

10. Mackie, *James IV*, 95–6.

11. *Cal. Docs. Scot.*, iv, Nos. 1671, 1672.

12. Rymer, *Foedera*, xii, 793, 797.

13. Lesley, *History*, 69.

14. Chrimes, *Henry VII*, 284–5.

15. *Ibid.*, 285.

16. *Cal. Docs. Scot.*, iv, App. 1, No. 37. Rymer, *Foedera*, xiii, 12, mistakenly dates this exchange of letters to 1502; and R.L. Mackie follows Rymer in this error: Mackie, *James IV*, 100. From the internal evidence of James's letter, the date can only be 1503.

17. John Leland, *Collectanea* (Lond., 1774), iv, 265–300.

18. Hall, *Chronicle*, 498.

19. *T.A.*, ii, 451–455.

20. For the details of 'days of truce', and border administration in general, see Thomas I. Rae, *The Administration of the Scottish Frontier, 1513–1603* (Edin., 1966), esp. 21–25, 47–51.

21. *James IV Letters*, No. 171.

22. *Ibid.*, No. 560. The exact date of Sir Robert Ker's death is unknown. Alone among the sixteenth-century Scottish chroniclers, Buchanan describes his slaying at some length. Those responsible were three Englishmen, John Heron, Lilburn, and Starhead. The English king's response to King James's demands for redress, according to Buchanan, was to hand over Lord Heron, brother of the killer, and Lilburn to the Scots, who imprisoned them in Fast Castle, where Lilburn died and Heron was incarcerated until 1513. Starhead was subsequently pursued and killed on the orders of Andrew Ker, son of the murdered Scottish warden; but the Bastard Heron escaped: Buchanan, *History*, ii, 246–7. This story may be substantially correct. Sir Robert Ker is described by Buchanan as master of the Scottish ordnance, and the records reveal him in that role in the campaign of 1497: *T.A.*, i, Pref., cl, clv, 329. Buchanan correctly names Robert's son as Andrew, who succeeded his father sometime before 1505: *E.R.*, xii, 387. If Buchanan's story is correct, therefore, the slaying of Sir Robert Ker must have occurred — at the latest – only three years after the 1502 treaty.

23. *T.A.*, iv, 72; Lesley, *History*, 76; *James IV Letters*, No. 171.

24. *James IV Letters*, Nos. 115, 136.

25. *Ibid.*, Nos. 126, 138.

26. *Ibid.*, Nos. 138, 139, 140.

27. *Ibid.*, No. 142.

28. *Cal. Docs. Scot.*, iv, No. 1742.

29. *Ibid.*, Nos. 1744, 1747.

30. For the details of Wolsey's visit to Scotland in March-April 1508, see *James IV Letters*, No. 171.

31. *R.M.S.*, ii, Nos. 3214, 3215.

32. *James IV Letters*, No. 171.

33. *Ibid.*, Nos. 175, 178.

34. *Ibid.*, No. 177 and n.l.
35. *T.A.*, iv, 125; *James IV Letters*, Nos. 180, 181.
36. Lesley, *History*, 79.
37. *Ibid.*; *James IV Letters*, Nos. 220, 221.
38. *Cal. Docs. Scot.*, iv, No. 1751.
39. Chrimes, *Henry VII*, 314.
40. *James IV Letters*, Nos. 250, 251.
41. *Ibid.*, Nos. 280, 281.
42. Nicholson, *Later Middle Ages*, 595.
43. Mackie, *James IV*, 201.
44. Scarisbrick, *Henry VIII*, 23.
45. *Letters and Papers Henry VIII*, i, pt. i, No. 5 (ii).
46. *Ibid.*, No. 406; *Cal. State Papers (Spain)*, ii, No. 44.
47. *Letters and Papers Henry VIII*, i, pt. i, No. 842.
48. Peter Iver Kaufman, 'Piety and Proprietary Rights: James IV of Scotland, 1488–1513', *The Sixteenth Century Journal*, xiii (1982), 83–99, at 96.
49. Scarisbrick, *Henry VIII*, 27.
50. *James IV Letters*, No. 543.
51. *Letters and Papers Henry VIII*, i, pt. i, No. 1297.
52. Scarisbrick, *Henry VIII*, 32–3.
53. *James IV Letters*, Nos. 443, 444.
54. *Flodden Papers*, 79–83.
55. *Ibid.*
56. *Letters and Papers Henry VIII*, i, pt. ii, No. 2157.
57. *Flodden Papers*, 79–83.
58. West's embassy is described in considerable detail in two letters which he wrote to Henry VIII on 1 and 13 April 1513: *James IV Letters*, No. 539, App. II.
59. *James IV Letters*, No. 544.
60. *Flodden Papers*, 79–83.
61. *James IV Letters*, App. II.
62. *Ibid.*, No. 552; *T.A.*, iv, 418.
63. *James IV Letters*, No. 394.
64. *Statutes of the Realm*, 3 Henry VIII, c. 23.
65. For the general context, see David M. Head, 'Henry VIII's Scottish Policy: a Reassessment', *S.H.R.* lxi (April 1982), 1–24, at 2–4.
66. *T.A.*, iv, 333; *James IV Letters*, No. 427.
67. Head, *op. cit*, 4.
68. And as early as 11 September 1512, John Anislow (Annesley), constable of Norham and the man who would be on the receiving end of James IV's successful siege in August 1513, had advised Thomas Ruthal, bishop of Durham, that it would be wise to take precautions against the Scots the following year: *James IV Letters*, No. 481.
69. Scarisbrick, *Henry VIII*, 38; *James IV Letters*, No. 568.
70. *Ibid.*, No. 478.
71. *See above*, Chapter 6.
72. For the details of the Cadiz and Fuentarrabia expeditions, see Scarisbrick, *Henry VIII*, 27–31.
73. Spont, *op. cit.*, xxv–xxvii.
74. *Letters and Papers Henry VIII*, i, pt. i, No. 1703.
75. *Ibid.*, i, pt. i, No. 1736.
76. Spont, *op. cit.*, xxxviii–xxxix, Nos. 72, 77.
77. *James IV Letters*, No. 550.
78. *Ibid.*, App. II.

79. *T.A.*, iv, Pref., lxiii–lxxv. On the subject of royal artillery in general see David H. Caldwell, 'Royal Patronage of Arms and Armour Making in Fifteenth and Sixteenth-Century Scotland', in David H. Caldwell (ed.), *Scottish Weapons and Fortifications 1100–1800* (Edin., 1981), 73–93.

80. *T.A.*, iv, 508–522.

81. *Ibid.*, iv, 507.

82. Pitscottie, *Historie*, i, 260–1.

83. *Ibid.*, i, 261; *Scots Peerage*, i, 21.

84. Pitscottie, *Historie*, i, 258–9; Buchanan, *History*, ii, 250–1. The queen went to Linlithgow on 6 August 1513, and James may have accompanied her: *T.A.*, iv, 418. Sir David Lindsay is first mentioned at court in October 1511, receiving a pension of £40: *T.A.*, iv, 269; by 17 November, 1512, he was usher to the infant prince James: *Ibid.*, iv, 441. He apparently resided at Linlithgow at this period: *Ibid.*, iv, 523. John Inglis may be an error for James Inglis, chaplain to the infant prince: *Ibid.*, iv, 441.

85. Mackie, *James IV*, 243–4.

86. Boece, *Bishops of Mortlach and Aberdeen*, 105.

87. Buchanan, *History*, ii, 253–5.

88. Pitscottie, *Historie*, i, 261–2.

89. *James IV Letters*, No. 559.

90. Spont, *French War of 1512–13*, No. 96.

91. Scarisbrick, *Henry VIII*, 27–8.

92. *R.M.S.*, ii, No. 3586. Those who witnessed the Irish alliance were: Alexander Stewart, archbishop of St Andrews; James, archbishop of Glasgow; David, bishop of Galloway, dean of the Chapel Royal; the Earls of Angus, Argyll, Lennox, Arran, Eglinton, and Glencairn; Lords Seton, Lindsay of Byres, Sinclair; John Hepburn, prior of St Andrews; George Crichton, abbot of Holyrood; James Stewart, abbot of Culross; Gavin Dunbar, archdeacon of St Andrews, clerk register; Patrick Paniter, Secretary; Robert Forman, dean of Glasgow; and Robert Colville of Ochiltree, director of chancery. This remarkable list, by far the longest *R.M.S.* sederunt for the entire reign, includes no less than eleven witnesses who do not appear on any other 1513 sederunt.

93. *James IV Letters*, No. 536 and n.l.

94. *R.M.S.*, ii, No. 3586; *T.A.*, iv, 527.

95. *T.A.*, iv, 527.

96. *Annals of Ulster*, iii, 506–7.

97. *T.A.*, iv, 413–4.

98. *James IV Letters*, No. 559.

99. *Ibid.*

100. *James IV Letters*, No. 565.

101. *Ibid.*, Nos. 564, 567; Spont, *op. cit.*, xliv, Nos. 85, 86, 87, 88, 89, 92, 94.

102. The size of the Scottish fleet is inferred from the 1513 Shipbuilding Accounts in *T.A.*, iv, 482–507.

103. Ian H. Stewart, *The Scottish Coinage* (Lond., 1966), 74.

104. Lesley, *History*, 87. Contemporary confirmation that James sailed as far as the Isle of May is to be found in *T.A.*, iv, 501.

105. *Annals of Ulster*, iii, 507, 509.

106. Pitscottie, *Historie*, i, xcvii, cix–cxii.

107. *Ibid.*, i, 256.

108. Buchanan, *History*, ii, 245.

109. Pitscottie, *Historie*, i, 257–8.

110. *R.S.S.*, i, No. 2550.

111. *T.A.*, iv, 416–7.

112. *Flodden Papers*, No. xviii; Spont, *French War of 1512–13*, No. 96.

113. *Ibid.*, No. 95.

114. *Ibid.*, No. 81.

115. For details of the English campaign, see Scarisbrick, *Henry VIII*, 35–7.

116. *Letters and Papers Henry VIII* (Brewer edn.), i, Nos. 4405, 4407.

117. Scarisbrick, *Henry VIII*, 36.

118. *James IV Letters*, No. 563.

119. For details, see Scarisbrick, *Henry VIII*, 50–56.

120. *T.A.*, iv, 416–7; *James IV Letters*, No. 560.

121. *Letters and Papers Henry VIII*, i, pt. ii, Nos. 2279, 2283; Lesley, *History*, 92; Hall, *Chronicle*, 555–6.

122. *T.A.*, iv, 419.

123. *Letters and Papers Henry VIII* (Brewer edn.), i, No. 4403.

124. There are many huge estimates of the size of the Scottish host, including Pitscottie's impossible figure of 100,000: Pitscottie, *Historie*, i, 262. A contemporary English report put the Scots army at 80,000 at the battle itself, far too high if the fairly reliable figure for Surrey's army — around 20,000 — is to be accepted: *Letters and Papers Henry VIII*, i, pt. ii, Nos. 2246, 2651 (3). On 20 September, Bishop Ruthal of Durham reported to Wolsey that, after the capture of Norham castle, 20,000 Scots had deserted James IV: *Ibid.*, i, pt. ii, No. 2283. This is probably too high a figure; but given that the armies at Flodden were roughly equal in size, and that James IV had twelve earls with him, somewhere between 30,000 — 40,000 is a likely figure for the Scottish host at the outset of the campaign. For the Scottish guns, see W. Mackay Mackenzie, *The Secret of Flodden* (Edin., 1931), 59–60.

125. *Ibid.*; Caldwell, *Scottish Weapons and Fortifications*, 76–7.

126. Pitscottie, *Historie*, i, 259–60; *Letters and Papers Henry VIII*, i, pt. ii, No. 2651 (3); *Cal. State Papers (Venice)*, ii, No. 341.

127. *T.A.*, iv, 515.

128. *Cal. State Papers (Venice)*, ii, No. 341; *Letters and Papers Henry VIII*, i, pt. ii, No. 2313.

129. *A.P.S.*, ii, 278.

130. Mackie, *James IV*, 248.

131. *Letters and Papers Henry VIII*, i, pt. ii, Nos. 2279, 2283.

132. *T.A.*, iv, 522.

133. *P.S.A.S.* vii (1866–7), 141–152, at 143 (for James IV at Ford). Etal lies only a few miles away, on the Scottish route south down the Till.

134. *Letters and Papers Henry VIII* (Brewer edn.), i, No. 4406.

135. *Edinburgh Burgh Records*, i, 143.

136. It may however have been easier to keep the service of contingents provided by the royal burghs for the full forty days; for example, on 2 August 1513, Aberdeen burgh council authorised the raising of a tax of £400 Scots to provide a small force 'to pas with our souerane lord in his weres in Ingland, for the space of xl dais efter thair cuming to his grace': *Aberdeen Council Register*, 85. The factor of payment may have encouraged loyalty for the full forty days in some cases — though certainly not in all, as the Edinburgh desertions suggest.

137. *P.S.A.S.* vii, 143; Hall, *Chronicle*, 557.

138. For Surrey's challenges, and James IV's responses, see *P.S.A.S.* vii, 143, 146; *Letters and Papers Henry VIII*, i, pt. ii, No. 2239.

139. *P.S.A.S.* vii, 146–7.

140. *Ibid.*, vii, 147–8.

141. There is a vast Flodden literature, ranging from contemporary accounts of the battle to Sir Walter Scott's *Marmion* and *Tales of a Grandfather*. Probably the most reliable, though hardly to be taken as gospel on such subjects as numbers involved and the death roll on the Scottish side, are a contemporary description of the battle, the 'Trewe Encountre', printed, with an introduction, in *P.S.A.S.* vii (1866–7), 141–152; the 'Articles of the bataill', in *Letters and Papers Henry VIII*, i, pt. ii, No. 2246; and

two letters by Thomas Ruthal, bishop of Durham, to Wolsey, on 20 September: *Ibid.*, i, pt. ii, Nos. 2283–4. Good modern accounts of the battle are in Mackie, *James IV*, 252–269; and Nicholson, *Later Middle Ages*, 600–606. W. Mackay Mackenzie, *The Secret of Flodden* (Edin., 1931), addresses himself to the crucial problems presented by the battle with considerable success, and prints a contemporary Italian poem, based on an English source, about the battle: 'La Rotta de Scocesi'.

142. Mackenzie, *Secret of Flodden*, 65–9, 70–72, 73–4.

143. *Letters and Papers Henry VIII*, i, pt. ii, No. 2283.

144. *Ibid.*, i, pt. ii, No. 2246.

145. Pitscottie, *Historie*, i, 271–2.

146. Mackenzie, *Secret of Flodden*, 84–5; *Letters and Papers Henry VIII*, i, pt. ii, No. 2283.

147. *Ibid.*

148. The most accurate Flodden death roll is in Emond, op. cit., Appendix A.

149. Philippe de Commynes, *The Universal Spider* (trans. and edited by P.M. Kendall, Lond. 1973), 212.

150. Lesley, *History*, 96.

151. *Letters and Papers Henry VIII*, i, pt. ii, No. 2283.

11

The Legend and the King

One of the minor tragedies of late medieval Scottish historical literature is the lack of any surviving contemporary chronicle of the life and reign of James IV. What might have been is well illustrated by a letter from Polydore Vergil, the Italian author of the *Historia Anglica*, to the Scottish king, written in London on 13 December 1509. Vergil, who had lived in England since 1502, informed James IV that he had undertaken the composition of a history of the Britons, followed by that of the Angles, and that he had nearly finished this task. He wished now to turn his attention to the Scots, and in order to assist him in his work, he asked King James to send him any existing Scottish annals, or a list of the kings in order, and particularly a description of his own achievements and those of his people.[1] No reply from King James survives, and perhaps there was none. In any event, Vergil's history of the Scots does not appear to have progressed beyond the planning stage, though his enquiry places him amongst the select few historians based in England who had — or have — the remotest knowledge of, or interest in, Scottish history.

A man rather better placed than Vergil in this respect, and one with more sympathy towards the Scots, was Don Pedro de Ayala, the Spanish ambassador to Scotland for a little over a year, summer 1496 to 1497, and one of the negotiators of the Peace of Ayton in September of the latter year. De Ayala did not write a chronicle; but his long letter to Ferdinand and Isabella, written from London at the end of July 1498,[2] contains a great deal of information about James IV and his people. For this reason, parts of the letter have been seized upon and treated as gospel by generations of historians. Certainly it has great value as a portrait of the king as a young man by a foreigner at his court who knew him well, who accompanied him on the campaigns of 1496 and 1497, and who was in many respects a shrewd observer of James and his subjects.

Much of what Ayala says must however be treated with caution. He was after all a Spaniard in London seeking to recollect his observations made during a single year spent in Scotland; and his purpose seems to have been not so much to impress Ferdinand and Isabella with the virtue of the Scots and their king, as to demonstrate his own worth as the architect of Anglo-Scottish peace, even in the face of fierce hostility from his compatriot and rival in London, De Puebla. It is important, therefore, not to tear Ayala's comments about Scotland out of context, for they refer only to 1496–7, a highly untypical year, and much of what the ambassador says is surely designed to underline Anglo-Scottish enmity and the difficulty of making peace between two realms which, in his letter, appear to be of equal size and strength.

We may rapidly discount some of Ayala's statements, for example the hugely exaggerated figures which he cites for James's annual revenue, the size of the Scottish host (120,000 horse), Ayala's belief that its rank-and-file soldiers were paid, and his tally of the Scottish peerage — 'five-and-thirty great barons in the Kingdom, without counting the smaller ones.' But some of his other remarks, based on direct experience, command more respect. According to Ayala, 'the prelates are very much revered; they have the larger share in the Government.' Such a view might be expected from an ambassador who had come to Scotland as a direct result of Archbishop Blacader's embassies to Spain, who saw Elphinstone entrenched as Privy Seal, the elevation to St Andrews of the king's brother, and — in the year of Perkin Warbeck — King James's heavy reliance on Andrew Forman, the future Bishop of Moray. Equally interesting are Ayala's views on how government was run. 'Spiritual as well as secular lords', he says, 'belong to the General Council. It meets four times a year in order to administer justice. It is a very good institution.' Ayala may of course be confusing General Councils with sittings of the Lords of Council; but it is significant that he does not mention parliaments — there were none during his stay in Scotland — and sees government as being the business of the first two estates in General Council. Such a view would fit the evidence of the third estate's complaint in 1504 that its members were not being consulted when taxation was authorised.[3] But of course General Councils were not held four times a year; indeed there appear to have been no General Councils in 1496, and the only recorded meeting in 1497 was in October[4] — that is, after Ayala had left Scotland. So his knowledge of the workings of Scottish royal government is probably based on hearsay, imperfectly recalled in London almost a year after his departure.

Ayala is however most quoted as a contemporary source for the appearance, education, habits, and character of James IV, and it is in this context that he is indispensable. 'The King', he remarks, 'is of noble stature, neither tall nor short, and as handsome in complexion and shape as man can be. . .He never cuts his hair or his beard. It becomes him very well.' The king's beard did not, however, last; on 9 August 1503, the day after his marriage to Margaret Tudor, James had his beard 'clippit' by the Countess of Surrey and her daughter at the exorbitant cost of £180 Scots,[5] and duly appears clean-shaven in all his portraits.

As to King James's education, Ayala is clearly most impressed by the king's command of languages: 'he speaks the following foreign languages; Latin, very well; French, German, Flemish, Italian, and Spanish. . .he likes, very much, to receive Spanish letters'. In addition, Ayala notes that the king could speak 'the language of the savages who live in some parts of Scotland and on the islands.' He was also well read in the Bible and in some other devout books, was a good historian, and had a very good memory. All this has the ring of truth; for more than any other medieval Stewart king, with the possible exception of James I, James IV had the time to learn. He was not thrust in his teens into the business of government like his father and grandfather, or for that matter his son. The rebellion of 1488, though in itself a traumatic experience for James, was followed, as it had been preceded, by a long period of tutelage. Indeed, when Ayala met the king in 1496, James at twenty-three had little more than a year's personal rule behind him. This late development meant that he was subject to a number of widely differing educational influences, some of them highly beneficial, both before and after he became king. Until her death in 1486, Queen Margaret of Denmark was in charge of James's education;[6] and she may have been assisted in this task by the royal Secretary Archibald Whitelaw, James III's tutor and a noted humanist, while John Ireland, the royal confessor who was to present the new king with 'The Meroure of Wyssdome' in 1490,[7] may also have had a hand in James's upbringing. There need be no doubt that King James received an excellent formal education, above all in Latin; and if Margaret of Denmark's biographer Sabadino, writing in 1492, is correct, the queen had more aptitude than James III for ruling the kingdom,[8] and may have passed her skills on to her eldest son.

After 1488 James had a further five years' service from Archibald Whitelaw; his Keepers of the Privy Seal were John Hepburn, prior of St Andrews, and from 1492 William Elphinstone, bishop of Aberdeen, both of them noted educationists, the latter joining with the king in supplicating the pope to found Aberdeen university before James had emerged from tutelage, the former the co-founder of St Leonard's College at St Andrews with James's son, the archbishop-Chancellor, in 1512. Following the Angus coup in 1492–3, the king came into closer contact with the earl's third son, the poet Gavin Douglas, who completed his Master's degree at St Andrews in 1494, was of an age with the king, and received rapid ecclesiastical preferment, presumably not only because he was a magnate's son but also because of Angus's influence with King James.[9] Though Hepburn opposition kept Gavin Douglas out of the coveted deanery of Dunkeld, he was supported in his right to the teinds of Monymusk in Aberdeenshire by the king in September 1497, he was presented to the parsonage of Glenholm in May 1498, and became rector of Linton or Hauch in East Lothian around 1504. Royal influence certainly secured for Douglas his most valuable benefice during this reign, the provostry of St Giles, Edinburgh, by March 1503. Evidence of Douglas as a royal familiar is in fact to be found as early as 11 April 1495, when in the king's chamber at Holyrood, Gavin Douglas witnessed a resignation of lands to the Crown together with John Ireland and Walter Chapman, at a time when he appears to have had no benefice, being described simply as Chancellor Angus's son.[10] Perhaps in gratitude for royal support in the ensuing years, and no doubt in expectation of further ecclesiastical preferment, Douglas dedicated 'The Palice of Honour' to James IV in 1501. His fortunes, however, to some extent mirrored those of his father, and Angus's long wardship on Bute between 1502 and 1509[11] may well have prevented Gavin Douglas from reaching the episcopate before 1513,

or even from achieving the intimacy with James IV that fell to Andrew Forman
— whom Douglas despised — and to the humanist and subtle diplomat, James's
Secretary from 1505, Patrick Paniter.

Clearly, however, the king in his formative years was surrounded by
a host of able tutors, enjoyed the company and the instruction of the
learned, and was interested enough to ensure that his sons, the Archbishop
of St Andrews and the Earl of Moray, had as good a formal education as was
available anywhere in Europe. Thus James IV's linguistic skill, as reported by
Ayala, hardly comes as a surprise. His knowledge of Latin and French might
perhaps be taken for granted; Flemish, German, and Spanish are altogether
more remarkable, though Ayala may be exaggerating James's ability in these,
going perhaps on a few words spoken by the king to his foreign gunners, or a
smattering of Spanish acquired to impress the ambassadors of Ferdinand and
Isabella, whose first embassy to Scotland arrived as early as July 1489,[12] seven
years before Ayala. As for James's Gaelic, his summer tours to Dunstaffnage, Dunaverty, Rarbert, and Mingary in 1493–5 had no doubt given him
some proficiency in the language, if only to communicate with the obsequious McIan of Ardnamurchan. It is possible, however, that James IV had
at least a reasonable knowledge of German. James's mother, his great-uncle
Gerhard von Oldenburg, his regular dealings with his uncle Hans, King of
Denmark — all these influences could have led to James's proficiency in
German.

Ayala's descriptions of James IV's piety are largely confirmed by contemporary
official records. The ambassador noted that the king observed all the precepts
of the Church, hearing regular masses, observing fast days, saying prayers,
and confessing with the Observantine Friars. All this is true — indeed Ayala
omits the king's predilection for regular pilgrimages — though there is a hint
of business, pleasure, and piety combined in the statement that 'after mass
[the king] has a cantata sung, during which he sometimes despatches very
urgent business.' Other virtues appear to have been based on a proper sense
of balance; the king, according to Ayala, was 'neither prodigal nor avaricious',
he was invariably truthful, he lent a willing ear to his counsellors, and he was
temperate in both eating and drinking. Ayala suggests rather less temperance
in James's sexual appetites, commenting on the efforts of those in power
during the minority to keep the king under their control by favouring his
love intrigues with their relatives — a clear reference to Angus and his niece
Marion Boyd.[13] But 'as soon as he came of age, and understood his duties,
he gave up these intrigues.' Ayala is less convincing here, for he immediately
goes on to say that when he arrived in Scotland — in the summer of 1496 —
the king was keeping a lady 'with great state' in a castle, an obvious reference
to Margaret Drummond at Stirling castle. 'Afterwards', claims Ayala, 'he sent
her to the house of her father, who is a knight, and married her' — that is,
married her off. As he is seeking to portray James IV in the most favourable
light possible, Ayala hurries on from his genteel description of King James's
affair with Margaret Drummond to suggest that 'it may be about a year since

he gave up, so at least it is believed, his lovemaking, as well from fear of God as from fear of scandal in this world, which is thought very much of here.'

The Spanish ambassador had of course no first-hand knowledge of James's sexual adventures after 1497; but he was certainly being optimistic if he believed that the Scottish king had given up his lovemaking. After Margaret Drummond came the lengthy liaison with Janet Kennedy, and a later association with Isabel Stewart, daughter of James, earl of Buchan, both of which produced children;[14] William Dunbar's poem 'The Wowing of the King quhen He wes in Dunfermeling' clearly reflects James's continued womanising;[15] and it is easy enough to imagine the role played by 'Janet bair ars', who received a number of royal gifts between 1508 and 1512.[16]

The most often quoted part of Ayala's letter concerns what appears a more serious flaw in James's character, namely his conduct of war. The Spanish ambassador had ample experience of Anglo-Scottish war; it began shortly after his arrival and did not end until some time after his departure. Hence his remark that the Scots 'spend all their time in wars.' Interestingly, given his visits to the host on the raid of Ellem in 1496 and the siege of Norham in 1497, Ayala commented that 'war is profitable to him [the king] and to the country.' James IV 'loves war so much that I fear. . .the peace will not last long.' However, 'he is not a good captain, because he begins to fight before he has given his orders. . .I have seen him often undertake most dangerous things in the last wars. I sometimes clung to his skirts, and succeeded in keeping him back. On such occasions he does not take the least care of himself.' Ayala is however fair enough to add James's justification for his recklessness: 'He said to me that his subjects serve him with their persons and goods, in just and unjust quarrels, exactly as he likes, and that, therefore, he does not think it right to begin any warlike undertaking without being himself the first in danger.' Such an attitude would hardly have surprised James's father or grandfather, both of whom had died on military campaigns; and it is hardly appropriate to relate Ayala's remarks, as many writers do, to the context of Flodden fifteen years later. The ambassador was after all only familiar with James's prowess at sieges, Heton castle and a number of towers in September 1496, Norham in July – August 1497. He saw no full-scale set-piece battle with the English, indeed none had taken place since Homildon Hill in 1402. When Flodden came, James IV would lose disastrously not because he thoughtlessly thrust himself into danger, but because his battle plan was inappropriate both to the terrain and the weather. Ironically, Ayala's strictures would probably have applied much more accurately to James's *successful* storming of Norham castle less than a fortnight before Flodden. The king's personal bravery in war, as described by Don Pedro, shows him amply fulfilling one of the key roles of a medieval monarch, a role which his young contemporary Henry VIII was anxious to play in France in 1513. Henry's death at Thérouanne or Tournai, and James IV's survival at Flodden — an alternative possible scenario for the summer of 1513 — would have altered radically the future histories of both England and Scotland.

If we are searching for alarming portents of disaster in Ayala's letter, we find rather more convincing material in his statement that 'on land they [the Scots] think themselves the most powerful kingdom that exists. . .no King can do her [Scotland] damage without suffering greater damages from her.' And in spite of making a virtue of James's temperance, Ayala is still moved to say that the king 'esteems himself as much as though he were Lord of the world.' This over-confidence, amounting frequently to arrogance, was at once a major strength and alarming weakness of James IV and the Scots. It was however something relatively new. Looking back, Ayala remarked that when there was no war, the Scots fought amongst themselves. However, 'it must be observed that since the present King succeeded to the throne they do not dare to quarrel so much with one another as formerly, especially since he came of age. They have learnt by experience that he executes the law without respect to rich or poor.' In these few words, Don Pedro sums up James III's failure to govern, above all his inability to halt the spread of feuds, and contrasts it with James IV's activity on the ayres and in the Lords of Council from the start of the reign.

Ayala's conclusion is that 'the King possesses great virtues, and no defects worth mentioning.' A rather different contemporary view is to be found in the poetry of William Dunbar. The great makar, a royal pensioner for at least thirteen years, might have been expected to provide us with revealing insights into the life of king and court. In fact, apart from some detailed information about Margaret Tudor's household, a complaint about the hangers-on one might expect to find at any court, an indictment of the Lords of Session, a lively assault on the lack of civic pride displayed by the merchants of Edinburgh, and two poems on Bernard Stewart of Aubigny — a welcome and an obituary[17] — Dunbar tells us little enough about James IV and those who habitually surrounded him. His first and last concern is for himself, and poems addressed directly to the king — and there are many — are punctuated throughout by the recurring theme of unrewarded service. A typical example is Dunbar's open reproof to King James in 'Schir, yit remembir as of befoir':

> 'How suld I leif and I not landit,
> Nor yit withe benefice am blandit?
> I say not, sir, yow to repreiff,
> Bot doutles I go rycht neir hand it. . .'[18]

At one level, the poet may have been doing little more than employing the normal medieval language of complaint and invective, choosing obvious targets such as undeserving familiars at court, enjoying his skill in varying his vituperative scorn.[19] Certainly he had little of substance to complain about in his own treatment by James IV. On 15 August 1500 Dunbar received a pension of £10 a year for life, or until he obtained a benefice worth an annual £40.[20] The king came to his first mass in March 1504, and gave him a gown worth £15 12/6d at Christmas 1511; most important of all, in November 1507 Dunbar's annual pension was officially increased to £20, and in August 1510 quadrupled to a handsome £80 a year.[21] This was double the sum received by the young poet David Lindsay from the autumn of 1511 — and from April 1512, on the birth of the future James V, Lindsay's role in the royal household, as chief servitor and personal attendant to the infant heir to the throne, was a highly responsible one.[22]

But the disadvantageous comparison which Dunbar himself made, in two fiercely satirical poems, was with John Damian, the 'French leech', abbot of Tongland, the most famous — or notorious — of James IV's alchemists, an individual whose expenses and royal gifts far outstripped anything given to Dunbar. In the six months following August 1503 Damian received no less than £150 from the royal Treasury; the previous year he had been granted the equivalent of £210 Scots in French money to travel abroad on his work; he was set up by the Crown in a research laboratory at Stirling castle, and sustained in his search for the quintessence by plentiful supplies of 'acqua vitae' — whisky; and, most offensive of all to Dunbar, Damian enjoyed an easy familiarity with James IV, with whom he played cards and took part in shooting contests in Holyrood Abbey close.[23] Even Damian's abortive flight from Stirling castle to France with a pair of manufactured wings in September 1507 — according to a gleeful Dunbar and Bishop Lesley, he plummetted into a midden[24] — did not end the alchemist's court career or his intimacy with the king. Dr Lyall has drawn attention to the fact that 'an attack on the proto-scientific world of alchemy. . .is not uncommon among medieval moralists', and cites Robert Henryson's 'Orpheus and Erudices' as revealing contemporary suspicion regarding astrology.[25] It is difficult, however, to read Dunbar's perennial complaints about court preferment without feeling that they are very personal, based on the fact that although he had finally received a handsome annual reward from James IV in 1510, he had had to wait an unconscionably long time for it — some nineteen years, if he was indeed the violently seasick William Dunbar on board the Earl of Bothwell's ship, the 'Katherine', on the French embassy of 1491.[26] Even then Dunbar had been a man of thirty, so that what he clearly regarded as modest preferment came to him only late in life. He lacked the advantages of birth enjoyed by his great rival, Walter Kennedy, or the aristocrat Gavin Douglas; and he failed to secure as firm a place at court as the young David Lindsay or the odious John Damian. Thus Dunbar's many addresses to the king, and his comments about the court and society in general, are tinged with bitterness. Perhaps there is some acceptance of his lot at the end, in 'The Petition of the Gray Horse, Auld Dunbar', when the king orders the Treasurer to 'tak in'the old horse and 'hows him now agenis this Yuill', decking him out for Christmas at royal expense — an order which it is tempting to relate to Dunbar's expensive Christmas gown of 1511.[27] For the most part, however, Dunbar's view of king, court, and the Scotland of his day is as bitter and jaundiced as Pedro de Ayala's is laudatory and optimistic. But Ayala, read carefully, tells us infinitely more about James IV and his times than Dunbar; and there can be little doubt that, from the king's point of view, the Spanish ambassador was better company than the disenchanted Scots makar.

The shortest of all accounts of the reign of James IV is to be found in the Asloan manuscript, where it forms the final chapter of 'Ane tractat drawin owt of the scottis cronikle', an anonymous description of the deeds of the Scots and their rulers from the origins of the kingdom down to the campaign of 1513. This brief chapter, which is presumably contemporary or nearly contemporary, tells us nothing new:

> 'The yere of god I^m iiij^c lxxxviij James the ferd
> was crovned at scone on sanct Jhon the baptistis day
> and apone the day of the decallacoun of sanct Jhon he
> wan norhame In the yere of god I^m v^c and xiij yeiris
> with mony diuerss strenthis and castellis on the yngliss
> bordour. . .'[28]

Twenty-five years are compressed into two sentences, and the 'tractat' serves only as an exercise in wish-fulfilment for the patriotic Scot. For the campaign of 1513 would appear to be a great success; there is no mention at all of Flodden.

Once Flodden had been fought, however, it coloured all subsequent accounts of James IV and his times, even those written by men who had lived in pre-1513 Scotland. For the disaster required to be explained, and explanations could only be provided by reference to the character of the king who had been responsible for it. Vices were sought — and easily found — to complement James IV's many admitted virtues; and flaws in the royal character — many of them very conventional — were enlisted to explain away the appalling end of the reign in terms to which a sixteenth-century audience would respond. A great deal of post-Flodden writing about James IV is rooted firmly in the *speculum principis* tradition; and it has exercised an enormous influence on historians down to the present day.

What might perhaps be described as the legend of Flodden — the view that James IV was doomed from the outset of the 1513 campaign through rejection of wise counsel — appears within a decade of the battle. In 1522 Hector Boece's *Lives of the Bishops of Mortlach and Aberdeen* was printed in Paris;[29] largely a hagiography of Bishop Elphinstone, who had appointed the author as Principal of his new University of Aberdeen, the work reduces James IV to little more than a cypher, guided through the reign by the wisdom of the bishop. Thus, according to Boece, 'whenever [the King] had any transaction with his subjects or with foreign princes, whenever a treaty had to be made with kings, or an alliance formed with provinces and states, our prelate was entrusted with these commissions. James took no step in any matter, discussed no question which had not been previously submitted to the bishop's judgment. Bishop William was thus beloved and venerated by the commons, dear to the nobles and a favourite with all.'[30] Yet this universal popularity failed to survive the test of giving unwelcome advice before the 1513 campaign. Elphinstone having spoken in the Council in favour of sending an embassy to advise Henry VIII not to make war on Scotland's French ally, and to wait for Henry's reply, he was faced with 'a tumult of opposition'. Insults were hurled at him, and he was accused of having spoken foolishly and thoughtlessly 'like a dotard' against the French alliance, the public interest, and the nation's honour. Elphinstone's efforts to prevent war were therefore rejected, in spite of the fact that his views were shared by 'the better part of the magnates of the country'[31] — a statement hardly borne out by the obvious popularity of the subsequent campaign. The sequel, the king having for the first time rejected the bishop's wise counsel, is 'a bitter ending', which Boece remarked that he hoped to incorporate into the history of Scotland which he was currently writing. However, when the first edition of that history appeared some five years later in 1527, James IV was relegated to only a brief mention towards the end of a table of Scottish kings from the nation's mythical beginnings down to James V.

This thumbnail sketch of James IV, incorporated into John Bellenden's translation of Boece,[32] made in the 1530s, is almost entirely about the 1513 campaign. The king is allowed only a single sentence to rule 'mony yeris in gret tranquillite', exercising firm and fair justice throughout the realm. Then 'fortoun began to invy his gret felicite', and he declared war against England, wholly in the interests of France, in order to 'draw the King of Ingland out of France'. According to Boece, James came to the borders with one hundred thousand men, won Norham and 'mony othir strenthis', stayed twenty days without battle, and 'scaled' — that is, disbanded — two-thirds of his army. Then on 9 September at Flodden, 'ruscheand ouir feirsly on his ennimes, but ordour', the king was killed with many of his nobles. There is no sign, in this account, of Bishop Elphinstone and the rejection of his wise advice; the king is rather the victim of fickle fortune and rashness on the day of the battle.

It is clear from Boece's eulogy of Elphinstone and from his brief sketch of the reign that the writer was remote from the political events which he describes in both. The conventional description of the Flodden campaign, complete with vastly exaggerated numbers, was circulating in English and foreign accounts of the battle very soon after it had taken place; and James is obliquely criticised by Boece for undertaking the war in the interests of France. In the *Lives of the Bishops*, the criticism is much more direct, and put into Elphinstone's mouth because Boece is not concerned to arrive at an accurate assessment of international diplomacy in the final years of the reign, but rather to eulogise his patron. With benefit of hindsight, he and everyone else could see Flodden as a disaster which needed to be explained. Elphinstone was invariably wise: therefore the bishop, in Boece's account, argued against the Flodden campaign, and was overruled by James IV in a classic rejection of wise counsel. We should not look in Boece's *Lives* for any deep insights into the world of politics and international diplomacy in which his patron was deeply involved;[33] indeed the book only really comes to life when he describes Elphinstone's good works within Aberdeen diocese, supporting these with a wealth of local detail. However, Boece is still close enough to the national events which he is describing not to fall into the trap of believing that the

Scottish king was motivated throughout by the desire to go on crusade, for there is not a hint of such a desire in either the *Lives* or the *History*.[34]

Elphinstone was not the only James IV bishop to benefit from a near-contemporary hagiography. In 1522 Alexander Myln, abbot of Cambuskenneth, completed his Latin *Lives of the Bishops of Dunkeld*,[35] the hero of which is Bishop George Brown, no favourite of James IV. Myln, like Boece, digresses from his eulogy of the bishop to point out the rejection of wise counsel by the Scottish king, rashly committing himself to the war of 1513 solely in the interests of the French, who were fickle allies.[36] Thus, in Myln's account, 'The French. . .gave assurances of aid in money and armed men, which they signally failed to observe.' But Myln then goes on immediately to say something extraordinary, namely that James IV 'invaded England, stormed Norhame Castle, and for fifteen days awaited the warriors of France, but all in vain.' The assertion that James's objective in remaining so long in England was not simply to draw home all, or at least part, of the English army in France, but also to await French reinforcements, is made by no other writer; but it may contain some elements of truth. The timing of the campaign in Myln's account is incorrect — there were eleven days between the fall of Norham and Flodden, and the entire campaign lasted twenty days — but more important, he may have misjudged the commitment of the French to the Scottish invasion. For on 22 September, less than a fortnight after Flodden, Brian Tuke, the English Clerk of the Signet in Henry VIII's army at Tournai, sent a lengthy report of the battle to Richard Pace, Cardinal Bainbridge's secretary. There is a wealth of detail, not all of it accurate, but convincing on the tactics adopted by both sides. At the end, Tuke noted that there was found, 'in the pouch of a noble Scot who perished', a written paper, rather in the manner of a receipt, declaring that 'to the western seaport of Dunbar the King of France sent to James IV, King of Scots: first, 25,000 gold crowns of full weight; also forty cartloads of powder; two pieces of great ordnance called cannons; 6,000 culverins with shot for them; a ship laden with bombards and other engines, including 6,000 spears, 6,000 maces, and the same number of pikes; as well as a knight, Dansi by name, with fifty men-at-arms in heavy armour, and forty captains to command the soldiers.'[37]

Tuke's list is interesting and suggestive: though he errs in naming the French port of entry as Dunbar when Dumbarton is obviously intended, his account leaves little room for doubt that King Louis sent substantial aid — ordnance, other weaponry, money, and troops — to assist James IV's war effort. That the French should reach Scotland late, after the departure of the royal army on the campaign, should come as no surprise. Louis was not after all bound by his May agreement with James to send material assistance to Scotland until the Scottish fleet had reached France. Presumably he sent his reinforcements shortly after 12 August, when he had definite news of the sailing of James IV's fleet,[38] and if so they must certainly have reached the east of Scotland — via Dumbarton — some time after the departure of the Scottish host from Edinburgh on 19 August. Thus it is tempting to identify the dead noble Scot in Tuke's account of the battle with Matthew Stewart, earl of Lennox, a man very close to James IV during the last ten years of the reign,[39] and who may well have been responsible for conducting the French, their arms, munitions, and money, from Dumbarton, at the heart of the Lennox, to the Scottish border. Thus a comparison of Myln, Tuke, and the available evidence concerning Louis XII's commitments, would suggest that the French arrived late in the Scottish host, though it is unlikely that James IV, after the storming of Norham on 29 August, was waiting in Northumberland only on their account.

In any event, there was no real possibility, in the early sixteenth century, that James IV would be absolved of guilt for the conduct of the entire 1513 campaign rather than simply for his personal rashness at Flodden. The view of the king which has to a greater or lesser extent influenced all subsequent writers is that of Sir David Lindsay of the Mount. Around 1530 Lindsay completed his 'Testament and Complaynt of Our Soverane Lordis Papyngo', a long vernacular poem (1190 lines) of conventional political advice directed to King James V, who had recently assumed control of government following a fifteen-year-long minority. The poem is interesting not so much for Lindsay's advice on government as for his thumbnail sketches of earlier rulers, among which that of James IV is of major importance because of the poet's presence in the royal household in the final years of the reign.

The reign of James IV is dealt with in some five stanzas, each of seven lines.[40] Lindsay begins by lamenting the passing of James IV, 'that potent prince', praising his virtues of humility and liberality, and concluding that 'Ane greater nobyll rang nocht in to the eird.' He then lists the king's achievements — the imposition of firm justice, so much so that 'the Savage Iles trymblit for terrour', and no-one on the borders, specifically in Eskdale, Ewesdale, Liddesdale, and Annandale, dared to rebel for fear of immediate royal retaliation; the winning of the support of the Scottish magnates; the king's ability to ride alone throughout the realm without fear of attack; and the European fame of James's court, acquired through the pursuit of sports appropriate to a king, 'tryumphand tornayis, justyng, and knychtly game'. In Lindsay's view, James IV was 'the glore of princelie governyng.'

The rest — almost half of the James IV part of the poem — is tragedy, brought about by the king's failure to use good counsel. Thus

> 'throuch the ardent lufe he had to France,
> Agane Ingland did move his ordinance.'

From this brief indication of James's motivation, Lindsay moves swiftly on to Flodden itself. The king is duly portrayed 'in his tryumphand glore' and is then swiftly brought low

> 'nocht be the vertew of Inglis ordinance,
> Bot be his awin wylfull mysgovernance.'

If he had used wise counsel, Lindsay claims, James would have won the battle. Instead:

> I never read in Tragedie nor storie,
> At one journaye, so mony nobyllis slane,
> For the defence and lufe of thair Soverane.'

Lindsay's 'Testament of the Papyngo' is fascinating in its treatment of James IV partly because of its relatively early date — 1530 — but also because it is an estimate of the king by someone who actually knew him — and knew him well enough at the end of the reign to be entrusted with the care of James's son and heir. There are, of course, limits to Lindsay's knowledge. As one of the custodians of the heir to the throne he was clearly not present at Flodden; his place would be at Linlithgow with the queen and the infant prince. Also, he is not writing a history of James IV, but rather a homily on the nature of good kingship, above all on the necessity for rulers to use wise counsel, and this certainly colours his view of the 1513 campaign. Furthermore, his lavish praise of James IV should to some extent be set against what Lindsay had experienced after 1513, that is, fifteen years of political instability, punctuated by palace revolutions and seizures of the boy king by warring magnate factions. Viewed against this background, James IV may indeed have seemed to Lindsay 'the glory of all princely governing'; and it may be that, for effect, the poet raises the king too high in order to underline the spectacular tragedy of his fall.

Yet what Lindsay has to say about James's achievements is of considerable interest. Passing over his conventional praise of royal humility and liberality, we come to the king's success in criminal justice. Here Lindsay is remarkably specific: James 'daunted' the Western Isles and the borders. In the case of the latter, the poet mentions only the West March, and he may indeed be referring to a single occasion — the Raid of Eskdale in the summer of 1504, when James IV, with the English warden Lord Dacre, was also to be found in Annandale, Liddesdale, and Ewesdale.[41] Likewise, the most committed royal onslaught on the Isles — though the king was not present — was in the late spring and early summer of 1504, with assaults on Eilean Donan, Strome, and Cairn-na-Burgh castles;[42] though it may be doubted that rebels in the Isles 'trembled for terror.' But Lindsay's purpose in drawing attention to the king's record in criminal justice is to make two further points — that he thereby earned the support of the nobility and made the country safe to ride through alone without risk. This last point was picked up more than a generation later by Bishop Lesley, who commented that 'the haill realme of Scotland wes in sic quietnes' that the king was able to ride great distances alone; and he cites an instance in 1507 when James journeyed 'with great deligens on ane day fra Striveling be Perth and Aberdene to Elgine in post, quhair he reposit him on ane hard burd ane certane space of the nycht in Mr Thomas Leslies hous, than parsoun of Kinguissie; and on the morn raid to Sanct Dutheis in Rosse by the messe, the last day of August, bot returnit agane to Striveling be jornay, accumpayneit with the nobilitie of these cuntries.'[43]

At first sight, this appears an unlikely tale, a story which, greatly embroidered, had come down to Lesley by way of his namesake in Elgin. But it is largely corroborated in the Treasurer's accounts. On 25 August 1507 many of the royal household had been sent over the Mounth 'to bide at post before the King.' Three days later, James IV took a purse of £26 'quhen he raid alane to the Month.' His route seems to have taken him first from Fife

— possibly via Stirling — to Perth, where we find him on 31 August. He did not stop long, for on the same day his horse required shoeing 'be the gait.' His movements thereafter are difficult to follow, and we lose sight of him until his return to Aberdeen four days later, on 4 September, and thence to Brechin and Perth the following day.[44] But there is one very significant entry, a payment of 14/- on the king's return to Perth, 'to Johne Dunlop he gaif for the Kingis fraucht at Ardroseir.'[45] The only possible reason that King James could have to use the Ardersier ferry at this time would be if he was coming west from Elgin on his way to the Black Isle and so north to St Duthac's at Tain. Thus Lindsay's hint, elaborated by Lesley, is largely confirmed by the records. In what must have been a deliberate attempt to set a record, perhaps even to prove his safety in far-flung areas of his kingdom, James IV sent household servants ahead of him to prepare the way for a very fast ride north to Tain, probably pausing for some sleep, as Lesley suggests, at Elgin en route, and returning at a more leisurely pace, via Aberdeen, to Brechin and Perth. Like James's pilgrimage on foot from Edinburgh to Whithorn in the spring of the same year, this was the sort of event which was likely to be remembered. It is a remarkable commentary on James's energy, a hectic ride even for this king, whose normal itinerary was physically punishing.

Chroniclers and official records alike comment at length on James's love of tournaments; there is ample evidence to support Lindsay's statement that the fame of King James's court spread throughout Europe on account of his 'tryumphand torneyis, justyng, and knychtly game'. Tournaments held in Scotland which attracted the attention of foreigners were nothing new — there are graphic contemporary accounts of the contest between Scots and Burgundian champions at Stirling, before James II, in February 1449[46] — but no Scottish king before James IV appears to have been so committed to the staging of tournaments and to taking part in them himself. Thus we find jousting in honour of Perkin Warbeck's marriage, early in 1496; a tournament to celebrate James's own wedding in August 1503 went on for three days in Holyrood palace courtyard; and — among others — there were spectacular jousts in June 1507 and May 1508, the latter to celebrate the arrival in Scotland of Bernard Stewart of Aubigny.[47] On both these occasions the king took an active part, playing the role in the former of the 'wild knycht',[48] entering combat with all comers. In 1507 and 1508, the 'knychtly game' had as its object a negress, the so-called 'black lady' who was brought to the tournament in a triumphal chair carried by two squires.[49] This may have been the 'Ladye with the mekle lippis' described by the poet William Dunbar, who claims that she 'landet furth of the last schippis' — presumably from Spain, like King James's Moorish drummers — and that she was the victor's prize at the tournament:

> 'Quhai for hir saek, with speir and scheld,
> Preiffis maest mychttelye in the feld,
> Sall kis and withe hir go in grippis;

and fra thyne furth hir luff sall weld:

My ladye with the mekle lippis.'[50]

Like hunting and hawking, jousting was a proper sport for king and nobility. Tournaments enabled James IV to display his warlike skills before a wide and approving public, skills which in 1496 he swiftly transferred from the Holyrood tiltyard to the seige of Heton castle. The ostentatious display, especially at the later tournaments, suitably impressed the Scottish magnates with the martial vigour of their king, channelled since 1497 into the relatively harmless pursuit of the chivalric ideal in jousting and pageantry. James's impressionable young brother-in-law, Henry VIII, soon followed suit, emulating James IV's disguise as the 'wild knycht' by appearing incognito in his first joust at Richmond in January 1510; thereafter he was a tireless devotee of the sport, challenging all and sundry to combat on horse or foot, and revelling in the elaborate chivalric ceremonial associated with jousting and tournaments.[51] The world of the young Henry VIII, like that of James IV, was one of knight errantry and militarism, born of the need to satisfy and entertain a military aristocracy for whom war was an essential part of life. If Bishop Lesley is correct, there may also have been an element of political calculation in the great Edinburgh tournament of May-June 1508; for although the tournament mainly involved Scots and French, there was elaborate 'counterfutting of the round tabill of King Arthour of Ingland.'[52] Only a year later, in October 1509, James IV and his queen would name their new-born son Arthur, a name recalling not so much the Arthur of English mythology as the deceased brother of the new King of England. The tournament ceremonial and the birth of a Scottish Prince Arthur were alike aggressive reminders of James IV's closeness to the English throne; and a spectacular tournament to impress the French may well have been a way of channelling Scottish hostility towards the English, which Wolsey had found rampant in the spring of 1508, into warlike sport rather than war itself. In the last analysis, however, it was not simply the Scottish nobility, but James himself, who looked beyond the tournament to the reality of conflict with England. As Don Pedro de Ayala had perceptively remarked, the king loved war.

A few years after Sir David Lindsay's 'Testament of the Papyngo', Adam Abell, an Observantine friar at Jedburgh, completed his vernacular 'Roit or Quheill of Tyme', an abridged version of a Latin original dealing with the history of the Scots from their mythological beginnings down to the author's own day.[53] Abell had not spent his entire life in Jedburgh; probably born around 1475, he was a distant kinsman of the Augustinian Robert Bellenden, abbot of Holyrood and translator of Boece. Not surprisingly, Abell became an Augustinian canon at Inchaffray in 1495, and probably remained there throughout the adult rule of James IV. The abbot of Inchaffray, Laurence Oliphant, was killed at Flodden, but it seems likely that by 1513 Abell had — perhaps fortunately for himself — moved to the stricter Observantine order at Jedburgh friary. Certainly his brief account of Flodden is unremarkable, and nothing in it suggests that he was personally present, as he might well have been if he had still been a canon at Inchaffray. Abell's account of the reign of James IV — the first of any length to survive — is therefore that of an Augustinian canon of Inchaffray, recollected in tranquillity at Jedburgh in 1533.[54]

Abell is concerned both to tell a moral tale and to glorify the order which he had eventually chosen to serve. Thus he remarks that James IV 'be ewill consall' took the field against his father in 1488; he comments on the new king's 'gret penance' without specifying what it was; and he extols James's founding of 'owr place of Striwiling' — the Observantine friary — and his endowment of 'outhir halie places', naming St Ninian's at Whithorn, St Duthac's at Tain, and Ladykirk. He emphasises the king's use of wise counsel, but erases the following clause which suggests that the royal advisers were mainly Observantine friars, perhaps feeling that he had gone too far. He comments on the sending of the Golden Rose to James by 'Pope Alexander VIII', and on Julius II's later gift of the Hat and Sword. And he remarks that the Scottish king was liberal, especially to foreigners, that in jousting and fighting either on foot or horseback 'he had few lik him in Scotland of his statuyr', and that he exercised firm justice, punishing thieves and reivers throughout the country.

All this is very conventional and unremarkable, a catalogue of kingly virtues. However, Abell does not leave James IV with an unblemished character. The king had apparently two vices. One of these is a conventional complaint: James IV 'wes gretumlie gewin to the plesour of the flesche and lechorie of it'. This is similar to Abell's complaint about James III, who 'wes gretumlie gewin to carnale plesour'; but in the case of James IV, the chronicler does not suggest that royal lechery was in any way connected with the king's final downfall. His other criticism has more substance: 'be prewat consall' — taking private, that is bad, counsel — King James 'maid a recognitioun of his baronis landis and the baronis for that taxat the pure lauboraris.'[55]

Abell is the first to describe recognition as an evil, but by no means the last. Bishop Lesley follows him in ascribing recognition not to the king directly, but to 'certane of his counsall', and is quick to absolve James of any blame, as 'the noble and gentle Prince, persavand his subjectis to gruge thairwith as ane new inventit maner to truble the estate of the cuntrey, did easely and gentlie aggre with the auld possessouris and awnaris, for the quhilk he conqueist gret favour of his people, and the inventouris of that practise greit hatrent.'[56] George Buchanan, whose Latin history appeared in 1582, sharply criticises a wide range of feudal casualties, claiming that they were introduced only because of royal extravagance, and describing them — incorrectly — as 'new' methods of raising money. Like Abell and Lesley, Buchanan concentrates on recognition, but goes further by ascribing its revival to Bishop Elphinstone, and ignoring the hardship imposed on lower orders of society; recognition was simply 'very oppressive to the whole nobility.' Grudgingly Buchanan admits that 'such was the love of those who suffered, and such their regard to their prince for his other virtues, that their dissatisfaction broke out into no sedition'[57] — a rather different version of events from Lesley, who claims that the king did something to mitigate the hardship which recognition caused. As for Buchanan's attack on Elphinstone, this may reflect little more than the chronicler's dislike of bishops — above all his detestation of Archbishop John Hamilton — in the 1570s, a fierce prejudice which runs throughout Buchanan's history, and causes him to criticise not only Elphinstone but also Bishop Kennedy of St Andrews.

Whatever their individual stories, however, all three chroniclers deal with recognition in essentially the same way; it was a device introduced not by the king, but by bad counsellors, and James IV, rightly or wrongly, managed to avoid much of the odium which recognition brought on these men. In a way, the chroniclers' treatment of this criticism of royal policy is a compliment to James's kingship; for as early as 1533, when Abell wrote, the popular view of James IV was that of a great and wise ruler, Lindsay's 'glory of all princely governing', a lost leader. So it was not only convention which made Abell and those who followed him ascribe the revival of recognition to evil counsellors rather than to James himself; for the royal character could not be sullied by total responsibility for a vice which brought obvious hardship to King James's people. As we have seen,[58] the reality was rather different, with free tenants having to assist their lords in the payment of huge royal compositions to recover estates which had fallen under recognition; and in the cases of other feudal casualties, such as non-entry, the Crown was unrelenting in its pursuit of cash returns. Only in some cases of royal feu-farm grants, for example in Menteith in 1510, do we find an enlightened Crown policy in operation towards sitting tenants. However, given James's public generosity, the logical targets at the time were his civil servants and lawyers, above all the royal advocate Master James Henryson, who must have been one of the most unpopular public figures of the reign.

Perhaps Abell's most significant contributions concern the end of the reign. Twenty years after the Flodden campaign, his view of the summer of 1513 clearly reflects the popular Scottish explanation of the disaster current in the minority of James V. Thus in conventional fashion Abell finds the necessary evil counsellor — Bishop Andrew Forman — and includes the popular view that James IV had somehow survived the battle. In the former case, the war with England is explained partly by 'unhappy fortune', partly by 'instigatioun of france men', but also by the influence of the protonotary, 'thain bischop of moraie remanend in france.'[59] The view of Forman as the architect of James IV's ruin was undoubtedly that of a faction which included Forman's rival Gavin Douglas, who had finally abandoned poetry for politics in the minority of James V; and Adam Abell may have absorbed Douglas's view of Forman as 'yon evyll myndyt Byschep of Morray'. Greatly elaborating on Abell's hints, Pitscottie gives the most colourful picture of Andrew Forman. The bishop was not only a royal familiar, but also a conjuror who performed such tricks as making the 'black lady' disappear at the banquet following the tournament of 1508.[60] In the course of Forman's shuttle diplomacy, according to Pitscottie, the bishop laid on a banquet for the pope 'and all his cardinallis', before which he was required to say grace. This upset Forman, who was 'not ane goode scholar and had not good latine', and he 'hapnit out in goode Scottis', saying "The Dewill tak yow all fallis cairllis, in nomine patris et filii spiritus sancti", to which the assembled company all replied 'Amen'.[61] Later Pitscottie makes Forman the agent of France, correctly stating that he obtained the archbishopric of Bourges in Berry, but hopelessly confusing the diplomatic manouevrings of the period, with Forman offered the 'priorie of Cowdibett' — the rectory of Cottingham, which Forman had in fact held since May 1501 — by Henry VIII in a vain effort to make the bishop use his influence with James IV not to support France in the forthcoming war of 1513.[62]

It is clear from all this that Pitscottie was drawing on stories about Forman's rise to power which were circulating after Flodden and which had also reached Abell at Jedburgh almost half-a-century earlier. Benefit of hindsight — the fact that Forman had done extremely well out of his diplomatic missions before 1513, although the results of his diplomacy had been disaster for the king and much of the political community — together with the political in-fighting of James V's minority, combined to produce the view of Andrew Forman as James IV's evil genius. Nor can the fact that Forman was one of the main architects of the English treaty of 1502 and an opponent of a Franco-Scottish alliance as late as 1508, yet a firm supporter of the French alliance in King James's last years, have helped his posthumous reputation.[63] But it is unthinkable that Forman was pushing James IV into a French treaty which the king did not want; and the fact that Forman hoped to receive substantial rewards for his services is hardly surprising. Blacader might well have received a Cardinal's hat if his Spanish diplomacy had borne fruit; Bainbridge of York in fact obtained one for performing similar diplomatic services for Henry VIII. Like these men, Andrew Forman was a career cleric pushing hard for rewards, and getting some largely because of his intimacy with the king. But James was the master and Forman the servant. It is understandable that the latter should have been condemned, above all by Protestant chroniclers more than sixty years later. Both Buchanan and Pitscottie must have relished the stories circulating about an evil prelate of the Old Faith whose counsel had led to the defeat and death of the king, though it must be said of Pitscottie that he accords Forman some sympathy — unlike Buchanan — and makes a joke of the bishop's scholarship. Unquestionably Forman came from a family endowed with more than its fair share of luck. As a royal familiar, he would certainly have accompanied James to Flodden if he had been in Scotland in the summer of 1513; and his brother Adam, who was not only at the battle but carried the royal banner there, survived the experience.[64]

Abell's 'Roit or Quheill of Tyme' is strangely inconsistent about James IV's death. He begins conventionally enough by remarking that when the Scottish king's army 'wes out of ordur' it was attacked by the 'haill power' of England, and in the battle that followed the king 'and amaist all the nobillis of Scotland wes slane.' However, he then continues: 'Of him [the king] diverss is opinion; ane is at he wes nocht slane in that feild of flowdone in inglis grund. Ane odir is at he wes slane in the feild. The first opinion I had maist trew for relation at

I haif hard in the ferms of our place of Jedwert.'⁶⁵ Thus Abell's initial certainty that the king had perished is immediately qualified, and on the strength of local Jedburgh gossip he ends up by taking the opposite view.

Other theories of James IV's survival, presumably originally based on the initial difficulty of the victors in identifying the king's naked corpse, and sustained by an understandable refusal by many Scots to accept that James was dead, soon surpassed Abell's modest suggestions. Thus Bishop Lesley claims that 'it is haldin for truth' that the body which the English recovered from the field was not that of the king, but 'ane vther Scottis man callit the laird of Bonehard quha wes slane in the saide feild.' He goes on to say that the king had been seen alive at Kelso on the evening after the battle, and that it 'wes commonlie haldin' that James was still alive — Lesley was writing in 1568, when the king would have been ninety-five — and that he had gone on pilgrimage to Jerusalem to spend the rest of his days in penance for 'his bygane and former offenceis.' In any event, 'howevir the matter come, he appeirit nocht in Scotland eftir as King.'⁶⁶

George Buchanan, who takes a much less favourable view of King James than Lesley, vies with the bishop in producing what he admits are doubtful tales of James's survival at Flodden. Thus he says that he has heard that many Scots wore the same coat-armour as the king, and that the body recovered by the English was that of 'Alexander Elphinstone' — Alexander, first Lord Elphinstone, raised to the peerage in 1511 and killed at Flodden — who, according to Buchanan, 'was very like the king in stature and appearance, and. . .clothed in royal insignia.' He goes on to say that the same sources claim that James himself recrossed the Tweed and was killed by the vassals of Hume near Kelso, either as an attempt to please Lord Hume, or on his direct orders, to avoid his being held accountable for his inactivity during the battle. Warming to his task, Buchanan recounts other conjectures — how on the night following Flodden, the abbey of Kelso was seized 'by Kerr, an intimate of Hume's, and the abbot ejected', an act which would not have been risked if James had still been alive. A further tale, supposedly from 1516 when Lord Hume was executed on the orders of the Governor, John, duke of Albany, has one David Galbraith, a kinsman of Hume, blaming the cowardice of his fellows for allowing Albany to behave in a tyrannical fashion towards the Hume family, when he, with six companions, had 'checked the insolence of the king at Kelso.' Buchanan is swift to point out that the charge of murdering King James after Flodden was never brought against the Humes at their trial in 1516; but he goes on to hedge his bets by remarking that he had heard personally from Lawrence Telfer, 'an honest and learned man', and a spectator of Flodden, that 'after the day was lost, he saw the king cross the Tweed upon horseback.'⁶⁷ Telfer, the vicar of Kirkpatrick in Glasgow diocese, was twenty-four in 1513, in the spring of which year he obtained a papal dispensation from taking holy orders for two years; and in fact his advancement in royal service would lead to his succeeding Paniter as Secretary in 1520.⁶⁸ He may indeed have been present at Flodden, as Buchanan claims, and have seen an individual dressed in James's coat-armour recross the Tweed. Buchanan concludes — clearly using the same source as Lesley — that amongst the slain, the English found the body either of King James or of 'Alexander Elphinstone'.

The ever-colourful Pitscottie has yet another tale, though it probably originates from the same or a similar source. Having described the removal of the king from the field accompanied by the mysterious four horsemen, he goes on to say that, ten years later, a man convicted of murder offered, in exchange for his life, to show the Duke of Albany where James IV was buried; the proof that the skeleton was indeed the king's would be his penitential iron belt lying beside him in the grave. However, according to Pitscottie, 'this man gat no awdience be thame that was about the Duik of Albanie, quho desyrit not at that tyme that sic thingis sould be knawin.' Having created a suitable air of mystery, Pitscottie then reverts to a well-worn theme, that of Scots wearing the king's livery; there were, he says, no less than ten clad in the royal coat-armour, among them two — Alexander McCulloch and the 'Squyer of Clesche' — who were similar in build to King James.[69] Alexander McCulloch is easily identifiable as a royal household servant;[70] and the 'Squyer of Clesche' is either the unfortunate individual who just missed sailing with the fleet on 25 July, or else he may be identified with William Meldrum 'of Cleische and Bynnis', the hero of Sir David Lindsay's 'Historie of Squyer Meldrum' who took part in the Carrickfergus raid and accompanied the Scottish expeditionary force to France.[71] If the latter is the case, then the 'Squyer of Clesche' cannot have perished at Flodden and Pitscottie, who names Lindsay as one of his sources, must have confused the information which he received about the squire's heroism. In any event his purpose was to show that the English failed to lay hands on the body of James IV; 'we knaw suirlie they gat not the king', he asserts, 'because they had nocht the taikin of his irone belt to schaw to no Scottisman.' Like the other chroniclers, however, Pitscottie is in no doubt that the king was killed — by somebody — around the time of the battle.

In fact, there is no room for doubt about the fate of James IV. Thomas, Lord Dacre, who had joined James in his hawking and hanging Raid of Eskdale in 1504, and who therefore knew the Scottish king well, identified 'the body of the King of Scots slain in the field . . . and thereupon . . . brought the corpse to Berwick.'[72] Subsequently the body was removed south to the Carthusian monastery of Sheen, seven miles from London, where it lay unburied for months because James had died excommunicate. On 12 October 1513 Henry VIII, in the course of a long letter to Pope Leo X in which he raised the spectre of the Archbishop of York's right to act as metropolitan for the entire Scottish church, also asked the pope to write to the Bishop of London to allow the body of the excommunicate King of Scots to be carried to London and buried with royal honours at St Paul's. On 29 November Leo X replied that as it was to be presumed that James IV had given some signs of repentance in his extremities, he might be buried with funeral honours.[73]

The Scottish chroniclers' obsession with James IV's supposed temporary survival, their need to believe that the English had not recovered their king's body, is in its way a striking tribute to James's popularity. For in spite of their widely varying backgrounds and attitudes — Bishop Lesley a Catholic exile and staunch defender of Mary Queen of Scots, George Buchanan a Protestant revolutionary and that queen's most bitter enemy, and Robert Lindsay of Pitscottie a Fife laird drawing mainly on local sources for his information — all three chroniclers had clearly absorbed the favourable stories about James IV which were circulating in the 1530s and which appear in embryo in Lindsay's 'Testament of the Papyngo' and Abell's 'Roit or Quheill of Tyme.' For the most part, then, they did not seek to alter the already established view of James IV's character and policies, but rather embroidered a wide variety of existing eulogies of the king. In his vernacular history,[74] Lesley is probably the most committed of all in his praise of King James, imbuing him with countless virtues and no real vices; even at Flodden, James's rashness is implied rather than openly condemned, and Lesley flies in the face of evidence which he must surely have possessed when he declares that 'thair wes in that battell ane griter nombre of the Inglis men slane nor of the Scottish men'.[75] The bishop's account of the reign, written in exile and therefore some distance removed from the Scottish public and archival sources which he cites to add authority to his history, is a curious blend of the severely annalistic and the colourfully anecdotal, drawing heavily on English sources such as Polydore Vergil and Hall, yet inclining in the end to an uncritical euology of James IV and all his works.[76] Perhaps Lesley was seeking to defend the sanctity of Scottish monarchy through praise of one of the country's most able kings; certainly he shows himself to be a committed supporter of the Hamilton family in the person of James's kinsman, the first Earl of Arran. And he concludes with unqualified praise, to the effect that if God had granted James longer life, he would have brought the realm of Scotland 'to sic flowrishinge estate, as the like in none of his prediscessors daies was never yit heard of.'[77]

George Buchanan's praise, by contrast, is shot through with criticism of James IV's vast expenditure on tournaments, the beautifying of royal palaces at Falkland and Stirling, and — above all — the construction of a royal navy, including a ship which far exceeded in size, cost, and equipment, any ship that had ever been seen on the ocean.' Thus, according to Buchanan, the treasury being exhausted, the king was advised to devise new means of raising money; and when these had been tried but were still inadequate because James would not set bounds to his expense nor listen to wise counsellors, the king 'determined to proceed to Syria' — a remarkable description of James's supposed crusading mania — in order to distract the Scots from his 'unbounded waste' at home. Thereafter Buchanan immediately goes on to describe the king's rigging out of a crusading fleet — presumably thereby compounding his 'unbounded waste' — and gives as a reason for the projected crusade James's desire to expiate the crime he had committed by bearing arms against his father. Preparations for a crusade were however interrupted by growing European tensions; and Buchanan thereafter abandons the subject altogether, and turns with relish to long descriptions of the causes of Anglo-Scottish war.[78] In their different ways, Andrew Forman and James Hamilton, earl of Arran, are seen by Buchanan as the incompetent or actively malicious counsellors who helped to bring the king to his ruin, while the wise advice of Archibald Douglas, earl of Angus, not to undertake war against England, is predictably rejected by the bellicose King James.[79] This combination of post-Reformation bias for or against specific families and misconceptions based on hearsay concludes with the remarkable statement that James was lucky to die when he did. Had he lived, Buchanan asserts, he might eventually have excited the hatred of his people through the imposition of new taxes, 'so that perhaps upon the whole, his death may be thought to have been for himself rather fortunate, than premature.'[80] Yet for all his criticism, Buchanan had absorbed the widely circulating favourable estimate of King James, and he admits: 'James, as he was greatly beloved while alive, so when dead, his memory was cherished with an affection beyond what I have ever read, or heard of being entertained for any other king.'[81]

When we turn to the *Historie* of Robert Lindsay of Pitscottie, completed in the late 1570s,[82] we are confronted with a string of anecdotes about the king and reign which, while they fail to provide any real motivation for the main events of the period, certainly make the most entertaining reading. Thus we are provided with tales of sea-fights in the Forth; of the vital roles played by Pitscottie's Lindsay of Byres ancestors before Sauchieburn and Flodden, in true *speculum principis* tradition giving wise counsel to kings who proceed to reject it out of hand; of the adventures of Andrew Forman at home and abroad; of King James's love of tournaments, and the precise way in which these were conducted; of the building and exact dimensions of the 'Great Michael'; and of the king's placing two infants on Inchkeith in the Firth of Forth in the charge of a dumb woman, to see what language they would speak when they grew up; Pitscottie, hedging his bets, cautiously comments 'sum sayis they spak good hebrew', and dates the experiment to 1493.[83] The story may be wishful thinking, an apocryphal tale which naturally attaches itself to a powerful and successful prince; very similar experiments are attributed to the thirteenth-century Emperor Frederick II and the sixteenth-century Akbar the Great in India;[84] and the idea may originate with Herodotus.

There is much in the official records which Pitscottie totally omits; indeed many central events of the reign, including the 1496–7 invasions, the 'daunting' of the Isles, European diplomatic manoeuvrings, and the business of James's few parliaments, are either confused or totally ignored. Pitscottie provides us only with a distant reflection of the reign as seen through the eyes of his Fife sources, none of whom were his contemporaries. This does not mean, however, that what he has to say on a number of subjects lacks value. For example, his information on the navy, which filtered through to him from the family of Sir Andrew Wood of Largo, is of considerable importance, some of it is not recorded elsewhere, and much of it is corroborated by official records; Sir William Scott of Balwearie, another of Pitscottie's sources, was for a time proprietor of the lands of Pitscottie, had witnessed James IV charters in 1503 and 1507, and had the remarkable distinction of having been taken prisoner at Flodden; and Sir David Lindsay of the Mount, a distant cousin of Pitscottie's whom the chronicler may well have met — Lindsay died in 1555 when Pitscottie was aged about twenty-three — is probably the source not only for the tale of the man in the blue gown at Linlithgow but also for the fleet's raid on Carrickfergus, which is dealt with at length in 'Squyer Meldrum.' Pitscottie's conclusion, that James was slain 'nocht be the manheid nor wisdome of Inglischemen bot be the kingis awin willfull misgovernance' is a clear echo of Lindsay's moralising in the 'Testament of the Papyngo.'[85]

By the close of the sixteenth century, then, the estimate of James IV broadly agreed upon by the chroniclers was that of an able ruler, much loved by his people, who at the end would not accept wise counsel; and disaster was the result. It is only this moralising, to accommodate the *speculum principis* genre in which the chroniclers were writing, which is significantly at odds with the surviving record evidence. In their overall portrayal of King James, Lesley, Buchanan, and Pitscottie all complement and in some respects enrich the official records; and they help to round out the contemporary picture of the character and policies of the king.

A review of widely varying source material — public records, contemporary comment, and later chronicle narratives — leaves no room for doubt that James IV was a ruler of great ability from the outset of his personal rule in 1495 to the day of his death at Flodden eighteen years later. It is perhaps a matter for little surprise that the king should receive such universal praise, if only because his character and — for the most part — his policies were so different from those of his father, which had produced palace revolutions, two major rebellions, and the alienation or elimination of the entire royal Stewart family. Yet by any standards the adult reign of James IV was remarkably peaceful, with a minimum of Crown-magnate conflict, none of which seriously threatened James's position as king.

This lengthy period of peace may partly be attributed to good luck. The rebellion of 1488 which had brought James the throne neither gave him real power at once nor settled the seething political unrest which had led to Sauchieburn. The domination of Scottish government by a faction holding the young king swiftly led, as we have seen, to widespread risings in 1489 and another parliamentary settlement in 1490. Thereafter a further five years of political adjustments at the centre and in the localities followed before King James at last asserted his authority. When he did so, therefore, he was untainted by too close adherence to any single faction during the minority, with the possible exception of a group associated with the Chancellor, Archibald, earl of Angus; and significantly, Angus's career went into a steep decline after 1497, while his former allies John Fresell and Cuthbert, Lord Kilmaurs, not only made their peace with the king but were duly rewarded, the former with a bishopric and the latter — eventually — with the restoration of the Cunningham earldom of Glencairn.[86]

The key to James IV's extraordinary success, therefore, is probably to be found in the skilful political balancing act which the king was able to pursue because by 1495 most of the really disruptive magnate struggles had worked themselves out. But James himself must be credited with a remarkable intelligence in choosing his counsellors, in knowing whom to trust. An early test for the king's 'natural' counsellors, the magnates, was of course the war against England in 1496–7; and it is interesting to see that feuding magnates — bitter rivals like Cunningham and Montgomery in Ayrshire — would both turn up for service in the Scottish host as a very public demonstration of their loyalty to King James. By the turn of the century, as Dr Trevor Chalmers has convincingly shown, the king's daily council contained magnates drawn from all over Scotland — Argyll and Lennox from the west, Bothwell and Hume from the south, Lundy of Balgonie from Fife, Huntly from the north-east, and amongst the clergy, Elphinstone of Aberdeen and the abbots of Holyrood and Scone.[87] The council's personnel changed considerably thereafter, but the same broad geographical base characterised its composition throughout, with the result that, as Dr Chalmers has observed, in theory at least, individuals from every locality might find a patron at court. No fifteenth-century Scottish king had James IV's initial advantages; but it took a highly intelligent ruler to make the most of these, and to sustain them for a generation.

For in addition to his very public display of the necessary trappings of medieval kingship — tournaments, hawking and hunting, liberal almsgiving, and frequent pilgrimages — King James was an extremely hard worker. His 'business' itinerary, drawn from charters issued under the great seal, reveals only the tip of the iceberg. From the earliest months of the reign he was personally active on justice ayres, and the records show him to have been present on ayres at Lanark, Dundee, Jedburgh, Kirkcudbright, Ayr, Wigtown, Dumfries, Lauder, Inverness, Elgin, Aberdeen, Perth, Peebles, and Edinburgh.[88] There appears to be some falling off in James's personal attendance on the ayres towards the end of the reign, but he would still turn up when he reckoned it necessary, as in the case of Jedburgh in November 1510, a punitive ayre remembered long afterwards by Bishop Lesley;[89] and summary justice was meted out to one Andrew Adamson at the Edinburgh ayre of 1512. For the crimes of murdering Thomas Peebles within Edinburgh castle, for theft, and for breaking ward, Adamson was sentenced to beheading, and thereafter to the fixing of his head on Edinburgh's West Port, and his hands and feet on the ports of the four burghs nearest to Edinburgh.[90] From beginning to end, James IV is to be found using the ayres to mete out summary justice for serious crimes. In many cases he might also grant remissions to make sizeable profits for the Crown, a custom for which his father had been much criticised in parliament, and for which he himself was mildly rebuked in 1504.[91] But there was a world of difference between the remote, aloof James III amassing money from profits of justice without moving from Edinburgh in the process, and his energetic son, who was to be seen by his subjects as far west as Mingary, as far north as Tain, and as far south as Whithorn, and who might be expected to appear very rapidly in any area in which unrest was likely to have damaging effects on Crown resources or prestige. Obvious examples are James's direct intervention in feuds in Cunningham, Strathearn, and Apnadull.[92]

The king was not, of course, successful in everything which he undertook, nor was the firm rule attributed to him by the chroniclers as widespread as they suggest. Inevitably, he delegated a great deal of authority to others, strikingly so in the cases of Archibald, second earl of Argyll and Alexander, third earl of Huntly, in the Highland west and vast areas north of the Mounth, both men acting as royal lieutenants from the turn of the century onwards. Of the two, Argyll, like his father before him, was the man of business at court, holding the office of Master of the Household from 1495 to his death at Flodden, the head of a family which had supported James IV from the beginning. Alexander, earl of Huntly, by contrast, held none of the major offices of state, and the Gordon family had wavered between lukewarm and openly hostile to the new regime in 1488; but Earl George had won the Chancellorship from Angus and at his death in 1501 passed on to his son Alexander a vast north-eastern empire in which Gordon interests stretched from Aberdeenshire in the east to Strome, Eilean Donan and even Stornoway in the west, and in which the Crown could only deal with trouble from disaffected Highland chiefs — for example Farquhar MacIntosh and Mackenzie of Kintail — with Huntly's support. No Scottish king could rule directly in the Highlands and Islands, and James had inherited major problems there, largely created for him by his father's initial assaults on the MacDonald hegemony in the Isles and Ross in 1475–6, and completed during his own minority by the Angus government's forfeiture of the Lordship of the Isles in 1493. The king was only partially and temporarily successful in solving these problems, and in the process seems to have alienated Argyll, who clearly resented Huntly's intrusion into the west and may seriously have considered joining his brother-in-law Torquil MacLeod in the Donald Dubh rebellion. In the last analysis, however, there was no alternative to Argyll as the crown policeman of the Highland west, though his lieutenancy was subject to review and criticism in a way that Huntly's never was; and it is significant that James IV sought to protect Huntly's position — and his own lands in Moray — by keeping Farquhar MacIntosh in ward, probably from 1498, to the end of the reign. When he escaped in 1502, he was hunted down by royal servants; and when, as late as 1512, his release from Dunbar castle was plotted by a group of Highlanders from Lochaber, its leaders were promptly arrested and hanged.[93] So the king might police the Highlands and Islands, and he might make the road to Tain in Easter Ross relatively safe for his annual pilgrimages to the shrine of St Duthac. But it is extremely unlikely that he won the hearts of many within the bounds of the forfeited lordship, or that Highlanders came in in any numbers to support the 1513 campaign. There must remain considerable doubt about the accuracy of Pitscottie's tale of Lachlan MacLean of Duart arriving — too late — to fight at Flodden, if only because the same Lachlan is to be found in rebellion against the Crown only a few years later. The genesis of Pitscottie's story is probably MacLean's subsequent ingratiation of himself with Governor Albany and the third Earl of Argyll, which may have given rise to later tales of his loyalty to the Crown.[94] But it seems likely that, at Flodden itself, the Highlanders who turned up to support King James were arrayed under the banners of the royal policemen, Argyll, Lennox, and Huntly.

Outwith the Highlands and Islands, there was little serious unrest. This is reflected in the fact that the only forfeitures pronounced throughout the reign — with the exception of those of the Lordship of the Isles and Torquil MacLeod — were speedily annulled or rescinded, for example in the cases of the 1489 rebels, Lennox, his son Matthew Stewart, and Robert Lord Lyle; indeed Matthew Stewart went on to become an important member of James's council, and as earl of Lennox died at Flodden. Forfeiture was also employed as a threat to bring disaffected magnates and their supporters into line, as in the case of Atholl, Stewart of Fortingall, Campbell of Glenorchy, and Robertson of Struan, over the Apnadull crisis in 1502–4. And the early forfeitures of Ross of Montgrenan and John Ramsay, Lord Bothwell, were annulled by 1490 and 1497 respectively. It is indeed both a measure of James IV's ability to attract support from former enemies, and a grim irony, that John Ramsay, who had advised Henry VII as late as 1496 how to catch and destroy the Scottish army, should rapidly thereafter switch allegiance to James IV and perish at Flodden in 1513, a victim of the tactics which he himself had counselled.

James's skill in preserving a political balance throughout the reign is reflected in his treatment of two major magnates — Patrick Hepburn, first earl of Bothwell, and Archibald Douglas, fifth earl of Angus. In the former case, Bothwell — the only 1488 rebel to be rewarded with an earldom — was head of the family which, more than any other, had risen to power on James IV's accession. The king remained grateful to him for the remainder of his life. Bothwell was an intimate of King James, who played cards with him, went hunting and hawking in his company, sent him to negotiate the French alliance of 1492, and promoted members of the Hepburn family to high office — William Hepburn became Clerk Register the day after Sauchieburn, Alexander Hepburn sheriff of Fife a few days later, John Hepburn Keeper of the Privy Seal in the same month.[95] King James visited Patrick Hepburn, earl of Bothwell, in his castle of Hailes about a year before his death in October 1508,[96] and continued to patronise Hepburns in the last years of the reign — Adam, second earl of Bothwell, and George, bishop of the Isles and Treasurer in 1508–10, both of whom fell at Flodden. Yet this extensive royal favour shown to a single family was not allowed to upset the balance within the royal government. The first Earl of Bothwell held no major office of state after 1494, and his uncle John Hepburn resigned the Privy Seal to Elphinstone in 1492; however, both men continued to serve regularly on the council, a fact which reveals not only their value to the king but also the Hepburn family's shrewd political intelligence.

If the Hepburns were not allowed to rise too high in the political firmament, so also the great maverick of the reign, Archibald, earl of Angus, was not permitted to sink too low. He was an obvious Hepburn rival on the borders and in the west of Scotland, and like the Earl of Bothwell an intimate of the king, to some extent basing his power on his kinship with James's first mistress Marion Boyd.[97] But his equivocal attitude towards England made him an unacceptable border magnate and an inappropriate Chancellor after 1497. When he fell, it may have been Bothwell's influence which brought him down, for Angus's long years of wardship — 1501–9 at Dumbarton and Rothesay — were not brought to an end while Patrick Hepburn was still alive. From 1510 onwards Angus reappears in government, though clearly bereft of the influence which he had wielded in the 'nineties and relentlessly pursued by royal officials for huge compositions for non-entry. He did not appear at Flodden, though it should be remembered that he was sixty-four in 1513 and that two of his sons died on the field.[98] Given his early treasons and his ambitions to recreate the former Black Douglas hegemony in the south-west, Angus might have been more harshly judged — and probably would have been by another Stewart king. But James IV, combining what was probably a residual liking for the earl with a shrewd sense of political balance, first warded Angus on Bute and only then granted Cuthbert Cunningham, Lord Kilmaurs, Angus's principal Ayrshire supporter, the title of earl of Glencairn, forfeited by the Cunningham family in 1488.

Even in Ayrshire, such sensible moderation did not always pay off. As late as March 1513, Angus, together with Cuthbert, earl of Glencairn, a royal herald, and a considerable body of armed men, attempted to force William Bunch, abbot of Kilwinning, to resign his abbacy in favour of their own nominee, John Forman, on the grounds that Forman had procured papal bulls of provision to Kilwinning. Bunch held his ground, refusing to open the abbey gates or yield any of his rights.[99] But there was no prospect that he would be able to function effectively at Kilwinning for any length of time so long as he was threatened by the two most powerful earls in the district, wrongly claiming royal and apostolic authority for their actions. So Bunch seems to have appealed to the king for support in the earliest and most public official forum he could find, that is, the Scottish host of 1513. Angus, as we know, left the host before Flodden, if indeed he was ever there; and his ally Glencairn may not have been present at all. Bunch was therefore in a good position to petition the king, and to demonstrate his loyalty by serving in the host. If this was indeed his idea, it was sound enough; but Bunch was killed at Flodden with his king.

The significance of the Kilwinning case is that Bunch's response to local magnate threats was to approach the king for justice; and this is in itself a tribute to James's authority. If he did not achieve permanent settlements of major feuds, he had the power to stop them during his lifetime; and his even-handedness in dealing with the problems of an unruly Ayrshire is most clearly seen in his gradual distribution of earldoms amongst the major families, Cunningham becoming earl of Glencairn in 1503, Montgomery earl of Eglinton in 1507, and Kennedy earl of Cassillis in 1509.

By the end of the reign, James had outlived many of his supporters of 1488; Bothwell, Blacader, and Argyll were all gone. Continuity was however provided by Elphinstone as Privy Seal; and the king increasingly placed a great deal of trust in Andrew Forman, bishop of Moray, in Patrick Paniter, Secretary from 1505, and probably also in his own son Alexander Stewart, Paniter's pupil whom he had made Archbishop of St Andrews and Chancellor. But there does not seem to have been a narrow clique at court, as one finds strikingly in the reign of James III. On the contrary, the Irish treaty of June 1513 was witnessed by both archbishops, one bishop, one prior, two abbots, six earls, three lords of parliament, and a further four royal officials including Secretary Paniter.[100] This was a king who consulted his magnates, and who, for the most part, was loyally supported by them.

This loyalty extended lower down the social scale, certainly to the vast array of craftsmen, shipwrights, and unskilled workmen who were employed on King James's extensive building programmes — sizeable additions to Holyrood, Stirling, and Linlithgow, improvements at Leith and the construction of two entirely new naval dockyards at Newhaven and Pool of Airth, the building, fitting out, maintaining, and repairing of ships owned or hired by the Crown; to seamen in royal service who received considerably more in pay than their English counterparts; and to gunners of every description, foreign and native, from the royal 'master meltar' down to the makers of arquebuses. For James IV's lavish expenditure in peace and war provided not only a great stimulus to the development of native crafts, but also a huge amount of paid labour for skilled and unskilled alike. To these sizeable benefits must be added the more elusive factor of charisma. The king was seen in far-flung parts of his kingdom not only on official business, when his presence may have been less than welcome to some, but also hunting, hawking, and on pilgrimage. James's subjects saw the private face of the sportsman or penitent as far afield as Lochmaben and Loch Rannoch; on the Glen Isla and Ardersier ferries; at the cobbler's in Penpont; and at Whitekirk and Whithorn. The invasion of the East March by the Earl of Surrey in August 1497 brought James in person to the front line, directing operations from a house in Cattleshiel. He was, in short, a man who appeared infinitely more approachable, infinitely more aware of his duties, than his father. He showed an instinctive grasp of the essentials of Scottish kingship, of the need above all to lead by example.

Thus the campaign of 1513 was no mad aberration on the part of an obstinate, but diplomatically naive, ruler dragging his people reluctantly after him on a doomed quixotic adventure. James IV was supported at the end, as he had been at the outset of his personal rule, by a very broad spectrum of the Scottish community because his interests coincided with theirs, because war with England was widely popular, and had been since at least 1508. And more than any earlier Scottish ruler, James IV had prepared for war. English naval attacks on the Forth early in the reign had been beaten off, and no others were advisable later because of the construction, from 1502 onwards, of the Scottish fleet, because of the fortifications at the Queensferry narrows, and because of the ominous presence of the 'Great Michael' off Inchkeith in the early summer of 1513. As for land warfare, the new weaponry — up-to-date artillery imported into, or cast in Scotland in the final years of the reign —

would assuredly bring success in a determined assault on Norham castle, the principal objective of the 1513 campaign. When Norham was taken by storm, after a lengthy bombardment, on 28–29 August, James IV's reputation with his subjects, already high, must have soared to new heights.

The death-roll at Flodden, less than a fortnight later, makes grim reading;[101] but it also reveals the extent of King James's support, even after the desertions which were to be expected after the fall of Norham. Nine earls were killed out of twelve who appear to have been present, and these included a wide geographical spectrum — Argyll and Lennox from the Highland west, Caithness from the extreme north, Erroll, Crawford, Montrose, and Rothes from the north-east, Cassillis from Ayrshire, and Bothwell from the south-east. Of those earls who survived, Huntly lost a brother and Marischal a son, while Angus, who was not present, lost two sons. Around fourteen lords of parliament fell; and of those who survived, many lost close relatives, including Lord Oliphant, whose son and heir Colin was killed in the battle together with his uncle Laurence, abbot of Inchaffray. The tally of dead lairds is, as far as later records reveal, equally impressive in its geographical distribution; and from the third estate, there fell burgesses of Ayr, Dundee, Glasgow, and Edinburgh, including Edinburgh's provost, Alexander Lauder of Blyth, and his brother George. When we add to these the casualties among the first estate — the archbishop-chancellor, the Hepburn bishop of the Isles, two abbots, and Thomas Dickson, dean of Restalrig, together with a host of lesser clergy, at least some of them from the diocese of Dunkeld — the breadth of James IV's support — from all three estates and from all over Scotland — becomes apparent. This was a popular king, joining his French ally in an effort to check the absurd European pretensions of England's bellicose and immature ruler, seeking at the same time to provide plunder for the host and a substantial strategic gain for himself.

He failed only at the very end. The English commanders who peered through the wind and rain on the late afternoon of 9 September 1513 and saw the five huge Scottish phalanxes begin their descent of Branxton Hill were in fact witnessing the last occasion on which a Scottish king, confidently and widely supported by his lieges, would offer battle in England. A few hours later James IV and most of his commanders were dead, the purpose, drive, and unanimity which he had instilled in the political community were shattered, and Scottish national self-confidence was lost for the remainder of the century. In death as in life, James did not lack admirers, including the great scholar Erasmus, whose eulogy stressed the Scottish king's vast knowledge and abundant generosity. But perhaps the most convincing epitaph for James IV is that of Sir David Lindsay of the Mount. Unlike William Dunbar, who about 1508 produced a 'Lament for the Makars', Lindsay, soon to become the greatest makar of his time, grieved over a lost golden age of Scottish government. For Lindsay, a courtier who lived through the trauma of 1513 and its aftermath at close quarters, James IV was 'the glore of princelie governyng', who had brought justice and peace to his country and European fame to his house. Lindsay's verdict is just. Far more than any of his Stewart predecessors, James IV understood the essentials of medieval Scottish kingship, and knew how to govern a country in which power was very widely decentralised. In sharp contrast to his father, he knew how to distribute patronage with an even hand, he found ways of raising large sums of money for the Crown without unduly alienating his lieges, and — most important of all — he understood the need to travel regularly from end to end of his kingdom. In the last analysis, formidable physical stamina was amongst the most impressive attributes of the kingship of James IV.

NOTES

1. *James IV Letters*, No. 282.
2. *Cal. State Papers (Spain)*, i, No. 210.
3. *A.P.S.*, ii, 245.
4. *A.D.C.*, ii, 81.
5. *T.A.*, ii, 314.
6. *See above*, Chapter 1.
7. *See above*, Chapter 4.
8. Chandler, S.B., 'An Italian Life of Margaret, Queen of James III', *S.H.R.*, xxxii (1953), 52–7, at 55.
9. For Gavin Douglas's life, see Priscilla Bawcutt, *Gavin Douglas* (Edin., 1976), 1–22.
10. *Prot. Bk. Young*, No. 790. For the Douglas-Hepburn contest over the deanery of Dunkeld, see Bawcutt, *op.cit.*, 6–7; Watt, *Fasti*, 105.
11. *See above*, Chapter 6.
12. *T.A.*, i, 117.
13. *See above*, Chapter 4.
14. By Janet Kennedy, the king had a son, James earl of Moray, born about 1500; by Isabel Stewart, he had a daughter Janet (or Jean): *Scots Peerage*, i, 22–3.
15. W. Mackay Mackenzie (ed.), *The Poems of William Dunbar* (Lond., 1970 edn.), 51–3.
16. *T.A.*, iv, 108, 358.
17. *Poems of William Dunbar*, passim.
18. *Ibid.*, 43.
19. See, in general, Roderick Lyall, 'Complaint, Satire and Invective in Middle Scots Literature', in Norman Macdougall (ed.), *Church, Politics, and Society: Scotland 1408–1929* (Edin., 1983), 44–64.
20. *R.S.S.*, i, No. 563.
21. *T.A.*, iii, 154, 181, 331, 361; iv, 69, 106, 127, 249–50; *R.S.S.*, i, No. 2119.
22. *The Poetic Works of Sir David Lyndsay*, ed. David Laing (Edin., 1879), i, pp. xii–xiii.
23. For Damian's career, see John Read, 'A Flying Alchemist', in *Humour and Humanism in Chemistry* (Lond., 1947), 16–36; and *T.A.*, ii, iii, iv, *passim*.
24. *Poems of William Dunbar*, 67–70; Lesley, *History*, 76.
25. Lyall, 'Complaint, Satire and Invective', 54.
26. For discussion of this, see Mackie, *James IV*, 61 and n.
27. *Poems of William Dunbar*, 46–8; *T.A.*, iv, 249–50.
28. *Asloan MS.*, i, 245–270, at 270.
29. Hector Boece, *Murthlacensium et Aberdonensium Episcoporum Vitae*, ed. and trans. James Moir (Aberdeen, 1894).

30. Boece, *Vitae*, 84.

31. *Ibid.*, 104–5.

32. Hector Boece, *The History and Chronicles of Scotland*, trans. John Bellenden (Edin. edn., 1821), ciii.

33. See, for example, his description of the Perkin Warbeck episode: Boece, *Vitae*, 81–83.

34. The best modern assessment of Boece, covering his life, career, and thought, is to be found in Macfarlane, *Elphinstone*, passim.

35. Alexander Myln, *Vitae Dunkeldensis Ecclesiae Episcoporum* (Bannatyne Club, 1837).

36. A translation of part of the *Vitae* is to be found in *Rentale Dunkeldense*. Myln's discussion of the 1513 campaign is on p. 315.

37. *Cal. State papers (Milan)*, No. 660.

38. *James IV Letters*, No. 564.

39. Lennox's attendance on the 'daily council' between 1503 and 1513 averaged more than 90% in spite of the fact that he held no official office: Chalmers, 'Council, Patronage, and Governance', 432–4.

40. *Lyndsay's Works* (ed. Laing), i, 79–80 (lines 486–520).

41. *See above*, Chapter 10.

42. *See above*, Chapter 7.

43. Lesley, *History*, 75–6.

44. *T.A.*, iii, Pref., xxxvi–xxxvii, 294, 412–16.

45. *Ibid.*, iii, 416.

46. Hume Brown, *Early Travellers in Scotland*, 37–8; *Asloan MS.*, i, 227.

47. For the 1507 and 1508 tournaments, see *T.A.*, iii, Pref., xlv–lii, 257–261; iv, Pref., lxxxiii–lxxxiv, 22, 119.

48. *T.A.*, iii, 258.

49. *Ibid.*

50. *Poems of William Dunbar*, 66–7 ('Of ane Blak-moir'). The poem is not to be taken literally, for according to Dunbar those who were defeated in the field had a rather different experience with the 'black lady':

> 'And quhai in felde receaves schaem,
> And tynis thair his knychtlie naem,
> Sall cum behind and kis hir hippis,
> And nevir to uther confort claem:
> My ladye with the mekle lippis.'

51. Scarisbrick, *Henry VIII*, 18–19.

52. Lesley, *History*, 78.

53. N.L.S., MS. 1746. The section on James IV is f.112 r–v.

54. For Abell's life, *see* Alasdair M. Stewart, 'Adam Abell's 'Roit or Quheill of Tyme'', *Aberdeen University Review* xliv (1972), 386–393.

55. N.L.S., MS. 1746, f.112 v; and *see above*, Chapter 6.

56. Lesley, *History*, 73.

57. Buchanan, *History*, ii, 241–2.

58. *See above*, Chapter 6.

59. N.L.S., MS. 1746, f.112 v.

60. Pitscottie, *Historie*, i, 244.

61. *Ibid.*, i, 249–50.

62. *Ibid.*, i, 250, 255–6.

63. Forman's biography — rather dated — is the subject of Herkless and Hannay, *Archbishops of St Andrews*, vol. ii. His employment, from the very beginning of the reign, as a diplomat at the Roman Curia, is the subject of an entertaining article by Dr Leslie Macfarlane: Leslie J Macfarlane, 'Precedence and protest at the Roman Curia, 1486–1493', in *Renaissance Studies* Vol. 2, No. 2 (Oxford, 1988), 222–230.

64. *Letters and Papers Henry VIII*, i, pt. ii, No. 2313.

65. N.L.S., MS. 1746, f.112 v.

66. Lesley, *History*, 95–6; Emond, 'Minority of James V', Appendix A.

67. Buchanan, *History*, ii, 258–260.

68. *James IV Letters*, xxvii, xxxii, No. 541.

69. Pitscottie, *Historie*, i, 272–3.

70. Not to be confused with his namesake, Sir Alexander McCulloch of Myreton, with whom indeed he is to be found in dispute before the Lords of Council on 14 November 1512, over the wardship of the lordship of Cardoness: S.R.O., A.D.C., xxiv, ff. 11v–12r.

71. *T.A.*, iv, 416; *Lyndsay's Works* (ed. Laing), i, 162; and for Laing's discussion of the identity of the squire of Cleish, see *Ibid.*, 308–9.

72. *Letters and Papers Henry VIII*, i, pt. ii, No. 2913.

73. Polydore Vergil, *Anglica Historia*, 221; *Letters and Papers Henry VIII*, i, pt. ii, Nos. 2355, 2469.

74. Lesley, *History*, 59–96.

75. *Ibid.*, 95.

76. For Lesley's sources, see Lesley, *History*, 7–9; and Lesley, *De Origine*, i, Pref., xvii–xxi.

77. Lesley, *History*, 96.

78. Buchanan, *History*, ii, 242–3.

79. *Ibid.*, ii, 243–5, 253–5.

80. *Ibid.*, ii, 261–2.

81. *Ibid.*, ii, 261.

82. The chapters on James IV are in Pitscottie, *Historie*, i, 213–276.

83. *Ibid.*, i, 237.

84. I am indebted for this information to Professor Robert Grieve of the University of Western Australia at Perth.

85. For Pitscottie's sources, see Pitscottie, *Historie*, i, civ–cxxi.

86. Fresell was elected to the bishopric of Ross — probably — before 10 September 1497 and certainly before 18 September 1497: Watt, *Fasti*, 269. Cuthbert, Lord Kilmaurs, was created Earl of Glencairn on 13 August 1503, at the time of the royal marriage: *Scots Peerage*, iv, 235.

87. Chalmers, 'Council, Patronage, and Governance', 431–2.

88. *T.A.*, i, ii, iii, iv, passim; Pitcairn, *Criminal Trials*, i, 14–124.

89. Lesley, *History*, 81–2; Pitcairn, *Criminal Trials*, i, 67–71.

90. *Ibid.*, i, 84.

91. *A.P.S.*, ii, 250 c.7.

92. *See above*, Chapters 5 and 6.

93. Pitcairn, *Criminal Trials*, i, 81.

94. Pitscottie, *Historie*, i, 274–6; Gregory, *History*, 120–122.

95. *See above*, Chapters 3 and 4.

96. *T.A.*, iv, Pref., xv.

97. *See above*, Chapter 4.

98. The sons of the fifth earl killed at Flodden were George, Master of Angus, and Sir William Douglas of Glenbervie: Fraser, *Douglas*, ii, 111–115, 125–139.

99. Fraser, *Douglas*, ii, 102–3.

100. *R.M.S.*, ii, No. 3856.

101. Emond, 'Minority of James V', Appendix A.

Appendix: The Itinerary of James IV

The map shows places where the king issued documents under the Great Seal and how many times he did so in each. It is thus mainly an itinerary of royal business rather than pleasure, though James IV, unlike his father, frequently managed to combine both, as illustrated, for example, in the entries for Darnaway and Glen Finglas. The map reveals, as might be expected, a heavy concentration on Edinburgh (1475 out of the 2152 registered Great Seal documents for the reign), but far more extensive royal travel than during the previous reign. No attempt has been made to plot in detail James IV's justice ayres or his Highland campaigns of the 1490s, which are unremarkable apart from his enthusiasm for, and three visits to, his new castle at Loch Kilkerran in Kintyre in 1498, and a single brief sojourn in Mingary castle in Ardnamurchan in 1495.

James IV's extensive itinerary outwith the confines of royal business included hunting in Perthshire and Fife, frequent pilgrimages to the shrines of St Duthac at Tain and St Ninian at Whithorn, and visits to mistresses as far apart as Duchal and Bothwell in the south and Darnaway in the north. All parliaments met in Edinburgh, while the annual exchequer audit alternated between Stirling, Edinburgh and Linlithgow.

Stornoway

TAIN 1
SPYNIE 2
DINGWALL 1 INNES 1
FORTROSE 1 ELGIN
Strome DARNAWAY 1
INVERNESS 7 Ardersier
Eilean Donan

ABERDEEN 15

MINGARY 1
BRECHIN 2 MONTROSE 2
Cairn-na-burgh Dunkeld
DUNSTAFFNAGE 1 SCONE 1 ARBROATH 5
METHVEN 1 DUNDEE 16
GLEN ARTNEY 1 PERTH 34 ST ANDREWS 15
GLEN FINGLAS 1 FALKLAND 19 CUPAR 7
DUMBARTON 10 STIRLING 306 ARDROSS 1
DUNGLAS 1 Sauchieburn DUNFERMLINE 5
NEWARK 1 LINLITHGOW 83 LEITH 2 HAILES 1
GREENOCK 1 Dunbar
ROTHESAY 1 GLASGOW 19 EDINBURGH 1475 COLDINGHAM 2
DUCHAL 1 PAISLEY 1 CORSTORPHINE 1
LANARK 6 Cattleshiel Ladykirk
PEEBLES 6 UPSETTLINGTON 1
KILMARNOCK 1 MELROSE 2 HUME 1 Norham
LOCH KILKERRAN 11 NEWARK 1 Flodden
AYR 9 KELSO 1
JEDBURGH 9
DURISDEER 1
Penpont
LOCHMABEN 1
PENNINGHAME 1 DUMFRIES 3
WIGTOWN 1 KIRKCUDBRIGHT 1
Carrickfergus WHITHORN 3

Source: R.M.S., ii, Nos. 1731-3883.

A total of 2152 registered documents covering 1488-1513. Of these, 43 indicate no place of issue. The remaining 2109 are distributed as follows:

Edinburgh	1475	Duchal	3	Glen Finglas	1
Stirling	306	Whithorn	3	Newark (Selkirk)	1
Linlithgow	83	Dumfries	3	Kelso	1
Perth	34	Dunglas	2	Elgin	1
Falkland	19	Spynie	2	Newark (Renfrews.)	1
Glasgow	19	Melrose	2	Castlemeary (Mingary)	1
Dundee	16	Montrose	2	Hume	1
St Andrews	15	Coldingham	2	Upsettlington	1
Aberdeen	15	Brechin	2	Greenock	1
Loch Kilkerran	11	Leith	2	Rothesay	1
Dumbarton	10	Wigtown	1	Scone	1
Ayr	9	Hailes	1	Darnaway	1
Jedburgh	9	Innes	1	Penninghame	1
Cupar	7	Kilmarnock	1	Lochmaben	1
Inverness	7	Methven	1	The Canonry in Ross	
Peebles	6	Ardross	1	(Fortrose)	1
Lanark	6	Dunstaffnage	1	Paisley	1
Arbroath	5	Durisdeer	1	Kirkcudbright	1
Dunfermline	5	Dingwall	1	Corstorphine	1
		Glenarthnay		Tain	1
		(Glen Artney)	1		

Bibliography

A. *Primary MS. Sources*
Edinburgh.
National Library of Scotland:
Adv. MS. 18.2.8. (John Ireland, 'The Meroure of Wyssdome').
        25.5.6. (Monynet MS.).
        34.7.3. (Gray MS.)
        35.5.9. (James IV Letters).
    MS 1746 (Adam Abell).
Dundas Charters.

Scottish Record Office:

Acts of the Lords of Council and Session.
Records of Parliament.
Accounts of the Lord High Treasurer.
MS. Treaties with France.
RH/1/1/3 (Commission from Prince James, May 1488).
RH/1/2 (Skene, 'Tabill and repertour of the Cheker rollis').
Airlie Charters.
Cunninghame–Grahame Muniments.
Dalhousie Muniments.
Eglinton Muniments.
Glencairn Muniments.
Gordon Castle Muniments.
Lennox Charters.

University Library.

MS Dc.7.63. (Law, 'De Cronicis Scotorum Brevia').

London
British Library:

Cotton MS. Vespasian Cxvi.
Royal MS. 17 Dxx.

Public Record Office:

Scots Docs. E. 39/92.

Blair Castle:

Atholl Royal Letters.

Dumbarton:

Burgh Records.

Copenhagen:

Danske Rigsarkiv: T.K.U.A. (Skotland), A.1.

The Vatican:

Registra Supplicationum (Vat. Reg. Supp.).
[Microfilms of supplications relating to Scotland, many of them calendared, are now stored in the Dept. of Scottish History, Glasgow University].

Vienna:

Österreichisches Nationalbibliothek Cod. Vinob. MS. 1897 (James IV — Margaret Tudor Book of Hours).

B. *Primary Printed Sources and Works of Reference.*

Aberdeen Council Register: *Extracts from the Council Register of the Burgh of Aberdeen* (Spalding Club, 1844–48).
Acts of the Lords Auditors of Causes and Complaints, 1466–1494 [*A.D.A.*], ed. T. Thomson (Edinburgh, 1839).
Acts of the Lords of Council in Civil Causes, 1478–1495 [*A.D.C., i*], ed. T. Thomson (Edinburgh, 1839).
Acts of the Lords of Council in Civil Causes, 1496–1501 [*A.D.C., ii*], edd. G. Neilson and H. Paton (Edinburgh, 1918).
Acts of the Lords of Council, 1501–1503 [*A.D.C., iii*], ed. J.A. Clyde (Stair Society, Edinburgh, 1942).
Acts of the Lords of Council in Public Affairs, 1501–1554 [*A.D.C.P.*], ed. R.K. Hannay (Edinburgh, 1932).
Acts of the Lords of the Isles, 1336–1493, edd. Jean Munro and R.W. Munro (S.H.S., Edinburgh, 1986).
Acts of the Parliaments of Scotland [*A.P.S.*], edd. T. Thomson and C. Innes (Edinburgh, 1814–75), vol. ii (1424–1567).
The Asloan Manuscript, vol. i, ed. W.A. Craigie (S.T.S., Edinburgh, 1923).
The Bannatyne Miscellany (Bannatyne Club, 1827–55).
Boece, Hector: *Hectoris Boetii Murthlacensium et Aberdonensium Episcoporum Vitae*, ed. J. Moir (New Spalding Club, Aberdeen, 1894).
Boece, Hector, *The History and Chronicles of Scotland*, trans. John Bellenden (Edinburgh edn., 1821).
Buchanan, George, *The History of Scotland*, trans. J. Aikman (Glasgow and Edinburgh, 1827–9).
Calendar of Documents relating to Scotland, vol. iv (1357–1509), ed. J. Bain (Edinburgh, 1888).
Calendar of Entries in the Papal Registers relating to Great Britain and Ireland, vol. xiv, ed. J.A. Twemlow; xv, ed. M.J. Haren (London, 1960 and 1978).
Calendar of the Patent Rolls, Edward IV, vol. iii (1476–85) (London, 1901).
Calendar of State Papers existing in the Archives and Collections of Milan, i, ed. A.B. Hinds (London, 1912).
Calendar of Letters, Despatches and State Papers relating to the negotiations between England and Spain, vol. i (1485–1509); vol. ii (1509–25); both ed. G. A. Bergenroth (London, 1862, 1866).

Calendar of State Papers and Manuscripts, relating to English affairs, existing in the Archives and Collections of Venice, vol. i (1202–1509); vol. ii (1509–19); both ed. R. Brown (London, 1864, 1867).

Commynes, Philippe de: *Mémoires de Philippe de Commynes*, ed. Mlle. Dupont (Société de l'Histoire de France, Paris, 1840–47).

Commynes, Philippe de, *The Universal Spider*, trans. and ed. P.M. Kendall (London, 1973).

Cowan, I.B., and Easson, D.E., *Medieval Religious Houses in Scotland* (London, 1976).

Drummond, William, of Hawthornden, *History of Scotland from the Year 1423 until the Year 1542* (London edn., 1681).

Dunbar, William: *The Poems of William Dunbar*, ed. W. Mackay Mackenzie (London, 1970).

Dunbar, William: *The Poems of William Dunbar*, ed. J. Small (S.T.S., Edinburgh, 1884–93).

Durkan, John, and Ross, Rev. Anthony, 'Early Scottish Libraries', *Innes Review*, ix (1), 1958.

Edinburgh City Charters: Charters and Other Documents relating to the City of Edinburgh (S.B.R.S., 1871).

The Exchequer Rolls of Scotland [E.R.], ed. J. Stuart and others (Edinburgh, 1878–1908).

Fasti Ecclesiae Scoticanae Medii Aevi ad annum 1638, ed. D.E.R. Watt (St Andrews, 1969).

Ferreri, Giovanni, *Appendix to Hector Boece's Scotorum Historiae*, second edn. (Paris, 1574).

Flodden Papers 1507–1517, ed. M. Wood (S.H.S., Edinburgh, 1933).

Foedera, Conventiones, Litterae et Cuiuscunque Generis Acta Publica, ed. T. Rymer (Record Commission, London, 1816–69).

Fraser, William, *The Book of Carlaverock* (Edinburgh, 1873).

Fraser, William, *The Douglas Book* (Edinburgh, 1885).

Fraser, William, *The Chiefs of Colquhoun and their Country* (Edinburgh, 1869).

Fraser, William, *The Lennox* (Edinburgh, 1874).

Fraser, William, *Memorials of the Montgomeries, Earls of Eglinton* (Edinburgh, 1859).

Fraser, William, *The Scotts of Buccleuch* (Edinburgh, 1878).

Fraser, William, *Memorials of the Family of Wemyss of Wemyss* (Edinburgh, 1888).

Glasgow Registrum: Registrum Episcopatus Glasguensis (Bannatyne and Maitland Clubs, 1843).

Hall, Edward, *Chronicle*, ed. Henry Ellis (London, 1809).

Handbook of British Chronology [H.B.C.], edd. F.M. Powicke and E.B. Fryde (London, 1961).

Henryson, Robert: *The Poems and Fables of Robert Henryson*, ed. H. Harvey Wood (New York, 1968).

Highland Papers, ed. J.R.N. Macphail (S.H.S., Edinburgh, 1914–1934).

Historical Manuscripts Commission: Reports of the Royal Commission on Historical Manuscripts [H.M.C.] (London, 1870–)

Hume, David, of Godscroft, *The History of the House and Race of Douglas and Angus* (4th edn., Edinburgh, 1748).

Hume Brown, P. (ed.), *Early Travellers in Scotland* (Edinburgh, 1891; facsimile, Edinburgh, 1978).

Ireland, John: *Johannes de Irlandia, The Meroure of Wyssdome*, vol. i, ed. C. Macpherson (S.T.S., Edinburgh, 1926); vol. ii, ed. F. Quinn (S.T.S., Edinburgh, 1965).

James IV: *The Letters of James the Fourth, 1505–1513*, ed. R.L. Mackie (S.H.S., Edinburgh, 1953).

The Knights of St. John of Jerusalem in Scotland, edd. I.B. Cowan, P.H.R. Mackay, and A. Macquarrie (S.H.S., Edinburgh, 1983).

Knox, John, *History of the Reformation in Scotland*, ed. W.C. Dickinson (Edinburgh, 1949).

Laing Charters: Calendar of the Laing Charters 854–1837, ed. J. Anderson (Edinburgh, 1899).

Leland, John, *De Rebus Britannicis Collectanea* (London, 1770), iv.

Letters and Papers illustrative of the Reigns of Richard III and Henry VII, ed. James Gairdner (London, 1861–3).

Letters and Papers, Foreign and Domestic, of the Reign of Henry VIII, vol. i (1509–1514), ed. J.S. Brewer (London, 1862).

Letters and Papers, Foreign and Domestic, of the Reign of Henry VIII, vol. i (2nd edn., revised R. H. Brodie), pts. i and ii (1509–1514), (London, H.M.S.O., 1920).

Letters and Papers relating to the War with France, 1512–1513, ed. Alfred Spont (Navy Records Society (x), 1897).

Lesley, John, *The History of Scotland from the Death of King James I in the Year 1436 to the Year 1561* (Bannatyne Club, 1830).

Lesley, John, *De Origine, Moribus et Rebus Gentis Scotorum* (S.T.S., Edinburgh, 1888 and 1895).

Lindsay, Sir David: *The Poetical Works of Sir David Lyndsay of the Mount*, ed. David Laing (Edinburgh, 1879).

Lindsay, Robert, of Pitscottie, *The Historie and Cronicles of Scotland* (S.T.S., Edinburgh, 1899).

MacCarthy, B (ed.), *Annals of Ulster*, iii (1379–1541) (Dublin, 1895).

Moray Registrum: Registrum Episcopatus Moraviensis (Bannatyne Club, 1879).

Myln, Alexander, *Vitae Dunkeldensis Ecclesiae Episcoporum* (Bannatyne Club, 1831).

Pitcairn, Robert (ed.), *Criminal Trials in Scotland from 1488 to 1624*, vol. i (Edinburgh, 1833).

Protocol Book of John Foular, 1501–1503, ed. M. Wood (S.R.S., Edinburgh, 1930).

Protocol Book of James Young, 1485–1515, ed. G. Donaldson (S.R.S., Edinburgh, 1952).

Registrum Magni Sigilli Regum Scotorum [R.M.S.], ii (1424–1513), ed. J.B. Paul (Edinburgh, 1882).

Registrum Secreti Sigilli Regum Scotorum [R.S.S.], i (1488–1529), ed. M. Livingstone (Edinburgh, 1908).

Reliquae Celticae, edd. A. MacBain and J. Kennedy (Inverness, 1894).

Renfrew: Archaeological and Historical Collections relating to the County of Renfrew, ed. A. Gardner (Paisley, 1885–90).

Rentale Dunkeldense 1505–1517, ed. R.K. Hannay (S.H.S., Edinburgh, 1915).

Rotuli Scotiae in Turri Londinensi et in Domo Capitulari Westmonasteriensi asservati [Rot. Scot.], ii (1399–1516), edd. D. Macpherson and others (London, 1819).

Scotichronicon, by Walter Bower: vol. 8 (books xv and xvi), ed. D.E.R. Watt (Aberdeen, 1987).

The Scots Peerage, ed. Sir J. Balfour Paul (Edinburgh, 1904–14).

The Sheriff Court Book of Fife, 1515–1522, ed. W.C. Dickinson (S.H.S., Edinburgh, 1928).

Spalding Miscellany: Miscellany of the Spalding Club (Spalding Club, Aberdeen, 1841–52).

Statutes of the Realm (Record Commission, 1810–1828).

Theiner, A., *Vetera Monumenta Hibernorum et Scotorum Historiam illustrantia* (Rome, 1864).

Treasurer's Accounts: Accounts of the Lord High Treasurer of Scotland [T.A.], i–iv (1473–1513), edd. T. Dickson and J.B. Paul (Edinburgh, 1877–1902).

Vergil, Polydore, *Anglica Historia*, ed. and trans. Denys Hay (Camden Society, London, 1950).

Wilkins, D. (ed.), *Concilia Magnae Britanniae et Hiberniae* (London, 1737).

C. *Secondary Sources*

Baldwin, John R., *Exploring Scotland's Heritage: Lothian and the Borders* (H.M.S.O., 1985).

Barron, Evan, *Inverness and the Macdonalds* (Inverness, 1930).

Bawcutt, Priscilla, *Gavin Douglas* (Edinburgh, 1976).

Briggs, Robin, *Early Modern France, 1560–1715* (Oxford, 1977).

Brown, Jennifer M. (ed.), *Scottish Society in the Fifteenth Century* (London, 1977).

Caldwell, David H. (ed.), *Scottish Weapons and Fortifications 1100–1800* (Edinburgh, 1981).

Chrimes, S.B., *Henry VII* (London, 1977).

Comrie, John D., *History of Scottish Medicine to 1860* (Wellcome Historical Medical Museum, London, 1927).

Conway, Agnes, *Henry VII's Relations with Scotland and Ireland, 1485–1498* (Cambridge, 1932).

Donaldson, Gordon, *Scotland: James V — James VII* (Edinburgh History of Scotland, vol. 3: 1965).

Donaldson, Gordon, *Scottish Kings* (London, 1967).

Dowden, John, *The Bishops of Scotland* (Glasgow, 1912).

Drummond, Hon. William (Viscount Strathallan), *The Genealogy of the most noble and ancient House of Drummond* (1681), Edinburgh edn. (1831).

Dunlop, Annie I., *The Life and Times of James Kennedy, Bishop of St. Andrews* (Edinburgh, 1950).

Falcon: The Autobiography of His Grace James the 4, King of Scots, presented by A.J. Stewart (London, 1970).

Fraser-Mackintosh, C., *Invernessiana* (Inverness, 1875).

Gairdner, James, *History of the Life and Reign of Richard III* (London, 1893).

Gilbert, John M., *Hunting and Hunting Reserves in Medieval Scotland* (Edinburgh, 1979).

Grant, Alexander, *Independence and Nationhood: Scotland 1306–1469* (London, 1984).

Gregory, D., *A History of the Western Highlands and Isles of Scotland, 1493–1625* (Edinburgh, 1836).

Halliwell, J.O., *Letters of the Kings of England* (London, 1846).

Herkless, John, and Hannay, Robert Kerr, *The Archbishops of St Andrews*, vols. i–iii (Edinburgh, 1907–10).

Hodgson, John, *History of Northumberland* (Newcastle, 1828).

Howard, Frank, *Sailing Ships of War, 1400–1800* (London, 1979).

Hume Brown, Peter, *History of Scotland to the Present Time* (Cambridge, 1911).

Lang, Andrew, *A History of Scotland from the Roman Occupation*, vol. i (Edinburgh, 1900).

Macdougall, Norman, *James III: A Political Study* (Edinburgh, 1982).

Macdougall, Norman, *Church, Politics and Society: Scotland 1408–1929* (Edinburgh, 1983).

Macfarlane, Leslie J., *William Elphinstone and the Kingdom of Scotland, 1431–1514* (Aberdeen, 1985).

Mackenzie, W. Mackay, *The Secret of Flodden* (Edinburgh, 1931).

Macquarrie, Alan, *Scotland and the Crusades, 1095–1560* (Edinburgh, 1985).

Mackie, R.L., *King James IV of Scotland: A Brief Survey of his Life and Times* (Edinburgh, 1958).

Nicholson, Ranald, *Scotland: The Later Middle Ages* (Edinburgh History of Scotland, vol. 2: 1974).

Nisbet, A., *A System of Heraldry* (new edn., Edinburgh, 1816).

Phillips, M. Mann, *The Adages of Erasmus: a study with translations* (Cambridge, 1964).

Pinkerton, J., *The History of Scotland from the Accession of the House of Stuart to that of Mary, with Appendices of Original Papers* (London, 1797).

Pollard, A.F., *The Reign of Henry VII from Contemporary Sources* (London, 1913).

Rae, Thomas I., *The Administration of the Scottish Frontier, 1513–1603* (Edinburgh, 1966).

Rait, R.S., *The Parliaments of Scotland* (Glasgow, 1924).

Read, John, *Humour and Humanism in Chemistry* (London, 1947).

Ross, Charles, *Edward IV* (London, 1974).

Scarisbrick, J.J., *Henry VIII* (London, 1968).

Scott, Sir Walter, *The Poetical Works of Sir Walter Scott* (London, Sands edn., 1899).

Scott, Sir Walter, *Tales of a Grandfather* (1828–9): (Edinburgh, Black edn., 1889).

Stewart, Ian H., *The Scottish Coinage* (London, 1966).

Stringer, K.J. (ed.), *Essays on the Nobility of Medieval Scotland* (Edinburgh, 1985).

Taylor, I.A., *The Life of James IV* (London, 1913).

Tytler, Patrick Fraser, *The History of Scotland from the Accession of Alexander III to the Union* (Edinburgh, 1868).

Wilson, Ian, *Reincarnation? The Claims Investigated* (London, 1982).

Wormald, Jenny, *Lords and Men in Scotland: Bonds of Manrent 1442–1603* (Edinburgh, 1985).

D. *Articles and Book Chapters*

Anderson, R.C., 'The 'Grace Dieu' of 1446–86', *E.H.R.*, xxxiv (1919), 584–6.

Arthurson, Ian, 'The King's Voyage into Scotland: The War that Never Was', in *England in the Fifteenth Century: Proceedings of the 1986 Harlaxton Symposium*, ed. Daniel Williams (Bury St Edmunds, 1987), 1–22.

Brown, A.L., 'The Cistercian Abbey of Saddell, Kintyre', *Innes Review*, xx (2), 1969, 130–137.

Brown, Jennifer M., 'The Exercise of Power', in *Scottish Society in the Fifteenth Century*, ed. Jennifer M. Brown (London, 1977), 33–65.

Burns, Rev. Charles, 'Papal Gifts to Scottish Monarchs: The Golden Rose and the Blessed Sword', *Innes Review*, xx (2), 1969, 150–194.

Burns, J.H., 'New Light on John Major', *Innes Review*, v (1954), 83–100.

Burns, J.H., 'John Ireland and 'The Meroure of Wyssdome'', *Innes Review*, vi (1955), 77–98.

Caldwell, David H., 'Royal Patronage of Arms and Armour Making in Fifteenth and Sixteenth Century Scotland', in David H. Caldwell (ed.), *Scottish Weapons and Fortifications 1100–1800* (Edinburgh, 1981), 73–93.

Chandler, S.B., 'An Italian Life of Margaret, Queen of James III', *S.H.R.*, xxxii (1952), 52–7.

Crawford, Barbara E., 'Scotland's Foreign Relations: Scandinavia', in J.M. Brown (ed.), *Scottish Society in the Fifteenth Century* (London, 1977), 85–100.

Dickinson, W.C., 'An Inquiry into the Origin of the Title Prince of Scotland', *Economica*, iv, 212–220.

Durkan, John, 'Archbishop Robert Blackadder's Will', *Innes Review*, xxiii (2), 1972, 138–148.

Easson, D.E., 'The Lollards of Kyle', *Juridical Review*, xlviii (1936), 123–8.

Flodden: 'A contemporary account of the battle of Flodden' ['Trewe Encountre'], *P.S.A.S.*, vii (1866–7), 141–152.

Graham, Angus, 'The Battle of 'Sauchieburn'', *S.H.R.*, xxxix (1960), 89–97.

Guthrie, Douglas, 'King James the Fourth of Scotland: His Influence on Medicine and Science', *Bulletin of the History of Medicine*, 21 (1947), 173–191.

Head, David M., 'Henry VIII's Scottish Policy: a Reassessment', *S.H.R.*, lxi (1982), 1–24.

Kaufman, Peter Iver, 'Piety and Proprietary Rights: James IV of Scotland, 1488–1513', *The Sixteenth Century Journal*, xiii (1982), 83–99.

Lyall, R.J., 'The Medieval Scottish Coronation Service: some seventeenth century evidence', *Innes Review*, xxviii (1), 1977, 3–21.

Lyall, R.J., 'Politics and Poetry in Fifteenth and Sixteenth Century Scotland', *Scottish Literary Journal*, 3(2), 1976, 5–29.

Lyall, R.J., 'Complaint, Satire and Invective in Middle Scots Literature', in Norman Macdougall (ed.), *Church, Politics and Society: Scotland 1408–1929* (Edinburgh, 1983), 44–64.

Macdougall, Norman, 'Crown versus Nobility: the struggle for the priory of Coldingham, 1472–1488', in K.J. Stringer (ed.), *Essays on the Nobility of Medieval Scotland* (Edinburgh, 1985), 254–269.

Macdougall, Norman, 'The greattest scheip that ewer saillit in England or France': James IV's "Great Michael", in Norman Macdougall (ed.), *Scotland and War AD 79–1918* (Edinburgh, 1991), 36–60.

Macfarlane, Leslie J., 'The Book of Hours of James IV and Margaret Tudor', *Innes Review*, xi (1960), 3–21.

Macfarlane, Leslie J., 'The Primacy of the Scottish Church, 1472–1521', *Innes Review*, xx (1969), 111–129.

Macfarlane, Leslie J., 'Precedence and Protest at the Roman Curia, 1486–1493', in *Renaissance Studies*, Vol. 2, No. 2 (Oxford, 1988), 222–230.

McRoberts, Rev. David, 'Hermits in Medieval Scotland', *Innes Review*, xvi (2), 1965, 199–216.

McRoberts, Rev. David, 'The Scottish Church and Nationalism in the Fifteenth Century', *Innes Review*, xix (1), 1968, 3–14.

McRoberts, Rev. David, 'Scottish Pilgrims to the Holy Land', *Innes Review*, xx(1), 1969, 80–106.

Madden, Craig, 'The Feuing of Ettrick Forest', *Innes Review*, xxvii(1), 1976, 70–84.

Madden, Craig, 'Royal Treatment of Feudal Casualties in Late Medieval Scotland', *S.H.R.*, lv (2), 1976, 172–194.

Mason, Roger, 'Kingship, Tyranny and the Right to Resist in Fifteenth Century Scotland', *S.H.R.*, lxvi (2), 1987, 125–151.

Munro, Jean, 'The Lordship of the Isles' in *The Middle Ages in the Highlands* (Inverness Field Club, 1981).

Neilson, George, "The Hede of Sant. . .': The Earl of Angus's Pilgrimage in 1489', *S.H.R.*, i (1904), 217–218.

Nicholson, Ranald, 'Feudal Developments in Late Medieval Scotland', *Juridical Review*, 1973 (1), 1–19.

Richmond, C.F., 'English Naval Power in the Fifteenth Century', *History*, lii (1967), 1–15.

Stevenson, R.B.K., 'The Return of Mons Meg from London, 1828–1829', in D.H. Caldwell (ed.), *Scottish Weapons and Fortifications 1100–1800* (Edinburgh, 1981), 419–436.

Stewart, Alasdair M., 'Adam Abell's "Roit or Quheill of Tyme" ', *Aberdeen University Review*, xliv (1972), 386–393.

Thomson, J.A.F., 'Innocent VIII and the Scottish Church', *Innes Review*, xix (1), 1968, 23–31.

Wormald, Jenny, 'Taming the Magnates?', in K.J. Stringer (ed.), *Essays on the Nobility of Medieval Scotland* (Edinburgh, 1985), 270–280.

E. *Theses*

Arthurson, Ian, '1497 and the Western Rising'
(Ph.D., Keele University, 1981).

Cardew, Anne, 'A Study of Society on the Anglo-Scottish Border, 1455–1502'
(Ph.D., St Andrews University, 1973).

Chalmers, Trevor M., 'The King's Council, Patronage, and the Governance of Scotland, 1460–1513'
(Ph.D., Aberdeen University, 1982).

Emond, William K., 'The Minority of King James V, 1513–1528'
(Ph.D., St Andrews University, 1988).

Kelham, Charles A., 'Bases of Magnatial Power in Later Fifteenth Century Scotland'
(Ph.D., Edinburgh University, 1986).

Kelley, Michael G., 'The Douglas Earls of Angus: A Study in the Social and Political Bases of Power of a Scottish Family from 1389 until 1557'
(Ph.D., Edinburgh University, 1973).

Madden, Craig, 'The Finances of the Scottish Crown in the Later Middle Ages'
(Ph.D., Glasgow University, 1978).

Murray, Athol L., 'Exchequer and Crown Revenue of Scotland, 1437–1542'
(Ph.D., Edinburgh University, 1961)

O'Brien, Irene, 'The Scottish Parliament in the Fifteenth and Sixteenth Centuries'
(Ph.D., Glasgow University, 1980).

Stevenson, A.W.K., 'Trade between Scotland and the Low Countries in the Later Middle Ages'
(Ph.D., Aberdeen University, 1982).

Index